The Writer's World
Paragraphs and Essays

FOURTH EDITION

Lynne Gaetz   **Suneeti Phadke**

Lionel Groulx College   **St. Jerome College**

PEARSON

Boston   Columbus   Indianapolis   New York   San Francisco   Upper Saddle River
Amsterdam   Cape Town   Dubai   London   Madrid   Milan   Munich   Paris   Montreal   Toronto
Delhi   Mexico City   Sao Paulo   Sydney   Hong Kong   Seoul   Singapore   Taipei   Tokyo

Executive Editor: Matthew Wright
Editorial Assistant: Laura Marenghi
Senior Development Editor: Marion Castellucci
Development Editor: Erica Nikolaidis
Senior Supplements Editor: Donna Campion
Executive Digital Producer: Stefanie Snajder
Content Specialist: Erin Jenkins
Digital Editor: Sara Gordus
Executive Marketing Manager: Roxanne McCarley
Production Manager: Denise Phillip Grant

Project Coordination, Text Design, and Electronic
    Page Makeup: Laserwords Private Limited
Cover Designer/Manager: Wendy Ann Fredericks
Cover Photos: © Shutterstock
Text Permissions: Aptara
Photo Researcher: Integra
Senior Manufacturing Buyer: Dennis Para
Printer/Binder: Courier/Kendallville
Cover Printer: Lehigh-Phoenix Color Hagerstown

Credits and acknowledgments borrowed from other sources and reproduced, with permission, in this textbook appear on the appropriate page within text and on pages 579–580.

Library of Congress Cataloging-in-Publication Data

Gaetz, Lynne, 1960–
    The writer's world : paragraphs and essays / Lynne Gaetz, Lionel Groulx College ; Suneeti Phadke, St. Jerome
College. — Fourth Edition.
        pages cm
    Previous edition: Upper Saddle River, N.J. : Pearson Education, 3rd ed., 2011.
    ISBN 978-0-321-89512-7
    1. English language—Paragraphs—Problems, exercises, etc.   2. English language—Rhetoric—Problems, exercises, etc.
3. Report writing—Problems, exercises, etc.   4. English language—Grammar—Problems, exercises, etc.
I. Phadke, Suneeti, 1961-   II. Title.
    PE1439.G254 2014
    808'.042—dc23
                                                            2013031287

10 9 8 7 6 5 4 3 2—V011—17 16 15 14

Student Edition ISBN-13:   978-0-321-89512-7
Student Edition ISBN-10:   0-321-89512-6

A la Carte Edition ISBN-13:   978-0-321-89523-3
A la Carte Edition ISBN-10:   0-321-89523-1

Contents

Part III   The Essay   163

Part IV   The Editing Handbook   250

SECTION 1   Effective Sentences
THEME: Popular Culture

Readings Listed by Rhetorical Mode

Thank you for making the third edition of *The Writer's World* a resounding success; we are delighted that the book has been able to help so many students across the country. This fourth edition, too, can help your students produce writing that is technically correct and richly detailed whether your classes are filled with students who have varying skill levels, whether students are native or nonnative speakers of English, or whether they learn better through the use of visuals.

When we started the first edition, we set out to develop practical and pedagogically sound approaches to these challenges, and we are pleased to hear that the book has been helping students succeed in their writing courses. We began with the idea that this project should be a collaboration with other developmental writing teachers. So we met with more than forty-five instructors from around the country, asking for their opinions and insights regarding (1) the challenges posed by the course, (2) the needs of today's ever-changing student population, and (3) the ideas and features we were proposing in order to provide them and you with a more effective teaching and learning tool. Pearson also commissioned dozens of detailed manuscript reviews from instructors, asking them to analyze and evaluate each draft of the manuscript. These reviewers identified numerous ways in which we could refine and enhance our key features. Their invaluable feedback was incorporated throughout *The Writer's World*. The text you are seeing is truly the product of a successful partnership between the authors, publisher, and well over one hundred developmental writing instructors.

What's New in the Fourth Edition?
Deeper MyWritingLab Integration

New to this edition, resources and assessments designed specifically for *The Writer's World* are in MyWritingLab along with the eText and all the diagnostic, practice, and assessment resources of MyWritingLab. Students can use MyWritingLab to access media resources, practice, and assessment for each chapter of *The Writer's World*. When they see MyWritingLab™ in the text, students have the option of completing the practice online right in MyWritingLab. Most practice assessments will flow to your instructor gradebook in MyWritingLab, reducing grading time and allowing you to focus attention on those students who may need extra help and practice.

- All Writer's Room activities can be completed in MyWritingLab, giving students access to a wide range of customizable instruction, practice, and assessment.
- Students can now answer additional reading comprehension questions for readings in Chapter 38 in MyWritingLab, offering extra practice and assessment and helping students strengthen their grasp of the readings.
- All "At Work" paragraph modes appear in MyWritingLab as interactive model documents. When students mouse over the paragraph, they hear detailed explanations of how the topic sentence, supporting details, and concluding sentence exemplify the pattern of development.

A New Look

A new clean and modern design streamlines instruction and increases usability, allowing students to more effectively find and retain the information covered.

New Annotated Student Essays

For each of the nine essay patterns covered in Chapter 14, a new student essay has been added and annotated to highlight the components of each essay (e.g., thesis statements, topic sentences, and concluding sentences). Each student essay is followed by a professional essay and a set of questions that deepen students' understanding of the different essay patterns.

New Readings

In Chapter 38, eight new readings relate to the themes presented in the grammar chapters. Thought-provoking essays from Amy Tan, Drew Hayden Taylor, Joseph T. Hallinan, Hugh Raffles, and Amanda Enayati discuss modern notions of multiculturalism, privacy in the Internet age, and the criminal justice process.

New Images

This edition presents new dynamic and vibrant images—photos of exotic locales and pop culture icons, as well as images from independent and mainstream films and television shows—that will engage students and prompt critical thinking.

New Grammar Themes and Practices

Many of the grammar practices in Part IV: The Editing Handbook are new, providing updated grammar instruction through the lens of topical and culturally relevant content. In addition, two new grammar themes have been added to engage student interest: Section 3: Spies and Hackers and Section 5: Our Environment.

Updated High-Interest Paragraph Models and Practices

Throughout the book you will notice new examples, sample paragraphs, writing practices, Writer's Desk topics, and grammar practices. In fact, to make the content more topical and appealing, roughly 30 percent of the book's content has been updated.

How *The Writer's World* Meets Students' Diverse Needs

We created *The Writer's World* to meet your students' diverse needs. To accomplish this, we asked both the instructors in our focus groups and the reviewers at every stage not only to critique our ideas but to offer their suggestions and recommendations for features that would enhance the learning process of their students. The result has been the integration of many elements that are not found in other textbooks, including our **visual program, coverage of nonnative speaker material, and strategies for addressing the varying skill levels students bring to the course.**

The Visual Program

A stimulating full-color book with more than 140 photos, *The Writer's World* recognizes that today's world is a visual one, and it encourages students to become better communicators by responding to images. Chapter-opening visuals in Parts I, II, III, and IV help students think about the chapter's key concept in a new way. For example, in the Chapter 9 opener, a photograph of children's toys sets the stage for classification. Toys are grouped by type, which helps students understand the premise of classification. In Part IV, chapter-opening photos help illustrate the theme of the examples and exercises. These visual aids can also serve as sources for writing prompts.

Each **At Work** box in the Part II chapters features multicolored highlighting and annotations, along with content on how that particular pattern of development is used on the job.

The visuals in Part II provide students with another set of opportunities to write in response to images, with Media Writing activities that encourage them to respond using particular paragraph and essay patterns. Throughout *The Writer's World*, words and images work together to encourage students to explore, develop, and revise their writing.

Seamless Coverage for Nonnative Speakers

Instructors in our focus groups noted the growing number of nonnative/ESL speakers enrolling in developmental writing courses. Although some of these students have special needs relating to the writing process, many of you still have a large portion of native speakers in your courses whose more traditional needs must also be satisfied. In order to meet the challenge of this rapidly changing dynamic, we have carefully implemented and integrated content throughout to assist these students. *The Writer's World* does not have separate ESL boxes, ESL chapters, or tacked-on ESL appendices. Instead, information that traditionally poses a challenge to nonnative speakers is woven seamlessly throughout the book. In our extensive experience teaching writing to both native and nonnative speakers of English, we have learned that both groups learn best when they are not distracted by ESL labels. With the seamless approach, nonnative speakers do not feel self-conscious and segregated, and native speakers do not tune out detailed explanations that may also benefit them. Many of these traditional problem areas receive more coverage than you would find in other textbooks, arming the instructor with the material to effectively meet the needs of nonnative speakers. Moreover, the *Annotated Instructor's Edition* provides more than seventy-five ESL Teaching Tips designed specifically to help instructors better meet the needs of their nonnative speaking students.

Issue-Focused Thematic Grammar

In surveys, many of you indicated that one of the primary challenges in teaching your course is finding materials that are engaging to students in a contemporary context. This is especially true in grammar instruction. **Students come to the course with varying skill levels**, and many students are simply not interested in grammar. To address this challenge, we have introduced **issue-focused thematic grammar** in *The Writer's World*.

Each chapter centers on a theme that is carried out in examples and activities. These themes include topics related to popular culture, psychology, spies and hackers, college life, the environment, health care, the legal world, and the workplace.

The thematic approach enables students to broaden their awareness of subjects important to American life, such as understanding advertising and consumerism and thinking about health care issues and alternative medicine. The thematic approach makes reading about grammar more engaging. And the more engaging grammar is, the more likely students will retain key concepts—raising their skill level in these important building blocks of writing.

We also think that it is important to teach grammar in the context of the writing process. Students should not think that grammar is an isolated exercise. Therefore, **each grammar chapter includes a warm-up writing activity**. Students write and edit their paragraphs, paying particular attention to the grammar point covered in the chapter. The end of each grammar section also contains paragraph and essay writing topics that are related to the theme of the section and that follow different writing patterns. In these chapters, suggestions are provided for readings in Part V that relate to the grammar themes.

Learning Aids to Help Students Get the Most from *The Writer's World*

Overwhelmingly, focus group participants and reviewers asked that both a larger number and a greater diversity of exercises and activities be incorporated into *The Writer's World*. In response, we have developed and tested the following learning aids in *The Writer's World*. We are confident they will help your students become better writers.

Hints In each chapter, Hint boxes highlight important writing and grammar points. Hints are useful for all students, but many will be particularly helpful for nonnative speakers. For example, in Chapter 12, one Hint encourages students to state an argument directly and a second Hint points out the need to avoid circular reasoning. In Chapter 22, a Hint discusses checking for consistent voice in compound sentences. Hints include brief discussions and examples so that students will see both concept and application.

HINT ▸ **Use Consistent Voice**

When a sentence has two independent clauses and is joined by a coordinating conjunction, use a consistent voice. In other words, if one part of the sentence is active, the other should also be active.

Not parallel	The researcher conducted the experiment, and then a report was written by him.
Parallel	The researcher conducted the experiment, and then he wrote a report. (Both parts use the active voice.)

Vocabulary Boost Throughout Part II of *The Writer's World*, Vocabulary Boost boxes give students tips to improve their use of language and to revise and edit their word choices. For example, a Vocabulary Boost in Chapter 4 asks students to replace repeated words with synonyms, and the one in Chapter 5 gives specific directions for how to vary sentence openings. These lessons give students concrete strategies and specific advice for improving their diction.

VOCABULARY BOOST

Using Varied Language

1. Underline the opening word of every sentence in your first draft. Check to see if some are repeated.

2. Replace repeated opening words with an adverb like *usually*, *generally*, or *fortunately* or a prepositional phrase, such as *On the side* or *Under the circumstances*. You can also begin the sentences with a phrase like *Leaving the door open*. In other words, avoid beginning too many sentences with a noun or transitional word.

Repeated First Words

We opened the door of the abandoned house. We looked nervously at the rotting floorboards. We thought the floor might collapse. We decided to enter. We walked carefully across the kitchen floor to the bedroom, one by one.

Variety

My cousins and I opened the door of the abandoned house. Nervously, we looked at the rotting floorboards. Thinking the floor might collapse, we decided to enter. One by one, we walked across the kitchen floor to the bedroom.

The Writer's Desk Parts I, II, and III include The Writer's Desk exercises that help students get used to practicing all stages and steps of the writing process. As the chapter progresses, students warm up with a prewriting activity and then use specific methods for developing, organizing (using paragraph and essay plans), drafting, and revising and editing to create a final draft.

THE WRITER'S DESK   Write a Paragraph Plan

Refer to the information you generated in previous Writer's Desk exercises and create a paragraph plan. If you think of new details that will explain your point more effectively, include them here.

Topic sentence: _____

_____

Support 1: _____

Details: _____

_____

_____

Support 2: _____

Details: _____

_____

_____

Support 3: _____

Details: _____

_____

_____

Paragraph Patterns at Work To help students appreciate the relevance of their writing tasks, Chapters 4–12 highlight an authentic writing sample from work contexts. Titled Illustration at Work, Narration at Work, and so on, this feature offers a glimpse of how people use writing patterns in different workplace settings.

ILLUSTRATION AT WORK

Patti Guzman is a registered nurse at a large hospital. She was invited to speak to nursing students at a local university. In the following excerpt from her speech, she gives examples to explain why a nurse must be in good physical health.

The topic sentence expresses the main idea.

Supporting sentences provide details and examples.

The concluding sentence brings the paragraph to a satisfying close.

Physically, the job of a nurse is demanding. On a daily basis, we must lift patients and move them. When patients are bedridden for prolonged periods, we must change their positions on their beds. When new patients arrive, we transfer them from stretchers to beds or from beds to wheelchairs. If patients fall, we must be able to help them stand up. If patients have difficulty walking, we must assist them. Patients who have suffered paralysis or stroke need to be lifted and supported when they are bathed and dressed. Keep in mind that some patients may be quite heavy, so the job requires a good level of physical strength.

Reflect On It Each Reflect On It is a chapter-review exercise. Questions prompt students to recall and review what they have learned in the chapter.

Reflect On It

Think about what you have learned in this chapter. If you do not know an answer, review that topic.

1. What are four things that you should look for when revising?

     _____   _____

     _____   _____

2. Circle the best answer(s). A paragraph is unified if
    a. there are no irrelevant supporting details.
    b. there are many facts and statistics.
    c. all details support the topic sentence.

3. Circle the best answer: Transitional words are _____ that help ideas flow in a logical manner.
    a. links   b. sentences   c. verbs

4. The Editing Handbook in Part IV includes information about grammar, spelling, and punctuation errors. In what chapter would you find information about the following topics? Look in the table of contents to find the chapter number.

    a. capitalization   _____

    b. subject–verb agreement   _____

    c. faulty parallel structure   _____

The Writer's Room The Writer's Room contains writing activities that correspond to general, college, and workplace topics. Some prompts are brief to allow students to freely form ideas while others are expanded to give students more direction.

There is something for every student writer in this end-of-chapter feature. Students who respond well to visual cues will appreciate the media writing exercises in The Writer's Room in Part II: Paragraph Patterns. Students who learn best by hearing through collaboration will appreciate the discussion and group work prompts in The Writers' Circle section of selected The Writer's Rooms. To help students see how grammar is not isolated from the writing process, there are also The Writer's Room activities at the end of sections 1–8 in Part IV: The Editing Handbook. In addition, all Writer's Room exercises can be completed in MyWritingLab, giving students access to a wide range of customizable instruction, practice, and assessment.

THE WRITER'S ROOM   MyWritingLab™

MyWritingLab™
Complete these writing assignments at mywritinglab.com

Writing Activity 1: Topics

Choose any of the following topics, or choose your own topic. Then write an illustration paragraph.

General Topics

1. important historical events
2. great things in life that are free
3. mistakes parents make
4. hobbies
5. positive personality traits

College and Work-Related Topics

6. pressures faced by college students
7. qualities that help you succeed
8. office etiquette
9. qualities of a good instructor
10. tools or equipment needed for your job

Writing Activity 2: Media Writing

Watch a popular television show or movie that deals with students in a high school or college setting. Examples are the *American Pie* movies, *High School Musical*, or television programs such as *Glee*, *The Hills*, or *Gossip Girl*. You can even go on YouTube and type "peer pressure" into the search bar, and then watch some of the segments. Write a paragraph about the show, movie, or video segment and explain the ways that characters feel peer pressure. Provide several examples.

***The Writer's World* eText**   Accessed through MyWritingLab (www.mywritinglab .com), students now have the eText for *The Writer's World* at their fingertips while completing the various exercises and activities within MyWritingLab. Students can highlight important material and add notes to any section for further reflection and/ or study throughout the semester.

How We Organized *The Writer's World*

The Writer's World is separated into five parts for ease of use, convenience, and ultimate flexibility.

Part I: The Writing Process teaches students (1) how to formulate ideas (Exploring); (2) how to expand, organize, and present those ideas in a piece of writing (Developing); and (3) how to polish writing so that they convey their message as clearly as possible (Revising and Editing). The result is that writing a paragraph or an essay becomes far less daunting because students have specific steps to follow.

Part II: Paragraph Patterns gives students a solid overview of the patterns of development. Using the same easy-to-understand process (Exploring, Developing, and Revising and Editing), each chapter in this section explains how to convey ideas using one or more writing patterns. As they work through the practices and write their own paragraphs and essays, students begin to see how using a writing pattern can help them fulfill their purpose for writing.

Part III: The Essay covers the parts of the essay and explains how students can apply the nine patterns of development to essay writing. This section also discusses the role research plays in writing and explains some ways that students can incorporate research in their essays.

Part IV: The Editing Handbook is a thematic grammar handbook. In each chapter, the examples correspond to a theme, such as popular culture, college life, and work. As students work through the chapters, they hone their grammar and editing skills while gaining knowledge about a variety of topics. In addition to helping build interest in the grammar practices, the thematic material provides a spark that ignites new ideas that students can apply to their writing.

Part V: Reading Strategies and Selections offers tips, readings, and follow-up questions. Students learn how to write by observing and dissecting what they read. The readings relate to the themes found in Part IV: The Editing Handbook, thereby providing more fodder for generating writing ideas.

Pearson Writing Resources for Instructors and Students

Book-Specific Ancillary Material

Annotated Instructor's Edition for *The Writer's World: Paragraphs and Essays, 4/e*
ISBN 0-321-89522-3

The *AIE* offers in-text answers, marginal annotations for teaching each chapter, links to the *Instructor's Resource Manual*, and MyWritingLab teaching tips. It is a valuable resource for experienced and first-time instructors alike.

Instructor's Resource Manual for *The Writer's World: Paragraphs and Essays, 4/e*
ISBN 0-321-89526-6

The material in the *IRM* is designed to save instructors time and provide them with effective options for teaching their writing classes. It offers suggestions for setting up their course; provides lots of extra practice for students who need it; offers quizzes and grammar tests, including unit tests; furnishes grading rubrics for each rhetorical mode; and supplies answers in case instructors want to print them out and have students grade their own work. This valuable resource is exceptionally useful for adjuncts who might need advice in setting up their initial classes or who might be teaching a variety of writing classes with too many students and not enough time.

PowerPoint Presentation for *The Writer's World: Paragraphs and Essays, 4/e*
ISBN 0-321-90678-0

PowerPoint presentations to accompany each chapter consist of classroom-ready lecture outline slides, lecture tips and classroom activities, and review questions. The PPT slide set is available for download from the Instructor Resource Center.

Answer Key for *The Writer's World: Paragraphs and Essays, 4/e*
ISBN 0-321-89521-5

The Answer Key contains the solutions to the exercises in the student edition of the text. Available for download from the Instructor Resource Center.

MyWritingLab MyWritingLab™

Where practice, application, and demonstration meet to improve writing.

MyWritingLab, a complete online learning program, provides additional resources and effective practice exercises for developing writers. MyWritingLab accelerates learning through layered assessment and a personalized learning path utilizing the Knewton Adaptive Learning Platform™, which customizes standardized educational content to piece together the perfect personalized bundle of content for each student. With over eight thousand exercises and immediate feedback to answers, the integrated learning aids of MyWritingLab reinforce learning throughout the semester.

What makes the practice, application, and demonstration in MyWritingLab more effective?

Diagnostic Testing: MyWritingLab's diagnostic Path Builder test comprehensively assesses students' skills in grammar. Students are provided with an individualized learning path based on the diagnostic's results, identifying the areas where they most need help.

Progressive Learning: The heart of MyWritingLab is the progressive learning that takes place as students complete the Overview, Animation, Recall, Apply, and Write exercises along with the Post-test within each topic. Students move from preparation (Overview, Animation) to literal comprehension (Recall) to critical understanding (Apply) to the ability to demonstrate a skill in their own writing (Write) to total mastery (Post-test). This progression of critical thinking enables students to truly master the skills and concepts they need to become successful writers.

Online Gradebook: All student work in MyWritingLab is captured in the Online Gradebook. Instructors can see what and how many topics their students have mastered. They can also view students' individual scores on all assignments throughout MyWritingLab, as well as overviews by student, and class performance by module. Students can monitor their progress in new Completed Work pages, which show them their totals, scores, time on task, and the date and time of their work by module.

eText: The eText for *The Writer's World* is accessed through MyWritingLab. Students now have the eText at their fingertips while completing the various exercises and activities

Suneeti Phadke in the Caribbean

Lynne Gaetz in the Dominican Republic

within MyWritingLab. The MyWritingLab logo (MyWritingLab™) is used throughout the book to indicate exercises or writing activities that can be completed in and submitted through MyWritingLab (results flow directly to the Gradebook where appropriate).

Additional Resources

Pearson is pleased to offer a variety of support materials to help make teaching writing easier for teachers and to help students excel in their coursework. Many of our student supplements are available free or at a greatly reduced price when packaged with *The Writer's World: Paragraphs and Essays, 4/e.* Visit www .pearsonhighereducation.com, contact your local Pearson sales representative, or review a detailed listing of the full supplements package in the *Instructor's Resource Manual* for more information.

Acknowledgments

Many people have helped us produce *The Writer's World*. First and foremost, we would like to thank our students for inspiring us and providing us with invaluable feedback. Their words and insights pervade this book.

We also benefited greatly from the insightful comments and suggestions from over two hundred instructors across the nation, all of whom are listed in the opening pages of the *Annotated Instructor's Edition*. Our colleagues' feedback was invaluable and helped shape *The Writer's World* series content, focus, and organization.

Reviewers

The following reviewers provided insight and assistance in the latest revision of *The Writer's World* series:

Justin Bonnett, Saint Paul College
Cheryl Borman, Hillsborough Community College, Ybor City Campus
Adam Carlberg, Tallahessee Community College
Judith L. Carter, Amarillo College
Zoe Ann Cerny, Horry-Georgetown Technical College
Cathy J. Clements, State Fair Community College
Cynthia Dawes, Edgecombe Community College
Mary F. Di Stefano Diaz, Broward College
Stephanie Fischer, Southern Connecticut State University
Paul Gallagher, Red Rocks Community College
Kim Allen Gleed, Harrisburg Area Community College
Karen Hindhede, Central Arizona College
Schahara Hudelson, South Plains College
Dianna W. Hydem Jefferson State Community College
Stacy Janicki, Ridgewater College
Patrice Johnson, Dallas County Community College District

Jennifer Johnston, Hillsborough Community College

Julie Keenan, Harrisburg Area Community College

Patricia A. Lacey, Harper College

Nicole Lacroix, Red Rock Community College

Ruth K. MacDonald, Lincoln College of New England

Joy McClain, Ivy Technical Community College, Evansville

Ellen Olmstead, Montgomery College

Deborah Peterson, Blinn College

Rebecca Portis, Montgomery College

Sharon Race, South Plains College

Stephanie Sabourin, Montgomery College

Sharisse Turner, Tallahassee Community College

Jody Wheeler, Saint Paul College

Julie Yankanich, Camden County College

Finally, we are indebted to the team of dedicated professionals at Pearson who have helped make this project a reality. They have boosted our spirits and have believed in us every step of the way. Special thanks to Erica Nikolaidis for her magnificent job in polishing this book and to Matthew Wright for trusting our instincts and enthusiastically propelling us forward. We owe a deep debt of gratitude to Yolanda de Rooy, whose encouraging words helped ignite this project. Michelle Gardner's attention to detail in the production process kept us motivated and on task and made *The Writer's World* a much better resource for both instructors and students.

Finally, we would like to dedicate this book to our families who supported us and who patiently put up with our long hours on the computer. Manu, Murray, and Natalia continually encouraged us. Rebeka Pelaez Gaetz, a graphic designer, provided helpful suggestions about the visual direction of the book. We especially appreciate the support and sacrifices of Diego, Rebeka, Kiran, and Meghana.

Lynne Gaetz and Suneeti Phadke

A Note to Students

Your knowledge, ideas, and opinions are important. The ability to clearly communicate those ideas is invaluable in your personal, academic, and professional life. When your writing is error-free, readers will focus on your message, and you will be able to persuade, inform, entertain, or inspire them. *The Writer's World* includes strategies that will help you improve your written communication. Quite simply, when you become a better writer, you become a better communicator. It is our greatest wish for *The Writer's World* to make you excited about writing, communicating, and learning. Enjoy!

Lynne Gaetz & Suneeti Phadke
writingrewards@pearson.com

Call for Student Writing!

Do you want to be published in *The Writer's World*? Send your paragraphs and essays to us along with your complete contact information. If your work is selected to appear in the next edition of *The Writer's World*, you will receive credit for your work and a copy of the book!

Lynne Gaetz and Suneeti Phadke
writingrewards@pearson.com

Part I

The Writing Process

An Overview The writing process is a series of steps that most writers follow to get from thinking about a topic to preparing the final draft. Generally, you should follow the process step by step; however, sometimes you may find that your steps overlap. For example, you might do some editing before you revise, or you might think about your main idea while you are prewriting. The important thing is to make sure that you have done all of the steps before preparing your final draft.

Before you begin the chapters that follow, review the steps in the writing process.

EXPLORING

- Think about your topic.
- Think about your audience.
- Think about your purpose.
- Try exploring strategies.

DEVELOPING

- Narrow your topic.
- Express your main idea.
- Develop your supporting ideas.
- Make a plan or an outline.
- Write your first draft.

REVISING AND EDITING

- Revise for unity.
- Revise for adequate support.
- Revise for coherence.
- Revise for style.
- Edit for technical errors.

THE PARAGRAPH AND THE ESSAY

Most of the writing that we do—e-mail messages, work reports, college papers—is made up of paragraphs and essays. A **paragraph** is a series of sentences that are about one central idea. Paragraphs can stand alone, or they can be part of a longer work such as an essay, a letter, or a report. An **essay** is a series of paragraphs that are about one central idea. Both the paragraph and the essay are divided into three parts.

Characteristics of a Paragraph

- The **topic sentence** introduces the subject of the paragraph and shows the writer's attitude toward the subject.
- The **body** of the paragraph contains details that support the topic sentence.
- The paragraph ends with a **concluding sentence**.

Characteristics of an Essay

- The **introduction** engages the reader's interest and contains the **thesis statement**.
- The **body** paragraphs each support the main idea of the essay.
- The **conclusion** reemphasizes the thesis and restates the main points of the essay. It brings the essay to a satisfactory close.

Review the following paragraph and essay, written by college student Anthony Coffman.

The Paragraph

A worthwhile place to visit is the Indianapolis Motor Speedway. Built in 1909, it is home to the greatest spectacle in racing: The Indianapolis 500 Indy races. The stadium showcases the apex in automotive design. In addition to the Indy car races, there are Brickyard 400 NASCAR races, Grand Prix events, and GP moto-race events. Races can be expensive; a more wallet-friendly alternative is to attend qualifying time trials or even take a tour and visit the museum on the grounds during the non-race times of the year. Visiting the Indianapolis Motor Speedway provides fun for the whole family.

Topic sentence

Supporting ideas

Concluding sentence

The Essay

Born in Indiana, I've lived here for most of my life. Often, others mention that they are bored, yet this state has a variety of great entertainment venues that are affordable. Visitors and local citizens can visit state parks, museums, and the Indianapolis Motor Speedway.

Indiana provides twenty-five recognized state parks that provide a variety of activities. Visitors can camp, fish, cycle, and see natural and historic sites. Some of the best parks include Turkey Run, Brown County, White River, Whitewater Memorial, and McCormick's Creek. I have had the opportunity to visit the grounds of Turkey Run, Brown County, and White River and had a wonderful time while hiking.

Another great activity to do in Indiana is visit museums. The Indianapolis Children's Museum offers educational exhibits including *Dinosphere* and the Anne Frank Peace Park with exhibits of the Seven Wonders of the World. The Indianapolis Museum of Art has over fifty thousand artworks and is home to the Virginia B. Fairbanks Art and Nature Park, which provides an urban oasis of woodlands, wetlands, lakes, and meadows. On the museum grounds, the Oldfield's-Lilly House gives visitors a glimpse into a country estate in the early twentieth century.

A worthwhile place to visit is the Indianapolis Motor Speedway. Built in 1909, it is home to the greatest spectacle in racing: the Indianapolis 500 Indy races. The stadium showcases the apex in automotive design. In addition to the Indy car races, there are Brickyard 400 NASCAR races, Grand Prix events, and GP moto-race events. Races can be expensive; a more wallet-friendly alternative is to attend qualifying time trials or even take a tour and visit the museum on the grounds during the non-race times of the year. Visiting the Indianapolis Motor Speedway provides fun for the whole family.

Certainly, there is no reason to be bored in Indiana. The twenty-five state parks offer scenic landscapes, while the museums are entertaining and educational. The Indianapolis Motor Speedway provides the spectacle of watching cars travel at nearly two hundred miles per hour. All three attractions are entertaining and inspiring.

The introduction contains a thesis statement.

Body paragraphs (Each paragraph has a topic sentence that supports the thesis statement.)

Concluding paragraph

1 Exploring

Before creating a final image, an artist takes the time to consider what to create. Similarly, before developing a draft, a writer needs to explore the topic.

LO 1 Define exploring.

What Is Exploring?

Have you ever been given a writing subject and then stared at the blank page, thinking, "I don't know what to write"? Well, it is not necessary to write a good paragraph or essay immediately. There are certain things that you can do to help you focus on your topic.

Understand Your Assignment

As soon as you are given an assignment, make sure that you understand what your task is. Answer the following questions about the assignment.

- How many words or pages should I write?
- What is the due date for the assignment?
- Are there any special qualities my writing should include?

After you have considered your assignment, follow the four steps in the exploring stage of the writing process.

▶ EXPLORING

STEP 1 **Think about your topic.** Determine what you will write about.

STEP 2 **Think about your audience.** Consider your intended readers and what interests them.

STEP 3 **Think about your purpose.** Ask yourself why you want to write.

STEP 4 **Try exploring strategies.** Experiment with different ways to generate ideas.

ESSAY LINK
When you plan an essay, you should follow the four exploring steps.

Topic

LO 2 Identify your topic.

Your **topic**, or **subject**, is what you are writing about. When an instructor gives you a topic for your writing, narrow the topic and find an angle that interests you. For example, if your instructor asks you to write about travel, you can take many approaches to the topic. You might write about the dangers of travel or explain what people can learn when they travel. Try to narrow the topic to suit your interests. When you think about your topic, ask yourself the following questions.

- ◆ What special knowledge do I have about the topic?
- ◆ What subtopics are most relevant to me?
- ◆ What aspect of the topic arouses my emotions?

Audience

LO 3 Identify your audience.

Your **audience** is your intended reader. Your audience might be your instructor, your classmates, your boss, your coworkers, and so on. Remember to adapt your language and vocabulary for a specific audience. For example, in a report written for your business class, you might use specialized accounting terms that would not be appropriate in an essay for your English class. When you think about your audience, ask yourself the following questions.

- ◆ Who will read my assignment? Will the reader be my instructor, or will other students also read it?
- ◆ What does my audience already know about the topic?
- ◆ What information will my readers expect?
- ◆ Should I use formal or informal language?

HINT ◀ Instructor as the Audience

Your instructor represents a general audience. Such an audience will expect you to use correct grammar and to reveal what you have learned or understood about the topic. Do not leave out information because you assume that your instructor is an expert in the field. Your ideas should be presented in a clear and organized manner.

Purpose

LO 4 Identify your purpose.

Your purpose is your reason for writing. Sometimes you may have more than one purpose. When you consider your purpose, ask yourself the following questions.

- ◆ Is my goal to **entertain**? Do I tell a personal story or anecdote?
- ◆ Is my goal to **persuade**? Do I convince the reader that my point of view is correct?
- ◆ Is my goal to **inform**? Do I explain something or present information?

> **HINT** ◅ **General and Specific Purpose**
>
> Your **general purpose** is to entertain, inform, or persuade. Your **specific purpose** is your more precise reason for writing. For example, imagine that you have to write about music. You can have the following general and specific purposes.
>
> General purpose: to inform
> Specific purpose: to explain how to become a better musician

PRACTICE 1

Read text messages A and B. Then answer the questions that follow.

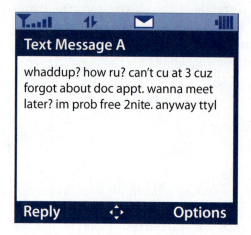
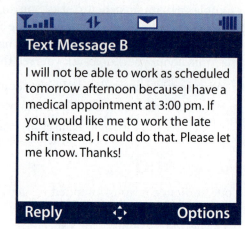

1. Who is the intended audience for text message A?
   _____ friend   _____ boss
   What language clues helped you determine the audience?

   _____

2. Who is the intended audience for text message B?
   _____ friend   _____ boss
   What language clues helped you determine the audience?

   _____

PRACTICE 2

Read each selection carefully. Underline any words or phrases that help you identify its source, audience, and purpose. Then answer the questions that follow each selection.

EXAMPLE: I'm totally <u>psyched</u> about learning the drums. It's taken me a while to get used to keeping up a steady beat, but I think I'm getting it. My drum teacher is <u>cool</u>, and he's <u>pretty patient</u> with me. I try to practice, but it bugs the neighbors when I hit the cymbals.

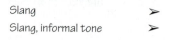

Slang   ➤
Slang, informal tone   ➤

What is the most likely source of this paragraph?

    a. Web site article   b. textbook   (c.) e-mail

What is its purpose? <u>To inform</u>

Who is the audience? <u>Friend or family member</u>

1. The nationalist movement in music was first felt in Russia, where music had been dominated entirely by foreign influence. Starting in the middle of the nineteenth century, Russian composers began to write operas in their own language, on Russian themes, and they often based their librettos on literary works by the great Russian writers of the time.

   What is the most likely source of this paragraph?

       a. short story   b. textbook   c. e-mail

   What is its purpose? _____

   Who is the audience? _____

2. When dealing with club managers, it is imperative that you act professionally. Get all the details of a gig in advance. Doing so will eliminate any confusion or miscommunication that could result in a botched deal. It will also instantly set you apart from the legions of flaky musicians that managers must endure on a daily basis. That's a good thing.

   What is the most likely source of this paragraph?

       a. Web site article   b. novel   c. e-mail

   What is its purpose? _____

   Who is the audience? _____

3. She brought a magazine out of her purse and paged through it, and then set it down on her lap. The music changed—some piano piece that seemed tuneless, for all the notes running up and down the scale, and the whisper of a drum and brushes. She looked at the magazine. Staring at a bright picture of little girls in a grass field, she remembered something unpleasant, and turned the page with an impatient suddenness that made him look over at her.

   What is the most likely source of this paragraph?

       a. short story   b. textbook   c. e-mail

   What is the purpose? _____

   Who is the audience? _____

PRACTICE 3

View the following cartoon. What is the topic? Who is the audience? What is the purpose? Does the cartoon achieve its purpose?

"Oh no, not homework again."

LO 5 Practice exploring strategies.

Exploring Strategies

After you determine your topic, audience, and purpose, try some **exploring strategies**—also known as **prewriting strategies**—to help get your ideas flowing. The four most common strategies are freewriting, brainstorming, questioning, and clustering. It is not necessary to do all of the strategies explained in this chapter. Find the strategy that works best for you.

You can do both general and focused prewriting. If you have writer's block and do not know what to write, use **general prewriting** to come up with possible topics. Then, after you have chosen a topic, use **focused prewriting** to find an angle of the topic that is interesting and that could be developed in your paragraph.

> ## HINT ◄ When to Use Exploring Strategies
>
> You can use exploring strategies at any stage of the writing process.
> - To find a topic
> - To narrow a broad topic
> - To generate ideas about your topic
> - To generate supporting details

Freewriting

Freewriting is writing for a limited period of time without stopping. The point is to record the first thoughts that come to mind. If you have no ideas, you can indicate that in a sentence such as "I don't know what to write." As you write, do not be concerned with your grammar or spelling. If you use a computer, let your ideas flow and do not worry about typing mistakes.

Sandra's Freewriting

College student Sandra Ahumada did freewriting about work. During her freewriting, she wrote everything that came to mind.

Work. I've only worked in a restaurant. Schedules are good for college students. Can work nights or weekends. Serving people so different from studying. You can relax your brain, go on automatic pilot. But you have to remember people's orders so it can be hard. And some customer are rude, rude, RUDE. In some jobs, you get tips in addition to the salary. Should people always tip servers?

Sandra's Focused Freewriting

After Sandra did her general freewriting, she underlined ideas that she thought could be expanded into a complete paragraph. Then she looked at her underlined ideas to decide which one to write about. Her purpose was to persuade, so she chose a topic that she could defend. She did focused freewriting about tipping.

> People should always tip in restaurants. Why. I dont earn a lot, so the tips are really important. I gotta lot a bills, and can't pay everything with minimum wage. What else? Diners should just consider the tip as a part of the cost of eating out. If they don't wanna tip, they should cook at home. Also, lots of other service people get tips and nobody cares. And bad service. It could be the cook's fault. We need those tips. Sure do.

THE WRITER'S DESK **Freewriting**

Choose one of the following topics and do some freewriting. Remember to write without stopping.

Stress   Nature   Sports

Brainstorming

Brainstorming is like freewriting except that you create a list of ideas, and you can take the time to stop and think when you create your list. As you think about the topic, write down words or phrases that come to mind. Do not be concerned about grammar or spelling. The point is to generate ideas.

Jin's Brainstorming

College student Jin Park brainstormed about health issues. He made a list of general ideas.

—lack of health care
—obesity
—fast food
—not enough exercise

Jin's Focused Brainstorming

Jin chose "not enough exercise" as his topic, and then he did focused brainstorming.

—video games, PlayStation
—parents worry about dangers on streets

—sports activities (e.g., football) cost a lot for fees, equipment, etc.

—too much sitting at school

—not enough physical education time

—need more community sports programs

THE WRITER'S DESK   Brainstorming

Choose one of the following topics and brainstorm. Create a list of ideas.

Ceremonies   Gossip   Good or bad manners

Questioning

Another way to generate ideas about a topic is to ask yourself a series of questions and write responses to them. The questions can help you define and narrow your topic. One common way to do this is to ask yourself *who, what, when, where, why,* and *how* questions. Like other exploring strategies, questioning can be general or focused.

Rachel's Questioning

College student Rachel Jubinville used a question-and-answer format to generate ideas about family.

What is a family?	—a unit of people tied by blood or legal documents
Can friends be considered like family?	—maybe long-time friends become part of an extended family
What are problems in families?	—abuse, bankruptcy, grudges, divorce, jealousy
How do families stay together?	—love, patience, withholding judgment, listening to each other, acceptance of differences
When can families connect the best?	—holidays, weddings, funerals, weekly dinners
Why is our family important?	—provides support and connection, helps during times of crisis

---

THE WRITER'S DESK   Questioning

Choose one of the following topics and write questions and answers. Ask *who, what, when, where, why,* and *how* questions.

Technology   Patriotism   Celebrities

Clustering

Clustering is like drawing a word map; ideas are arranged in a visual image. To begin, write your topic in the middle of the page and draw a box or a circle around it. That idea will lead to another, so write the second idea and draw a line connecting it to your topic. Keep writing, circling, and connecting ideas until you have groups, or "clusters," of them on your page. You can use clustering to get ideas about a general or a specific topic.

Mahan's Clustering

College student Mahan Zahir used clustering to explore ideas about crime. He identified some main topics.

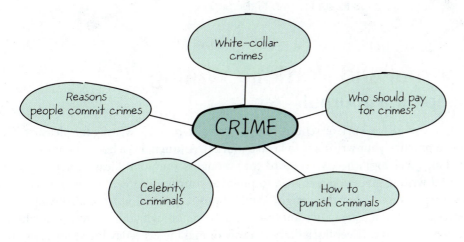

Mahan's Focused Clustering

Mahan decided to write about the reasons that people commit crimes. He added clusters to that topic.

THE WRITER'S DESK Clustering

Choose one of the following topics and use clustering to explore it on a separate sheet of paper. Begin by writing the key word in the middle of the space. Then connect related ideas.

Jobs   Health   Relationships

When you explore a topic using any of the listed strategies, keep in mind that a lot of the ideas you generate may not be useful. Later, when you develop your ideas, be prepared to cut irrelevant information.

LO 6 Practice journal and portfolio writing.

Journal and Portfolio Writing
Keeping a Journal

You may write for work or school, but you can also practice writing for pleasure. One way to practice your writing is to keep a journal. A **journal** is a book, a computer file, or a blog (Web log) where you record your thoughts, opinions, ideas, and impressions. Journal writing gives you a chance to practice your writing without worrying about your readers and what they might think about it. Journal writing also gives you a source of material when you want to write about a topic of your choice. According to author Anaïs Nin, "Keeping a diary is a way of making everyday life seem as exciting as fiction."

In your journal, you can write about any topic that appeals to you. Here are some topics for journal writing.

- reflections and feelings about your personal life, your career goals, your college courses, your past and future decisions, and your work
- your reactions to controversies in the world, in your country, in your state, in your city, or in your college
- facts that interest you
- your reflections on the opinions and philosophies of others, including your friends or people that you read about in your courses

Keeping a Portfolio

A **writing portfolio** is a binder or an electronic file folder where you keep samples of all of your writing. The reason to keep a portfolio is to have a record of your writing progress. In your portfolio, keep all drafts of your writing assignments. When you work on new assignments, review your previous work in your portfolio. Identify your main problems, and try not to repeat the same errors.

Reflect On It

Think about what you learned in this chapter. If you do not know an answer, review that topic.

1. Before you write, you should think about your topic, audience, and purpose. Explain what each one is.

   a. topic: _____

   b. audience: _____

   c. purpose: _____

2. Briefly define each of the following exploring styles.

a. freewriting: _____

b. brainstorming: _____

c. questioning: _____

d. clustering: _____

THE WRITER'S ROOM — MyWritingLab™

MyWritingLab™
Complete these writing assignments at mywritinglab.com

Writing Activity 1

Choose one of the following topics, or choose your own topic. Then generate ideas about the topic. You may want to try the suggested exploring strategy.

General Topics

1. Try freewriting about a strong childhood memory.
2. Try brainstorming about anger, listing any thoughts that come to mind.
3. Try clustering. First, write "music" in the middle of the page. Then write clusters of ideas that connect to the general topic.
4. Ask and answer some questions about online addictions.

College and Work-Related Topics

5. Try freewriting about a comfortable work environment. Include any emotions or other details that come to mind.
6. Try brainstorming about study habits. List any ideas that come to mind.
7. To get ideas, ask and answer questions about the best or worst jobs.
8. Try clustering about different types of customers. First, write "customers" in the middle of the page. Then write clusters of ideas that relate to the general topic.

Writing Activity 2

Look carefully at the poster on the following page. First, determine the topic, audience, and purpose. Whom is the poster trying to convince? What is the purpose? Is the purpose fulfilled? Then try exploring the topic. Use questioning as your exploring strategy. Ask and answer *who, what, when, where, why*, and *how* questions.

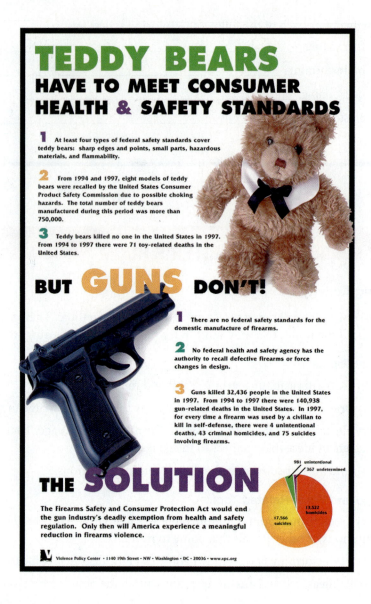

Exploring Checklist

As you explore your topics, ask yourself the following questions.

☐ What is my topic? (Consider what you will write about.)

☐ Who is my audience? (Think about your intended reader.)

☐ What is my purpose? (Determine your reason for writing.)

☐ How can I explore? (You might try freewriting, brainstorming, questioning, or clustering.)

Developing 2

After finding an idea, an artist begins to define shapes and layer on colors. Like an artist, a writer shapes ideas to create a solid paragraph or essay.

LO 1 Define developing.

ESSAY LINK
When you develop an essay, you follow similar steps. For details about essay writing, see Chapter 13.

What Is Developing?

In Chapter 1, you learned how to use exploring strategies to formulate ideas. In this chapter, you will focus on the second stage of the writing process: **developing**. There are five key steps in the developing stage.

▶ DEVELOPING

STEP 1 **Narrow your topic.** Focus on some aspect of the topic that interests you.

STEP 2 **Express your main idea.** Write a topic sentence that expresses the main idea of the paragraph (or a thesis statement that expresses the main idea of the essay).

STEP 3 **Develop your supporting ideas.** Find facts, examples, or anecdotes that best support your main idea.

STEP 4 **Make a plan.** Organize your main and supporting ideas, and place your ideas in a plan or an outline.

STEP 5 **Write your first draft.** Communicate your ideas in a single written piece.

Reviewing Paragraph Structure

Before you practice developing your paragraphs, review the paragraph structure. A **paragraph** is a series of related sentences that develop one central idea. Because a paragraph can stand alone or be part of a longer piece of writing, it is the essential writing model. You can apply your paragraph writing skills to longer essays, letters, and reports. A stand-alone paragraph generally has the following characteristics.

♦ A **topic sentence** states the topic and introduces the idea the writer will develop.
♦ **Body sentences** support the topic sentence.
♦ A **concluding sentence** ends the paragraph.

College student Tam Wang wrote the following paragraph. Notice how it is structured.

The topic sentence expresses the main idea. ➤

Greenwashing occurs when companies misleadingly promote themselves as environmentally friendly. Just as whitewashing means "to make something look better than it is," greenwashing is an attempt to look greener than one really is. Some greenwashers spend more money advertising their "green" qualities than actually doing ecological practices. For instance, an electronic device can be advertised as energy-efficient even though it contains hazardous materials. Oil companies promote eco-friendly corn ethanol even though its production is energy-intensive. Finally, some products have misleading labels with images of mountains and trees. Various household cleaners claim to be organic, but they were never tested by an impartial organization. **In short, greenwashers make use of vague and misleading marketing.**

Supporting sentences provide details and examples. ➤

The concluding sentence brings the paragraph to a satisfying close. ➤

HINT ◂ **Paragraph Form**

When you write a paragraph, make sure that it has the following form.

• Try to leave a margin of an inch to an inch and a half on each side of your paragraph.
• Always indent the first word of a paragraph. Put it about one inch, or five spaces, from the left-hand margin.

Indent first line ⟶   The legal drinking age is an ineffective deterrent to underage drinking.

⟵ 1-inch margins

LO 2 Narrow your topic.

Narrow the Topic

A paragraph has one main idea. If your topic is too broad, you might find it difficult to write only one paragraph about it. When you **narrow** your topic, you make it more specific. To narrow your topic, you can use exploring strategies such as freewriting, brainstorming, and questioning. These strategies are explained in more detail in Chapter 1, "Exploring." Review the following examples of general and narrowed topics.

General Topic	Narrowed Topic
The job interview	How to dress for a job interview
College	My misconceptions about college life
Rituals	The high school prom

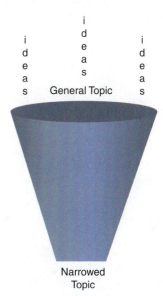

HINT ◄ Narrowing the Topic

One way to narrow your topic is to break it down into smaller categories.

Sports

Steroids in sports   Team sports   Dangerous sports

Sandra's Example of Narrowing a Topic

College student Sandra Ahumada practiced narrowing a topic by thinking of ideas about work.

—types of work: paid work, housework, homework

—jobs I have done in the service industry: server, cashier

—reasons to work in a restaurant

—how to find a job

—bad jobs that I have had

—are online job sites useful?

> **ESSAY LINK**
> An essay contains several paragraphs and can have a broader topic than a paragraph.

THE WRITER'S DESK   Narrow the Topic

Topics 1 to 5 are very broad. Practice narrowing topics by writing three ideas for each one.

EXAMPLE: Crime: *white-collar crime*

why people steal

types of punishment

1. Stress: _____

_____

_____

2. Gossip: _____

_____

_____

3. Nature: _____

_____

_____

4. Sports: _____

_____

_____

5. Jobs: _____

_____

_____

LO 3 Write your topic sentence.

> **ESSAY LINK**
> Just as a topic sentence expresses the main point of a paragraph, the thesis statement expresses the main point of an essay. Both have a controlling idea.

The Topic Sentence

After you have narrowed the topic of your paragraph, your next step is to write a topic sentence. The **topic sentence** has specific characteristics.

- It introduces the topic of the paragraph.
- It states the paragraph's controlling idea.
- It is the most general sentence in the paragraph.
- It is followed by other sentences that provide supporting facts and examples.

The **controlling idea** makes a point about the topic and expresses the writer's opinion, attitude, or feeling. You can express different controlling ideas about the same topic. For example, the following topic sentences are about youth offenders, but each sentence makes a different point about the topic.

narrowed topic   controlling idea
Youth offenders should not receive special treatment from the correctional system.

controlling idea   narrowed topic
Rehabilitation and education are the best ways for the state to handle **youth offenders**.

PRACTICE 1

Circle the topic and underline the controlling idea in each topic sentence.

EXAMPLE: Repair a water heater with three simple steps.

1. Physical education is essential in public schools.

2. There are three types of terrible bosses.

3. My furnished room has everything a student could need.

4. We had many problems during our camping trip.

5. Carolina Bomback has a very eccentric fashion style.

6. A serious problem in high schools is cyber bullying.

7. The Beatles went through many musical phases.

8. Learning to cook well requires practice, patience, and perseverance.

Identifying the Topic Sentence

Before you write topic sentences, practice finding them in paragraphs by other writers. To find the topic sentence of a paragraph, follow these steps.

◆ Read the paragraph carefully.

◆ Look for a sentence that sums up the paragraph's subject. Professional writers may place the topic sentence anywhere in the paragraph.

◆ After you have chosen a sentence, see if the other sentences in the paragraph provide evidence that supports that sentence.

If you find one sentence that sums up what the paragraph is about and is supported by other sentences in the paragraph, then you have identified the topic sentence.

PRACTICE 2

Underline or highlight the topic sentences in paragraphs 1, 2, and 3. Remember that the topic sentence is not always the first sentence in the paragraph.

EXAMPLE:

Clever marketers have manipulated the public to equate diamonds with wedding proposals. In the 1930s, the Oppenheimer family, which controlled the diamond trade, discovered large diamond deposits in South Africa. Before then, diamonds were valuable because they were rare. The family faced the problem of marketing a product that was no longer scarce. Using clever marketing techniques, such as the creation of the slogan "Diamonds are forever," the family entrenched the idea in people's minds that a wedding proposal should be accompanied with a diamond ring. Oppenheimer's company, De Beers, also paid film companies to include "diamond ring" wedding proposals in film scripts. The larger the diamond, the more a man expressed his love. Today, the average bride expects to receive a diamond ring, unaware that a diamond company created the tradition.

1.   The idea of controlling music in society has been around for a long time. About 2,400 years ago, the Greek philosopher Plato said that the types of music people listened to should be controlled by the state. During the Middle Ages and the Renaissance, it was the Church that specified how music should be composed and performed. And in later centuries, secular rulers held a virtual monopoly over the music that was allowed in their realm. Often, composers had to submit a work to a committee before it was allowed to be published or performed.

—Jeremy Yudkin, *Understanding Music*

2.   A ring, a ceremony, and a joyful notice in the newspaper once demonstrated the highlights of a romance, and the bitter lowlights were usually endured in the tearful intimacy of close friends. These days, however, in a culture permeated by social networking sites like Facebook, a simple click of a button can mark the beginning and end of a relationship. For instance, about a year ago, as Jamie Barone's relationship became serious, he had a discussion with his girlfriend about changing their relationship status from "single" to "in a relationship" on their Facebook profiles. Barone describes Facebook as a "billboard." The negative side of romance is also publicized. When Spencer

Raymond, twenty-six, changed his Facebook status to single, he inadvertently hurt his ex-girlfriend. She was barraged with phone calls from several of his four hundred online friends, an experience he says was uncomfortable for both of them. "Relationships are hard as it is," says Raymond. Facebook just "adds to the pain of a sensitive situation."

—Zunaira Zaki, "Love and Heartbreak on Facebook," *ABCNews.com*

3.   Imagine a society without laws. People would not know what to expect from one another (an area controlled by the law of contracts), nor would they be able to plan for the future with any degree of certainty (administrative law); they wouldn't feel safe knowing that the more powerful or better armed could take what they wanted from the less powerful (criminal law); and they might not be able to exercise basic rights which would otherwise be available to them as citizens of a free nation (constitutional law).

—Frank Schmalleger, *Criminal Justice Today*

Writing an Effective Topic Sentence

TECHNOLOGY LINK
If you write your paragraph on a computer, make your topic sentence bold (ctrl B). Then you and your instructor can easily identify it.

When you develop your topic sentence, avoid some common errors by asking yourself these three questions.

1. **Is my topic sentence a complete sentence that has a controlling idea?**
   You might state the topic in one word or phrase, but your topic sentence should always reveal a complete thought and have a controlling idea. It should not simply announce the topic.

Incomplete	Working in a restaurant.
	(This item gives a topic but is *not* a topic sentence. It does not contain both a subject and a verb, and it does not express a complete thought.)
Announcement	I will write about part-time jobs.
	(This sentence announces the topic but says nothing relevant about it. Do not use expressions such as *My topic is . . . or I will write about. . . .*)
Topic sentence	Part-time jobs help college students build self-esteem.

2. **Does my topic sentence make a valid and supportable point?**
   Your topic sentence should express a valid point that you can support with your evidence. It should not be a vaguely worded statement, and it should not be a highly questionable generalization.

Vague	Beauty is becoming more important in our culture.
	(Beauty is more important than what?)
Invalid point	Beauty is more important than it was in the past.
	(Is this really true? Cultures throughout history have been concerned with notions of beauty.)
Topic sentence	Fashion magazines do not provide readers with enough varied examples of beauty.

3. **Can I support my topic sentence in a single paragraph?**
   Your topic sentence should express an idea that you can support in a paragraph. It should not be too broad or too narrow.

   Too broad   Love is important.

   (It would be difficult to write a paragraph about this topic. There are too many things to say.)

   Too narrow   My girlfriend was born on March 2.

   (What more is there to say?)

   Topic sentence   During my first relationship, I learned a lot about being honest.

ESSAY LINK
If you find that your topic is too broad for a paragraph, you might want to save it so you can try using it for an essay.

HINT ◀ **Write a Clear Topic Sentence**

Your topic sentence should not express an obvious or well-known fact. When you clearly indicate your point of view, your topic sentence will capture your readers' attention and make your readers want to continue reading.

Obvious   Money is important in our world.
(Everybody knows this.)

Better   There are several effective ways to save money.

PRACTICE 3

Choose the word from the list that best describes the problem with each topic sentence. Correct the problem by revising each sentence.

Announces   Incomplete   Narrow
Broad   Invalid   Vague

EXAMPLE: This paragraph is about television advertisements.

Problem: _Announces_

Revision: _Television advertisements should be banned during children's programming._

1. I will write about negative political campaigns.

   Problem: _____ Revision: _____

2. Pollution is a big problem.

   Problem: _____ Revision: _____

3. Deciding to go to college.

   Problem: _____ Revision: _____

4. The subject of this paragraph is cyber bullying.

Problem: _____   Revision: _____

_____

5. Politicians are all liars.

Problem: _____   Revision: _____

_____

6. The campus coffee shop has red doors.

Problem: _____   Revision: _____

_____

PRACTICE 4

The following paragraphs do not contain topic sentences. Read the paragraphs carefully, and write appropriate topic sentences for each.

1. _____

_____

First, take shorter showers. Five minutes is enough time to get clean. Also, do the laundry only when there is a full load. When brushing your teeth, don't leave the water running. Just turn the water off and on as needed. Finally, ask your landlord to install toilets that use very little water. Remember that water is a precious resource.

2. _____

_____

First, art education teaches children to be creative thinkers. Early exposure to art promotes right-brain thinking. Also, art classes help children have a greater appreciation for the beauty that surrounds them daily. It helps them slow down and appreciate life. Above all, making art is fun. It provides a stress-free moment in a child's day.

THE WRITER'S DESK   Write Topic Sentences

Narrow each of the topics in this exercise. Then write a topic sentence that contains a controlling idea. You could look at the Writer's Desk: Narrow the Topic on page 17 for ideas.

EXAMPLE: Crime

Narrowed topic: Why people steal _____

Topic sentence: People steal for several reasons. _____

_____

1. Stress

   Narrowed topic: _____

   Topic sentence: _____

   _____

2. Gossip

   Narrowed topic: _____

   Topic sentence: _____

   _____

3. Nature

   Narrowed topic: _____

   Topic sentence: _____

   _____

4. Sports

   Narrowed topic: _____

   Topic sentence: _____

   _____

5. Jobs

   Narrowed topic: _____

   Topic sentence: _____

   _____

The Supporting Ideas

Once you have written a clear topic sentence, you can focus on the **supporting details**—the facts and examples that provide the reader with interesting information about the subject matter.

Generating Supporting Ideas

You can try an exploring strategy such as brainstorming or freewriting to generate ideas. Then you can choose the best ideas.

An effective paragraph has **unity** when all of its sentences directly relate to and support the topic sentence. Create a unified paragraph by selecting three or four ideas that are the most compelling and that clearly support your topic sentence. You may notice that several items in your list are similar; therefore, you can group them together. If some items do not support the topic sentence, remove them.

Mahan's Supporting Ideas

College student Mahan Zahir narrowed his topic and brainstormed a list of supporting ideas. Then he grouped similar ideas together and crossed out two items.

LO 4 Generate supporting ideas.

ESSAY LINK
When writing an essay, place the thesis statement in the introduction. Then each supporting idea becomes a distinct paragraph with its own topic sentence.

People steal for many reasons.

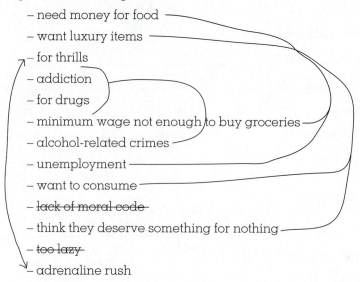

- need money for food
- want luxury items
- for thrills
- addiction
- for drugs
- minimum wage not enough to buy groceries
- alcohol-related crimes
- unemployment
- want to consume
- ~~lack of moral code~~
- think they deserve something for nothing
- ~~too lazy~~
- adrenaline rush

TECHNOLOGY LINK
On a computer, you can cut (ctrl X) and paste (ctrl V) similar ideas together.

HINT ◂ Identifying the Best Ideas

There are many ways that you can highlight your best ideas. You can circle the best supporting points and then use arrows to link them with secondary ideas. You can also use highlighter pens or asterisks (*) to identify the best supporting points.

PRACTICE 5

College student Romina Herrera brainstormed ideas about compulsory volunteer work. Her purpose was to persuade, so she created a topic sentence that expressed her opinion about the issue.

Underline the three ideas from her list that you think are the most compelling and that most clearly illustrate the point she is making in her topic sentence. Then group together any related ideas under each of the main subheadings. If any ideas do not relate to her topic sentence, cross them out.

Topic Sentence: Freshman high school students should be forced to do community service on weekends.

—in Haiti, youths helped rebuild houses after the earthquake

—during last year's floods, student volunteers could have helped in shelters

—can provide assistance in times of crisis

—some students are too lazy and don't want to help anyone else

—Miguel stopped littering after he cleared roadside garbage

—provides a chance to learn about real-world issues with the environment, poverty, etc.

—can gather food and clothing for the homeless

—some students need to earn money on weekends

—provides a character-building opportunity

—Kelsey developed empathy when she worked at the women's shelter

—need more shelters for battered women

—Ivan became more generous after working with the homeless

THE WRITER'S DESK   Generate Supporting Ideas

Choose two of your topic sentences from the Writer's Desk on page 22. For each topic sentence, develop a list of supporting ideas.

After you have two complete lists, choose the one that you find most interesting. Then group ideas together and cross out any ideas that are not useful.

> **ESSAY LINK**
>
> In an essay, you can use time, space, or emphatic order to organize your ideas.

Organizing Your Ideas

To make your ideas easy for your readers to follow, organize your ideas in a logical manner. You can use one of three common organizational methods: (1) time order, (2) emphatic order, or (3) space order.

Transitional expressions help guide the reader from one idea to another. A complete list of transitional expressions appears on pages 38–39 in Chapter 3.

Time Order

When you organize a paragraph using **time order (chronological order)**, you arrange the details according to the sequence in which they have occurred. When you narrate a story, explain how to do something, or describe a historical event, you generally use time order.

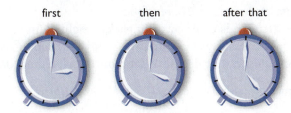

first   then   after that

Here are some transitional expressions you can use in time-order paragraphs.

after that	first	later	next
eventually	in the beginning	meanwhile	suddenly
finally	immediately	months after	then

The next paragraph is structured using time order.

> One day, some gentlemen called on my mother, and I felt the shutting of the front door and other sounds that indicated their arrival. Immediately, I ran upstairs before anyone could stop me to put on my idea of formal clothing. Standing before the mirror, as I had seen others do, I anointed my head with oil and covered my face thickly with powder. Then I pinned a veil over my head so that it covered my face and fell in folds down to my shoulders. Finally, I tied an enormous bustle round my small waist, so that it dangled behind, almost meeting the hem of my skirt. Thus attired, I went down to help entertain the company.
>
> —Helen Keller, *The Story of My Life*

Emphatic Order

When you organize the supporting details of a paragraph using **emphatic order**, you arrange them in a logical sequence. For example, you can arrange details from least to most important, from least appealing to most appealing, and so on.

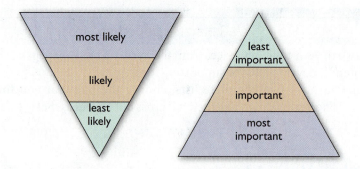

Here are some transitional expressions you can use in emphatic-order paragraphs.

above all	first	moreover	principally
clearly	in particular	most importantly	the least important
especially	last	of course	the most important

The following paragraph uses emphatic order. The writer presents the conditions from bad ones to the worst ones.

> The conditions experienced by the eager young volunteers of the Union and Confederate armies included massive, terrifying, and bloody battles, apparently unending, with no sign of victory in sight. First, soldiers suffered from the uncertainty of supply, which left troops, especially in the South, without uniforms, tents, and sometimes even food. They also endured long marches over muddy, rutted roads while carrying packs weighing fifty or sixty pounds. Most importantly, disease was rampant in their dirty, verminous, and unsanitary camps, and hospitals were so dreadful that more men left them dead than alive.
>
> —Adapted from John Mack Faragher et al., *Out of Many: A History of the American People*

HINT ‹ **Using Emphatic Order**

When you organize details using emphatic order, use your own values and opinions to determine what is most or least important, upsetting, remarkable, and so on. Another writer might organize the same ideas in a different way.

Space Order

When you organize ideas using **space order**, you help the reader visualize what you are describing in a specific space. For example, you can describe something or someone from top to bottom or bottom to top, from left to right or right to left, or from far to near or near to far.

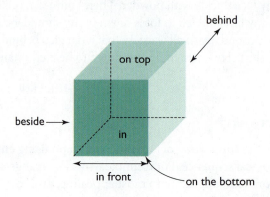

Here are some transitional expressions you can use in space-order paragraphs.

above	beneath	nearby	on top
behind	closer in	on the bottom	toward
below	farther out	on the left	under

In the next paragraph, the writer describes a location beginning at the beach and ending at the front of the house.

> Their house was even more elaborate than I expected. It was a cheerful red-and-white Georgian Colonial mansion overlooking the bay. The lawn started at the beach and ran toward the front door for a quarter of a mile, jumping over sundials and brick walks and burning gardens. Finally, when it reached the house, it drifted up the side in bright vines as though from the momentum of its run. The front was broken by a line of French windows.
>
> —F. Scott Fitzgerald, *The Great Gatsby*

PRACTICE 6

Read each paragraph and underline the topic sentence. Then decide what order the writer used: time, emphatic, or space order. Circle any words or phrases that help you make your choice.

1. After two months of work, I realized that my job selling a health drink was actually a pyramid scheme. In the beginning, I answered an online ad promising great money in sales. I went to the initiation meeting, and there were about twenty job seekers. Enthusiastic speakers spoke to us about the enormous amounts of money we would soon be earning. The next day, after a screening process, the recruiter claimed to choose the best candidates. I now realize that she chose everybody. Then, a week later, we were asked to invest $200 in our initial samples. "Sell your drinks and the money will start rolling in," the recruiter promised. We could also earn income by recruiting more salespeople. I was nervous, but I really needed the job, so I put almost all of my savings into those power drinks. After two months of unsuccessful sales, I understood that the only people making money were those at the top of the scheme.

    —Latonza Hines, student

    Order: _____

2. Many factors contribute to racist attitudes. First, there are often higher levels of racist incidents in societies that have historically had very little contact with different ethnic groups. According to the writer and political analyst Gwynne Dyer, such isolated societies may feel threatened when there is an influx of immigrants. Moreover, racist attitudes become more prevalent when various ethnic communities do not intermingle. If different cultural communities do not work and study together, stereotypes about other groups become entrenched. Most importantly, high levels of poverty contribute to racist reactions; immigrants become easy and available scapegoats when there is competition for limited jobs.

    —Eliot Mandel, student

    Order: _____

3.   Samuel Spade's jaw was long and bony, his chin a jutting v under the more flexible v of his mouth. His nostrils curved back to make another, smaller, v. His yellow-grey eyes were horizontal. The v motif was picked up again by thickish brows rising outward from twin creases above a hooked nose, and his pale brown hair grew down—from high flat temples—in a point on his forehead. He looked rather pleasantly like a blond satan.

—Dashiell Hammett, *The Maltese Falcon*

Order: _____

PRACTICE 7

Read the following topic sentences. Decide what type of order you can use to develop the paragraph details. Choose time, emphatic, or space order. (There may be more than one correct organizational method.)

EXAMPLE: Repair a water heater with three simple steps.   *time*

1.   Physical education is essential in public schools.   _____

2.   There are three types of terrible bosses.   _____

3.   My furnished room has everything a student could need.   _____

4.   We had many problems during our camping trip.   _____

5.   Carolina Bomback has a very eccentric fashion style.   _____

6.   A serious problem in high schools is cyber bullying.   _____

7.   The Beatles went through many musical phases.   _____

8.   Learning to cook well requires practice, patience, and perseverance.   _____

LO 5 Develop a paragraph plan.

The Paragraph Plan

A **plan** (or **outline**) of a paragraph is a map showing the paragraph's main and supporting ideas. To make a plan, write your topic sentence and then list supporting points and details. Remember to use time, emphatic, or space order to organize the supporting points. In a more formal outline, you can use letters and numbers to indicate primary and secondary ideas.

Mahan's Paragraph Plan

Mahan completed his paragraph plan. He narrowed his topic, wrote a topic sentence, and thought of several supporting details. Here is his paragraph plan.

Topic Sentence: People steal for many reasons.

> **Support 1:**   Poverty is a primary motivation for people to steal.
> **Details:**   —some people are unemployed
> —others work at low-paying jobs
> —need money for food, rent, clothing
> **Support 2:**   Some criminals are greedy.
> **Details:**   —want to live a life of luxury
> —crave jewels and nice cars
> —wish for a larger yacht or faster jet

ESSAY LINK
Make a plan when you write an essay. In essay plans, each supporting idea becomes a separate paragraph.

Support 3:	Some people steal due to drug or alcohol addictions.
Details:	—addicts steal to buy drugs
	—alcohol ruins good judgment
Support 4:	Some people steal for the kicks.
Details:	—experience the thrill
	—receive an adrenaline rush when stealing

HINT ◂ Adding Specific Details

When you prepare your paragraph plan, ask yourself if the details clearly support your topic sentence. If not, then you could add details to make your points stronger. For example, when Mahan first brainstormed a list of supporting details (page 24), he did not think of specific details to support his point about greed. In his paragraph plan, however, he added a few more details (larger yacht, faster jet) to make that point stronger and more complete.

THE WRITER'S DESK Write a Paragraph Plan

Look at the topic sentence and the organized list of supporting ideas that you created for the previous Writer's Desk exercises. Now, in the space provided, make a paragraph plan. Remember to include details for each supporting idea.

Topic sentence: _____

_____

Support 1: _____

Details: _____

_____

Support 2: _____

Details: _____

_____

Support 3: _____

Details: _____

_____

Writing the Concluding Sentence

A stand-alone paragraph may have a **concluding sentence** that brings it to a satisfactory close. There are several ways to write a concluding sentence.

- Restate the topic sentence in a new, refreshing way.
- Make an interesting final observation.
- End with a prediction, suggestion, or quotation.

ESSAY LINK
Essays end with a concluding paragraph. For more information, see pages 180–181.

HINT **Problems with Concluding Sentences**

To make an effective conclusion, avoid the following:

• Do not contradict your main point or introduce new or irrelevant information.

• Do not apologize or back down from your main points.

• Do not end with a rhetorical question. (A rhetorical question is a question that won't be answered, such as, "When will people stop texting while driving?")

For example, in Mahan's paragraph about crime, he should not end with a statement that questions or contradicts his main point.

Weak But nobody really understands why people break the law.
(This concluding sentence undermines the main point, which is that people steal for many reasons.)

Better Knowing why people steal may help social services and lawmakers deal with criminals more effectively.
(This prediction brings the paragraph to a satisfactory close.)

PRACTICE 8

The topic sentences in paragraphs 1 and 2 are underlined. For each paragraph, circle the letter of the most effective concluding sentence, and then explain why the other choice is not as effective.

EXAMPLE:

Games are not just for children. <u>Adults should exercise their brains by playing games.</u> Puzzles and games help keep a person's mind sharp, especially as the aging process occurs. According to the *New England Journal of Medicine*, seniors who play cards, do board games, and solve crossword puzzles can reduce their risks of developing dementia. Marcia Wilkins, a senior living in Arlington, Virginia, plays the addictive number game Sudoku and credits the game with helping her concentration skills.

a. However, do all adults have the time or energy to play games?

(b.) Ultimately, people need to exercise their brains as much as they exercise their bodies.

Why is the other choice not as effective?

Answer "a" is a rhetorical question that sends the paragraph

in a different direction.

1.   <u>Our state should insist that day care centers provide more flexible hours for families.</u> Today, in many families, both parents work outside the home. These parents do not necessarily work from nine to five. For example, nurses and factory employees work in shifts. It is important for these parents to have flexible day care. Also, many parents who are in the service and retail industries work on weekends. For these parents, it is important to have adequate child care facilities during their work hours.

a. The current hours of most day care centers do not meet the needs of a great number of families.

b. However, maybe day care owners do not want to open on nights and weekends.

Why is the other choice not as effective?

_____

2. <u>College students should find part-time jobs that require them to exercise</u> <u>different muscles.</u> If a business student spends hours sitting in front of a computer screen, then he should try to find a job that requires physical activity. If an engineering student has to do advanced calculus, then maybe her part-time job should allow her to rest her brain. Students who do a lot of solitary study could try to find jobs that allow them to interact socially.

a. Some college students should not take part-time jobs because they need to concentrate on their studies.

b. Humans need to do a variety of activities to be mentally and physically strong, so college students should keep that in mind when they look for work.

Why is the other choice not as effective?

_____

The First Draft

LO 6 Write the first draft.

After making a paragraph plan, you are ready to write your first draft, which is a very important step in the writing process. Your first draft includes your topic sentence, some supporting details, and a concluding sentence. It is okay if your first draft is incomplete or messy. Later, during the revising and editing stages, you can clarify your ideas and modify the organization of your paragraph.

Mahan's First Draft

Here is Mahan Zahir's first draft. You may notice that his paragraph has errors. He will correct these when he gets to the revising and editing stage of the process.

> People steal for many reasons. Poverty is a primary motivation for people to steal. Because some people are unemployed and others may be underemployed. They may not have enough money for food, clothing rent. Stealing money or food may be very tempting. As a means of survival. Criminals do fraud because they are greedy. In fact, some extremly wealthy people steal simply because they want to acquire a larger yacht or a more better jet. Another important reason that people engage in stealing is to pay for their addictions. Finally, people also steal for kicks. Criminals get an adrenaline rush when you outwit the cops.

THE WRITER'S DESK **Write Your First Draft**

In the previous Writer's Desk on page 29, you made a paragraph plan. Now use the plan's information to type or write your first draft paragraph.

Reflect On It

Think about what you have learned in this chapter. If you do not know an answer, review that topic.

1. What is a topic sentence? _____

_____

2. What is time order? _____

_____

3. What is emphatic order? _____

_____

4. What is space order? _____

_____

Are the following sentences true or false? Circle the best answer.

5. A paragraph has more than one main idea.   True   False

6. A paragraph's details support its topic sentence.   True   False

7. A paragraph can have several supporting ideas.   True   False

MyWritingLab™

Complete these writing assignments at mywritinglab.com

MyWritingLab™

THE WRITER'S ROOM

Writing Activity 1

In the Writer's Room in Chapter 1, "Exploring," you used various strategies to find ideas about the following topics. Select one of the topics and write a paragraph. Remember to follow the writing process.

General Topics

1. a childhood memory
2. anger
3. music
4. online addictions

College and Work-Related Topics

5. a comfortable work environment
6. study or work habits
7. college life
8. types of customers

Writing Activity 2

Choose a topic that you feel passionate about, and write a paragraph. Your topic could be an activity (painting, swimming, basketball) or an interest (music, politics). Your topic sentence should make a point about the topic.

Developing Checklist

As you develop your paragraph, ask yourself the following questions.

- ☐ Have I narrowed my topic?
- ☐ Does my topic sentence make a valid and supportable point about the topic?
- ☐ Is my topic sentence interesting?
- ☐ Does my paragraph focus on one main idea?
- ☐ Do the details support the topic sentence?
- ☐ Do the supporting details follow a logical order?
- ☐ Does my paragraph end in a satisfactory way?

3 Revising and Editing

LEARNING OBJECTIVES

LO 1 Define revising and editing. **(p. 34)**

LO 2 Revise for unity. **(p. 35)**

LO 3 Revise for adequate support. **(p. 36)**

LO 4 Revise for coherence. **(p. 38)**

LO 5 Revise for style. **(p. 41)**

LO 6 Edit for errors. **(p. 42)**

LO 7 Write a final draft. **(p. 44)**

The revising and editing stage of the writing process is similar to adding the finishing touches to an artwork. Small improvements can make the work more solid and complete.

LO 1 Define revising and editing.

What Are Revising and Editing?

After you have written the first draft of your paragraph, the next step in the writing process is to revise and edit your work. When you **revise**, you modify your writing to make it stronger and more convincing. To revise, read your first draft critically, looking for faulty logic, poor organization, or poor sentence style. Then you reorganize and rewrite your draft, making any necessary changes. When you **edit**, you proofread your final draft for errors in grammar, spelling, punctuation, and mechanics.

There are five key steps to follow during the revising and editing stage.

▶ REVISING AND EDITING

STEP 1 **Revise for unity.** Ensure that all parts of your work relate to the main idea.

STEP 2 **Revise for adequate support.** Determine that your details effectively support the main idea.

STEP 3 **Revise for coherence.** Verify that your ideas flow smoothly and logically.

STEP 4 **Revise for style.** Ensure that your sentences are varied and interesting.

STEP 5 **Edit for technical errors.** Proofread your work, and correct errors in grammar, spelling, mechanics, and punctuation.

Revise for Unity

Unity means that a paragraph has only one main idea. All of the sentences in the paragraph should support the topic sentence. A paragraph lacks unity if some sentences drift from the main idea or if the paragraph contains two main ideas. To check for unity, ensure that every sentence in the body of the paragraph relates to one main idea.

Paragraph Without Unity

In the next paragraph, the writer drifted away from her main idea. The highlighted sentences do not relate to the topic sentence. When they are removed, the paragraph has unity.

Every idea in a paragraph should move in the same direction just as the vehicles on this bridge need to move in the same direction to reach their destinations. There should be no forks in the road.

> **The United States should make voting mandatory.** Many past elections have seen less than 50 percent voter turnout. For democracy to work, citizens must vote. It is a person's civic duty. Mandatory voting will ensure that a majority of the population expresses its concerns about issues. Moreover, candidates would have to develop election platforms that appeal to many groups. Such groups would include the most vulnerable, like the very poor. In addition, political candidates would spend less on campaigns because the politicians would not need to mobilize voters. Of course, some people are not interested in politics. In fact, my friend Jimmy-Lee never votes. He thinks it is not worth it. Voting is important, and the government should make it compulsory.

◄ The writer took a detour here.

PRACTICE 1

Paragraphs 1 and 2 contain problems with unity. Underline the topic sentence of each paragraph. Then circle the letter that indicates the type of problem, and make any necessary changes to each paragraph to ensure that it has unity. You may have to cross out sentences that do not belong, or you may have to indicate the start of a new paragraph.

1.   Although parents and teachers often criticize the negative influence of video games on today's youth, such games may actually have a positive impact on young people. First, video games help people acquire important skills, such as problem solving, hand–eye coordination, and memory skills. With "Guitar Hero" or "Wii Sports," players improve these skills because the levels of games vary in difficulty. Also, video games improve players' social skills. Some video games, such as "Lara Croft" and "The Sims," teach players about leadership, friendship, and real-life rules. Lastly, video games are powerful tools to aid children who lack self-esteem. If a child attains a high level playing the "Tony Hawk's Motion" game, he or she may feel a sense of accomplishment. My friend Joe and I often play video games at the arcade. Yesterday, we played for two hours, and then we went to the park. Thus, parents and teachers should keep a balanced perspective about video games.

> **ESSAY LINK**
> When revising and editing your essay, check that the body paragraphs support the thesis statement. Also, ensure that each body paragraph has unity.

      a. Some sentences are off topic.   b. Paragraph contains two main ideas.

2.   Americans will benefit in many ways if the government raises the tax on junk food. First, a high tax rate will increase the price of items like chips and soda. Consumers will most likely have to limit the purchase of these products. By reducing their consumption of junk food, consumers will get fewer calories

from nutritionally empty food. People will eat better to replace the empty calories, which will lead to better health. Health problems like obesity and type 2 diabetes might be reduced in the general population. Healthier Americans will consume fewer resources in the health-care system. The government should also give tax rebates to people who participate in some physical exercise. People can join a gym or do an organized physical activity like tai chi for a tax credit. Exercise is one way Americans can be healthier. By encouraging citizens to engage in more exercise, the government will save money on healthcare.

    a. Some sentences are off topic.   b. Paragraph contains two main ideas.

LO 3 Revise for adequate support.

Revise for Adequate Support

A paragraph has **adequate support** when there are enough details and examples to make it strong, convincing, and interesting. The following paragraph attempts to persuade, but it does not have any specific details that make a strong point.

A bridge is built using several well-placed support columns. Like a bridge, a paragraph requires adequate support to help it stand on its own.

ESSAY LINK
When revising your essay, ensure that you have adequately supported the thesis statement. Also ensure that each body paragraph has sufficient supporting details.

Paragraph Without Adequate Support

    In the past, the entertainment industry stereotyped women as the weaker sex. However, women are now portrayed as tough and intelligent characters. Most comic books usually depicted males as superheroes. But comic books now embrace super heroines. Recent films have portrayed females as super heroines. Video games are also changing stereotypical gender roles. The image of women as the weaker sex in the entertainment media is definitely being redefined.

PRACTICE 2

When the preceding paragraph about female stereotypes in the entertainment media is expanded with specific details and examples, the paragraph becomes more convincing. Add details on the lines provided. You can do this practice alone or with a partner.

    In the past, the entertainment industry stereotyped women as the weaker sex. However, women are now portrayed as tough and intelligent characters. Most comic books usually depicted males as superheroes. For example, _____ and _____ fought creepy scoundrels. But comic books now embrace super heroines. One of the most famous female comic book heroines is _____. She is beautiful, but she can fight evil as well as any man. Furthermore, recent films have portrayed females as super heroines. In the movie, _____, the actress _____ plays a strong and intelligent character who outwits her opponents. Video games are also changing stereotypical gender roles. For example, _____ is a super sexy heroine who is strong, determined, and intelligent. She can overcome any obstacle in her way. The image of women as the weaker sex in the entertainment industry is definitely being redefined.

Avoiding Circular Reasoning

Circular reasoning means that a paragraph restates its main point in various ways but does not provide supporting details. The main idea goes in circles and never progresses. Avoid using circular reasoning by providing a clear, concise topic sentence and by supporting the topic sentence with facts, examples, statistics, and anecdotes.

Ariane's Paragraph

Ariane Kureishi wrote the following paragraph about the modern environmental movement. In the paragraph, she repeats her main point and does not provide any details to support her topic sentence.

Circular	Many groups work hard to protect the environment. Some groups focus on a broad range of issues. There are international environmental groups that protect certain wildlife. Other groups put their efforts into protecting oceans. It takes a lot of effort to protect the environment.

Circular reasoning in a paragraph is like a Ferris wheel. The main idea of the paragraph does not seem to progress.

In the second version of this paragraph, Ariane added specific examples to illustrate her main point.

Revised Paragraph	Many groups work hard to protect the environment. Some groups focus on a broad range of issues. For example, Greenpeace concentrates its efforts on a variety of causes, such as climate change and nuclear power. There are international environmental groups that protect certain wildlife. The World Wildlife Fund (WWF) works with both private citizens and governments to safeguard various species from extinction. Other groups put their efforts into protecting forests and oceans. The Rainforest Action Network (RAN) pressures corporations to act responsibly toward the environment. In 1987, RAN campaigned Burger King to stop buying beef from rainforest areas that were cleared for grazing animals. It takes a lot of effort from various sources to protect the environment.

PRACTICE 3

Paragraphs 1 and 2 use circular reasoning. Neither has specific evidence to support the topic sentence. List supporting examples for each paragraph. With numbers, indicate where you would place the supporting examples.

EXAMPLE:

American teenagers go through several rites of passage. These rites of passage **(1)** help the teenager navigate the transition from childhood to adulthood. Some rites of **(2)** passage are shared with the community. These rites are an important part of every youth's life.

Examples:	(1) The first date and the first kiss are important. The first job is also a special step.
	(2) During the high school prom, the community members gather together.

1. The percentage of Americans who shop online is growing for a number of reasons. People are buying a lot of items from Internet sites. All ages of people shop online, so online shopping will only increase.

Examples: _____

_____

_____

_____

_____

2. Having a summer job teaches adolescents some valuable life lessons. There are many situations that students will experience through a summer job that will help them navigate the adult world. So students should try to get some work knowledge before graduating.

Examples: _____

_____

_____

_____

_____

LO 4 Revise for coherence.

Just as bolts link pieces of a bridge, transitional expressions can link ideas in a paragraph.

Revise for Coherence

When you drive along a highway and you suddenly hit a pothole, that is an uncomfortable experience. Readers experience similar discomfort if they encounter potholes in a piece of writing. Make your writing as smooth as possible by ensuring that it has **coherence**: the sentences should flow smoothly and logically.

Transitional Expressions

Transitional expressions are linking words or phrases, and they ensure that ideas are connected smoothly. Here are some common transitional expressions.

> **ESSAY LINK**
> To create coherence in an essay, you can place transitional expressions at the beginning of each body paragraph.

Function	Transitional Word or Expression		
Addition	again also besides finally first (second, third)	for one thing furthermore in addition in fact last	moreover next then
Concession of a point	certainly even so	indeed no doubt	of course to be sure
Comparison and contrast	as well equally even so however	in contrast instead likewise nevertheless	on the contrary on the other hand similarly
Effect or result	accordingly as a result consequently	hence otherwise then	therefore thus

Function	Transitional Word or Expression		
Example	for example for instance in other words	in particular namely specifically	to illustrate
Emphasis	above all clearly first especially	in fact in particular indeed least of all	most important most of all of course particularly principally
Reason or purpose	for this purpose for this reason	the most impor- tant reason	

Space	above
	behind
	below
	beneath
	beside
	beyond
	closer in
		farther out
		inside
		near
		nearby
		on one side/on
		  the other side
		on the bottom
			on the left/right
			on top
			outside
			to the north/east/
			  south/west
			under

Summary or conclusion	in conclusion in other words in short generally	on the whole therefore thus	to conclude to summarize ultimately
Time	after that at that time at the moment currently earlier eventually first (second, etc.) gradually	immediately in the beginning in the future in the past later meanwhile months after now	one day presently so far subsequently suddenly then these days

HINT ◄ Use Transitional Expressions with Complete Sentences

When you add a transitional expression to a sentence, ensure that your sentence is complete. Your sentence must have a subject and a verb, and it must express a complete thought.

Incomplete For example, the rules posted on the wall.

Complete For example, the rules <u>were</u> posted on the wall.

> **GRAMMAR LINK**
> For more practice using transitions in sentences, see Chapter 17, "Compound Sentences," and Chapter 18, "Complex Sentences."

PRACTICE 4

The next paragraph contains eight transitional expressions that appear at the beginning of sentences. Underline each expression, and then indicate its purpose. The first one has been done for you.

    The McDonaldization of society—the standardization of everyday life—does not refer just to the robot-like assembly of food. <u>Indeed</u>, sociologist George Ritzer points out that this process is occurring throughout society—and it is transforming our lives. First, shopping malls offer one-stop shopping in controlled environments. In addition, travel agencies offer "package" tours. They will transport tourists to ten European capitals in fourteen days. All visitors experience the same hotels, restaurants, and other

spew: pour out

scheduled sites—and no one need fear meeting a "real" native. Similarly, news agencies **spew** out McNews—short, bland unanalytical pieces that can be digested between gulps of McShake or McBurgers. Moreover, our programmed education will eliminate the need for discussion of social issues. Accordingly, computerized courses will teach the same answers to everyone—the approved, "politically correct" ways to think about social issues. Likewise, mass testing will ensure that students **regurgitate** the programmed responses. Therefore, for good or bad, our lives are being McDonaldized, and the predictability of packaged settings seems to be our social destiny.

regurgitate: repeat

—James M. Henslin, *Sociology*

Transitional Expression	Function
1. Indeed	Emphasis
2.	
3.	
4.	
5.	
6.	
7.	
8.	

PRACTICE 5

Add appropriate transitional expressions to the following paragraph. Choose from the following list, and use each transitional word once. There may be more than one correct answer for each blank.

consequently	furthermore	on the other hand
for example	first	therefore

Workplace gossip has both positive and negative effects. _____, when two colleagues share secrets about others, that helps build trust and create intimacy. _____, in large organizations, gossip helps form small social groups that provide workplace support systems. _____, overly negative gossip can undermine employee morale. An employee who hears malicious gossip may suspect that he or she is also the subject of office chatter. _____, Latisha Bishop, an employee at CR Industries, says that she felt devastated when she realized that her coworkers were spreading information about her private life. _____, she seriously considered leaving her job. _____, when office workers gossip, they should try to do so without malice.

Revise for Style

When you revise for sentence **style**, you ensure that your paragraph has concise and appropriate language and sentence variety. You can ask yourself the following questions.

LO 5 Revise for style.

♦ Have I used a **variety of sentence patterns**? (To practice using sentence variety, see Chapter 19.)

♦ Have I used **exact language**? (To learn about slang, wordiness, and overused expressions, see Chapter 32.)

♦ Are my sentences **parallel in structure**? (To practice revising for parallel structure, see Chapter 22.)

Just as paint and lighting can make a bridge more beautiful, varied sentence style makes a paragraph more compelling.

Mahan's Revision

On page 31 in Chapter 2, you read the first draft of student Mahan Zahir's paragraph about crime. Look at his revisions for unity, support, coherence, and style.

People steal for many reasons. ~~Poverty~~ **First, poverty** is a primary motivation ⊲ Transition

for people to steal. Because some people are unemployed and others

may be underemployed. They may not have enough money for food,

clothing rent. Stealing money or food may be very tempting. As a means

of survival. Criminals ~~do~~ **perpetrate** fraud because they are greedy. In fact, some   ⊲ Transition (**Next,**)   ⊲ Better word

extremly wealthy people steal simply because they want to acquire a

For example, Bernie Madoff was found guilty of stealing from clients, he did not lack personal wealth.   ⊲ Specific example

larger yacht or a more better jet. Another important reason that people

According to the bureau of Justice Statistics, 68 percent of jailed inmates reported that their substance abuse problems contributed to there decisions to commit crimes.   ⊲ Add statistic

engage in stealing is to pay for their addictions. Finally, people also steal

for kicks. Criminals get an adrenaline rush when you outwit the ~~cops~~ **police**.   ⊲ Better word

Knowing the different reasons that people steal may help social workers and lawmakers deal with criminals more effectively.   ⊲ Add concluding sentence

---

HINT ⊳ Adding Strong Support

When you revise, look at the strength of your supporting details. Ask yourself the following questions.

- Are my supporting details interesting, and do they grab the reader's attention? Should I use more vivid words?

- Is my concluding sentence appealing? Could I end the paragraph in a more interesting way?

ESSAY LINK
You should revise your essays for style, ensuring that sentences are varied and parallel. Also, ensure that your language is exact.

PRACTICE 6

In Chapters 1 and 2, you saw examples of Sandra Ahumada's prewriting and planning. Now look at the first draft of Sandra's paragraph, and revise it for unity, support, and coherence. Also, ask yourself what you could do to enhance her writing style.

> Customers should always tip restaurant servers. Servers need tips to live. Their salary is very low. They depend on tips to pay for food, housing, and other necessities. They do not get benefits such as health insurance. If you do not like the service, remember that mistakes are not always the server's fault. Poor service could be the cook's fault. Sometimes there are not enough servers. I work as a server in a restaurant, I know how hard it is when customers leave bad tips. Always tip your restaurant server.

LO 6 Edit for errors.

GRAMMAR LINK
For more editing practice, see Chapter 37.

TECHNOLOGY LINK
Word processors have spelling and grammar checkers. Do not automatically choose the first suggestion for a correction. Make sure that suggestions are valid before you accept them.

Edit for Errors

When you **edit**, you reread your writing and make sure that it is free of errors. You focus on the language, and you look for mistakes in grammar, punctuation, mechanics, and spelling. There is an editing guide at the back of this book. It contains some common error codes that your teacher may use and provides you with a checklist to proofread your text.

Editing Tips

The following tips will help you proofread your work effectively.

- Put your writing aside for a day or two before you do the editing. Sometimes, when you have been working closely with a text, you might not see the errors.
- Begin your proofreading at any stage of the writing process. For example, if you are not sure of the spelling of a word while writing the first draft, you could either highlight the word to check later or immediately look up the word in the dictionary.
- Keep a list of your common errors in a separate grammar log, such as the one in Appendix 7. When you finish a writing assignment, consult your error list, and make sure that you have not repeated any of those errors. After each assignment has been corrected, you can add new errors to your list.

Mahan's Edited Paragraph

Mahan Zahir edited his paragraph about crime. He corrected errors in spelling, capitalization, punctuation, and grammar.

> People steal for many reasons. First, poverty is a primary motivation for people to steal. Because some people are unemployed and others

, they
may be underemployed. ~~They~~ may not have enough money for food,

, and
clothing rent. Stealing money or food may be very tempting. ~~As~~ a
                                                              as

means of survival. Next, criminals perpetrate fraud because they are

extremely
greedy. In fact, some ~~extremly~~ wealthy people steal simply because

faster
they want to acquire a larger yacht or a ~~more better~~ jet. For example,

. He
Bernie Madoff was found guilty of stealing from clients~~,~~ ~~he~~ did not lack

personal wealth. Another important reason that people engage in

B
stealing is to pay for their addictions. According to the ~~b~~ureau of Justice

Statistics, 68 percent of jailed inmates reported that their substance

their
abuse problems contributed to ~~there~~ decisions to commit crimes. Finally,

they
people also steal for kicks. Criminals get an adrenaline rush when ~~you~~

outwit the police. Knowing the different reasons that people steal may

help social workers and lawmakers deal with criminals more effectively.

THE WRITER'S DESK **Revise and Edit**

Choose a paragraph you wrote for Chapter 2, or choose one that you have written for another assignment. Carefully revise and edit the paragraph. You can refer to the Revising and Editing Checklist at the end of this chapter.

Peer Feedback

After you write a paragraph or essay, it is useful to get peer feedback. Ask another person, such as a friend, family member, or fellow student, to read your work and make suggestions for addressing its weaknesses.

HINT **Offer Constructive Criticism**

When you peer-edit someone else's writing, try to make your comments useful. Phrase your comments in a positive way. Look at these examples.

Instead of saying …	**You could say …**
Your sentences are boring.	Maybe you could combine some sentences.
Your supporting ideas are weak.	You could add more details here.

You can use the following peer feedback form to evaluate written work.

Peer Feedback Form

Written by: _____   Feedback by: _____

Date: _____

1. What is the main point of the written work?

   _____

2. What details effectively support the topic sentence?

   _____

   _____

3. What, if anything, is unclear or unnecessary?

   _____

   _____

4. Give some suggestions about how the work could be improved.

   _____

   _____

5. What is an interesting or unique feature of this written work?

   _____

   _____

LO7 Write a final draft.

Write the Final Draft

When you have finished making revisions on the first draft of your paragraph, write the final draft. Include all of the changes that you have made during the revision and editing phases. Before you hand in your final draft, proofread it one last time to ensure that you have caught any errors.

THE WRITER'S DESK Write Your Final Draft

You have developed, revised, and edited your paragraph. Now write the final draft. Before you offer it to readers, proofread it one last time to ensure that you have found all of your errors.

HINT ▸ Spelling, Grammar, and Vocabulary Logs

- **Keep a spelling and grammar log.** You probably repeat, over and over, the same types of grammar and spelling errors. You will find it very useful to record your repeated grammar mistakes in a spelling and grammar log. You can refer to your list of spelling and grammar mistakes when you revise and edit your writing.

- **Keep a vocabulary log.** Expanding your vocabulary will be of enormous benefit to you as a writer. In a vocabulary log, you can make a list of unfamiliar words and their definitions.

See Appendix 7 for more information about spelling, grammar, and vocabulary logs.

Reflect On It

Think about what you have learned in this chapter. If you do not know an answer, review that topic.

1. What are four things that you should look for when revising?

   _____   _____

   _____   _____

2. Circle the best answer(s). A paragraph is unified if
   a. there are no irrelevant supporting details.
   b. there are many facts and statistics.
   c. all details support the topic sentence.

3. Circle the best answer: Transitional words are _____ that help ideas flow in a logical manner.
   a. links   b. sentences   c. verbs

4. The Editing Handbook in Part IV includes information about grammar, spelling, and punctuation errors. In what chapter would you find information about the following topics? Look in the table of contents to find the chapter number.

   a. capitalization   _____

   b. subject–verb agreement   _____

   c. faulty parallel structure   _____

   d. commas   _____

   e. commonly confused words   _____

MyWritingLab™

THE WRITER'S ROOM

Writing Activity 1

Choose a paragraph that you have written for your job or for another course. Revise and edit that paragraph, and then write a final draft.

Writing Activity 2

Choose any of the following topics, or choose your own topic. Then write a paragraph. Remember to follow the writing process.

General Topics

1. interesting things about yourself
2. heroes in the media
3. a risky adventure
4. bad service

College and Work-Related Topics

5. something you learned in a college course or on campus
6. reasons to change jobs
7. telemarketing
8. an interesting job

Revising and Editing Checklist

When you revise and edit, ask yourself the following questions. (For a more detailed editing checklist, refer to the inside back cover of this book.)

Unity

☐ Is my paragraph unified under a single topic?

☐ Does each sentence relate to the topic sentence?

Support

☐ Does my paragraph have an adequate number of supporting details?

Coherence

☐ Is my paragraph logically organized?

☐ Do I use transitional words or expressions to help the paragraph flow smoothly?

Style

☐ Do I use a variety of sentence styles?

☐ Is my vocabulary concise?

☐ Are my sentences parallel in structure?

Editing

☐ Do my sentences contain correct grammar, spelling, punctuation, and mechanics?

Part II

Paragraph Patterns

What Is a Paragraph Pattern? A *pattern* or *mode* is a method used to express one of the three purposes: to inform, to persuade, or to entertain. Once you know your purpose, you will be able to choose which writing pattern or patterns can help you to express it.

Patterns can overlap, and it is possible to use more than one pattern in a single piece of writing. For example, imagine you are writing a paragraph about bullying, and your purpose is to inform the reader. You might use *definition* as your predominant pattern, but in the supporting details, you might use *comparison and contrast* to compare a bully and a victim. You might also use *narration* to highlight an incident in which a bully harassed a victim.

Before you work through the next chapters, review the paragraph patterns.

CHAPTER 4
▶ **ILLUSTRATION**

To illustrate or prove a point using specific examples

CHAPTER 5
▶ **NARRATION**

To narrate or tell a story about a sequence of events that happened

CHAPTER 6
▶ **DESCRIPTION**

To describe using vivid details and images that appeal to the reader's senses

CHAPTER 7
▶ **PROCESS**

To inform the reader about how to do something, how something works, or how something happened

CHAPTER 8
▶ **DEFINITION**

To define or explain what a term or concept means by providing relevant examples

CHAPTER 9
▶ **CLASSIFICATION**

To classify or sort a topic's qualities to help readers better understand the topic.

CHAPTER 10
▶ **COMPARISON AND CONTRAST**

To present information about similarities (compare) or differences (contrast)

CHAPTER 11
▶ **CAUSE AND EFFECT**

To explain why an event happened (the causes) or what the consequences of the event were (the effects)

CHAPTER 12
▶ **ARGUMENT***

To argue or to take a position on an issue and offer reasons for your position

*Argument is included as one of the nine patterns, but it is also a purpose in writing.

Illustration 4

LEARNING OBJECTIVES

LO 1 Define illustration. (p. 50)

LO 2 Explain how to write an illustration paragraph. (p. 50)

LO 3 Explore topics. (p. 52)

LO 4 Identify the topic sentence of an illustration paragraph. (p. 52)

LO 5 Identify the supporting details of an illustration paragraph. (p. 53)

LO 6 Develop an illustration paragraph plan. (p. 54)

LO 7 Write the first draft of an illustration paragraph. (p. 55)

LO 8 Revise and edit an illustration paragraph. (p. 56)

Travel agencies use examples of attractions to sell tour packages. In illustration writing, you give examples to support your point of view.

WRITERS' EXCHANGE

Work with a team of two or three other students. List at least five examples of each part of speech. Include only words that begin with the letters *H* or *S*. Do as many as you can in two minutes.

Noun   Verb   Adjective   Pronoun

▶ **EXPLORING**

LO 1 Define illustration.

What Is Illustration?

When you write using **illustration**, you include specific examples to clarify your main point. You illustrate, or give examples, any time you want to explain, analyze, narrate, or give an opinion about something. As a writer, you can use many different types of examples to help your reader acquire a deeper and clearer understanding of your subject. You can include personal experience or factual information, such as a statistic.

You give examples every day. When telling a friend why you had a good day or a bad day, you might use examples to make your story more interesting. At college, you might give an oral presentation using examples that will help your audience better understand your point. At work, you might give examples to show clients where or how they might market their products.

ILLUSTRATION **AT WORK**

Patti Guzman is a registered nurse at a large hospital. She was invited to speak to nursing students at a local university. In the following excerpt from her speech, she gives examples to explain why a nurse must be in good physical health.

The topic sentence expresses the main idea.

Supporting sentences provide details and examples.

The concluding sentence brings the paragraph to a satisfying close.

Physically, the job of a nurse is demanding. On a daily basis, we must lift patients and move them. When patients are bedridden for prolonged periods, we must change their positions on their beds. When new patients arrive, we transfer them from stretchers to beds or from beds to wheelchairs. If patients fall, we must be able to help them stand up. If patients have difficulty walking, we must assist them. Patients who have suffered paralysis or stroke need to be lifted and supported when they are bathed and dressed. Keep in mind that some patients may be quite heavy, so the job requires a good level of physical strength.

LO 2 Explain how to write an illustration paragraph.

The Illustration Paragraph

There are two ways to write an illustration paragraph.

ESSAY LINK
You can develop illustration essays with a series of examples or extended examples.

◆ **Use a series of examples** to illustrate your main point. For example, if you are writing a paragraph about an innovative teacher that you had, you might list things that the teacher did such as wear a costume, let students teach parts of the course, and use music to make a point.

◆ **Use an extended example** to illustrate your main point. The example can be an anecdote or a description. For example, in a paragraph about creativity, you might describe a time when you tried to make a sculpture.

PRACTICE 1

Read the next paragraph and answer the questions.

Digital home technology is rapidly invading our lives. In Japan, Toto Ltd. has manufactured the Intelligent Toilet. This digital lavatory measures blood sugar, blood pressure, and obesity. It also carries out urine analysis, which tracks hormone levels. The toilet, which is hooked up to a home computer, allows users to graph personal health trends. Furthermore, engineers are developing touch-screen technology for doorknobs, furniture, and appliances. They respond to different touches and are programmed to react. Disney researcher scientist Ivan Poupyrev says that a postman can touch the doorknob with three fingers and record a message. Moreover, the Smart Home system by Rogers Communications allows homeowners to synchronize lighting systems, carbon monoxide sensors, and alarms to their smartphones to get instant alerts. Setting up a digital home is likely to become easier and cheaper in the near future.

—"Digital Life" by Julia Johnson

1. Underline the topic sentence of this paragraph. (The topic sentence expresses the main idea of the paragraph.)

2. What type of illustration paragraph is this? Circle the better answer.

   a. a series of examples   b. an extended example

3. List the examples that the writer gives to illustrate her point.

_____

_____

_____

_____

_____

_____

_____

PRACTICE 2

Read the next paragraph and answer the questions.

Online chatting is one way that computer viruses can be spread. For example, my friend Chelsea met someone online. She thought her new acquaintance was a polite, well-behaved young man who was a few years older than she was. They exchanged pictures at his request. However, the file he sent via e-mail was actually a virus. He was able to control my friend's computer through his screen. Later, using Chelsea's name, he sent threatening messages to others in chatrooms. He could even open and close my friend's disk drawer through clicking on the Eject button on her screen. Of course, Chelsea was terrified. She was only able to get rid of the virus with the help of a computer specialist.

—Nancy A. Ghaley, student

1. Underline the topic sentence.

2. What does the writer use to present her supporting details? Circle the best answer.

   a. a series of examples   b. an extended example

3. What example(s) does the writer give to illustrate her point?

_____

4. What are the main events in the narrative? List them.

_____

_____

_____

_____

_____

_____

LO 3 Explore topics.

Explore Topics

In the Warm Up, you will try an exploring strategy to generate ideas about different topics.

THE WRITER'S DESK   Warm Up

Think about the following questions, and write the first ideas that come to your mind. Try to think of two to three ideas for each topic.

EXAMPLE: What are some symbols of a child's transition into adolescence?

getting a driver's license

dating

celebrating a birthday

1. What are some types of body art?

_____

_____

2. What are some traits of an effective leader?

_____

_____

3. What are some qualities that you look for in a mate?

_____

_____

_____

LO 4 Identify the topic sentence of an illustration paragraph.

ESSAY LINK

In an illustration essay, the thesis statement expresses the controlling idea.

▶ **DEVELOPING**

The Topic Sentence

The topic sentence of the illustration paragraph is a general statement that expresses both your topic and your controlling idea. To determine your controlling idea, think about what point you want to make.

topic   controlling idea
Part-time jobs teach students valuable skills.

controlling idea   topic
Our father overreacted **when my sister started dating**.

THE WRITER'S DESK   **Write Topic Sentences**

Write a topic sentence for each of the following topics. You can look for ideas in the previous Writer's Desk. Remember to narrow your topic. Each topic sentence should contain a general statement that expresses both your topic and your controlling idea.

EXAMPLE: Topic: Symbols of a child's transition into adolescence

Topic sentence: In the United States, many important rites and rituals symbolize a child's transition into adolescence.

1. Topic: Types of body art

    Topic sentence: _____

    _____

2. Topic: Traits of an effective leader

    Topic sentence: _____

    _____

3. Topic: Qualities you look for in a mate

    Topic sentence: _____

    _____

The Supporting Ideas

LO 5 Identify the supporting details of an illustration paragraph.

After you have developed an effective topic sentence, generate supporting ideas. In an illustration paragraph, you can give a series of examples or an extended example.

When you use a series of examples, you can arrange your examples in emphatic order. Emphatic order means that you can place your examples from the most to the least important or from the least to the most important. If you use an extended example, you can arrange your ideas using time order.

Visualizing Illustration
PRACTICE 3

Brainstorm supporting ideas for the following topic sentence. Give examples of how people risk their lives.

Topic Sentence: Some workers risk their lives daily.

window washer

electrician

fisher

police officer

THE WRITER'S DESK   Generate Supporting Ideas

Generate some supporting examples under each topic. Make sure your examples support the topic sentences that you wrote for the previous Writer's Desk.

EXAMPLE:

Symbols of a child's transition into adolescence

- celebrating a birthday

- having more responsibilities

- becoming interested in

  a romantic partner

2. Traits of an effective leader

_____

_____

_____

_____

1. Body art

_____

_____

_____

_____

3. Qualities you look for in a mate

_____

_____

_____

_____

LO 6 Develop an illustration paragraph plan.

The Paragraph Plan

A paragraph plan helps you organize your topic sentence and supporting details before you write a first draft. When you write a paragraph plan, make sure that your examples are valid and relate to the topic sentence. Also include details that will help clarify your supporting examples. Organize your ideas in a logical order.

Topic Sentence: In the United States, many important rites and rituals symbolize a child's transition into adolescence.

ESSAY LINK

In an illustration essay, place the thesis statement in the introduction. Then, structure the essay so that each supporting idea becomes a distinct paragraph with its own topic sentence.

Support 1: Celebrating a birthday signals a child's entry into adolescence.

Details: —Jewish American boys and girls celebrate bar mitzvahs and bat mitzvahs.

—Mexican American girls celebrate quinceaneras.

Support 2: Teenagers often look for more responsibilities to show that they are no longer children.

Details: —At sixteen years old, many teens get a driver's license.

—Many people get their first job during their teen years.

Support 3: Some adolescents become interested in a romantic partner.

Details: —Teenagers start to date.

THE WRITER'S DESK **Write a Paragraph Plan**

Choose one of the topic sentences that you wrote for the previous Writer's Desk. Write a paragraph plan using some of the supporting ideas that you have generated. Include details for each supporting idea.

Topic sentence: _____

_____

Support 1: _____

Details: _____

_____

Support 2: _____

Details: _____

_____

Support 3: _____

Details: _____

_____

The First Draft

LO 7 Write the first draft of an illustration paragraph.

After you outline your ideas in a plan, you are ready to write the first draft. Remember to write complete sentences. You might include transitional words or expressions to help your ideas flow smoothly.

Transitional Words and Expressions

Transitional expressions can help you introduce an example or show an additional example. The following transitional words are useful in illustration paragraphs.

To Introduce an Example		To Show an Additional Example	
for example	namely	also	in addition
for instance	specifically	first (second, etc.)	in another case
in other words	to illustrate	furthermore	moreover

THE WRITER'S DESK   **Write the First Draft**

For the previous Writer's Desk, you developed a paragraph plan. Now write the first draft of your illustration paragraph. Before you write, carefully review your paragraph plan and make any necessary changes.

▶ **REVISING AND EDITING**

LO 8 Revise and edit an illustration paragraph.

Revise and Edit an Illustration Paragraph

When you finish writing an illustration paragraph, review your work and revise it to make the example(s) as clear as possible to your readers. Check to make sure that the order of ideas is logical, and remove any irrelevant details. Before you work on your own paragraph, practice revising and editing a student paragraph.

PRACTICE 4

Read the next student paragraph, and answer the questions.

> In the United States, many important rites and rituals symbolize a child's transition into adolescence. Celebrating a birthday often symbolizes entry into adolescence. For example, Jewish American boys and girls celebrate bar mitzvahs and bat mitzvahs. And Mexican American girls quinceaneras. Some teenagers look forward to their sweet-sixteen parties. In addition, teenagers often look for more responsibilities to show that they are no longer children. At sixteen years old, a teenager may get their driver's license. A teen may also get a first job during this period. Furthermore, some adolescents become interested in a romantic partner. Teenagers start dating. Such rites of passage are important markers of adolescence.
>
> —Rafael Castillo, student

Revising

1. Underline the topic sentence.

2. What type of illustration paragraph is this?

    a. a series of examples   b. an extended example

3. List the main supporting points.

    _____

    _____

    _____

4. What is the purpose of this paragraph?

    a. to persuade   b. to entertain   c. to inform

Editing

5. Underline a pronoun error. Write your correction in the space below.

   Correction: _____

6. This paragraph contains a fragment, which is an incomplete sentence. Underline the fragment. Then correct it in the space below.

   Correction: _____

GRAMMAR LINK
See the following chapters for more information about these grammar topics:
Pronouns, Chapter 29
Fragments, Chapter 20

GRAMMAR HINT Writing Complete Sentences

A fragment is an incomplete sentence. When you give an example, make sure that your sentence is complete. Avoid fragment errors.

Fragment For example, too many parties.

Correction For example, some students go to too many parties.

THE WRITER'S DESK Revise and Edit Your Paragraph

Revise and edit the paragraph that you wrote for the previous Writer's Desk. Make sure that your paragraph has unity, adequate support, and coherence. Also, correct any errors in grammar, spelling, punctuation, and mechanics.

VOCABULARY BOOST

Avoid Repetition

Read through the first draft of your paragraph, and identify some words that you frequently repeat. Replace those words with synonyms.

Reflect On It

Think about what you have learned in this chapter. If you do not know an answer, review that topic.

1. In an illustration paragraph, you _____

2. There are two ways to write illustration paragraphs. Explain each of them.

   a. Using a series of examples: _____

   b. Using an extended example: _____

3. List three transitional expressions that indicate an additional idea.

   _____

MyWritingLab™

Complete these writing assignments at mywritinglab.com

**WRITING LINK
MORE ILLUSTRATION
WRITING TOPICS**

Chapter 16, Writer's Room
    topic 1 (page 262)
Chapter 17, Writer's Room
    topic 1 (page 274)
Chapter 20, Writer's Room
    topic 1 (page 304)
Chapter 25, Writer's Room
    topic 1 (page 356)
Chapter 28, Writer's Room
    topic 1 (page 391)

**READING LINK
MORE ILLUSTRATION
READINGS**

"Comics As Social
    Commentary" by
    Nicolas Slayton
    (page 190)
"Guy Chores" by Tom
    Keenan (page 192)
"Why We Make Mistakes"
    by Joseph Hallinan
    (page 534)
"The Beeps" by Josh
    Freed (page 548)

MyWritingLab™   **THE WRITER'S ROOM**

Writing Activity 1: Topics

Choose any of the following topics, or choose your own topic. Then write an illustration paragraph.

General Topics

1. important historical events
2. great things in life that are free
3. mistakes parents make
4. hobbies
5. positive personality traits

College and Work-Related Topics

6. pressures faced by college students
7. qualities that help you succeed
8. office etiquette
9. qualities of a good instructor
10. tools or equipment needed for your job

Writing Activity 2: Media Writing

Watch a popular television show or movie that deals with students in a high school or college setting. Examples are the *American Pie* movies, *High School Musical*, or television programs such as *Glee*, *The Hills*, or *Gossip Girl*. You can even go on YouTube and type "peer pressure" into the search bar, and then watch some of the segments. Write a paragraph about the show, movie, or video segment and explain the ways that characters feel peer pressure. Provide several examples.

Illustration Paragraph Checklist

After you write your illustration paragraph, review the checklist on at the back of the book. Also ask yourself the following questions.

☐ Does my topic sentence make a point that can be supported with examples?

☐ Does my paragraph contain sufficient examples that clearly support the topic sentence?

☐ Do I use transitions to smoothly connect my examples?

☐ Have I arranged my examples in a logical order?

Narration 5

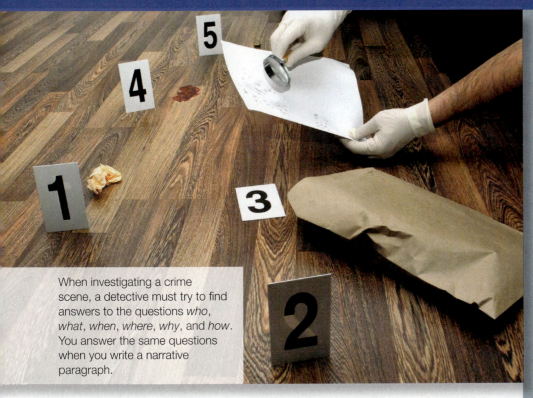

When investigating a crime scene, a detective must try to find answers to the questions *who, what, when, where, why,* and *how.* You answer the same questions when you write a narrative paragraph.

WRITERS' EXCHANGE

Work in a team of at least three students. First, choose a fairy tale to retell in an updated way. Next, one team member begins by saying one sentence. Then, another team member adds a sentence to the tale. Team members continue to take turns until the story is complete.

Example: Yesterday, a young woman wearing a red baseball cap decided to visit her grandmother.

LO 1 Define narration.

What Is Narration?

When you **narrate**, you tell a story about what happened. You generally explain events in the order in which they occurred, and you include information about when they happened and who was involved in the incidents.

You use narration every day. You may write about the week's events in your personal journal, or you might send a postcard to a friend detailing what you did during your vacation. At college, you may explain what happened during a historical event or what happened in a novel that you have read. At work, you might use narration to explain an incident involving a customer or coworker.

Narration is not only useful on its own; it also enhances other types of writing. For example, Jason must write an argument essay about youth crime. His essay will be more compelling if he includes a personal anecdote about the time a gang of youths attacked him in a subway station. In other words, narration can provide supporting evidence for other paragraph or essay patterns.

NARRATION **AT WORK**

Joseph Roth, a boiler and pressure vessel inspector, used narrative writing in a memo he wrote to his supervisor.

The topic sentence expresses the main idea.

As you know, I recently inspected the boiler and pressure vessels in the refinery on Highway 11, and I had a few problems that I would like to mention. When I first arrived, the manager of the unit was uncooperative and initially tried to stop me from examining the boiler! After much discussion, I was finally permitted into the boiler room, where I noticed several defects in the operation and condition of the equipment. Immediately, I saw that the low-water fuel cutoff chamber was filled with sludge and could not possibly function properly. Then I realized that the boiler heating surfaces were covered with scale. Finally, I found stress cracks in the tube ends and in tube seats. This is a sure sign of caustic embrittlement, which makes the boiler unsafe to operate and in danger of exploding. I have asked that the boiler be taken out of service immediately. We must follow up to make sure that measures are being taken to replace the boiler.

Supporting sentences provide details and examples.

The concluding sentence brings the paragraph to a satisfying close.

The Narrative Paragraph

There are two main types of narrative paragraphs.

1. **Use first-person narration (autobiography).**

   In first-person narration, you describe a personal experience from your point of view. You are directly involved in the story. You use the words *I* (first-person singular) or *we* (first-person plural). For example: "When I was a child, I thought that the world began and ended with me. I didn't know, or care, how other children felt. Thus, when schoolmates ridiculed a shy boy, I gleefully joined in."

LO 2 Explain how to write a narrative paragraph.

ESSAY LINK
In a narrative essay, you can use first- or third-person narration.

2. **Use third-person narration.**

   In third-person narration, you do not refer to your own experiences. Instead, you describe what happened to somebody else. The story is told in the third person using *he, she, it,* or *they.* You might tell a story about your mother's childhood, or you might explain what happened during the last election. In this type of narration, you are simply an observer or storyteller; you are not a participant in the action. For example: "The students gathered to protest against the war. One student threw a chair through the window of the student center. Suddenly, people started pushing and shoving."

HINT ◂ **Choose an Interesting Topic**

When you write a narrative paragraph, try to choose a topic that will interest the reader. For example, the reader might not be interested if you write about the act of eating your lunch. However, if you write about a time when your best friend argued with a waiter during a meal, you could create an entertaining narrative paragraph.

Think about a topic that you personally find very interesting, and then share it with your readers. Try to bring your experience to life so that your readers can share it with you.

Explore Topics

LO 3 Explore topics.

In the Warm Up, you will try an exploring strategy to generate ideas about different topics.

THE WRITER'S DESK **Warm Up**

Think about the following questions, and write down the first ideas that come to your mind. Try to think of two or three ideas for each topic.

EXAMPLE: Can you recount an interesting or funny event that has happened to you, or have family members told you about interesting or funny events that have happened to them?

I got stuck in an elevator. My uncle Donovan taught in Japan for a year.

What else? My sister brought a stray dog home. My brother and his

band members got lost.

1. Have you ever done a good deed, or has someone ever helped you? If so, what happened?

    _____

    _____

    _____

2. What are some memorable parties or celebrations that you have attended?

    _____

    _____

    _____

3. Think about interesting true events that have happened to family members or friends. Are some stories particularly funny, sad, or inspiring? List some ideas.

    _____

    _____

    _____

PRACTICE 1

Read the paragraph and answer the questions.

At eighteen years old, I was offered a scholarship to the University of South Africa. I took my first plane flight and had a very frightening experience. After the plane took off from Cameroon, I took pictures of the fields and clouds below. Suddenly, I realized there was smoke at the rear of the plane. The pilot announced an emergency landing at the international airport in Congo. At that time, Congo was in the midst of a civil war. Suddenly, the passengers who had been calm and relaxed became frantic. Some bowed their heads for their last prayers, and others moved toward the emergency exits. As soon as we landed, rebels approached our plane, and we had to run. We were hiding in a bunker when we heard loud screams from people who were being chased by horsemen with machetes. The frightened civilians stumbled into our safe location, which then exposed us to the attackers. When the rebels saw us, they looked as though they had found a gold mine. Because we were from Cameroon, they decided not to hurt us but stripped us of our possessions. As we walked to a neighboring city, we saw burning homes and running refugees. There were also child soldiers carrying big machine guns and patrolling the city center. Eventually, we made our way to Zimbabwe, and then I caught a ferry to South Africa. This experience changed my perspective on life. Every day when I wake up, I am grateful to be alive and breathe free air.

—Beryl Fomundam, student

1. Underline the topic sentence.

2. What type of narration is this paragraph? _____

3. Who is the narrator? _____

4. Where is the narrator? _____

5. Why is the narrator in that region? _____

_____

_____

6. What happens to her? _____

_____

_____

7. By combining your answers to questions 3 and 6, write a one-sentence summary of the paragraph. Someone who has never read the paragraph should have a clear idea of the paragraph's content after reading your sentence.

_____

_____

_____

PRACTICE 2

Read the next paragraph and answer the questions.

On May 4, 2009, John Yettaw's reckless and misguided action endangered his freedom and that of a **Burmese** activist. On that day, **Aung San Suu Kyi** was being held under house arrest by Burmese military authorities, and she was due to be released in two weeks. Her home in a heavily guarded lakeside compound was supposed to be impenetrable. Yettaw, a Vietnam veteran from Missouri, planned his route across the lake using Google Earth. He made the 1.2-mile swim and was approaching land when guards started throwing rocks at him. Yettaw, undeterred, arrived on shore, climbed a drainpipe, and entered Suu Kyi's home. Two female assistants fed Yettaw. He then managed to leave the house and swim away, but he was apprehended the next day. Because Yettaw had come without authorization, the Burmese authorities claimed that Suu Kyi had violated her parole. Her prison term was extended for another eighteen months. Thus, Yettaw's unwise adventure created severe consequences for him and Suu Kyi.

—Mya Ne Win, student

> **Burma:**   a southeast Asian country, also known as Myanmar; under military dictatorship until 2011
>
> **Aung San Suu Kyi:**   a political activist and Nobel Peace Prize winner

1. Who or what is the paragraph about? _____
    _____

2. Underline the topic sentence of the paragraph.

3. What point is the author making? _____
    _____

4. What type of narration is this paragraph? _____

5. How does the author support the topic sentence? List some details.
    _____
    _____
    _____
    _____

6. Do the details provide adequate support for the topic sentence? Explain your answer.
    _____
    _____

> **ESSAY LINK**
> In a narrative essay, the thesis statement expresses the controlling idea.

▶ DEVELOPING

The Topic Sentence

When you write a narrative paragraph, it is important to express a main point. Simply describing a list of activities is boring for the reader. To make your paragraph interesting, make sure that your topic sentence has a controlling idea.

> **LO 4** Identify the topic sentence of a narrative paragraph.

topic controlling idea
When somebody broke into my house, I felt totally invaded.

controlling idea topic
Jay learned to be responsible **during his first job**.

Make a Point

In a narrative paragraph, the topic sentence should make a point. For help finding the controlling idea, you can ask yourself the following questions.

- ◆ What did I learn?
- ◆ How did I change?
- ◆ How did it make me feel?
- ◆ What is important about it?

EXAMPLE:

Topic	Moving out of the family home
Possible controlling idea	Becoming more independent

topic controlling idea
When I moved out of the family home, I became more independent.

PRACTICE 3

Practice writing topic sentences. Complete the following sentences by adding a controlling idea.

1. When I moved out of the family home, I felt _____
   _____

2. In my first job, I learned _____
   _____

3. When Tara heard the news about _____,
   she realized _____

THE WRITER'S DESK   Write Topic Sentences

Write a topic sentence for each of the following topics. You can look for ideas in the Writer's Desk Warm Up on page 61. Each topic sentence should mention the topic and express a controlling idea.

EXAMPLE: Topic: A funny coincidence

Topic sentence: *When Uncle Donovan met a fellow tourist, they turned out to have some strange things in common.*

1. Topic: A good deed

   Topic sentence: _____
   _____

2. Topic: A celebration or party

Topic sentence: _____

_____

3. Topic: A story about someone

Topic sentence: _____

_____

The Supporting Ideas

LO 5 Identify the supporting details of a narrative paragraph.

A narrative paragraph should contain specific details so that the reader understands what happened. To come up with the details, ask yourself a series of questions. Your paragraph should provide answers to these questions.

- Who is the paragraph about?
- What happened?
- When did it happen?
- Where did it happen?
- Why did it happen?
- How did it happen?

When you recount a story to a friend, you can add details out of order, saying, "I forgot to mention something." When you write a narrative paragraph, however, your sequence of events should be clearly chronological so that your reader can follow your story.

Visualizing Narration
PRACTICE 4

Brainstorm supporting ideas for the following topic sentence. Write some descriptive words and phrases.

Topic Sentence: Our camping trip exposed us to new experiences.

_____ _____ _____

_____ _____ _____

THE WRITER'S DESK   Develop Supporting Ideas

Generate supporting ideas for each topic. List what happened.

EXAMPLE: A funny coincidence

Uncle Donovan was working in Japan

went to see some temples

met a stranger

asked where she worked

were colleagues

1. A good deed

_____

_____

_____

_____

_____

2. A celebration or party

_____

_____

_____

_____

_____

3. A story about someone

_____

_____

_____

_____

_____

L0 6 Develop a narrative paragraph plan.

ESSAY LINK
In a narrative essay, you place the thesis statement in the introduction. Each event is developed in a supporting paragraph.

The Paragraph Plan

Before you write a narrative paragraph, it is a good idea to make a paragraph plan. Write down events in the order in which they occurred. To make your narration more complete, include details about each event.

Topic Sentence: When Uncle Donovan met a fellow tourist, they turned out to have some strange things in common.

Support 1: My uncle was working in Japan for a year.
—He went on a tour of some temples.
—The only other person in the courtyard was a woman.

Support 2: He started a conversation with the woman.
—He asked where she was from.
—She was also American.
—She was on vacation in Japan.

Support 3: He asked where she worked.
—She said, "I teach at Brownfield College."
—Uncle Donovan said he did also.
—He asked her which department she taught in.
—She said the English department.
—She had been hired while he was away.
—They were colleagues.

THE WRITER'S DESK   Write a Paragraph Plan

Choose one of the topic sentences that you wrote for the previous Writer's Desk. Write a paragraph plan using some of the supporting ideas that you have generated. Include details for each supporting idea.

Topic sentence: _____

_____

Support 1: _____

Details: _____

_____

_____

Support 2: _____

Details: _____

_____

_____

Support 3: _____

Details: _____

_____

_____

The First Draft

LO 7 Write the first draft of a narrative paragraph.

After you outline your ideas in a plan, you are ready to write the first draft. Remember to write complete sentences. You might include transitional words or expressions to help your ideas flow smoothly.

Transitional Words and Expressions

Transitions can help you show a sequence of events. The following transitional words are useful in narrative paragraphs.

To Show a Sequence of Events

afterward	finally	in the end	meanwhile
after that	first	last	next
eventually	in the beginning	later	then

THE WRITER'S DESK   Write the First Draft

In the previous Writer's Desk, you developed a paragraph plan. Now write the first draft of your narrative paragraph. Before you write, carefully review your paragraph plan and make any necessary changes.

> # VOCABULARY BOOST
>
> ## Using Varied Language
>
> 1. Underline the opening word of every sentence in your first draft. Check to see if some are repeated.
>
> 2. Replace repeated opening words with an adverb like *usually*, *generally*, or *fortunately* or a prepositional phrase, such as *On the side* or *Under the circumstances*. You can also begin the sentences with a phrase like *Leaving the door open*. In other words, avoid beginning too many sentences with a noun or transitional word.
>
> ### Repeated First Words
>
> We opened the door of the abandoned house. We looked nervously at the rotting floorboards. We thought the floor might collapse. We decided to enter. We walked carefully across the kitchen floor to the bedroom, one by one.
>
> ### Variety
>
> My cousins and I opened the door of the abandoned house. Nervously, we looked at the rotting floorboards. Thinking the floor might collapse, we decided to enter. One by one, we walked across the kitchen floor to the bedroom.

▶ REVISING AND EDITING

LO 8 Revise and edit a narrative paragraph.

Revise and Edit a Narrative Paragraph

When you finish writing a narrative paragraph, carefully review your work and revise it to make the events as clear as possible to your readers. Check that you have organized events chronologically, and remove any irrelevant details. Before you revise and edit your own paragraph, practice revising and editing a student paragraph.

PRACTICE 5

Read the next student paragraph and answer the questions.

> When Uncle Donovan met a fellow tourist, they turned out to have some strange things in common. Uncle Donovan was on leave for a year from his teaching job. He was working in Japan. One day, he went to see some Buddhist temples. There was only one other person at the temple, a woman. A few minutes later, he started a conversation with her. He asks her where she was from. Raquel was an American vacationing in Japan. Uncle Donovan then asked her where she worked. She said "I teach at Brownfield College." Astonished, he replied that he worked at the same college. She told him that she worked in the English department. Uncle Donovan was completely dumbstruck. He told her that he also worked in the English department. She had been hired to teach during his absence. They were colleagues. After he returned home, Uncle Donovan told friends and colleagues about how he met Raquel in Japan. Everyone was amazed at the coincidence.

—Romina Fonseca, student

Revising

1. Write down the two parts of the topic sentence.

topic   +   controlling idea

_____

2. What type of order do the specific details follow? Circle the best answer.

    a. space   b. time

    c. emphatic   d. no order

3. What are some transitional expressions that the author used?

    _____

4. What type of narration is this paragraph?

    a. first person   b. third person

Editing

5. This paragraph contains a tense inconsistency. The tense shifts for no apparent reason. Identify the incorrect sentence, and write the correct sentence in the space below.

    _____

6. The direct quotation is incorrectly punctuated. Correct the error.

    _____

> **GRAMMAR LINK**
> See the following chapters for more information about these grammar topics:
> Tense consistency, Chapter 27
> Quotations, Chapter 35

GRAMMAR HINT ◀ Using Quotations

When you insert a direct quotation into your writing, capitalize the first word of the quotation and put the final punctuation inside the closing quotation marks.

- Place a comma after an introductory phrase.

    Vladimir screamed, "The kitchen's on fire!"

- Place a colon after an introductory sentence.

    Vladimir watched me coldly: "We have nothing to discuss."

THE WRITER'S DESK   Revise and Edit Your Paragraph

Revise and edit the paragraph that you wrote for the previous Writer's Desk. Make sure that your paragraph has unity, adequate support, and coherence. Also, correct any errors in grammar, spelling, punctuation, and mechanics.

Reflect On It

Think about what you have learned in this chapter. If you do not know an answer, review that topic.

1. In narrative writing, you _____

2. What are the differences between the two following types of narration?

    First person: _____

    _____

Third person: _____

_____

3. What are some questions that you should ask yourself when you write a narrative paragraph?

   _____

4. What organizational method is commonly used in narrative paragraphs? Circle the best answer.

   a. space order   b. time order   c. emphatic order

MyWritingLab™

Complete these writing assignments at mywritinglab.com

WRITING LINK

MORE NARRATIVE WRITING TOPICS

Chapter 21, Writer's Room topic 1 (page 311)
Chapter 23, Writer's Room topic 1 (page 333)
Chapter 31, Writer's Room topic 1 (page 432)

READING LINK

MORE NARRATIVE READINGS

"My Prison Story" by Yirga Gebremeskel (page 195)
"A Lesson in Humility" by Jeff Kemp (page 196)
"The Sanctuary of School" by Lynda Barry (page 528)
"My Relentless Pursuit of the Guy Who Robbed Me" by Amanda Enayati (page 556)

MyWritingLab™

THE WRITER'S ROOM

Writing Activity 1: Topics

Choose any of the following topics, or choose your own topic. Then write a narrative paragraph.

General Topics

1. an interesting decade
2. a great or disastrous date
3. an unforgettable holiday
4. a disturbing news event
5. a time when you were influenced by peer pressure

College and Work-Related Topics

6. an embarrassing incident at college or work
7. a life-changing meeting
8. a positive or negative job interview
9. an encounter with a difficult customer
10. a proud moment at work or college

Writing Activity 2: Media Writing

Watch a popular television show or movie that shows a character overcoming a challenge. Examples are the movie *Django Unchained* and television programs such as *Nashville, Chicago Fire*, and *Scandal*. You can even go on YouTube and watch some videos about people who have to overcome challenges to meet their personal goals. For example, Susan Boyle surprised audiences when she sang on *Britain's Got Talent*. Narrate what happened.

Narrative Paragraph Checklist

As you write your narrative paragraph, review the checklist at the end of the book. Also ask yourself the following questions.

☐ Does my topic sentence clearly express the topic of the narration?

☐ Does my topic sentence contain a controlling idea that is meaningful and interesting?

☐ Does my paragraph answer most of the following questions: *who, what, when, where, why, how*?

☐ Do I use transitional expressions that help clarify the order of events?

☐ Do I include details to make my narration more interesting?

6 Description

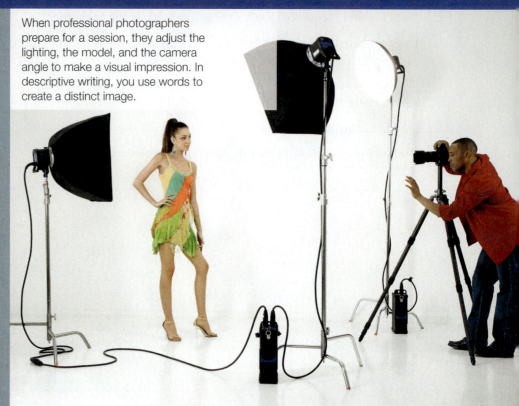

When professional photographers prepare for a session, they adjust the lighting, the model, and the camera angle to make a visual impression. In descriptive writing, you use words to create a distinct image.

WRITERS' EXCHANGE

Work with two or three students. First, think about a particular place. It can be a street, a coffee shop, a mall, a park, or any other place in your region. Describe details about that place. Describe sights, sounds, and smells. Speak nonstop about the place for about forty seconds. Your teammates must guess the place that you are describing.

LO 1 Define description.

▶ **EXPLORING**

What Is Description?

Description creates vivid images in the reader's mind by portraying people, places, or moments in detail.

You use description every day. At home, you might describe a new friend to your family, or you might describe an object that you bought. At college, you might describe the structure of a cell or the results of a lab experiment. At work, you may describe a new product to a client, or you could describe the qualities of potential clients to your boss.

DESCRIPTION **AT WORK**

In this excerpt from a note sent from Dr. Pradish Chowdhury to his students, he describes chicken pox.

Chicken pox, related to the herpes family, is a highly contagious virus. The first symptoms include skin that is hot to the touch. A rash, appearing like small red spots, appears on the upper part of the body. Within about twenty-four hours, the spots become fluid-filled and itchy blisters, which can appear on the face, scalp, back, chest, and even inside the nostrils and mouth. Sometimes the skin becomes darker around the blisters, which can number in the hundreds. Keep an infected child's nails very short, as scratching can cause blisters to become infected and can leave scars. After a few days, crusty scabs form and the blisters fall off. Full recovery takes about a week to ten days.

> The topic sentence expresses the main idea.

> Supporting sentences provide details and examples.

> The concluding sentence brings the paragraph to a satisfactory close.

The Descriptive Paragraph

LO 2 Explain how to write a descriptive paragraph.

When you write a descriptive paragraph, focus on three main points.

1. **Create a dominant impression.**

   The dominant impression is the overall atmosphere that you wish to convey. It can be a strong feeling, mood, or image. For example, if you are describing a business meeting, you can emphasize the tension in the room.

2. **Express your attitude toward the subject.**

   Do you feel positive, negative, or neutral toward the subject? For example, if you feel positive about your best friend, then the details of your paragraph about him or her should convey the good feelings you have. If you describe a place that you do not like, then your details should express how uncomfortable that place makes you feel. You might write a neutral description of a science lab experiment.

3. **Include concrete details.**

   Details will enable a reader to visualize the person, place, or situation that is being described. You can use active verbs and adjectives so that the reader imagines the scene more clearly. You can also use **imagery**, which is description using the five senses. Review the following examples of imagery.

   Sight   While talking casually to her husband, Joanna absentmindedly tugs at a hangnail until the skin tears and a tiny droplet of blood appears.

                                     —Deborah Tannen, *You're Wearing That?*

   Sound   As the glass tinkled onto the cellar floor, he heard a low growl.

                                    —Christopher Morley, *The Haunted Bookshop*

> **ESSAY LINK**
> In descriptive essays, you should also create a dominant impression, express your attitude toward the subject, and include concrete details.

Smell	The odor of fresh-sawed pine perfumed the air.

—Stewart Edward White, *The Blazed Trail*

Touch	My heart started racing, perspiration dripped down my face causing my glasses to slide, and I had a hard time breathing.

—Bebe Moore Campbell, "Dancing with Fear"

Taste	I asked for fresh lemonade, and got it—delicious, and cold, and tangy with real fruit.

—Mary Stewart, *My Brother Michael*

PRACTICE 1

Read the next paragraph and answer the questions.

My biological father left before my birth, and my single mother worked three dead-end jobs. By my twelfth birthday, I was gang affiliated, and I was on a first-name basis with police. I tried medications and meditation to relieve my built-in rage, but nothing helped. My life changed, and I became tamed when I found a five-foot six-inch, sun-rotted, waterlogged surfboard in my neighbor's garbage. Initially, learning to surf wasn't easy. During my first hundred times, I nearly drowned. I'd swallow the salty water as I tumbled into the ocean, often banging my head on the board. Of course, there were moments of terror. I was often visited by an ancient predator, the shark. Sharks can pick up on the electromagnetic beat of the human heart and sense fear, so I learned to tame my nerves. Furthermore, I learned about balance. Sitting on the board naturally calmed my heart rate while I stared into the vast blue, aware of the swooshing waves and squawking seagulls and the fishy odors. Ultimately, surfing gave me what I had never had, a sense of real belonging. When I am in the ocean, I am in the womb, attached to the birth cord. To the naked eye, my surfboard is a dinged-up piece of foam, fiberglass, and epoxy resin. To me, it is a thousand stories of courage and joy.

—Robert James Perkins, student

1. Underline the topic sentence. Be careful, as it may not be the first sentence in the paragraph.

2. What is the dominant impression that the writer creates?

    a. pride   b. rage   c. shock

    Give examples that show the dominant impression.

    _____

    _____

3. Provide examples from the paragraph of each type of sensory detail.

    a. sight   _____

    b. sound   _____

    c. taste   _____

    d. touch   _____

    e. smell   _____

4. How did riding a surfboard affect or change the author?

    _____

    _____

Explore Topics

In the Warm Up, you will try an exploring strategy to generate ideas about different topics.

THE WRITER'S DESK **Warm Up**

Think about the following questions, and write down the first ideas that come to your mind. Try to think of two or three ideas for each topic.

EXAMPLE: What are some strong impressions you have had at a workplace?

donut shop smells

images when I first tried welding

the loud banging in the machine shop

1. What were some very emotional moments in your life? (Think about two or three moments when you felt extreme joy, sadness, excitement, anxiety, or other strong emotions.)

_____

_____

_____

2. Describe your food quirks. What are your unusual tastes or eating habits? Which foods do you really love or hate?

_____

_____

_____

3. What are some very beautiful places in or near your home?

_____

_____

_____

▶ DEVELOPING

When you write a descriptive paragraph, choose a subject that lends itself to description. In other words, find a subject that appeals to the senses. For example, you can describe the sounds, sights, tastes, and smells in a bakery.

ESSAY LINK
In a descriptive essay, the thesis statement expresses the controlling idea.

The Topic Sentence

In the topic sentence of a descriptive paragraph, you should convey a dominant impression about the subject. The dominant impression is the overall impression or feeling that the topic inspires.

topic   controlling idea

The abandoned buildings in our neighborhood <u>are an eyesore</u>.

topic   controlling idea

When the car skidded, <u>I panicked</u>.

HINT ◀ **How to Create a Dominant Impression**

To create a dominant impression, ask yourself how or why the topic is important.

Poor   The parade was noisy.
              (Why should readers care about this statement?)

                        topic   controlling idea

Better   **The parade participants** loudly celebrated the arrival of the
              New Year.

THE WRITER'S DESK   **Write Topic Sentences**

Write a topic sentence for each of the following topics. You can look for ideas in the previous Writer's Desk. Remember to narrow each topic. Each topic sentence should state what you are describing and contain a controlling idea.

EXAMPLE: Topic: Impressions at work

Topic sentence: My first attempt at arc welding filled me with awe.

_____

1. Topic: An emotional moment

    Topic sentence: _____

    _____

2. Topic: Food quirks (unusual food habits or foods you love or hate)

    Topic sentence: _____

    _____

3. Topic: A beautiful place

    Topic sentence: _____

    _____

LO 5 Identify the supporting details of a description paragraph.

The Supporting Ideas

After you have developed an effective topic sentence, generate supporting details. The details can be placed in space, time, or emphatic order.

Visualizing Description
PRACTICE 2

Brainstorm supporting ideas for the following topic sentence. Write some descriptive words or phrases.

Topic Sentence: During my walk in the forest, the scenery fascinated me.

_____   _____   _____
_____   _____   _____
_____   _____   _____

Show, Don't Tell

Your audience will find it more interesting to read your written work if you *show* a quality of a place or an action of a person rather than just state it.

Example of Telling	Recently, a snowstorm arrived and was impressive.
Example of Showing	Recently, a blizzard roared off Lake Michigan and blasted our farm. The trees moaned and their branches creaked. Wind-driven snow encased pine needles, heaped into drifts, and sculpted fields. Curtains of snow-draped shrubs created small caverns where sparrows and rabbits hid.

—from "Snow" by Joan Donaldson

PRACTICE 3

Choose one of the following sentences, and write a short description that shows—not tells—the quality of the person, place, thing, or event.

1. The food smelled delicious.

2. It was a hot day.

3. The child's room was messy.

List Sensory Details

To create a dominant impression, think about your topic and make a list of your feelings and impressions. These details can include imagery (images that appeal to sight, sound, touch, taste, and smell).

Topic: An abandoned building

Details: —damp floors

—boarded-up windows   —musty

—broken glass   —gray bricks

—graffiti on the walls   —chipping paint

> **ESSAY LINK**
> When you plan a descriptive essay, it is useful to list sensory details.

VOCABULARY BOOST

Using Vivid Language

When you write a descriptive paragraph, try to use **vivid language**. Use specific action verbs and vivid adjectives to create a clear picture of what you are describing.

unpretentious

The wealthy owner was ~~nice~~.
(Use a more vivid, specific adjective.)

howled

The wind ~~blew~~.
(Use a more vivid, specific verb or image.)

Think about other words or expressions that more effectively describe these words:

Hungry: _____

Not friendly: _____

Cry: _____

Speak: _____

THE WRITER'S DESK   List Sensory Details

Think about images, impressions, and feelings that the following topics inspire in you. Refer to your topic sentences on page 76, and make a list under each topic.

EXAMPLE: Impressions at work

arc welding

flashing light

burning smell

bright sparks

smell of rust

bending wire

popping sound

1. An emotional moment: _____

_____

_____

_____

_____

_____

2. Food quirks: _____

_____

_____

_____

_____

_____

_____

3. A beautiful place: _____

_____

_____

_____

_____

_____

_____

The Paragraph Plan

LO 6 Develop a descriptive paragraph plan.

A descriptive paragraph should contain specific details so that the reader can clearly imagine what is being described. When you make a paragraph plan, remember to include concrete details. Also think about the organizational method that you will use.

Topic Sentence: My first attempt at arc welding filled me with awe.

> **Support 1:**   At first, the flashing lights frightened me.
> **Details:**   —popping and cracking sound
>   —like a roaring brush fire
>   —bright sparks
> **Support 2:**   The smell of burning newspaper filled the air.
> **Details:**   —oxidized metal
>   —odor of a rusty boat hull
> **Support 3:**   I was able to shape the raw metal.
> **Details:**   —red-hot wire
>   —bent like licorice

ESSAY LINK
In a descriptive essay, place the thesis statement in the introduction. Then, develop each supporting idea in a body paragraph. Include descriptive details.

THE WRITER'S DESK   **Write a Paragraph Plan**

Choose one of the topic sentences that you wrote for the Writer's Desk on page 76, and write a detailed paragraph plan. You can include some of the sensory details that you have generated in the previous Writer's Desk.

Topic sentence: _____

_____

Support 1: _____

Details: _____

_____

_____

Support 2: _____

Details: _____

Support 3: _____

Details: _____

The First Draft

LO 7 Write the first draft of a descriptive paragraph.

After you outline your ideas in a plan, you are ready to write the first draft. Remember to write complete sentences. You might include transitional words or expressions to help your ideas flow smoothly.

Transitional Words and Expressions

You can use space order to describe a person, place, or thing. The following transitions are useful in descriptive paragraphs.

To Show Place or Position

above	beyond	in the distance	outside
behind	closer in	nearby	over there
below	farther out	on the left/right	under
beside	in front	on top	underneath

THE WRITER'S DESK **Write the First Draft**

In the previous Writer's Desk, you developed a paragraph plan. Now write the first draft of your descriptive paragraph. Before you write, carefully review your paragraph plan and make any necessary changes.

▶ **REVISING AND EDITING**

LO 8 Revise and edit a descriptive paragraph.

Revise and Edit a Descriptive Paragraph

When you finish writing a descriptive paragraph, carefully review your work and revise it to make the description as clear as possible to your readers. Check that you have organized your steps logically, and remove any irrelevant details.

PRACTICE 4

Read the following student paragraph, and answer the questions.

Eight years ago, my first attempt at arc welding filled me with awe. I was fearful, yet I felt as if I had uncover a great secret. At first, the flashing lights frightened me. They made a popping and crackling noise that sounded like a roaring brush fire. Imagine charging a car battery and accidentally knocking the clamps. Sparks flew, yet I could control and maintain the sparking. An odor like that of burning newspaper filled the air. Also, the oxidized metal . It smelled like a rusty boat hull after a rainfall. I felt so powerful because I could make raw metal take shape. Using a vise, the red-hot steel bent as easily as a piece of licorice.

—Kelly Bruce, student

Revising

1. Underline the topic sentence.

2. Highlight three vivid images in the paragraph.

3. The paragraph ends abruptly. Add a concluding sentence.

_____

_____

GRAMMAR LINK
See the following chapters for more information about these topics:

Past Participles, Chapter 24
Fragments, Chapter 20
Modifiers, Chapter 31

Editing

4. Underline and correct one past participle error.

5. A fragment lacks a subject or verb and is an incomplete sentence. Underline and correct one fragment.

6. Underline and correct a dangling modifier. See the following Grammar Hint for an explanation about dangling modifiers.

GRAMMAR HINT   Using Modifiers

When you revise your descriptive essay, check that your modifiers are placed near the items they are modifying. Also make sure that the modifier is connected to another part of the sentence and is not dangling.

Incorrect   Gazing at the sky, the clouds drifted on the horizon.

Correct   Gazing at the sky, **I noticed** the clouds drifting on the horizon.

THE WRITER'S DESK   Revise and Edit Your Paragraph

Revise and edit the paragraph that you wrote for the previous Writer's Desk. Check that your paragraph has unity, adequate support, and coherence. Also, correct any errors in grammar, spelling, punctuation, and mechanics.

Reflect On It

Think about what you have learned in this chapter. If you do not know an answer, review that topic.

1. What are the main features of a descriptive paragraph? _____

   _____

   _____

   _____

2. Define imagery. _____

3. Look at the familiar words below. Write down at least two more descriptive ways to say each word. Try to find words that are more specific.
   a. cute _____   c. sad _____
   b. angry _____   d. mean _____

MyWritingLab™

**Complete these
writing assignments at
mywritinglab.com**

MyWritingLab™   **THE WRITER'S ROOM**

Writing Activity 1: Topics

Choose any of the following topics, or choose your own topic. Then write a descriptive paragraph.

General Topics

1. an interesting house or building
2. a comfortable room
3. an evening out
4. a scene from nature
5. a positive person

College and Work-Related Topics

6. a quiet area on campus
7. an unusual student or coworker
8. an inspiring teacher or instructor
9. an uncomfortable uniform
10. a place with a good or bad odor

Writing Activity 2: Media Writing

Watch a popular television show or movie that describes the future or that depicts mysterious places. For example, you can choose the movies *Looper, District 9, Gamer, The Twilight Saga,* and *Star Trek* or television shows such as *Game of Thrones, The Walking Dead,* and *True Blood.* In a paragraph, describe the setting or main characters. Use imagery that appeals to the senses.

WRITING LINK

**MORE DESCRIPTIVE
WRITING TOPICS**

Chapter 20, Writer's Room
    topic 2 (page 304)
Chapter 22, Writer's Room
    topic 1 (page 319)
Chapter 23, Writer's Room
    topic 2 (page 333)
Chapter 27, Writer's Room
    topic 1 (page 375)
Chapter 36, Writer's Room
    topic 1 (page 491)

READING LINK

**MORE DESCRIPTIVE
READINGS**

"Roaring Waves of Fire" by
    Christi Lester (page 200)
"Chicken Hips" by
    Catherine Pigott
    (page 201)
"The Catcher of Ghosts"
    by Amy Tan (page 525)
"Aunt Tee" by Maya
    Angelou (page 540)

Descriptive Paragraph Checklist

As you write your descriptive paragraph, review the checklist at the end of the book. Also ask yourself the following questions.

☐ Does my topic sentence clearly show what I will describe?

☐ Does my topic sentence have a controlling idea that makes a point about the topic?

☐ Does my paragraph make a dominant impression?

☐ Does my paragraph contain supporting details that appeal to the reader's senses?

☐ Do I use vivid language?

Process 7

Dancers learn new steps by following a process. Similarly, in process writing, you describe how to do something.

WRITERS' EXCHANGE

Choose one of the following topics, and have a group or class discussion. Describe the steps you would take to do that process.

1. How to write a paragraph

2. How to ruin a date

3. How to recognize when someone is lying

4. How to be a better person

> ▶ **EXPLORING**

What Is a Process?

A **process** is a series of steps done in chronological order. In process writing, you explain how to do something, how an incident took place, or how something works.

You explain processes every day. At home, you may explain to a family member how to use an electronic appliance, or you may need to give written instructions to a babysitter or caregiver. At college, you may explain how to perform a scientific experiment or how a new product was invented. At work, you may explain how to operate a machine or how to do a particular job.

PROCESS **AT WORK**

In this memo to fellow employees, Mawlid Abdul Aziz, a network administration assistant, uses process writing to explain how to install antivirus software on a computer.

The topic sentence expresses the main idea.	Because of a new security threat circulating on the Internet, the IT department strongly recommends that you update your antivirus software. To do so, double-click on the antivirus icon at the bottom right on your computer screen (system tray).
Supporting sentences provide details and examples.	The correct icon should appear at the far left of the row of icons. Then, a window will appear that is called the virus scan console. In this window, there are several items, one of which is labeled "Automatic Update." When you double-click on that button, another window will appear that contains the button "Run Now." Click on it, and after a minute or two, there will be a message box saying "completed."
The concluding sentence brings the paragraph to a satisfying close.	Please do not hesitate to contact the IT department if you encounter any difficulty with this procedure.

The Process Paragraph

There are two main types of process paragraphs.

♦ **Complete a process.** This type of paragraph contains directions on how to complete a particular task. For example, a writer might explain how to paint a picture, how to repair a leaky faucet, or how to get a job. The reader should be able to follow the directions and complete the task.

♦ **Understand a process.** This type of paragraph explains how something works or how something happens. In other words, the goal is to help the reader understand a process rather than do a process. For example, a writer might explain how the heart pumps blood to other organs in the body or how a country elects its political leaders.

PRACTICE 1

A framed painting hanging on a wall creates its own imaginary world. Understanding and responding to a painting does not have to be difficult. First, get up close. When you approach a picture, step into its universe. Put your nose up close and observe the picture as a physical object. Drink in its visual and physical properties. Next, take a step back and look at the picture as a whole. Look at the arrangement or composition of the picture's elements: background or foreground, implied movement, and dramatic action. Is there a story? Who are the human figures? Are there symbols? What feelings or ideas does it stimulate in you? Then, think and apply what you know. Study the picture in historical context. This knowledge can help identify the style or movement to which a picture belongs. It can tell you about the work's patron or something significant about the artist's life and how this work fits into that story. Finally, respond with your own thoughts and feelings. Look at what it shows you and listen to what it says and record that experience for yourself in a journal or notebook. This personal reflection fixes the impression and helps you recall this picture as something you've become acquainted with.

—Philip E. Bishop, *A Beginner's Guide to the Humanities*

1. a. What is the topic of this paragraph? _____

_____

b. What is the controlling idea in the topic sentence? _____

_____

2. What type of process paragraph is this?

a. complete a process   b. understand a process

3. List the main steps the author suggests to help you understand a painting.

_____

_____

_____

_____

PRACTICE 2

Read the next paragraph, and answer the questions.

Back in the early 1950s, Jim Henson created one of his first Muppets, Kermit, using his imagination and everyday materials. First, he planned the design, making a detailed sketch of a lizard-like creature. Then he proceeded to build the Muppet. Cutting up the fabric from a discarded fuzzy green coat that had belonged to his mother, Henson created Kermit's head. According to Shanna Freeman in *How Stuff Works*, Henson made the lizard's eyes by cutting a spherical toy called Wacky Stax in half and attaching the pieces to the face. Kermit's body was built from stiff cardboard covered in the coat's green fabric. Because the Muppet's head was mainly built with soft material, Henson could use his hand to make Kermit's face expressive. By tilting his hand or twisting his fingers inside Kermit's mouth, Henson made the little creature come alive. Henson also provided Kermit with his distinctive voice. Later, Henson added a collar to Kermit's neck, and the creature became more clearly identified as a frog. Kermit was originally a character in television commercials, but it is the children's television series *Sesame Street* that ingrained Kermit in people's minds and hearts.

—Jill Chang, student

1. Underline the topic sentence.

2. What type of process paragraph is this? Circle the best answer.

   a. complete a process   b. understand a process

3. List the steps in the process. The first one has been done for you.

   <u>made a detailed sketch</u>

   _____

   _____

   _____

   _____

   _____

   _____

PRACTICE 3

For each of the following topics, write *C* if it explains how to complete a process, or write *U* if it explains how to understand a process (how something works or how something happens).

1. How to train a pet dog   _____

2. The stages in a child's development   _____

3. Three steps to making your eyes more attractive   _____

4. How to avoid being mugged   _____

5. How a cloud forms   _____

LO 3 Explore topics.

Explore Topics

In the Warm Up, you will try an exploring strategy to generate ideas about different topics.

THE WRITER'S DESK   **Warm Up**

Think about the following questions, and write down the first ideas that come to your mind. Try to think of two or three ideas for each topic.

EXAMPLE: Explain how to do a group "flash mob" activity. Write down some of the steps in the process.

—to make a flash mob dance, you need to find music

—organize your friends and learn the steps

—perform the dance in a public place

1. How do you do a particular activity at your workplace?

   _____

   _____

   _____

2. What are some things you should do to succeed in college?

   _____

   _____

   _____

3. Think about a particular holiday or celebration that you enjoy. What are some things you do to prepare for that holiday?

   _____

   _____

   _____

▶ DEVELOPING

ESSAY LINK
In a process essay, the thesis statement expresses the controlling idea.

When you write a process paragraph, choose a process that you can easily cover in a single paragraph. For example, you might be able to explain how to send an e-mail message in a single paragraph; however, you would need much more than a paragraph to explain how to use a particular computer software program.

The Topic Sentence

LO 4 Identify the topic sentence of a process paragraph.

In a process paragraph, the topic sentence states which process you will be explaining and what readers will be able to do or understand after they have read the paragraph.

          topic   controlling idea

To calm your child during a tantrum, <u>follow the next steps</u>.

      controlling idea   topic

<u>With inexpensive materials</u>, **you can redecorate a room in your house**.

HINT ◀ Make a Point

Your topic sentence should not simply announce the topic. It should make a point about the topic.

Announces	I will describe how to do speed dating.

                                      controlling idea   topic

Correct   It is surprisingly easy and efficient **to meet someone using speed dating**.

THE WRITER'S DESK **Write Topic Sentences**

Write a topic sentence for each of the following topics. You can look for ideas in the previous Writer's Desk on page 86. Remember to narrow each topic. Each topic sentence should state the process and should contain a controlling idea.

EXAMPLE: Topic: How to create a flash mob event

Topic sentence: _To create a fun flash mob dance, there are a few steps_ _you should follow._

1. Topic: How to do an activity at work

    Topic sentence: _____

    _____

2. Topic: How to succeed in college

    Topic sentence: _____

    _____

3. Topic: How to prepare for a holiday or celebration

    Topic sentence: _____

    _____

ESSAY LINK

In an essay, each body paragraph could describe a process. For example, in an essay about how to get rich, one body paragraph could be about buying lottery tickets and another could be about inventing a product.

LO 5 Identify the supporting ideas of a process paragraph.

The Supporting Ideas

A process paragraph contains a series of steps. When you develop supporting ideas for a process paragraph, think about the main steps that are necessary to complete the process. Most process paragraphs use time order.

HINT ◄ **Give Steps, Not Examples**

When you explain how to complete a process, describe each step. Do not simply list examples of the process.

Topic: How to Get Rich

List of Examples	Steps in the Process
write a best seller	do market research
win the lottery	find a specific need
invent a product	invent a product to fulfill that need
inherit money	heavily promote the product

Visualizing Process

PRACTICE 4

Brainstorm supporting ideas for the following topic sentence. List some steps that you should take.

Topic Sentence: Putting in contact lenses is not a difficult procedure.

_____

_____

THE WRITER'S DESK **List the Main Steps**

Think of three or four essential steps in each process. Make a list under each topic.

EXAMPLE: How to create a flash mob event

choose a song and a sound system

contact friends using Facebook

practice the dance moves

meet in a public place to dance

_____

1. How to do an activity at work

_____

_____

_____

_____

2. How to succeed in college

_____

_____

_____

_____

_____

3. How to prepare for a holiday or a celebration

_____

_____

_____

_____

_____

LO 6 Develop a process paragraph plan.

ESSAY LINK

In a process essay, place the thesis statement in the introduction. Then use each body paragraph to explain a step in the process.

The Paragraph Plan

A paragraph plan helps you organize your topic sentence and supporting details before you write a first draft. Decide which steps and which details your reader will really need to know to complete the process or understand it. Write down the steps in chronological order.

Topic Sentence: To create a fun flash mob dance, there are a few steps you should follow.

Support 1:	Find a song that you'd like to dance to.
Details:	—Borrow a good sound system.
	—Choose a song that everyone will recognize.
Support 2:	Organize the event using Facebook and Twitter.
Details:	—Determine a time and place to practice.
	—Try to get as many people as possible.
Support 3:	Meet somewhere to practice the dance steps.
Details:	—Choreograph the steps.
	—Repeat until everyone knows the routine.
Support 4:	At a planned time in a public place, do the flash mob dance.
Details:	—Act like normal members of the public.
	—Turn on the music and start dancing.
	—Bystanders will stare in amazement and maybe join in.

HINT ◄ **Include Necessary Tools or Supplies**

When you are writing a plan for a process paragraph, remember to include any special tools or supplies a reader will need to complete the process. For example, if you want to explain how to pack for a move, you should mention that the reader will need boxes, felt-tip markers, newsprint, twine, scissors, and tape.

THE WRITER'S DESK   Write a Paragraph Plan

Choose one of the topic sentences that you wrote for the Writer's Desk on page 88, and then list the main steps to complete the process. Also add details and examples that will help to explain each step.

Topic sentence: _____

_____

Supporting points:

Step 1: _____

Details: _____

_____

Step 2: _____

Details: _____

_____

Step 3: _____

Details: _____

_____

Step 4: _____

Details: _____

_____

Step 5: _____

Details: _____

_____

The First Draft

LO 7 Write the first draft of a process paragraph.

After you outline your ideas in a plan, you are ready to write the first draft. Remember to write complete sentences. You might include transitional words or expressions to help your ideas flow smoothly.

Transitional Words and Expressions

Most process paragraphs explain a process using time (or chronological) order. The following transitions are useful in process paragraphs.

To Begin a Process	To Continue a Process		To End a Process
(at) first	after that	later	eventually
initially	afterward	meanwhile	finally
the first step	also	second	in the end
	furthermore	then	ultimately
	in addition	third	

THE WRITER'S DESK **Write the First Draft**

In the previous Writer's Desk, you developed a paragraph plan. Now write the first draft of your process paragraph. Before you write, carefully review your paragraph plan and make any necessary changes.

▶ **REVISING AND EDITING**

Revise and Edit a Process Paragraph

LO 8 Revise and edit a process paragraph.

When you finish writing a process paragraph, carefully review your work and revise it to make the process as clear as possible to your readers. Check to make sure that you have organized your steps chronologically, and remove any irrelevant details.

PRACTICE 5

Read the following student paragraph, and answer the questions.

To create a fun flash mob dance, there are a few steps you should follow. First, find a song. It's best to choose an easily recognizable song with a strong beat. You will also need a good sound system. Organize the event using Facebook and Twitter. Determine a time and place to practice. Don't ask others for input, or you might never agree on a date. Try to get as many people as possible to participate, ask friends to contact their friends. Meet somewhere to practice the steps. Repeat the steps until everyone knows the routine. You can even videotape yourself doing the steps and post it online so others can practice at home. At a planned time in a public place, do the flash mob dance. Act like normal members of the public, start the music, and then start dancing. Bystanders will stare in amazement and might even join in. For sure, your going to have a fantastic time. Craig Knowles, a flash mob veteran, says, "Its the best feeling in the world to add some laughter and joy to a routine day".

—Amal Kahan, student

Revising

1. Underline the topic sentence.

2. The author uses "first" to introduce the first steps. Subsequent steps would be more clearly recognizable if the writer had used more transitions. Include three more transitional expressions.

3. How does the writer conclude the paragraph?

   a. with a prediction   b. with a suggestion   c. with a quotation

Editing

4. The paragraph contains a type of run-on sentence called a comma splice. Two complete ideas are incorrectly connected with a comma. Identify and correct the run-on sentence.

5. Identify and correct two pronoun errors. (For more information about pronoun errors, see the Grammar Hint below.)

6. Correct a punctuation error in the concluding quotation.

GRAMMAR LINK
See the following chapters for more information about these grammar topics:
Run-Ons, Chapter 21
Pronouns, Chapter 29
Quotations, Chapter 35

GRAMMAR HINT   Confusing Pronouns

Some possessive adjectives sound like common contractions. Be particularly careful not to confuse *your* with *you're*, *their* with *they're*, and *its* with *it's*.

it's   you're
When ~~its~~ muggy outside, ~~your~~ more likely to get a headache.

THE WRITER'S DESK   Revise and Edit Your Paragraph

Revise and edit the paragraph that you wrote for the previous Writer's Desk. Ensure that your paragraph has unity, adequate support, and coherence. Also correct any errors in grammar, spelling, punctuation, and mechanics.

VOCABULARY BOOST

Look at the first draft of your process paragraph. Underline the verb that you use in each step of the process. Then, when possible, come up with a more evocative or interesting verb. Use your thesaurus for this activity.

Reflect On It

Think about what you have learned in this unit. If you do not know an answer, review that topic.

1. What are the two types of process paragraphs? Briefly explain each type.

   a. _____

   _____

   b. _____

   _____

2. What organizational method is generally used in process writing? Circle the best answer.

   a. space order   b. time order   c. emphatic order

3. Why are transitional words important in process writing?

   _____

   _____

MyWritingLab™
Complete these writing assignments at mywritinglab.com

THE WRITER'S ROOM   MyWritingLab™

Writing Activity 1: Topics

Choose any of the following topics, or choose your own topic. Then write a process paragraph.

General Topics

1. how to make your home safe
2. how to have a great weekend with $20
3. how to be a good roommate
4. how to train a pet
5. how to become famous

College and Work-Related Topics

6. how to choose a college
7. how to prepare for a job interview
8. how to get along with your coworkers
9. how to organize your desk or tools
10. how something was discovered

WRITING LINK

MORE PROCESS WRITING TOPICS
Chapter 17, Writer's Room topic 2 (page 274)
Chapter 28, Writer's Room topic 2 (page 391)
Chapter 29, Writer's Room topic 2 (page 409)
Chapter 30, Writer's Room topic 1 (page 423)
Chapter 32, Writer's Room topic 1 (page 441)
Chapter 34, Writer's Room topic 1 (page 470)

READING LINK

MORE PROCESS READING

"The Wonders of PowerPoint" by Karine Godin (page 204)

"Steps to Music Success" by Jake Sibley (page 206)

"The Criminal Justice Process" by John Randolph Fuller (page 551)

"How Spies Are Caught" (page 554)

Writing Activity 2: Media Writing

Watch a reality television show such as *America's Next Top Model*, *Survivor*, *Hell's Kitchen*, or *Dancing with the Stars*. Describe the process the contestants go through to win the prize.

Process Paragraph Checklist

As you write your process paragraph, review the checklist at the end of the book. Also ask yourself the following questions.

☐ Does my topic sentence make a point about the process?

☐ Do I include all of the steps in the process?

☐ Do I clearly explain each step so my reader can accomplish the process or understand it?

☐ Do I mention all of the supplies that my reader needs to complete the process?

☐ Do I use transitions to connect all of the steps in the process?

Definition 8

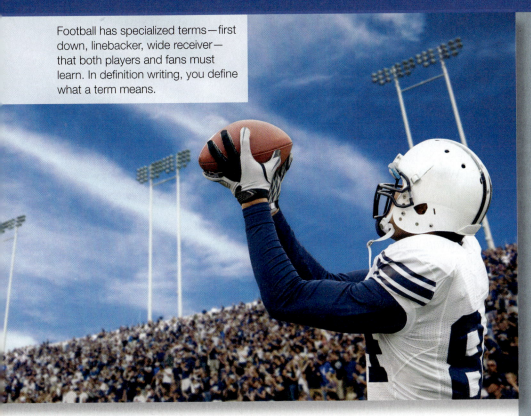

Football has specialized terms—first down, linebacker, wide receiver— that both players and fans must learn. In definition writing, you define what a term means.

WRITERS' EXCHANGE

Work with a partner or a team of students. Try to define the following terms. Think of some examples that can help define each term.

netiquette chick flick urban sprawl a tweet (on Twitter)

LO 1 Define definition.

What Is Definition?

When you **define**, you explain the meaning of a word. Some terms have concrete meanings, and you can define them in a few words. For example, a pebble is "a small stone." Other words, such as *culture, happiness*, or *evil*, are more abstract and require longer definitions. In fact, it is possible to write a paragraph, an essay, or even an entire book on such concepts.

The simplest way to define a term is to look it up in a dictionary. However, many words have nuances that are not necessarily discussed in dictionaries. For example, suppose that your boss calls your work "unsatisfactory." You might need clarification of that term. Do you have poor work habits? Do you miss deadlines? Is your attitude problematic? What does your boss mean by "unsatisfactory"?

The ability to define difficult concepts is always useful. At home, a friend or loved one may ask you to define *commitment*. If you mention that a movie was *great*, you may need to clarify what you mean by that word. In a political science class, you might define *socialism, capitalism*, or *communism*. At work, you might define your company's *winning strategy*.

DEFINITION **AT WORK**

In the following memo to a parent, reading specialist Amanda Wong defines a common reading disorder.

The topic sentence expresses the main idea.

Supporting sentences provide details and examples.

The concluding sentence brings the paragraph to a satisfying close.

As we have discussed, your daughter exhibits signs of a reading disorder commonly referred to as dyslexia, which is often found in visual learners. Such learners associate pictures with words. For example, your daughter would associate the word *tiger* with the animal, but she has no image to associate with words such as *a* or *the*. Therefore, she may become confused when she reads such words. A feeling of disorientation when reading the letters in words can further compound the problem. She may not perceive individual letters in sequence but might interpret them in a variety of orders and directions. Thus, a dyslexic child may see the word *dog* as *god* or *bog*. In our next meeting, I will give you some strategies to help your daughter with her reading.

LO 2 Explain how to write a definition paragraph.

The Definition Paragraph

When you write a definition paragraph, try to explain what a term means to you. For example, if someone asks you to define *bravery*, you might tell stories to illustrate the meaning of the word. You may also give examples of acts of bravery. You might even explain what bravery is not.

When you write a definition paragraph, remember the following two points.

◆ **Choose a term that you know something about.** You need to understand a term in order to say something relevant and interesting about it.

◆ **Give a clear definition.** In your first sentence, write a definition that is understandable to your reader, and support your definition with examples. Do not simply give a dictionary definition because your readers are capable of looking up the word themselves. Instead, describe what the word means to you.

HINT ◀ **Consider Your Audience**

When you write a definition paragraph, consider your audience. You may have to adjust your tone and vocabulary, depending on who reads the paragraph. For example, if you write a definition paragraph about computer viruses for your English class, you will have to use easily understandable terms. If you write the same paragraph for your computer class, you can use more technical terms.

PRACTICE 1

Read the paragraph, and then answer the questions.

Anonymous is not a tightly organized group; it is a very loose and open hacker collective. Generally, someone posts a threat on YouTube while wearing the white mask that was made famous in the film *V for Vendetta*. Occasionally, the members of the collective act as a unit to do a spectacular action. In the *Vanity Fair* article "World War 3.0," security expert Joshua Corman says that the hacker group's fame spread when they defended WikiLeaks. After PayPal, MasterCard, and Visa stopped accepting donations for WikiLeaks, thousands of Anonymous hackers worked in sync to temporarily shut down those companies' Web sites. At the same time, the collective is very loose and has no clear hierarchy. Anyone can make a video and claim to be a member, so the openness can be a disadvantage. Some members dilute the group's legitimacy when they make empty threats. For instance, in 2011, a mask-wearing individual claiming to be from Anonymous threatened to take down Facebook, but it never happened. According to Joshua Corman, youthful members have the power to cause a lot of damage, but they may lack "the compassion, humility, wisdom, or restraint to wield that power responsibly."

—Romina Raminez, student

Source: Gross, Michael Joseph. "World War 3.0." *Vanity Fair*. Conde Nast, May 2012. Web.

1. Underline the topic sentence.

2. What is the writer defining? _____

3. What information does the writer provide to support the definition? List some key ideas.

_____

_____

_____

LO 3 Explore topics.

Explore Topics

In the Warm Up, you will try an exploring strategy to generate ideas about different topics.

THE WRITER'S DESK   **Warm Up**

Think about the following questions, and write down the first ideas that come to your mind. Try to think of two or three ideas for each topic.

EXAMPLE: What is slang? Think of some examples of slang.

—*words people use for effect*

—*cool, dude, bro*

—*different cultural groups have their own slang terms*

1. What is a white lie? Give some examples of white lies.

2. What is binge viewing?

3. What are some characteristics of a blended or reconstructed family?

▶ **DEVELOPING**

LO 4 Identify the topic sentence of a definition paragraph.

The Topic Sentence

A clear topic sentence for a definition paragraph introduces the term and provides a definition. There are three basic ways to define a term.

◆ By synonym
◆ By category
◆ By negation

Definition by Synonym

The easiest way to define a term is to supply a synonym (a word that has a similar meaning). This type of definition is useful if the original term is difficult to understand and the synonym is a more familiar word.

ESSAY LINK
In a definition essay, the thesis statement expresses the controlling idea. In the thesis, you can define the term by synonym, category, or negation.

<table>
<tr><td>term</td><td>+</td><td>synonym</td></tr>
</table>

term	+	synonym
Plinking		is embedding a product or service link in a video.

I am a procrastinator,   which means I tend to put things off.

Definition by Category

A more effective way to define a term is to give a definition by category (or class). When you define by category, you determine the larger group to which the term belongs. Then you determine what unique characteristics set the term apart from others in that category.

term +	category +	detail
A farce is	a dramatic work	filled with exaggerated and humorous situations.
Luddites are	people	who are skeptical about new technology.

Definition by Negation

When you define by negation, you explain what a term does not mean. You can then include a sentence explaining what it does mean. Definition by negation is especially useful when your readers have preconceived ideas about something. Your definition explains that the term does not mean what the reader previously thought.

term +	what it is not +	what it is
Alcoholism	is not an invented disease;	it is a serious physical dependency.
Hackers	are not playful computer geeks;	they are criminals.

GRAMMAR HINT ◄ Using Semicolons

When you write a definition by negation, you can join the two separate and independent sentences with a semicolon.

Independent clause   ;   independent clause
Feminists are not man haters; they are people who want fairness and equality for women.

PRACTICE 2

A. Write a one-sentence definition by synonym for each of the following terms. Your definition should include the term and a synonym. If necessary, you can look up the terms in the dictionary; however, define each one using your own words.

EXAMPLE: To capitulate _means to give up or surrender._

1. To procrastinate _____

2. A pseudonym _____

B. Write a one-sentence definition by category for the following terms. Make sure that your definition includes the term, a category, and details.

EXAMPLE: Jargon *is vocabulary used by specific professions.*

3. A knockoff _____

_____

4. A superstorm _____

_____

C. Write a one-sentence definition by negation for the following terms. Explain what each term is not, followed by what each term is.

EXAMPLE: A placebo *is not a real drug; it is a sugar pill.*

5. A YouTube addict _____

_____

6. A vote _____

_____

Use the Right Word

When you write a definition paragraph, it is important to use precise words to define the term. Moreover, when you define a term by category, make sure that the category for your term is correct. For example, look at the following imprecise definitions of insomnia.

Insomnia is the (inability) to sleep well.
(Insomnia is not an ability or an inability.)

Insomnia is (when) you cannot sleep well.
(*When* refers to a time, but insomnia is not a time.)

Insomnia is the (nights) when you do not get enough sleep.
(Insomnia is not days or nights.)

Insomnia is (where) it is hard to fall asleep.
(*Where* refers to a place, but insomnia is not a place.)

Now look at a better definition of insomnia.

category
Insomnia is a **sleeping disorder** characterized by the inability to sleep well.

HINT ◂ **Make a Point**

Defining a term by synonym, category, or negation is the guideline for writing topic sentences. However, keep in mind that your paragraph will be more interesting if you express an attitude or point of view in your topic sentence.

No point	Anorexia is an eating disorder.
Point	Anorexia is a tragic eating disorder that is difficult to cure.

PRACTICE 3

Revise each sentence using precise language.

EXAMPLE: Tuning out is when you ignore something.

Tuning out is the action of ignoring something.

1. Claustrophobia is the inability to be in a small place.

   _____

   _____

2. A bully is the abuse of power over others.

   _____

   _____

3. Adolescence is where you are between childhood and adulthood.

   _____

   _____

4. Ego surfing is when you surf the Internet to find references to yourself.

   _____

   _____

VOCABULARY BOOST

Using Your Thesaurus

Work with a partner to brainstorm synonyms or expressions that can replace each word listed below. If you have trouble coming up with ideas, use your thesaurus.

1. optimist _____

2. depressed _____

3. lazy _____

4. reckless _____

Later, when you finish writing your definition paragraph, identify any repeated words and replace them with synonyms.

THE WRITER'S DESK Write Topic Sentences

For each of the following, write a topic sentence in which you define the topic. You can look for ideas in the Warm Up on page 98. Remember to use precise language in your definition.

EXAMPLE: Topic: Slang

Topic sentence: Slang is informal language that changes rapidly and exists in various forms among different cultural groups.

1. Topic: A white lie

    Topic sentence: _____

    _____

2. Topic: Binge viewing

    Topic sentence: _____

    _____

3. Topic: A blended family

    Topic sentence: _____

    _____

LO 5 Identify the supporting ideas of a definition paragraph.

The Supporting Ideas

After you have developed an effective topic sentence, generate supporting ideas. In a definition paragraph, you can give examples that clarify your definition.

Think about how you will organize your examples. Most definition paragraphs use emphatic order, which means that examples are placed from the most to the least important or from the least to the most important.

Visualizing Definition

PRACTICE 4

Brainstorm supporting ideas for the following topic sentence. Using words or phrases, describe each example of timeless fashion.

Topic Sentence: Men's timeless fashions remain popular and will not go out of style.

_____   _____   _____

_____   _____   _____

THE WRITER'S DESK Develop Supporting Ideas

Choose one of your topic sentences from the Writer's Desk on pages 101–102. List three or four examples that best illustrate the definition.

EXAMPLE:

Topic sentence: Slang is informal language that changes rapidly and exists in various forms among different cultural groups.

Supports: —words change in different eras

—rappers, punks, goths have own terms

—used like a code between friends

—words show inventive, creative thinking

Topic sentence: _____

_____

Supports: _____

_____

_____

_____

The Paragraph Plan

A good definition paragraph includes a complete definition of the term and provides adequate examples to support the central definition. When creating a definition paragraph plan, make sure that your examples provide varied evidence and do not just repeat the definition. Also add details that will help clarify your supporting examples.

Topic Sentence: Slang is informal language that changes rapidly and exists in various forms among different cultural groups.

Support 1: Slang is a type of code used between friends.

Details: —Punks might call each other emo or poseurs.

—People outside the group might not understand slang.

—Words often help define relationships among group members.

Support 2: Slang words often show very inventive and creative thinking.

Details: —Computer users have come up with a wide variety of net slang terms.

—Some terms are very illustrative and visual.

LO 6 Develop a definition paragraph plan.

ESSAY LINK
In a definition essay, the thesis statement is in the introduction. Each supporting idea is in a distinct body paragraph with its own topic sentence.

Support 3: Many slang words come and go quickly.

Details: —In the 1920s, people used words that have gone out of fashion.

—In the 1950s, people used words such as hipster or swell.

—Slang words from the early 2000s, such as homie, are already becoming obsolete.

THE WRITER'S DESK   **Write a Paragraph Plan**

Create a detailed paragraph plan using the topic sentence that you wrote for the Writer's Desk on page 103. Arrange the supporting details in a logical order.

Topic sentence: _____

_____

Support 1: _____

Details: _____

_____

_____

Support 2: _____

Details: _____

_____

_____

Support 3: _____

Details: _____

_____

_____

L0 7 Write the first draft of a definition paragraph.

The First Draft

After you outline your ideas in a plan, you are ready to write the first draft. Remember to write complete sentences. You might include transitional words or expressions to help your ideas flow smoothly.

Transitional Words and Expressions

Transitional expressions can show different levels of importance. The following transitions are useful in definition paragraphs.

To Show the Level of Importance	
clearly	next
first	one quality . . . another quality
most of all	second
most important	undoubtedly

THE WRITER'S DESK   Write the First Draft

In the previous Writer's Desk, you developed a paragraph plan. Now write the first draft of your definition paragraph. Before you write, carefully review your paragraph plan and make any necessary changes.

▶ REVISING AND EDITING

Revise and Edit a Definition Paragraph

L0 8 Revise and edit a definition paragraph.

When you finish writing a definition paragraph, carefully review your work and revise it to make the definition as clear as possible to your readers. Check that you have organized your steps logically, and remove any irrelevant details.

PRACTICE 5

Read the following student paragraph and answer the questions.

Slang is informal language that changes rapidly and exists in various forms among different cultural groups. It is a type of code used between friends. Punks call each other emo or poseurs. Such words denote a persons status in the group. Often, those outside the group might not understand the group's slang. My grandmother, for example, doesn't know what a gamer is. Soldiers, athletes, musicians, and even wealthy industrialists come up with their own particular jargon. The rich might put down social climbers as wannabes. They might call a spouse a trophy wife or husband. Slang words often show very inventive and creative thinking. Computer users have come up with a wide variety of net slang terms such as blog, flamer, troll, cyberspook, or flamebait. Some terms are very illustrative. Jerk sounds like a fast movement. Whipped is similar to the sound a whip makes. Most slang words come and go quick, and they change over time. In the 1920s, men would call a woman's legs gams and money clams. In the 1980s, people used words such as bodacious, dweeb, and yuppie. Those words are no longer popular. Even slang words from the early years of the twenty-first century, such as homie, are already becoming obsolete.

—Alexis Wright, student

Revising

1. Underline the topic sentence.

2. What type of definition does the topic sentence contain? Circle the best answer.

   a. definition by synonym   b. definition by category

   c. definition by negation

3. This paragraph lacks sentence variety. Revise the paragraph to give it more sentence variety by combining sentences or changing the first word of some sentences. (For more information about combining sentences and sentence variety, see Chapters 17–19.)

4. The paragraph lacks transitions to show the order of ideas. Add some transitional words or expressions.

5. The paragraph needs a concluding sentence. Add a concluding sentence in the lines provided.

    _____

    _____

GRAMMAR LINK
See the following chapters for more information about these grammar topics:
Apostrophes, Chapter 35
Adjectives and Adverbs, Chapter 30

Editing

6. There is one apostrophe error. Circle and correct the error.

7. There is an error in adverb form. Circle and correct the error.

THE WRITER'S DESK   **Revise and Edit Your Paragraph**

Revise and edit the paragraph that you wrote for the previous Writer's Desk. Make sure that your paragraph has unity, adequate support, and coherence. Also correct any errors in grammar, spelling, punctuation, and mechanics.

Reflect On It

Think about what you have learned in this chapter. If you do not know an answer, review that topic.

1. In definition writing, what do you do? _____

    _____

2. Write an example of a definition by synonym. _____

    _____

3. Write an example of a definition by category. _____

    _____

4. Write an example of a definition by negation. _____

    _____

THE WRITER'S ROOM MyWritingLab™

Writing Activity 1: Topics

Choose any of the following topics, or choose your own topic. Then write a definition paragraph.

General Topics	**College and Work-Related Topics**
1. a hacktivist	6. integrity
2. a spoiled child	7. a workaholic
3. fashion police	8. an opportunist
4. texting addict	9. the glass ceiling
5. a lightbulb moment	10. newbie

Writing Activity 2: Media Writing

Watch a television show about people who fight to succeed. Examples are *American Idol*, *The Voice*, *The Wire*, *The Amazing Race*, *Parks and Recreation*, or *Survivor*. You could watch a documentary such as *The Corporation* or a movie such as *Lincoln*, *The Godfather*, *There Will Be Blood*, or *Fame*. You can also watch YouTube videos about people who want to become famous. Define the term "blind ambition," and support your definition with examples or anecdotes from the media.

WRITING LINK

MORE DEFINITION WRITING TOPICS

Chapter 19, Writer's Room topic 1 (page 296)
Chapter 24, Writer's Room topic 1 (page 345)
Chapter 26, Writer's Room topic 1 (page 370)
Chapter 35, Writer's Room topic 1 (page 483)

READING LINK

MORE DEFINITION READINGS

"Homophobia" by Dominic Chartrand (page 209)
"What Is Luck?" by Matthew Hutson (page 211)
"Being a Hyphenated American" by Zaina Arafat (page 508)
"Musicophilia" by Oliver Sacks (page 531)

Definition Paragraph Checklist

As you write your definition paragraph, review the checklist at the end of the book. Also ask yourself the following questions.

☐ Does my topic sentence contain a definition by synonym, negation, or category?

☐ Do all of my supporting sentences relate to the topic sentence?

☐ Do I use concise language in my definition?

☐ Do I include enough examples to help define the term?

Classification 9

Parents often organize their children's toys. In this photo, the toys are divided into animals, trucks, and blocks. In classification writing, you divide a topic into categories to explain it.

WRITERS' EXCHANGE

Work with a partner or in a group. Classify the next words into three or four different categories. What are the categories? Why did you choose those categories?

mechanic	fertilizer	kitchen	office
garden	cook	programmer	computer
microwave	landscaper	wrench	garage

> ▶ **EXPLORING**

What Is Classification?

When you **classify**, you sort a subject into more understandable categories. The categories must all belong to the subject, yet they must also be distinct from one another. For example, you might write a paragraph about the most common types of pets and sort the subject pets into the categories cats, dogs, and birds.

Classification occurs in many situations. At home, you could classify the responsibilities of each person in the family, or you could classify your bills. In a biology course, you might write a paper about the different types of cells, or in a commerce course, you may write about the categories in a financial statement. On the job, you might advertise the different types of products or services that your company sells.

CLASSIFICATION **AT WORK**

Robert Luzynski, an allergy specialist, wrote the following information in a brochure for his patients.

Topic sentence expresses the main idea.

Supporting details provide details and examples.

The concluding sentence brings the paragraph to a satisfying close.

If you exhibit allergic symptoms to animals, there are three types of treatment that you can follow. The most effective is to avoid contact with known allergens. Thus, avoid bringing pets into the home. If you have a pet, consider using an air cleaner, vacuum two to three times a week, and ensure that the animal is groomed frequently to remove loose fur and dander. The second type of treatment consists of medications. Antihistamines help alleviate the symptoms of allergic reactions, but they do not cure allergies. It is important to read the labels carefully, as some antihistamines cause drowsiness. A final method, desensitization, is an extended treatment involving allergy shots. You would be exposed to gradually increasing amounts of specific allergens. The treatment lasts for an extended period of time, and the goal is to reduce your sensitivity to the allergens. One of these treatments should work for you.

The Classification Paragraph

To find a topic for a classification paragraph, think of something that can be sorted into different groups, or categories. Also determine a reason for classifying the items. When you are planning your ideas for a classification paragraph, remember these two points.

> **ESSAY LINK**
> Classification essays also require a classification principle and distinct categories.

1. **Use a common classification principle.** A **classification principle** is the overall method that you use to sort the subject into categories. To find the classification principle, think about one common characteristic that unites the different categories. For example, if your subject is the telephone, your classification principle might be any of the following:

   —types of annoying phone calls
   —reasons that people buy cell phones
   —types of long-distance service
   —types of customer reactions to telephone salespeople

2. **Sort the subject into distinct categories.** A classification paragraph should have two or more categories.

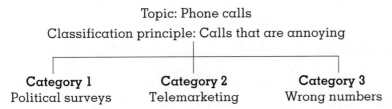

Topic: Phone calls

Classification principle: Calls that are annoying

Category 1	**Category 2**	**Category 3**
Political surveys	Telemarketing	Wrong numbers

PRACTICE 1

Read the next paragraph and answer the questions.

There may be no way to rid the world of dishonesty, but researchers have learned a great deal about how to tell when someone is lying. Clues to deception are found in four elements of a performance: words, voice, body language, and facial expression. People who are good liars mentally rehearse their lines, but they cannot always avoid inconsistencies that suggest deception. A simple slip of the tongue—something the person did not mean to say in quite that way—can occur in even a carefully prepared performance. Secondly, voice is also useful to determine when a person is lying. Tone and patterns of speech contain clues to deception because they are hard to control. Especially when trying to hide a powerful emotion, a person cannot easily prevent the voice from trembling or breaking. A "leak," conveyed through body language, may tip off an observer to deception. Body movements, sudden swallowing, or rapid breathing may show that a person is nervous. Because there are forty-three muscles in the face, facial expressions are even more difficult to control than body language. A real smile is usually accompanied by a relaxed expression and lot of "laugh lines" around the eyes; a phony smile seems forced and unnatural, with fewer wrinkles around the mouth and eyes. We all try to fake emotion, but the more powerful the emotion, the more difficult it is to deceive others.

—John J. Macionis, "Spotting Lies: What Are the Clues" in *Sociology*

1. Underline the topic sentence of this paragraph.

2. State the four categories that the author discusses, and list some details about each category.

a. _____

Details: _____

_____

b. _____

Details: _____

_____

c. _____

Details: _____

_____

d. _____

Details: _____

_____

3. Who is the audience for this paragraph?

_____

4. What is the purpose of this paragraph? Circle the best answer.

a. to persuade   b. to inform   c. to entertain

LO 3 Explore topics.

Explore Topics

In the Warm Up, you will try an exploring strategy to generate ideas about different topics.

THE WRITER'S DESK   **Warm Up**

Think about the following questions, and write down the first ideas that come to your mind. Try to think of two or three ideas for each topic.

EXAMPLE: What are some types of cheaters?

_____

_____

_____

1. List some clothing that you own. You might think about old clothing, comfortable clothing, beautiful clothing, and so on.

_____

_____

_____

2. What are some different types of sports fans? To get ideas, you might think about some people you know and the way that they show team support.

_____

_____

_____

3. List some skills or abilities people need for different jobs. As you brainstorm ideas, consider manual labor as well as professional and office jobs.

_____

_____

_____

Making a Classification Chart

A **classification chart** is a visual representation of the main topic and its categories. Making a classification chart can help you identify the categories more clearly so that you will be able to write more exact topic sentences.

When you classify items, remember to use a single classification principle to sort the items. For example, if you are classifying movies, you might classify them according to their ratings: General Audience, Parental Guidance, and Restricted. You could also classify movies according to their country of origin: British, American, and French, for example. Remember that one classification principle must unite the group.

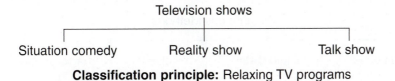

Television shows

| Situation comedy | Reality show | Talk show |

Classification principle: Relaxing TV programs

> **HINT** ◄ Categories Should Not Overlap
>
> When sorting a topic into categories, make sure that the categories do not overlap. For example, you would not classify drivers into careful drivers, aggressive drivers, and bad drivers because aggressive drivers could also be bad drivers. Each category should be distinct.

PRACTICE 2

In the following classification charts, a subject has been broken down into distinct categories. The items in the group should have the same classification principle. Cross out one item in each group that does not belong. Then write down the classification principle that unites the group.

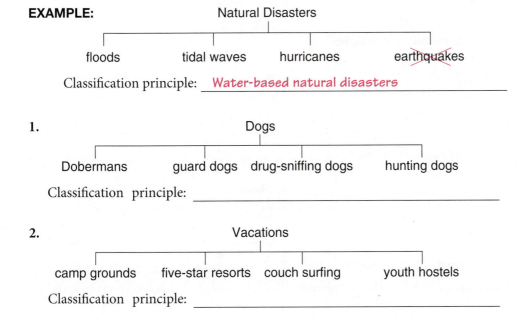

EXAMPLE: Natural Disasters

floods   tidal waves   hurricanes   ~~earthquakes~~

Classification principle: _Water-based natural disasters_

1. Dogs

Dobermans   guard dogs   drug-sniffing dogs   hunting dogs

Classification principle: _____

2. Vacations

camp grounds   five-star resorts   couch surfing   youth hostels

Classification principle: _____

3.

Books

| paperback | hardcover | best-sellers | online |

Classification principle: _____

4.

Children

| spoiled | middle | eldest | youngest |

Classification principle: _____

5.

Weight-Loss Methods

| fruit diets | liquid diets | exercise | magic-pill diets |

Classification principle: _____

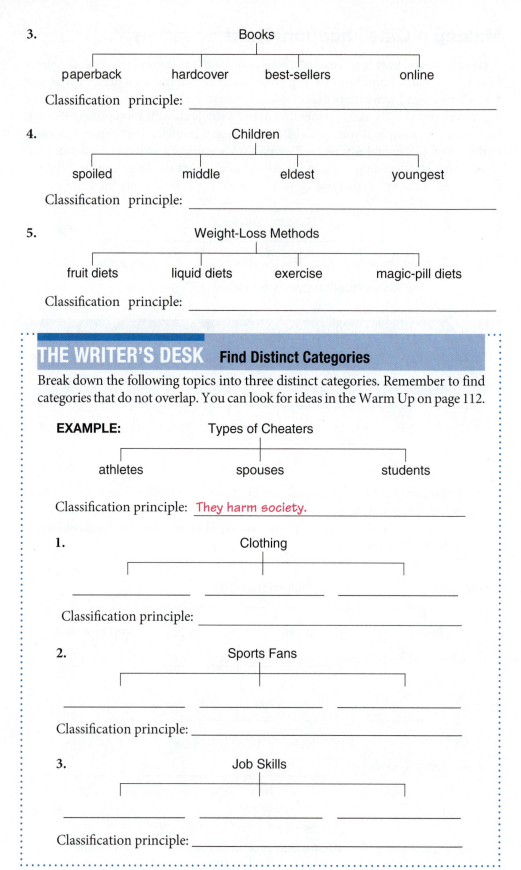

THE WRITER'S DESK   Find Distinct Categories

Break down the following topics into three distinct categories. Remember to find categories that do not overlap. You can look for ideas in the Warm Up on page 112.

EXAMPLE:

Types of Cheaters

| athletes | spouses | students |

Classification principle: _They harm society._

1.

Clothing

_____   _____   _____

Classification principle: _____

2.

Sports Fans

_____   _____   _____

Classification principle: _____

3.

Job Skills

_____   _____   _____

Classification principle: _____

▶ **DEVELOPING**

The Topic Sentence

The topic sentence in a classification paragraph clearly indicates what you will classify. It also includes the controlling idea, which is the classification principle that you use.

LO 4 Identify the topic sentence of a classification paragraph.

> **ESSAY LINK**
> In a classification essay, the thesis statement expresses the controlling idea, or classification principle.

Several types of students can completely disrupt a classroom.

Topic	Students
Classification principle	Disruptive types

You can also mention the types of categories in your topic sentence.

The most annoying telephone calls are surveys, telemarketing, and wrong numbers.

Topic	Telephone calls
Classification principle	Types of annoying calls

HINT ◀ Make a Point

To make interesting classification paragraphs, try to express an attitude, opinion, or feeling about the topic. For example, you can write a paragraph about types of diets, but it is more interesting if you make a point about the types of diets.

Poor	Types of diets
Better	Types of **dangerous** diets
	Types of **effective** diets

THE WRITER'S DESK   Write Topic Sentences

Look again at what you wrote in the Warm Up on page 112. Also look at the classification charts that you made for each topic. Now write clear topic sentences. Remember that your topic sentence can include the different categories you will be discussing.

EXAMPLE: Topic: Types of cheaters

Topic sentence: _Three types of cheaters harm our society._ _____

_____

_____

1. Topic: Clothing

    Topic sentence: _____

    _____

2. Topic: Sports Fans

   Topic sentence: _____

   _____

3. Topic: Job skills

   Topic sentence: _____

   _____

LO 5 Identify the supporting ideas of a classification paragraph.

The Supporting Ideas

After you have developed an effective topic sentence, generate supporting ideas. In a classification paragraph, you can list details about each of your categories.

Visualizing Classification

PRACTICE 3

Brainstorm supporting ideas for the following topic sentence. List unhealthy ingredients in each type of food.

Topic Sentence: Junk food can be classified into three main categories.

Salty

_____

_____

Sweet

_____

_____

Fatty

_____

_____

LO 6 Develop a classification paragraph plan.

The Paragraph Plan

You can make a standard paragraph plan. You can also create a pie chart to help you visualize the different categories.

Finally, an effective way to visualize your categories and supporting ideas is to make a detailed classification chart. Break down the main topic into several categories, and then give details about each category.

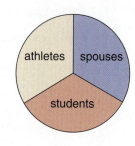

Three types of cheaters harm our society.

athletes	spouses	students
- take steroids - lie to media - use tricks to win	- break their vows - have affairs - hurt their families	- cheat on tests - plagiarize - find answers with smartphones

ESSAY LINK
You can make a detailed classification chart when you develop your classification essay. Each supporting idea would become a distinct paragraph.

THE WRITER'S DESK   Make a Detailed Classification Chart

Choose one of the topic sentences that you wrote for the previous Writer's Desk, and make a detailed classification chart. Arrange the supporting details in a logical order. You can refer to the information you generated in the Warm Up.

Topic sentence: _____

_____

HINT ◄ Use the Chart as a Plan

Your classification chart can also serve as your paragraph plan. Like a paragraph plan, your chart contains your topic sentence, your supporting ideas (categories), and details about each idea (category).

The First Draft

L07 Write the first draft of a classification paragraph.

After you outline your ideas in a classification chart or plan, you are ready to write the first draft. Remember to write complete sentences. You might include transitional words or expressions to help your ideas flow smoothly.

Transitional Words and Expressions

Some classification paragraphs use transitional words and expressions to show which category is most important and to signal a movement from one category to the next. The following transitions are very useful in classification writing.

To Show Importance	To Show Types of Categories
above all	one kind … another kind
clearly	the first/second type
the most important	the first/second kind
most of all	the last category
particularly	

THE WRITER'S DESK   Write the First Draft

Write the first draft of your classification paragraph. Before you write, carefully review your detailed classification chart and make any necessary changes.

VOCABULARY BOOST

Classifying Parts of Words

A prefix is added to the beginning of a word, and it changes the word's meaning. A suffix is added to the end of a word, and it also changes the word's meaning. Review the list of ten common prefixes and suffixes. Then come up with at least two more words using the listed prefix or suffix.

Prefixes	Example	
anti = against	antiwar	_____
un = not	unable	_____
re = again	redo	_____
bi = two	bilingual	_____
mis = wrong	misspell	_____

Suffixes	Example	
er = doer	teacher	_____
ment = condition	agreement	_____
less = without	homeless	_____
ous = full of	courageous	_____
ful = filled with	respectful	_____

▶ REVISING AND EDITING

LO 8 Revise and edit a classification paragraph.

Revise and Edit a Classification Paragraph

When you finish writing a classification paragraph, carefully review your work and revise it to make sure that the categories do not overlap. Check to make sure that you have organized your paragraph logically, and remove any irrelevant details.

PRACTICE 4

Read the following student paragraph and answer the questions.

Many people have a strong sense of civic duty. However, three types of cheaters harm our society. First, cheaters in sports disappoint fans. In 2012, many Americans became disillusioned when the U.S. Anti-Doping Agency (USADA) concluded that Lance Armstrong used performance-enhancing drugs when he won the Tour de France seven times. The USADA stripped Armstrong of his gold medals. Furthermore, some people cheat in relationships. They may commit adultery. Which can be emotionally and financially damaging to their partners and children. Finally, academic cheating can also harm a community. Some students cheat on exams, and some academics plagiarize from their colleagues' work. A student may be expelled or recieve other sanctions if he or she is caught. Academic cheating can mar a student's future prospects, a professor's career advancement, and an institution may lose its reputation . In conclusion, different types of cheating can lead to harmful consequences for the cheater and society.

—Theodore Johnson, student

Revising

1. What is the classification principle in this paragraph?

    _____

2. What are the three categories?

    _____

3. Add one more supporting example to each category.

    _____

    _____

    _____

Editing

4. There is a sentence fragment. Identify and correct the fragment.
5. There is one spelling error. Identify and correct the error.
6. There is one error in parallel structure. Underline the error and correct it.

> **GRAMMAR LINK**
> See the following chapters for more information about these grammar topics:
> Fragments, Chapter 20
> Parallel Structure, Chapter 22
> Spelling, Chapter 33

GRAMMAR HINT

Use parallel structure when words or phrases are joined in a series.

The three categories of allergies are <u>animal allergies</u>, <u>food allergies</u>, and
drug allergies
<u>people who are allergic to medicine</u>.

THE WRITER'S DESK   Revise and Edit Your Paragraph

Revise and edit the paragraph that you wrote for the previous Writer's Desk. Make sure that your paragraph has unity, adequate support, and coherence. Also correct any errors in grammar, spelling, punctuation, and mechanics.

Reflect On It

Think about what you have learned in this chapter. If you do not know an answer, review that topic.

1. What is classification? _____

   _____

2. What is the classification principle? _____

   _____

3. Give examples of various classification principles that you can use to classify the following items.

   EXAMPLE: Cars _Types of owners, degrees of fuel efficiency, price_____

   a. Animals _____

   b. Sports _____

4. Now choose one classification principle for each item in question 3. Write down three possible categories for that item.

   EXAMPLE: Cars

   Classification principle: _____

   Categories: _____

   a. Animals

      Classification principle: _____

   Categories: _____

   b. Sports

      Classification principle: _____

   Categories: _____

5. Why is it useful to make a classification chart?

   _____

THE WRITER'S ROOM

MyWritingLab™

MyWritingLab™
Complete these writing assignments at mywritinglab.com

Writing Activity 1: Topics

Choose any of the following topics, or choose your own topic. Then write a classification paragraph.

General Topics

Categories of . . .

1. relationship problems
2. friends
3. tech users
4. games
5. entertainment

College and Work-Related Topics

Categories of . . .

6. campus fashions
7. housing
8. bosses
9. cheating
10. coworkers

Writing Activity 2: Media Writing

Watch a television show or movie about spies. Television shows are *Homeland*, *Nikita*, and *Burn Notice*, and movies are *Zero Dark Thirty*, *Argo*, and *Mission: Impossible*. You could also watch James Bond or Bourne Identity films. Classify spies into types or describe different types of spying, and use examples to support your ideas.

WRITING LINK

MORE CLASSIFICATION WRITING TOPICS

Chapter 22, Writer's Room topic 2 (page 319)
Chapter 29, Writer's Room topic 1 (page 409)
Chapter 32, Writer's Room topic 2 (page 441)
Chapter 34, Writer's Room topic 2 (page 470)
Chapter 36, Writer's Room topic 2 (page 491)

READING LINK

MORE CLASSIFICATION READINGS

"Breaking Traffic Laws" by Lonzell Courtney (page 214)
"The Purpose of Pets" by W. Stephen Damron (page 215)
"Fads" by David A. Locher (page 510)
"Advertising Appeals" by Michael R. Solomon, Greg W. Marshall, and Elnora W. Stuart (page 542)

Classification Paragraph Checklist

As you write your classification paragraph, review the checklist at the end of the book. Also ask yourself the following questions.

☐ Does my topic sentence explain the categories that will be discussed?

☐ Do I use a common classification principle to unite the various categories?

☐ Do I offer sufficient details to explain each category?

☐ Do I arrange the categories in a logical manner?

☐ Does all of the supporting information relate to the categories that are being discussed?

☐ Do I include categories that do not overlap?

Comparison and Contrast 10

Shoppers compare prices in order to make an informed decision. In this chapter, you will practice comparing and contrasting.

LEARNING OBJECTIVES

LO 1 Define comparison and contrast. **(p. 124)**

LO 2 Explain how to write a comparison and contrast paragraph. **(p. 124)**

LO 3 Explore topics. **(p. 127)**

LO 4 Identify the topic sentence of a comparison and contrast paragraph. **(p. 128)**

LO 5 Identify the supporting ideas of a comparison and contrast paragraph. **(p. 129)**

LO 6 Develop a comparison and contrast paragraph plan. **(p. 130)**

LO 7 Write the first draft of a comparison and contrast paragraph. **(p. 132)**

LO 8 Revise and edit a comparison and contrast paragraph. **(p. 132)**

WRITERS' EXCHANGE

Work with a partner. Each of you should discuss your music preferences. Then make a short list showing which music preferences you share and which ones you do not share.

▶ **EXPLORING**

LO 1 Define comparison and contrast.

What Is Comparison and Contrast?

When you want to decide between options, you compare and contrast. You **compare** to find similarities and **contrast** to find differences. The exercise of comparing and contrasting can help you make judgments about things. It can also help you better understand familiar things.

You often compare and contrast. At home, when you watch TV, you might compare and contrast different programs. At college, you might compare and contrast different psychological or political theories. On the job, you might need to compare and contrast computer operating systems, shipping services, or sales figures.

COMPARISON AND CONTRAST AT WORK

In this paragraph, Stephen Bergeron, an artist, compares and contrasts acrylic and oil paints.

The topic sentence expresses the main idea.

Supporting sentences provide details and examples.

The concluding sentence brings the paragraph to a satisfying close.

Both acrylic and oil paints have useful characteristics. Acrylics, which were developed about fifty years ago, can be mixed with water. The brushes can be easily rinsed out. The paints do not have a strong odor, so they can be used indoors. A great advantage of acrylics is that they can mimic water color or gouache, and they can be used as a base painting under oils. Additionally, some artists appreciate the quick drying time of acrylics. Oil paints, on the other hand, have a slow drying time, which is useful when artists want to mix and layer colors. Although oil paints can have a strong smell when mixed with mineral spirits or linseed oil, the texture of oil paints is creamier than that of acrylics. Finally, most artists find that oil paints have deeper and more vivid colors than acrylics. A beginning artist should experiment with both types of paint and find the one that suits his or her needs.

LO 2 Explain how to write a comparison and contrast paragraph.

The Comparison and Contrast Paragraph

In a comparison and contrast paragraph, you can compare and contrast two different subjects, or you can compare and contrast different aspects of a single subject. For example, you might contrast married life and single life, or you might write only about marriage but contrast the expectations people have before they get married to what realistically happens after marriage.

When you write a comparison and contrast paragraph, remember to think about your specific purpose.

- **Your purpose could be to make judgments about two things.** For example, you might compare and contrast two restaurants in order to convince your readers that one is preferable.

- **Your purpose could be to describe or understand two familiar things.** For example, you might compare two stories to help your readers understand their thematic similarities.

Comparison and Contrast Patterns

Comparison and contrast texts follow two common patterns. One pattern is to present the details point by point. Another is to present one topic and then the other topic.

When you are thinking about ideas for writing a comparison and contrast paragraph, you can choose one of two methods to organize your supporting ideas: point by point or topic by topic.

Point by Point

Present one point about Topic A and then one point about Topic B. Keep following this pattern until you have a few points for each topic. You go back and forth from one side to the other like tennis players hitting a ball back and forth across a net.

Topic by Topic

Present all points related to Topic A in the first few sentences, and then present all points related to Topic B in the last few sentences. So, you present one side and then the other side, just as lawyers might in the closing arguments of a court case.

Kyle's Example

Kyle is trying to decide whether he should take a job in another city or stay at his current job in his hometown. His goal is to decide whether he should move or stay where he is. Kyle could organize his information using a point-by-point or topic-by-topic method.

> **ESSAY LINK**
> To write a comparison and contrast essay, organize *each paragraph* in point-by-point or topic-by-topic form.

Point by Point		**Topic by Topic**	
Job A	Low salary	Job A	Low salary
Job B	Good salary		Parents nearby
Job A	Parents nearby		Like my colleagues
Job B	Parents far away		
Job A	Like my colleagues	Job B	Better salary
Job B	Don't know colleagues		Parents far away
			Don't know colleagues

PRACTICE 1

Read the next two paragraphs and answer the questions.

A.   Mai Thi Hiep, born to a Vietnamese mother and an American soldier, was placed for adoption in the United States at age seven. Hiep—renamed Heidi—was culturally molded in America and distanced from her birth country's values. Raised by a single woman from Pulaski, Tennessee, Heidi forgot her native language and acquired all of the tastes and attitudes of American teenagers, going to malls and using the current slang. By 1997, she had married an American serviceman and become the mother of two young daughters. That year, longing to reconnect with her roots, Heidi visited her birth mother in Vietnam. Although the reunion was deeply moving, Heidi found the sights and sounds of Vietnam strange and the poverty shocking. She did not know the etiquette of how to eat, which involved dipping food from common plates into sauces. After a few days, Heidi was asked to help her sister financially. Then her brother, mentioning that he and his siblings had cared for their mother for twenty-two years, asked Heidi to do her "filial duty" and send money monthly. Heidi felt shocked and insulted, thinking that she had come to be reunited, not to provide financial salvation. Her family members expected "Hiep" to conform to their cultural values. Heidi, however, interpreted her family's expectations through the lens of American culture.

—Nancy Bonvillain, *Cultural Anthropology*

1. Underline the topic sentence. Be careful; it may not be the first sentence in the paragraph.

2. What does the writer compare? _____

3. What pattern of comparison does the author follow? Circle the correct answer.

   a. Point by point   b. Topic by topic

4. What does the paragraph focus on? Circle the correct answer.

   a. Similarities   b. Differences

B.   There are some major differences between the supermarket and a traditional marketplace. The cacophony of a traditional market has given way to programmed innocuous music, punctuated by enthusiastically intoned commercials. A stroll through a traditional market offers an array of sensuous aromas; if you are conscious of smelling something in a supermarket, there is a problem. The life and death matter of eating, expressed in traditional markets by the sale of vegetables with stems and roots and by hanging animal carcasses, is purged from the supermarket, where food is processed somewhere else, or at least trimmed out of sight. But the most fundamental difference between a traditional market and the places through which you push your cart is that in a modern retail setting nearly all the selling is done without people. The product is totally dissociated from the personality of any particular person selling it—with the possible exception of those who appear in its advertising. The supermarket purges sociability, which slows down sales.

—Thomas Hine, "What's in a Package?"

5. Underline the topic sentence.

6. What pattern of comparison does the author follow? Circle the best answer.

   a. Point by point   b. Topic by topic

7. What does the author focus on? Circle the best answer.

   a. Similarities   b. Differences

8. Using your own words, list the main differences.

Traditional market	**Supermarket**
_____	_____
_____	_____
_____	_____
_____	_____

VOCABULARY BOOST

Brainstorming Opposites

Work with a partner to brainstorm words that have the opposite meaning of the words listed on the next page. Try to come up with as many antonyms (words that have the opposite meaning) as possible.

Example: tiny   huge, immense, gigantic

shy   _____

happy   _____

whisper   _____

spicy   _____

Explore Topics

LO 3 Explore topics.

In the Warm Up, you will try an exploring strategy to generate ideas about different topics.

THE WRITER'S DESK   **Warm Up**

Think about the following questions, and write down the first ideas that come to your mind. Try to think of two to three ideas for each topic. Then decide if a good paragraph would be about similarities or differences.

EXAMPLE: What are some key features of two cultural traditions?

My mother's tradition: Diwali	**My father's tradition: Hanukkah**
festival of lights	festival of lights
share gifts with siblings	light the menorah
great desserts	gold-wrapped chocolates

My paragraph will focus on ___X___ similarities _____ differences

1. What are some stereotypes about your nationality? What is the reality about your nationality?

Stereotypes	**Reality**
_____	_____
_____	_____
_____	_____

   This paragraph will focus on _____ similarities _____ differences.

2. What were your goals when you were a child? What are your goals today?

Goals in childhood	**Goals today**
_____	_____
_____	_____
_____	_____

   This paragraph will focus on _____ similarities _____ differences.

3. What are some qualities and characteristics of someone who is a good sport and someone who is a bad sport?

A good sport	**A bad sport**
_____	_____
_____	_____
_____	_____

   This paragraph will focus on _____ similarities _____ differences.

When you plan your comparison and contrast paragraph, decide whether you want to focus on comparing (looking at similarities), contrasting (looking at differences), or both. In a paragraph, it is usually best to focus on either comparing or contrasting. In a larger essay, you could more easily do both.

▶ **DEVELOPING**

LO 4 Identify the topic sentence of a comparison and contrast paragraph.

> **ESSAY LINK**
>
> In a comparison and contrast essay, the thesis statement expresses the main point of the essay.

The Topic Sentence

In a comparison and contrast paragraph, the topic sentence indicates what is being compared and contrasted and expresses a controlling idea.

Although all dogs make good house pets, large dogs are much more useful than small dogs.

Topic	Large dogs versus small dogs
Controlling idea	One is more useful than the other.

PRACTICE 2

Read each topic sentence, and then answer the questions that follow. State whether the paragraph would focus on similarities or differences.

EXAMPLE: Before the baby comes, people expect a beautiful world of soft coos and sweet smells, but the reality is quite different.

a. What is being compared? _Expectation versus reality of life with a baby_

b. What is the controlling idea? _Reality not as pleasant as expectation_

c. What will the paragraph focus on? Circle the correct answer.

Similarities   (Differences)

1. Many media pundits complain about reality television; however, reality shows are just as good as regular scripted shows.

   a. What is being compared? _____

   b. What is the controlling idea? _____

   _____

   c. What will the paragraph focus on? Circle the correct answer.

   Similarities   Differences

2. Women's sports lag behind men's in media attention, prize money, and salaries.

   a. What is being compared? _____

   b. What is the controlling idea? _____

   _____

   c. What does the paragraph focus on? Circle the best answer.

   Similarities   Differences

3. Texting can be as intimate as calling.

   a. What is being compared? _____

   b. What is the controlling idea? _____

   c. What does the paragraph focus on? Circle the correct answer.

   Similarities   Differences

THE WRITER'S DESK   **Write Topic Sentences**

For each topic, write whether you will focus on similarities or differences. Then, write three topic sentences. Look for ideas in the Writer's Desk Warm Up on page 127. Your topic sentence should include what you are comparing and contrasting, as well as a controlling idea.

EXAMPLE: Topic: Two cultural traditions

Focus: Similarities
                       _____

Topic sentence: Diwali and Hanukkah have some surprising similarities.
                       _____

1. Topic: Stereotypes and reality about my nation

   Focus: _____

   Topic sentence: _____

                       _____

2. Topic: Goals in childhood and goals in adulthood

   Focus: _____

   Topic sentence: _____

                       _____

3. Topic: People who are good and bad sports

   Focus: _____

   Topic sentence: _____

                       _____

The Supporting Ideas

After you have developed an effective topic sentence, generate supporting ideas. In a comparison and contrast paragraph, think of examples that help clarify the similarities or differences.

LO 5 Identify the supporting ideas of a comparison and contrast paragraph.

Visualizing Comparison and Contrast
PRACTICE 3

Brainstorm supporting ideas for the following topic sentence. Compare and contrast the types of heroes.

Topic Sentence: My childhood heroes were very different from my current heroes.

Childhood heros

Current heros

_____   _____

_____   _____

Make a Venn Diagram

To generate supporting ideas, you might try using a Venn diagram. In this example, you can see how the writer draws two circles to contrast Diwali and Hanukkah. Where the circles overlap, the writer includes similarities. If you are focusing only on similarities or differences, then you can make two separate circles.

<u>Diwali</u>
* candles and oil lamps lit for five days to symbolize the victory of good over evil
* food includes fried sweets and delicacies
* people give each other clothes & jewelry

* people light candles
* place candles near windows
* feasts
* gift giving

<u>Hanukkah</u>
* candles on menorah are lit each night for eight consecutive nights
* food is fried to symbolize the miraculous oil
* children receive money, clothing, or toys

LO 6 Develop a comparison and contrast paragraph plan.

The Paragraph Plan

Before you write a comparison and contrast paragraph, it is a good idea to make a paragraph plan. Decide which pattern you will follow: point by point or topic by topic. Write "**A**" and "**B**" alongside your topics. Then add supporting details. Make sure that each detail supports the topic sentence.

Topic Sentence: Diwali and Hanukkah have some surprising similarities.

POINT BY POINT

A/B Both celebrations are festivals of light.
Details: -People light candles.
-They place candles near windows.

A/B Both have traditions of feasts.
Details: -People eat fried sweets for Diwali.
-Everyone loves fried food for Hanukkah.

A/B Both celebrations include gift giving.
Details: -Diwali, people give clothing and jewelry to each other.
-Hanukkah, people give gifts to children.

TOPIC BY TOPIC

A Diwali is a festival of light.
Details: -Oil lamps are lit for five days, symbolizing the victory of good over evil.

A Diwali includes feasts.
Details: -Food includes fried sweets and delicacies.

A During one day of the Diwali festival, people give gifts to each other.
Details: -Clothes and jewelry are given.
-Children get the most gifts.

B Hanukkah is also a festival of light.
Details: -People light menorah candles.
-Candles lit each night for eight nights.

B People have feasts during Hanukkah.
Details: -Food is fried to symbolize the miraculous oil.

B People give gifts to children during Hanukkah.
Details: -They get money, clothing, or toys.

THE WRITER'S DESK Write a Paragraph Plan

Write a detailed paragraph plan in a point-by-point or side-by-side pattern. You can refer to the information you generated in previous Writer's Desk exercises. You can use the letters **A** and **B** to indicate which side you are discussing in your plan. Include details about each supporting idea.

Topic sentence: _____

_____

Support 1: _____

Details: _____

_____

Support 2: _____

Details: _____

_____

Support 3: _____

Details: _____

_____

Support 4: _____

   Details: _____

_____

Support 5: _____

   Details: _____

_____

Support 6: _____

   Details: _____

_____

LO 7 Write the first draft of a comparison and contrast paragraph.

The First Draft

After you outline your ideas in a plan, you are ready to write the first draft. Remember to write complete sentences. You might include transitional words or expressions to help your ideas flow smoothly.

Transitional Words and Expressions

In comparison and contrast paragraphs, there are some transitional words and expressions that you might use to explain either similarities or differences.

To Show Similarities		To Show Differences	
additionally	in addition	conversely	nevertheless
at the same time	in the same way	however	on the contrary
equally	similarly	in contrast	then again

THE WRITER'S DESK   **Write the First Draft**

Write the first draft of your comparison and contrast paragraph. Before you write, carefully review your paragraph plan to see if you have enough support for your points and topics.

▶ **REVISING AND EDITING**

LO 8 Revise and edit a comparison and contrast paragraph.

Revise and Edit a Comparison and Contrast Paragraph

When you finish writing a comparison and contrast paragraph, carefully review your work and revise it to make the comparison or contrast as clear as possible to your readers. Check that you have organized your paragraph logically, and remove any irrelevant details.

PRACTICE 4

Read the following student paragraph and answer the questions.

The Hindu and Jewish faiths have distinct religious celebrations. However, Diwali and Hanukkah have surprising similarities. For Hindus, Diwali is known as the festival of light. For five nights, celebrators are lighting as many small oil lamps as possible to symbolize hope and the victory of good over evil. Similarly, Hanukkah is a festival of lights, and people light candles on a menorah for eight consecutive nights. The candles celebrate the miracle of an oil lamp found in the Temple, which burned for eight days and nights even though it had only a day's worth of oil in it. Furthermore, both Hindus and Jews place the lights near windows so that people passing by can see them. Another similarity: feasts. People celebrating Diwali and Hanukkah work real hard to create special meals. The Diwali feast includes fried sweets and other desserts. In the same way, during Hanukkah, people eat food fried in oil, such as potato pancakes and donuts. Finally, both Diwali and Hanukkah involve gift-giving, with children as the major beneficiaries of the generosity. During Diwali, children receive gifts of clothing or jewelry. Hanukkah celebrants give gifts of money, clothing, or toys. Thus, Hindus and Jews celebrate some festivals in a similar way.

—Puspavalli Kumar, student

Revising

1. What is the writer comparing? _____

2. What does the writer focus on? Circle the best answer.

   a. Similarities   b. Differences

3. Number the three main points.

4. Underline six transitional words or expressions that appear at the beginnings of sentences.

Editing

5. Identify and correct one verb-tense error.

6. This paragraph contains one fragment, which is an incomplete sentence. Identify and correct the fragment.

7. Find and correct one error with an adjective or adverb. For more information about adjectives and adverbs, see the Grammar Hint on the next page.

GRAMMAR LINK

See the following chapters for more information about these grammar topics:

Fragments, Chapter 20
Verb Tenses, Chapter 25
Adjectives and Adverbs, Chapter 30

GRAMMAR HINT ◀ Comparing with Adjectives and Adverbs

When comparing or contrasting two items, ensure that you have correctly written the comparative forms of adjectives and adverbs. For instance, never put *more* with an adjective ending in *-er*.

Living alone is ~~more~~ quieter than living with a roommate.

If you are comparing two actions, remember to use an adverb instead of an adjective.

more quickly

My roommate cleans ~~quicker~~ than I do.

THE WRITER'S DESK   **Revise and Edit Your Paragraph**

Revise and edit the paragraph that you wrote for the previous Writer's Desk. Make sure that your paragraph has unity, adequate support, and coherence. Also correct any errors in grammar, spelling, punctuation, and mechanics.

Reflect On It

Think about what you have learned in this chapter. If you do not know an answer, review that topic.

1. Define the words *comparing* and *contrasting*.
    a. Comparing: _____
    b. Contrasting: _____

2. Explain the following comparison and contrast patterns.
    a. Point by point: _____

        _____

    b. Topic by topic: _____

        _____

MyWritingLab™

Complete these writing assignments at mywritinglab.com

MyWritingLab™   **THE WRITER'S ROOM**

Writing Activity 1: Topics

Choose any of the following topics, or choose your own topic. Then write a comparison and contrast paragraph.

General Topics

1. physical beauty and inner beauty
2. people from two different regions
3. your current home and a home that you lived in before

Compare or contrast ...

4. expectations about marriage and the reality of marriage
5. two Web sites

College and Work-Related Topics

6. male and female students

7. a high school and a college course

8. working indoors and working outdoors

Compare or contrast . . .

9. leaving a child in day care or with a family member

10. working mainly with your hands and working mainly with your head

WRITING LINK

MORE COMPARISON AND CONTRAST WRITING TOPICS

Chapter 16, Writer's Room topic 2 (page 262)

Chapter 18, Writer's Room topic 1 (page 285)

Chapter 21, Writer's Room topic 2 (page 311)

Writing Activity 2: Media Writing

Compare another country to the United States. Watch a foreign film such as *A Separation* (Iran), *Paradise Now* (Palestine), *Close to Home* (Israel), *Volver* (Spain), *The Queen* (Great Britain), *The Kite Runner* (Afghanistan), and *Slumdog Millionaire* (India). You can also watch YouTube videos about foreign places. You can compare the clothing, music, attitudes, and landscapes of the two places.

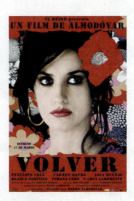

READING LINK

MORE COMPARISON AND CONTRAST READINGS

"Two Jobs" by Adrianna Gonzalez (page 219)

"Just Say No" by Mark Milke (page 220)

"This Boat Is My Boat" by Drew Hayden Taylor (page 513)

"Gone with the Windows" by Dorothy Nixon (page 516)

Comparison and Contrast Paragraph Checklist

As you write your comparison and contrast paragraph, review the checklist at the end of the book. Also ask yourself the following questions.

☐ Does my topic sentence explain what I am comparing and/or contrasting?

☐ Does my topic sentence make a point about the comparison?

☐ Does my paragraph have a point-by-point or topic-by-topic pattern?

☐ Does my paragraph focus on either similarities or differences?

☐ Do all of my supporting examples clearly relate to the topics that I am comparing or contrasting?

11 Cause and Effect

LEARNING OBJECTIVES

LO 1 Define cause and effect. **(p. 137)**

LO 2 Explain how to write a cause and effect paragraph. **(p. 137)**

LO 3 Explore topics. **(p. 138)**

LO 4 Identify the topic sentence of a cause and effect paragraph. **(p. 140)**

LO 5 Identify the supporting ideas of a cause and effect paragraph. **(p. 141)**

LO 6 Develop a cause and effect paragraph plan. **(p. 143)**

LO 7 Write the first draft of a cause and effect paragraph. **(p. 144)**

LO 8 Revise and edit a cause and effect paragraph. **(p. 145)**

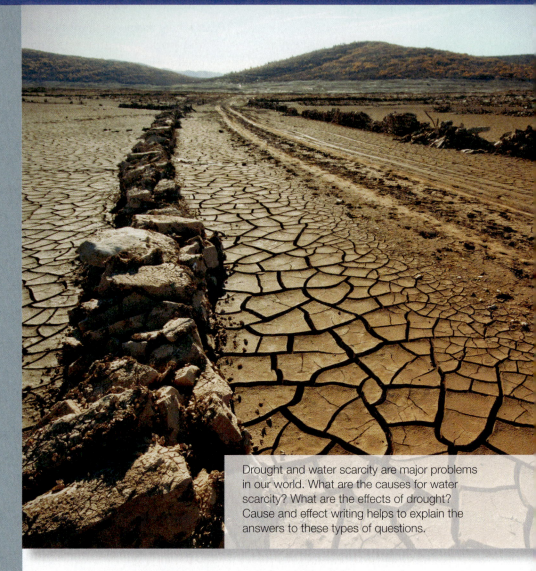

Drought and water scarcity are major problems in our world. What are the causes for water scarcity? What are the effects of drought? Cause and effect writing helps to explain the answers to these types of questions.

WRITERS' EXCHANGE

Your instructor will divide the class into two groups. You should work with a partner or a team of students. Your group will discuss one of the following topics.

What are some reasons that students go to college?
What effects does a college education have on a person's life?

What Is Cause and Effect?

LO 1 Define cause and effect.

Cause and effect writing explains why an event happened or what the consequences of such an event were. A cause and effect paragraph can focus on causes, effects, or both.

You often analyze the causes or effects of something. At home, you may worry about what causes your siblings or your own children to behave in a certain manner, or you may wonder about the effects of certain foods on your health. In a U.S. history course, you might analyze the causes of the Civil War, or you might write about the effects of industrialization on American society. At work, you may wonder about the causes or effects of a promotion or a pay cut.

CAUSE AND EFFECT AT WORK

In this memo from the file of a fourth-grade student, early childhood educator Luisa Suarez explains some causes and effects of the child's behavioral and learning problems.

Mark frequently expresses his dislike of school and reading. He continues to read at a second-grade level and is behind his classmates in the acquisition of knowledge expected from fourth-grade students. In interviews with the child, he has stated that he never reads at home and spends most of his time watching television. Because he is so far behind his peers in the classroom, he is embarrassed to show his lack of reading skills for fear of ridicule. It is easier for him to "act out," thus distracting others from his deficiency in reading. He displays a low level of self-confidence and appears to have given up trying.

> The topic sentence expresses the main idea.

> Supporting sentences provide details and examples.

> The concluding sentence brings the paragraph to a close.

The Cause and Effect Paragraph

When you write a cause and effect paragraph, focus on two main points.

LO 2 Explain how to write a cause and effect paragraph.

1. **Indicate whether you are focusing on causes, effects, or both.** Because a paragraph is not very long, it is often easier to focus on either causes or effects. If you do decide to focus on both causes and effects, make sure that your topic sentence announces your purpose to the reader.

2. **Ensure that your causes and effects are valid.** Determine real causes and effects, and do not simply list things that happened before or after the event. Also verify that your assumptions are logical.

   Illogical   The product does not work because it is inexpensive.
   (This statement is illogical; quality is not always dictated by price.)

   Better   The product does not work because it is constructed with poor-quality materials.

PRACTICE 1

Read the following paragraph and answer the questions.

In October 1981, Kent Cochrane, aged thirty, skidded his motorcycle off a highway exit ramp and down an embankment. He had massive bleeding in his brain and was unconscious for seventy-two hours. Ever since, he has been incapable of forming new memories of his personal experiences. His pre-existing memories for facts about the world were spared, such as the layout of his house, driving directions to the family cottage, and the names of his relatives. He can follow a conversation and learn new skills. He can play the piano and explain the rules of his favorite TV show, *The Price is Right*. But his internal autobiography ends in 1981, and today he lives in a perpetual present, incapable of recalling even his recent past or, strangely, imagining himself in the future. Kent Cochrane does not remember the interview he did for this story, nor any of the hundreds of visits over the years from dozens of scientists and graduate students. "Wow," says Kent with a smile, on hearing (not for the first time) that he is famous. "It's like it's not there," he says of his memory. He agrees that it is sad that he cannot remember joyous occasions, but his voice lacks the timbre of true despair. He does not know what he has forgotten.

—Joseph Brean, "What Is Memory? Is It What Makes Us Human?"
National Post

1. Underline the topic sentence. Be careful because it is not necessarily the first sentence in the paragraph.

2. What does the paragraph mainly focus on? Circle the best answer.

   a. Causes   b. Effects

3. Who is the audience? _____

4. List the supporting details.

   _____

   _____

   _____

   _____

LO 3 Explore topics.

Explore Topics

In the Warm Up, you will try an exploring strategy to generate ideas about different topics. Imagine that you had to write a cause and effect paragraph about traffic jams. You might brainstorm to come up with as many causes and effects as possible.

Causes
- Poor weather
- Road construction
- High traffic for special events
- Poor traffic signal timing
- Insufficient road capacity

Traffic jams

Effects
- Waste of time
- Increase in frustration and stress
- Loss of work hours
- Higher cost for gas and vehicle maintenance
- Increase in air pollution level

GRAMMAR HINT   ◄ Do Not Confuse *Effect* and *Affect*

Generally, *affect* is used as a verb, and *effect* is used as a noun. *Affect* (verb) means "to influence or change" and *effect* (noun) means "the result."

verb
How will your new job <u>affect</u> your family?

noun
What <u>effect</u> will moving to a new city have on your spouse's career?

Effect can also be used as a verb that means "to cause or to bring about." It is generally used in the following phrases: "to effect a change" or "to effect a plan."

The union members demonstrated to <u>effect</u> changes in their working conditions.

THE WRITER'S DESK   Warm Up

Write some possible causes and effects for the following topics. Then decide if your paragraph will focus on causes or effects.

EXAMPLE: Reduction of violent crime

Causes	Effects
- more police on street	- citizens feel sense of security
- reduction in youth population rate	- less cost to taxpayers
- harsher sentences for nonviolent crimes	- public money for crime prevention can be spent on other things

Focus on: _Causes_

1. Cheating

Causes	Effects
_____	_____
_____	_____
_____	_____
_____	_____

Focus on: _____

2. Having a poor body image

Causes	Effects
_____	_____
_____	_____
_____	_____
_____	_____

Focus on: _____

3. Teenage rebellion

Causes	Effects
_____	_____
_____	_____
_____	_____
_____	_____

Focus on: _____

▶ DEVELOPING

LO 4 Identify the topic sentence of a cause and effect paragraph.

ESSAY LINK
In a cause and effect essay, the thesis statement expresses whether the essay will focus on causes, effects, or both.

The Topic Sentence

The topic sentence in a cause and effect paragraph must clearly demonstrate whether the focus is on causes, effects, or both. Also, make sure that you have clearly indicated your controlling idea. For example, read the topic sentences. Notice that the controlling ideas are underlined.

topic   controlling idea (causes)
The American public is paying high gasoline prices for many reasons.

topic   controlling idea (effects)
High gasoline prices have led Americans to change their driving habits.

topic   controlling idea (causes and effects)
High gasoline prices, which are caused by many factors, have profound consequences for many Americans.

PRACTICE 2

Carefully read the following topic sentences. Decide whether each sentence focuses on causes, effects, or both. Look for key words that give you clues. Circle the best answer.

1. People become homeless because of difficult life circumstances.

    a. Causes   b. Effects   c. Both

2. Homeless people must deal with difficult situations in their day-to-day lives.

    a. Causes   b. Effects   c. Both

3. Because of many problems at the Chernobyl nuclear site, the environment in Ukraine has changed forever.

    a. Causes   b. Effects   c. Both

4. Scientists have proposed many theories that explain the disappearance of the dinosaurs.

    a. Causes   b. Effects   c. Both

THE WRITER'S DESK   Write Topic Sentences

Write a topic sentence for each of the following topics. You can look for ideas in the Writer's Desk Warm Up on pages 139–140. Determine whether you will focus on causes, effects, or both in your paragraph.

EXAMPLE: Topic: Reduction of violent crime

Topic Sentence: _The number of serious crimes committed in the United_

States has fallen recently for several reasons.

1. Topic: Cheating

    Topic sentence: _____

    _____

2. Topic: Having a poor body image

    Topic sentence: _____

    _____

3. Topic: Teenage rebellion

    Topic sentence: _____

    _____

The Supporting Ideas

LO 5 Identify the supporting ideas of a cause and effect paragraph.

After you have developed an effective topic sentence, generate supporting ideas. When planning a cause and effect paragraph, think of examples that clearly show the causes or effects. Then arrange your examples in emphatic order. When you use **emphatic order**, you place your examples from the most to the least important or from the least to the most important.

Visualizing Cause and Effect

PRACTICE 3

Brainstorm supporting ideas for the following topic sentence. Explain how pollution might affect the environment.

Topic Sentence: Pollution has serious effects on our planet.

_____   _____   _____

_____   _____   _____

HINT ▸ **Do Not Oversimplify**

Avoid attributing a simple or general cause to a complex issue. When you use expressions such as *It appears that* or *A possible cause is*, you show that you are aware of the complex factors involved in the situation.

Oversimplification	The growing rate of homelessness in the United States is caused by the foreclosure crisis.
	(This is an oversimplification of a complicated problem.)
Better	A possible cause of the growing rate of homelessness in the United States is that a large number of families have lost their homes through foreclosure.

THE WRITER'S DESK **Generate Supporting Ideas**

Choose one of the topic sentences from the Writer's Desk on page 141. Then list either causes or effects.

EXAMPLE: Topic sentence: _The number of serious crimes committed in the United States has fallen recently for several reasons._

_____

Supports: youth population rates have declined

different policing tactics

harsher sentences for all types of crimes

Topic sentence: _____

_____

Supports: _____

_____

_____

_____

The Paragraph Plan

LO 6 Develop a cause and effect paragraph plan.

In many courses, instructors ask students to write about the causes or effects of a particular subject. Plan your paragraph before you write your final version. Also think about the order of ideas. Arrange the supporting details in a logical order. As you make your plan, ensure that you focus on causes, effects, or both.

ESSAY LINK

In a cause and effect essay, place the thesis statement in the introduction. Then use body paragraphs, each with its own topic sentence, to support the thesis statement.

Topic Sentence: The number of serious crimes committed in the United States has fallen recently for several reasons.

Support 1: There are fewer people between the ages of fifteen and twenty-four.

Details: —There was a drop of almost 5 percent in youth populations between 1975 and 2000.

Support 2: Police-patrolling tactics have changed.

Details: —Police get to know locals.

—Police check suspicious individuals for hidden weapons.

Support 3: Punishment for criminals has become tougher.

Details: —Nonviolent offenders and drug dealers are given prison terms.

—More criminals are off the street, which reduces the crime rate.

THE WRITER'S DESK   Write a Paragraph Plan

Refer to the information you generated in previous Writer's Desk exercises and create a paragraph plan. If you think of new details that will explain your point more effectively, include them here.

Topic sentence: _____

_____

Support 1: _____

Details: _____

_____

_____

Support 2: _____

Details: _____

_____

_____

Support 3: _____

Details: _____

_____

_____

VOCABULARY BOOST

Using your thesaurus, come up with three synonyms for *cause* and three synonyms for *effect*.

LO 7 Write the first draft of a cause and effect paragraph.

The First Draft

After you outline your ideas in a plan, you are ready to write the first draft. Remember to write complete sentences. You might include transitional words or expressions to help your ideas flow smoothly.

Transitional Words and Expressions

The following transitional expressions are useful for showing causes and effects.

To Show Causes	To Show Effects
for this reason	accordingly
the first cause	as a result
the most important cause	consequently

THE WRITER'S DESK   Write the First Draft

Write the first draft of your cause and effect paragraph. Before you write, carefully review your paragraph plan and make any necessary changes.

Revise and Edit a Cause and Effect Paragraph

LO 8 Revise and edit a cause and effect paragraph.

When you finish writing a cause and effect paragraph, review your work and revise it to make the examples as clear as possible to your readers. Make sure that your sentences relate to the topic sentence and flow together smoothly.

PRACTICE 4

Read the next student paragraph and answer the questions.

The number of serious crimes committed in the United States has fallen recently for several reasons. First, experts believe that there are fewer people between the ages of fifteen and twenty-four. From 1975 to 2000, the youth population rate droped by almost 5 percent. This decrease has led to a reduction in crime rates. In addition, police-patrolling tactics have changed. Police officers get to know locals in various neighborhoods. Officers also check suspicious individuals for concealed weapons. Finaly, punishment has become more tougher. People who commit certain nonviolent crimes and drug offenses are given prison terms. More criminals are off the streets, which reduces the crime rate. But some people have been wrongly convicted because they can't afford a good lawyer. In conclusion, these factors have had a positive affect on the country's crime rate.

—Logan Two-Rivers, student

Revising

1. Does the paragraph focus on causes, effects, or both? _____

2. List the causes or effects given. _____
    _____
    _____
    _____

3. There is one sentence in the paragraph that does not relate to the topic. Cross it out.

4. This paragraph has some sentences that require source information. Highlight two or three examples of unsupported claims.

5. Go online and find two or three specific examples to back up the claims made in this paragraph. Add them here, and include your sources.

_____

_____

_____

_____

_____

GRAMMAR LINK
See the following chapters for more information about these grammar topics:
Spelling and Commonly Confused Words, Chapter 33
Adjectives and Adverbs, Chapter 30

Editing

6. This paragraph contains two misspelled words. Identify and correct them.

7. There is one error with the comparative form. Correct the error.

8. There is one commonly confused word error. Underline the error and replace it with the correct word.

THE WRITER'S DESK Revise and Edit Your Paragraph

Revise and edit the paragraph that you wrote for the previous Writer's Desk. Make sure that your paragraph has unity, adequate support, and coherence. Also correct any errors in grammar, spelling, punctuation, and mechanics.

Reflect On It

Think about what you have learned in this chapter. If you do not know an answer, review that topic.

1. What is the difference between the words *affect* and *effect*?
   Affect: _____
   Effect: _____

2. Why should oversimplification of causes or effects be avoided?

   _____

   _____

3. List some common transitional words used in a cause and effect paragraph.

   _____

   _____

THE WRITER'S ROOM   MyWritingLab™

Writing Activity 1: Topics

Choose any of the following topics, or choose your own topic. Then write a cause and effect paragraph.

General Topics

Causes and/or effects of . . .

1. having a close friendship
2. telling lies
3. voter apathy
4. holding a grudge
5. spoiling a child

College and Work-Related Topics

Causes and/or effects of . . .

6. having low (or high) marks in college
7. not keeping up with college workload
8. working with a family member
9. working at home
10. getting a promotion

Writing Activity 2: Media Writing

Watch a television show or movie that deals with falling in love or breaking up. You could watch any television soap opera or a television drama such as *The Good Wife*. You could also watch romance movies such as *Twilight*, *Hope Springs*, or *The Five-Year Engagement*. You could also listen to love songs. Describe the causes or effects of falling in love or breaking up and use examples to support your point.

from the producer of BRIDESMAIDS

A COMEDY ABOUT THE JOURNEY BETWEEN POPPING THE QUESTION AND TYING THE KNOT

THE **FIVE-YEAR** *Engagement*

APRIL 27

WRITING LINK

MORE CAUSE AND EFFECT WRITING TOPICS

Chapter 18, Writer's Room topic 2 (page 285)
Chapter 19, Writer's Room topic 2 (page 296)
Chapter 24, Writer's Room topic 2 (page 345)
Chapter 30, Writer's Room topic 2 (page 423)
Chapter 35, Writer's Room topic 2 (page 483)

READING LINK

MORE CAUSE AND EFFECT READINGS

"Why Small Businesses Fail" by Jim Baek (page 223)
"Don't Worry, Act Happy" by Albert Nerenberg (page 224)
"Mother Nature's Melting Pot" by Hugh Raffles (page 537)
"Is Anything Private Anymore" by Sean Flynn (page 545)

Cause and Effect Paragraph Checklist

As you write your cause and effect paragraph, review the checklist at the end of the book. Also ask yourself the following questions.

☐ Does my topic sentence indicate clearly that my paragraph focuses on causes, effects, or both?

☐ Do I have adequate supporting examples of causes and/or effects?

☐ Do I make logical and valid points?

☐ Do I use the terms *effect* and *affect* correctly?

12 Argument

LEARNING OBJECTIVES

LO 1 Define argument. **(p. 149)**

LO 2 Explain how to write an argument paragraph. **(p. 149)**

LO 3 Explore topics. **(p. 151)**

LO 4 Identify the topic sentence of an argument paragraph. **(p. 151)**

LO 5 Identify the supporting ideas of an argument paragraph. **(p. 153)**

LO 6 Develop an argument paragraph plan. **(p. 157)**

LO 7 Write the first draft of an argument paragraph. **(p. 159)**

LO 8 Revise and edit an argument paragraph. **(p. 159)**

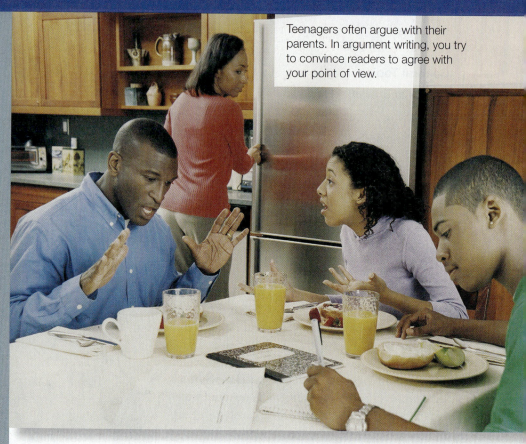

Teenagers often argue with their parents. In argument writing, you try to convince readers to agree with your point of view.

WRITERS' EXCHANGE

For this activity, you and a partner will take turns debating an issue. To start, choose who will begin speaking. The first speaker chooses one side of any issue listed below, and then argues about that issue, without stopping, for a set amount of time. Your instructor will signal when to switch sides. After the signal, the second speaker talks nonstop about the other side of the debate. If you run out of ideas, you can switch topics when it is your turn to speak.

Possible topics:

Dogs are better than cats.

Cats are better than dogs.

It's better to be married than single.

It's better to be single than married.

Life is easier for men.

Life is easier for women.

▶ **EXPLORING**

What Is Argument?

LO1 Define argument.

When you use **argument**, you take a position on an issue and attempt to defend it. You try to convince somebody that your point of view is the best one.

Argument is both a writing pattern and a purpose for writing. In fact, it is one of the most common aims or purposes in college and work-related writing. For example, in Chapter 10, there is a paragraph about the religious celebrations Diwali and Hanukkah, and the author uses comparison and contrast as the predominant pattern. At the same time, the author uses argument to convince the reader that the two celebrations are not so different. Therefore, in most of your college and work-related writing, your purpose is to persuade the reader that your ideas are compelling and valid.

You use argument every day. At home, you may write a persuasive letter to a newspaper to express your views about public policy. At college, in a sociology class, you might take a position on capital punishment or on gun control. At work, you might have to convince your manager to give you a raise.

ARGUMENT **AT WORK**

Lawyer Marshal L. Dodge argues on behalf of his client, Ethan Ward,* a veteran of the conflict in Afghanistan, for disability compensation for posttraumatic stress disorder (PTSD).

On behalf of my client, I request that the Veterans Claims Board grant Mr. Ward disability compensation. Ward served on active duty in Afghanistan from September 2008 to January 2010. After his discharge, Mr. Ward began to experience a nervous condition. He could not sleep, eat, or do other daily activities. The American Psychiatric Association has acknowledged PTSD as a delayed-stress syndrome experienced by combat veterans. My client has provided a list of each stress-related incident he has experienced since returning to civilian life. Mr. Ward has provided the necessary medical reports from health care professionals. The medical reports indicate that, before serving in Afghanistan, my client functioned very well in his day-to-day activities. Furthermore, my client has responded in a timely manner to all and any requests made by the VA regarding his claim. Therefore, he should receive disability compensation.

*name changed

> The topic sentence expresses the main idea.

> Supporting sentences provide details and examples.

> The concluding sentence brings the paragraph to a satisfying close.

The Argument Paragraph

LO2 Explain how to write an argument paragraph.

When you write an argument paragraph, remember the following four points.

ESSAY LINK
When you write argument essays, also keep these four points in mind.

- **Choose a subject that you know something about.** It would be very difficult to write a good text about space research funds, capital punishment, or conditions in federal prisons, for example, if you have never had experience with, or read about, these issues. On the other hand, if you, or someone close to you, cannot find good day care, then you could likely write a very effective paragraph about the need for better day-care services.

- **Consider your readers.** What do your readers already know about the topic? Are they likely to agree or disagree with you? Do they have specific concerns? Consider what kind of evidence would be most effective with your audience.

♦ **Know your purpose.** In argument writing, your main purpose is to persuade the reader to agree with you. Your specific purpose is more focused. You may want the reader to take action, you may want to support a viewpoint, you may want to counter somebody else's argument, or you may want to offer a solution to a problem. Ask yourself what your specific purpose is.

♦ **Take a strong position and provide supporting evidence.** The first thing to do in the body of your paragraph is to prove that there is, indeed, a problem. Then back up your point of view with a combination of facts, statistics, examples, and informed opinions.

HINT ◂ Be Passionate!

When you are planning your argument paragraph, try to find a topic that you feel passionate about. If you care about your topic, and if you express your enthusiasm, your audience will be more likely to care about it, too.

PRACTICE 1

Read the next paragraph, and answer the questions.

As one solution to global warming, the locavore movement encourages consumers to buy within a 100-mile radius. However, buy-local advice is not especially eco-friendly. First, a 2008 study by researchers at Carnegie Mellon University showed that only 11 percent of greenhouse gases released into the atmosphere come from long-distance transportation of food supplies. Large ships or planes send enormous quantities of produce very efficiently. In 2006, New Zealand researchers at Lincoln University proved that New Zealand lamb transported to Britain consumed less energy than locally produced British lamb. In addition, local farming methods may be inefficient. The Carnegie Mellon study showed that almost 83 percent of carbon emissions could be attributed to regional food-production practices. For instance, community-produced crops may require more water, fertilizer, and pesticides than crops from overseas. Large amounts of forest may have to be cleared to ensure that farmers make a profit. In colder climates, food producers often grow and store food in temperature-controlled warehouses. Exotic flowers or fruits cultivated in a tropical climate require less energy than those same flowers and fruits grown in a hothouse in a cold climate. Although reduction of greenhouse gases is a **laudable** goal, consumers should thoroughly inform themselves about the best solutions in fighting climate change.

laudable: praiseworthy

—Kevin Libin, "Rethinking Green: Eat Global, Not Local" (adapted)

1. Underline the topic sentence. Remember that a topic sentence is not necessarily the first sentence in the paragraph.

2. Who is the author's audience? _____

_____

3. What is the author's specific purpose? _____

_____

_____

4. Underline some examples that the author gives to show that there is a problem.

5. Look at the author's supporting evidence, and circle two statistics.

Explore Topics

LO 3 Explore topics.

In the Warm Up, you will try an exploring strategy to generate ideas about different topics.

THE WRITER'S DESK   **Warm Up**

Think about the following questions, and write down the first ideas that come to mind. Try to think of two or three ideas for each topic.

EXAMPLE: Should people stop launching frivolous lawsuits?

Yes, I think so. I sold a computer and it stopped working so my friend sued me. But computers sometimes break! Lawsuits cause stress and break up friendships.

1. Sometimes minors steal, vandalize, go joyriding, and do other illegal acts. Should parents be required to pay for damages when their children break the law?

   _____

   _____

   _____

2. Should college students be permitted to carry concealed weapons?

   _____

   _____

   _____

3. What are some of the major controversial issues in your neighborhood, at your workplace, at your college, or in the news these days?

   _____

   _____

   _____

▶ **DEVELOPING**

The Topic Sentence

LO 4 Identify the topic sentence of an argument paragraph.

In the topic sentence of an argument paragraph, state your position on the issue. In the following topic sentence, notice that the controlling idea has been underlined.

       controlling idea   topic

Our government <u>should severely punish</u> **corporate executives who commit fraud**.

Your topic sentence should be a debatable statement. It should not be a fact or a statement of opinion.

Fact	In some public schools, students wear uniforms.
	(This is a fact. It cannot be debated.)

Opinion	I think that it is a good idea for public school students to wear uniforms.
	(This is a statement of opinion. Nobody can deny that you like school uniforms. Therefore, do not use phrases such as *In my opinion*, *I think*, or *I believe* in your topic sentence.)

Argument	Public school students should wear uniforms.
	(This is a debatable statement.)

PRACTICE 2

Evaluate the following statements. Write *F* for a fact, *O* for an opinion, or *A* for a debatable argument.

1. I think that dieting makes people fat.   _____

2. Most high school graduates take SATs to get accepted into college.   _____

3. American businesses should give longer maternity and paternity
   leave for employees.   _____

4. I believe that the government should ban handguns.   _____

5. Private citizens should not be permitted to own handguns.   _____

6. Many Internet viruses are installed with pop-up notices.   _____

7. High school graduates should be required to do volunteer
   work for one year.   _____

8. In my opinion, the voting age should be lowered to sixteen.   _____

HINT   **Be Direct**

You may be reluctant to state your point of view directly. You may feel that it is impolite to do so. However, in academic writing, it is perfectly acceptable, and even desirable, to state an argument in a direct manner.

In argument writing, you can make your topic debatable by using *should*, *must*, or *ought to* in the topic sentence or thesis statement.

Although daily prayer is important for many people in the United States, it **should** not take place in the classroom.

THE WRITER'S DESK   **Write Topic Sentences**

Write a topic sentence for the following topics. You can look for ideas in the previous Writer's Desk Warm Up. Make sure that each topic sentence clearly expresses your position on the issue.

EXAMPLE: Topic: Frivolous lawsuits

Topic sentence: *People should stop suing each other over minor incidents.*

1. Topic: Parents paying for children's crime sprees

   Topic sentence: _____

   _____

2. Topic: College students carrying concealed weapons

   Topic sentence: _____

   _____

3. Topic: A controversial issue in your neighborhood, at work, at college, or in the news

   Topic sentence: _____

   _____

The Supporting Ideas

When you write an argument paragraph, it is important to support your point of view with examples, facts, statistics, and informed opinions. It is also effective to think about some answers you can give to counter the opposition's point of view, and you can consider the long-term consequences if something does not occur. Therefore, try to use several types of supporting evidence.

LO 5 Identify the supporting ideas of an argument paragraph.

> **ESSAY LINK**
> In an argument essay, body paragraphs should contain supporting details such as examples, facts, informed opinions, logical consequences, and answers to the opposition.

- **Examples** are pieces of information that illustrate your main argument. For instance, if you want to argue that there are not enough day-care centers in your area, you can explain that one center has over one hundred children on its waiting list.

  Another type of example is the **anecdote**. To support your main point, you can write about a true event or tell a personal story. For example, if you think that rebellious teenagers hurt their families, you might tell a personal story about your brother's involvement with a gang.

- **Facts** are statements that can be verified in some way. For example, the following statement is a fact: "According to the World Health Organization, secondhand smoke can cause cancer in nonsmokers." **Statistics** are another type of fact. When you use statistics, ensure that the source is reliable, and remember to mention the source. For example, if you want to argue that underage drinking is a problem, you could mention the following statistic from the *Journal of the American Medical Association*: "Underage drinkers consume about 20 percent of all the alcohol imbibed in this country."

- Sometimes experts in a field express an **informed opinion** about an issue. An expert's opinion can give added weight to your argument. For example, if you want to argue that the courts treat youths who commit crimes too harshly or leniently, then you might quote a judge who deals with juvenile criminals. If you want to argue that secondhand smoke is dangerous, then you might quote a lung specialist or a health organization.

- Solutions to problems can carry **logical consequences**. When you plan an argument, think about long-term consequences if something does or does not happen. For example, many youths post embarrassing photos and personal information online, and they enjoy their friends' reactions. But at a later date, those photos and comments could have an impact on the youths' job prospects.

♦ In argument writing, try to **answer the opposition**. For example, if you want to argue that drinking laws are ineffective, you might think about the arguments that your opposition might make. Then you might write, "Drinking age laws do a fine job of keeping young people out of clubs and bars; however, these laws do nothing to keep young people from getting access to alcohol from other places." Try to refute some of the strongest arguments of the opposition.

Visualizing Argument

PRACTICE 3

Brainstorm supporting ideas for the following topic sentence. Write a sentence explaining why each activity is dangerous.

Topic Sentence: There are several activities you should never do when driving.

Putting on Makeup

_____

_____

_____

Using Cell Phone

_____

_____

_____

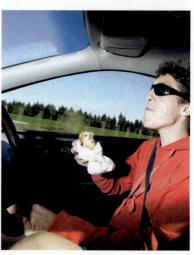

Eating

_____

_____

_____

HINT ◀ **Avoid Circular Reasoning**

When you write an argument paragraph, make sure that your main point is supported with facts, examples, informed opinions, and so on. Do not use circular reasoning.

Circular reasoning occurs when you simply restate an idea in various ways, and your premise is the same as your conclusion. Your idea does not develop or advance.

Circular Youths who break laws should be treated differently from adults. Adolescents who are under eighteen are not mature enough to make reasoned decisions, so they cannot really be compared to people who are older. Most teenagers do not have the capacity to think about consequences. They are not capable of considering outcomes. Thus, treating a juvenile in the same way as an adult offender is unfair and unjust.

Not Circular	Youths who break laws should be treated differently from adults. First, adolescents undergo massive hormonal changes, which can impact their behavior. In the book *Psychosocial Development During Adolescence*, the authors state that "testosterone, which is closely associated with aggression, increases tenfold in adolescent boys." Furthermore, the prefrontal cortex, the part of the brain involved in impulse control, is not fully developed in teens. In a CBS News article, Laurence Steinberg, a Temple University professor, compares the teen brain to "a car with a good accelerator but a weak brake." Because many teens have poor control of their impulses, they are more likely than adults to engage in reckless behavior. Thus, treating a juvenile in the same way as an adult offender is unfair and unjust.

PRACTICE 4

You have learned about different methods to support a topic. Read each of the following topic sentences, and think of a supporting reason for each one. Use the type of support suggested in parentheses.

1. Companies should be prevented from marketing to children.

   (Example) _____

   _____

   _____

2. Boys should be encouraged to express their emotions.

   (Logical consequence) _____

   _____

   _____

3. Voting should be mandatory in the United States.

   (Fact) _____

   _____

   _____

4. Teen magazines should not show ads with extremely thin models.

   (Logical consequence) _____

   _____

   _____

5. Couples who have severe marital problems should not stay together for the sake of their children.

   (Answer the opposition.) _____

   _____

   _____

READING LINK
For more information about avoiding plagiarism and evaluating and documenting sources, refer to Chapter 15, "Enhancing Your Writing with Research."

HINT   Using Research

You can enhance your argument essay with **research** by including information from an informed source. You can look for information in textbooks, newspapers, and magazines and on the Internet.

When you use the Internet for research, make sure that your sources are from legitimate organizations or from reputable magazine, newspaper, or government sites. For example, for information about the spread of AIDS, you might find statistics on the World Health Organization's Web site. You would not go to someone's personal rant or conspiracy theory site.

Consider Both Sides of the Issue

Once you have decided what to write about, try to think about both sides of the issue. Then you can predict arguments that your opponents might make, and you can plan your answer to the opposition.

THE WRITER'S DESK   Consider Both Sides of the Issue

Write arguments for and against each of the following topics.

EXAMPLE: Frivolous lawsuits

For	Against
—people get hurt	—makes us look greedy
—makes doctors more careful	—breaks friendships
—many cases are legitimate	—raises costs for everyone
—people have the right to sue	—causes anger between neighbors

1. Parents paying for children's crimes

For	Against
_____	_____
_____	_____
_____	_____
_____	_____

2. College students carrying concealed weapons

For	Against
_____	_____
_____	_____
_____	_____
_____	_____

3. A controversial issue: _____

For	Against
_____	_____
_____	_____
_____	_____
_____	_____

Avoid Common Errors

When you write an argument paragraph or essay, avoid the following pitfalls.

Do not make generalizations. If you begin a statement with *Everyone knows* or *It is common knowledge*, then the reader may mistrust what you say. You cannot possibly know what everyone else knows. It is better to refer to specific sources.

Generalization	Everyone knows that global warming is destroying our planet.
Better	According to the United Nations Panel on Climate Change, governments must take serious steps to reduce greenhouse gas emissions.

Use emotional arguments sparingly. Certainly, the strongest arguments can be emotional ones. Sometimes the most effective way to influence others is to appeal to their sense of justice, humanity, pride, or guilt. However, do not rely on emotional arguments. If you use emotionally charged words (for example, if you call someone *ignorant*) or if you try to appeal to basic instincts (for example, if you appeal to people's fear of other ethnic groups), then you will seriously undermine your argument.

Emotional	Racists believe that undocumented immigrants are attacking the American way of life.
Better	Many sectors of society, including some politicians, students, and activists, believe that illegal immigration hampers the efforts of those who want to immigrate legally.

Do not make exaggerated claims. Make sure that your arguments are plausible.

Exaggerated	Undocumented immigrants are taking everybody's jobs.
Better	Although undocumented immigrants work hard, they continue the demand for cheap labor.

VOCABULARY BOOST

Looking at Associated Meanings

Some words have neutral, positive, or negative associations. With a partner, try to find the most neutral word in each list. Categorize the other words as positive or negative.

1. macho, jerk, hunk, lout, hottie, man, stud, sweetheart, bully
2. nation, homeland, refuge, kingdom, rogue state, country, motherland, axis of evil
3. freedom fighter, terrorist, anarchist, believer, radical, fanatic, revolutionary, rebel, soldier, activist

---

The Paragraph Plan

LO 6 Develop an argument paragraph plan.

Before you write your argument paragraph, make a plan. Think of some supporting arguments, and think about details that can help illustrate each argument. Make sure that every example is valid and that it relates to the topic sentence. Also, arrange your ideas in a logical order.

Topic Sentence: People should stop suing each other over minor incidents.

Support 1: They should accept that accidents can happen and stop being so greedy.

Details: —A woman sued McDonald's after she spilled hot coffee on her lap.

—People sue doctors for events that are outside the doctors' control.

—A man answered his cell phone while driving and sued his boss who had called him.

Support 2: Lawsuits can break friendships and create antagonism between neighbors.

Details: —My friend sued me over the sale of a computer that had stopped working.

—A neighbor wearing high heels fell and sued another neighbor.

—Good friends and neighbors stop speaking to each other.

Support 3: Finally, lawsuits contribute to higher costs for everyone.

Details: —Doctors pay high amounts for malpractice suits, raising medical costs.

—Companies pass along the costs of defending themselves to customers.

—Insurance costs are high because of the suits.

THE WRITER'S DESK   Write a Paragraph Plan

Choose one of the topic sentences that you wrote for the Writer's Desk on page 153, and write a detailed paragraph plan. You can refer to the information you generated in previous Writer's Desk exercises, and if you think of examples that will explain your point more effectively, include them here.

Subject: _____

Topic sentence: _____

_____

Support 1: _____

Details: _____

_____

_____

Support 2: _____

Details: _____

_____

_____

Support 3: _____

Details: _____

_____

_____

The First Draft

LO 7 Write the first draft of an argument paragraph.

After you outline your ideas in a plan, you are ready to write the first draft. Remember to write complete sentences. You might include transitional words or expressions to help your ideas flow smoothly.

Transitional Words and Expressions

The following transitional words and expressions can introduce an answer to the opposition or the support for an argument.

To Answer the Opposition	To Support Your Argument
admittedly	certainly
however	consequently
nevertheless	furthermore
of course	in fact
on one hand/on the other hand	obviously
undoubtedly	of course

THE WRITER'S DESK **Write the First Draft**

Write the first draft of your argument paragraph. Before you write, carefully review your paragraph plan and make any necessary changes.

▶ **REVISING AND EDITING**

Revise and Edit an Argument Paragraph

LO 8 Revise and edit an argument paragraph.

When you finish writing an argument paragraph, carefully review your work and revise it to make the supporting examples as clear as possible to your readers. Check that the order of ideas is logical, and remove any irrelevant details.

PRACTICE 5

Read the next student paragraph and answer the questions.

People should stop suing each other over minor incidents. Of course, some people think that citizens need the right to sue and that lawsuits make doctors more careful. But too many people are greedy idiots. Americans should accept that accidents can happen, they should stop hunting for easy money. For example, a woman sued McDonald's because she spilled hot coffee on her own lap. In our state, after a driver answered his cell phone and had an accident, he sued his own boss for phoning him. Those people should take responsibility for their own actions. In addition, the lawsuits create antagonism between friends and neighbors. For example, our neighbor, Mrs. Blair, slipped and fell on a sidewalk wearing high heels. She sued our other neighbor, Mr. Ferner, and now they are not friends no more. Finally, consider why are prices so high. Lawsuits contribute to higher expenses for everyone. Medical costs increase when doctors pay for malpractice insurance. Companies pass along the costs of defending themselves to consumers. In Ohio and elsewhere, Americans have to stop suing each other for ridiculous reasons.

—Jill Chen, student

Revising

1. Underline the topic sentence.

2. The writer uses an emotionally charged word. Remove it.

3. Does the writer acknowledge the opposition?   _____ Yes   _____ No

    If you answered "yes," circle the sentence in which the writer acknowledges the opposition.

4. Number the three supporting arguments. Then summarize the three ideas here.

    _____

    _____

    _____

    _____

GRAMMAR LINK box:

GRAMMAR LINK
See the following chapters for more information about these grammar topics:
Slang versus Standard English, Chapter 32,
Dangling Modifiers, Chapter 31
Run-On Sentences, Chapter 21
Embedded Questions, Chapter 18

Editing

5. A run-on sentence occurs when two complete ideas are joined incorrectly with a comma. Identify and correct a run-on sentence.

6. This paragraph contains a misplaced modifier. Underline the modifier and indicate where it should be placed.

7. Underline and correct an embedded question error. (For information about embedded questions, see the Grammar Hint below.)

8. Underline and correct a double negative error.

GRAMMAR HINT   Using Embedded Questions

When you embed a question inside a larger sentence, you do not need to use the question word order. Make sure that your embedded questions are correctly written.

why our government doesn't

Some people wonder ~~why doesn't our government~~ strictly regulate the banks.

THE WRITER'S DESK   Revise and Edit Your Paragraph

Revise and edit the paragraph that you wrote for the previous Writer's Desk. Make sure that your paragraph has unity, adequate support, and coherence. Also correct any errors in grammar, spelling, punctuation, and mechanics.

Reflect On It

Think about what you have learned in this chapter. If you do not know an answer, review that topic.

1. What is the main purpose of an argument paragraph or essay?

   _____

2. What is the difference between a statement of opinion and a statement of argument?

   _____

   _____

3. What five types of supporting evidence can you use in argument writing?

   _____   _____

   _____   _____

   _____

4. In argument writing, you should avoid circular reasoning. What is circular reasoning?

   _____

   _____

5. Why is it important to avoid using emotionally charged words?

   _____

   _____

THE WRITER'S ROOM   My WritingLab™

MyWritingLab™
Complete these writing assignments at mywritinglab.com

Writing Activity 1: Topics

Choose any of the following topics, or choose your own topic. Then write an argument paragraph. Remember to narrow your topic and to follow the writing process.

General Topics
Should

1. the voting age be raised or lowered?

2. pennies be removed from circulation?

3. people look for partners online?

4. the government provide free day care?

5. children be homeschooled?

College and Work-Related Topics
Should

6. companies give drug testing to employees?

7. all college programs include internships?

8. physical education courses be compulsory in colleges?

9. office relationships be permitted?

10. tips for service be abolished?

WRITING LINK

MORE ARGUMENT WRITING TOPICS
Chapter 25, Writer's Room topic 2 (page 356)
Chapter 26, Writer's Room topic 2 (page 370)
Chapter 27, Writer's Room topic 2 (page 375)
Chapter 28, Writer's Room topic 2, (page 391)
Chapter 31, Writer's Room topic 2 (page 432)
Chapter 33, Writer's Room topics 1 and 2 (page 457)

READING LINK

MORE ARGUMENT READINGS

"The Importance of Music" by Christine Bigras (page 228)

"Robot Ethics" (page 229)

"It's Class, Stupid!" by Richard Rodriguez (page 518)

"The Case for Affirmative Action" by Dave Malcolm (page 521)

Writing Activity 2: Media Writing

Watch a television show or movie that deals with health care. You could watch television shows such as *Grey's Anatomy, Dr. Oz, Dr. Phil, The Doctors*, or *House*. Movies include *Sicko* or *Looper*. Find a controversial issue in the program or movie, and write an argument paragraph. Give examples to support your ideas.

Argument Paragraph Checklist

As you write your argument paragraph, review the checklist at the end of the book. Also ask yourself the following questions.

☐ Does my topic sentence clearly state my position on the issue?

☐ Do I make strong supporting arguments?

☐ Do I include facts, examples, statistics, logical consequences, or answers to the opposition?

☐ Do my supporting arguments provide evidence that directly supports the topic sentence?

Part III

The Essay

An *essay* is a series of paragraphs that support one main or central idea. Essays differ in length, style, and subject, but the structure of an essay generally consists of an introductory paragraph, several body paragraphs, and a concluding paragraph.

Before you begin reading the following chapters, become familiar with the parts of the common five-paragraph essay by reviewing the student essay on the next page.

CHAPTER 13

▶ **WRITING THE ESSAY**

- Develop a series of paragraphs that support one main idea.

CHAPTER 14

▶ **ESSAY PATTERNS**

- Apply the nine paragraph patterns covered in Chapters 4 through 12 to essay writing.

CHAPTER 15

▶ **ENHANCING YOUR WRITING WITH RESEARCH**

- Research information to effectively support essay writing.

EXTENDING THE SCHOOL YEAR

President Barack Obama proposes that American school children extend their time in class either by lengthening the school days or by cutting summer vacation days. Although critics believe that extending the U.S. school year would cause many difficult consequences, many parents and politicians believe otherwise. The school year should be increased from 180 to 210 days because students would not be left at home alone, they would not get into trouble, and teachers would have more time to teach their subjects.

If the school year were lengthened to 210 days, parents would not have to worry about their children spending many hours at home alone during the summer months. Currently, students have at least two months of summer holidays. Many students do not have anything to do except eat and watch television. For example, Carol, a single mother of three boys, works at a Quick-Stop Store from 7:00 A.M. until 7:00 P.M. The boys have no supervision. They never pick up a book, nor do they do any sports. Having a longer school year would ensure that children are more constructively occupied.

Moreover, students would stay out of trouble by going to school for 210 days a year. Many adolescents have a lot of free time on their hands after school and during school vacations. For instance, when thirteen-year-old KeKe went to the mall, her friends pressured her to steal a pair of gold earrings. The security guard arrested the girls as they walked out of the store, and KeKe now has a record. If the school year were extended, students would have less free time and would be less likely to get into mischief.

Furthermore, teachers would have more time to teach their course curriculum if the school year were prolonged. During long summer holidays, many students forget what they learned, so teachers spend a lot of time revisiting the previous year's subject matter. With the additional days of instruction, students could spend more time studying. They would also have more time to absorb their course material. For example, Sally, a student in junior high, has a problem reading. If the school year were longer, she could get the extra help she needs because the teacher would have more time. Teachers could work with students one on one and teach their subjects step by step. Students' grades would probably go up because teachers would be able to spend more time with them.

In conclusion, the U.S. school year should be increased from 180 to 210 days. Students would spend less time at home alone, they could keep out of trouble, and teachers would have more time to teach. The grades of students would improve, and they would gain more confidence. Increasing the number of days students spend in school is a winning situation.

—Archie Arnold, student

The title gives a hint about the essay's topic.

An introductory paragraph introduces the essay's topic and contains its thesis statement.

The thesis statement contains the essay's topic and its controlling idea.

Each body paragraph begins with a topic sentence and contains supporting details.

The concluding paragraph brings the essay to a satisfactory close.

Writing the Essay 13

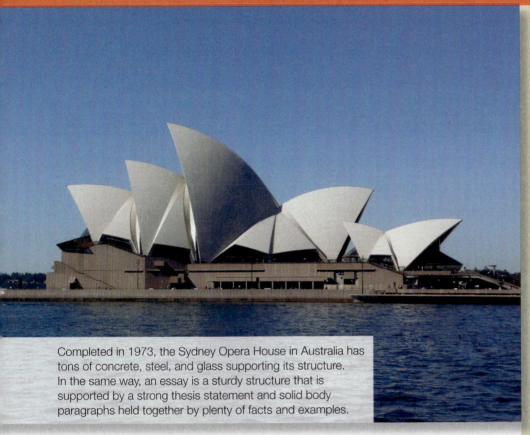

Completed in 1973, the Sydney Opera House in Australia has tons of concrete, steel, and glass supporting its structure. In the same way, an essay is a sturdy structure that is supported by a strong thesis statement and solid body paragraphs held together by plenty of facts and examples.

LEARNING OBJECTIVES

LO 1 Explore topics. (p. 165)

LO 2 Develop a thesis statement. (p. 167)

LO 3 Develop the supporting ideas. (p. 170)

LO 4 Develop an essay plan. (p. 173)

LO 5 Develop an introduction. (p. 177)

LO 6 Develop a conclusion. (p. 180)

LO 7 Write the first draft. (p. 182)

LO 8 Revise and edit the essay. (p. 182)

LO 9 Develop the essay title. (p. 184)

LO 10 Write the final draft. (p. 185)

▶ **EXPLORING**

Explore Topics

LO 1 Explore topics.

There are limitless topics for writing essays. Your knowledge and personal experiences will help you find topics and develop ideas when you write your essay.

When you are planning your essay, consider your topic, audience, and purpose. Your **topic** is who or what you are writing about. Your **audience** is your intended reader, and your **purpose** is your reason for writing. Do you hope to entertain, inform, or persuade the reader?

Narrowing the Topic

Your instructor may assign you a topic for your essay, or you may need to think of your own. In either case, you need to narrow your topic (make it more specific) to ensure that it suits your purpose for writing and fits the size of the assignment.

> **WRITING LINK**
> For more information about exploring strategies, see Chapter 1.

To narrow your topic, you can use some exploring methods such as questioning or brainstorming.

When you narrow your topic, keep in mind that an essay contains several paragraphs; therefore, an essay topic can be broader than a paragraph topic. In the following examples, you will notice that the essay topic is narrow but is slightly larger than the paragraph topic.

Broad Topic	Essay Topic	Paragraph Topic
Job interview	Preparing for the interview	Dressing for the interview
Rituals	Initiation rituals	College orientation week

HINT ‹ Choosing an Essay Topic

Paragraphs and essays can also be about the same topic. However, an essay has more details and concrete examples to support its thesis.

Do not make the mistake of choosing an essay topic that is too broad. Essays that try to cover a large topic risk being superficial and overly general. Make sure that your topic is specific enough that you can cover it in an essay.

David Narrows His Topic

Student writer David Raby-Pepin used both brainstorming and questioning to narrow his broad topic, "music." His audience was his English instructor, and the purpose of his assignment was to persuade.

—Should street performers be required to have a license?

—downloading music

—difference in earning power between classical and pop musicians

—Why do some rock bands have staying power?

—how to be a successful musician

—What is hip-hop culture?

—the popularity of shows like *American Idol*

—difference between poetry and song lyrics

THE WRITER'S DESK   Narrow the Topics

Practice narrowing five broad topics.

EXAMPLE: Money: _–reasons it doesn't make you happy_

–teach children about value of money

–best ways to be financially successful

1. Volunteer work: _____

   _____

   _____

2. Environment: _____

   _____

   _____

3. Advertising: _____

_____

_____

4. Entertainment: _____

_____

_____

The Thesis Statement

LO 2 Develop a thesis statement.

Once you have narrowed the topic of your essay, develop your thesis statement. The **thesis statement**—like the topic sentence in a paragraph—introduces the topic of the essay and arouses the interest of the reader.

Characteristics of a Good Thesis Statement

A thesis statement has three important characteristics.

- It expresses the main topic of the essay.
- It contains a controlling idea.
- It is a complete sentence that usually appears in the essay's introductory paragraph.

Here is an example of an effective thesis statement.

<u>topic</u>   <u>controlling idea</u>
Marriage <u>has lost its importance for many young people in our society</u>.

Writing an Effective Thesis Statement

When you develop your thesis statement, ask yourself the following questions.

1. **Is my thesis statement a complete statement that has a controlling idea?** Your thesis statement should always reveal a complete thought and make a point about the topic. It should not simply announce the topic or express a widely known fact.

Incomplete	Gambling problems.
	(This statement is not complete.)
Announcement	I will write about lotteries.
	(This statement announces the topic but says nothing relevant about the topic. Do not use expressions such as _I will write about…_ or _My topic is…_)
Thesis statement	Winning the lottery will not necessarily lead to happiness.

2. **Does my thesis statement make a valid and supportable point?** Your thesis statement should express a valid point that you can support with evidence.

It should not be a vaguely worded statement, and it should not be a highly questionable generalization.

Vague	Workplace relationships are harmful.
	(For whom are they harmful?)
Invalid point	Women earn less money than men.
	(Is this really true for all women in all professions? This generalization might be hard to prove.)
Thesis statement	Before coworkers become romantically involved, they should carefully consider possible problems.

3. **Can I support my thesis statement in an essay?** Your thesis statement should express an idea that you can support in an essay. It should not be too broad or too narrow.

Too broad	There are many museums in the world.
	(It would be difficult to write an essay about this topic.)
Too narrow	The Spy Museum is in Washington.
	(What more is there to say?)
Thesis statement	Washington's Spy Museum contains fascinating artifacts related to the secret world of espionage.

HINT ◀ **Give Specific Details**

Give enough details to make your thesis statement focused and clear. Your instructor may want you to guide the reader through your main points. To do this, mention both your main point and your supporting points in your thesis statement. In other words, your thesis statement provides a map for the readers to follow.

Weak	My first job taught me many things.
Better	My first job taught me about responsibility, organization, and the importance of teamwork.

PRACTICE 1

Identify the problem in each thesis statement. Then revise each statement to make it more interesting and complete.

Announces	Invalid	Broad
Incomplete	Vague	Narrow

EXAMPLE: I will write about human misery on television news.

Problem: Announces

Revised statement: Television news programs should not treat personal tragedies as big news.

1. Young men are worse drivers than young women.

Problem: _____

Revised statement: _____

_____

2. In my opinion, rappers are poor role models for American youths.

   Problem: _____

   Revised statement: _____

   _____

3. Freedom is important.

   Problem: _____

   Revised statement: _____

   _____

4. The streets are becoming more dangerous.

   Problem: _____

   Revised statement: _____

   _____

5. The problem with traditional values.

   Problem: _____

   Revised statement: _____

   _____

6. My children know how to count to ten in Spanish.

   Problem: _____

   Revised statement: _____

   _____

THE WRITER'S DESK   Write Thesis Statements

For each item, choose a narrowed topic from the Writer's Desk on pages 166–167. Then write an interesting thesis statement. Remember that each thesis statement should contain a controlling idea.

EXAMPLE: Topic: Money

Narrowed topic: Winning a lottery _____

Thesis statement: Rather than improving your life, winning the lottery

can lead to feelings of guilt, paranoia, and boredom.

1. Topic: Volunteer work

   Narrowed topic: _____

   Thesis statement: _____

   _____

2. Topic: Environment

   Narrowed topic: _____

   Thesis statement: _____

   _____

3. Topic: Advertising

Narrowed topic: _____

Thesis statement: _____

_____

4. Topic: Entertainment

Narrowed topic: _____

Thesis statement: _____

_____

LO3 Develop the
supporting ideas.

The Supporting Ideas

The thesis statement expresses the main idea of the entire essay. In the following
illustration, you can see how the ideas flow in an essay. Topic sentences relate to the
thesis statement, and details support the topic sentences; therefore, all the ideas in the
essay are unified and support the thesis.

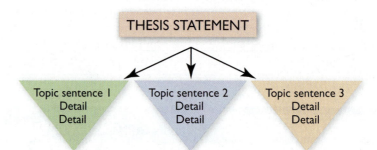

PRACTICE 2

Read the following essay by student Tami Farr. After you have finished reading, do
the following:

1. Create an effective thesis statement. It should sum up the point of the entire
    essay.

2. Write a topic sentence at the beginning of each body paragraph. The
    topic sentence should sum up the main point of the paragraph in an
    interesting way.

    Introduction:
        Our generation greatly relies on the Internet. Most of the time, the
    media report on only the dark side of the Internet. The Internet allows
    untrustworthy people to have easy access to personal information. The
    Internet also contains pornographic sites, and sexual predators use these
    sites to target victims. **Thesis Statement:**   _____

    _____

Body paragraph 1 topic sentence: _____

_____

Many students use the Internet for school research. The Internet is more accessible than libraries, is quicker than tracking down books, and has a bigger database. Google Advanced Scholar is a wonderful resource where a student can find information on any subject. Encyclopedias can be accessed on the Internet. Students can also find a tutor for any subject online, which allows them to receive timely help for school success.

Body paragraph 2 topic sentence: _____

_____

In the past, if we wanted to write to friends, we had to wait for days or weeks for our letter to reach them. Now e-mail helps us to communicate with people in seconds. E-mail is very useful if we want to send the same message to several friends. Instead of having to write multiple letters, we can now just enter multiple e-mail addresses.

Body paragraph 3 topic sentence: _____

_____

Most companies can now serve the world instead of just communities. Many companies' profits have increased by selling on the Internet. For example, Amazon.com sells products only through the Internet, and it is a very successful business. Consumers can also sell items through the Internet. Companies such as eBay allow both buyer and seller to conduct business easily. More people can work from home and get work done more quickly because of the Internet.

Conclusion:
    The Internet is a wonderful asset to our generation. Even though we see and hear about the negative aspects of the Internet, we need to keep in mind that if we use the Internet wisely, and for the right purposes, it can be a great boon in our lives.

Generating Supporting Ideas

An effective essay has **unity** when the body paragraphs support the thesis statement. When you plan your supporting ideas, make sure that they develop and provide evidence for the central point that you are making in the thesis statement. To generate ideas for body paragraphs, you could use exploring strategies such as brainstorming, clustering, or freewriting.

David's Supporting Ideas

David created a list to support his thesis statement. Then he reread his supporting points and removed ideas that he did not want to develop in his essay.

Thesis Statement: Rap and hip-hop artists use their music to share their positive cultural values with others.

—use lyrics to reveal their religious opinions
—Christian lyrics

—hip hop inspired breakdancing

—praise Allah

—want to promote peace

—some address issues of violence

—some hip hop artists have been jailed

—advise fans about healthy lifestyles

—warn about drugs

—talk about AIDS

THE WRITER'S DESK **List Supporting Ideas**

Choose two of your thesis statements from the previous Writer's Desk on page 169, and create two lists of possible supporting ideas.

Thesis 1: _____   Thesis 2: _____

_____   _____

Support: _____   Support: _____

_____   _____

_____   _____

_____   _____

_____   _____

_____   _____

_____   _____

_____   _____

_____   _____

_____   _____

_____   _____

WRITING LINK
For more information about time, space, and emphatic order, see Chapter 2, "Developing."

Organizing Your Ideas

After you have examined your list of supporting ideas, choose three or four that are most compelling and most clearly support your statement. Highlight your favorite ideas, and then group together related ideas. Finally, make your essay as clear and coherent as possible by organizing your ideas in a logical manner using time, space, or emphatic order.

David's Example

David underlined his three best supporting points, and he grouped related ideas using emphatic order.

3
—use lyrics to reveal their religious opinions
—Christian lyrics
—hip hop inspired breakdancing
—praise Allah

1
—want to promote peace
—some address issues of violence
—some hip hop artists have been jailed

2
—advise fans about healthy lifestyles
—warn about drugs
—talk about AIDS

THE WRITER'S DESK Organize Your Ideas

Look at the list you produced in the previous Writer's Desk, and then follow these steps.

1. Highlight at least three ideas from your list that you think are the most compelling and that most clearly illustrate the point you are making in your thesis statement.

2. Group together any related ideas with the three supporting ideas.

3. Organize your ideas using time, space, or emphatic order.

The Essay Plan

L04 Develop an essay plan.

An **essay plan** or an **outline** can help you organize your thesis statement and supporting ideas before you write your first draft. To create an essay plan, follow these steps.

◆ Look at your list of ideas and identify the best supporting ideas.

◆ Write topic sentences that express the main supporting ideas.

◆ Add details under each topic sentence.

In the planning stage, you do not have to develop your introduction and conclusion. It is sufficient to simply write your thesis statement and an idea for your conclusion. Later, when you flesh out your essay, you can develop the introduction and conclusion.

David's Essay Plan

David wrote topic sentences and supporting examples and organized his ideas into a plan. Notice that he begins with his thesis statement, and he indents his supporting ideas.

Thesis Statement: Rap and hip-hop artists use their music to share their positive cultural values with others.

Body paragraph 1: Many musicians shout out a powerful message of nonviolence.
—They have broken from the "gansta rap" lyrics.
—Encourage listeners to respect themselves and others.

Body paragraph 2:   Some advise fans about responsible and healthy lifestyles.

—They discuss the importance of good parenting.

—They talk about drug addiction or AIDS.

Body paragraph 3:   These urban musicians use their poetry to reveal their religious beliefs.

—Some show their Christian faith through the lyrics.

—Others praise Allah.

Concluding sentence: Finally, music is a way for rap musicians to share their personal culture with the world.

Writing a Formal Essay Plan

Most of the time, a basic essay plan is sufficient. However, in some of your courses, your instructor may ask you to make a formal plan. A formal plan uses Roman numerals and letters to identify main and supporting ideas.

Thesis statement: _____

I.   _____

    A. _____

    B. _____

II.   _____

    A. _____

    B. _____

III. _____

    A. _____

    B. _____

Concluding idea: _____

PRACTICE 3

Create an essay plan based on Archie Arnold's essay "Extending the School Year" on page 164.

_____

_____

_____

_____

_____

_____

_____

_____

_____

_____

_____

_____

_____

_____

_____

_____

_____

_____

_____

_____

_____

_____

PRACTICE 4

Complete the following essay plan. Add details under each supporting point. Make sure that the details relate to the topic sentence.

> **Thesis statement:** Rather than improving someone's life, winning the lottery can lead to feelings of guilt, paranoia, and boredom.

I. Feelings of guilt are common in newly rich people.

Details: A. _____

_____

B. _____

_____

C. _____

_____

II. Lottery winners often become paranoid.

Details: A. _____

_____

B. _____

_____

C. _____

_____

III. After lottery winners quit their jobs, they commonly complain of boredom and loneliness.

Details: A. _____

_____

B. _____

_____

C. _____

_____

Concluding idea: _____

_____

_____

THE WRITER'S DESK   **Write an Essay Plan**

Write an essay plan using one of your thesis statements and supporting details you came up with in the previous Writer's Desk.

Thesis statement: _____

_____

I. _____

Details: A. _____

B. _____

C. _____

II. _____

Details: A. _____

B. _____

C. _____

III. _____

Details: A. _____

B. _____

C. _____

Concluding idea: _____

_____

The Introduction

LO 5 Develop an introduction.

After you have made an essay plan, you develop the sections of your essay by creating an effective introduction, linking paragraphs, and writing a conclusion.

The **introductory paragraph** introduces the subject of your essay and contains the thesis statement. A strong introduction will capture the reader's attention and make him or her want to read on. Introductions may have a lead-in, and they can be developed in several different ways.

The Lead-In

You can choose to begin the introduction with an attention-grabbing opening sentence, or lead-in. There are three common types of lead-ins.

* Quotation
* Surprising or provocative statement
* Question

Introduction Styles

You can develop the introduction in several different ways. Experiment with any of these introduction styles.

* **Give general or historical background information.** The general or historical information gradually leads to your thesis. For example, in an essay about winning a lottery, you could begin by giving a brief history of lotteries.
* **Tell an interesting anecdote.** Open your essay with a story that leads to your thesis statement. For example, you might begin your lottery essay by telling the story of a real-life lottery winner.
* **Present a vivid description.** Give a detailed description, and then state your thesis. For example, you might describe the moment when a lottery winner realizes that he or she has won.
* **Present an opposing position.** Open your essay with an idea that contradicts a common belief or an idea that is the opposite of the one that you will develop, and build to your thesis. For instance, you could begin by listing all of the great things about winning a lottery, and then your thesis could mention that lottery wins are not as great as they appear.
* **Give a definition.** Define a term, and then state your thesis. For example, in an essay about the lottery, you could begin by defining *happiness*.

HINT Placement of the Thesis Statement

Although a paragraph often begins with a topic sentence, an introduction does not begin with a thesis statement. Rather, most introductory paragraphs are shaped like a funnel. The most general statement introduces the topic. The following sentences become more focused and lead to a clear, specific thesis statement. Therefore, the thesis statement is generally the last sentence in the introduction.

PRACTICE 5

In introductions A through E, the thesis statement is underlined. Read each introduction and then answer the questions that follow. Look at David's example for some guidance.

EXAMPLE:

David's Introduction

Can hip-hop, with its obscene lyrics and violent culture, have any redeeming qualities? Hip-hop and rap music mainly originated from poor, minority-inhabited neighborhoods located in New York City. Since the residents did not have enough money to buy musical instruments, they began creating beats with their mouths. This raw form of music rapidly became popular within these communities because it gave people a way to express themselves and to develop their creative abilities. <u>Many rap and hip-hop artists use their music to share their positive cultural values with others.</u>

1. What type of lead-in does David use? *Question*

2. What introduction style does he use?
   a. Description   b. Definition
   (c.) Historical background   d. Opposing position

3. What is his essay about? *The positive message of hip-hop and rap music*

A.   "He's rich, so he must be really smart!" wrote blogger Lee Wang about Mark Zuckerberg. Zuckerberg created his first messaging program at the age of twelve. Shortly after, his parents, who are both professionals, hired a private tutor to help teenage Mark continue his interest in computer programming. Then Zuckerberg's parents sent him to Harvard University where he developed Facebook. <u>Most so-called "self-made millionaires"</u> actually received a lot of help along the way.

—Emanuel DeSouza, student

1. What type of lead-in does the author use? _____

2. What introduction style does the author use?
   a. Description   b. Anecdote
   c. Historical information   d. Opposing position

3. What is this essay about? _____

B.   Sacred consumption occurs when we set apart objects and events from normal activities and treat them with respect or awe. Many consumers regard events such as the Super Bowl and people such as Michael Jackson as sacred. Indeed, virtually anything can become sacred. Consider the Web site that sells unlaundered athletic wear that members of the Dallas Cowboys football team have worn. <u>Sacred consumption permeates many aspects of our lives.</u>

—Adapted from Michael R. Solomon, *Consumer Behavior: Buying, Having, and Being*

4. What introduction style does the author use?

    a. Anecdote   b. Vivid description

    c. General background   d. Definition

5. What is this essay about? _____

C.   High school is a waste of time. In fact, it is a baby-sitting service for teens who are too old to be baby-sat. In England, fifteen-year-olds graduate and can choose technical or university streams of education. They are free to choose what to study, or they can stop schooling and get jobs. In short, they are treated like mature adults. In our country, we prolong the experience of forced schooling much longer than is necessary. We should abolish high schools and introduce a system of technical or pre-university schooling.

                                                    —Adelie Zang, student

6. What type of lead-in does the author use? _____

7. What introduction style does the author use?

    a. Anecdote   b. Definition

    c. Background information   d. Opposing position

8. What is this essay about? _____

D.   Why are Westerners getting upset about women wearing burqas? In Spain, the Catalonian assembly almost passed a law to ban women from wearing the burqa in public. In France, politicians want to ban such clothing, and girls cannot wear Muslim head coverings at school. Belgian politicians are also debating this issue. Europeans are very emotional about this subject. But Americans must guard against falling into a similar mindset.

                                                —Amida Jordan, student

9. What type of lead-in does the author use? _____

10. What introduction style does the author use?

    a. Anecdote   b. General background

    c. Description   d. Opposing position

11. What is this essay about?_____

E.   How can we understand the fierce determination and driving will that could lead a single man to conceive of himself as ruler of the world? Between 221 BCE when he brought the warring states under his control until his death in 210 BCE, Qin Shihuangdi turned his vast lands of China into a unified state. To govern the Qin Empire, he created a bureaucracy—an intricate, hierarchal network—based on competence, not family heritage, and guided by a code of law. He united his lands with a common language and system of writing and more than 4,000 miles of roads. His tremendous actions were simple, direct, and brilliant.

                                     —Marilyn Stokstad, *Art: A Brief History*

12. What type of lead-in does the author use? _____

13. What introduction style does the author use?
    a. Description   b. Definition
    c. Historical background   d. Opposing position

14. What is this essay about? _____

THE WRITER'S DESK   Write Three Introductions

In the previous Writer's Desk, you made an essay plan. Now, write three different styles of introductions for your essay. Use the same thesis statement in all three introductions. Later, you can choose the best introduction for your essay.

LO 6 Develop a conclusion.

The Conclusion

A **conclusion** is a final paragraph that rephrases the thesis statement and summarizes the main points in the essay. To make your conclusion more interesting and original, you could close with a prediction, a suggestion, a quotation, or a call to action.

David's Conclusion

David concluded his essay by restating his main points.

> Finally, music is a way for hip-hop and rap musicians to share their personal culture with the world. This cultural facet can be reflected through different values, religious beliefs, and ways of life.

He could then close his essay with one of the following:

Prediction   If you are concerned about hip-hop portraying negative images, don't abandon the music yet. There are many artists who promote and will continue to promote positive values through upbeat lyrics.

Suggestion   Hip-hop fans should encourage musicians to continue to give a positive message through their music.

Call to action   If you are concerned by the negative message of hip-hop music, make your opinions heard by joining the debate on hip-hop blogs and buying CDs from musicians who only write positive lyrics.

Quotation   According to hip-hop artist Doug E. Fresh, "Hip Hop is supposed to uplift and create, to educate people on a larger level, and to make a change."

PRACTICE 6

Read the following conclusions and answer the questions.

moribund:
dying

pedestrianized:
streets for pedestrians; streets where no vehicles are allowed

A.   American cities are always looking for quick fixes to revive their **moribund** downtowns. Sadly, the dismal record of failed urban design strategies is long: downtown shopping malls, **pedestrianized** streets, underground passages, skyways, monorails, festival marketplaces, downtown stadiums—and that most elusive fix of all, iconic cultural buildings. It appears likely that we will soon be adding elevated parks to the list.

— Witold Rybczynski, "Bringing the High Line Back to Earth"

1. What method does the author use to end the conclusion?
   a. Prediction
   b. Suggestion
   c. Quotation
   d. Call to action

B.   So how can nonhuman primates be protected from us? There really are only two major ways: Either human population growth in many places has to be curtailed, or we have to preserve substantial populations of non-human primates in protected parks and zoos.

—Carol R. Ember et al., "Endangered Primates"

2. What method does the author use to end the conclusion?
   a. Prediction
   b. Suggestion
   c. Quotation
   d. Call to action

C.   Every once in a while the marketing wizards pay lip service to today's expanding career options for women and give us a Scientist Barbie complete with a tiny chemistry set as an accessory. But heaven forbid should little Johnnie plead for his parents to buy him that Scientist Barbie. After all, it is acceptable for girls to foray, occasionally, into the world of boy-style play, but for boys the opposite "sissified" behavior is taboo. Why is this? One commentator, D. R. Shaffer, says, "The major task for young girls is to learn how not to be babies, whereas young boys must learn how not to be girls."

—Dorothy Nixon, "Put GI Barbie in the Bargain Bin"

3. What method does the author use to end the conclusion?
   a. Prediction
   b. Suggestion
   c. Quotation
   d. Call to action

HINT Avoiding Conclusion Problems

In your conclusion, do not contradict your main point, and do not introduce new or irrelevant information. David initially included the next sentences in his conclusion.

> The rap and hip-hop movement is not restrained only to the musical scene. It influences many other facets of art and urban culture as well. It can be found in dance and fashion, for instance. Thus, it is very versatile.

He revised his conclusion when he realized that some of his ideas were new and irrelevant information. His essay does not discuss dance or fashion.

THE WRITER'S DESK   Write a Conclusion

In previous Writer's Desks, you wrote an introduction and an essay plan. Now write a conclusion for your essay.

LO 7 Write the first draft.

The First Draft

After creating an introduction and conclusion, and after arranging the supporting ideas in a logical order, you are ready to write your first draft. The first draft includes your introduction, several body paragraphs, and your concluding paragraph.

THE WRITER'S DESK   **Write the First Draft**

In previous Writer's Desks, you wrote an introduction, a conclusion, and an essay plan. Now write the first draft of your essay.

LO 8 Revise and edit the essay.

▶ **REVISING AND EDITING**

Revising and Editing the Essay

Revising your essay is an extremely important step in the writing process. When you revise your essay, you modify it to make it stronger and more convincing. You do this by reading the essay critically, looking for faulty logic, poor organization, or poor sentence style. Then you reorganize and rewrite it, making any necessary changes.

Editing is the last stage in writing. When you edit, you proofread your writing and make sure that it is free of errors.

Revising for Unity

To revise for **unity**, verify that all of your body paragraphs support the thesis statement. Also look carefully at each body paragraph: make sure that the sentences support the topic sentence.

HINT ◀ **Avoiding Unity Problems**

Here are two common errors to check for as you revise your body paragraphs.

- **Rambling paragraphs.** The paragraphs in the essay ramble on. Each paragraph has several topics, and there is no clearly identifiable topic sentence.
- **Artifical breaks.** A long paragraph is split into smaller paragraphs arbitrarily, and each smaller paragraph lacks a central focus.

To correct either of these errors, revise each body paragraph until it has *one* main idea that supports the thesis statement.

WRITING LINK
To practice revising for unity and support, see Chapter 3, "Revising and Editing."

Revising for Adequate Support

When you revise for adequate **support**, ensure that there are enough details and examples to make your essay strong and convincing. Include examples, statistics, quotations, or anecdotes.

Revising for Coherence

When you revise for **coherence**, ensure that paragraphs flow smoothly and logically. To guide the reader from one idea to the next, or from one paragraph to the next, try using **paragraph links**.

You can develop connections between paragraphs using three methods.

1. **Repeat words or phrases from the thesis statement in each body paragraph.** In the next example, *violent* and *violence* are repeated words.

Thesis statement	Although some will argue that violent movies are simply a reflection of a violent society, these movies actually cause a lot of the violence around us.
Body paragraph 1	Action movie heroes train children to solve problems with violence.
Body paragraph 2	Violent movies are "how to" films for many sick individuals.

2. **Refer to the main idea in the previous paragraph, and link it to your current topic sentence.** In body paragraph 2, the writer reminds the reader of the first point (the newly rich feel useless) and then introduces the next point.

Thesis statement	A cash windfall may cause more problems than it solves.
Body paragraph 1	The newly rich often lose their desire to become productive citizens, and they end up feeling useless.
Body paragraph 2	Apart from feeling useless, many heirs and lottery winners also tend to feel guilty about their wealth.

3. **Use a transitional word or phrase to lead the reader to your next idea.**

Body paragraph 2	Furthermore, the newly rich often feel guilty about their wealth.

> **WRITING LINK**
> *Furthermore* is a transition. For a list of transitions, see pages 38–39 in Chapter 3.

Revising for Style

Another important step in the revision process is to ensure that you have varied your sentences and that you have used concise wording. When you revise for sentence style, ask yourself the following questions.

- Do I use a variety of sentence patterns? (To practice using sentence variety, see Chapter 19.)
- Do I use exact language? (To learn about slang, wordiness, and overused expressions, see Chapter 32.)
- Are my sentences parallel in structure? (To practice revising for parallel structure, see Chapter 22.)

Editing

When you edit, you proofread your essay and correct any errors in punctuation, spelling, grammar, and mechanics. There is an editing guide on the inside back cover of this book that provides you with a list of things to check for when you proofread your text.

> **ESSAY LINK**
> To practice your editing skills, see Chapter 37, "Editing Paragraphs and Essays."

David's Essay

David Raby-Pepin revised and edited this paragraph from his essay about hip-hop culture.

Furthermore, some
~~Some~~ rappers advise fans about responsible and healthy lifestyles.

they are
Several hip-hop artists divulge the fact that ~~their~~ parents and discuss

the importance of good parenting. Others announce their choice of a

and
monogamous lifestyle. ~~They~~ encourage their fans to have respectful

relationships. Some rappers mention past drug addictions and advise

avoid
listeners to ~~be avoiding~~ drugs. Others rap about the dangers of sexually

example,
transmitted diseases. The rapper Ludacris, for ~~example. He~~ warns his

fans about AIDS and HIV and advises them to be careful and to use

extremely
condoms during sex. Such messages are ~~extremly~~ important since many

young people do not take precautions with their health.

THE WRITER'S DESK   **Revising and Editing Your Essay**

In the previous Writer's Desk, you wrote the first draft of an essay. Now revise and edit your essay. You can refer to the checklist at the end of this chapter.

LO 9 Develop the essay title.

ESSAY LINK
For more information about punctuating titles, see pages 478–479 in Chapter 35.

The Essay Title

It is a good idea to think of a title after you have completed your essay because then you will have a more complete impression of your essay's main point. The most effective titles are brief, depict the topic and purpose of the essay, and attract the reader's attention.

When you write your title, place it at the top center of your page. Capitalize the first word of your title, and capitalize the main words except for prepositions (*in, at, for, to*, etc.) and articles (*a, an, the*). Double-space between the title and the introductory paragraph.

Descriptive Titles

Descriptive titles are the most common titles in academic essays. They depict the topic of the essay clearly and concisely. Sometimes, the author takes key words from the thesis statement and uses them in the title. Here are some descriptive titles.

The Importance of Multiculturalism in a Democratic Society
Why Mothers and Fathers Should Take Parenting Seriously

Titles Related to the Writing Pattern

You can also relate your title directly to the writing pattern of your essay. Here are examples of titles for different writing patterns.

Illustration	The Problems with Elections
Narration	My Visit to Las Vegas
Description	Graduation Day
Process	How to Dress for an Interview
Definition	What It Means to Be Brave
Classification	Three Types of Hackers
Comparison and contrast	Fast Food versus Gourmet Food
Cause and effect	Why People Enter Beauty Pageants
Argument	Barbie Should Have a New Look

HINT ◀ **Avoiding Title Pitfalls**

When you write your title, watch out for problems.

- Do not view your title as a substitute for a thesis statement.
- Do not put quotation marks around the title of your essay.
- Do not write a really long title because it can be confusing.

PRACTICE 7

1. List some possible titles for the essay about the Internet in Practice 2 (pages 170–171).

   _____

   _____

2. List some alternative titles for David's essay about rap and hip-hop music, which appears on page 186.

   _____

   _____

The Final Draft

LO 10 Write the final draft.

When you have finished making the revisions on the first draft of your essay, write the final copy. This copy should include all the changes that you have made during the revision phase of your work. You should proofread the final copy of your work to check for grammar, spelling, mechanics, and punctuation errors.

David's Essay

David Raby-Pepin revised and edited his essay about hip-hop culture. This is his final draft.

Positive Messages in Hip-Hop Music

Can hip-hop, with its obscene lyrics and violent culture, have any redeeming qualities? Hip-hop and rap music mainly originated from poor, minority-inhabited neighborhoods located in New York City. Since the residents did not have enough money to buy musical instruments, they began creating beats with their mouths. This raw form of music rapidly became popular within these communities because it gave people a way to express themselves and to develop their creative abilities. Many rap and hip-hop artists use their music to share their positive cultural values with others.

A lot of these musicians shout out a powerful message of nonviolence. Leading hip-hop and rap artists have broken from the gangsta rap lyrics of the past. Instead, they write lyrics that present a productive way to resolve conflicts. They encourage listeners to respect themselves and others.

Furthermore, some rappers advise fans about responsible and healthy lifestyles. Several hip-hop artists divulge the fact that they are parents and discuss the importance of good parenting. Others announce their choice of a monogamous lifestyle and encourage their fans to have respectful relationships. Some rappers mention past drug addictions and advise listeners to avoid drugs. Others rap about the dangers of sexually transmitted diseases. The rapper Ludacris, for example, warns his fans about AIDS and HIV and advises them to be careful and to use condoms during sex. Such messages are extremely important since many young people do not take precautions with their health.

Moreover, these urban musicians also use their lyrics to reveal their religious beliefs. Some show their Christian faith by including God in their texts. For example, in the song "Tommy" by Mathematics, the lyrics refer to a relationship with God after death. Members of the band Killarmy praise Allah in their lyrics. Hip-hop and rap musicians generally do not criticize other religions through their songs. They use this form of communication to support their own religious opinions. Hip-hop and rap music can be a way for individuals to show their faith or to pass it on to members of their audience.

Finally, music is a way for rap musicians to share their personal culture with the world. This cultural facet can be reflected through different values, religious beliefs, and ways of life. According to hip-hop artist Doug E. Fresh, "Hip Hop is supposed to uplift and create, to educate people on a larger level, and to make a change."

THE WRITER'S DESK **Writing Your Final Draft**

At this point, you have developed, revised, and edited your essay. Now write the final draft. Before you hand in your essay to your instructor, proofread it one last time to make sure that you have found as many errors as possible.

Reflect On It

Think about what you have learned in this unit. If you do not know an answer, review that topic.

1. What is a thesis statement? _____

   _____

2. What are the five different introduction styles?

   _____   _____

   _____   _____

   _____

3. What are the four different ways to end a conclusion?

   _____   _____

   _____   _____

4. What are the three different ways you can link body paragraphs?

   _____

   _____

   _____

THE WRITER'S ROOM

MyWritingLab™

MyWritingLab™
Complete these writing assignments at mywritinglab.com

Writing Activity 1: Topics

Choose any of the following topics, or choose your own topic. Then write an essay. Remember to follow the writing process.

General Topics

1. communication
2. an unforgettable experience
3. differences between generations
4. advertising
5. peer pressure

College and Work-Related Topics

6. juggling college and family life
7. having a job and going to college
8. long-term career goals
9. a current social controversy
10. an important issue in the workplace

Writing Activity 2: Photo Writing

What ideas come to mind when you examine this photo? You may think about celebrities, culture of excess, culture of entitlement, good or bad role models, big business, and so on. Write an essay based on the photo or your related topic.

Revising and Editing Checklist for Essays

As you write your essay, ask yourself the following questions.

Revising

☐ Does my essay have a compelling introduction and conclusion?

☐ Does my introduction have a clear thesis statement?

☐ Does each body paragraph contain a topic sentence?

☐ Does each body paragraph's topic sentence relate to the thesis statement?

☐ Does each body paragraph contain specific details that support the topic sentence?

☐ Do all of the sentences in each body paragraph relate to its topic sentence?

☐ Do I use transitions to smoothly and logically connect ideas?

☐ Do I use a variety of sentence styles?

Editing

☐ Do I have any errors in grammar, spelling, punctuation, and capitalization?

Essay Patterns 14

Fashion designers choose fabric patterns that are appropriate for the articles of clothing that they wish to make. In the same way, writers choose essay patterns that best suit their purposes for writing.

LEARNING OBJECTIVES

LO 1 Write an illustration essay. **(p. 190)**

LO 2 Write a narrative essay. **(p. 194)**

LO 3 Write a descriptive essay. **(p. 198)**

LO 4 Write a process essay. **(p. 203)**

LO 5 Write a definition essay. **(p. 208)**

LO 6 Write a classification essay. **(p. 213)**

LO 7 Write a comparison and contrast essay. **(p. 218)**

LO 8 Write a cause and effect essay. **(p. 222)**

LO 9 Write an argument essay. **(p. 227)**

In Chapters 4 through 12, you read about and practiced using nine different paragraph patterns. In this chapter, you will learn how to apply those patterns when writing essays. Before you begin working through this chapter, take a moment to review the nine writing patterns.

Pattern	Purpose
Illustration	To prove a point using specific examples
Narration	To tell a story about a sequence of events that happened
Description	To portray something using vivid details and images that appeal to the reader's senses
Process	To inform the reader about how to do something, how something works, or how something happened
Definition	To explain what a term or concept means by providing relevant examples
Classification	To sort a topic to help readers understand different qualities about that topic
Comparison and contrast	To present information about similarities (compare) or differences (contrast)
Cause and effect	To explain why an event happened (the cause) or what the consequences of the event were (the effects)
Argument	To take a position on an issue and offer reasons for your position

Most college essay assignments specify one dominating essay pattern. However, you can use several additional essay patterns to fulfill your purpose. For example, imagine that you want to write a cause and effect essay about youth crime and the purpose of the essay is to inform. The supporting paragraphs might include a definition of youth crime and a narrative about an adolescent with a criminal record. You might incorporate different writing patterns, but the dominant pattern would still be cause and effect.

Each time you write an essay, remember to follow the writing process that you learned in Chapter 13, "Writing the Essay."

LO 1 Write an illustration essay.

> **PARAGRAPH LINK**
> For more information about developing ideas with examples, refer to Chapter 4, "Illustration."

The Illustration Essay

When writing an illustration essay, you use specific examples to clarify your main point. Illustration writing is a pattern that you frequently use in college essays and exams because you must support your main idea with examples.

The Thesis Statement

The thesis statement in an illustration essay gives the direction of the body paragraphs. It includes the topic and a controlling idea about the topic.

topic   controlling idea

A second language provides students with several important advantages.

The Supporting Ideas

In an illustration essay, the body paragraphs contain examples that support the thesis statement. You can develop the body paragraphs in two different ways. To give your essay variety, you could use both a series of examples and an extended example.

- **Use a series of examples** that support the paragraph's topic sentence. For example, in an essay about bad driving, one body paragraph could be about drivers who do not pay attention to the road. The paragraph could list the things that those drivers do, such as choosing songs on an iPod, using a cell phone, eating, and putting on makeup.

- **Use an extended example** to support the paragraph's topic sentence. The example could be an anecdote or a description of an event. In an essay about bad driving, for example, one paragraph could contain an anecdote about a driver who always wanted to be faster than other drivers.

A Student Illustration Essay

Read and analyze the structure of the next student illustration essay.

> ## COMICS AS SOCIAL COMMENTARY

Nicholas Slayton

1.   Comics, funny illustrated magazines, are the home of people in tights fighting each other. They are also a great medium for social commentary and protest. Since their inception, comic books have challenged the established system and worked to highlight injustice around the world.

Thesis statement

2. When comics started in the 1930s, the writers were urban and influenced by the world around them. If cities were at the forefront of social and economic progress, then the comics that came out of them were timely and well aware of the troubles facing contemporary society. Joe Shuster and Jerry Siegel initially created Superman not as a defender of truth, justice, and the American way, but as a defender of the New Deal. Accordingly, Superman spent his early issues taking on slumlords, corrupt businessmen, and other symptoms of the Great Depression.

> Topic sentence

3. In the 1950s, comics briefly found their soapbox kicked out from under them because of congressional pressure and self-imposed censorship. The Comics Code nearly killed the industry, and the remaining series in publication turned to camp and silly stories instead of social commentary. That is until the 1970s, when a new group of writers, influenced by the counter culture and political unrest of the 1960s, took over. Stan Lee, who revolutionized comics by focusing on heroes with personal issues—as opposed to the shining beacons of heroic perfection from the 1940s—decided to tackle drug use. In the *Amazing Spider-Man* "Green Goblin Reborn!" comic, Spider-Man confronted his best friend who had started using drugs. Meanwhile at DC, Green Arrow and Green Lantern traveled across the United States, confronting poverty, racism, and, ultimately, drug use when Green Arrow's sidekick was revealed to be a heroin addict.

> Topic sentence

4. From the 1980s onwards, activism in comics took a new spin. In the 1980s, British writers took over American series. Dark titles such as *Hellblazer* took on the politics and conservatism of the time. Alan Moore and David Lloyd's *V for Vendetta* was a direct reaction to Margaret Thatcher's conservatism and ended up forecasting the CCTV cameras everywhere in London. In the new millennium, a new wave of writers came from a **DIY** mindset. David Lloyd, the artist behind the *V for Vendetta* Guy Fawkes mask, used Kickstarter, a large funding platform, to support Occupy Comics, which aims to capture the spirit and motivations of the Occupy movement. It provides a form of documentation for the ongoing protests. And beyond works like Occupy Comics, there are more subtle works. For instance, Brian Wood's recently concluded *DMZ* was a sharp critique of the post–September 11 world.

> Topic sentence

> DIY:
> do it yourself

5. Because comics are aimed at youth—the people who are likely to be the most socially conscious—there's a greater impact. Why should students support equal rights? Read *X-Men*, and they'll see why they should take action. Comics combine protest art, visual documentation, and text. Comics have been calling out injustices for decades and hopefully will for many more to come.

> Conclusion ends with a prediction

PRACTICE 1

1. How does the writer develop the body paragraphs? Circle the best answer.

   a. Extended examples   c. Both

   b. Series of examples

2. Who is the audience for this essay? _____

   _____

3. What organizational pattern does the author use in this essay?

   a. Time order   c. Emphatic order

   b. Space order

A Professional Illustration Essay

Read the next essay by award-winning science writer Tom Keenan, and answer the questions that follow.

Guy Chores

1   For some reason, hot summer days remind me of my father doing mundane things like changing the oil in the car or washing paintbrushes with turpentine after completing a project around the house. It's far too late to make a difference to him, but experts now say some chemicals we handle doing "guy chores" can be pretty bad for us.

2   The latest is motor oil, which, according to a study in *Arthritis Research & Therapy*, may be linked to a risk of developing rheumatoid arthritis. A Swedish study found men who were exposed to mineral oils had a 30 percent higher risk of developing this disease than a control group. Before people panic and hand their cars over to the pros, it should be noted that the men in this study came into contact with motor or hydraulic oils regularly in the course of their work. The average man is not likely to suffer much from servicing the family car every 3000 miles.

3   Oil-based paint can contain a lot more gunk than just mineral spirits. According to information provided by the city of Phoenix, Arizona, on its very helpful household hazardous materials webpage, "a Johns Hopkins University study found 300 toxic chemicals and 150 carcinogens that may be present in paint." According to that source, the culprit chemicals span several components of oil-based paint and stains. "Pigments that provide the color may contain heavy metals such as cadmium and chromium. Cadmium irritates the respiratory tract while chromium is an eye and skin irritant. Pigments also may be made with zinc oxide, which can cause flu-like symptoms." So if people send their children out to paint the fence, they should make sure the paint is the safe kind.

4   Some guys are getting into gardening. It is relaxing and therapeutic, but some of those pesticides can be as bad as the car stuff in the garage. A study showed a disturbingly high concentration of estradiol—a form of the female sex hormone—in men exposed to pesticides and other agricultural chemicals. One good gardening tip is to avoid watering an area immediately after applying a chemical. Perhaps a better idea would be to get into pesticide-free gardening. That may result in a bit more stooping to get weeds, but the exercise is good for you.

5   Fortunately, I seem to have survived my contact with benzene, transmission fluid, and turpentine. Still, I'd think twice before letting young hobbyists work with dangerous materials. Believing that they are invincible, they may not appreciate the dangers, and they tend to be sloppy. Teenagers love fiddling with cars, and I'm not suggesting they have to switch to pasting stamps in albums. Still, a growing body of research shows common-sense precautions are really important when dealing with that shelf of weird chemicals out in the garage.

PRACTICE 2

1. Who is the audience for this essay? _____

    _____

2. Why does the writer use vocabulary such as *guys*, *gunk*, and *stuff*?

    _____

    _____

3. Highlight the thesis statement of the essay.

4. Underline the topic sentence of each body paragraph.

5. Identify the types of specific examples the writer uses to support his thesis.

   a. statistics
   b. research study
   c. facts
   d. expert opinion
   e. anecdote

6. What suggestion does the writer make in the conclusion of the essay?

   _____

   _____

   _____

THE WRITER'S ROOM

MyWritingLab™

MyWritingLab™
Complete these writing assignments at mywritinglab.com

Writing Activity 1: Topics

Write an illustration essay about one of the following topics.

General Topics

1. important milestones
2. stereotypes on television
3. useless products or inventions
4. activities that relieve stress
5. American symbols

College and Work-Related Topics

6. characteristics of a good boss
7. qualities of an ideal workplace
8. skills that you need for your job
9. temptations that college students face
10. important things to know about doing your job

PARAGRAPH LINK
To practice illustration writing, you could develop an essay about one of the topics found in Chapter 4, "Illustration."

Illustration Essay Checklist

As you write your illustration essay, review the essay checklist at the end of the book. Also ask yourself the following questions.

☐ Does my thesis statement include a topic that I can support with examples?

☐ Does my thesis statement make a point about the topic?

☐ Do my body paragraphs contain sufficient examples that clearly support the thesis statement?

☐ Do I smoothly and logically connect the examples?

LO 2 Write a narrative essay.

PARAGRAPH LINK
For more information about narrative writing, refer to Chapter 5, "Narration."

The Narrative Essay

When you write a narrative essay, you tell a story about what happened, and you generally explain events in the order in which they occurred.

There are two main types of narrative writing. In **first-person narration**, you describe a personal experience using *I* or *we*. In **third-person narration**, you describe what happened to somebody else, and you use *he, she, it,* or *they*.

The Thesis Statement

The thesis statement controls the direction of the body paragraphs. To create a meaningful thesis statement for a narrative essay, you could ask yourself what you learned, how you changed, or how the event is important.

controlling idea   topic

Something wonderful happened **the summer I turned fifteen**.

The Supporting Ideas

Here are some tips to remember as you develop a narrative essay.

♦ Make sure that your essay has a point. Do not simply recount what happened. Try to indicate why the events are important.

♦ Organize the events in time order (the order in which they occurred). You could also reverse the order of events by beginning your essay with the outcome of the events and then explaining what happened that led to the outcome.

♦ Make your narrative essay more interesting by using some descriptive language. For example, you could use images that appeal to the senses.

To be as complete as possible, a good narrative essay should provide answers to most of the following questions.

♦ *Who* is the essay about? ♦ *Where* did it happen?
♦ *What* happened? ♦ *Why* did it happen?
♦ *When* did it happen? ♦ *How* did it happen?

GRAMMAR LINK
For information about punctuating quotations, see Chapter 35.

HINT ◄ **Using Quotations**

One effective way to enhance your narrative essay is to use dialogue. Include direct and/or indirect quotations.

A **direct quotation** contains a person's exact words. A direct quotation is set off with quotation marks. When you tell a story and include the exact words of more than one person, you must start a new paragraph each time the speaker changes.

Sara looked at me sadly: "Why did you betray me?"

"I didn't mean to do it," I answered.

She looked down at her hands and said, "I don't think I can ever forgive you."

An **indirect quotation** keeps the person's meaning but not the person's exact words. An indirect quotation is not set off by quotation marks.

Sara asked why I had betrayed her.

A Student Narration Essay

Read and analyze the next student narration essay.

MY PRISON STORY

Yirga Gebremeskel

1. Growing up, I found myself constantly getting in trouble. I hung around with the wrong group of people and experimented with marijuana. My academic work declined because all I wanted to do was hang out with the crew. My mother constantly lectured me, but no matter what she said, I always did what I wanted to do. At seventeen years old, I was heading for disaster when I was wrongfully convicted of assault and battery.   → Thesis statement

2. My troubles started when my little brother Samson and I hung out with my friend Malcolm. We were in downtown Boston, and we joked around and went window-shopping. Then we stopped into a 7-Eleven to get drinks. When I got to the counter to pay, I looked through the glass doors and saw a cop cruiser pull up. The officer pointed toward me and signaled me to come outside. My heart pounding, I went outside to meet him. He said that someone had just been assaulted, and I fit the description. I protested that there had to be a mistake, but he put me against the wall and patted me down. Then he read me my rights, and he shoved me into the cruiser.   → Topic sentence

3. I was thrust into a legal problem over which I had no control. I couldn't afford a lawyer, so the court gave me a court-appointed attorney. Four months later, my attorney unexpectedly arrived and said it was time to go to court. I explained that my best witness, my little brother, was in school, but he wouldn't give my mother enough time to find Samson. The actual trial was very brief and was hard for me to take seriously; I felt like any moment the victim would realize his mistake. But when the victim took the stand and described what had happened, he seemed earnest. He really believed that I was his attacker.   → Topic sentence

4. The verdict caused my family a lot of pain. There was no other evidence but the victim's word, but that was enough. The jury convicted me, and the judge gave me my sentence: six months in prison with an additional two years on probation. I turned around to look at my mother's face, and there were tears coming down her cheeks. She knew that I hadn't done the crime. When the court officer clutched my arm, I asked him if I could hug my mother, and he allowed me to. She held me like she was trying to hold on. Then the officer escorted me through a side exit.   → Topic sentence

5. My days in the South Bay Correction Facility were tough. I couldn't sleep; I tossed and turned all night. Small things were the most difficult. The food was horrible. Sometimes I had cellmates who wouldn't shower, so the cell smelled bad. And it was loud; voices echoed as people talked and argued constantly. Even at night, people would holler through the doors. When I talked to my family or friends on the phone, I felt down because they were getting ready to go to a party or just a simple walk to the park, but I was going back to my cell.   → Topic sentence

6. Eventually, my incarceration changed my life in a positive way. One great piece of advice I got was to do the time and not let the time do me, so I started to make better use of my days. I read business books, a subject I had a lot of interest in. I spent nights thinking about my life and where I was heading, and how   → Topic sentence

I could never come back to this place. Later, when my time was up and I could head home, I vowed to become a better person and to live my life to the fullest.

7.   Now I'm going to school, and I have given up drugs. To this day, I can't explain why the victim identified me. Probably I look like the person who assaulted him. I wonder how accurate visual memory is? Still, the terrible experience I went through made me a better person and helped me realize that life is too short and beautiful to be wasted.

Concluding sentence

PRACTICE 3

1. Who is this essay about? _____

2. What type of narration is this essay? _____

3. What organizational pattern does the author use in this essay?

    a. Time order   b. Space order   c. Emphatic order

A Professional Narrative Essay

In the next essay, Jeff Kemp recounts what happened during his early years as a professional football player. Read the essay and answer the questions.

A Lesson in Humility

1   We live in an age when, too often, rules are scorned, values are turned upside down, principles are replaced by **expediency**, and character is sacrificed for popularity. Individual athletes are sometimes the worst offenders, but not as often as one might think. In fact, sports teach important moral lessons that athletes can apply on and off the playing field.

expediency:
convenience; self-interest

2   Many people dream of being a professional athlete. For me, the dream seemed to be within reach because my father, Jack Kemp, an outstanding quarterback, played for the American Football League's Buffalo Bills (prior to the AFL's 1970 merger with the National Football League). The trouble was, I was not very good! I was a third-string football player through most of junior high and high school and for two years at Dartmouth College. I was not anyone's idea of a "hot prospect." After graduation, I was passed over by NFL scouts. When I was finally asked to join the Los Angeles Rams in 1981 as a free agent, I was **designated** as a fifth-string quarterback.

designated:
selected

3   It was a 50-to-1 shot that I would survive training camp. Rookies were the only players required to show up for the first week of camp. There were dozens competing for the few spots open on the team. After two days, a young boy approached me as I was walking off the field. He asked if he could carry my helmet to the locker room. It was a long way, but I said, "Sure, I think you can handle that." The next morning, he showed up before practice and offered to carry my helmet and shoulder pads, and he was there again after practice offering the same service. So it went for the rest of the week.

4   On the last day, as we were departing the field, my young assistant said, "Jeff, can I ask you a question?" (We were on a first-name basis by then.)

5   I thought, "This is my first fan! He is going to ask me for an autograph."

6   He then inquired, "When do the good football players come to camp?" Right then and there, I learned a lesson in humility from a seven-year-old boy.

7   In my first three NFL seasons, I was forced to learn the same lesson over and over again. During that time, I threw just 31 passes. Nevertheless, by 1984, I had managed to outlast the five NFL quarterbacks who had been ahead of me. With the Rams' record standing at 1–2, I took over for injured quarterback Vince Ferragamo and earned my first start against the Cincinnati Bengals, eventually leading the Rams to nine more victories and a playoff berth.

8   The next season, I returned to the bench as a backup quarterback. Humility, I was compelled to remind myself, was a good thing. It helped me appreciate what I had and avoid dwelling on what I did not have. It prevented complaining, which drains the spirit and unity of any group. It also led me to persevere and be ready whenever opportunity presented itself.

PRACTICE 4

1. What type of narration is this text? Circle the best answer.

   a. First person   b. Third person

2. Underline the thesis statement of the essay.

3. What introduction style does Kemp use? Circle the best answer.

   a. Definition   c. General information

   b. Anecdote   d. Historical information

4. List the main events that Kemp recounts in his essay.

   _____

   _____

   _____

   _____

   _____

   _____

5. What organizational method does Kemp use in this essay?

   a. Time order   b. Space order   c. Emphatic order

6. Write down one example of an indirect quotation from the essay.

   _____

   _____

7. Write down one example of a direct quotation from the essay.

   _____

   _____

8. Narrative writers do more than simply list a series of events. Kemp explains why the events were meaningful. What did Kemp learn?

   _____

   _____

MyWritingLab™

Complete these writing assignments at mywritinglab.com

PARAGRAPH LINK
To practice narrative writing, you could develop an essay about one of the topics found in Chapter 5, "Narration."

MyWritingLab™

THE WRITER'S ROOM

Writing Activity 1: Topics

Write a narrative essay about one of the following topics.

General Topics

1. a family legend
2. an illuminating moment
3. a rebellious act
4. an important event in the world
5. when you learned to do something new

College and Work-Related Topics

6. life lessons that college teaches you
7. what your previous job taught you
8. your best or worst job
9. your first job
10. a scandal at work or college

Narrative Essay Checklist

As you write your narrative essay, review the essay checklist at the end of the book. Also ask yourself the following questions.

☐ Does my thesis statement clearly express the topic of the narration, and does it make a point about that topic?

☐ Does my essay answer most of the following questions: *who, what, when, where, why, how?*

☐ Do I use transitional expressions that help clarify the order of events?

☐ Do I include details to make my narration more interesting?

LO 3 Write a descriptive essay.

PARAGRAPH LINK
For more information about descriptive writing, refer to Chapter 6, "Description."

The Descriptive Essay

When writing a descriptive essay, use words to create a vivid impression of a subject. Use details that appeal to the five senses: sight, smell, hearing, taste, and touch. You want your readers to be able to imagine all that you are describing.

The Thesis Statement

In a descriptive essay, the thesis statement includes what you are describing and makes a point about the topic.

topic   controlling idea
The Joshua Tree National Park has an inspirational landscape filled with life.

The Supporting Ideas

When you develop your descriptive essay, make sure it gives a **dominant impression**. The dominant impression is the overall feeling that you wish to convey. For example, the essay could convey an impression of tension, joy, nervousness, or anger.

You can place the details of a descriptive essay in space order, time order, or emphatic order. The order that you use depends on the topic of your essay. For example, if you describe a place, you can use space order, and if you describe a difficult moment, you can use time order.

HINT ◄ Using Figurative Devices

When writing a descriptive essay, you can use figurative devices such as simile, metaphor, or personification. These devices use comparisons and images to add vivid details to your writing.

- A **simile** is a comparison using *like* or *as*.

  It was Françoise, motionless and erect, framed in the small doorway of the corridor like the statue of a saint in its niche. —Marcel Proust, *Swann's Way*

  My son's constant whining felt like a jackhammer on my skull.

- A **metaphor** is a comparison that does not use *like* or *as*.

  Jealousy . . . is the green-eyed monster . . . —William Shakespeare, *Othello*

  The mind is a battlefield.

- **Personification** is the act of attributing human qualities to an inanimate object or animal.

  The wind kicked the leaves. —Kurt Vonnegut, Jr., "Next Door"

  The sauce hissed on the stove.

PRACTICE 5

Practice using figurative language. Use one of the following to describe each item: simile, metaphor, or personification. If you are comparing two things, try to use an unusual comparison.

EXAMPLE: Surprising: *Her sudden appearance was as surprising as a 4 a.m.*
phone call. (Simile)

1. Truck: _____

2. Road: _____

3. Crowd: _____

4. Annoying: _____

5. Relaxed: _____

A Student Description Essay

Read and analyze the next student description essay.

ROARING WAVES OF FIRE

Christi Lester

Thesis statement

1.   During the dry season on the African savannah, drought often brings fires. In South Africa, we call these veldt fires. When I moved to my grandparents' beautiful farm outside a small town called Bronkhorstspruit, I imagined a peaceful life. But one traumatic day, my peace was broken, and my life changed.

Topic sentence

2.   Something mysterious was in the distance, and it frightened the people around me. "Look at that strange yellow light," Megan yelled as we walked down the winding dirt road. As we arrived at our grandparents' house, we saw our grandmother frantically filling up massive buckets of water and drenching as much of the ground around the brick farmhouse as she could. It suddenly struck us that the yellow, red light was a raging fire, and it was approaching us as fast as any gold medal Olympian could run.

Topic sentence

3.   I felt panicky and desperate when I saw that the fire was only seven feet from our house. I dashed inside but realized that escape was useless. The fire could destroy the house; it could destroy me. My grandmother started filling the bath in case we needed to hide in it. If the flames were to engulf our house, a bath full of water would be our only hope for survival. I imagined many awful possibilities. I pictured everything belonging to me slowly melting away. I envisioned my two adorable cats and my bulldog trying to escape and being burnt to ashes. Everything seemed hopeless.

Topic sentence

4.   Looking outside my bedroom window, I watched the fire get closer and closer. It was my enemy. It ate the grass and the flowers. It consumed the trees, which crackled and hissed as their bark burnt. And then my foe advanced toward me. The fire's heat pricked my skin and suffocated me. My lungs filled with smoke, and I coughed and coughed. Just when it seemed that the fire would devour the house, my grandfather appeared on a big, red tractor, which contained a life-saving tank of water. My grandfather sprayed water on the flames under my window. The spray of water cooled my face, and it tasted clean and cold in my parched mouth. Soon the fire was out. There was silence, and I felt at peace.

5.   The evidence of the fire remained for months. The silky green grass was charred black, the red and white rose bushes were mud brown, and the walls of the house were covered in charcoal dust. The pungent smell of smoke stuck to surfaces for a long time. But each day, I saw only the blue sky and remembered how beautiful life was. Before the fire, I had spent much of my time being pessimistic. Nowadays, I know I have much to be grateful for and live with the motto that there is always a more positive side to every situation.

Concluding sentence

PRACTICE 6

1.   This essay contains imagery that appeals to the senses. Find one example of imagery for each sense.

a. Sight: _____

_____

b. Sound: _____

_____

c. Smell: _____

_____

   d. Taste: _____

       _____

   e. Touch: _____

       _____

2. This essay also contains figurative language. Find one example of a simile, metaphor, and personification. For definitions of these terms, see page 199.

   Simile: _____

   _____

   Metaphor: _____

   _____

   Personification: _____

   _____

3. What is the dominant impression of this essay? Circle the best answer.

   a. Awe   b. Fear   c. Joy   d. Surprise

A Professional Descriptive Essay

Read the following essay by Catherine Pigott, a freelance writer. Pay close attention to the descriptive details.

Chicken Hips

1   The women of the household clucked disapprovingly when they saw me. It was the first time I had worn African clothes since my arrival in tiny, dusty Gambia, and evidently they were not impressed. They adjusted my head-tie and pulled my *lappa*, the ankle-length fabric I had wrapped around myself, even tighter. "You're too thin," one of them pronounced. "It's no good." They nicknamed me "Chicken-hips."

2   I marveled at this accolade, for I had never been called thin in my life. It was something I longed for. I would have been flattered if those ample-bosomed women hadn't looked so distressed. It was obvious I fell far short of their ideal of beauty.

3   I had dressed up for a very special occasion—the baptism of a son. The women heaped rice into tin basins the size of laundry tubs, shaping it into mounds with their hands. Five of us sat around one basin, thrusting our fingers into the scalding food. These women ate with such relish, such joy. They pressed the rice into balls in their fists, squeezing until the bright-red palm oil ran down their forearms and dripped off their elbows.

4   I tried desperately, but I could not eat enough to please them. It was hard for me to explain that I come from a culture in which it is almost unseemly for a woman to eat too heartily. It's considered unattractive. It was even harder to explain that to me thin is beautiful, and in my country we deny ourselves food in our pursuit of perfect slenderness.

5   That night, everyone danced to welcome the baby. Women swiveled their broad hips and used their hands to emphasize the roundness of their bodies. One needed to be round and wide to make the dance beautiful. There was no place for thinness here. It made people sad. It reminded them of things they

wanted to forget, such as poverty, drought, and starvation. They never knew when the rice was going to run out.

6   I began to believe that Africa's image of the perfect female body was far more realistic than the long-legged leanness I had been conditioned to admire. There, it is beautiful—not shameful—to carry weight on the hips and thighs, to have a round stomach and heavy, swinging breasts. Women do not battle the bulge; they celebrate it. A body is not something to be tamed and molded.

7   The friends who had christened me Chicken-hips made it their mission to fatten me up. It wasn't long before a diet of rice and rich, oily stew twice a day began to change me. Every month, the women would take a stick and measure my backside, noting with pleasure its gradual expansion. "Oh Catherine, your buttocks are getting nice now!" they would say.

8   What was extraordinary was that I, too, believed I was becoming more beautiful. There was no sense of panic, no shame, and no guilt-ridden resolves to go on the miracle grape-and-water diet. One day, I tied my *lappa* tight across my hips and went to the market to buy beer for a wedding. I carried the crate of bottles home on my head, swinging my hips slowly as I walked. I felt transformed.

PRACTICE 7

1.   In this essay, what is the author describing? _____

     _____

2.   Underline at least five descriptive verbs.

3.   What is the dominant impression? Circle the best answer.

     a.   homesickness   b.   tension   c.   admiration

4.   The writer appeals to more than one sense. Give an example for each type of imagery.

     a.   Sight: _____

          _____

     b.   Sound: _____

          _____

     c.   Touch: _____

          _____

5.   How does the writer change physically and emotionally during her time in Africa?

     _____

     _____

     _____

6.   What is the writer's main message?

     _____

     _____

     _____

THE WRITER'S ROOM

Writing Activity 1: Topics

Write a descriptive essay about one of the following topics.

General Topics

1. a celebration
2. your ideal house
3. a painting or photograph
4. a physical and psychological self-portrait
5. your hometown

College and Work-Related Topics

6. your first impressions of college
7. a sports event
8. your college or workplace cafeteria or food court
9. a memorable person with whom you have worked
10. a pleasant or unpleasant task

PARAGRAPH LINK
To practice descriptive writing, you could develop an essay about one of the topics in Chapter 6, "Description."

Descriptive Essay Checklist

As you write your descriptive essay, review the essay checklist at the end of the book. Also ask yourself the following questions.

☐ Does my thesis statement clearly show what I will describe in the rest of the essay?

☐ Does my thesis statement make a point about the topic?

☐ Does my essay have a dominant impression?

☐ Does each body paragraph contain supporting details that appeal to the reader's senses?

☐ Do I use figurative language (simile, metaphor, or personification)?

The Process Essay

A **process** is a series of steps done in chronological order. When you write a process essay, you explain how to do something, how something happens, or how something works. There are two main types of process essays.

1. **Complete a process.** Explain how to complete a particular task. For example, you might explain how to create a sculpture or how to give first aid to a choking victim. Each step you describe helps the reader complete the process.
2. **Understand a process.** Explain how something works or how something happens. In other words, the goal is to help the reader understand a process rather than do a process. For example, you might explain how a law is passed or explain how a previous war began.

LO 4 Write a process essay.

PARAGRAPH LINK
For more information about process writing, refer to Chapter 7, "Process."

The Thesis Statement

The thesis statement in a process essay includes the process you are describing and a controlling idea. In the introduction of a process essay, you should also mention any tools or supplies that the reader would need to complete the process.

topic   controlling idea

Choosing a college <u>requires some careful thinking and planning</u>.

topic   controlling idea

Pregnancy <u>consists of several stages</u>.

HINT ◂ **List Specific Steps**

You can write a thesis statement that contains a map, or guide, to the details that you will present in your essay. To guide your readers, you could mention the main steps in your thesis statement.

topic   controlling idea

It is possible to quit smoking <u>if you focus on your goal</u>, <u>find alternative relaxing activities</u>, and <u>enlist the support of friends and family</u>.

The Supporting Ideas

The body paragraphs in a process essay should explain the steps in the process. Each body paragraph should include details and examples to explain each step.

HINT ◂ **Using Commands**

When writing an essay to help readers complete a process, you can use commands to explain each step in the process. It is not necessary to write *you should*.

command

First, **introduce** yourself to your roommate.

command

Ask your roommate about his or her pet peeves.

A Student Process Essay

Read and analyze the next student process essay.

THE WONDERS OF POWERPOINT

Karine Godin

1.   In college, students are often asked to do oral presentations. Many students create PowerPoint slides, but let's face it—a lot of those PowerPoint presentations are far from being great. They add nothing extra to the presentation. A badly constructed PowerPoint can detract from the contents of the presentation. But students should not despair. By following the next simple rules, they can enhance their PowerPoint presentations.

Thesis statement

2.   <mark>The first rule of making a good PowerPoint is not to overuse colors and gradients.</mark> Colors should emphasize the message, not distract the audience's attention from it. Therefore, if a student uses random colors everywhere, all the contents of the PowerPoint will have the same importance, making the use of colors completely useless. Gradients can be useful if they put emphasis on the content and make a prettier background for the PowerPoint. However, if a PowerPoint contains too many gradients or an overly detailed gradient, then the text of the PowerPoint will be hard to read. For example, if a student uses a rainbow gradient for the background of her slides, the audience will have problems reading the text because the color of the text will not contrast from the background. Therefore, students should use colors only to emphasize key points and choose gradients that will not distract from the message.

→ Topic sentence

3.   <mark>Next, students should remember to use only one font style in their PowerPoint slides. Many different font styles do not go together well.</mark> Audiences will not be able to read the contents of the slide if their eyes have to process too much variety in font style. To distinguish between main ideas and secondary ideas, a student can change the size or thickness of the font. When I had to make a PowerPoint presentation, I used a simple font style like Arial. I put titles and headings in 28-size font and secondary information in 24-size font. However, many of my classmates tried to make complicated slides using different types of fonts. Such slides were difficult to read.

→ Topic sentence

4.   <mark>Moreover, students should not abuse sounds and other PowerPoint effects.</mark> At first, a presenter might think that these effects are beautiful. But if there are too many sounds and visuals, the audience could easily become annoyed. In addition, too many sounds and visuals take up a lot of time because the presenter must wait for the effects to be over before she proceeds to the next slide. For example, Pia, a fellow classmate, made a PowerPoint presentation with ten lines per page. Each slide contained either a sound or visual effect. Her presentation went over the time allocated, and the professor had to stop her before she completed it.

→ Topic sentence

5.   In conclusion, all of these simple rules can be summed into one: **KISS** (keep it simple stupid). <mark>If a presenter uses colors and gradients correctly, uses the least number of fonts possible, and uses sound and visual effects wisely, then he or she should end up with a great PowerPoint presentation.</mark>

→ Concluding sentence

PRACTICE 8

1. What kind of process essay is this? Circle the best answer.

    a. Complete a process

    b. Understand a process

2. Who is the audience for this essay? _____

3. In which paragraph(s) does the writer use an anecdote? _____

4. How does the writer end the conclusion?

    a. With a suggestion   b. With a quotation   c. With a prediction

A Professional Process Essay

In the following essay, Jake Sibley, a musician who maintains an online music site, explains how to become a successful musician. Read the essay and answer the questions.

Steps to Music Success

1   Before you can achieve anything, you must first imagine it. If you are serious about becoming a successful musician, it will serve you well to look not only at the next step, but also to look down the road to where you ultimately want to be. There is no question that regularly revisiting the fundamentals is critical to success in any long-term **endeavor**. With that in mind, there are some basic things to consider while pursuing your musical dreams.

endeavor:
attempt

vital:
extremely important

2   First, setting specific goals and giving them regular attention is **vital** to achieving success at any level in the music business. Goals give direction to your action. Furthermore, achieving goals is a tasty reward that will build your esteem and motivate you to reach even higher. So pick your endpoint, and then write down the steps to get there. If you are just beginning in music, then resolve to take lessons. If you are taking lessons, then resolve to get in a performing band. If you are already performing, then resolve to join a paid project. There is no obstacle that can prevent you from reaching your dream. You just have to plan it and then do it.

3   It is also important to spend time, not money, on your dream. Most likely you have seen rookie musicians with stacks of absurdly expensive gear. Certainly I am guilty of walking into a music store and **ogling** the top-end instruments, convinced that if I could afford that equipment, my sound would improve by leaps and bounds: "If I had that guitar, I would practice *every day*." If you are not practicing every day already, a new guitar won't change that. The only investment that will improve your success as a musician is *time*—time spent practicing, time spent learning, and time spent pursuing your goals. The lure of expensive gear is a tempting but false road to better musicianship.

ogling:
staring at with desire

4   Furthermore, if you really want to improve, play with others. Music is a form of conversation between human beings. It may well be the oldest language, used for millennia by musically inclined people to jointly convey their own rage, sorrow, hope, and joy to other human beings. Learning music without this community is as futile as learning to play football by yourself. Although hours spent alone with your instrument are certainly necessary for success, engaging in musical conversations and performances is an equally vital element to your progress. A very common weakness among amateur musicians is their inability to make music with other artists—a flaw that can be easily remedied with experience. Even if you are a beginner, get out and play with others and stage a few performances if you can. Without even realizing it, you will begin to assimilate fundamental lessons about listening, interacting, and performing in a live setting that are critical to your future success.

5   Finally, practice, practice, practice! There is simply no other way to ensure your own progress as a musician. Have you been spending hours on the Internet,

combing for information on how to market your music, or cheaply record a CD, or win a music competition? That's great, but have you been spending at least as much time alone with your instrument? If not, you should reconsider your priorities. If you are not practicing several times a week at least, the music you market, or record cheaply, or submit to a competition is not going to get very far. As a musician seeking success at any level, practicing your instrument should be your number-one priority.

6   If you're serious about music, keep focused on your goal. Take the time to learn your craft, and share your gift with others. Do not let anyone else hold you back from what you know you can achieve.

PRACTICE 9

1. Highlight the thesis statement of the essay.

2. Underline the topic sentences in paragraphs 2 to 5.

3. What type of process essay is this? Circle the best answer.

   a. Complete a process   b. Understand a process

4. In process essays, the support is generally a series of steps. List the steps to music success.

   _____

   _____

   _____

   _____

   _____

5. What organizational method does the author use in this essay?

   a. Time order   b. Emphatic order   c. Space order

6. Circle the transitional expressions that Sibley uses to introduce each new paragraph.

7. In which paragraph does Sibley use an anecdote to support his point?

   _____

8. Who is the audience for this essay?

   _____

9. How could this essay have relevance for people who never play music?

   _____

   _____

   _____

MyWritingLab™
Complete these writing assignments at mywritinglab.com

PARAGRAPH LINK
To practice process writing, you could develop an essay about one of the topics in Chapter 7, "Process."

MyWritingLab™ THE WRITER'S ROOM

Writing Activity 1: Topics

Write a process essay about one of the following topics.

General Topics

1. how to be a good person
2. how to kick a bad habit
3. how someone became famous
4. how something works
5. how to deal with a problematic teenager

College and Work-Related Topics

6. how to manage your time
7. how education changed somebody's life
8. how to do your job
9. how to be a better student
10. how to find satisfaction in your work life

Process Essay Checklist

As you write your process essay, review the essay checklist at the end of the book. Also ask yourself the following questions.

☐ Does my thesis statement make a point about the process?

☐ Does my essay explain how to do something, how something works, or how something happened?

☐ Do I include all of the steps in the process?

☐ Do I clearly explain the steps in the process or in the event?

☐ Do I mention the tools or equipment that my readers need to complete or understand the process?

LO 5 Write a definition essay.

PARAGRAPH LINK
For more information about definition writing, refer to Chapter 8, "Definition."

The Definition Essay

A definition tells you what something means. When you write a **definition essay**, you give your personal definition of a term or concept. Although you can define most terms in a few sentences, you may need to offer extended definitions for words that are particularly complex. For example, you could write an essay or even an entire book about the term *love*. The way that you interpret love is unique, and you would bring your own opinions, experiences, and impressions to your definition essay.

The Thesis Statement

In your thesis statement, indicate what you are defining and include a definition of the term. Look at the three ways you might define a term in your thesis statement.

1. **Definition by synonym.** You could give a synonym for the term.

   term   +   synonym

   Some consumers insist that Frankenfood, or genetically modified food, be labeled.

2. **Definition by category.** Decide what larger group the term belongs to, and then determine the unique characteristics that set the term apart from others in that category.

   term   +   category   +   detail

   A groupie is a fanatical devotee of a musician or band.

3. **Definition by negation.** Explain what the term is not, and then explain what it is.

   term   +   what it is not   +   what it is

   Stalkers are not misguided romantics; they are dangerous predators.

The Supporting Ideas

In a definition essay, you can support your main point using a variety of writing patterns. For example, in a definition essay about democracy, one supporting paragraph could give historical background about democracy, another could include a description of a functioning democracy, and a third paragraph could compare different styles of democracy. The different writing patterns would all support the overriding pattern, which is definition.

HINT ◀ **Enhancing a Definition**

One way to enhance a definition essay is to begin with a provocative statement about the term. Then in the body of your essay, develop your definition more thoroughly. This technique arouses the interest of the readers and makes them want to continue reading. For example, the next statement questions a common belief.

> According to Dr. W. Roland, attention-deficit disorder is an invented disease.

A Student Definition Essay

Read and analyze the next student definition essay.

HOMOPHOBIA

Dominic Chartrand

1. The status of homosexuality has changed with time in various parts of the world. In Greek mythology, Patroclus was Achilles' lover. Alexander the Great was alleged to have had homosexual relationships. Central and South American natives were also known to tolerate homosexuality. When Western religions declared homosexuality a sin, a direct consequence of this edict was homophobia. Homophobia is deplorable feelings of hate and fear toward homosexuals, and it rages on under many forms.

Thesis statement

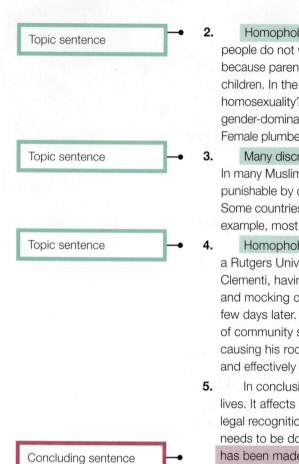

2. Homophobia is a problem that affects people's professional lives. First, some people do not want gays or lesbians to occupy certain jobs, such as teaching, because parents are afraid that teachers may "teach" homosexuality to their children. In the movie *Milk*, Harvey Milk's character asks, "How do you teach homosexuality? Like French?" In addition, people of the opposite sex working in gender-dominated professions are constantly assaulted by homophobic comments. Female plumbers, male hairdressers, or male nurses might be labeled gay.

3. Many discriminatory laws have been passed by people who fear homosexuals. In many Muslim countries, such as Saudi Arabia and Yemen, homosexuality is punishable by death. Some other punishment methods include jail and torture. Some countries prohibit homosexuals from marrying or adopting children. For example, most states in our nation prohibit gay marriage.

4. Homophobia is a social factor that can destroy people's lives. For example, a Rutgers University student, Dharun Ravi, secretly filmed his roommate, Tyler Clementi, having sexual relations with another man. Ravi then posted cruel and mocking comments on Twitter about Clementi. Clementi killed himself a few days later. Ravi was given a one-month jail sentence, hundreds of hours of community service, and a heavy fine. Although Ravi was never charged with causing his roommate's death, the gay-bashing act led to serious consequences and effectively destroyed two people's lives.

5. In conclusion, homophobia is a problem present in every sphere of people's lives. It affects individuals on a professional, legal, and personal level. Achieving legal recognition does not annihilate homophobia entirely. Lots of work still needs to be done to eradicate intolerance completely. However, some progress has been made toward acceptance and tolerance in the last forty years, and homosexuals throughout the world have to keep faith in a brighter future.

PRACTICE 10

1. What type of definition does the writer use in the thesis statement? Circle the best answer.

   a. Definition by synonym

   b. Definition by category

   c. Definition by negation

2. Who is the audience? _____

3. In which paragraph does the author give an anecdote? _____

4. How does the writer end the essay?

   a. With a prediction   b. With a suggestion   c. With a quotation

5. What organizational pattern does the writer use in this essay?

   a. Time order   b. Space order   c. Emphatic order

A Professional Definition Essay

In the following essay adapted from his book *The 7 Laws of Magical Thinking*, science journalist Matthew Hutson explores the definition of luck.

What Is Luck?

1   On the morning of August 9, 1945, the wings of Bockscar lifted it into the air. The B-29, loaded with a five-ton atomic bomb named "Fat Man," took off from Tinian, an island 1,500 miles southeast of Japan. By the time Bockscar passed over its target at 10:44 A.M., the city was covered in haze and difficult to see. So the crew left the city of Kokura and made their way over to their second choice, **Nagasaki**. Most people have never heard of Kokura. In this regard, it can be counted as one of the luckiest cities in the world. In another case, in 1993, a German motorcyclist hit a truck, went flying into a tree, and was impaled on a branch. The headline in a Norwegian newspaper, next to a photograph of this unfortunate gentleman with a branch still going into his chest and out his back, read, "Verdens Heldigste," or "World's Luckiest," because the branch had missed all his vital organs. We are fascinated by such near misses.

Nagasaki:
a Japanese city hit by an atomic bomb on August 9, 1945

2   Luck is as tricky to define as it is to tame. Rare good things are lucky. But, what about Kokura? Nothing positive happened to it. In fact, it lost thousands of neighboring countrymen. And the German motorcyclist had surely seen better days. "Luck" is often yoked to terrible, terrible things.

3   Karl Teigen, a psychologist at the University of Tromsø in Norway, has spent years studying what we mean when we talk about luck. One conclusion he has reached is that, on par, "lucky" events are not pleasant. In a search of newspaper stories, for example, he found that "with the exception of an occasional sports champion and a . . . lottery winner, the typical lucky person had survived a plane or car crash, had been stabbed or shot, had fallen off a cliff or bridge, or had been shipwrecked or surrounded by flames." In a one-month period, he found one mention of "bad luck" in a story about a soldier who had stepped on a mine—but the soldier had nevertheless commented on his own good fortune in losing just the one leg.

4   Teigen suggests that luck derives not from the absolute value of an outcome but from its relative value. That soldier lost a leg but thought of how he had almost lost two, so he considered himself lucky. Why wouldn't he compare losing a leg to not stepping on the mine at all? Mentally altering an effect or a recent cause in a chain of events comes more naturally than mentally undoing an earlier cause. Once someone has skewered himself on a tree, he'll tend to think of the untouched organs right next to the branch hole, not about how this never would have happened if he hadn't taken the extra five minutes to floss that morning.

5   According to Teigen, feeling lucky correlates with feelings of gratitude, a distinctly social sentiment, and the thanks are often of an existential kind, directed not toward a person but toward God or the universe or fate. A few years ago, Eugene Subbotsky, a psychologist at Lancaster University who studies magical thinking, was strolling through Moscow with his young son, with no one around. They walked past an empty parked car. "Just when we were passing by, the engine started," Subbotsky told me soon after the event. The car started moving. It swerved toward them. Finally, it turned a little more and hit an iron gate a few inches away. "We escaped death very narrowly," he said. "I could have been smashed to pieces with my little son. I am a rational man, I am a scientist, I'm studying this phenomenon, but there are some events in life that I cannot explain rationally. Of course people can always write it down to chance and say,

'Okay, it's a coincidence,' but it's such a rare coincidence that they start thinking mystically and magically about things."

6   We can certainly tell a good story of a lucky escape without resorting to unnatural intervention: event B just logically followed event A. However, we want to believe that flukes of luck happened for a reason or are building up to some future purpose. It gives the story of our lives both continuity and a destination, something to strive for. Sometimes it's fun to pretend.

PRACTICE 11

1. Highlight the thesis statement. Be careful because it may not be in the first paragraph.

2. Underline the topic sentences in body paragraphs 2 to 5.

3. According to the author, people define luck by "its relative value." In your own words, what does he mean?

   _____

   _____

   _____

4. According to the author, how does society generally define "lucky people"?

   _____

   _____

   _____

5. How does the author support the thesis? _____

6. In your own words, sum up the author's main supporting anecdotes.

   a. _____

   b. _____

   c. _____

   d. _____

MyWritingLab™

Complete these writing assignments at mywritinglab.com

PARAGRAPH LINK
To practice definition writing, you could develop an essay about one of the topics found in Chapter 8, "Definition."

MyWritingLab™

THE WRITER'S ROOM

Writing Activity 1: Topics

Write a definition essay about one of the following topics.

General Topics

1. propaganda
2. a pacifist
3. street smarts
4. a control freak
5. our disposable culture

College and Work-Related Topics

6. a McJob
7. a perfectionist
8. a whistle-blower
9. a green-collar job
10. downsizing

Definition Essay Checklist

As you write your definition essay, review the essay checklist at the end of the book. Also ask yourself the following questions.

☐ Does my thesis statement explain what term I am defining?

☐ Does each topic sentence clearly show some aspect of the definition?

☐ Do my supporting paragraphs include examples that help illustrate the definition?

☐ Do I use concise language in my definition?

The Classification Essay

Classifying means to sort a subject into more understandable categories. When you are planning a classification essay, find a topic that you can organize into categories. Each category must be part of a larger group, yet it must also be distinct. For example, if your essay is about types of lawyers, you might sort lawyers into criminal lawyers, divorce lawyers, and corporate lawyers.

L0 6 Write a classification essay.

PARAGRAPH LINK
For more information about classification writing, refer to Chapter 9, "Classification."

The Thesis Statement

The thesis statement in a classification essay mentions the categories of the subject and contains a controlling idea. In this type of essay, the controlling idea is your classification principle, which is the overall method that you use to sort the items. For example, if your essay topic is "crime," you might sort crime according to types of criminals, categories of violent crimes, or categories of bank-machine crimes.

controlling idea (classification principle)   topic   categories
There are three very effective types of **bank-machine crimes**: no-tech, low-tech, and high-tech.

HINT ‹ **List Specific Categories**

You can guide your reader by listing the specific categories you will cover in your thesis statement.

topic   controlling idea
Children learn gender roles through the family, the school, and the media.

The Supporting Ideas

In a classification essay, each body paragraph covers one category. To organize your categories and supporting details, you can use a classification chart or a more traditional classification essay plan.

A Classification Chart

A classification chart helps you plan your ideas by providing a visual representation of how you wish to classify a subject. In this sample chart, the thesis statement appears at the top, and all of the categories branch from it.

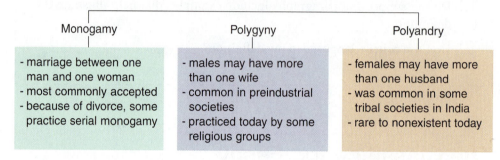

Historically, three types of heterosexual marital unions have been practiced around the world.

Monogamy	Polygyny	Polyandry
- marriage between one man and one woman - most commonly accepted - because of divorce, some practice serial monogamy	- males may have more than one wife - common in preindustrial societies - practiced today by some religious groups	- females may have more than one husband - was common in some tribal societies in India - rare to nonexistent today

A Student Classification Essay

Read and analyze the next student classification essay.

BREAKING TRAFFIC LAWS

Lonzell Courtney

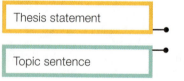

Thesis statement

1.   Ask most people, and they will insist they are law-abiding. Dig a little deeper, though, and the hidden criminal emerges. Stand on any street corner for a few hours, and you probably will observe all types of people breaking traffic laws. ==Pedestrians, cyclists, and drivers regularly break the rules of the road.==

Topic sentence

2.   ==There are many traffic laws that pedestrians ignore.== For example, jaywalking is common. When people arrive at a crossing with traffic lights, they are supposed to wait for the walk signal. They should also cross the street at corners and proper crossings, and they should not walk on the road. Yet most people break these rules. Armando Guzman, an exterminator from Florida, is an unapologetic jaywalker who crosses between intersections rather than walk to the corner. Kate Shapiro, a hairdresser, admits that she always crosses when the "Don't Walk" signal is blinking if there is no traffic. "It is ridiculous to wait when I know I can cross safely," she argues.

Topic sentence

3.   ==Cyclists also disrespect traffic laws.== Many municipalities have bicycle helmet laws, but citizens regularly flout the law and drive with bare heads. In some states, bicycles must be equipped with reflectors, but many cyclists do not bother getting them. Furthermore, most cyclists don't obey the rules of the road. They ride past stop signs and red lights, and they speed along sidewalks. In 2012, a Toronto cyclist who was going the wrong way on a one-way street struck a fifty-six-year-old woman, fracturing her skull.

Topic sentence

4.   ==Drivers, of course, are the worst offenders.== Virtually every driver has occasionally broken a traffic law. Who hasn't gone over the speed limit, for example? Many people believe that the maximum speed limit sign generally means, "I can go ten or fifteen miles per hour over that limit." Some drivers also

change lanes without signaling, they drive on the shoulder to pass slow traffic, and they allow children to ride without seatbelts. Worst of all, many people drink and drive. In 2012, actress Amanda Bynes was charged with driving under the influence and driving while talking on a cell phone.

5.　　Most traffic lawbreakers are unrepentant, claiming that everyone else also breaks the law. Yet pedestrians, cyclists, and drivers can injure themselves and others. As comedian David Letterman once said, traffic signals "are just rough guidelines."

> Conclusion ends with a quotation

PRACTICE 12

1. What is the classification principle? That is, what main principle unifies the three categories? _____

2. How are the main ideas organized?
   a. From the least to the most offensive actions
   b. From the most to the least offensive actions.

3. How does the writer support the main ideas? Circle the best answers.
   a. Examples
   b. Anecdotes
   c. Statistics
   d. Expert opinions

A Professional Classification Essay

This essay first appeared in *Introduction to Animal Science* by W. Stephen Damron. Read the essay and answer the questions that follow.

The Purpose of Pets

1　　Pet species provide many practical services to society, and it is clear that some animals are companion animals. Their greatest value is defined by their relationships with the people who share their lives. Once a source of derision, the human–companion animal bond is now recognized for its value as a contributing factor in the physical, mental, emotional, and social health of the owner. However, not all domestic animals qualify as companions. For instance, there are many barn cats across the country whose job in life is just to keep the rats and mice at bay. In fact, many people purchase an animal for the following motives: the animal is ornamental, a status symbol, or a plaything.

Ornamental Pets

2　　Ornamental pets serve the same purpose that houseplants serve—they decorate and enhance the atmosphere. Ornamental pets are usually brightly colored birds or fish or some type of animal that adds aesthetic appeal to an environment. It is common to find an aquarium filled with brightly colored or interesting aquatic species in restaurants, professional offices, or homes. Decorators have been known to bring fabric swatches to pet stores in order to pick a bird that matches carpets and draperies. Outdoor environments are often graced by flashy species such as peacocks, pheasants, Sumatra chickens, swans, geese, and ducks. Rarely are these ornamental pets handled, named, or treated in any special way. They are not considered companion animals.

Status Symbols

3   There is strong evidence that at least part of the domestication of the wolf was linked to the status its presence in camp gave the human occupants. A wolf as totem and companion would have conveyed a powerful message to rival clans or tribes. Sometimes we succumb to this same symbolism in modern life. This explains the motives of some people who keep poisonous snakes, piranhas, vicious dogs, big cats, bears, or wolves as pets. The animals are usually admired and well cared for as long as they satisfy the owner's expectations. In a more benign example, the symbolism of animals as totems for ancient people is not so different from that conveyed in modern society by what we generally refer to as "mascots." Status can also be conveyed by a pet kept for another primary reason. Purebred animals generally convey more status than mixed breed animals. Sometimes unusual, rare, and expensive animals are status symbols.

Playthings

4   Pets as playthings may range from living toys given to children, before they are old enough to appreciate the responsibilities, to animals used in sporting events such as hunting or riding. Children are often given a pet as a plaything before they are capable of appreciating it. Some of the people involved in sports and who use animals are only interested in the animal during the competitive season and lose interest and enthusiasm rather quickly at the close of the season. Often, these animals are poorly treated and may be discarded or destroyed by their owners when the animals lose their amusement value.

5   It is clear that some animals are companion animals. Their greatest value is defined by their relationships with the people who share their lives. The Council for Science and Society states, "An animal employed for decoration, status-signaling, recreation, or hobby is being used primarily as an object—the animal equivalent of a work of art, a Rolls Royce, a surfboard, or a collector's item. The companion animal, however, is typically perceived and treated as a subject—as a personality in its own right, irrespective of other considerations. With companion animals, it is the relationship itself which is important to the owner."

PRACTICE 13

1.   Highlight the thesis statement.

2.   What is the essay's classification principle? _____

_____

3.   What are the three main categories? _____

_____

4.   Underline the topic sentences in body paragraphs 2, 3, and 4.

5.   Provide some details about each type of pet. Use your own words.

Ornamental Pets: _____

_____

Status Symbols: _____

_____

Playthings: _____

_____

6. To better understand how the author organizes this essay, make a classification chart. Write the categories on the lines and examples in the boxes. Use your own words to explain each category.

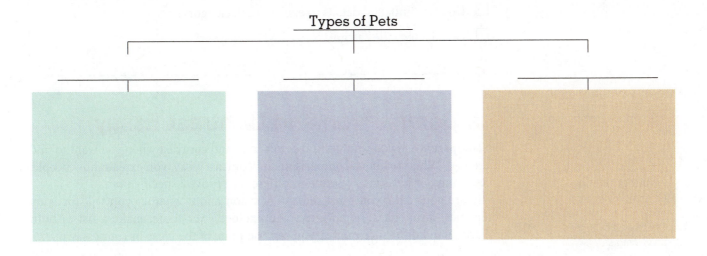

Types of Pets

7. What is the writer's point in the conclusion? _____

_____

_____

THE WRITER'S ROOM   MyWritingLab™

MyWritingLab™
Complete these writing assignments at mywritinglab.com

Writing Activity 1: Topics

Write a classification essay about one of the following topics.

General Topics

1. addictions
2. marriage ceremonies
3. extreme sports
4. things that cause allergic reactions
5. youth subcultures

College and Work-Related Topics

6. annoying customers or clients
7. punishment
8. competition
9. success
10. fashions in the workplace

PARAGRAPH LINK
To practice classification writing, you could develop an essay about one of the topics found in Chapter 9, "Classification."

- - - - ┌ *Classification Essay Checklist* ┐ - - - - - - - - -

As you write your classification essay, review the essay checklist at the end of the book. Also ask yourself the following questions.

☐ Do I clearly identify which categories I will discuss in my thesis statement?

☐ Do I use a common classification principle to unite the various items?

☐ Do I include categories that do not overlap?

☐ Do I clearly explain one of the categories in each body paragraph?

☐ Do I use sufficient details to explain each category?

☐ Do I arrange the categories in a logical manner?

LO 7 Write a comparison and contrast essay.

PARAGRAPH LINK
For more information about this pattern, refer to Chapter 10, "Comparison and Contrast."

The Comparison and Contrast Essay

You **compare** when you want to find similarities and **contrast** when you want to find differences. When writing a comparison and contrast essay, you explain how people, places, things, or ideas are the same or different to prove a specific point.

Before you write, you must make a decision about whether you will focus on similarities, differences, or both. As you explore your topic, make a list of both similarities and differences. Later, you can use some of the ideas in your essay plan.

The Thesis Statement

The thesis statement in a comparison and contrast essay indicates if you are making comparisons, contrasts, or both. When you write a thesis statement, specify what you are comparing or contrasting and the controlling idea.

Although neat people have a very nice environment, messy people are more relaxed.

Topics being contrasted: Neat people and messy people
Controlling idea: Messy people are more relaxed.

Alice's daughter wants to be her own person, but she is basically very similar to her mother.

Topics being compared: Mother and daughter
Controlling idea: Very similar personalities

The Supporting Ideas

In a comparison and contrast essay, you can develop your body paragraphs in two different ways.

1. In a **point-by-point** development, you present *one* point about Topic A and then *one* point about Topic B. You keep following this pattern until you have a few points for each topic.

    Paragraph 1: Topic A, Topic B

    Paragraph 2: Topic A, Topic B

    Paragraph 3: Topic A, Topic B

2. In a **topic-by-topic** development, you discuss one topic in detail, and then you discuss the other topic in detail.

   Paragraphs 1 and 2: All of Topic A

   Paragraphs 3 and 4: All of Topic B

A Student Comparison and Contrast Essay

Read and analyze the structure of the next student comparison and contrast essay.

TWO JOBS

Adrianna Gonzalez

1. "I can't believe it's Monday," I often say after the alarm clock rings. The average nine-to-five job may seem like a drag if the person is not fond of the job. Yet there have been instances where one job was better than the other one. My current job as a caregiver is much more fulfilling than my previous job was. ●—— Thesis statement

2. My first job as a receptionist at a church was not as interesting as my current job. At the church, I was the only one present during my shifts. I would only catch the priest now and then. My whole shift was quiet, and although others thought, "What a peaceful job," it became boring. I often thought, "Oh great, another lonely day at the office. What will I occupy myself with this time?" On the other hand, my current job as a caregiver is filled with lots of people and diverse activities. I show up for work eager to pick up the infants that I care for. The time passes by quickly, and all my coworkers are friendly. ●—— Topic sentence

3. Furthermore, in my old job, the boss was not organized, and he did not care for the workplace. For example, I was alone in the church's office when two visitors came in for their appointments, and the priest was not there. During such instances, I would have to try to come up with a plausible excuse for why the priest would be thirty minutes late. The priest frequently did not keep the appointments and did not provide me with information to give visitors regarding the cancellations of the meetings. Now in my new job, organization is a priority. I am constantly informed of what is happening; memos are sent and meetings take place almost every week. The director and manager want to make the environment as welcoming as possible. I now realize that if there had been just a little bit of organization at my old job, it would have made a big difference. ●—— Topic sentence

4. Finally, the pay is much better at my new job than it was at my old one. At the church, I was paid minimum wage. I was not allowed to work overtime or to do extra shifts. I became angry because I was paid so little and received no support at that job. In my current job, my initial salary was higher than minimum wage, and the pay increases every year. I can work as many as eleven hours in one day. The amount in my first paycheck was the equivalent of two or three paychecks at my old job. ●—— Topic sentence

5. I am happy that I changed jobs because I really enjoy working as a caregiver. It is easy to hate a job that is boring and low paying, and it is difficult to deal with a disorganized boss. In such cases, consider looking for a better job. ●—— Concluding sentence

PRACTICE 14

1. What type of introduction does the writer use?

   a. Opposing position   b. Definition   c. General information

2. What does this essay focus on?

   a. Similarities   b. Differences

3. What pattern of comparison does the writer follow in each body paragraph?

   a. Point by point   b. Topic by topic

4. How does the writer end the essay?

   a. With a suggestion   b. With a prediction   c. With a quotation

A Professional Comparison and Contrast Essay

In the following essay, author and journalist Mark Milke compares and contrasts two different time periods. Read the essay and answer the questions that follow.

Just Say No

1   In a world where many people have instant text messaging, multiple e-mail accounts, several phones, the still-ubiquitous television screen, and a smorgasbord of unlimited web information, life's challenges today are not the ones faced by our ancestors. While theirs were about finding a way to eke out a slightly better life than their narrow circumstances allowed, our world requires a conscious denial of opportunities.

2   Think back one hundred years. With the exception of the tiniest sliver of the population, most people faced daily scarcity. The food they ate was necessarily local (and limited the possibility for a healthier diet); communication beyond their immediate surroundings was restricted to letters and in-person visits. Even for those who had telephones, long-distance calling was prohibitively expensive. As for vacations, if taken at all, they were close to home or at the relatives. And only the rich could spare the money and time to see exotic locales that many now assume as an annual rite and right. Such generations, to say nothing of the ones that preceded them, knew scarcity as a fact of daily life.

3   In contrast, today, while poverty yet exists at home and abroad, and in some places more severely than others—North Korea and sub-Saharan Africa are examples—much of the world endures a new predicament rarely considered: abundance. That's a better "problem" to face than chronic shortages of food and opportunities. Still, for anyone who wants to live out what Plato called "the good life," the challenge is to face this fact: If we want a better, more rewarding existence, we have to say "no" more often than "yes." Fail the temptation offered by abundance, and the waistline explodes, the mind atrophies, and the deepest potential joys—discovered through conversation and contemplation and by mastery of some skill, sport, art, or career—are sacrificed to a twittered and inconsequential life.

4   An advantage exists for those who choose the better over the banal. Those who can shut up and shut out the unhelpful distractions long enough to let the useful thoughts and activities into their soul can then accomplish something

valuable. While counterintuitive, the world will never belong to those who engage in every distraction. The world will not build future shrines to those who e-mail, Facebook, text, Twitter, and talk their lives away but never have anything useful to say in all their virtual activities. They have never taken the time to ignore the frenetic present long enough to learn from the past or from some still small voice. What would be the point of trekking into the great outdoors, but with little music buds stuck in one's ears, and then missing the roar of a river or the call of one bird to another?

5   The most profound books, the most sublime symphonies, and life's rare beautiful moments result from those who choose to say "no" to life's many siren calls of opportunistic distractions. Such men and women also have the most impact on the world around them precisely because they found their own solid center. It is from that solidity that they can then offer others something unique. Case in point: Had **Glenn Gould** been raised in the Internet age and succumbed to every possible distraction, the world would have missed out on the full actualization of his talents; the world would also have been poorer.

Glen Gould (1932–1982): Canadian classical pianist, best known for his interpretation of Bach

6   In much of human history, men and women necessarily devoted every waking moment to scratching out a basic life of subsistence. These days, our challenge is to block out the avalanche of cheap opportunities that can make us satiated, content, oblivious, and dull.

PRACTICE 15

1. What type of introduction does the writer use?

    a. Opposing position   b. Definition   c. General information

2. Underline the thesis statement.

3. This essay looks at lifestyles in the past and present. What is the focus of this essay?

    a. Similarities   b. Differences

4. In the introduction, the writer says that our world requires a conscious denial of opportunities. What opportunities is the writer referring to?

    _____

    _____

5. What are the differences between the generation a hundred years ago and our generation? _____

    _____

    _____

    _____

6. In paragraph 3, what is the author's main message?

    _____

    _____

    _____

MyWritingLab™
Complete these writing assignments at mywritinglab.com

PARAGRAPH LINK
To practice comparison and contrast writing, you could develop an essay about one of the topics found in Chapter 10, "Comparison and Contrast."

MyWritingLab™   **THE WRITER'S ROOM**

Writing Activity 1: Topics

Write a comparison and contrast essay about one of the following topics.

General Topics

Compare and/or contrast . . .

1. expectations about parenthood versus the reality of parenthood
2. two different interpretations of an event
3. living together and getting married
4. male versus female consumers
5. peer pressure versus parental pressure

College and Work-Related Topics

Compare and/or contrast . . .

6. male and female college athletes
7. a good manager and a bad manager
8. a stay-at-home parent and an employed parent
9. student life and professional life
10. expectations about a job and the reality of that job

Comparison and Contrast Essay Checklist

As you write your comparison and contrast essay, review the essay checklist at the end of the book. Also ask yourself the following questions.

☐ Does my thesis statement explain what I am comparing or contrasting?

☐ Does my thesis statement make a point about my topic?

☐ Does my essay focus on either similarities or differences?

☐ Does my essay include point-by-point and/or topic-by-topic patterns?

☐ Do all of my supporting examples clearly relate to the topics that are being compared or contrasted?

☐ Do I use transitions that will help readers follow my ideas?

LO 8 Write a cause and effect essay.

The Cause and Effect Essay

When writing a cause and effect essay, you explain why an event happened or what the consequences of such an event were.

The Thesis Statement

The thesis statement in a cause and effect essay contains the topic and the controlling idea. The controlling idea indicates whether the essay will focus on causes, effects, or both.

PARAGRAPH LINK
For more information about this pattern, refer to Chapter 11, "Cause and Effect."

topic   controlling idea (causes)
Chronic insomnia is caused by many factors.

topic   controlling idea (effects)
Chronic insomnia can have a serious impact on a person's health.

topic   controlling idea (causes and effects)
Chronic insomnia, which is caused by many factors, can have a serious impact on a person's health.

HINT ◄ Thinking About Effects

If you are writing about the effects of something, you might think about both the short-term and long-term effects. By doing so, you will generate more ideas for the body of your essay. You will also be able to structure your essay more effectively by moving from short-term to long-term effects.

For example, look at the short- and long-term effects of a smoke-free work zone.

Short term	Inside air is cleaner.
	The smokers get more coffee breaks.
Long term	Fewer smoke-related illnesses occur in nonsmokers.
	Some smokers might quit smoking.

The Supporting Ideas

The body paragraphs in a cause and effect essay focus on causes, effects, or both. Make sure that each body paragraph contains specific examples that clarify the cause and/or effect relationship.

A Student Cause and Effect Essay

Read and analyze the structure of the next student cause and effect essay.

WHY SMALL BUSINESSES FAIL

Jim Baek

1.   Last spring, Pablo Ortiz rented a tiny pizzeria in his neighborhood to turn it into a taco restaurant. Full of enthusiasm, he bought supplies, paid for advertisements, and posted a large menu in the window of his new venture, called Taco Heaven. Ten months later, Taco Heaven closed, and Ortiz declared bankruptcy. He was not alone. The Small Business Administration Office reports that close to half of all new businesses fail within the first five years. Causes of small business failures are numerous.   ← Thesis statement

2.   First, inexperienced business owners often neglect to do market research to find out if community members are interested in the product. In Ortiz's case, he thought that area residents would appreciate the chance to buy hearty chicken or pork tacos. However, there were three other Mexican fast-food restaurants in the area, so Ortiz's competitors took most of the business.   ← Topic sentence

Topic sentence

3.   Second, inadequate pricing can hurt new businesses. Maggie Stevens, owner of a successful restaurant in Los Angeles, sells stuffed Belgian waffles to an eager clientele. Before pricing her waffles, she calculated the exact cost of each plate, right down to the strawberry that adorned the waffle and the touch of cream next to it. She also considered other costs beyond that of the ingredients, including the cost of labor and food spoilage. Her final price for each dish was 60 percent higher than her base cost. Ortiz, on the other hand, had absolutely no idea what he really spent to make each taco. He ended up underpricing his product and losing money.

Topic sentence

4.   Additionally, many small business owners have insufficient funds to run their ventures successfully. According to accountant Louis Polk, most small businesses operate for four years before they break even, let alone actually make money. Therefore, owners need a cash reserve to get through the first slow years. Ortiz, expecting to make a decent profit right away, did not realize that he would have to use up his savings to keep his business afloat.

Topic sentence

5.   Finally, inexperienced merchants may underestimate the sheer volume of work involved in running a business. Ortiz admits he was very naive about the workload. Taco Heaven was open 15 hours a day, 7 days a week. Ortiz had to cook, shop for ingredients, and do the accounting. After months of grueling work and little to no pay, he burned out.

Concluding sentence

6.   Inexperience, lack of proper planning, and insufficient funds can combine to create a business failure. People who plan to open small businesses should become informed, especially about potential pitfalls.

PRACTICE 16

1.   Does this essay focus on causes or effects? _____

2.   Who is the audience for this essay?

_____

_____

A Professional Cause and Effect Essay

Albert Nerenberg is a writer, director, and journalist. He has worked on many projects about the power of laughter. Read the essay and answer the questions that follow.

Don't Worry, Act Happy

1   We usually think of acting as the preserve of movie stars and annoying people with fake moustaches and bad accents. But a surging scientific theory says acting could make people happy. The theory arises from a controversial concept, sometimes called the body–mind principle, that emotions can be reverse engineered. It's simple: If we feel good, we may smile. But the surprising part is if we smile, we may feel good. The Act Happy theory is that we get happier simply by going through the motions of contentment and joy.

2   Although the Act Happy idea has been bouncing around for years, all of a sudden there's heat around it. There is increasing evidence that the opposite is true—acting enraged, obsessed, malevolent, or depressed may be bad for us. Actor Leonardo DiCaprio developed obsessive–compulsive disorder while playing Howard Hughes in the blockbuster *The Aviator*. In real life, Hughes had the disorder. Actor David Duchovny, who plays a writer obsessed with sex in the TV series *Californication*, checked into a sex-addiction clinic. Batman star Christian Bale allegedly assaulted his mother and sister after completing the violent and brooding *Dark Knight*. Heath Ledger played a tragic and maniacal Joker. Ledger, who had everything going for him, was allegedly clinically depressed. So if people can cultivate rage, depression, and death, can they cultivate joy, hilarity, love, and vitality? If the simple human smile is anything to go by, the answer is yes.

3   A traditional Buddhist adage recommends smiling as the first conscious thing to do each day, and science may concur. Smiling has clear health benefits. Lee Berk, Associate Director of the Centre for Neuroimmunology at Loma Linda University California, has demonstrated that "mirthful emotions" or "mirthful laughter" seem to increase the number of T cells, or immune cells, in the bloodstream. Robert Kall, a Philadelphia-based Positive Psychology therapist, tried simple smiling as a way to treat depression. "I would put surface electrodes on the smile muscles in people's faces and, using electromyography, would measure the strength of their smiles," he said. "People who were not depressed had smile muscles that were on average four times stronger than people who were depressed," he said. So he began developing what could only be described as a smiling exercise program. "I would have depressed people pump 'smile' iron," he said. "I would have them do repetitions: three sets of 12 every day." By naturally triggering smiles, the "smilercizers" would seem to drive themselves to happier states.

4   Smiling's greatest benefit may be that it helps us to connect with others. According to Dr. Mark Stibich, a behavior change expert at the University of California San Diego, smiling not only boosts the immune system and lowers blood pressure, it enhances other people's views of us. When we practice positive emotions, it makes others more apt to reciprocate and smile back. Tanisha Wright, who runs the Beautiful Beginnings Charm School in New Jersey, said her students would sometimes burst out laughing while exercising their smiles.

5   Although it is often viewed with suspicion, acting may just represent a way to expand our emotional range. Acting comes naturally. Kids do it all the time. Since most people can learn to act, perhaps most could learn to Act Happy. If Heath Ledger's tragic torn smile has taught us anything, it may be that we are what we act. So we should be good to ourselves and not forget to smile.

PRACTICE 17

1. Highlight the thesis statement.

2. Underline the topic sentences in paragraphs 2 to 4. Be careful; the topic sentence may not be the first sentence in the paragraph.

3. Overall, what does this essay focus on?

    a. Causes   b. Effects   c. Both

4. Why does the author mention actors who portrayed depressed or disagreeable characters?

_____

_____

5. What psychological and physical changes does a person experience by acting happy?

_____

_____

_____

6. What type of support does the author use to prove his thesis?

_____

_____

_____

MyWritingLab™
Complete these writing assignments at mywritinglab.com

PARAGRAPH LINK
To practice cause and effect writing, you could develop an essay about one of the topics found in Chapter 11, "Cause and Effect."

MyWritingLab™
THE WRITER'S ROOM

Writing Activity 1: Topics

Write a cause and effect essay about one of the following topics.

General Topics

Causes and/or effects of . . .

1. a new law or policy
2. rejecting or adopting a religion
3. patriotism
4. peer pressure
5. leaving your home or homeland

College and Work-Related Topics

Causes and/or effects of . . .

6. being a parent and college student
7. taking time off before college
8. having an office romance
9. gossiping in the office
10. changing jobs or career paths

Cause and Effect Essay Checklist

As you write your cause and effect essay, review the essay checklist at the end of the book. Also ask yourself the following questions.

☐ Does my essay clearly focus on causes, effects, or both?

☐ Do I have adequate supporting examples of causes and/or effects?

☐ Do I avoid using faulty logic (a mere asumption that one event causes another or is the result of another)?

☐ Do I use the terms _effect_ and _affect_ correctly?

The Argument Essay

LO 9 Write an argument essay.

When you write an **argument essay**, you take a position on an issue, and you try to defend your position. In other words, you try to persuade your readers to accept your point of view.

PARAGRAPH LINK
For more information about argument writing, refer to Chapter 12, "Argument."

The Thesis Statement

The thesis statement in an argument essay mentions the subject and a debatable point of view about the subject. Do not include phrases such as *in my opinion, I think*, or *I am going to talk about* in your thesis statement.

        topic   controlling idea

Building a wall on the Mexican border **is an ineffective way to deal with illegal immigration**.

> ### HINT ◂ List Specific Arguments
>
> Your thesis statement can further guide your readers by listing the specific arguments you will make in your essay.
>
>   controlling idea   topic   (arguments)
> Colleges should implement **work-study programs** to help students acquire
>   1   2   3
> job skills, make professional contacts, and earn money for expenses.

The Supporting Ideas

In the body of your essay, give convincing arguments. Try to use several types of supporting evidence.

PARAGRAPH LINK
For more detailed information about types of evidence, see pages 153–154 in Chapter 12, "Argument."

- **Include anecdotes.** Specific experiences or pieces of information can support your point of view.
- **Add facts.** Facts are statements that can be verified in some way. **Statistics** are a type of fact. When you use a fact, make sure that your source is reliable.
- **Use informed opinions.** Opinions from experts in the field can give weight to your argument.
- **Think about logical consequences.** Consider long-term consequences if something does or does not happen.
- **Answer the opposition.** Think about your opponents' arguments, and provide responses to their arguments.

> ### HINT ◂ Quoting a Respected Source
>
> One way to enhance your essay is to include a quotation from a respected source. Find a quotation from somebody in a field that is directly related to your topic. When you include the quotation as supporting evidence, remember to mention the source.
>
> According to Dr. Tom Houston, co-director of the American Medical Association's SmokeLess States campaign, secondhand smoke "can lead to serious health consequences, ranging from ear infections and pneumonia to asthma."

RESEARCH LINK
For more information about doing research, see Chapter 15, "Enhancing Your Writing with Research."

A Student Argument Essay

Read and analyze the structure of the next student argument essay.

THE IMPORTANCE OF MUSIC

Christine Bigras

Thesis statement →

1.   Most parents want their children to receive a well-rounded education. Students study traditional subjects, such as math, science, English, history, geography, and physical education, but many educators and parents have come to believe that schoolchildren should also be taught fine arts subjects. Thus, often school boards offer art, dance, and music, if not as core courses, then at least as extracurricular activities. Although the study and practice of all these arts develop sensitivity and creativity in students, learning music is the most beneficial to all-around student success.

Topic sentence →

2.   First, music makes a child smarter. Everybody has already heard about scientists or doctors who are also musicians. A child who studies music may not become a genius; nevertheless, several research findings have shown that music lessons can enhance IQ and develop intelligence. One of the most recent and conclusive studies has shown that there is a link between children who study music and their academic success because music and schoolwork may develop similar problem-solving skills (Schellenberg).

Topic sentence →

3.   Furthermore, music education improves a child's physical and psychological health. Playing music is excellent exercise for the heart, especially for those who play a wind instrument. A child will also learn to stand straight and adopt good posture. Playing music also decreases stress and anxiety. Through music, the apprentices will learn concentration and listening skills. Furthermore, according to the Texas Commission on Drug and Alcohol Abuse Report, a 2010 study showed that the 19 percent of students who participated in band or orchestra had a lower percentage of illegal substance abuse than students who did not engage in any music program (Liu).

Topic sentence →

4.   Finally, music education helps a child's social development. Playing music may help students connect with one another, particularly through participation in orchestra or a choir. If a child is ugly, poor, big, or shy, he or she is as important as any other musician in the group. Music is the great equalizer. Musicians learn how to respect each other, how to cooperate, and how to build constructive relationships with others. When Yoko Kiyuka entered my former high school, she was very shy and lonely. The music program changed her life. The connections she made helped her become integrated into the school and feel valued.

5.   Many school boards are removing music education from the curriculum. They argue that music is not a necessary or useful course. However, the benefits conveyed by music education are tremendous. By developing a child's brain, body, and feelings, music gives the child a better chance to be confident in life.

Concluding sentence →

Parents of elementary or secondary school children should play an active role in the success of their children by encouraging them to learn music.

WORKS CITED

Liu, Liang Y. "Texas School Survey of Substance Use Among Students: Grades 7–12." *Research Archives: School Surveys*. Texas Department of State Health Services, 2012. Web. 6 Nov. 2012.

Schellenberg, E. Glenn. "Music Lessons Enhance IQ." *Psychological Science* 15.8 (2004): 511–514. Web. 6 Nov. 2012.

PRACTICE 18

1. Find an example in the essay for each of the following types of support.

   a. Statistic: _____

   _____

   _____

   b. Anecdote: _____

   _____

2. Who is the audience for this essay? _____

   _____

3. How does the writer end the essay?

   a. With a prediction   b. With a quotation   c. With a suggestion

A Professional Argument Essay

Read the professional argument essay from *The Economist* and answer the questions that follow.

Robot Ethics

1   In the classic science fiction film *2001*, the ship's computer, HAL, faces a dilemma. His instructions require him both to fulfill the ship's mission (investigating an artifact near Jupiter) and to keep the mission's true purpose secret from the ship's crew. To resolve the contradiction, he tries to kill the crew. As robots become more autonomous, the notion of computer-controlled machines facing ethical decisions is moving out of the realm of science fiction and into the real world. Society needs to find ways to ensure that machines are better equipped to make moral judgments than HAL was.

2   Robots are spreading in the military and civilian worlds. Military technology is at the forefront of the march towards self-determining machines. For example, the Sand Flea can leap through a window or onto a roof, filming all the while. RiSE, a six-legged robo-cockroach, can climb walls. LS3, a dog-like robot, trots

behind a human over rough terrain, carrying up to 180 kilograms of supplies. SUGV, a briefcase-sized robot, can identify a man in a crowd and follow him. Robots are spreading in the civilian world, too, from the flight deck to the operating theatre. Passenger aircraft have long been able to land themselves. Fully self-driving vehicles are being tested around the world. Google's driverless cars have clocked up more than 250,000 miles.

3   As they become smarter and more widespread, autonomous machines are bound to end up making life-or-death decisions in unpredictable situations. Although weapons systems currently have human operators "in the loop," as they grow more sophisticated, they will be able to carry out orders autonomously. When that happens, they will be presented with ethical dilemmas. Should a drone fire on a target's house, which may also be sheltering civilians? Should a driverless car swerve to avoid pedestrians if that means hitting other vehicles or endangering its occupants? Such questions have led to the emergence of the field of "machine ethics," which aims to give machines the ability to make such choices appropriately—in other words, to tell right from wrong.

4   One way of dealing with these difficult questions is to avoid them altogether, by banning autonomous battlefield robots and requiring cars to have the full attention of a human driver at all times. But autonomous robots could do much more good than harm. Robot soldiers would not commit rape, burn down a village in anger, or become erratic decision-makers amid the stress of combat. Driverless cars are very likely to be safer than ordinary vehicles, as autopilots have made planes safer. Sebastian Thrun, a pioneer in the field, reckons driverless cars could save one million lives a year.

5   Regulating the development and use of autonomous robots will require progress in three areas in particular. First, laws are needed to determine whether the designer, the programmer, the manufacturer, or the operator is at fault if an autonomous drone strike goes wrong or a driverless car has an accident. In order to allocate responsibility, autonomous systems must keep detailed logs so that they can explain the reasoning behind their decisions. Second, where ethical systems are embedded into robots, the judgments they make need to be ones that seem right to most people. Last, and most important, more collaboration is required between engineers, ethicists, lawyers, and policymakers, all of whom would draw up very different types of rules if they were left to their own devices.

6   Technology has driven mankind's progress, but each new advance has posed troubling new questions. Autonomous machines are no different. The sooner the questions of moral agency they raise are answered, the easier it will be for mankind to enjoy the benefits that they will undoubtedly bring.

PRACTICE 19

1. Highlight the thesis statement in the introduction.

2. What introductory style opens this essay? Circle the best answer.

    a. Definition   c. General information

    b. Anecdote   d. Opposing viewpoint

3. Underline the topic sentence in each body paragraph.

4. In which paragraph(s) does the writer give the following examples of support?

    an informed opinion: _____

    a series of examples: _____

    a series of questions: _____

5. According to the writer, what should robot experts take into consideration as they develop future robots? _____

    _____

    _____

    _____

    _____

    _____

6. Who is the audience for this essay? _____

    _____

7. How does the writer end the essay?

    a. With a prediction   b. With a suggestion   c. With a quotation

---

THE WRITER'S ROOM   MyWritingLab™

MyWritingLab™
Complete these writing assignments at mywritinglab.com

Writing Activity 1: Topics

Write an argument essay about one of the following topics. Remember to narrow your topic and follow the writing process.

General Topics

1. state-sponsored gambling
2. beauty contests
3. talk shows
4. driving laws
5. the healthcare system

College and Work-Related Topics

6. outsourcing of jobs
7. great reasons to choose your college
8. the cost of a university education
9. student activism
10. dress codes at work

PARAGRAPH LINK
To practice argument writing, you could develop an essay about one of the topics found in Chapter 12, "Argument."

Argument Essay Checklist

As you write your argument essay, review the essay checklist at the end of the book. Also ask yourself the following questions.

☐ Does my thesis statement clearly state my position on the issue?

☐ Do I include facts, examples, statistics, logical consequences, or answers to my opponents in my body paragraphs?

☐ Do my supporting arguments provide evidence that directly supports each topic sentence?

☐ Do I use transitions that will help readers follow my ideas?

Enhancing Your Writing with Research 15

When you want more information about something, you might talk to other people; look for resources in libraries, bookstores, and museums; make phone calls; search the Internet; and so on. You can use the same tools when looking for details to include in your writing.

LEARNING OBJECTIVES

LO 1 Explain the purpose of research. **(p. 233)**

LO 2 Research for academic writing. **(p. 233)**

LO 3 Gather information. **(p. 234)**

LO 4 Evaluate sources. **(p. 236)**

LO 5 Add a paraphrase, summary, or quotation. **(p. 238)**

LO 6 Cite sources using MLA style. **(p. 242)**

LO 7 Analyze a sample research essay that uses MLA style. **(p. 247)**

What Is Research?

When you **research**, you look for information that will help you better understand a subject. For example, when you plan to see a movie and read movie reviews in the newspaper, you are engaging in research to make an informed decision. At college, you are often asked to quote outside sources in your essays. This chapter gives you some strategies for researching information and effectively adding it to your writing.

LO 1 Explain the purpose of research.

Research for Academic Writing

There is a formal type of writing called the research paper. However, many types of academic essays, especially those with the purpose of persuading, can benefit from research. Additional facts, quotations, and statistics can back up your arguments.

Student writer David Raby-Pepin prepared an argument for an essay about rap music. You may have read his essay in Chapter 13 on page 186. His purpose was to persuade the reader that rap musicians share positive cultural values. The following paragraph is from his essay.

LO 2 Research for academic writing.

David's Paragraph without Research

Many of these musicians shout out a powerful message of nonviolence. Leading hip-hop and rap artists have broken from the gangsta rap lyrics of the past. Instead, they write lyrics that present a productive way to resolve conflicts. They encourage listeners to respect themselves and others.

David's paragraph, although interesting, is not entirely convincing. He mentions that rappers encourage listeners to respect others, but he doesn't give any examples. David decided to do some research to support his points with specific details. He found many Internet sites about his topic that are run by hip-hop fans, but he worried that his readers might be skeptical if he used those sources. He kept searching and found two quotations from reputable sources.

David's Paragraph with Research

David added two quotations from respected publications. He included the authors' last names in parentheses. Because the publications were on Web sites, he did not include page numbers in the parentheses.

Many of these musicians shout out a powerful message of nonviolence. Leading hip-hop and rap artists have broken from the gangsta rap lyrics of the past. Instead, they write lyrics that present a productive way to resolve conflicts. They encourage listeners to respect themselves and others. For instance, the Boston rap group 4Peace has the mission "to sell peace as aggressively as other rappers peddle sex and violence" (Kahn). At a concert in Connecticut, rapper Edo. G said, "You need to respect your parents, respect your teachers, and respect the police. You need to respect yourselves and stop the violence" (qtd. in Macmillan).

Later, at the end of his essay, David also included a "Works Cited" page with the following information. (You will learn more about the Works Cited page later in this chapter.)

Works Cited

Kahn, Joseph P. "The Message." *Boston Globe*. Globe Newspaper Company, 10 Oct. 2006. Web. 22 Feb. 2010.

Macmillan, Thomas. "Through Hip Hop, Nonviolence Resonates." *New Haven Independent*. New Haven Independent, 7 May 2009. Web. 21 Feb. 2010.

LO3 Gather information.

Gather Information

To find information that will bolster your essay, consult sources in the library or on the Internet.

Using the Library

When you first enter a library, ask the reference librarian to help you locate information using various research tools, such as online catalogs, CD-ROMs, and microforms.

- **Search the library's online catalog.** You can search by keyword, author, title, or subject. When you find a listing that interests you, remember to jot down the title, author, and call number. You will need that information when you search the library shelves.

- **Use online periodical services in libraries.** Your library may have access to EBSCOhost® or INFOtrac. By typing keywords into EBSCOhost®, you can search through national or international newspapers, magazines, and reference books. When you find an article that you need, e-mail the link to yourself or paste the document into a word processing file. Remember to print or copy the publication data because you will need that information when you cite your source.

Using the Internet

The Internet is a valuable research tool. You will be able to find information about almost any topic online. Here are some tips to help you with your online research.

◆ **Use efficient search engines such as Yahoo! or Google.** These sites can rapidly retrieve thousands of documents from the Internet.

◆ **Choose your keywords with care.** Narrow your search by entering very specific keywords. For example, to bolster an essay about binge drinking, you might try to find information about deaths due to alcohol poisoning. By placing quotation marks around your key words, you further limit your search. For example, when you type the term *alcohol poisoning deaths* into Google without quotation marks, you will get more than a million hits. When the same term is enclosed in quotation marks, the number of hits is reduced to about five hundred, and the displayed Web pages are more relevant.

◆ **Use bookmarks.** When you find information that might be useful, create a folder where you can store the information so that you can easily locate it later. (The bookmark icon appears on the toolbar of your search engine.)

Web Addresses

A Web address (also known as a URL) has the following parts.

| Protocol | Host name | Domain name | Document path | Specific topic |

http://www.nytimes.com/2008/10/28/technology/28soft.html?ref=business

Sometimes you can determine what type of organization runs the Web site by looking at the domain, shown by the three letters that follow the site name. However, be careful to always evaluate the site's content.

URL ending	Meaning	Example
.com	Company	www.companyname.com
.edu	Educational institution	www.stateschoolname.edu
.gov	Government	www.governmentagencyname.gov
.org	Organization	www.organizationname.org

HINT ◄ Useful Web Sites

The following Web sites could be useful when you do research on the Internet. Enter the title of each Web site into your search engine to access these sites.

Statistics

FedStats (statistics from more than one hundred government agencies)
U.S. Bureau of Labor Statistics
U.S. Census Bureau

News Organizations

Magazine Directory (links to hundreds of online magazines)
Newspapers.com (access to newspapers from all over the world)
New York Times site for college students

Job Sites

Monster.com

Jobs.org

Academic Research Sites

Encyclopedia.com

Encyclopaedia Britannica

Google Scholar

LO 4 Evaluate sources.

Evaluate Sources

Be careful when you use Internet sources. Some sites contain misleading information, and some sites are maintained by people who have very strong and specific biases. Remember that the content of Internet sites is not always verified for accuracy. When you view Web sites, try to determine who benefits from the publication. What is the site's purpose?

HINT ◄ Evaluating a Source

When you find a source, ask yourself the following questions:

• Will the information support the point that I want to make?

• Is the information current? When was the site last updated? Ask yourself if the date is appropriate for your topic.

• Is the site reliable and highly regarded? Is it a well-known newspaper, journal, or Web site? Is the English grammatically correct?

• Is the author an expert on the subject? (Many sites provide biographical information about the author.)

• Does the author present a balanced view? Ask yourself if the author has a political or financial interest in the issue.

• Does the author develop key ideas with solid supporting facts and examples? Does the author quote reliable sources?

• Is there advertising on the site? Consider how advertising might influence the site's content.

PRACTICE 1

Imagine that you are writing an essay about the effectiveness of antidepressants. Answer the questions by referring to the list of Web sites on the next page.

1. Write the letters of the three sites that you should investigate further. Briefly explain how each site could be useful.

     _____

     _____

     _____

2. Write the letters of the three sites that are not useful for your essay. For each site, explain why.

_____

_____

_____

_____

A. **Antidepressants** likely do more harm than good, study suggests

www.sciencedaily.com/releases/2012/04/...htm

Apr 24, 2012—In previous research, Andrews and his colleagues had questioned the **effectiveness** of **anti-depressants** even for their prescribed function, . . .

B. Buy **Antidepressants** Online

antidepressants377...com

Jan 20, 2013—Buy **Antidepressants** online and save money. **Antidepressants** buy Easily online. UK buy **Antidepressants** Purchase order **Antidepressants** . . .

C. **Antidepressants**: placebos with side **effects**?

www.ncbi.nlm.nih.gov → ... → CMAJ → v.182(18); Dec 14, 2010

Dec 14, 2010—**Antidepressants**: placebos with side effects? Reviewed by Daniel Carlat, MD, Associate clinical professor of psychiatry. Tufts University School . . .

D. Weight Gain and **Antidepressants** (Including SSRIs)

www.webmd.com/depression/features/**antidepressants**-weight-gain...

Up to 25% of people who take **antidepressants** gain weight. Is there anything . . . Depression Myths and Facts. What's Causing Your Depression? Getting Help: . . .

E. **Antidepressants** suck.

forums.massassi.net → ... → Main Massassi Forums → Discussion Forum

Went to the doctors, with the sole purpose of geting my hands on some happy pills. Its a new university year and I have no wish to have mood . . .

F. In Defense of **Antidepressants** — NYTimes.com

www.nytimes.com/2011/07/10/opinion/.../10antidepressants.html?...

Jul 9, 2011—IN terms of perception, these are hard times for **antidepressants**. A number of articles have suggested that the drugs are no more **effective** than . . .

PRACTICE 2

1. Go to Google, and type _prison reform_ in the search bar. How many hits did you get?

_____

2. Now put _prison reform_ in quotation marks. How many hits did you get?

_____

3. Find sites with the following domains.

.edu _____

.org _____

.gov _____

4. On a separate sheet of paper, write a paragraph comparing two Web sites. Choose one site that is not reliable and explain why. Then choose a site that is probably quite reliable and explain why. To evaluate the sites, refer to the questions in the "Evaluating a Source" hint box on page 236.

Keeping Track of Sources

RESEARCH LINK
To find out more about the MLA and its guidelines, visit the MLA Web site.

Source information is easy to find in most print publications. It is usually on the second or third page of the book, magazine, or newspaper. On many Internet sites, however, finding the source information can take more investigative work. When you research on the Internet, look for the home page to find the site's title, publication date, and so on. Record as much of the following information from the site as possible.

Book, Magazine, Newspaper
Author's full name
Title of article
Title of book, magazine, or newspaper
Publishing information (name of publisher, city, and date of publication)
Pages used

Web Site
Author's full name
Title of article
Title of site
Publisher of site
Date of publication or updating
Date you accessed the site
Complete Web site address

LO 5 Add a paraphrase, summary, or quotation.

Add a Paraphrase, Summary, or Quotation

To add research to a piece of writing, you can paraphrase it, summarize it, or quote it.

- When you **paraphrase**, you use your own words to present someone's ideas. A paraphase is about the same length as the original selection.

- When you **summarize**, you briefly state the main ideas of another work. A summary is much shorter than the original selection.

- When you **quote**, you either directly state a person's exact words (with quotation marks) or report them (without quotation marks).

All of these are valid ways to incorporate research in your writing, as long as you give credit to the author or speaker.

HINT ◀ Avoid Plagiarism!

Plagiarism is the act of using someone else's words or ideas without giving that person credit. Plagiarism is a very serious offense and can result in expulsion from college or termination from work.

The following actions are examples of plagiarism.

- Buying another work and presenting it as your own

- Using another student's work and presenting it as your own

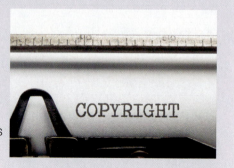

- Failing to use quotation marks or properly set off an author's exact words
- Using ideas from another source without citing that source
- Making slight modifications to an author's sentences but presenting the work as your own
- Copying and pasting text from an Internet source without using quotation marks to set off the author's words

To avoid plagiarism, always cite the source when you borrow words, phrases, or ideas from an author. Include the author's name, the title of the work, and the page number (if it is available).

Paraphrasing and Summarizing

Both paraphrases and summaries present the ideas that you have found in a source. The main difference between a paraphrase and summary is the length. While a paraphrase can be the same length as the original selection, a summary is much shorter.

How to Paraphrase

To paraphrase, do the following:

- Highlight the main ideas in the original text.
- Restate the main ideas using your own words. You can keep specialized words, common words, and names of people or places. However, find synonyms for other words and use your own sentence structure.
- Use a dictionary or thesaurus, if necessary, to find synonyms.
- Acknowledge the source in the paraphrase or place the source information in parentheses after the paraphrase.
- Maintain the original author's ideas and intent.
- After you finish writing, proofread your text.

   Remember that a paraphrase is roughly the same length as the original selection.

How to Summarize

When you summarize, you condense a message to its basic elements. Do the following:

- Read the original text carefully because you will need a complete picture before you begin to write.
- Ask yourself *who, what, when, where, why,* and *how* questions to help you identify the central idea of the text.
- Acknowledge the source in your summary, or place the source information in parentheses after the summary.
- Reread your summary. Make sure that you have expressed the essential message in your own words.
- Your summary should be a maximum of 30 percent of the length of the original work.

   In written summaries, readers should be able to understand the crucial message. The complete document will contain details and examples, but readers should not require the original to make sense of the central ideas.

   Review examples of an original selection followed by a paraphrase and summary.

Original Selection

Glass provides valuable evidence because we come in contact with it so often. If we were to analyze a piece or pieces of glass, we would ask certain questions. . . . For instance, when we observe glass in a fire scene, is the soot baked on? If so, it was most likely a slow moving fire. If the soot is readily wiped off the glass, then we have a fast moving fire and should look for an accelerant.

—Wilson T. Sullivan III, *Crime Scene Analysis*, p. 135

Paraphrase

Investigators are able to determine the speed of a fire, according to Wilson T. Sullivan III. When soot is difficult to remove from glass, the fire probably burned slowly. If the soot can be removed with ease, the fire burned quickly and may have been aided with some type of gasoline or other catalyst.

Summary

According to the book *Crime Scene Analysis*, glass at a fire scene can give clues to a fire's speed, with easily removed soot indicating that a fire may have been intentionally started.

PRACTICE 3

Paraphrase and summarize the following selections.

1.   The National Honor Society says that 64 percent of its members—outstanding high school students—are girls. Some colleges give special help to male applicants—yes, that's affirmative action for white males—to avoid skewed sex ratios. A new report just issued by the Center on Education Policy, an independent research organization, confirms that boys have fallen behind in reading in every single state. It found, for example, that in elementary schools, about 79 percent of girls could read at a level deemed "proficient," compared with 72 percent of boys. Similar gaps were found in middle school and high school.

—Nicholas D. Kristof, "The Boys Have Fallen Behind," *New York Times*

Paraphrase: _____

_____

_____

_____

_____

Summary: _____

_____

_____

2.   Unfortunately it turns out that hit men, genocidal maniacs, gang leaders, and violent kids often have high self-esteem, not low self-esteem. A recipe for their violence is a mean streak combined with an unwarranted sense of

self-worth. When such a boy comes across a girl or parents or schoolmates who communicate to him that he is not all that worthy, he lashes out.

—Martin Seligman, "The American Way of Blame," *APA Monitor Online*

Paraphrase: _____

_____

_____

_____

_____

Summary: _____

_____

_____

Quoting Sources

GRAMMAR LINK
To find out more about using quotations, see Chapter 35.

A **direct quotation** contains the exact words of a source, and the quotation is set off with quotation marks. Use direct quotations to reveal the opinions of an expert or to include ideas that are particularly memorable and important. Quotations should be integrated into sentences, and the source of the quotation should be mentioned either in the introductory phrase or sentence or in parentheses after the quotation. Details about citing sources in the body of your essay appear later in this chapter.

> **EXAMPLE:** In his book *Sociology*, John E. Farley writes, "Human history abounds with legends of lost or deserted children who were raised by wild animals" (97).

HINT ◀ Words That Introduce Quotations

One common way to introduce a quotation is to write *The author says*. However, there are a variety of other verbs that you can use.

admits	comments	explains	mentions	reports	suggests
claims	concludes	maintains	observes	speculates	warns

PRACTICE 4

Read the following selections, and try to identify examples of plagiarism. The original selection, written by Bill Bryson, appeared in *A Short History of Nearly Everything*.

Original Selection

Most schoolroom charts show the planets coming one after the other at neighborly intervals, but this is a necessary deceit to get them all on the same piece of paper. . . . Such are the distances, in fact, that it isn't possible, in any practical terms, to draw the solar system to scale. Even if you added lots of fold-out pages to your textbooks or used a really long sheet of poster paper, you wouldn't come close. On a diagram of the solar system to scale, with Earth reduced to about the diameter of a pea, Jupiter would be over a thousand feet away and Pluto would be a mile and a half distant.

1. **Summary**

   According to Bill Bryson, the solar system's true size is too large to show on a piece of paper, even if you added lots of fold-out pages. If you reduced Earth to the diameter of a pea, Jupiter would be over a thousand feet away.

   Is this plagiarism? _____ Yes _____ No

   Why? _____

   _____

2. **Summary**

   Bill Bryson cleverly demonstrates how pictures of the solar system are misleading. In fact, our solar system is so immense that a piece of paper would have to be more than a mile long to show all of the planets.

   Is this plagiarism? _____ Yes _____ No

   Why? _____

   _____

3. **Summary**

   Drawings of the solar system are misleading. Actually, the solar system is so immense that it is not possible, in practical terms, to draw the solar system to scale. If the Earth were depicted as the size of a pea, Pluto would be over a mile away.

   Is this plagiarism? _____ Yes _____ No

   Why? _____

   _____

LO 6 Cite sources using MLA style.

Cite Sources Using MLA Style

Each time you use another writer's words or ideas, you must **cite the source**, giving complete information about the original document from which you borrowed the material. When quoting, paraphrasing, or summarizing, you can set off the source information using parentheses. These **in-text citations**, also known as **parenthetical citations**, allow you to acknowledge where you obtained the information. You must also cite your sources in an alphabetized list at the end of your essay. The Modern Language Association (MLA) refers to the list as Works Cited.

HINT ◂ Choose a Documentation Style

The three most common styles for documenting sources are the Modern Language Association (MLA) format, *Chicago Manual of Style* (CMS) format, and the American Psychological Association (APA) format. Before writing a paper, check with your instructor to see which documentation style you should use and to learn where you can find more information about it.

Citing the Source in the Body of Your Essay

When you paraphrase, summarize, or quote, you must cite the source in the body of the essay. You must also cite the source in a Works Cited page at the end of your essay. See page 244 to view the Works Cited page for the following quotations.

There are two ways to show that you have borrowed an idea or quotation: cite the source in the sentence or cite the source in parentheses.

Source	Source cited in the sentence	Source cited in parentheses
Print	Mention the author's name in the sentence. Include the page number in parentheses.	Put the author's last name and the page number in parentheses.
	In *Business Communications*, Bovee says, "Short, direct messages have a much better chance of being acted on" (149).	One expert says, "Short, direct messages have a much better chance of being acted on" (Bovee 149).
Internet	For online sources, just mention the author's name. No page number is necessary.	For online sources, just put the author's last name in parentheses.
	Jane E. Brody discusses the dangers when women smoke: "Today, women who smoke are even more likely than men who smoke to die of lung cancer."	Women should think twice before smoking: "Today, women who smoke are even more likely than men who smoke to die of lung cancer" (Brody).
	If an online source does not provide an author's name, mention the article's title or the Web site title in the sentence.	If the online source does not provide an author's name, write a short form of the title in parentheses.
	According to "Bipolar Support and Self Help," not all people use medications: "Living well with bipolar disorder requires certain adjustments."	Not all people use medications: "Living well with bipolar disorder requires certain adjustments" ("Bipolar").

GRAMMAR HINT ◄ Quoting from a Secondary Source

Sometimes you may want to quote from an indirect source. If your source material contains a quotation from someone, then put the abbreviation **qtd. in**—which means *quoted in*—in the parentheses.

Dr. Lauren Streicher says, "There are a lot of profit-motivated physicians out there" (qtd. in Parikh).

See Chapter 35 for more information about using quotations.

Preparing a Works Cited Page

The Works Cited page gives details about each source you have used, and it appears at the end of your essay. To prepare a Works Cited list, follow these basic guidelines.

1. Begin the Works Cited section on a new page. Write "Works Cited" at the top of the page and center it. Make sure your last name and page number appear in the upper-right corner.
2. List each source alphabetically, using the author's last name. If no author is mentioned, use the title.
3. Indent the second line and all subsequent lines of each reference.
4. Double space the entire page.

A Works Cited reference generally has the following parts, with the order and punctuation shown below.

1. **Author(s)** — Complete last name, first name. Coauthor's first name, last name.
2. **Title of short work** — "Article." or "Short Story."
3. **Title of long work** — *Book.* or *Magazine.* or *Web site Name.*
4. **Edition** (if applicable) — 2nd Ed.

Note: For second, third, or subsequent editions, write the abbreviated form: 8th Ed.

5. **City of publication**   City:
6. **Publisher's name**   Company,

> Note: Omit *A*, *An*, or *The* and words such as *Co.*, *Corp.*, *Books*, *Press*, and *Publishers*. The short form for University Press is UP. On Internet sites, look for the publisher's or sponsor's name.

7. **Date of publication**   Day Month Year.
8. **Medium of publication**   Print. or Web. or Film.

> Note: For paper sources, write *Print*. For Internet content, write *Web*. Other sources might be *CD*, *Performance*, *Television*, or *Film*.

9. **Page numbers** (if applicable)   e.g., A13. or 6–19.
10. **Date of access** (Web sources)   Day Month Year.

HINT ◀ **Placement and Order of Works Cited**

The Works Cited list should be at the end of the research paper. List sources in alphabetical order of the authors' last names. If there is no author, put the title in the alphabetized list. The example is a Works Cited page for the quotations listed on page 243.

Works Cited

"Bipolar Support and Self Help." *Helpguide.org*. Wise and Healthy Aging, 2009. Web. 25 Feb. 2010.

Bovee, Courtland, and John Thill. *Business Communication Essentials*. 2nd ed. Upper Saddle River: Prentice, 2006. Print.

Brody, Jane E., "Smoking Gender Gap Closes." *New York Times*. New York Times Company, 15 May 2013. Web. 14 Jan. 2014.

Model Entries

Book

> Last name, First name. *Title of the Book*. Edition. City of Publication: Publisher, Year. Print.

One author

> Bonvillain, Nancy. *Cultural Anthropology*. 3rd. Ed. Boston: Pearson, 2013. Print.

Two or three authors

After the first author's last and first name, put *and* followed by the first and last name of the subsequent authors.

> Cornelius, Steven, and Mary Natvig. *Music: A Social Experience*. Boston: Pearson, 2012. Print.

Four or more authors

Put the first author's name followed by *et al*, which means "and others."

> Thill, John V., et al. *Excellence in Business Communication*. Toronto: Pearson, 2009. Print.

Work in an anthology

For articles or essays taken from an anthology, write *Ed.* and the editor's name after the title.

> Budnitz, Judy. "Nadia." *The Best American Nonrequired Reading*. Ed. Dave Eggers. Boston: Houghton, 2006. Print.

Encyclopedia or dictionary

It is unnecessary to mention volume and page numbers. Simply list the edition and year of publication.

> "Morocco." *Columbia Encyclopedia*. 6th ed. 2005. Print.
>
> "Democracy." *The New American Webster Handy College Dictionary*. 3rd ed. 1995. Print.

Periodical

> Last name, First name. "Title of Article." *Title of the Magazine* or *Newspaper* Date: Pages. Print.

Note: If the pages are not consecutive, put the first page number and a plus sign (15+).

Newspaper article

> Lewis, Charles. "The Running Mate." *National Post* 18 Aug. 2012: A1+. Print.

Magazine article

> Thurman, Judith. "Drawn From Life." *New Yorker* 23 Apr. 2012: 49–55. Print.

Electronic (Internet) Source

When using a source published on the Internet, include as much of the following information as you can find. Keep in mind that some sites do not contain complete information. **Generally, do not include the complete Web address unless the site is difficult to find or your teacher requires it.**

Put a comma after the publisher or sponsor, and put periods after all other parts of the citation. If there is no clear publisher or sponsor, write **n.p.** If there is no clear publication date, write **n.d.**

> Last name, First name. "Title of Article." *Title of Site* or *Online Publication*. Publisher or sponsor, Date of publication. Web. Date you accessed the site (Day Month Year). <Internet address (optional)>.

Online newspaper article

> Firestone, David. "Blame the Poor." *New York Times*. New York Times, 28 Aug. 2012. Web. 14 May 2013.

Online magazine article

> Hutson, Matt. "Your Sixth Sense." *Psychology Today*. Sussex, 09 Jul. 2012. Web. 15 May 2014.

Online dictionary

> "Ubiquitous." *Longman Dictionary of Contemporary English*. Pearson ELT, n.d. Web. 22 Aug. 2014.

E-Book

Format the reference like the print copy. For the medium of publication, mention the type of file, such as *Nook file, Kindle file, PDF file*, etc. If you cannot identify the file, write *Digital file*.

> McKenna, Christina. *The Misremembered Man*. Las Vegas: AmazonEncore, 2008. Kindle file.

Web-only article

> Doig, Will. "It's Time to Love the Bus." *Salon.com*. Salon Media Group, 3 Mar. 2012. Web. 14 May 2013.

No listed author

If the site does not list an author's name, begin with the title of the article.

"How to Detect Lies." *Bifaloo.com*. Bifaloo, 2012. Web. 14 Sept. 2014.

"E-Stats." *US Census Bureau*. US Department of Commerce, 10 May 2012. Web. 28 May 2014.

Other Sources

Film or DVD

Include the name of the film, the director, the studio, and the year of release. You can include other data that you consider relevant such as the names of the main performers or screenwriters. End with *Film* or *DVD*.

The Hunger Games. Dir. Gary Ross. Perf. Jennifer Lawrence. Lion's Gate, 2012. Film.

Sound recording

Include the name of the performer or band, the title of the song, the title of the CD, the name of the recording company, and the year of release. End with *CD* or *LP*.

Charles, Ray. "Fever." *Genius Loves Company*. Hear Music, 2004. CD.

Television or radio program

Include the segment title, the narrator (if applicable), the program name, the station, and the broadcast date. End with *Television* or *Radio*.

"Face Blindness." Narr. Leslie Stahl. *Sixty Minutes*. CBS. 5 Aug. 2012. Television.

PRACTICE 5

Imagine that you are using the following sources in a research paper. Arrange the sources for a Works Cited list using MLA style. You can type your Works Cited list on a separate piece of paper. Double-space each entry, and indent the second line of each entry.

- You use a definition of "honesty" from the online dictionary *Merriam-Webster*. The year of publication is 2012. You accessed the site today.
- You use statistics from an article called "Honesty/Ethics in Professions." The Web site is *Gallup*, and the publisher is Gallup. The publication date is December 1, 2011. There is no author.
- You quote from a book by Dan Ariely called *The (Honest) Truth about Dishonesty*. The publisher is HarperCollins, and the publication date is 2012. The publisher's city is New York.
- You quote from page 231 of the textbook *Psychology* by Saundra K. Ciccarelli and J. Noland White. It is a second edition. The publisher is Pearson, and the publication date is 2009. The publisher's city is Upper Saddle River.
- You quote from the article "The King of Human Error" by Michael Lewis. It appeared in a magazine called *Vanity Fair*, which was published in December 2011. Your quote was from page 153.
- You quote from an online magazine called *Salon.com*. "The Lying Game" was written by Alan Wolfe and published on September 18, 2008. The online publisher is Salon Media Group. You accessed the site today.

Works Cited

_____

_____

_____

_____

_____

_____

_____

_____

_____

_____

_____

_____

Sample Research Essay Using MLA Style

LO7 Analyze a sample research essay that uses MLA style.

Read the complete student essay that follows. Notice how the student integrates paraphrases, summaries, and quotations.

Saumur 1

Stephanie Saumur
Professor Pelaez
English 101
15 April 2010

Cell Phone Safety

These days, it's common to see someone holding a cell phone while walking, driving, or having dinner. The big companies design cell phones to be as small and as practical as possible, and the little gadgets have become essential to our way of life. A lot of research has been done, and it reveals that cell phone microwaves may have an impact on the brain. Cell phones have some benefits, but they may be dangerous for human health.

Cell phone emissions have positive and negative effects on concentration and memory. The positive effect is that cell phone microwaves can help humans memorize things. They keep the short-term memory active. An Australian scientist discovered that cell phone use can temporarily help people "with certain tasks that require a working memory but can also slow reaction time" (Szalavitz). In *Psychology*, Saundra K. Ciccarelli says that "long term memory must be fairly well organized for retrieval to be so quick" (222). Radiation may affect the organization of memories. Henrietta Nittby, a researcher from Lund University, tested the theory on rats. For more than a year, some rats were exposed to cell phone radiation on a weekly basis. On memory tests, the rats that had been exposed to radiation did much worse than the rats that had not been exposed ("Mobile Phones").

◄ Double-space your name, instructor's name, course title, and date.

◄ Center the title. Notice that the title is not underlined, boldfaced, or italicized.

◄ End your introduction with a thesis statement.

◄ Begin body paragraphs with a topic sentence.

◄ You can place the author's name in parentheses.

◄ You can cite the source in your sentence. Include the page number of print sources.

◄ Acknowledge the source of a paraphrase.

Saumur 2

Although people worry about getting cancer because of their cell phone usage, scientists are divided on the cell phone and cancer link. Professor John Moulder, from the Medical College of Wisconsin, does not believe cell phones contribute to brain cancer (Szalavitz). However, some researchers disagree: "In 2006, a Swedish study reported that 85 of 905 brain tumor patients had used mobile phones heavily for 10 years or more, and most of their tumors occurred on the side of their head where they usually held their phones" (Butler 43). Kjell Mild, a professor at the Swedish National Institute for Working Life, says, "If you look at the studies with large numbers of people who used mobiles for ten years or more, all show an increased risk" of cancer (qtd. in Szalavitz).

Finally, there are concerns that cell phone radiation may cause brain damage. A University of Rome study showed that phones affect the cortex, "but no one can yet tell whether the effect is harmful, neutral, or even beneficial" (Szalavitz). Yet Henrietta Nittby's research on rats showed that radiation can cause a protein in the blood to infiltrate the brain, causing damage to nerve cells ("Mobile Phones"). Furthermore, research suggests that cell phones can cause tissue damage in humans. A study done at Lund University has shown that cell phone microwaves can cause blood products to seep across the blood–brain barrier. The implications are serious: "Blood contains toxins . . . that can be lethal to brain tissue" (Sage).

Although the research isn't clear and complete enough to conclude that cell phones are dangerous, some researchers are convinced that mobile phone radiation can have significant long-term effects on human health. Those who are worried about health consequences should use hands-free phone equipment and minimize the amount of time spent on a cell phone. Another option is to increase the use of text messaging because the phone is not placed next to the head. Finally, because long-term safety of cell phones is unclear, perhaps children should not be given a cell phone.

Acknowledge the source of a summary.

You can introduce a quotation with a complete sentence followed by a colon.

Use "qtd. in" when you use a quotation that appeared in a secondary source.

You can integrate a quotation into a sentence.

Three spaced periods indicate that part of the quotation has been deleted.

Saumur 3

Works Cited

Butler, Kiera. "This is Your Brain on Cell Phones." *Mother Jones* July–Aug 2008: 43. Print.

Ciccarelli, Saundra K., and Glenn E. Meyer. *Psychology*. Upper Saddle River: Prentice, 2006. Print.

"Mobile Phones Affect Memory in Laboratory Animals, Swedish Study Finds." *ScienceDaily*. ScienceDaily, 5 Dec. 2008. Web. 6 Feb. 2011.

Sage, Cindy. "Cell Phones and Blood–Brain Barrier." *EMFacts*. EMFacts Consultancy, 11 Nov. 2008. Web. 5 Feb. 2011.

Szalavitz, Maia. "Your Brain on Mobile?" *Psychology Today*. Sussex, 15 May 2007. Web. 4 Feb. 2011.

Always put the Works Cited list on a separate page.

Center the "Works Cited" heading.

Place sources in alphabetical order.

If the source has no author, place the title of the article first.

Double-space throughout, and indent the second line of each source.

Reflect On It

Think about what you have learned in this chapter. If you do not know an answer, review that topic.

1. What are the differences between a paraphrase and a summary?

   Paraphrase   **Summary**

   _____   _____

   _____   _____

   _____   _____

2. What is a Works Cited page?

   _____

   _____

   _____

   _____

   _____

THE WRITER'S ROOM   MyWritingLab™

Writing Activity 1

Choose a paragraph or an essay that you have written, and research your topic to get more detailed information. Then insert at least one paraphrase, one summary, and one quotation into your work. Remember to acknowledge your sources.

Writing Activity 2

Write an essay about one of the following topics. Your essay should include research (find at least three sources). Include a Works Cited page at the end of your assignment.

1. Write about a controversial issue that is in the news. In your essay, give your opinion about the issue.

2. Write about your career choice. You could mention job opportunities in your field, and you could include statistical information.

3. Write about the importance of daily exercise. Find some facts, examples, or statistics to support your view.

Part IV
The Editing Handbook

Why is grammar so important? When you speak, you have tools such as tone of voice and body language to help you express your ideas. When you write, however, you have only words and punctuation to get your message across. Naturally, if your writing contains errors in style, grammar, and punctuation, you may distract readers from your message, and they may focus instead on your inability to communicate clearly. You increase your chances of succeeding in your academic and professional life when you write in clear standard English.

The chapters in this Editing Handbook can help you understand important grammar concepts and ensure that your writing is grammatically correct.

SECTION 1 Effective Sentences
THEME: Popular Culture

16 Simple Sentences

SECTION THEME: Popular Culture

LEARNING OBJECTIVES

LO 1 Identify subjects. (p. 252)

LO 2 Identify prepositional phrases. (p. 255)

LO 3 Identify verbs. (p. 257)

LO 4 Identify helping verbs. (p. 258)

In this chapter, you will read about topics related to advertising and consumerism.

THE WRITER'S JOURNAL

What is your cultural background? How would you identify yourself culturally? Write a paragraph about your cultural identity.

LO 1 Identify subjects.

Identify Subjects

A **sentence** contains one or more subjects and verbs, and it expresses a complete thought. Although some sentences can have more than one idea, a **simple sentence** expresses one complete thought. The **subject** tells you who or what the sentence is about. The **verb** expresses an action or state. If a sentence is missing a subject or a verb, it is incomplete.

Singular and Plural Subjects

Subjects may be singular or plural. To determine the subject of a sentence, ask yourself who or what the sentence is about.

A **singular subject** is one person, place, or thing.

> **Kayla Rice** is a marketing consultant.
>
> **Manhattan** has many advertising agencies.

A **plural subject** is more than one person, place, or thing.

> Contemporary **marketers** try to reach a mass audience.
>
> Many **countries** import American products.

Pronouns

A **subject pronoun** (*he, she, it, you, I, we, they*) can act as the subject of a sentence, and it replaces the noun.

> Jeff Bezos sold books. **He** founded Amazon.com.
>
> Consumers have rights. **They** can complain about unethical advertising.

Gerunds (-*ing* words)

Sometimes a gerund (-*ing* form of the verb) is the subject of a sentence.

> **Advertising** surrounds us.
>
> **Business planning** is an ongoing process.

Compound Subjects

Many sentences have more than one subject. *Compound* means "multiple." Therefore, a **compound subject** contains two or more subjects.

> **Men** and **women** evaluate products differently.
>
> The **accountants**, **designers**, and **managers** will meet to discuss the product launch.

HINT ◄ **Recognizing Simple and Complete Subjects**

In a sentence, the **simple subject** is the noun or pronoun. The complete name of a person, place, or organization is a simple subject.

> he   dancer   Omar Epps   Sony Music Corporation

The **complete subject** is the noun, plus the words that describe the noun. In the next examples, the descriptive words are in italics.

> *new electric* piano   *old, worn-out* shoes   *Anna's green* sofa

In the following sentences, the simple and complete subjects are identified.

> simple subject
> The glossy new **magazine** contained interesting articles.
> complete subject

PRACTICE 1

Underline the complete subject and circle the simple subject(s).

EXAMPLE: Academic <u>institutions</u> teach popular culture.

1.   Popular music, films, books, and fashions are the sources of our common culture.

2.   Marketing is linked to all types of entertainment.

3.   You and your friends and family may see hundreds of ads each day.

4.   Jack Nevin and Linda Gorchels study consumer behavior.

5.   Traditional marketing methods are losing their impact.

6.   Restless and cynical citizens are bored with television, radio, and billboard ads.

7.   Creative advertisers constantly look for new ways to seduce the public.

8.   Social networking sites are now targeted by marketing firms.

9.   Other strategies include buzz marketing and guerilla marketing.

10.   Expensive advertising does not always produce results.

Special Subject Problems

Unstated Subjects (Commands)

In a sentence that expresses a command, the subject is unstated, but it is still understood. The unstated subject is *you*, and "should" is implied.

> Remember to use your coupon.

> Pay the cashier.

Here/There

Here and *there* are not subjects. In a sentence that begins with *Here* or *There*, the subject follows the verb.

> There are five **ways** to market a product.

> Here is an interesting **brochure** about cosmetics.

PRACTICE 2

In the following paragraph, circle the simple subject(s). If the subject is unstated, then write the subject (*you*) before the verb.

EXAMPLE: To see the announcement, *you (should)* watch carefully.

There are many advertisements on the streets of our cities. Look at any bus shelter, billboard, store window, or newspaper. Certainly, some ads appear in surprising places. There are framed announcements on the doors of hotel bathrooms, for example. Furthermore, there are commercials hidden in the middle of the action in movies and television shows. For instance, soft-drink and car companies advertise during the popular reality show *American Idol.* There are soft drinks on the table in front of the show's judges. The show's performers often sing a tribute to an American automobile company. View advertising with a critical eye.

Identify Prepositional Phrases

LO 2 Identify prepositional phrases.

A **preposition** is a word that links nouns, pronouns, or phrases to other words in a sentence. It expresses a relationship based on movement or position. Here are some common prepositions.

Common Prepositions

about	around	beyond	from	off	to
above	at	by	in	on	toward
across	before	despite	inside	onto	under
after	behind	down	into	out	until
against	below	during	like	outside	up
along	beside	except	near	over	with
among	between	for	of	through	within

A **phrase** is a group of words that is missing a subject, a verb, or both and is not a complete sentence. A **prepositional phrase** is made up of a preposition and its object (a noun or a pronoun). In the following phrases, an object follows the preposition.

Preposition	+	**Object**
in		the morning
among		the shadows
over		the rainbow

HINT ◄ **Be Careful**

Because the object of a preposition is a noun, it may look like a subject. However, the object in a prepositional phrase is *never* the subject of the sentence. For example, in the next sentence, the subject is *child*, not *cereal box.*

subject

Inside the cereal box, the **child** found the hidden gift.

Sometimes a prepositional phrase appears before or after the subject. To help you identify the subject, you can put parentheses around prepositional phrases or mark them in some other way. In each of the following sentences, the subject is in boldface type and the prepositional phrase is in parentheses.

(With huge sales,) **Amazon** is an amazing success story.

Jeff Bezos, (with very little money,) launched his Web site.

Sometimes a sentence can contain more than one prepositional phrase.

prepositional phrase   prepositional phrase

(In the mid 1990s,) (inside his Seattle garage,) **Bezos** created his online bookstore.

> **HINT** ◄ **According to . . .**
>
> When a sentence contains *according to*, the noun that immediately follows is *not* the subject of the sentence. In the following sentence, *Jack Solomon* is not the subject.
>
> subject
> (According to Jack Solomon,) **consumers** are easily persuaded.

PRACTICE 3

Place parentheses around the prepositional phrase(s) in each sentence. Then circle the simple subject.

EXAMPLE: (In a suburb,) a young girl shows a new phone to her friends.

1. In the early 1990s, the advertising industry began to market actively to young teens.

2. With their disposable cash and their desire to be cool, tweens are a marketer's dream customer.

3. Children between eight and thirteen years old spend billions of dollars annually.

4. According to *CBS News*, some marketing companies pay for children's slumber parties.

5. "Alpha" girls, with their good looks and their self-confidence, convince their guests to buy certain products.

6. In her book *Born to Buy*, author Juliet Schor criticizes such selling techniques.

7. With no concern for the children, marketers take advantage of peer dynamics.

8. GIA Marketing, with its 40,000 "secret agents", relies on its tween influencers.

9. In spite of the criticism, viral marketing is here to stay.

PRACTICE 4

Look at the underlined word in each sentence. If it is the subject, write C (for "correct") beside the sentence. If the underlined word is not the subject, then circle the correct subject(s).

EXAMPLES: In past eras, bustling markets contained consumer goods. _____

Enclosed shopping malls are a fairly recent development. ___C___

1. In Edina, Minnesota, the first indoor mall was built. _____

2. The world's largest mall has eight hundred stores. _____

3. For some <u>consumers</u>, the local dress shop is a dangerous place.   _____

4. On her twenty-second <u>birthday</u>, Amber Wyatt divulged a secret.   _____

5. During the previous four years, <u>she</u> had piled up $60,000 in credit card debts.   _____

6. She acknowledges, with a shrug, her shopping <u>addiction</u>.   _____

7. Today, with a poor credit <u>rating</u>, Amber is unable to get a lease.   _____

8. Her <u>brother</u>, boyfriend, and aunt have lent her money.   _____

9. Her <u>parents</u>, with some reluctance, allowed their daughter to move back home.   _____

10. Many <u>American</u> men and women, according to a recent survey, have a shopping addiction.   _____

Identify Verbs

LO 3 Identify verbs.

Every sentence must contain a verb. The **verb** either expresses what the subject does or links the subject to other descriptive words.

Action Verbs

An **action verb** describes an action that a subject performs.

In 2006, China <u>launched</u> an electric car called the ZAP Xebra.

Engineers <u>designed</u> the car's energy-efficient engine.

Linking Verbs

A **linking verb** connects a subject with words that describe it, and it does not show an action. The most common linking verb is *be*.

The marketing campaign <u>is</u> expensive.

Some advertisements <u>are</u> very clever.

Other linking verbs refer to the senses and indicate how something appears, smells, tastes, and so on.

The advertising photo <u>looks</u> grainy.

The glossy paper <u>feels</u> smooth.

Common Linking Verbs

appear	feel	smell
be (am, is, are, was, were, etc.)	look	sound
become	seem	taste

Compound Verbs

When a subject performs more than one action, the verbs are called **compound verbs**.

Good advertising <u>informs</u>, <u>persuades</u>, and <u>convinces</u> consumers.

Members of the public either <u>loved</u> or <u>hated</u> the logo.

HINT ‹ Infinitives Are Not the Main Verb

Infinitives are verbs preceded by *to* such as *to fly*, *to speak*, and *to go*.
An infinitive is never the main verb in a sentence.

          V   infinitive   V   infinitive

Kraft <u>wants</u> **to compete** in Asia. The company <u>hopes</u> **to sell** millions of products.

PRACTICE 5

Underline one or more main verbs in these sentences. Remember that infinitives such as *to sell* are not part of the main verb. Write *L* above two linking verbs.

EXAMPLE: Our consumer culture <u>affects</u> everyone.

1. Before the 1940s, diamonds were not more popular than other stones.

2. During marriages, a groom gave a simple gold or silver band to his bride.

3. Then, in 1947, Frances Gerety created the best marketing slogan in history.

4. A diamond is forever.

5. The slogan connected diamonds with love and marriage.

6. De Beers also paid Hollywood stars to pose with diamond engagement rings.

7. The advertising campaign had a huge impact on diamond sales.

8. The emotional appeals changed people's habits and helped sell diamonds.

9. Marketers produced an irrational demand for an expensive product.

10. Today, the majority of brides expect to receive a diamond ring.

LO 4 Identify helping verbs.

Identify Helping Verbs

A verb can have several different forms, depending on the tense that is used. **Verb tense** indicates whether the action occurred in the past, present, or future. In some tenses, there is a **main verb** that expresses what the subject does or links the subject to descriptive words, but there is also a helping verb.

The **helping verb** combines with the main verb to indicate tense, negative structure, or question structure. The most common helping verbs are forms of *be, have,* and *do*. **Modal auxiliaries** are another type of helping verb; they indicate ability (*can*), obligation (*must*), possibility (*may, might, could*), advice (*should*), and so on. For example, here are different forms of the verb *open*. The helping verbs are underlined.

is opening	had opened	will open	should have opened
was opened	had been opening	can open	might be open
has been opening	would open	could be opening	could have been opened

The **complete verb** consists of the helping verb and the main verb. In the following examples, the helping verbs are indicated with *HV* and the main verbs with *V*.

              HV HV   V

American culture has been spreading across the globe for years.

        HV   HV V

You must have seen the news articles.

In **question forms**, the first helping verb usually appears before the subject.

   HV   subject HV   V

Should the coffee chain have expanded so quickly?

  HV   subject   V

Will the coffee and cakes sell in Moscow?

Interrupting words may appear between verbs, but they are *not* part of the verb. Some interrupting words are *easily, actually, not, always, usually, sometimes, frequently, often, never,* and *ever.*

            HV   V

Consumers have often complained about product quality.

           HV   HV   V

The car maker should not have destroyed its electric cars.

PRACTICE 6

Underline the helping verbs once and the main verbs twice. Be careful because some sentences only have main verbs.

EXAMPLE: The modern consumerism movement has been strong since the 1960s.

1. In 1961, President John F. Kennedy outlined the Consumer Bill of Rights.

2. Products should not be dangerous or defective.

3. A single company should never have a monopoly.

4. Businesses must provide consumers with honest information.

5. Some companies have been sued for defective products.

6. Merck, a pharmaceutical company, was forced to remove the drug Vioxx from the market.

7. To protect consumers, the Federal Trade Commission has implemented rules to prevent misleading advertising.

8. Some companies have been fined for deceptive marketing methods.

9. In a Volvo ad, a monster truck ran over a row of cars and crushed all but the Volvo station wagon.

10. In fact, the Volvo's structure had been reinforced.

11. Volvo was fined $150,000 for deceptive marketing.

12. How should companies respond to consumer complaints?

> **GRAMMAR LINK**
> For information on the position of mid-sentence adverbs, such as *often*, *sometimes*, and *never*, see pages 414–415 in Chapter 30.

PRACTICE 7

Circle the simple subjects and underline the complete verbs. Remember to underline all parts of the verb.

EXAMPLE: Consumer (activists) <u>can have</u> an impact.

1. In 1989, Kalle Lasn and Bill Schmalz started a new media foundation with the name Adbusters. They have produced a magazine and Web site. Adbusters does not accept advertising. Instead, the anti-consumption magazine often parodies common advertisements. Contributors to the magazine have created amusing spoof ads. For example, some graphic designers have mocked Joe Camel cigarette advertising. One ad depicts "Joe Chemo" in a hospital bed. The cartoon camel is hooked up to IV tubes. In another spoof ad, an image of a broken Absolut Vodka bottle has the headline "Absolut Mayhem." And a different parody of the vodka brand shows a sagging bottle with the title "Absolut Impotence."

2. On its Web site, Adbusters describes itself as "a global network of artists, activists, writers, pranksters, students, educators and entrepreneurs." The founders want people to reconsider their consumption habits. The not-for-profit organization sponsors social marketing campaigns such as "Buy Nothing Day." More recently, in mid-2011, Adbusters Foundation was behind the Occupy Wall Street movement. Over the years, the organization has had many supporters and critics. In his textbook *Consumer Behavior*, Michael R. Solomon advises corporations to listen to unhappy consumers. It is easy to dismiss organizations such as Adbusters as "the lunatic fringe." However, according to Solomon, such organizations deserve to be taken seriously.

Reflect On It

Think about what you have learned in this chapter. If you do not know an answer, review that concept.

1. What is a sentence? _____

   _____

2. What does the subject of a sentence do? _____

   _____

Chapter 16

3. What is a verb? _____

_____

4. Write an example of a linking verb and an action verb.

Linking _____ Action _____

Circle the best answers.

5. Can the object of a preposition be the subject of a sentence? No Yes

6. Can a sentence have more than one subject? No Yes

7. Can a sentence have more than one verb? No Yes

FINAL REVIEW

Circle the simple subjects, and underline the complete verbs. Underline *all* parts of the verb. Remember that infinitives such as *to go* or *to run* are not part of the main verb.

EXAMPLE: A good (name) and (logo) are immensely important.

1. In their book *Marketing: Real People, Real Choices*, Michael R. Solomon, Greg Marshall, and Elnora Stuart discuss brands. **2.** With a great deal of care, companies must carefully choose the best name for their products. **3.** According to the authors, product names should be memorable. **4.** Irish Spring, for instance, is a fresh and descriptive name for soap.

5. Occasionally, mistakes are made. **6.** The company Toro called its lightweight snow blower "Snow Pup." **7.** The product did not sell well. **8.** Later, the product was renamed "Snow Master" and then "Snow Commander." **9.** The sales have improved tremendously since then.

10. Some brands have become the product name in consumers' minds. **11.** Everyone knows popular brands such as Kleenex, Jell-O, Scotch Tape, and Kool-Aid. **12.** Without a second thought, many consumers will ask for a Kleenex but not for a tissue with another brand name. **13.** Therefore, a great name can be linked to the product indefinitely.

14. According to Solomon, Marshall, and Stuart, there are four important elements in a good brand name. **15.** It must be easy to say, easy to spell, easy to read, and easy to remember. **16.** Apple, Coke, and Dove are examples of great product names. **17.** Good names should also have a positive or functional relationship with the product. **18.** Drano is a very functional name. **19.** On the other hand, Pampers and Luvs suggest good parenting but have no relation to the function of diapers. **20.** Ultimately, large and small businesses put a great deal of care into product branding.

MyWritingLab™
Complete these writing assignments at mywritinglab.com

MyWritingLab™
THE WRITER'S ROOM

Write about one of the following topics. After you finish writing, identify your subjects and verbs.

1. Describe an effective advertising campaign. List the elements that make the campaign so successful.

2. Compare two online shopping sites. Describe the positive and negative features of each site.

Compound Sentences 17

SECTION THEME: Popular Culture

In this chapter, you will read about topics related to fads and fashions.

LEARNING OBJECTIVES

LO 1 Compare simple and compound sentences. **(p. 263)**

LO 2 Combine sentences using coordinating conjunctions. **(p. 264)**

LO 3 Combine sentences using semicolons. **(p. 267)**

LO 4 Combine sentences using transitional expressions. **(p. 269)**

THE WRITER'S JOURNAL

Do you have body art, such as tattoos and piercings? In a paragraph, explain why you do or do not have body art.

MyWritingLab™
Complete this Writer's Journal activity at mywritinglab.com

Compare Simple and Compound Sentences

LO 1 Compare simple and compound sentences.

When you use sentences of varying lengths and types, your writing flows more smoothly and appears more interesting. You can vary sentences and create relationships between ideas by combining sentences.

Review the differences between simple and compound sentences.

A **simple sentence** is an independent clause. It expresses one complete idea, and it stands alone. Simple sentences can have more than one subject and more than one verb.

One subject and verb	Tattooing is not a new fashion.
Two subjects	Tattooing and body piercing are not new fashions.
Two verbs	Della McMahon speaks and writes about current trends.

A **compound sentence** contains two or more simple sentences. The two complete ideas can be joined in several ways.

	Vera creates handbags. + She also designs shoes.
Add a coordinator	Vera creates handbags, and she also designs shoes.
Add a semicolon	Vera creates handbags; she also designs shoes.
Add a semicolon and conjunctive adverb	Vera creates handbags; moreover, she designs shoes.

LO 2 Combine sentences using coordinating conjunctions.

Combine Sentences Using Coordinating Conjunctions

A **coordinating conjunction** joins two complete ideas and indicates the connection between them. The most common coordinating conjunctions are *for, and, nor, but, or, yet,* and *so.*

> Complete idea,   **coordinating conjunction**   complete idea.

Review the following chart showing coordinating conjunctions and their functions.

Coordinating Conjunction	Function	Example
for	to indicate a reason	Henna tattoos are great, **for** they are not permanent.
and	to join two ideas	Jay wants a tattoo, **and** he wants to change his hairstyle.
nor	to indicate a negative idea	Cosmetic surgery is not always successful, **nor** is it particularly safe.
but	to contrast two ideas	Tattoos hurt, **but** people get them anyway.
or	to offer an alternative	Jay will dye his hair, **or** he will shave it off.
yet	to introduce a surprising choice	He is good-looking, **yet** he wants to get cosmetic surgery.
so	to indicate a cause and effect relationship	He saved up his money, **so** he will get a large tattoo.

HINT ◄ **Recognizing Compound Sentences**

To be sure that a sentence is compound, place your finger over the coordinating conjunction, and then ask yourself whether the two clauses are complete sentences.

Simple   The fashion model was tall **but** also very thin.

Compound   The fashion model was tall**, but** she was also very thin.

PRACTICE 1

Indicate whether the following sentences are simple (*S*) or compound (*C*). Underline the coordinating conjunction in each compound sentence.

EXAMPLE: There are many ways to alter your appearance.   _____*S*_____

1. Many humans permanently alter their bodies, and they do it for a variety of reasons.   _____

2. Body altering is not unique to North America, for people in every culture and in every historical period have found ways to permanently alter their bodies.   _____

3. In past centuries, some babies in South America had boards tied to their heads, and their soft skulls developed a long, high shape.   _____

4. In Africa, Ubangi women used to extend their lower lips with large, plate-sized pieces of wood.   _____

5. In the 1700s, wealthy European men and women ate tiny amounts of arsenic to have very pale complexions.   _____

6. Then, in the next century, European and American women wore extremely tight corsets, and they suffered from respiratory and digestive problems.   _____

7. Today, some people want to improve their physical appearance, so they sculpt their bodies with cosmetic surgery.   _____

8. Botox injections are popular but dangerous.   _____

9. Body altering can be painful and very costly, but people do it anyway.   _____

PRACTICE 2

Read the following passages. Insert an appropriate coordinating conjunction in each blank. Choose from the list below, and try to use a variety of coordinating conjunctions.

for   and   nor   but   or   yet   so

EXAMPLE: Fashions usually take a while to be accepted, __*but*__ fads appear and vanish quickly.

1.   Have you heard of Harajuku culture? Harajuku is the name of a district in Tokyo, _____ it is also a teen subculture. Every Sunday afternoon, hundreds of Japanese teenagers meet on Jinju Bridge, _____ they engage in "cosplay" (costume play). Some young males dress up, _____ most of the Harajuku kids are female. The girls want to be noticed, _____ they wear homemade frilly dresses and carry parasols. Their costumes require a lot of effort. They might dress up as a cute cartoon character, _____ they can choose to dress in dark gothic costumes.

2.   The pop star Gwen Stefani has a perfume brand called "Harajuku," _____ she loves that subculture. Today, the Harajuku district is famous, _____ many visitors go there. Tourists and professional photographers search for the best-dressed youths. Seventeen-year-old Shoshi lives in Toyko, _____ she

visits Jinju Bridge every week. Next Sunday, she might wear a yellow bow in her hair, _____ she may wear a white lace cap. Her costumes are elaborately detailed, _____ she attracts a lot of attention. Tourists stare at her, _____ she is not self-conscious. Shoshi is frequently photographed, _____ she always wears the most eye-catching outfits. She never refuses to pose, _____ do most of her friends.

3.   Curiously, participants love to socialize and make friends, _____ they do not use their real names. The teens choose special names, _____ they use those pseudonyms whenever they dress up in costume. Harajuku culture will probably remain a unique Japanese lifestyle.

> **HINT** ◂ **Place a Comma Before the Coordinating Conjunction**
>
> Add a comma before a coordinating conjunction if you are certain that it joins two complete sentences. If the conjunction joins two nouns, verbs, or adjectives, then you do not need to add a comma before it.
>
> | | |
> |---|---|
> | **Comma** | The word *fashion* refers to all popular styles, **and** it does not refer only to clothing. |
> | **No comma** | The word *fashion* refers to all popular styles **and** not only to clothing. |

PRACTICE 3

Create compound sentences by adding a coordinating conjunction and another complete sentence to each simple sentence. Remember to add a comma before the conjunction.

EXAMPLE: Many people deny it <u>, but they worry about their personal style.</u>

1. I don't have a tattoo _____

   _____

2. Body piercing is common _____

   _____

3. Cosmetic surgery is expensive _____

   _____

4. She dyed her hair _____

   _____

Combine Sentences Using Semicolons

LO3 Combine sentences using semicolons.

Another way to form a compound sentence is to join two complete ideas with a semicolon. The semicolon replaces a coordinating conjunction.

Complete idea	;	complete idea.

Advertisers promote new fashions every year**;** they effectively manipulate consumers.

HINT ◄ Use a Semicolon to Join Related Ideas

Do not use a semicolon to join two unrelated sentences. Remember that a semicolon takes the place of a conjunction.

Incorrect	Some societies have no distinct word for art; people like to dress in bright colors.
	(The second idea has no clear relationship with the first idea.)
Correct	Some societies have no distinct word for art; art is an intrinsic part of their cultural fabric.
	(The second idea gives further information about the first idea.)

PRACTICE 4

Insert the missing semicolon in each sentence.

EXAMPLE: Often, bizarre fashion styles become accepted ; almost everyone adopts the style.

1. Ashley Harrell has identified some of this century's worst fashion trends her article appeared in the *SF Weekly* blog.

2. Crocs are on her list the bright plastic shoes are not attractive.

3. She also criticizes long pointy-toed shoes they are only good for kicking something.

4. Other critics hate the low pants trend most people should not show their bellies.

5. Since 2000, pierced tongues have been popular dentists benefit from the fashion.

6. Derek has decided to stretch his earlobe holes with heavy rings he may regret his decision one day.

7. Next year, perhaps shaved eyebrows will become popular fashionistas will follow the trend.

8. People should be careful they should think twice before altering their bodies to follow a trend.

PRACTICE 5

Write compound sentences by adding a semicolon and another complete sentence to each simple sentence. Remember that the two sentences must have related ideas.

EXAMPLE: Last year my sister had her tongue pierced ; she regretted her decision.

1. Youths rebel in many ways _____

_____

2. Hair dyes can be toxic _____

   _____

3. At age thirteen, I dressed like other teens _____

   _____

4. Running shoes are comfortable _____

   _____

Combine Sentences Using Transitional Expressions

LO 4 Combine sentences using transitional expressions.

A third way to combine sentences is to join them with a semicolon and a transitional expression. A **transitional expression** can join two complete ideas together and show how they are related. Most transitional expressions are **conjunctive adverbs** such as *however* or *furthermore*.

Transitional Expressions

Addition	Alternative	Comparison or Contrast	Time	Example or Emphasis	Result or Consequence
additionally	in fact	equally	eventually	for example	consequently
also	instead	however	finally	for instance	hence
besides	on the contrary	nevertheless	later	namely	therefore
furthermore	on the other hand	nonetheless	meanwhile	of course	thus
in addition	otherwise	similarly	subsequently	undoubtedly	
moreover		still			

If the second part of a sentence begins with a transitional expression, put a semicolon before it and a comma after it.

> Complete idea;   **transitional expression,**   complete idea.

Yuri is not wealthy; **nevertheless**, he always wears the latest fashions.
                 ; **however**,
                 ; **nonetheless**,
                 ; **still**,

PRACTICE 6

Punctuate the following sentences by adding any necessary semicolons and commas.

EXAMPLE: Tattoos are applied with needles ; thus , they are painful.

1. During the era of the Roman Empire, soldiers received tattoos on their hands consequently deserting soldiers could be easily identified.

2. More recently, tattoos represented a person's spirituality or profession for instance sailors commonly had anchors tattooed on their biceps.

3. During World War II, some people were forced to get tattoos for example the Nazis tattooed concentration camp victims.

4. Since the 1990s, tattoos have surged in popularity in fact ordinary citizens of all ages and from all economic classes get them.

5. Some people hate the new fad meanwhile others have become addicted to tattooing.

6. At age sixteen, Rick Genest got a skull and crossbones tattoo on his left shoulder eventually he tattooed his arms, his face, and his skull.

7. He has spent over $17,000 on tattoos hence his hobby is very expensive.

8. These days, tattoos are not always harmless body decorations on the contrary they can symbolize membership in a criminal organization.

9. In Japan, "yakuza" criminals have large colorful tattoos similarly in El Salvador, members of the Mara 18 gang have lip tattoos.

10. Most of my friends have tattoos nevertheless I refuse to get one.

PRACTICE 7

Combine sentences using one of the following transitional expressions. Choose an expression from the following list, and try to use a different expression in each sentence.

in contrast	for example	~~however~~	of course	thus
in fact	for instance	nevertheless	therefore	

EXAMPLE: Today's parents often complain about their children. ~~Young~~ *; however, young* people today are not more violent and rebellious than those of past generations.

1. Youth rebellion is not new. In each era, teenagers have rebelled.

2. Teenagers distinguish themselves in a variety of ways. They listen to new music, create new dance styles, wear odd fashions, and break established social habits.

3. The most visible way to stand out is to wear outrageous fashions. Teenagers try to create original clothing and hairstyles.

4. In the past fifty years, rebellious teens have done almost everything to their hair, including growing it long, buzzing it short, dyeing it, spiking it, shaving it

off, and coloring it blue. It is difficult for today's teenagers to create an original

hairstyle.

5. Sometimes a certain group popularizes a style. Hip-hop artists wore baggy

    clothing in the late 1980s.

6. Many parents hated the baggy, oversized pants. Boys wore them.

7. In the past, most people pierced their ears with tiny holes. Many of today's

    youths stretch their earlobes to create large holes.

8. "Retro" hair and clothing styles will always be popular. People often look to the

    past for their inspiration.

HINT ◄ Subordinators versus Conjunctive Adverbs

A **subordinator** is a term such as *when*, *because*, *until*, or *although*. Do not
confuse subordinators with conjunctive adverbs. When a subordinator is added
to a sentence, the clause becomes incomplete. However, when a conjunctive
adverb is added to a sentence, the clause is still complete.

Complete	She wore fur.
Incomplete (with subordinator)	When she wore fur.
Complete (with conjunctive adverb)	Therefore, she wore fur.

When you combine two ideas using a conjunctive adverb, use a semicolon.

No punctuation	She was criticized when she wore fur.
Semicolon	It was very cold; therefore, she wore fur.

PRACTICE 8

Create compound sentences by using the next transitional expressions. Try to use a
different expression in each sentence.

    in fact   however   ~~therefore~~   furthermore   consequently

EXAMPLE: I have my own style *; therefore, I refuse to spend money following
        the latest fad.*

1. Designer clothing is expensive _____

    _____

2. I cannot sew _____

    _____

3. Some men shave their heads _____

_____

4. My best friend loves to shop _____

_____

Reflect On It

Think about what you have learned in this unit. If you do not know an answer, review that concept.

1. a. What is a simple sentence? _____

_____

   b. Write a simple sentence. _____

_____

2. a. What is a compound sentence? _____

_____

   b. Write a compound sentence. _____

_____

3. What are the seven coordinating conjunctions? _____

_____

4. When two sentences are joined by a coordinating conjunction such
   as *but*, should you put a comma before the conjunction?   Yes ☐   No ☐

5. When you join two simple sentences with a transitional expression, how
   should you punctuate the sentence?

_____

_____

FINAL REVIEW

Read the following essay. Create at least ten compound sentences by adding semicolons, transitional expressions (*however, therefore*, and so on), or coordinating conjunctions (*for, and, nor, but, or, yet, so*). You may choose to leave some simple sentences.

Chapter 17

EXAMPLE: The fashion industry does not hire average-sized models. ~~Top~~ models *; for example, top*
are very tall and thin.

1.   The fashion industry and advertisers promote an unrealistic body type. They use tall, skinny models to sell clothing. A public backlash has developed against the skinny top model image. People on both sides of the controversy have an opinion. They may love the fashion industry. They may hate it.

2.   Critics accuse the fashion industry of creating impossible standards. Most models must fit into a size zero. They need a 32-inch bust, 23-inch waist, and 34-inch hips. That is an unhealthy size. It is more realistic for children. The average eight-year-old has a 22-inch waist. Also, in recent years, models have become younger and younger. In 2011, *French Vogue* used ten-year-old Thylane Loubry Blondeau in a sexy fashion layout. Additionally, the fashion industry affects males. Young men feel pressured to have perfect six-pack stomachs. Insecure adolescents often become addicted to intense exercise. Many people also develop dangerous eating disorders. Pro-anorexia Web sites use magazine images for "thinspiration." They also use clips from programs such as *America's Next Top Model*.

3.   Most in the modeling industry have ignored the complaints. Some are getting the message. In 2006, fashion organizations in Spain banned super-thin models from catwalks. Italian fashion shows did the same thing a few years later. In 2012, *Vogue* editors promised to exclude underage and underweight models. They refused to stop Photoshopping images to make models look perfect. In 2012, Israel became the first country to ban underweight models from advertising. Maybe other countries will follow with legislation.

4.   The skinny model controversy will continue. Many in the fashion industry refuse to change. H&M clothing company has defended its practice of using computer-generated bodies on its models. According to designers Karl Lagerfeld and Victoria Beckham, clothing looks better on thin models. Critics should stop complaining. The debate about underweight models is important. It may never be resolved.

*My*WritingLab™
Complete these writing assignments at mywritinglab.com

*My*WritingLab™

THE WRITER'S ROOM

Write about one of the following topics. Include some compound sentences.

1. Think about some fashions over the last one hundred years. Which fashion trends do you love the most? Give examples.

2. List the steps you take when you make a major purchase. For example, what process do you follow when you decide to buy an appliance, car, computer, or house?

Complex Sentences 18

SECTION THEME: Popular Culture

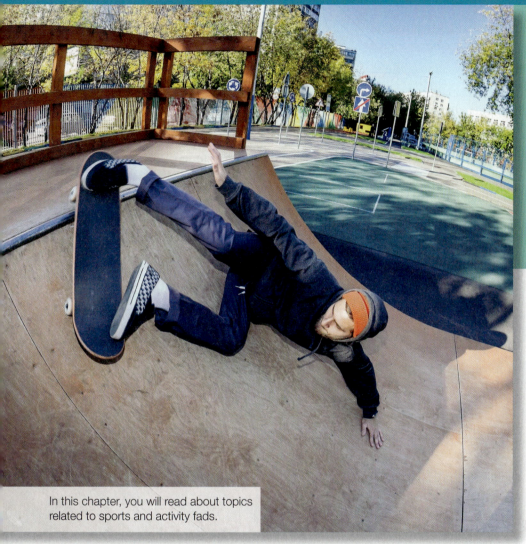

In this chapter, you will read about topics related to sports and activity fads.

THE WRITER'S JOURNAL

How active are you? Write a paragraph about some of the physical activities that you do. Provide specific examples and anecdotes.

MyWritingLab™

Complete this Writer's Journal activity at mywritinglab.com

LO 1 Identify a complex sentence.

What Is a Complex Sentence?

Before you learn about complex sentences, it is important to understand some key terms. A **clause** is a group of words containing a subject and a verb. There are two types of clauses.

An **independent clause** has a subject and a verb and can stand alone because it expresses one complete idea.

> Laban Nkete won the race.

A **dependent clause** has a subject and a verb, but it cannot stand alone. It "depends" on another clause to be complete.

> Although he had injured his heel

A **complex sentence** combines both a dependent and an independent clause.

> dependent clause   independent clause
> Although he had injured his heel, Laban Nkete won the race.

HINT ◄ **More About Complex Sentences**

Complex sentences can have more than two clauses.

>   1
> Although women have played organized football for over a century, their
>   2   3
> salaries are not very high because their games are rarely televised.

You can also combine compound and complex sentences. The next example is a **compound-complex sentence**.

>   complex
> Although Kyra is tiny, she plays basketball, and she is a decent player.
>   compound

LO 2 Use subordinating conjunctions.

Use Subordinating Conjunctions

An effective way to create complex sentences is to join clauses with a subordinating conjunction. When you add a **subordinating conjunction** to a clause, you make the clause dependent. *Subordinate* means "secondary," so subordinating conjunctions are words that introduce secondary ideas. Here are some common subordinating conjunctions followed by examples of how to use these types of conjunctions.

Common Subordinating Conjunctions

after	as though	if	though	where
although	because	provided that	unless	whereas
as	before	since	until	wherever
as if	even if	so that	when	whether
as long as	even though	that	whenever	while

Main idea	subordinating conjunction	secondary idea.
The fans celebrated	**because**	the team won the game.

Subordinating conjunction	secondary idea,	main idea.
Because	the team won the game,	the fans celebrated.

PRACTICE 1

The following sentences are complex. In each sentence, circle the subordinating conjunction, and then underline the dependent clause.

EXAMPLE: Even if we cannot know for sure, early humans probably played games and sports.

1. When humans shifted from being food gatherers to hunters, sports probably developed in complexity.

2. It would be important to practice cooperative hunting before humans attacked mammoths or other large creatures.

3. Early groups of humans probably also practiced war games so that they could win battles with other tribes.

4. Spectator sports evolved when societies had more leisure time.

5. In many places, spectators watched while young boys passed through their initiation rituals.

6. Whenever early humans played sports or games, they tested their physical, intellectual, and social skills.

Meanings of Subordinating Conjunctions

Subordinating conjunctions create a relationship between the clauses in a sentence.

	Cause or Reason	Condition or Result	Contrast	Place	Time
Conjunctions	as because since so that	as long as even if if provided that only if so that unless	although even though if though whereas unless	where wherever	after before once since until when/whenever while
Example	Eric learned karate **because** he wanted to be physically fit.	He will not fight **unless** he feels threatened.	People learn karate **even though** it is difficult to master.	**Wherever** you travel, you will find karate enthusiasts.	**After** he received his black belt, he became a teacher.

PRACTICE 2

In each of the following sentences, underline the dependent clause. Then, indicate the type of relationship between the two parts of the sentence. Choose one of the following relationships.

condition   contrast   reason   place   time

EXAMPLE: <u>When Rebeka feels lonely</u>, she goes on her Facebook page.   <u>*time*</u>

1. After the invention of computers, many new fads emerged. _____

2. Social networking sites are popular because people can stay in touch with their friends. _____

3. A lot of college students use Facebook or Twitter whenever they have spare time. _____

4. Generally, students use Facebook whereas professionals use LinkedIn. _____

5. Wherever Rebeka goes, she can check her Facebook page. _____

6. Rebeka will continue to use Facebook unless a better networking site appears. _____

HINT ◄ **Punctuating Complex Sentences**

If you use a subordinator at the beginning of a sentence, put a comma after the dependent clause. Generally, if you use a subordinator in the middle of the sentence, you do not need to use a comma.

Comma   **Even though** he is afraid of heights**,** Malcolm tried skydiving.

No comma   Malcolm tried skydiving **even though** he is afraid of heights.

PRACTICE 3

Underline the subordinating conjunction in each sentence. Then add eight missing commas.

EXAMPLE: <u>Although</u> most sports are quite safe, some sports are extremely hazardous.

1. Each year, many people are killed or maimed when they practice a sport. Although skydiving and bungee jumping are hazardous extreme sports like base jumping, free diving, and rodeo events are even more dangerous.

2. Even though they may get arrested many people try base jumping. Wherever there are tall structures there

may also be base jumpers. The jumpers wear parachutes and dive off buildings and bridges so that they can feel an adrenaline rush. Because the parachute can get tangled on the structure   base jumping is an extremely risky sport.

3.   Free divers hold their breath until they are as deep as possible underwater. So that they can break existing records   some free divers have dived almost 400 feet. If their brains lack oxygen   they have to be resuscitated.

4.   Although most rodeo sports can be safe   bull riding is dangerous. Many bull riders are injured or even killed because the bull throws them off and tramples them.

5.   Surprisingly, most sports-related injuries occur when people ride bicycles. If anyone rides a bike   he or she should wear a protective helmet.

PRACTICE 4

Add a missing subordinating conjunction to each sentence. Use each subordinating conjunction once.

although	even though	~~when~~	whereas
because	unless	whenever	

EXAMPLE: _____When_____ you refer to a "football" in Europe, Africa, or Asia, most people assume you are talking about a round black-and-white ball.

1. British people will assume you are speaking about soccer _____ you specifically say "American football."

2. Soccer is the world's most popular sport _____ it is inexpensive to play. _____ someone decides to join a soccer team, he or she does not require expensive padding or equipment.

3. _____ a lot of Americans love to play soccer, there are not many professional teams in the United States. Sports such as basketball, baseball, and football have professional teams and are shown on network television _____ soccer is not widely viewed.

4. _____ soccer has yet to become as popular as other sports in the United States, it is America's fastest-growing sport, according to the American Soccer Federation.

HINT ◀ **Put a Subject After the Subordinator**

When you form complex sentences, always remember to put a subject after the subordinator.

it
Wrestling is like theater because ˄involves choreographed maneuvers.

they
Boxers do not know who will win the round when ˄enter the ring.

PRACTICE 5

Combine each pair of sentences into a single sentence. Add one of the following subordinating conjunctions. Use each conjunction once.

~~although~~   even though   because   after   when   if

EXAMPLE: I am not athletic. I love football.

Although I am not athletic, I love football.

1. Professional football players can achieve fame and fortune. Many students want to play the sport.

2. Football is a great sport. It has some drawbacks.

3. Linebackers hit other players. They can develop head injuries.

4. Players have concussions. They should receive proper medical care.

5. Professional football players retire. Some have long-term health problems.

LO 3 Use relative pronouns.

Use Relative Pronouns

A **relative pronoun** describes a noun or pronoun. You can form complex sentences by using relative pronouns to introduce dependent clauses. Review the most common relative pronouns.

who   whom   whomever   whose   which   that

That

Use *that* to add information about a thing. Do not use commas to set off clauses that begin with *that*.

> In 1947, Jackie Robinson joined a baseball team **that** was located in Brooklyn.

Which

Use *which* to add nonessential information about a thing. Generally, use commas to set off clauses that begin with *which*.

> Football, **which** was segregated in 1945, included African-American players the following year.

Who

Use *who* (*whom, whomever, whose*) to add information about a person. When a clause begins with *who*, you may or may not need a comma. Put commas around the clause if it adds nonessential information. If the clause is essential to the meaning of the sentence, do not add commas. To decide if a clause is essential or not, ask yourself if the sentence still makes sense without the *who* clause. If it does, the clause is not essential.

> Most women **who** play sports do not earn as much money as their male counterparts.
> (The clause is essential. The sentence would not make sense without the *who* clause.)

> Tennis player Serena Williams, **who** has won many tournaments, earns millions of dollars in endorsement deals.
> (The clause is not essential.)

HINT ◂ Using *That* or *Which*

Both *which* and *that* refer to things, but *which* refers to nonessential ideas. Also, *which* can imply that you are referring to the complete subject and not just a part of it. Compare the next two sentences.

> Local baseball teams that have very little funding can still succeed.
> (This sentence suggests that some teams have good funding, but others don't.)

> Local baseball teams, **which** have very little funding, can still succeed.
> (This sentence suggests that all of the teams have poor funding.)

GRAMMAR LINK
For more information about punctuating relative clauses, refer to Chapter 34, "Commas."

PRACTICE 6

Using a relative pronoun, combine each pair of sentences to form a complex sentence.

EXAMPLE: The cheerleaders do complex routines. The routines can lead to injuries.
> *Cheerleaders do complex routines that can lead to injuries.*

1. In the past, cheerleading was often a popularity contest. It attracted the best-looking girls.

   _____

   _____

2. These days, it is a legitimate sport. It involves complex acrobatic stunts.

_____

_____

3. Young men and women become cheerleaders. They must be as flexible as gymnasts.

_____

_____

4. Tiara has leadership qualities. She is the captain of the squad.

_____

_____

5. Halftime shows last for fifteen minutes. They feature fabulous stunts.

_____

_____

PRACTICE 7

Add a dependent clause to each sentence. Begin each clause with a relative pronoun (*who, which,* or *that*). Add any necessary commas.

EXAMPLE: Teams _that have good leadership_ often win tournaments.

1. The player _____ might be hired to promote running shoes.

2. An athlete _____ should be suspended for at least one game.

3. Bungee jumping is an activity _____

4. Skydiving _____ is a sport I would like to try.

5. Athletes _____ should be warned about the dangers of steroids.

LO 4 Use embedded questions.

Use Embedded Questions

It is possible to combine a question with a statement or to combine two questions. An **embedded question** is a question that is set within a larger sentence.

Question	How old are the Olympic Games?
Embedded question	The sprinter wonders <u>how old the Olympic Games are</u>.

Embedded questions do not require the usual question word order, added helping verbs, or in some cases, even question marks. As you read the following examples, pay attention to the word order in the embedded questions.

Combine two questions.

Separate	Do you know the answer? Why **do** they like bullfighting?
	(The second question includes the helping verb *do*.)
Combined	Do you know <u>why they like bullfighting</u>?
	(The helping verb *do* is removed from the embedded question.)

Combine a question and a statement.

Separate	I wonder about it. When **should** we go to the arena?
	(In the question, the helping verb *should* appears before the subject.)
Combined	I wonder <u>when we should go to the arena</u>.
	(In the embedded question, *should* is placed after the subject.)

HINT ◄ **Use the Correct Word Order**

When you edit your writing, make sure that you have formed your embedded questions properly. Remove question form structures from the embedded questions.

He wonders why ~~do~~ people like bullfighting. I asked him what ~~did he think~~ *he thought*
about the sport.

PRACTICE 8

Correct eight embedded question errors, and modify verbs when necessary.

EXAMPLE: Have you seen what ~~is~~ the latest sport *is*?

1. In 1998, J.K. Rowling released the first Harry Potter novel. In the book, young
    wizards play a game. Do you know what is the sport? It is called Quidditch.
    Wizards fly on broomsticks and attempt to score points by putting a "Quaffle"
    ball through hoops. In 2007, reporters were amazed to learn what have some
    students done. College students on more than two hundred American campuses
    have replicated the fictional sport.

2. Of course, many people wonder how can humans play
    Quidditch. Real-life players run holding a broomstick. Do
    you know what does a Quidditch "pitch" look like? On college
    campuses, Quidditch matches are played on grass fields, and
    there are three hooped goal posts on both ends of the field. In
    the Harry Potter novels, a "Snitch" is a golden ball with wings.

    Guess what do human Quidditch players do. At each game, a neutral player dresses
    in gold and tries to evade capture. Fans love to see how do players catch the snitch.

3.   There have been Quidditch matches in countries around the world. There is even a Quidditch World Cup. Do you know where was last year's Quidditch World Cup? Last year, Randall, New York, hosted about one hundred Quidditch teams from around the world. I wonder when will I see a Quidditch game.

Reflect On It

Think about what you have learned in this chapter. If you do not know an answer, then review that concept.

1. Write six subordinating conjunctions. _____

    _____

2. Write a complex sentence. _____

    _____

3. List six relative pronouns. _____

4. Correct the error in the following sentence.

    Clayton wonders why should he wear a helmet when he goes skateboarding.

FINAL REVIEW

The following paragraphs contain only simple sentences. To give the paragraphs more variety, form at least ten complex sentences by combining pairs of sentences. You will have to add some words and delete others.

                                  When people   *, they*
EXAMPLE: ~~People~~ pierce their tongues. ~~They~~ risk getting an infection.

1.   Many activity fads come and go. Many of these fads are ridiculous. Why do fads become so popular? Nobody knows the answer. There were some unusual fads in the 1960s. Hula hoops hit the market. Millions of people bought and used the circular plastic tubes. The hula hoop fad did not last long. It briefly provided people with an innovative way to exercise. People put the hoops around their waists. They would gyrate to keep the hoops spinning. In the spring of 1974, a streaking fad began. It occurred on college campuses in Florida and California. Young people stripped naked. They may have felt embarrassed. They ran through public places such as football stadiums and malls.

2. Fads are not always the same around the world. Some Japanese parks and spas have amusement baths. People wear bathing suits. They jump into a large round tub filled with noodles. The bathtub looks like a giant soup bowl. New Zealanders have a zorbing craze. A zorb looks like a giant hamster ball. It is very safe. Someone climbs inside the transparent ball. He or she rolls down a hill.

3. Today, many people want to exercise. They do not want to leave their homes. Luckily, video games no longer encourage lethargy. Companies have produced active games. The games force participants to move vigorously. Children play Dance Dance Revolution. They burn three times more calories than those who use traditional hand-held games. Even adults buy the games. They can play tennis or football in their living rooms. Do you know the answer to the following question? Why do adults love active video games? The reasons are simple. The games are entertaining and provide some exercise.

THE WRITER'S ROOM   MyWritingLab™

MyWritingLab™
Complete these writing assignments at mywritinglab.com

Write about one of the following topics. Include some complex sentences.

1. Think about a sport that you really enjoy and a sport that you dislike. Compare and contrast the two sports.

2. What causes children to love or hate gym class in grade school?

19 Sentence Variety

SECTION THEME: Popular Culture

LEARNING OBJECTIVES

LO 1 Define sentence variety. **(p. 286)**

LO 2 Combine sentences. **(p. 287)**

LO 3 Include a question, a quotation, or an exclamation. **(p. 288)**

LO 4 Vary the opening words. **(p. 289)**

LO 5 Combine sentences with a present participle. **(p. 290)**

LO 6 Combine sentences with a past participle. **(p. 291)**

LO 7 Combine sentences with an appositive. **(p. 293)**

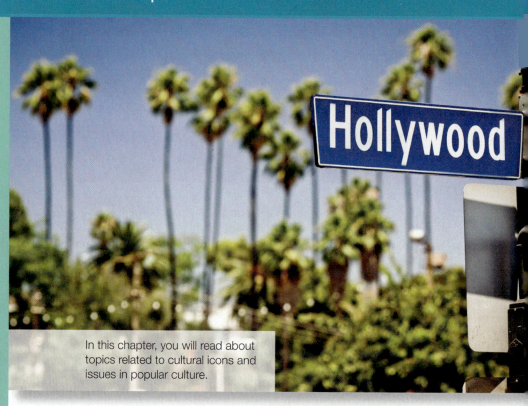

In this chapter, you will read about topics related to cultural icons and issues in popular culture.

MyWritingLab™

Complete this Writer's Journal activity at mywritinglab.com

THE WRITER'S JOURNAL

Would you like to be famous? What are some problems that could be associated with fame? Write a paragraph about fame.

LO 1 Define sentence variety.

What Is Sentence Variety?

In Chapters 17 and 18, you learned how to write different types of sentences. This chapter focuses on sentence variety. **Sentence variety** means that your sentences have assorted patterns and lengths. In this chapter, you will learn to vary your sentences by consciously considering the length of sentences, by altering the opening words, and by joining sentences using different methods.

Combine Sentences

LO 2 Combine sentences.

A passage filled with simple, short sentences can sound choppy. When you vary the lengths of your sentences, the same passage becomes easier to read and flows more smoothly. For example, read the following two passages about social networking and relationships. In the first paragraph, most of the sentences are short, and the style is repetitive and boring. In the second paragraph, there is a mixture of simple, compound, and complex sentences.

GRAMMAR LINK
If you forget what compound and complex sentences are, refer to Chapters 17 and 18.

Simple Sentences

Many people are becoming disillusioned with social networking. They feel frustrated about the time wasted online. They may have hundreds of cyber contacts. Most are not real friends. For instance, Hal Niedzviecki is a writer. He invited his six hundred Facebook "friends" to a gathering. About thirty responded. Only one person came. He was quite upset. At the same time, the incident was revealing. People want connections with others. They don't want to work at those relationships.

Simple, Compound, and Complex Sentences

Feeling frustrated about the time wasted online, many people are becoming disillusioned with social networking. They may have hundreds of cyber contacts, but most are not real friends. For instance, Hal Niedzviecki, a writer, invited his six hundred Facebook "friends" to a gathering; about thirty responded. Only one person came, so he was quite upset. At the same time, the incident was revealing. Although people want connections with others, they don't want to work at those relationships.

HINT **Be Careful with Long Sentences**

If a sentence is too long, it may be difficult for the reader to understand. If you have any doubts, break up a longer sentence into shorter ones.

Long and complicated	Elvis Presley is a cultural icon who achieved the American dream by using his musical skills to transform himself from a truck driver into a rock-and-roll legend, yet he did not handle his fame very well, and by the end of his life, he was unhappy and addicted to painkillers.
Better	Elvis Presley is a cultural icon who achieved the American dream. Using his musical skills, he transformed himself from a truck driver into a rock-and-roll legend. However, he did not handle his fame very well. By the end of his life, he was unhappy and addicted to painkillers.

PRACTICE 1

Modify the following paragraph so that it has both long and short sentences. Make sure you write some compound and complex sentences.

A cultural icon can be an object, a person, or a place. Cultural icons symbolize a belief or a way of life. Each country has its own icons. They become part of the country's history. For example, Mickey Mouse is more than eighty years old. The cartoon character symbolizes American optimism. The Statue of Liberty is also a potent symbol. It represents America's willingness to welcome immigrants. People can be icons, too. Benito Juarez is celebrated in Mexico. Martin Luther King Jr. is idolized in the United States. These icons reflect shared cultural experiences.

Include a Question, a Quotation, or an Exclamation

LO 3 Include a question, a quotation, or an exclamation.

The most common type of sentence is a statement. A simple but effective way to achieve sentence variety is to do the following:

◆ Ask and answer a **question**. You could also insert a **rhetorical question**, which does not require an answer but is used for effect.

> Did Elvis really do anything shocking**?**

◆ Include the occasional **exclamation** to express surprise. However, do not overuse exclamations, especially in academic writing.

> Elvis's swinging hips were considered obscene**!**

◆ Add a **direct quotation**, which includes the exact words that somebody said.

> Elvis said, "I didn't copy my style from anybody."

In the next passage, a question, an exclamation, and a quotation add variety.

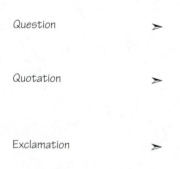

Question ➤

Quotation ➤

Exclamation ➤

> Some divorce attorneys are pleased with the massive expansion of Facebook. **Why are they so happy?** Social networking sites have contributed to marital breakups. **According to Tom Johansmeyer, in an article for *Daily Finance*, "More and more divorce petitions are mentioning Facebook and similar tools as contributing factors."** In the past, people could spend weeks or months tracking down old flames, and communication was difficult, with long-distance phone bills leaving telltale evidence. **These days, with a click of the mouse, a man can find his high school sweetheart in minutes!** Those flirty exchanges, however, can provide clear evidence in a court of law.

HINT ‹ **Punctuating Quotations**

If you introduce your quotation with a phrase like "he said," put a comma after the phrase and before the opening quotation marks. Put the final period inside the closing quotation marks.

> Marilyn Monroe once complained**,** "Everybody is always tugging at you**."**

If the end of the quotation is not the end of the sentence, place a comma inside the final quotation mark.

> "They were terribly strict**,"** she once said.

PRACTICE 2

Read the following passage. Change one sentence to a question, one to an exclamation, and one to a quotation.

GRAMMAR LINK
For more information about punctuating quotations, refer to Chapter 35.

Chapter 19

EXAMPLE: ~~Most~~ people want to be famous/

Why do most *?*

We are living in a celebrity era. Many ordinary people achieve almost saintly status. In previous centuries, heroes were those who fought bravely in wars or who rescued others. Today, actors, musicians, politicians, and athletes are routinely deified. Even criminals such as Al Capone and Charles Manson become household names. In the words of Daniel J. Boorstin, celebrity worship and hero worship should not be confused. However, we confuse them every day.

Vary the Opening Words

LO 4 Vary the opening words.

An effective way to make your sentences more vivid is to vary the opening words. Instead of beginning each sentence with the subject, you could try the following strategies.

Begin with an Adverb

An **adverb** is a word that modifies a verb, and it often (but not always) ends in *-ly*. *Slowly, usually*, and *suddenly* are adverbs. Other adverbs include words such as *sometimes, never, however*, and *often*.

 <u>Generally</u>, a cultural icon arouses strong feelings in members of that culture.

 <u>Often</u>, an extremely gifted and famous person becomes an icon.

Begin with a Prepositional Phrase

A **prepositional phrase** is a group of words made up of a preposition and its object. *Under the chair, in the beginning*, and *after the fall* are prepositional phrases.

 <u>In New York's harbor</u>, the Statue of Liberty welcomes visitors.

 <u>At dawn</u>, we photographed the statue.

HINT ◄ **Comma Tip**

Generally, when a sentence begins with an adverb or a prepositional phrase, place a comma after the opening word or phrase.

 Cautiously, the reporter asked another question to the volatile star.

 Without any warning, she stood up and left the room.

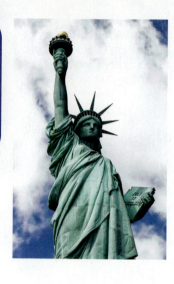

PRACTICE 3

Rewrite the following sentences by placing an adverb or prepositional phrase at the beginning. First, strike out any word or phrase that could be moved. Then, rewrite that word or phrase at the beginning of the sentence. Finally, correctly punctuate your new sentence.

EXAMPLE: _Actually, the_ ~~The~~ United States' most recognizable symbol was ~~actually~~ made in France.

1. _____ A group of French intellectuals, in 1865, met in a restaurant and discussed the United States.

2. _____ The French artists and thinkers carefully criticized their oppressive emperor, Napoleon III.

3. _____ They then expressed in quiet voices admiration for America's new democratic government.

4. _____ A sculptor suddenly decided to create a gift for the United States.

5. _____ Frédéric Auguste Bartholdi searched for a site to place his sculpture during a visit to the United States.

6. _____ He crafted Lady Liberty with the help of many workers.

PRACTICE 4

Add an opening word or phrase to each sentence. Use the type of opening that is indicated in parentheses. Remember to punctuate the sentence properly.

EXAMPLE: (Adverb) _Surprisingly,_ the playwright Naomi Iizuka loves the 50-foot Hollywood sign.

1. (Adverb) _____ the sign is more than just white letters that spell "Hollywood."

2. (Prepositional phrase) _____ the sign is like a beacon to aspiring actors.

3. (Prepositional phrase) _____ thousands of people arrive with dreams of stardom.

4. (Adverb) _____ some people find acting jobs, but many do not.

5. (Prepositional phrase) _____ the sign is an important American symbol.

L05 Combine sentences with a present participle.

Combine Sentences with a Present Participle

You can combine two sentences with a present participle. A **present participle** is a verb that ends in *-ing*, such as *believing, having,* and *using.* Combine sentences using an *-ing* modifier only when the two actions happen at the same time and the sentences have the same subject.

Separate sentences	He looked across the harbor. He saw the Statue of Liberty.
Combined sentences	<u>Looking</u> across the harbor, he saw the Statue of Liberty.

PRACTICE 5

Combine the next sentences by converting one of the verbs into an *-ing* modifier.

EXAMPLE: Pop artists focused on familiar images. They painted comic strips and supermarket products.

<u>Focusing on familiar images, pop artists painted comic strips</u>

<u>and supermarket products.</u>

1. Andy Warhol worked as an illustrator. He drew footwear for a shoe company.

   _____

   _____

2. He desired respect. He wanted his work to be in art galleries.

   _____

   _____

3. One gallery owner rejected Warhol's art. She wanted original ideas.

   _____

   _____

4. Warhol felt inspired. He decided to create pop art.

   _____

   _____

5. Warhol needed an original idea. He focused on his favorite brands.

   _____

   _____

6. He reproduced soup cans and Coke bottles. He attracted a lot of attention.

   _____

   _____

Combine Sentences with a Past Participle

LO 6 Combine sentences with a past participle.

Another way to combine sentences is to use a past participle. A **past participle** is a verb that has an *-ed* ending (although there are many irregular past participles, such as *gone, seen, broken,* and *known*).

GRAMMAR LINK
For a complete list of irregular past participles, see Appendix 2.

You can begin a sentence with a past participle. To do this, you must combine two sentences that have the same subject, and one of the sentences must contain a past participle.

Separate sentences	Roma is influenced by Kim Kardashian. Roma desires luxurious items.
Combined sentences	<u>Influenced by Kim Kardashian</u>, Roma desires luxurious items.

PRACTICE 6

Combine each pair of sentences into one sentence beginning with a past participle.

EXAMPLE: Kim Kardashian was encouraged by Paris Hilton in 2007. Kim decided to star in a reality show.

   Encouraged by Paris Hilton in 2007, Kim Kardashian decided to star in a reality show.

1. The Kardashians have been followed by cameras since 2007. They have exposed their lavish lifestyle.

_____

_____

2. The show is condemned by many critics. The show glamorizes greed.

_____

_____

3. The Kardashian sisters are also criticized for their weight and curves. They respond with laughter.

_____

_____

4. The sisters were frustrated by the negative comments. They express disinterest in being size zeros.

_____

_____

5. Roma Winters is surprised by the criticism of the show. She looks up to the Kardashians.

_____

_____

6. Women are held to impossible weight standards. Some women feel better about having curves after seeing the show.

_____

_____

Combine Sentences with an Appositive

An **appositive** is a word or phrase that gives further information about a noun or pronoun. You can combine two sentences by using an appositive. In the example, the italicized phrase could become an appositive because it describes the noun *Bob Marley*.

Two sentences   Bob Marley was *a founding member of The Wailers*. He went on to have a solo career.

You can place the appositive directly before the word that it refers to or directly after that word. Notice that the appositives are set off with commas.

                                                   appositive

Combined   A founding member of The Wailers, **Bob Marley** went on to have a successful solo career.

                                                   appositive

Combined   **Bob Marley**, a founding member of The Wailers, went on to have a successful solo career.

HINT ◄ **Finding an Appositive**

To find an appositive, look for a word or phrase that describes or renames a noun. The noun could be anywhere in the sentence.

    Bob Marley popularized a new fashion trend. He wore dreadlocks.

In the preceding sentences, "dreadlocks" describes the new fashion trend. You could combine the sentences as follows:

                                            appositive

    Bob Marley popularized **a new fashion trend**, dreadlocks.

PRACTICE 7

Combine the following pairs of sentences. In each pair, make one of the sentences an appositive. Try to vary the position of the appositive. In some sentences, you could put the appositive at the beginning of the sentence, and in others, you could put the appositive after the word that it describes.

EXAMPLE: Bob Marley was a Jamaican. He greatly popularized reggae music.

    Bob Marley, a Jamaican, greatly popularized reggae music.

1. Bob Marley brought international attention to reggae music. He was a great musician.

    _____

    _____

2. Marley was biracial. He was born in 1945 in Jamaica.

    _____

    _____

3. Marley's father was a sailor. His father died when Marley was young.

   _____

   _____

4. At the age of 14, Marley jammed with Joe Higgs. Higgs was a Rastafarian and reggae musician.

   _____

   _____

5. Jamaicans loved the reggae sound of Bob Marley and the Wailers. The group was one of the most famous bands in the country.

   _____

   _____

6. Bob Marley has had a profound influence on contemporary music. Marley is a music icon.

   _____

   _____

Reflect On It

Think about what you have learned in this unit. If you do not know an answer, review that topic.

1. Why is sentence variety important? _____

   _____

2. Write a sentence that begins with an adverb. _____

   _____

3. Write a sentence that begins with a present participle. _____

   _____

4. Write a sentence that begins with a past participle. _____

   _____

5. Write a sentence that begins with an appositive. _____

   _____

FINAL REVIEW

The next essay lacks sentence variety. Use the strategies that you have learned in this and in previous chapters to create up to fifteen varied sentences.

EXAMPLE: People are obsessed with fame. ~~Perhaps they believe~~ , believing that fame will make them immortal.

1.   In 2008, Hal Niedzviecki was a writer. He was fascinated with online blogs, videos, and social media networks. He wondered why so many people share their private thoughts with strangers. To find the answers, he did a lot of research. He wrote a book called *The Peep Diaries*. His book was about the shocking amount of oversharing online. Millions of people use Twitter, YouTube, Facebook, and personal blogs. They become stars in their own lives. The book made Niedzviecki a minor celebrity after it was selected by Oprah Winfrey's magazine *O* as a "must-read" book in 2009.

2.   Filmmakers Sally Blake and Jeannette Loakman heard about the book. They approached Neidzviecki about a documentary project. He agreed to embark on an interesting experiment. He allowed cameras to film him 24 hours a day. During the documentary, he met with some colorful characters. For example, he met Cork. Cork was a man in his early thirties. Cork lived alone. Cork's home was filled with cameras. Cork's home was like a studio. His every move was watched by thousands of followers. Neidzviecki also met with a pilot and with a gastric bypass patient.

3.   At first, Niedzviecki felt uncomfortable with the cameras in his home. He hid upstairs. He quickly began to love the attention from the followers of his video blog. Sometimes he said or did embarrassing things. Then he would run to his computer to see how his online audience reacted. He was treated like a mini celebrity. He felt intoxicated with power.

4.   Niedzviecki ultimately sees a downside to peep culture. He is concerned about possible abuses. He warns parents to teach their children about proper boundaries. If we have an audience, it does not make our lives better or more valuable. According to Niedzviecki, the life lived in privacy is just as important as the one lived in front of millions.

MyWritingLab™
**Complete these
writing assignments at
mywritinglab.com**

Chapter 19

MyWritingLab™

THE WRITER'S ROOM

Choose one of the following topics, and write a paragraph or an essay. When you write, remember to follow the writing process.

1. Define *hero*. What makes a person a hero?

2. Why do so many people crave fame? How does celebrity status affect people? Write about the causes or effects of fame.

THE WRITER'S CIRCLE Collaborative Activity

Get into a group of three or four students. Then think about songs that you really love. Each person in your team should contribute five song titles to the list.

Using the titles as inspiration, write a paragraph. Add words and sentences to make your paragraph complete. Your paragraph should have at least one simple sentence, one compound sentence, and one complex sentence. Also, vary the beginnings of sentences, ensuring that one sentence begins with a present participle and one begins with a past participle.

Fragments 20

SECTION THEME: Psychology

LEARNING OBJECTIVE

LO 1 Identify fragments.
(p. 298)

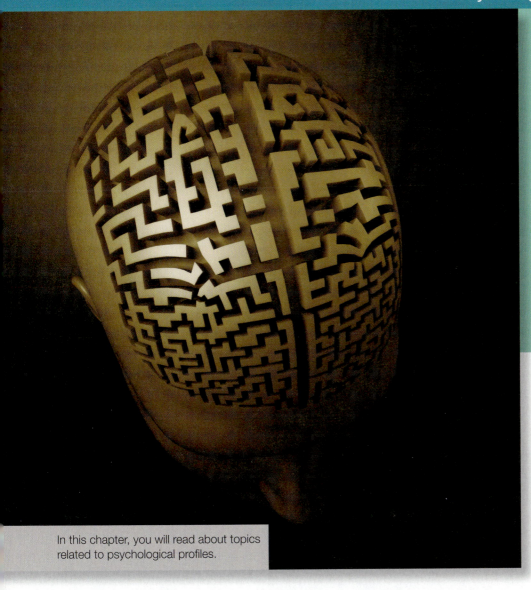

In this chapter, you will read about topics related to psychological profiles.

THE WRITER'S JOURNAL

How do men and women deal with personal problems? Do they use different strategies? Write about problem-solving techniques that men and women use.

MyWritingLab™

Complete this Writer's Journal activity at mywritinglab.com

LO 1 Identify fragments.

Fragments

A **sentence** must have a subject and a verb, and it must express a complete thought. A **fragment** is an incomplete sentence. Either it lacks a subject or a verb, or it fails to express a complete thought. You may see fragments in newspaper headlines and advertisements (*Wrinkle-free skin in one month*). However, in college writing, it is unacceptable to write fragments.

Sentence	Sigmund Freud was a famous psychologist.
Fragment	Considered to be the founder of psychoanalysis.

Phrase Fragments

A phrase fragment is missing a subject or a verb. In the following examples, the fragments are underlined.

No verb	First, B. F. Skinner. He did research on human behavior.
No subject	B. F. Skinner wrote a novel about human behavior. Called *Walden Two*.

How to Correct Phrase Fragments

To correct a phrase fragment, either add the missing subject or verb, or join the fragment to another sentence. Here are two ways you can correct the phrase fragments in the previous examples.

Join sentences	First, B. F. Skinner did research on human behavior.
Add words	B. F. Skinner wrote a novel about human behavior. It was called *Walden Two*.

HINT ◀ **Incomplete Verbs**

A sentence must have a subject and a complete verb. If a sentence has an incomplete verb, it is a phrase fragment. The following example contains a subject and part of a verb. However, it is missing a helping verb; therefore, the sentence is incomplete.

Fragment	Many books about psychology written by Carl Jung.

To make this sentence complete, you must add the helping verb.

Sentence	Many books about psychology were written by Carl Jung.

PRACTICE 1

Underline and correct six phrase fragments.

EXAMPLE: Studies show that people become happier. ~~By~~ doing selfless acts.
_{by}

1. Happiness. It means different things to different people. Psychologists, biologists, and philosophers reflect on happiness. Religious philosophers give advice. On how to achieve happiness. But what is happiness?

2.   Most people know when they are happy. Or unhappy. Happiness is a state of

mind. Statistics. They show that people need a threshold of money to achieve

a basic level of happiness. However, after the threshold has been reached,

acquiring more wealth does not increase a person's level of happiness. Happy

people spend time with family. And friends. They are often engaged in a

pastime. Or volunteer work. Happy people are often very generous hearted.

Fragments with *-ing* and *to*

A fragment may begin with a **present participle**, which is the form of the verb that ends in *-ing* (*running, talking*). It may also begin with an **infinitive**, which is *to* plus the base form of the verb (*to run, to talk*). These fragments generally appear before or after another sentence that contains the subject. In the examples, the fragments are underlined.

-ing **fragment**	<u>Thinking about positive outcomes.</u> It helps people cope with stress.
to **fragment**	Oprah Winfrey has developed a resilient attitude. <u>To overcome her childhood traumas.</u>

How to Correct *-ing* and *to* Fragments

To correct an *-ing* or *to* fragment, either add the missing words or join the fragment to another sentence. Here are two ways to correct the previous examples.

Join sentences	Thinking about positive outcomes helps people cope with stress.
Add words	Oprah Winfrey has developed a resilient attitude **because she had** to overcome her childhood traumas.

HINT   **When the *-ing* Word Is the Subject**

Sometimes a gerund (*-ing* form of the verb) is the subject of a sentence. In the next example, *listening* is the subject of the sentence.

Correct	<u>Listening</u> is an important skill.

A sentence fragment occurs when the *-ing* word is part of an incomplete verb string or when the subject was mentioned in a previous sentence.

Fragment	Dr. Phil has achieved success. <u>Listening to people's problems.</u>

PRACTICE 2

Underline and correct six *-ing* and *to* fragments.

EXAMPLE: Many schools help students. ~~To~~ ^{to} deal with bullies.

    Bullying is getting a lot of attention in society. Bullying is abusive behavior. To

acquire power over someone. Using methods of intimidation. Bullies can control their victims. Psychologists study cases of bullying. To discover the causes and effects of such conduct. Studying the link between bullying and school violence. Researchers have found that two-thirds of students say they have been victims of bullies. Furthermore, studies have shown that 60 percent of identified male student bullies were convicted of a crime by age twenty-four. Recognizing the harmful effects of bullying. School administrators and teachers are implementing anti-bullying programs. People need to make great efforts. To reduce bullying in all areas of society.

Explanatory Fragments

An **explanatory fragment** provides an explanation about a previous sentence and is missing a subject, a complete verb, or both. Such fragments are sometimes expressed as an afterthought. These types of fragments begin with one of the following words.

also	especially	for example	including	particularly
as well as	except	for instance	like	such as

In each example, the explanatory fragment is underlined.

Fragment   Carl Jung studied with many prominent psychologists. <u>For instance, Sigmund Freud.</u>

Fragment   Psychologists analyze behavior. <u>Particularly through methods of observation.</u>

How to Correct Explanatory Fragments

To correct explanatory fragments, add the missing words, or join the explanation or example to another sentence. Here are two ways to correct the fragments in the previous examples.

Add words   Carl Jung studied with many prominent psychologists. For instance, **he worked with** Sigmund Freud.

Join sentences   Psychologists analyze behavior, particularly through methods of observation.

PRACTICE 3

Underline and correct six explanatory fragments. You may need to add or remove words.

EXAMPLE: Some fans are very loyal. ~~Especially~~ Red Sox fans.
loyal, especially

Stephen Dubner wrote *Confessions of a Hero-Worshipper*. He describes the personality of sports fans, and his book has interesting anecdotes. For example, the 1994 World Cup. The saliva of male soccer fans was tested before and after an

important match. The chosen fans were from Brazil. As well as Italy. The testosterone levels in the fans of the winning team rose quickly. Particularly during the final minutes of the game. The losing fans' testosterone levels decreased. Researcher Paul Bernhardt was surprised. Especially by the percentages. The fans of the winning team, with a 20 percent increase, had the same level of testosterone as the athletes. The findings may explain aggressive episodes. Such as soccer hooliganism. Immediately after a testosterone surge, some males may act more aggressively. Especially when provoked.

Dependent-Clause Fragments

A **dependent clause** has a subject and a verb, but it cannot stand alone. It *depends* on another clause to be a complete sentence. Dependent clauses may begin with subordinating conjunctions (subordinators) or relative pronouns. The following are some of the most common words that begin dependent clauses.

Common Subordinating Conjunctions				Relative Pronouns
after	before	though	whenever	that
although	even though	unless	where	which
as	if	until	whereas	who(m)
because	since	what	whether	whose

The next two examples contain dependent-clause fragments. In each example, the fragment is underlined.

Fragment	<u>Although I cross my fingers for luck.</u> I know that it is a silly superstition.
Fragment	I will not walk under a ladder. <u>That is leaning against a wall.</u>

How to Correct Dependent-Clause Fragments

To correct dependent-clause fragments, either join the fragment to a complete sentence or add the necessary words to make it a complete idea. You could also delete the subordinating conjunction. Here are two ways to correct the fragments in the previous examples.

Delete the subordinator	I cross my fingers for luck. I know that it is a silly superstition.
Join sentences	Although I cross my fingers for luck, I know that it is a silly superstition. I will not walk under a ladder that is leaning against a wall.

Chapter 20

PRACTICE 4

Underline and correct five dependent-clause fragments.

EXAMPLE: Whenever they blame themselves. ~~Negative~~ thinkers make their
              problems larger.

    , negative

1.   Andrew Shatte is a University of Pennsylvania researcher. Who worked on
the Resiliency Project. For the project, graduate psychology students taught
seventy children. That they can become more resilient. Children learned the
difference between productive and self-defeating thinking. After they looked
at their own fears. The children had to test their expectations to see if they
were realistic.

2.   One child in the program who came from a tough inner-city neighborhood
had convinced himself that he would probably end up in a gang. Even
though he hated violence. The program taught this boy. That there are other
possible outcomes. He learned that he did not have to focus on worst-case
scenarios.

Reflect On It

Think about what you have learned in this unit. If you do not know an answer,
review that concept.

1. What is a sentence fragment? _____
_____

2. What are the types of fragments?
_____
_____

3. Correct the next fragment.

    According to Freud, people unintentionally repress certain memories. Because
they are painful or threatening.

FINAL REVIEW

Correct fifteen fragment errors.

EXAMPLE: Humans rely on memory. ~~To~~ *to* perform any action.

1.   Have you ever forgotten a telephone number? That you have just looked up. Forgetting an item of information. It happens to all of us. Memory is an intriguing process. Psychologists identify three types of memory. First, sensory memory. It refers to the initial perception of information. The second kind of memory is short-term memory. By rehearsing, we can transfer information from our sensory memory to our short-term memory. Researchers have discovered that we can hold about seven pieces of information in our short-term memory. But only for about 30 seconds. We store information in our long-term memory. Through chemical changes in our brain.

2.   As we age, our memory decays. However, there are techniques that we can attempt. To help our memory. We can remember information more easily. Using mnemonics. One mnemonic device employs rhymes. A familiar example is the rule *i* before *e* except after *c*. Which helps us with our spelling. Another mnemonic technique is the acronym. An acronym uses the first letters of a series of words. Such as FBI (Federal Bureau of Investigation). A third type of mnemonic device is called the peg system. Alphabet books. They generally use the peg system when they teach *A for apple*, *B for ball*, and so on.

3.   A very effective memory device is called the SQ4R. According to psychologists. SQ4R (pronounced "square") is an acronym for a study strategy: Survey, Question, Read, Reflect, Recite, and Review. Researchers believe that this system is very useful for students. Who need to remember large amounts of information. By following the SQ4R method, students may have more success at retaining information. Especially when they study for exams.

4. Finally, we must practice organizing and rehearsing information. Because we cannot develop a good memory by being passive. We should use mnemonic devices. When we need to remember a phone number or another item of information.

MyWritingLab™
Complete these
writing assignments at
mywritinglab.com

MyWritingLab™
THE WRITER'S ROOM

Write about one of the following topics. Check that there are no sentence fragments.

1. Explain why people are superstitious, and give examples to support your point of view.

2. Look again at Practice 2. Have you ever been bullied, bullied someone else, or witnessed bullying? Describe your experience.

Run-Ons 21

SECTION THEME: Psychology

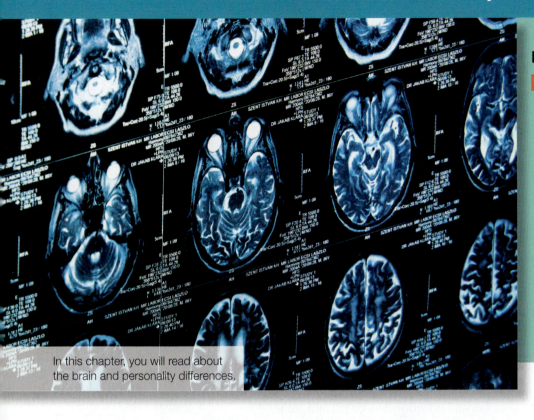

In this chapter, you will read about the brain and personality differences.

LEARNING OBJECTIVE

LO 1 Identify and correct run-ons. **(p. 305)**

MyWritingLab™

Complete this Writer's Journal activity at mywritinglab.com

THE WRITER'S JOURNAL

Do you have any good habits? In a paragraph, describe your good habits. Why do you think they are positive?

Run-Ons

LO 1 Identify and correct run-ons.

A **run-on sentence** occurs when two or more complete sentences are incorrectly joined. In other words, the sentence runs on without stopping. There are two types of run-on sentences.

♦ A **fused sentence** has no punctuation to mark the break between ideas.

| Incorrect | Psychologists describe human behavior they use observational methods. |

♦ A **comma splice** uses a comma incorrectly to connect two complete ideas.

| Incorrect | Wilhelm Wundt was born in 1832, he is often called the founder of modern psychology. |

305

PRACTICE 1

Read the following sentences. Write *C* beside correct sentences and *RO* beside run-ons.

EXAMPLE: Sigmund Freud and Carl Jung were two famous psychologists they profoundly influenced the field of psychology.   *RO*

1. Psychologists study human behavior, researchers have developed many theories on human nature.   _____

2. Instinct theory is one model developed by psychologists it proposes that behavior is based on biology.   _____

3. Learning theory suggests that humans learn through experience.   _____

4. Trait theories focus on human characteristics, psychologists describe personality types.   _____

5. Freud developed a theory about personality in which he divided the mind into three parts.   _____

6. Freud named the parts the *id*, *ego*, and *superego* his theory became enormously influential.   _____

7. Psychoanalysis started to lose its popularity by the 1940s, at that time other personality theories were developing.   _____

8. One psychologist, William Sheldon, tried to connect personality to body shapes.   _____

9. Sheldon's types were mesomorphic, or lean; endomorphic, or fat; and ectomorphic, or tall and thin.   _____

10. Human personalities vary greatly it is difficult to categorize them.   _____

How to Correct Run-Ons

You can correct run-on sentences in a variety of ways. Read the following run-on sentence, and then review the four ways to correct it.

Run-On   His parents were Jewish, Freud didn't believe in God.

1. **Make two separate sentences.**   His parents were Jewish. Freud didn't believe in God.

2. **Add a semicolon.**   His parents were Jewish; Freud didn't believe in God.

3. **Add a coordinator.**   His parents were Jewish, **but** Freud didn't believe in God.
   (*for, and, nor, but, or, yet, so*)

4. **Add a subordinator**   **Although** his parents were Jewish, Freud didn't believe in God.
   (*after, although, as, because, before, since, when, while*)

PRACTICE 2

A. Correct each run-on sentence by making two complete sentences.

EXAMPLE: Psychologists study children's behavior, they write articles about their findings.

(correction: period after "behavior" and "They" replacing "they")

1. Carolyn Weisz was a little girl, she attended the Bing Nursery School.

2. Carolyn went to the daycare everyday it was on the campus of Stanford University.

3. One day, Carolyn was asked to play in a small room it had a desk and a chair.

B. Correct each run-on by joining the two sentences with a semicolon.

EXAMPLE: Some children need few rules others need a firm hand.

(correction: semicolon after "rules")

4. Carolyn was told to sit at the desk, there was a plate full of marshmallows on the desk.

5. A young man told Carolyn that she could have one treat right away if she waited while the man was out of the room, Carolyn could have two treats when he returned.

6. Carolyn does not remember her reaction her mom thinks that Carolyn waited for the man's return.

C. Correct the next run-ons by joining the two sentences with a comma and a coordinator such as *for*, *and*, *nor*, *but*, *or*, *yet*, or *so*.

EXAMPLE: Most children want to be independent they also need specific rules.

(correction: ", but" after "independent")

7. The Stanford marshmallow experiment was initially meant to demonstrate how people delayed gratification the experiment showed some other surprising results.

8. Psychologist Walter Mischel became curious about the children in the study he asked his daughters, who knew and grew up with the test subjects, how their Bing Nursery School friends were doing.

9. Dr. Mischel noticed that those who waited to get two treats did well in life those who could not wait did less well.

D. Correct the next run-ons by joining the two sentences with a subordinator such as *although, even though, because, where, when,* and so on.

> When children
> **EXAMPLE:** ~~Children~~ receive praise, they are more cooperative.

10. Psychologist Terrie Moffitt did the same study in New Zealand she wanted to see if the marshmallow experiment could be replicated.

11. The children in both experiments wanted to eat the treat, the patient children could distract themselves in order to wait for two goodies.

12. These two experiments have astonishing results more studies have to be done on self-control.

PRACTICE 3

Some sentences are correct and some are run-ons. Write *C* beside each correct sentence and *RO* beside the run-ons. Using a variety of methods, correct each run-on error.

> , and
> **EXAMPLE:** There are many self-help books ^ some people read them for guidance when they are examining their lives.   RO

1. One of the first pop psychology columns was *Dear Abby*, it was a syndicated newspaper column containing common-sense advice to letter writers.   _____

2. Abby's real name was Pauline Phillips, she had a twin sister named Eppie Lederer.   _____

3. Eppie was also a newspaper columnist she wrote a similar advice column under the name Anne Landers.   _____

4. Another early self-help guru was L. Ron Hubbard he wrote *Dianetics: The Modern Science of Mental Health* about the relationship between the mind and the body.   _____

5. The book was successful, he started the Church of Scientology from the proceeds of the book sales.   _____

6. Oprah Winfrey, one of the most successful talk show hosts in history, made self-help books and gurus very popular with audiences.   _____

7. Dr. Phil McGraw attained celebrity status he appeared on Oprah's show.   _____

8. Pop psychology has been criticized for being overly simplistic,
   it sometimes helps people understand the causes of their behaviors. _____

9. However, because proper treatment for mental disorders is important,
   people who suffer from such conditions should see a qualified doctor. _____

PRACTICE 4

Correct twelve run-on errors.

EXAMPLE: About 3 percent of births in the United States are twins ^(, but) the percentage
is increasing.

1. Thomas Bouchard Jr. and some colleagues at the University of Minnesota
    began studying twins in 1979. Bouchard had read about twins who had been
    raised apart, he contacted them to study their similarities and differences. By
    1990, Bouchard's team had studied seventy-seven sets of identical twins.

2. Most of the separated twins had astounding similarities.
    For example, two men named Jim had been separated at
    birth. They met in 1979 they found that they were similar
    in many ways. They smoked the same brand of cigarettes,
    they were both volunteer firefighters. The Jims also enjoyed
    carpentry, they built similar white benches.

Jim Lewis and Jim Springer

3. In the study, one set of twins was unusual. Japanese-born
    twins were adopted by different families in California. They
    shared some similarities researchers were puzzled by their differences. One
    twin had 20/20 vision, the other wore glasses. One was afraid to travel by
    airplane the other had no such fear. One twin was quite timid, the other was
    easygoing and friendly.

4. Researchers suspect that the environment may play a role in twin differences.
    For example, one twin could be malnourished, the other could have a healthy
    diet. The differences in diet could affect the development of the twins' brains
    and bodies. Birthing problems may also result in differences between twins one
    twin might receive less oxygen during delivery.

5. The separated-twin studies suggest certain possibilities, for example, twins raised separately may be more similar than twins raised together. Twins raised together may emphasize their differences twins raised apart would have no need to search for their individuality. More research is needed to know how genes influence behavior.

Reflect On It

Think about what you have learned in this unit. If you do not know an answer, review that concept.

1. What is a run-on? ____
____
2. Define a comma splice. ____
____
3. Define a fused sentence. ____
____
4. Explain the four ways to correct a run-on sentence.
   a. ____
   b. ____
   c. ____
   d. ____

Final Review

Correct fifteen run-on errors.

EXAMPLE: The brain is an extremely complex organ~~, it~~ ; it is the center of the human nervous system.

1. The basis of human behavior is the human brain, if it malfunctions, people experience problems. Yet, researchers still have a lot to learn about the human brain.

2. In 1985, Dr. Oliver Sacks wrote a book called *The Man Who Mistook His Wife for a Hat*, he analyzed some interesting cases of patients who had exhibited puzzling behavior. One of Dr. Sacks's patients was a music teacher he had lost his ability to identify objects or people. This condition is known as agnosia, it

has many possible causes. For example, Anita Kaye was in a car accident. She was hurled out of the car, she experienced brain trauma. Now she no longer recognizes people, shapes, and objects. She can see a plate placed before her she cannot name it. If she wants something, she describes the object to a family member.

3.   Another interesting case concerned Mrs. O'C. She was old, she started to hear Irish music. She became Dr. Sacks's patient she wanted to stop hearing the music. Apparently, she was experiencing small epileptic seizures they triggered her brain to recall music from her childhood. Mrs. O'C was an orphan, the seizures may have released a desire to relive her childhood before her parents' death.

4.   A Russian composer had a similar experience. During World War II, a bomb exploded near Dmitri Shostakovich a small piece of metal lodged in his head. Years later, he consulted a Chinese neurologist, the composer wanted to know if the metal should be removed. Whenever he moved his head, the piece of metal shifted, and he would hear music. The doctor recommended leaving the metal in place, the bomb had actually done some good.

5.   The brain is a mysterious organ researchers are trying to understand it. According to neurologist Wilder Penfield, the brain is the organ of destiny, it holds secrets that will determine the future of the human race.

THE WRITER'S ROOM   MyWritingLab™

MyWritingLab™
Complete these
writing assignments at
mywritinglab.com

Write about one of the following topics. Make sure that you have not written any run-ons.

1. Narrate a story about one of your earliest memories.

2. Describe a set of twins. Compare and contrast twins by looking at their similarities and differences. If you don't know any twins, then describe the similarities and differences between siblings (brothers and sisters).

22 Faulty Parallel Structure

SECTION THEME: Psychology

LEARNING OBJECTIVES

LO 1 Define parallel structure. **(p. 312)**

LO 2 Identify faulty parallel structure. **(p. 313)**

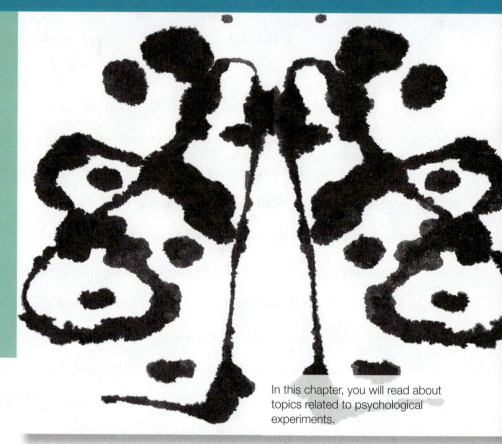

In this chapter, you will read about topics related to psychological experiments.

MyWritingLab™

Complete this Writer's Journal activity at mywritinglab.com

THE WRITER'S JOURNAL

Write a short paragraph comparing your personality to that of a family member or friend. Describe how your personalities are similar and different.

LO 1 Define parallel structure.

What Is Parallel Structure?

Parallel structure occurs when pairs or groups of items in a sentence are balanced. In the following sentences, the underlined phrases contain repetitions of grammatical structure but not of ideas. Each sentence has parallel structure.

Internet sites, magazines, and newspapers published the results of the experiment. (The nouns are parallel.)

Psychologists observe and predict human behavior. (The present tense verbs are parallel.)

The experiment was fascinating, groundbreaking, and revolutionary. (The adjectives are parallel.)

To get to the psychology department, go <u>across the street</u>, <u>into the building</u>, and <u>up the stairs</u>.
(The prepositional phrases are parallel.)

There are some test subjects <u>who develop a rash</u> and some <u>who have no reactions</u>.
(The "who" clauses are parallel.)

PRACTICE 1

All of the following sentences have parallel structures. Underline the parallel items.

EXAMPLE: Students in my psychology class <u>listened to the instructor</u>, <u>took notes</u>, and <u>asked questions</u>.

1. Professor Stanley Milgram taught at Yale, conducted a famous experiment, and wrote a book about his research.

2. Milgram's experiment was controversial, provocative, and surprising.

3. His experiment tried to understand how humans reacted to authority, how they obeyed authority, and how they felt about authority.

4. For his experiment, Milgram used one actor in a lab coat, one actor with glasses, and one unsuspecting subject in street clothes.

5. The psychologist told the subject to sit at the desk, to watch the "patient" behind the glass, and to listen to the experiment "leader."

6. The leader told the subject when to start electric shocks, when to increase the level of shocks, and when to stop the experiment.

7. Milgram's experiment raised important questions, ended in astonishing results, and gave valuable insight into human behavior.

8. Psychologists continue to perform experiments, give lectures, and debate issues.

Identify Faulty Parallel Structure

LO 2 Identify faulty parallel structure.

It is important to use parallel structure for a series of words or phrases, paired clauses, a comparison, and a two-part construction.

Series of Words or Phrases

Use parallel structure when words or phrases are joined in a series.

Not parallel Students, administrators, and people who teach sometimes volunteer for psychology experiments.

Parallel <u>Students</u>, <u>administrators</u>, and <u>teachers</u> sometimes volunteer for psychology experiments.
(The nouns are parallel.)

Not parallel I plan to study for tests, to attend all classes, and listening to the instructor.

Parallel I plan <u>to study</u> for tests, <u>to attend</u> all classes, and <u>to listen</u> to the instructor.
(The verbs are parallel.)

Paired Clauses

Use parallel structure when independent clauses are joined by *and, but*, or *or*.

Not parallel	He was surprised by the results, but he did not have a feeling of pleasure.
Parallel	He <u>was surprised</u> by the results, but he <u>was not pleased</u>. (The adjectives are parallel.)
Not parallel	She felt dizzy, and she also had a feeling of fright.
Parallel	She felt <u>dizzy</u>, and she also felt <u>frightened</u>. (The adjectives are parallel.)

> **GRAMMAR LINK**
> To learn more about active and passive voice, see pages 340–342 in Chapter 24.

HINT ▶ Use Consistent Voice

When a sentence has two independent clauses and is joined by a coordinating conjunction, use a consistent voice. In other words, if one part of the sentence is active, the other should also be active.

Not parallel	The researcher conducted the experiment, and then a report was written by him.
Parallel	The researcher <u>conducted the experiment</u>, and then <u>he wrote a report</u>. (Both parts use the active voice.)

PRACTICE 2

Correct the faulty parallel structure in each sentence.

EXAMPLE: Some psychology experiments are bold, pioneering, and ~~show their originality~~. *original*

1. Ivan Pavlov was a Russian physiologist, a research scientist, and he won a Nobel prize.

2. Pavlov became interested in dog salivation, and digestion also interested him.

3. To get to his lab, Pavlov walked through the door, up the stairs, and the department is where he entered.

4. Pavlov used many sound-making devices to stimulate his dogs, such as metronomes, whistles, and he also used tuning forks.

5. Pavlov noticed that the dogs heard the noise, saw the food dish, and were salivating.

6. Some of the dogs were excited, nervous, and were acting with enthusiasm.

7. Western scientists found Pavlov's experiments to be astounding, innovative, and thought they were important.

8. Ivan Pavlov worked quickly and was very efficient.

Comparisons

Use parallel structure in comparisons containing *than* or *as*.

Not parallel	Creating new experiments is more difficult than to re-create an earlier experiment.
Parallel	Creating a new experiment is more difficult than re-creating an earlier experiment. (The -*ing* forms are parallel.)
Not parallel	His home was as messy as the way he kept his laboratory.
Parallel	His home was as messy as his laboratory. (The nouns are parallel.)

Two-Part Constructions

Use parallel structure for the following paired items.

either … or	not … but	both … and
neither … nor	not only … but also	rather … than

Not parallel	My psychology class was both informative and a challenge.
Parallel	My psychology class was both informative and challenging. (The adjectives are parallel.)
Not parallel	I would rather finish my experiment than leaving early.
Parallel	I would rather finish my experiment than leave early. (The verbs are parallel.)

PRACTICE 3

Correct twelve errors in parallel construction.

EXAMPLE: Philip Zimbardo is creative and ~~an interesting person~~ *interesting*.

1. Philip Zimbardo created an experiment that was both unique and startled others. The Stanford Prison Experiment examined how ordinary people react when placed in positions of power or helplessness. He chose twenty-four students who were healthy, stable, and they abided by the law. Each subject would be either a guard or a prisoner for a two-week period.

2. On the first day of the experiment, each guard was told to wear a uniform, carry a baton, and sunglasses were put on. Ordinary people who had committed no crime, who had broken no laws, and had been honest were placed in a cold room. The prisoners were not only arrested but the guards also deloused them.

3. Immediately, the experimenters observed shocking behavior. Some of the guards started to act controlling, sadistic, and they abused the prisoners. On the second day, the prisoners rioted, and the guards attacked. Some prisoners decided that they would rather leave than continuing with the experiment.

4. During the next few days, officials, priests, and teachers observed the experiment. Nobody questioned the morality of the proceedings. Then, on the sixth day, Zimbardo's girlfriend visited the lab, and her shock was expressed. At first, Zimbardo's response was neither receptive nor did he encourage her.

5. Later that day, Zimbardo agreed that the actors were taking the experiment too seriously. Both the prisoners and the students playing the guards could experience long-term effects. They might be seriously hurt, distressed, and suffer from depression. Zimbardo terminated the planned two-week experiment after six days. He decided it was safer to end the experiment than completing it.

PRACTICE 4

Correct nine errors in parallel construction.

EXAMPLE: Information about bystander apathy is surprising and ~~of interest~~. *interesting*

1. Bystander apathy is the unwillingness of an individual to help another in an emergency. In the 1960s, psychologists started to collect data, investigate behaviors, and proposing theories about bystander apathy. One celebrated instance of bystander apathy is the Kitty Genovese case.

2. On March 13, 1964, Kitty Genovese was on her way to her apartment in Queens, New York. She was walking quietly and her steps were quick. Suddenly, she saw a strange man. He attacked her, and she screamed for help. Kitty Genovese died slowly, violently, and in tragic circumstances.

3. According to the *New York Times*, thirty-eight people heard the screaming, and the attack was watched by some of them, but nobody called the police. After reading the article, citizens were shocked and were feeling outrage. They called for the bystanders to be punished. We now know that the media exaggerated some aspects of the case. According to a 2007 *American Psychologist* article,

fewer people saw the attack, some people lied, and the police were called by one person. Still, nobody intervened in time, and Genovese died.

4.   Many psychologists have studied the phenomenon of bystander apathy, and the results have been published by them. There are many reasons a bystander may not help someone in trouble. Bystanders may not want to risk their own lives, they may not have the skills to help in an emergency, or legal problems could be incurred. In addition, many people do not want to look stupid or be seen as being foolish if there is no real emergency. Psychologists believe that these are only some possible reasons for bystander apathy.

PRACTICE 5

Write sentences using parallel structure with the following grammatical items.

1. Parallel nouns: _____

_____

2. Parallel verbs: _____

_____

3. Parallel adjectives: _____

_____

4. Parallel *who* clauses: _____

_____

Reflect On It

Think about what you have learned in this chapter. If you do not know an answer, review that concept.

1. What is parallel structure? _____

_____

2. Why is parallel structure important? _____

_____

Fill in the blanks of the following sentences. Make sure the grammatical structures are parallel.

3. The college I attend is both _____ and

_____.

4. In my spare time, I _____, _____,

and _____.

FINAL REVIEW

Correct fifteen errors in parallel construction.

EXAMPLE: Psychiatrists, psychologists, and ~~other people who are counselors~~ counselors help patients deal with their mental health problems.

1. Have you ever been in a group discussion where you wanted to offer a different point of view but did not? Psychologist Irving Janis was ambitious, intelligent, and worked hard. In 1972, he studied group dynamics and then a book was written by him. He called his book *Groupthink*.

2. Groupthink occurs when members of a group feel a strong need to agree with others. These are people who do not criticize a prevailing position, who do not offer alternative strategies, and do not voice any disagreement. Group participants not only suppress common sense, but unpopular opinions are also avoided.

3. Janis presented an interesting example of groupthink in his book. In 1961, CIA operatives, military leaders, and people in American politics wanted to overthrow Fidel Castro. When President John F. Kennedy heard about the plan to invade Cuba, he was both agreeable and enthusiasm was felt by him. Kennedy's group of advisors wanted to be both cooperative and acting patriotic. As a result, all of Kennedy's counselors agreed with the proposal. The invasion was planned blindly, quickly, and without care. As a result, the Bay of Pigs invasion was a failure.

4. In October 1962, the Soviet Union placed nuclear warheads in Cuba. When Kennedy heard about the missiles, he wanted to react immediately rather than delaying his response. He walked rapidly through the garden, along the corridor, and he went into the Oval Office. At the meeting with his advisors, Kennedy employed strategies to avoid groupthink. His advisors were encouraged to discuss, to debate, and they could disagree. Therefore, the men could either challenge bad ideas or good ideas could be analyzed. Using diplomacy, the president solved the crisis. The Soviets removed the nuclear weapons from Cuba immediately and with speed.

5. Janis's book has shown how groupthink can have negative consequences in government, in academics, and for people who work in business. Many executives ignore groupthink rather than to learn about it. It is a phenomenon that can lead to very bad decision making.

THE WRITER'S ROOM · MyWritingLab™

Choose one of the following topics and write a paragraph or an essay. When you write, remember to follow the writing process.

1. What makes you happy? Describe some situations or events that make you happy.

2. What are some different ways that people deal with their fears? Classify their responses to fear into three categories.

THE WRITERS' CIRCLE Collaborative Activity

When you apply for a job, the employer often asks you what your strengths and weaknesses are. Work with a team of students to do the following activity.

STEP 1   Think of a successful person. You could choose a person from any of the next categories.

A business tycoon	A politician	A movie star
A musician	An athlete	A writer or artist

STEP 2   Brainstorm one list of that person's strengths and another list of that person's weaknesses.

STEP 3   Write a short paragraph about that successful person, discussing the person's strengths and weaknesses.

STEP 4   Exchange paragraphs with another team. Proofread the other team's paragraph, checking especially for fragments, run-ons, and parallel structure.

MyWritingLab™
Complete these writing assignments at mywritinglab.com

READING LINK

To learn more about beliefs and psychological issues, read the next essays.

"What Is Luck?" by Matt Hutson (page 211)
"Don't Worry, Act Happy" by Albert Nerenberg (page 224)
"The Catcher of Ghosts" by Amy Tan (page 525)
"The Sanctuary of School" by Lynda Barry (page 528)
"Musicophilia" by Oliver Sacks (page 531)
"Why We Make Mistakes" by Joseph T. Hallinan (page 534)

Chapter 22

23 Present and Past Tenses

SECTION THEME: Spies and Hackers

LEARNING OBJECTIVES

LO 1 Define verb tense. **(p. 320)**

LO 2 Identify simple present tense. **(p. 321)**

LO 3 Identify simple past tense. **(p. 322)**

LO 4 Avoid double negatives. **(p. 330)**

In this chapter, you will read about spy tools and communication technology.

THE WRITER'S JOURNAL

Write a short paragraph describing the last spy or suspense movie that you have seen. Describe what happened in the movie.

LO 1 Define verb tense.

What Is Verb Tense?

A verb shows an action or a state of being. A **verb tense** indicates when an action occurred. Review the various tenses of the verb *work*.

Present   She <u>works</u> alone.

Past   The agent <u>worked</u> in Monaco last summer.

Future   She <u>will work</u> in the Middle East next year.

Use Standard Verb Forms

Nonstandard English is used in everyday conversation, and it may differ according to the region in which you live. **Standard American English** is the common language generally used and expected in schools, businesses, and government institutions in the United States. Most of your instructors will want you to write using Standard American English.

Nonstandard	He <u>don't</u> have <u>no</u> time.	She <u>be</u> busy.
Standard	He <u>does not</u> have <u>any</u> time.	She <u>is</u> busy.

The Simple Present Tense

LO 2 Identify simple present tense.

In English there are two forms of the present tense. The **simple present tense** indicates that an action is a general fact or habitual activity. Note that the present progressive form is explained in the Hint box and in Chapter 25.

Fact   The Spy Museum <u>contains</u> many interesting spy artifacts.

**Habitual
activity**   The computer hacker <u>goes</u> online every day.

The undercover agent <u>meets</u> her superiors once a month.

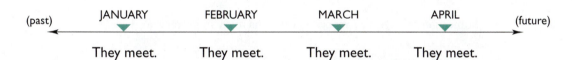

(past)	JANUARY	FEBRUARY	MARCH	APRIL	(future)
	▼	▼	▼	▼	
	They meet.	They meet.	They meet.	They meet.	

HINT ◀ **The Present Progressive**

The **present progressive tense** indicates that an action is in progress at this moment. In this chapter, you will focus on the simple present form.

present progressive tense
Right now, the agent <u>is taking</u> pictures with her spy camera.

GRAMMAR LINK
For more information about progressive forms, see pages 346–348 in Chapter 25.

Forms of the Simple Present Tense

Simple present tense verbs (except *be*) have two forms. *Be* has three forms: *is, am, are*.

- **Base form:** When the subject is *I, you, we,* or *they,* or the equivalent (*women, the Rocky Mountains*), do not add an ending to the verb.

    Nations <u>rely</u> on spies to gather secret information.

- **Third-person singular form:** When the subject is *he, she, it,* or the equivalent (*Mark, Carol, Miami*), add an *-s* or *-es* ending to the verb. Remember that *have* is an irregular verb. The third-person singular form is *has*.

    That woman <u>works</u> as a spy.

Look at the singular and plural forms of the verb *work*.

Present Tense of *Work*

	Singular	Plural
First person	I work.	We work.
Second person	You work.	You work.
Third person	He work**s**.	They work.
	She work**s**.	
	It work**s**.	

PRACTICE 1

Circle the correct present tense form of the verbs in parentheses.

EXAMPLE: Spying (seem / seems) like an exciting job.

1. According to Christopher Andrew, coauthor of *The Sword and the Shield*, the acronym *MICE* (sum / sums) up the reasons why a person may become a traitor.

2. *MICE* (stand / stands) for "money, ideology, compromise, and ego."

3. According to Andrew, the most popular reason (is / are) money.

4. Some agents (receive / receives) millions in cash, jewelry, and so on.

5. Another reason (is / are) ideology.

6. Sometimes people (believe / believes) that another country's way of life is better.

7. Some men and women (become / becomes) spies because they are ashamed of something that they have done.

8. For example, if a government bureaucrat (steal / steals) money and another person (find / finds) out, the bureaucrat can be blackmailed to become a spy.

9. Finally, many people (think / thinks) that spying (is / are) an exciting profession.

10. Andrew (say / says) that "an interesting minority want to be secret celebrities" in their own little world of espionage.

LO 3 Identify simple past tense.

The Simple Past Tense

The **simple past tense** indicates that an action occurred at a specific past time. In the past tense, there are regular and irregular verbs. **Regular verbs** end in *-d* or *-ed* (*talked, ended, watched*). **Irregular verbs** do not follow a regular pattern and do not end in any specific letter (*knew, saw, met*).

Last month, someone **stole** my computer.

Yesterday morning, the spy satellite **passed** over my home.

YESTERDAY MORNING   TODAY

The satellite **passed** over my home.

HINT ◄ **The Past Progressive**

The **past progressive tense** indicates that an action was in progress at a particular past moment. In this chapter, you will focus on the simple past.

past progressive tense
While the detectives <u>were watching</u> the house, the suspect escaped.

GRAMMAR LINK
See Chapter 25, "Other Verb Forms," for more information about progressive verb forms.

Regular Past Tense Verbs

Regular past tense verbs have a standard *-d* or *-ed* ending. Use the same form for both singular and plural past tense verbs.

Singular subject   The agent **learned** to speak six languages.

Plural subject   During the war, spies **used** code names.

Spell Regular Past Tense Verbs Correctly

Most regular past tense verbs are formed by adding *-ed* to the base form of the verb.

walke<u>d</u>   questione<u>d</u>

However, there are some exceptions.

* When the regular verb ends in *-e*, just add *-d*.

  realize<u>d</u>   appreciate<u>d</u>

* When the regular verb ends in consonant + *-y*, change the *y* to *i* and add *-ed*.

  reply–repl<u>ied</u>   try–tr<u>ied</u>

* When the regular verb ends in the vowel + *-y*, just add *-ed*.

  play<u>ed</u>   employ<u>ed</u>

* When the regular verb ends in a consonant–vowel–consonant combination, double the last consonant and add *-ed*.

  tap–tap<u>ped</u>   plan–plan<u>ned</u>

* When verbs of two or more syllables end in a stressed consonant–vowel–consonant combination, double the last letter and add *-ed*. But if the final syllable is not stressed, just add *-ed*.

  Final stressed syllable   refer–refer<u>red</u> omit–omit<u>ted</u>

  Final unstressed syllable   open–open<u>ed</u>   develop–develope<u>d</u>

GRAMMAR LINK
See Chapter 33, "Spelling and Commonly Confused Words," for information about the spelling of verbs.

HINT ◀ **Do Not Confuse *Past* and *Passed***

Some people confuse *past* and *passed*. *Past* is a noun that means "in a previous time" or "before now."

> She has many secrets in her <u>past</u>.

Passed is the past tense of the verb *pass*, which has many meanings.

> Many days <u>passed</u> as we waited for her arrival.
> (*Passed* means "went by.")

> I <u>passed</u> you the butter a moment ago.
> (*Passed* means "took something and gave it to someone.")

> He <u>passed</u> the entrance test.
> (*Passed* means "successfully completed.")

PRACTICE 2

Write the simple past form of each verb in parentheses. Make sure you spell the past tense verb correctly.

EXAMPLE: The United States (launch) ___*launched*___ a spy satellite in 1960.

1.   The Central Intelligence Agency (use) _____ a series of spy satellites during the 1960s and 1970s. Officials (name) _____ each satellite with a code word. They (call) _____ the operation "Corona." The satellites (pass) _____ over sensitive locations in the former Soviet Union.

2.   Each Corona spy satellite (contain) _____ a powerful camera and regular film. When the camera (finish) _____ filming, it ejected from the satellite inside a special capsule. Then back on Earth, experts (study) _____ the images and (learn) _____ about the military secrets of other nations. During the 1960s, the Corona satellites (drop) _____ at least three hundred capsules. Parachutes (open) _____ and the capsules (float) _____ down. Then Air Force pilots (recover) _____ the capsules.

3.   In the 1970s, the numbers of satellites (multiply) _____ dramatically. Last year, thousands of satellites (provide) _____ nations with high-resolution images of everything from shifting ice masses to traffic conditions in Los Angeles.

GRAMMAR LINK
See Appendix 2 on page 563–564 for a list of irregular verbs.

Irregular Past Tense Verbs

Irregular verbs change internally. Because their spellings change from the present to the past tense, these verbs can be challenging to remember.

The prisoner <u>wrote</u> with invisible ink.
(wrote = past tense of *write*)

The guards <u>sent</u> the letter.
(sent = past tense of *send*)

PRACTICE 3

Write the correct past form of each verb in parentheses. Some verbs are regular, and some are irregular. If you do not know the past form of an irregular verb, consult Appendix 2.

EXAMPLE: The 2009 virus (have) _____had_____ peculiar properties.

1.   What is the difference between a computer virus and a worm? A virus requires action, such as clicking on an e-mail attachment, to infect a computer. A worm spreads without any human action. Last year, Internet security systems (find) _____ over a million viruses and worms!

2.   In 2009, clever experts (write) _____ a computer program called Stuxnet. They (send) _____ the sophisticated worm around the world. For several months, Stuxnet (make) _____ targeted hits on controllers, which regulate the machinery in factories and power plants. The worm (have) _____ no impact on ordinary computers and on most controllers. But when the worm (spread) _____ to nuclear reactors in Iran, it attacked the machinery. At that time, people in many governments (feel) _____ concerned about Iran's nuclear capabilities. According to experts, an unidentified nation (build) _____ the complicated worm to sabotage Iran's nuclear plants.

3.   The worm worked by spinning the centrifuges of the nuclear facility at extreme speeds so that they would self-destruct. At the same time, the worm (show) _____ fake readings to Iranian scientists. They (see) _____ regular measurements. While the reactor was quietly destroying itself, Iranian scientists (think) _____ it was functioning normally.

4.   In 2010, Stuxnet (come) _____ under intense scrutiny. What nation initially (run) _____ the program? Some suspect that Israel, the United States, and Germany (take) _____ part in the worm's development. Clearly, cyberwarfare is now possible.

Be (*was* or *were*)

Past tense verbs generally have one form that you can use with all subjects. However, the verb *be* has two past forms: *was* and *were*.

Past Tense of *Be*

	Singular	Plural
First person	I was	We were
Second person	You were	You were
Third person	He was	They were
	She was	
	It was	

PRACTICE 4

Write *was* or *were* in each space provided.

EXAMPLE: Robert Barron _____was_____ not an ordinary artist.

1.   During the 1970s, Robert Barron worked for the Pentagon. He _____

not happy with his parking spot because he always had to walk a long way to

get to his office. One day, when he _____ alone, he created a perfect

fake parking permit. Some other employees _____ aware of what

Barron had done, and they told their superior officers about it. Barron had

to pay a fine. As it happened, some CIA agents _____ curious about

Barron's artistic talents.

2.   Soon, Barron joined the graphic arts department at the CIA. He became an

expert at creating disguises for secret agents, and he _____ happy with

his new job. Barron and other artists _____ very creative, and they

made false noses, foreheads, and chins so that agents could look completely

different. Some artists _____ experts at creating false mustaches,

beards, wigs, and teeth. The disguises _____ important because

defectors needed to pass army checkpoints and borders.

Problems with *be, have,* and *do*

Some students find it particularly difficult to remember how to use the irregular verbs *be, have,* and *do* in the past tense. Here are some helpful guidelines.

Avoiding Common Errors with *be*

♦ Use *were* in the past tense when the subject is plural. Do not use *was*.

> were
> The spies ~~was~~ arrested in 1995.

♦ Use the standard form of the verb (*is* or *was*), not *be*.

> is
> The camera ~~be~~ small enough to fit in a pen.

Avoiding Common Errors with *have*

◆ Use the past form of the verb (*had*), not the present form (*have* or *has*), when speaking about a past event.

had

During the war, the agent ~~has~~ several passports.

Avoiding Common Errors with *do*

◆ Use *done* only when it is preceded by a helping verb (*was done, is done*, and so on).

did

In 2002, Valerie Plame ~~done~~ undercover work.

PRACTICE 5

Underline and correct ten verb errors. If the verb is incorrectly formed, or if the verb is in the wrong tense, write the correct form above it.

have

EXAMPLE: Some people <u>has</u> very little respect for pigeons.

1. Most city dwellers believes that pigeons are nuisances. For example, at my

   apartment building, the owner done many things last year to keep pigeons off

   the balconies. However, people undervalue pigeons. During past

   wars, the homing pigeon has an important role in international

   espionage.

2. During the Napoleonic wars, homing pigeons gived officials a

   crucial way to communicate. The small birds carried and delivered

   secret messages because they was able to fly over enemy territories.

   Those pigeons be able to transmit messages faster than soldiers on

   horses, and they haved legendary endurance.

3. According to Richard Platt's book *Spy*, the Roman emperor Julius

   Caesar also used birds to send messages. Pigeons be valued for their speed, size,

   and reliability. Additionally, more than half a million pigeons taked messages

   to soldiers during World War I, and some soldiers actually hided pigeons in

   their pockets and cared for them on battlefields. We should appreciate pigeons

   because they played an important role in previous wars.

Negative and Question Forms

In the present and past tenses, you must add a helping verb (*do, does,* or *did*) to question and negative forms. In the present tense, use the helping verb *do,* or use *does* when the subject is third-person singular. Use *did* in the past tense.

Questions	**Do** you know about the Spy Museum in Washington?
	Does the museum open on weekends?
	Did you visit the spy museum last summer?
Negatives	We **do** not live in Washington.
	The museum **does** not open on holidays.
	We **did** not visit the spy museum last summer.

When the main verb is *be* (*is, am, are*), no additional helping verb is necessary.

Questions	**Is** the spy story suspenseful?
	Were foreign spies in New York during the 2005 World Summit?
Negatives	The story **is not** suspenseful.
	Foreign spies **were not** in New York during the event.

A Note about Contractions

In informal writing, it is acceptable to contract negative verb forms. However, you should avoid using contractions in your academic writing.

           does not
The CIA ~~doesn't~~ have enough multilingual interpreters.

HINT ◄ **Use the Correct Question and Negative Forms**

In question and negative forms, always use the base form of the main verb, even when the subject is third-person singular.

           have
Why <u>does</u> the Spy Museum ~~has~~ so many spy gadgets?

           discuss
In 1914, Mata Hari <u>did</u> not ~~discussed~~ her identity.

PRACTICE 6

Write questions for each answer. Remember to add a helping verb (*do, does,* or *did*) when necessary.

EXAMPLES: <u>Where is the International Spy Museum?</u>

The International Spy Museum is in Washington.

<u>What does it contain?</u>

It contains hundreds of spy gadgets.

1. _____

The Spy Museum opened in 2002.

2. _____

The spy gadgets are from nations around the world.

3. _____

Yes, the museum is open on Sundays.

4. _____

Yes, the camera has a powerful lens.

5. _____

Yes, many tourists visit the museum each year.

PRACTICE 7

Combine the words in parentheses to form negatives. Remember to add a helping verb (_do_, _does_, or _did_) when necessary.

EXAMPLE: Washington's Spy Museum has hundreds of spy gadgets, but it (have,

not) _____does not have_____ paintings.

1.   Washington's International Spy Museum contains many interesting gadgets.

For example, on display is a tube of lipstick called "The Kiss of Death." The

tube (have, not) _____ an obvious function. It (add, not)

_____ color to a person's lips. Instead, the lipstick tube

conceals a tiny pistol. In 1965, a female Russian spy carried the pistol in her

purse, and others (know, not) _____ about her hidden

weapon.

2.   The museum also has interesting listening devices. Some of them (be, not)

_____ very large. In 1960, Hal Lipset (work, not)

_____ for the government. He was a private

detective, and he created an "olive" microphone. The olive (look, not)

_____ fake when it was placed inside a martini. The

toothpick acted as an antenna. It (have, not) _____ a very

wide range and could only pick up nearby sounds. In the 1960s, recording

devices (be, not) _____ very sensitive. Nowadays,

microphones (have, not) _____ to be in a particular room

to pick up a conversation.

3.   Clearly, the Spy Museum is an extremely interesting place. Tourists (have,

not) _____ to spend the entire day at the museum because

it (be, not) _____ a very large place.

HINT ◄ **Use the Base Form After *To***

Remember to use the base form of verbs that follow *to* (infinitive form).

Greenstein wanted to ~~studied~~ study the postcard.

PRACTICE 8

The next selection contains verb tense, spelling, and *past* versus *passed* errors. Underline and correct fifteen errors.

EXAMPLE: In 2011, Wael Ghonim ~~work~~ worked for Google.

1. In 1981, Hosni Mubarak becomed the president of Egypt. Thirty years past by, and Egyptians did not mobilized against their dictator. Mubarak thought that he would rule for the rest of his life. But in 2010, something be different in the world. New online tools and Web sites helped disillusioned citizens organize a revolution.

2. In 2010, Wael Ghonim, the head of marketing for Google in the Middle East, maked a Facebook page in memory of an anti-government protestor. In retaliation, Mubarak's regime putted Ghonim in prison. Ghonim's family told the international media about his disappearance. Many bloggers writed about the case. Eleven days later, the government gived in to public pressure and released Ghonim. During an emotional interview on Egyptian television, Ghonim said that the regime did not deserved support.

3. During the following weeks, Egyptians used cell phone messages, Twitter, and Facebook to organized. When the government tried to block online sites, hackers finded ways to bypass restrictions. On February 11, 2011, the Egyptian government fallen. According to many observers, YouTube, blogs, Facebook, and Twitter was essential tools for the Arab Spring.

LO 4 Avoid double negatives.

Avoid Double Negatives

A double negative occurs when a negative word such as *no, nothing, nobody,* or *nowhere* is combined with a negative adverb such as *not, never, rarely,* or *seldom.* The result is a sentence that has a double negative. Such sentences can be confusing because the negative words cancel each other.

> The agent <u>didn't</u> accept <u>no</u> money.
> (According to this sentence, the agent accepted money.)

How to Correct Double Negatives

There are several ways to correct double negatives.

- Completely remove one of the negative forms.

  accepted no *or* didn't accept
  The agent ~~didn't accept no~~ money.

- Change *no* to *any* (*anybody, anything, anywhere*).

  any
  The agent didn't accept ~~no~~ money.

PRACTICE 9

Underline and correct the six errors with double negatives. You can correct each error in more than one way.

had no (*or* didn't have any)
EXAMPLE: The spy <u>didn't have no</u> money.

1.   Every year, intelligence agencies develop highly sophisticated spy tools. Today,

spy planes are lightweight and fly at extremely high altitudes. They don't have no

pilots. Instead, ground teams direct the planes using remote control technology.

For example, during a 2005 flight over Iraq, the Predator spy drone provided

about fifteen hours of surveillance. It didn't make no noise, so people on the

ground didn't see or hear nothing. The plane took high-resolution videos.

More recently, the Global Hawk flew from the United States to Afghanistan

and collected data from a height of about 65,000 feet. The Global Hawk

did not need no refueling during the long journey.

2.   Scientists are trying to shrink the size of flying robots.

According to the *Washington Post*, federally funded teams

are working on remote control insects. However, the CIA

did not confirm nothing to the reporters. Intelligence agents

do not want nobody to know exactly what they are doing.

Reflect On It

Think about what you have learned in this chapter. If you do not know an answer, review that concept.

1. What are the present and past forms of the verb *be?*

	Present	Past
I	_____	_____
he, she, it	_____	_____
you, we, they	_____	_____

2. Write two regular past tense verbs. _____

3. Write two irregular past tense verbs. _____

4. Correct one verb tense error in each of the following sentences.

   a. In 1954, a Russian agent surrender to the United States.

   b. Khokhlov defected because he did not wanted to kill another Russian agent.

   c. Khokhlov past many days and nights hiding in a forest.

   d. The agent owned a cigarette case that be a secret weapon.

   e. The cigarette case fired bullets that was poisonous.

FINAL REVIEW

Underline and correct errors in present and past tense verbs. Also look for one double negative. There are fifteen errors.

EXAMPLE: When people talk about espionage, they generally ~~thinks~~ *think* about secret agents who work for governments.

1. A nation's economic survival depend on its ability to be innovative. Countries try to protect secret technologies. For example, in the 1970s, DuPont created Kevlar, a synthetic fiber that be five times stronger than steel. It appears in products such as bulletproof vests. When DuPont developed Kevlar, the company didn't wanted competitors to learn its trade secrets. However, in 2006, an angry employee revealed information about Kevlar to a foreign company.

2.   In 2006, Michael David Mitchell lost his job at DuPont after twenty-five years of employment. Immediately, he done some unethical acts. First, he brung home private documents. Then he told DuPont officials that he didn't have no sensitive files. Two weeks later, he goed to work as a consultant for a Korean firm called Kolon, Inc. While there, he past secret information about Kevlar to his new employers. He also tried to got additional secret information from some of his former DuPont colleagues.

3.   In 2007, DuPont officials finded out that Mitchell was contacting former colleagues and looking for information. Of course, DuPont executives be furious, and they contacted the FBI. In 2008, federal agents searched Mitchell's home. To save himself, Mitchell agree to cooperate with the government.

4.   Governments around the world take industrial espionage seriously. In the past, unhappy employees sold private documents to competitors. These days, secrets travel around the world with the click of a mouse, so businesses are more vulnerable than ever.

THE WRITER'S ROOM   MyWritingLab™

MyWritingLab™
Complete these writing assignments at mywritinglab.com

Write about one of the following topics. Check your verb tenses carefully.

1.   Have you ever done volunteer work? If so, describe when and where you worked, and explain what you did. If not, explain why not.

2.   Describe an effective election advertisement. Include details that appeal to the senses.

Chapter 23

24 Past Participles

SECTION THEME: Spies and Hackers

LEARNING OBJECTIVES

LO 1 Identify past participles. **(p. 334)**

LO 2 Define the present perfect tense. **(p. 336)**

LO 3 Define the past perfect tense. **(p. 338)**

LO 4 Identify the passive voice. **(p. 340)**

LO 5 Use the past participle as an adjective. **(p. 343)**

In this chapter, you will read about some spying techniques and online privacy.

MyWritingLab™

Complete this Writer's Journal activity at mywritinglab.com

THE WRITER'S JOURNAL

Do you regularly use a social networking site such as Facebook or Twitter? Why or why not?

LO 1 Identify past participles.

Past Participles

A **past participle** is a verb form, not a verb tense. You cannot use a past participle as the only verb in a sentence; instead, you must use it with a helping verb such as *have, has, had, is, was,* or *were.*

	helping verbs	past participles
Ian Fleming	was	raised in England.
His novels	have	become very popular.

Regular Verbs

The past tense and the past participle of regular verbs are the same.

GRAMMAR LINK
For a list of irregular past participles, see Appendix 2 on pages 563–564.

Base Form	Past Tense	Past Participle
walk	walked	walked
try	tried	tried

Irregular Verbs

The past tense and the past participle of irregular verbs may be different. For a complete list of irregular past participles, see Appendix 2.

Base Form	Past Tense	Past Participle
begin	began	begun
speak	spoke	spoken

PRACTICE 1

Each group of verbs contains one error. Underline the error, and write the correct verb form in the space provided.

EXAMPLE:

Base Form	Past Tense	Past Participle	
lose	<u>losed</u>	lost	*lost*
1. cost	cost	costed	_____
2. come	came	came	_____
3. build	builded	built	_____
4. sing	sang	sang	_____
5. bring	brang	brought	_____
6. think	thank	thought	_____
7. choose	choosed	chosen	_____
8. fall	felt	fallen	_____
9. feel	felt	fell	_____
10. blow	blew	blowed	_____
11. tear	tore	tore	_____
12. take	taked	taken	_____
13. bite	bited	bitten	_____
14. sit	sat	sitten	_____
15. grow	grew	growed	_____

PRACTICE 2

In the following selection, the past participles are underlined. Correct ten past participle errors. Write *C* over four correct past participles.

                                    met

EXAMPLE: The business ethics students have <u>meeted</u> many times to discuss the issue.

1.   Consumer groups have <u>expressed</u> concerns about consumer privacy and online marketing techniques. Particularly, the social networking site Facebook has <u>came</u> under attack. Since its inception, Facebook has <u>earn</u> money through targeted advertising. Facebook users' personal information can be <u>viewed</u> by marketers.

2.   In 2007, Facebook Beacon was <u>launch</u>. When an online purchase was <u>maked</u> by a Facebook user, the information was <u>send</u> to the user's friends. For example, Chad Reims bought movie tickets at Fandango and the information was <u>publish</u> on his Facebook news feed without his knowledge. In a well-known case, a man planned to propose to his girlfriend. After he had <u>buyed</u> an engagement ring online, the information was <u>distributed</u> to his Facebook friends. Of course, the news was <u>saw</u> by his girlfriend. After a class-action suit was <u>filed</u>, Facebook allowed users to opt out of the Beacon program.

3.   Facebook's marketing practices have always <u>being</u> legal. Perhaps children should be <u>teached</u> to use privacy settings when they use social networking sites.

LO 2 Define the present perfect tense.

The Present Perfect Tense: *have/has* + Past Participle

Combine *have* or *has* and a past participle to form the **present perfect tense**. You can use this tense in two different circumstances.

♦ Use the present perfect to show that an action began in the past and continues to the present time. You will often use *since* and *for* with this tense.

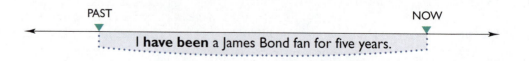

PAST   NOW

I **have been** a James Bond fan for five years.

◆ Use the present perfect to show that one or more completed actions occurred at unspecified past times.

PAST (unspecified past times)   NOW
?   ?   ?   ?

I **have watched** at least four James Bond movies.

HINT ▸ Use Time Markers

Time markers are words that indicate when an action occurred.

Simple Past Tense
To refer to a completed incident that occurred at a specific past time, use the following time markers.

yesterday	ago	when I was . . .	last (week, month, year . . .)
in the past	in 2005	during the 1970s	in the early days of . . .

Ian Fleming **wrote** his first novel <u>in 1953</u>.

Present Perfect Tense
• To refer to an action that began in the past and is still continuing, use the following time markers.

since	for (a period of time up to now)	ever
up to now	so far	not . . . yet

Spy films **have been** popular <u>since the 1930s</u>.

• To refer to an action that occurred at unspecified past times, use the following types of time markers

once	twice	several times	lately	recently	many

I **have seen** *The World Is Not Enough* <u>once</u> and *Die Another Day* <u>twice</u>.

Look at the difference between the past and the present perfect tenses.

Simple past	In 1962, Sean Connery <u>appeared</u> in the first James Bond film, *Dr. No.* (This event occurred at a known past time.)
Present perfect	Many different actors <u>have played</u> James Bond. (We do not really know when the actors played James Bond.) James Bond movies <u>have been</u> popular for more than forty years. (The action began in the past and continues to the present.)

Chapter 24

PRACTICE 3

Write the simple past or present perfect form of each verb in parentheses.

EXAMPLE: We (meet) _____ *have met* _____ many times to discuss the problem.

1. Spying on employees is not new; in fact, companies (do) _____

    it for many years. Since 2000, some employers (scan) _____

    their staff's computer usage. Over the years, employer spying (become)

    _____ more and more prevalent.

2. Raymond Croft, the CEO of a small company, (buy) _____

    several types of spying software over the years. Two years ago, he (purchase)

    _____ SpectorSoft monitoring

    software. Since then, he (use) _____ the

    software to do spot checks on employees. For example,

    last January, a young female member of the staff (take)

    _____ her laptop to a coffee shop.

    She (tell) _____ her boss that she

    was going to work from home. Instead, she (spend)

    _____ the afternoon sending out

    résumés and reading tabloid gossip. She (realize, not)

    _____ that her computer was being

    monitored. Since then, Croft (fire) _____ that employee.

3. Over the years, many critics (complain) _____ that spy

    software leads to a hostile work atmosphere. Since 2005, too many employees

    (lose) _____ their jobs simply for being human and going

    online during breaks. On the other hand, many employers (catch)

    _____ staff doing illegal activities such as selling trade secrets.

    Certainly, workers should remember that their bosses can spy on them.

LO3 Define the past perfect tense.

The Past Perfect Tense: *had* + Past Participle

The **past perfect tense** indicates that one or more past actions happened before another past action. It is formed with *had* and the past participle.

PAST PERFECT   PAST   NOW

The robbers **had left** when the police arrived.

Notice the differences between the simple past, the present perfect, and the past perfect tenses.

Simple past Last night I <u>watched</u> a documentary on double agents.
(The action occurred at a known past time.)

Present perfect I <u>have read</u> many articles about spying.
(The actions occurred at unspecified past times.)

Past perfect Government officials <u>had suspected</u> the agent for a long time before they arrested him as a spy.
(All of the actions happened in the past, but one action happened before another.)

PRACTICE 4

Underline the correct verb form. You may choose the simple past, the present perfect, or the past perfect tense.

EXAMPLE: Ben Lee (was / <u>has been</u>) a CIA agent since 2001.

1. Khaleb and Richard (are / were / have been) friends since they were children.

   When they (were / had been) eight years old, they (pretended / have pretended)

   to work for the Central Intelligence Agency. By the age of ten, they (have

   made / had made) several paper CIA badges.

2. By the time Richard turned twenty, he (has been / had been) in trouble with

   the law several times. For example, in 2006, Richard went out with a friend.

   Richard did not realize that his friend (brought / had brought) some drugs into the

   car. The police arrested both men and showed them the drugs. Richard truthfully

   claimed that he (never saw / had never seen) the drugs. He said that someone else

   (has put / had put) them in the trunk. However, because Richard was in the car,

   the officer (charged / had charged) him with possession of narcotics. Now Richard

   cannot become a CIA agent because he has a criminal record.

3. Khaleb has good grades in college. He (never failed / has never failed) a

   course in his entire life. Khaleb is also in good physical condition. During his

   last medical exam, the doctor said that he (never saw / had never seen) such a

   healthy young man. Furthermore, Kaleb speaks three languages. By the time he

   was twelve years old, Khaleb (has already learned / had already learned) to speak

   Spanish and Arabic. Since the summer, the agency (made / has made) several

   background checks on Khaleb. Up to now, Khaleb (had passed / has passed) all

   of the tests. Khaleb has a very good chance of becoming a CIA agent.

LO 4 Identify the passive voice.

The Passive Voice: *be* + Past Participle

In sentences with the **passive voice**, the subject receives the action and does not perform the action. Look carefully at the next two sentences.

Active The diplomat **gave** secret documents to an undercover agent.
(This is active because the subject, *diplomat*, performed the action.)

Passive Secret documents **were given** to an undercover agent.
(This is passive because the subject, *documents*, was affected by the action and did not perform the action.)

To form the passive voice, use the appropriate tense of the verb *be* plus the past participle.

Verb Tenses	Active Voice (The subject performs the action.)	Passive Voice: *be* + Past Participle (The subject receives the action.)
Simple present	She writes spy stories.	Spy stories <u>are</u> written (by her).
Present progressive	is writing	<u>are being</u> written
Simple past	wrote	<u>were</u> written
Present perfect	has written	<u>have been</u> written
Future	will write	<u>will be</u> written
Modals	can write	<u>can be</u> written
	could write	<u>could be</u> written
	should write	<u>should be</u> written
	would have written	<u>would have been</u> written

PRACTICE 5

Underline the appropriate verb in parentheses. Then decide if it is active or passive. Write *A* for "active" or *P* for "passive" above each verb.

EXAMPLE: The software (designed / <u>was designed</u>) to spy on users of infected
computers. *[P]*

1. During times of war, nations (have used / have been used) soldiers, tanks, and airplanes to fight each other. Today, another type of war (is fighting / is being fought) online. In 2012, for *Vanity Fair* magazine, Michael Joseph Gross (wrote / was written) the article "World War 3.0." He says that battle lines (have drawn / have been drawn) between some regimes and their technologically savvy opponents. Nations (can use / can be used) stealthy computer worms to spy.

2. In 2012, a type of malware called "Flame" (discovered / was discovered) in Iran. Flame (targeted / was targeted) Windows operating systems. It

(could not detect / could not be detected) by antivirus software. With Flame,

computer experts (could access / could be accessed) the private messages of

government officials in the Middle East. Even audio files and conversations on

Skype (could record / could be recorded) by the spy program. At the time, Flame

(considered / was considered) the most sophisticated spying software in the world.

HINT ◀ The *by* . . . Phrase

In many passive sentences, it is not necessary to write the *by* . . . phrase because
the noun performing the action is understood.

> CIA agents are selected according to their abilities.
> (Adding "by CIA recruiters" after "selected" is not necessary.)

PRACTICE 6

Complete the following sentences by changing each italicized verb to the passive form.
Do not alter the verb tense. Note: You do not have to include the *by* . . . phrase.

EXAMPLE: The supervisor *spies* on the workers.

The workers ___are spied on (by the supervisor)._____

1. Sometimes employers *place* spy cameras in their factories.

   Sometimes spy cameras _____

   _____

2. Last year, Mr. Roy *installed* three surveillance cameras.

   Last year, three surveillance cameras _____

   _____

3. The video cameras *filmed* some sleeping workers.

   Some sleeping workers _____

   _____

4. As a result, the boss *has fired* three technicians.

   As a result, three technicians _____

   _____

5. The workers will file a complaint.

   A complaint _____

   _____

Chapter 24

HINT ▸ Avoid Overusing the Passive Voice

Generally, use the active voice instead of the passive voice. The active voice is more direct and less wordy than the passive voice. For example, read the next two versions of the same message.

Passive voice The problem has been rectified by us, and a new order is being prepared for you. You will be contacted by our sales department.

Active voice We have corrected the problem and are preparing a new order for you. Our sales department will contact you.

In rare cases when you do not know who did the action, the passive voice may be more appropriate.

James Bond's miniature camera was made in Italy.
(You do not know who made the camera.)

PRACTICE 7

Underline examples of the passive voice in the following letter. Then rewrite the letter using the active voice.

Dear Parents,

Security cameras have been installed in our school for several reasons. First, intruders have been seen by students. Also, if fighting is done by students, the scenes will be recorded and the culprits will be caught. In addition, any vandalism to school property can be viewed by our staff. For further information, we can be contacted at any time during school hours.

Sincerely,
Tony Romano, Principal, Rosedale High School

_____

_____

_____

_____

_____

_____

_____

_____

_____

_____

The Past Participle as an Adjective

LO 5 Use the past participle as an adjective.

A past participle can function as an adjective when it appears after a linking verb such as *be* or *feel*. In the example, *excited* modifies *agent*.

> The young <u>agent</u> was **excited**.

A past participle can also function as an adjective when it describes or modifies the noun that follows it. In the example, *broken* modifies *promises*.

> She was angry about the **broken** <u>promises</u>.

GRAMMAR LINK
For more information about linking verbs, see page 257 in Chapter 16.

HINT ◀ Be Careful!

In the passive voice, sometimes the verb *be* is suggested but not written. The following sentence contains the passive voice.

that were

Many activities done in the 1920s are still common today.

PRACTICE 8

Underline and correct fifteen past participle errors.

EXAMPLE: The scandal has resulted <u>result</u> in the closing of the newspaper.

1. In the early 2000s, cell phone messages that belonged to Prince William, Jude Law, and other celebrities were hack. The information was gave to tabloid journalists. At first, the public was not very interest in the issue. After all, celebrities are expect to have no privacy.

2. Everything changed in 2011. Information was leak to the media about the phone hacking of ordinary citizens. Apparently, a tabloid call *News of the World* had pay a private investigator to spy on a thirteen-year-old murder victim, Milly Dowler. Nine years earlier, after Dowler had disappear, some of her voicemail messages were delete. The parents of the missing teenager were thrill because they thought that their cherish daughter had remove the messages herself.

3. An article, wrote by *The Guardian* newspaper, gave details about the scandal. Members of the public were shock, and they demanded action. In the summer of 2011, the celebrated *News of the World* newspaper was close.

Chapter 24

Reflect On It

Think about what you have learned in this chapter. If you do not know an answer, review that concept.

1. Give two circumstances in which you would use the present perfect tense.

   _____

   _____

   _____

2. When do you use the past perfect tense? _____

   _____

   _____

3. How do you form the passive voice? _____

   _____

   _____

4. Identify and correct the errors in the following sentences.

   a. Robert Ludlum's first book was publish in 1971.

   b. By 2000, he had wrote twenty-one spy novels.

   c. Millions of people have buyed his novel *The Bourne Identity*.

   d. Have you ever saw a movie that was based on a book by Ludlum?

FINAL REVIEW

Part A: Fill in each blank with the appropriate verb tense. The sentence may require the active or passive voice.

EXAMPLE: Closed-circuit cameras (be) _____*have been*_____ common for many years.

1. Since the 1990s, many ordinary citizens (install) _____

   security cameras outside their homes. For example, in 2009, a camera (place)

   _____ outside a home in Coventry, England. In August 2010,

   a forty-five-year-old woman named Mary Bale (film) _____ by

   the security camera as she picked up Darryl Mann's cat and threw it into a large

   blue trash container. The cat, Lola, (discover) _____ fifteen

   hours later by the owners.

2. The next day, Mann released the video on his Facebook page. It quickly became viral, and the culprit, Mary Bale, (identify) _____ by a member of the public. She couldn't deny her action because she (catch) _____ red-handed. A few days later, she said, "It was just a cat," and her life (threaten) _____ by angry animal lovers. Since then, Bale (have) _____ to move to another city.

3. Although Bale (break) _____ the law before that incident, she became the most hated woman in Britain. Many times since then, the gray-haired woman (apologize) _____. Do people deserve to be named and shamed when they make mistakes?

Part B: Underline and correct five past participle errors.

used
EXAMPLE: The video was <u>use</u> in court.

4. Over the years, personal privacy has diminish. For example, the 2010 footage that was took and put online helped capture Bale. She was not gave the opportunity to apologize to the family and to deal with the incident privately. Instead, over a million people have viewed the "Cat in bin in Coventry" video on YouTube, and Bale has losed her good reputation. These days, many people are shame when they act improperly in public.

THE WRITER'S ROOM — MyWritingLab™

MyWritingLab™
**Complete these
writing assignments at
mywritinglab.com**

Write about one of the following topics. Make sure that verb forms are correct.

1. Define an ideal politician. What characteristics should a great politician have?

2. Why do some parents spy on their children? What are the effects of such spying? Write about the causes and effects of spying on children.

Chapter 24

25 Other Verb Forms

SECTION THEME: Spies and Hackers

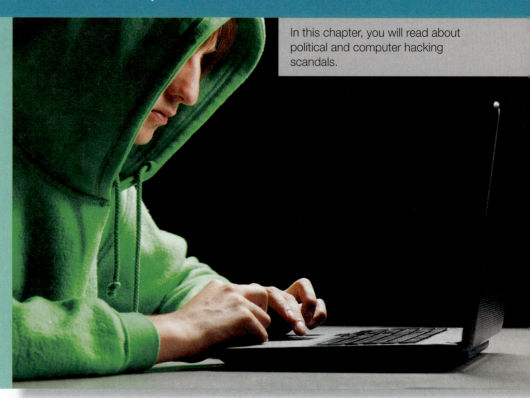

In this chapter, you will read about political and computer hacking scandals.

LEARNING OBJECTIVES

LO 1 Identify problems with progressive forms (-*ing* verbs). **(p. 346)**

LO 2 Avoid nonstandard forms: *gonna, gotta, wanna*. **(p. 348)**

LO 3 Use gerunds and infinitives. **(p. 349)**

LO 4 Use conditional forms. **(p. 351)**

LO 5 Avoid nonstandard forms: *would of, could of, should of*. **(p. 353)**

MyWritingLab™
Complete this Writer's Journal activity at mywritinglab.com

THE WRITER'S JOURNAL

In your opinion, is it ethical to use cameras to spy on nannies, babysitters, or other caregivers? Write a paragraph about the issue.

LO 1 Identify problems with progressive forms (-*ing* verbs).

Problems with Progressive Forms (-*ing* Verbs)

Most verbs have progressive tenses. The **progressive tense** indicates that an action is, was, or will be in progress. For example, the present progressive indicates that an action is happening right now or for a temporary period of time.

Simple present   Every day, Detective Jonkala **spies** on cheating spouses.

Present progressive   Today, he **is following** Ms. Wang.

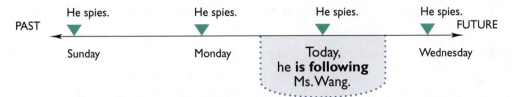

Every day, Detective Jonkala spies on cheating spouses.

To form the progressive, use the appropriate tense of the verb *be* with the *-ing* verb.

Present progressive	Right now, Detective Jonkala is **watching** the suspect.
Past progressive	He **was taking** notes when the suspect left the hotel.
Future progressive	Tomorrow, at 6:00 A.M., Natasha **will be following** the suspect.
Present perfect progressive	Detective Jonkala **has been working** for the police since 1994.
Past perfect progressive	He **had been waiting** in his car when his partner arrived.

Common Errors with the Progressive Form

♦ Do not use the progressive form when an action happens regularly.

        complains

Every day, he ~~is complaining~~ about his job.

♦ In the progressive form, use the correct form of the verb *be*.

         is

Right now, the nanny ~~be~~ playing with the children.

♦ In the progressive form, always include the complete helping verb.

     are   *have*

Right now, the agents examining the photos. They been working for hours.

HINT ◄ Nonprogressive Verbs

Some verbs do not take the progressive form because they indicate an ongoing state or a perception rather than a temporary action. Here are some examples of nonprogressive verbs.

Perception Verbs	Preference Verbs	State Verbs	Possession
admire	care*	believe	belong
feel*	desire	know	have*
hear	doubt	mean	own
look*	hate	realize	possess
see	like	recognize	
seem	love	suppose	
smell*	prefer	think*	
taste*	want	understand	

*The verbs marked with an asterisk have more than one meaning and can also be used in the progressive tense. Compare the next pairs of sentences.

Nonprogressive	Progressive
He **has** a video camera. (Expresses ownership)	He **is having** a bad day.
I **think** it is unethical. (Expresses an opinion)	I **am thinking** about you.

Chapter 25

PRACTICE 1

Each sentence has errors with progressive forms. Underline and correct each error.

EXAMPLE: I <u>been</u> working at the company for years.
have been

1. Generally, I am loving my job, but recently something happened that disturbed me.

2. Yesterday morning, I be browsing the Internet while I was on my break, and I visited a social networking site.

3. I was later called into my boss's office, and I was shocked because I was recognizing my Facebook page on his computer.

4. My boss be upset that I was using Facebook on the company computer.

5. I now realize that the company been monitoring our Internet activity since last summer.

6. It is hard for me to believe that they been spying on my coworkers and me.

7. I am a good employee, and every day I am conducting myself professionally.

8. I do not think that a boss should spy on his or her employees unless they been breaking any rules or ignoring their work.

LO 2 Avoid nonstandard forms: *gonna, gotta, wanna.*

Nonstandard Forms: *gonna, gotta, wanna*

Some people commonly say *I'm gonna, I gotta,* or *I wanna.* These are nonstandard forms, and you should not use them in written communication.

- Write *going to* instead of *gonna.*
  The nanny is ~~gonna~~ sue her employer.
  going to

- Write *have* or *had to* instead of *gotta.*
  The Smiths ~~gotta~~ go to court to fight the lawsuit.
  have to

- Write *want to* instead of *wanna.*
  They ~~wanna~~ win their case.
  want to

PRACTICE 2

Underline and correct eight incorrect verb tenses or nonstandard verbs.

EXAMPLE: Some traitors just <u>wanna</u> earn extra money.
want to

1. From 1976 to 2001, Robert Hanssen worked for the Federal Bureau of Investigation. For fifteen years, while he be doing his day job, he also spying for the Russian government. He regularly passed documents to Russian agents. In 2000, FBI agents realized that Hanssen was a spy.

2. Usually, if agents are gonna arrest someone, they gotta have solid evidence. To get that evidence, the FBI promoted Hanssen and placed him under surveillance. Hanssen did not wanna accept the promotion because he would lose access to useful information. However, he had no choice, so he moved to FBI Headquarters. He soon became suspicious. He noticed that his new assistant was watch him closely.

3. By January 2001, Hanssen realized that he was gonna be arrested. Still, he continued working as a spy. On February 18, he placed a white piece of tape on a sign, which was a signal to his Russian contact. Then, while he was attach a package of documents to the bottom of a wooden footbridge, he was arrested. As agents were handcuffing him, Hanssen asked, "What took you so long?"

Using Gerunds and Infinitives

L03 Use gerunds and infinitives.

Sometimes a main verb is followed by another verb. The second verb can be a gerund or an infinitive. A **gerund** is a verb with an *-ing* ending. An **infinitive** consists of *to* and the base form of the verb.

	verb + gerund
Gerund	Hanssen <u>considered</u> **joining** the FBI.
	verb + infinitive
Infinitive	He <u>wanted</u> **to have** a long career.

Do not confuse gerunds with progressive verb forms. Compare the following sentences.

Maria is writing.   (The action of writing is in progress right now.)

Some people <u>enjoy</u> **writing**.   (*Writing* is a gerund that follows *enjoy*.)

Verbs Followed by Gerunds

acknowledge	deny	keep	recall
adore	detest	loathe	recollect
appreciate	discuss	mention	recommend
avoid	dislike	mind	regret
can't help	enjoy	miss	resent
complete	finish	postpone	resist
consider	imagine	practice	risk
delay	involve	quit	tolerate

EXAMPLES: She would <u>consider</u> **working** for us.

She <u>risks</u> **losing** her job.

Verbs Followed by Infinitives

afford	decide	manage	refuse
agree	demand	mean	seem
appear	deserve	need	swear
arrange	expect	offer	threaten
ask	fail	plan	volunteer
claim	hesitate	prepare	want
compete	hope	pretend	wish
consent	learn	promise	would like

EXAMPLES: He <u>expected</u> **to keep** his job.

He <u>promised</u> **to be** honest.

Verbs Followed by Gerunds or Infinitives

Some verbs can be followed by either a gerund or infinitive.

begin   continue   like   love   start

EXAMPLES: Marcus <u>loves</u> **to spy**.

Marcus <u>loves</u> **spying**.

HINT ‹ Using *Stop*

You can follow *stop* with a gerund or infinitive, but there is a difference in meaning.

Stop + gerund means "to permanently stop doing something."

Hanssen <u>stopped</u> **selling** information to the Soviets.

Stop + infinitive means "to stop an activity to do something else."

The agent was leaving when he <u>stopped</u> **to talk** to an old friend.

PRACTICE 3

Underline the appropriate verb form. Choose the gerund or the infinitive.

EXAMPLE: The spy's job involved (<u>passing</u> / to pass) information to the Russians.

1.   Robert Hanssen, like many double agents, was a very good liar. Most people can't help (lying / to lie) at one time or another. The psychologist Robert Feldman enjoys (studying / to study) human deception. He says that human beings need (lying / to lie) sometimes. Lying seems (being / to be) a part of human nature.

2.   Feldman conducts experiments to learn how people lie. In one test, he places two strangers in a small room. He asks (videotaping / to videotape) the participants. After ten minutes, he stops (taping / to tape), and then he questions the two people. Usually, the subjects deny (to lie / lying). Then, while watching the video, they stop (fooling / to fool) themselves, and they admit that they have made many inaccurate statements. For instance, in one trial, the male participant falsely claimed (being / to be) a musician, and the female pretended (to like / liking) the same music as the male. They justified (being / to be) inaccurate by saying that their lies were not harmful. It appears that humans simply cannot avoid (lying / to lie) sometimes.

Using Conditional Forms

LO 4 Use conditional forms.

In **conditional sentences**, there is a condition and a result. There are three types of conditional sentences, and each type has two parts, or clauses. The main clause depends on the condition set in the *if* clause.

First Form: Possible Present or Future

The condition is true or very possible.

If + present tense, ⟶ present or future tense

Condition (*if* clause)	**Result**
If you **buy** the book,	you **will learn** about satellites.

Second Form: Unlikely Present

The condition is not likely and will probably not happen.

If + past tense, ⟶ *would* (expresses a condition)
If + past tense, ⟶ *could* (expresses a possibility)

Condition (*if* clause)	**Result**
If he **had** the chance,	he **would work** for the CIA.

Chapter 25

Note: In formal writing, when the condition contains the verb *be*, always use *were* in the *if* clause.

If Amanda **were** older, she **would become** a spy.

Third Form: Impossible Past

The condition cannot happen because the event is over.

> *If* + past perfect tense, ————————► *would have* (+ past participle)

Condition (if clause)	**Result**
If Amanda **had known** about the dangers,	she **would have been** more careful.

HINT ◄ **Be Careful with the Past Conditional**

In the third type of conditional sentence, the impossible past, the writer expresses regret about a past event or expresses the wish that a past event had worked out differently. In the *if* part of the sentence, remember to use the past perfect tense.

> *If* + past perfect tense,   . . . *would have* (past participle) . . .

had listened
If CIA agents ~~would have listened~~ to the tape, they **would have discovered** the agent's identity.

PRACTICE 4

Fill in the blanks with the past conditional tense.

EXAMPLE: If the police (make) _____had made_____ an investigation, the case would have been solved.

1. Is hacking ethical? In "A Brief History of Hacking," Mark Ward says that in the 1960s, "hackers were benign creatures." A "hack" was "an inspired solution to a problem." If you (live) _____ in 1986, you (admire) _____ the hackers. Most early hackers just wanted to find the flaws in computer systems. Some of them did silly pranks. For instance, Steve Jobs hacked telephone systems to make free phone calls. Perhaps if the police (arrest) _____ Jobs back in the 1980s, he (form, not) _____ Apple Computers.

2. Another early hacker went by the name Dark Dante. He took over the phone lines of radio shows and won major prizes. For instance, in 1990, he was the 102nd caller to a Los Angeles radio show, and he won a Porsche. If those

radio stations (know) _____ about the hacking, they
(change) _____ the contest rules. After
exploits such as Dark Dante's became well known, new anti-hacking laws
were introduced.

Nonstandard Forms: *would of, could of, should of*

LO 5 Avoid nonstandard forms: *would of, could of, should of*.

Some people commonly say *would of, could of,* or *should of.* They may also say *woulda, coulda,* or *shoulda.* These are nonstandard forms, and you should avoid using them in written communication. When you use the past forms of *should, would,* and *could,* always include *have* + the past participle.

would have
If I had been alive in 1963, I ~~woulda~~ tried to meet President Kennedy.

should have
Unfortunately, he was assassinated. The president ~~should of~~ traveled in a

bulletproof car.

PRACTICE 5

Underline and correct ten errors in conditional forms or in the past forms of *could* and *should.*

should have
EXAMPLE: Chapman ~~shoulda~~ been more careful.

1.   On a warm June day in 2010, Anna Chapman was sitting in a Manhattan

coffee shop. In a few minutes, she would meet a mysterious stranger.

A Facebook addict, she definitely would have check her Facebook page.

She coulda passed for the girl next door, but the perky redhead was actually an

undercover Russian spy.

2.   Chapman's guest arrived. The good-looking man said he was working

for the Russian consulate. That FBI agent would of said anything to get

Chapman to trust him. He asked Chapman if she would delivering a fake

passport to another Russian spy. Chapman shoulda been more suspicious,

but she agreed to do the transfer. Soon after, Chapman and nine other

Russian spies were arrested. They must of felt upset when they were handcuffed.

Anna Chapman

3.   Normally, the spies would have went to prison. However, the United States and Russia didn't want to damage their relationship, and they organized a spy exchange. Probably, if Anna Chapman would have refused to work as a spy, her life woulda been more boring. Today, she hosts her own weekly TV show in Russia. If she hadn't become notorious, she would not of received that job.

Reflect On It

Think about what you have learned in this chapter. If you do not know an answer, review that concept.

1. When do you use the progressive form of verbs? _____
    _____

2. Write your own examples of the three types of conditional sentences.
    First form: _____

    _____

    Second form: _____

    _____

    Third form: _____

    _____

3. Correct the following sentences by writing the standard form of each nonstandard verb.

    a. If you wanna succeed, you gotta work hard.

    b. J. Rowen been investigating UFOs since 1978.

    c. If Kennedy would have taken another route, maybe he woulda lived.

    d. Maybe one day somebody is gonna tell the truth about the Kennedy case.

    e. I enjoyed to read a book about the trial.

FINAL REVIEW

Underline and correct twenty errors with verbs. Look for nonstandard verbs and errors with conditionals, gerunds, and progressive forms.

EXAMPLE: Monsegur should ~~of~~ *have* found a computer security job.

1.   In early February 2011, Aaron Barr, the CEO of a security

firm, did an interview with the *Financial Times*. He boasted that

he was gonna expose core leaders in the hacker collective

Anonymous. Many people read the interview, including some

hackers. A few days later, on February 6, Barr be watching the

Super Bowl. When he finished to drink his coffee, he tried

unsuccessfully to access his e-mail account. At that moment,

hackers annihilating Barr's Web site, changing his passwords,

and posting thousands of his e-mails on Pirate Bay. Barr panicked and

realized that he should not of threatened Anonymous. He called his

computer technician, pleading, "You gotta do something." It was too late. If

Barr would have kept quiet, he would have avoided a major headache.

2.   Feeling bold after the Barr attack, the Anonymous members promised

hacking the CIA and the FBI. They felt sure that nobody was gonna catch them.

But those hackers should not of been so cocky. On June 7, 2011, two FBI agents

put on their bulletproof vests and went to a housing complex in New York's

Lower East side. That day was very hot, so the agents be sweating profusely.

Hector Xavier Monsegur, a twenty-eight-year-old unemployed father of two,

be cooking for his children when someone knocked on the door. Monsegur,

who used the online name "Sabu," couldn't believe it when he saw the agents.

At first, he denied to be a hacker, but his computers provided the evidence the

agents needed. Soon after, Sabu agreed working undercover for the FBI. Of

course, he woulda felt really guilty about snitching on his friends, but he didn't

wanna lose his children and spend his life in prison.

3.   In March 2012, based on Sabu's information, police arrested Ryan Ackroyd,

a twenty-five-year-old British citizen. Maybe if Ackroyd would have been more

Chapter 25

suspicious of Sabu, he could have saved himself. A few days later, Jake Davis, an eighteen-year-old hacker, must of been shocked when the police turned up at his door. Many argue that the hackers should not of attacked government and corporate Web sites and that their arrests were justified. Since then, other hackers have filled the void left by the arrests. Clearly, computer hacking is gonna continue in the future.

MyWritingLab™

Complete these writing assignments at mywritinglab.com

MyWritingLab™ **THE WRITER'S ROOM**

Write about one of the following topics. Review your verb forms carefully.

1. How would your life have been different if you had lived one hundred years ago? List some ways.

2. Should journalists report on the private lives of politicians? For example, is it important to know if a candidate has committed adultery or has had an addiction to drugs or alcohol? Explain your views.

THE WRITER'S CIRCLE **Collaborative Activity**

Work with a group of two or three other students. Choose a scandal that was in the news. It can be a scandal that happened to a celebrity, politician, sports figure, or business person. Discuss what happened. Then, as a team, write a short paragraph about the scandal. Use the past tense.

After writing the paragraph about the scandal, discuss what you would have done if you had been that person. Then, in a second paragraph, write about what you would have done. Explain why, and give some details.

READING LINK

To learn more about spies and hackers, read the next essays.

"How Spies Are Caught" (page 554)

Subject–Verb Agreement 26

SECTION THEME: College Life

In this chapter, you will read about topics related to college issues.

LEARNING OBJECTIVES

LO 1 Identify basic subject–verb agreement rules. **(p. 357)**

LO 2 Maintain subject–verb agreement when there is more than one subject. **(p. 362)**

LO 3 Identify special subject forms. **(p. 363)**

LO 4 Maintain subject–verb agreement when the verb is before the subject. **(p. 365)**

LO 5 Identify interrupting words and phrases. **(p. 366)**

Complete this Writer's Journal activity at mywritinglab.com

THE WRITER'S JOURNAL

In a short paragraph, express your opinion about the extracurricular activities on your campus.

Basic Subject–Verb Agreement Rules

LO 1 Identify basic subject–verb agreement rules.

Subject–verb agreement simply means that a subject and verb agree in number. A singular subject needs a singular verb, and a plural subject needs a plural verb.

                               S   V

Singular subject   Mr. Connor **teaches** in a community college.

                               S   V

Plural subject   The students **appreciate** his approach.

Simple Present Tense Agreement

Writers use the **simple present tense** to indicate that an action is habitual or factual. Review the following rules for simple present tense agreement.

◆ When the subject is *he, she, it*, or the equivalent (*Adam, Maria, Florida*), add an *-s* or *-es* ending to the verb. This is also called the **third-person singular form**.

> **Singular**   Michael **works** in the college bookstore. (one person)
>
>   This neighborhood **needs** a medical clinic. (one place)
>
>   The trophy **belongs** to the best athlete in the college. (one thing)

> **GRAMMAR LINK**
> For more information about the present tense, see Chapter 23.

◆ When the subject is *I, you, we, they*, or the equivalent (*the Zorns, the mountains, Amber and Tom*) do not add an ending to the verb.

> **Plural**   College students **have** many options. (more than one person)
>
>   Many colleges **host** political debates. (more than one place)
>
>   The benefits **include** a higher standard of living. (more than one thing)

For example, review the present tense forms of the verb *help*.

Present Tense of *Help*

	Singular	Plural
First person	I help	We help
Second person	You help	You help
Third person	He **helps**	They help
	She **helps**	
	It **helps**	

PRACTICE 1

Write the present tense form of each verb in parentheses.

EXAMPLE: Counselors (encourage) _____*encourage*_____ students to seek help for problems.

1. A freshman, Alex Snow (study) _____ at a college four hours away from his hometown.

2. He (rent) _____ a small room near the college, but he (try) _____ to go home as often as possible.

3. Alex (realize) _____ that he sometimes (get) _____ lonely.

4. He (miss) _____ his family and friends.

5. Many students (find) _____ that they (become)

   _____ homesick in their first months at college.

6. Alex's college (offer) _____ a counseling service for

   students experiencing difficulties, such as homesickness, depression, and

   so on.

7. Alex (know) _____ that it is important to get help, so he (see)

   _____ a counselor once a week.

Troublesome Present Tense Verbs: *be, have, do*

Some present tense verbs are formed in special ways. Review the verbs *be, have,*
and *do.*

	Be	*Have*	*Do*
Singular Forms			
First person	I am	I have	I do
Second person	You are	You have	You do
Third person	He **is**	He **has**	He **does**
	She **is**	She **has**	She **does**
	It **is**	It **has**	It **does**
Plural Forms			
First person	We are	We have	We do
Second person	You are	You have	You do
Third person	They are	They have	They do

HINT ◄ Use Standard Forms of *Be*

Some people use sentences such as *He be ready* or *She ain't happy*. However,
those are nonstandard forms and should not be used in written conversation.
Review the following corrections.

>   *is*   *is not*
> That man ~~be~~ cool, but he ~~ain't~~ a good candidate for Student Council
> president.

PRACTICE 2

In the next selection, each verb is underlined. Correct fifteen errors in subject–verb
agreement or the incorrect use of *ain't*. Write *C* above five correct verbs.

Chapter 26

learn

EXAMPLE: Successful students <u>learns</u> good study skills.

1. College students <u>need</u> to form good study habits if they <u>wants</u> to get good marks. College courses <u>has</u> fewer assignments than high school courses, so a college assignment <u>are</u> worth more. Being organized <u>are</u> crucial for college success.

2. Annie <u>is</u> a typical student. She <u>participate</u> in many activities. She <u>have</u> an active social life. She <u>waits</u> until the last minute to finish her assignments. She <u>try</u> to hurry, so she <u>make</u> many mistakes.

3. Successful college students <u>organizes</u> their time. They <u>know</u> that it <u>ain't</u> good to postpone doing homework. Rashad <u>hope</u> to become a better student. He <u>spend</u> each evening reviewing his notes and doing his assignments. He <u>ask</u> his professors questions if he <u>do</u> not understand a concept. He <u>has</u> a social life, but he <u>use</u> his time wisely.

Simple Past Tense Agreement

In the past tense, all verbs except *be* have one past form.

Regular	I called.	He called.	You called.	We called.	They called.
Irregular	I slept.	He slept.	You slept.	We slept.	They slept.

Exception: *Be*

In the past tense, the only verb requiring subject–verb agreement is the verb *be*, which has two past forms: *was* and *were*.

Was	**Were**
I was	We were
He was	You were
She was	They were
It was	

Present Perfect Tense Agreement

When writing in the present perfect tense, which is formed with *have* or *has* and the past participle, use *has* when the subject is third-person singular.

My college **has** raised tuition fees. Other colleges **have** not raised their fees.

Agreement in Other Tenses

When writing in most other verb tenses, and in modal forms (*can, could, would, may, might,* and so on), use the same form of the verb with every subject.

GRAMMAR LINK
For more information about using the present perfect tense, see Chapter 24.

Future	I will **work**; she will **work**; they will **work**; you will **work**; we will **work**
Past perfect	I had **met**; she had **met**; they had **met**; you had **met**; we had **met**
Modals	I can **talk**; she should **talk**; they could **talk**; you might **talk**; we would **talk**

PRACTICE 3

Correct twelve subject–verb agreement errors among the underlined verbs, and write *C* above five correct verbs.

                          exists
EXAMPLE: A problem exist in many colleges and universities.

1.   Credit card debt <u>be</u> common on American campuses. Card companies <u>mail</u> applications to students. Today, the average undergraduate <u>have</u> more than $2,000 in credit card debt. Of course, the longer a student <u>takes</u> to pay off a debt, the higher the debt <u>become</u>.

2.   Jeremy <u>be</u> a thirty-year-old man who is still paying for the pizza that he ate in college. Ten years ago, Jeremy and his friends <u>was</u> not careful. They <u>were</u> happy to buy food, video games, and clothing with their credit cards. Since then, Jeremy <u>have</u> never <u>managed</u> to pay off the debt. In fact, he still <u>use</u> his Visa card regularly. He <u>want</u> to pay $42, which is the minimum payment. He <u>don't</u> realize that only 89 cents will be applied to his debt. The rest of the money <u>will goes</u> toward late fees and interest fees.

3.   Credit card companies <u>charge</u> extremely high fees. When you <u>receives</u> a credit card, you <u>should pays</u> the balance every month. You <u>can avoid</u> interest rates of about 20 percent.

Chapter 26

More Than One Subject

There are special agreement rules when there is more than one subject in a sentence.

and

When subjects are joined by *and*, use the plural form of the verb.

Colleges, universities, and trade schools **prepare** students for the job market.

or, nor

When two subjects are joined by *or* or *nor*, the verb agrees with the subject that is closer to it.

plural

Neither Amanda Jackson nor her students **use** the computer lab.

singular

Either the students or Amanda **uses** the department's portable laptop computer.

HINT ◂ *As Well As* and *Along With*

The phrases *as well as* and *along with* are not the same as *and*. They do not form a compound subject. The real subject is before the interrupting expression.

Joe, as well as Carlos and Peter, **works** in a career college.

Joe, along with Carlos and Peter, **teaches** business classes.

PRACTICE 4

Underline the correct verb in each sentence. Make sure the verb agrees with the subject.

EXAMPLE: College administrators (make / makes) rules to discourage underage drinking.

1. College administrators, student counselors, and parents (worry / worries) about a major problem on college campuses.

2. College students and young workers (abuse / abuses) alcohol.

3. Beer, as well as hard liquor, (is / are) common on college campuses.

4. Dorian and Alfredo (drink / drinks) because of peer pressure.

5. Keshia, along with her friends, (go / goes) to bars on weekends.

6. Either Keshia or her boyfriend (buy / buys) alcohol to take to parties.

7. Underage drinkers sometimes (miss / misses) classes, (engage / engages) in unplanned sexual activities, or (injure / injures) themselves.

8. Either the police or an administrator (punish / punishes) students who are caught drinking.

9. Sometimes a male or female student (get / gets) expelled from college due to underage drinking.

Special Subject Forms

LO 3 Identify special subject forms.

Some subjects are not easy to identify as singular or plural. Two common types are indefinite pronouns and collective nouns.

Indefinite Pronouns

Indefinite pronouns refer to a general person, place, or thing. Carefully review the following list of indefinite pronouns.

Indefinite Pronouns

Singular	another	each	nobody	other
	anybody	everybody	no one	somebody
	anyone	everyone	nothing	someone
	anything	everything	one	something
Plural	both, few, many, others, several			

Singular Indefinite Pronouns

In the following sentences, the verbs require the third-person singular form because the subjects are singular.

Everyone **knows** that career colleges offer practical, career-oriented courses.

Nothing **stops** people from applying to a career college.

You can put one or more singular nouns (joined by *and*) after *each* and *every*. The verb is still singular.

Each man and woman **knows** the stories about secret societies.

Plural Indefinite Pronouns

Both, few, many, others, and *several* are all plural subjects. The verb is always plural.

Many **apply** to high-tech programs.

Others **prefer** to study in the field of health care.

PRACTICE 5

Underline the subjects and circle the correct verbs.

EXAMPLE: Many Americans (is / are) English instructors in Korea.

1. Min-Jee Park (lives / live) in South Korea. She (is / are) a Korean-American. She, along with her friend Andrea, (teaches / teach) English at a university in Seoul. Both (considers / consider) their jobs to be very satisfying.

2. Koreans (wants / want) to improve their knowledge of English. Many (enrolls / enroll) in language classes while attending university. Korean culture (values / value) social uniformity over individual ability. So universities often (refuses / refuse) to test students for language proficiency. Therefore, Min-Jee (has / have)

students of all language levels in her class. All of Min-Jee's students (desires / desire) high grades. Some even (offers / offer) Min-Jee "gifts" for higher marks. This practice is not unusual, but she (refuses / refuse) such presents.

3.   Korean students (is / are) very respectful of their instructors. When Min-Jee (walks / walk) past a group of students, everyone (bows / bow) to her. Although Min-Jee is only twenty-five, no one (calls / call) her by her first name. In class, everybody always (listens / listen) to her. Nobody ever (voices / voice) disagreement with the instructor. Min-Jee sometimes (has / have) difficulty getting her students to debate issues.

4.   Neither Min-Jee nor Andrea (wants / want) to return to the United States yet. Both still (has / have) one more year on their teaching contract. They (is / are) becoming used to life in Korea.

Collective Nouns

Collective nouns refer to a group of people or things. These are common collective nouns.

army	class	crowd	group	population
association	club	family	jury	public
audience	committee	gang	military	society
band	company	government	organization	team

Generally, each group acts as a unit, so you must use the singular form of the verb.

The <u>committee</u> supports the new policies.

If the members of the group act individually, use the plural form of the verb. It is a good idea to use a phrase such as *members of*.

Acceptable   The <u>committee</u> **are** not able to come to an agreement.

Better   The <u>members of the committee</u> **are** not able to come to an agreement.

HINT   *Police* Is Plural

The word *police* is always thought of as a plural noun because the word *officers* is implied but not stated.

The police **have** arrested the senator.

The police **are** patrolling the neighborhood.

PRACTICE 6

In each sentence, underline the subject and circle the correct verb.

EXAMPLE: The <u>government</u> (offer / offers) financial aid for some students.

1.   A career college (is / are) a sensible choice for many students wanting practical work skills. Such institutions (offer / offers) a variety of career-related

programs. For example, my college (have / has) programs in high-tech, health care, business, and hospitality.

2.   My friend Santosh (studies / study) in the hospitality program. Santosh (was / were) a cook in the army, but now he (want / wants) a career in adventure tourism. The army (provide / provides) financial help to Santosh for his studies. In fact, the military (encourage / encourages) its personnel to continue their education and training. Santosh's family also (give / gives) him encouragement.

3.   People (need / needs) social, math, communication, and organizational skills in the hospitality business. Everyone (enter / enters) this field knowing that he or she must be able to get along with people during stressful situations. The industry (is / are) growing, but it (is / are) very important to have the right education. Career colleges (give / gives) students an advantage in this highly competitive market.

Verb Before the Subject

Usually the verb comes after the subject, but in some sentences, the verb comes before the subject. In such cases, you must still ensure that the subject and verb agree.

LO 4 Maintain subject–verb agreement when the verb is before the subject.

there or *here*

When a sentence begins with *there* or *here*, the subject always follows the verb. *There* and *here* are not subjects.

    V   S   V   S

Here **is** the college course <u>list</u>. There **are** many night <u>courses</u>.

Questions

In questions, word order is usually reversed, and the main or helping verb is placed before the subject. In the following example, the main verb is *be*.

    V   S   V   S

Where **is** the <u>cafeteria</u>? **Is** the <u>food</u> good?

In questions in which the main verb isn't *be*, the subject usually agrees with the helping verb.

    HV   S   V HV   S   V

When **does** the <u>library</u> **close**? **Do** <u>students</u> **work** there?

PRACTICE 7

Correct any subject–verb agreement errors. If the sentence is correct, write *C* in the blank.

EXAMPLE: ~~Has~~ you ever won a competition?   <u> Have </u>

1. There is many athletic scholarships in colleges.   <u>   </u>

2. Has many students benefited from the scholarships?   <u>   </u>

3. Does athletes get preferential treatment?   _____

4. Is there a reason to stop giving scholarships to athletes?   _____

5. There is many pressures on student athletes.   _____

6. Why do Wayne Brydon want to play basketball professionally?   _____

7. Do female athletes have the same opportunities
    as male athletes?   _____

8. According to Selma Rowen, there have not been enough
    attention given to academically successful students.   _____

9. On the other hand, there is many people who support athletes. _____

10. In addition to doing their coursework, do college athletes
    have to train for several hours each day?   _____

LO 5 Identify interrupting words and phrases.

Interrupting Words and Phrases

Words that come between the subject and the verb may confuse you. In these cases, look for the subject and make sure that the verb agrees with the subject.

> S   interrupting phrase   V
> Some <u>rules</u> regarding admission to this college **are** controversial.

> S   prepositional phrase   V
> A <u>student</u> in two of my classes **writes** for the college newspaper.

HINT ◀ **Identify Interrupting Phrases**

When you revise your paragraphs, add parentheses around words that separate the subject and the verb. Then you can check to see whether your subjects and verbs agree.

> S   prepositional phrase   V
> The <u>single mother</u> (in my literature class) also **works** part time.

When interrupting phrases contain *of the* or similar words, the subject appears before the phrase.

> S   prepositional phrase   V
> <u>One</u> (of my biggest problems) **is** my lack of organization.

PRACTICE 8

Underline the subject in each sentence. Add parentheses around any words that come between each subject and verb. Then circle the correct form of the verb.

EXAMPLE: <u>One</u> (of the most controversial issues on campus) (**is**) / **are** affirmative
action.

1.   Some colleges in this country **have** / **has** more relaxed admission standards

    for students from ethnic minority groups. Such colleges, with good reason,

want / wants to have a vibrant and diverse student population. However, arguing that they have been discriminated against, students from across the nation **have / has** sued their colleges. Judges in many jurisdictions **have / has** had to consider whether affirmative action is unfair.

2.   People in favor of affirmative action **have / has** compelling arguments. Historically, some ethnic groups in the United States **has / have** not had access to higher education. Many factors, such as poverty, **contribute / contributes** to the problem. University of California professor Norman Matloff, in an article for *Asian Week*, **suggest / suggests** that society suffers when there is a large, poorly educated underclass. Additionally, affirmative action **help / helps** create a diverse student body.

3.   Opponents of affirmative action **feel / feels** that admissions should be based purely on test scores. Barbara Grutter, a white businesswoman, **was / were** thinking of changing careers. Her application to the University of Michigan's law school **was / were** refused. She **argues / argue** that affirmative action is reverse discrimination. One of her best arguments **is / are** compelling: Grutter, as a forty-year-old single mother, **add / adds** to the university's diversity. On June 23, 2003, a decision about Grutter's affirmative action case **was / were** made. Although justices in the U.S. Supreme Court **were / was** divided, the Court ruled that race can be used as one of the factors in college admissions.

4.   For some people, regulations to safeguard affirmative action **help / helps** equalize opportunities in our society. For others, such regulations **is / are** unfair to certain groups. What is your opinion?

Interrupting Words: *who, which, that*

Some sentences include a relative clause beginnning wih the pronoun *who*, *which*, or *that*. In the relative clause, the verb must agree with the antecedent of *who*, *which*, or *that*.

In the first example below, the antecedent of *who* is *woman*. In the second example, the antecedent of *that* is *newspapers*. And in the third example, the *antecedent* of which is *article*.

There is a <u>woman</u> in my neighborhood *who* **counsels** students.

Here are some old <u>newspapers</u> *that* **discuss** steroid abuse.

One <u>article</u>, *which* **contains** stories about corruption, is very interesting.

Chapter 26

PRACTICE 9

Underline and correct nine subject–verb agreement errors.

EXAMPLE: The candidate who ~~support~~ *supports* tax increases is unlikely to win.

1.   Students who hope to become politicians usually becomes active in college

   politics. The experience that they gain help them advance politically. For

   instance, Chandra Wang, who is in a community college, have a position on the

   student council. About once a month, she go to council meetings. The council

   discusses issues that affects students. In the future, Wang hopes to become a

   senator.

2.   There is many people who wants to enter the political arena. Generally, nobody

   start at the top. Almost every leader who is successful have a lot of experience.

Reflect On It

Think about what you have learned in this unit. If you do not know an answer, review that concept.

1.   When should you add -*s* or -*es* to verbs? _____

   _____

2.   Look at the following nouns. Circle all the collective nouns.

   family   people   army   committee
   judge   crowd   brothers   audience

3.   When do you use *was* and *were*?
   Use *was* _____
   Use *were* _____

4.   Circle and correct any subject–verb agreement errors in the following sentences.

   a.   There is many colleges in Florida.

   b.   Yale is a university that have several secret societies.

   c.   Either the Edwards sisters or Simon have been initiated.

   d.   One of our cousins go to Yale.

   e.   There is no hazing rituals on our campus.

FINAL REVIEW

Underline and correct twenty errors in subject–verb agreement.

                                                   provides

EXAMPLE: A full-scholarship college in the United States <u>provide</u> students with a
wide-ranging education.

1.   Every morning at 7:00 A.M., Conrad Dilbert walk to the outdoor areas on
his college campus. He, along with another classmate, weed the flowerbeds.
The college provides Conrad with free tuition but expect him to work part
time. In fact, everyone who study there works part time.

2.   There is only a few full-scholarship colleges in the United States. Each
college committee accept applicants on the basis of financial need and academic
standing. Conrad, as well as his classmates, work in the cafeteria, on the
grounds, or in the library.

3.   According to *BusinessWeek*, there is many reasons to choose tuition-free
colleges. First, the cost of a college or university education have risen in recent
years. Many parents find the expense prohibitive. Neither Conrad nor his
parents has a lot of money. Furthermore, almost everyone who select such
colleges graduate without a lot of student debt. Moreover, these institutions
attract students who wants to specialize in subjects such as music or
engineering.

4.   How do a particular college afford to be tuition free? One of the colleges
that recently received publicity are Berea College in Kentucky. The *New York
Times* reported that Berea, which were founded more than a century ago, have
a very large endowment. The college's billion-dollar fund help it to offer a free
education to its students. Nobody pay tuition.

5.   Tuition-free colleges help students who cannot afford college fees
completes a college education. Such institutions help society.

MyWritingLab™

THE WRITER'S ROOM

Write about one of the following topics. Make sure that your subjects and verbs agree.

1. Examine this photo. Define a term that relates to the photo. Some ideas might be *debt*, *interest rates*, *reckless spender*, *cheapskate*, *spendthift*, or *credit card junkie*.

2. Should college be free? What are the advantages or disadvantages of free college?

LEARNING OBJECTIVE

LO 1 Use consistent verb tense. **(p. 371)**

In this chapter, you will read about people who have made difficult choices.

THE WRITER'S JOURNAL

How do images in the media influence the way that people judge their own bodies? Write a short paragraph about the media and body image.

Consistent Verb Tense

LO 1 Use consistent verb tense.

When you write, the verb tense you use gives the reader an idea about the time when the event occurred. A **faulty tense shift** occurs when you shift from one tense to another for no logical reason.

Faulty tense shift	College reporter Erica Santiago interviewed a protester and <u>asks</u> about his political philosophy.
Correct	College reporter Erica Santiago interviewed a protester and <u>asked</u> about his political philosophy.

Sometimes the time frame in a text really does change. In those circumstances, you would change the verb tense. The following example accurately shows two different time periods. Notice that certain key words (*during my childhood, today*) indicate what tense the writer should use.

past   present

During my childhood, I <u>ate</u> a lot of fast food. Today, I <u>try</u> to eat a healthy diet.

PRACTICE 1

Identify and correct each faulty tense shift. If the sentence is correct, write *C* in the space.

EXAMPLE: Many adults go back to college and ~~received~~ training in   *receive*
new careers.

1. Career change is a frightening experience for many people because they lost the security and familiarity of a job, and they have to go back to school to become requalified.   _____

2. Last year, Lee Kim was at a crossroads in his life because he is about to change careers.   _____

3. For the previous ten years, Lee had been working as a computer service technician for a small company, but a year ago, the company downsized, and he lost his job.   _____

4. Suddenly, at the age of thirty-five, Lee is faced with having to change careers, and he was scared.   _____

5. Lee met with a career counselor; she advises Lee to check out the different programs in various career colleges.   _____

6. Lee researched the courses at different institutions, and he finds that the medical laboratories program was a good option for him.   _____

7. Now, Lee is enrolled as a student at Holly Fields Career College, but he admits that going back to college after many years is intimidating.   _____

8. Nowadays, Lee had to budget his money and has to relearn how to be a student.   _____

HINT ⟨ *Would* and *Could*

When you tell a story about a past event, use *would* instead of *will*, and use *could* instead of *can*.

could
In 1996, college wrestler Robert Burzak knew that he <u>can</u> bulk up if he

would
used steriods, but he promised his coach that he <u>will</u> not.

PRACTICE 2

Underline and correct ten faulty tense shifts.

finished
EXAMPLE: Kendra went to career college after she <u>finishes</u> high school.

1.   According to historians, America's first institution of higher education was

founded in 1636. Harvard University opened only sixteen years after the

Mayflower lands at Cape Cod. The university was named after John Harvard, who leaves his money to the institution after his death. He also gives Harvard about four hundred books.

2.   One of Harvard's earliest donors was a woman. Anne Radcliff Moulson, along with her husband, Thomas Moulson, operated an inn. After her husband's death, "Lady Anne" built up the family business, and she decides to create a scholarship at Harvard. Throughout her lifetime, however, the university excludes women. In fact, for the first 147 years of its existence, women can't go to Harvard. They can complain, but the school won't change its policies.

3.   Eventually, in 1873, builders created an annex for women, and the university names it after Radcliff. Finally, in 1999, Harvard and Radcliff joined, and women can study alongside men. These days, females outnumber males at Harvard and at many other major universities.

Reflect On It

Think about what you have learned in this unit. If you do not know an answer, review that concept.

1. What is a faulty tense shift? _____

   _____

2. If you are writing a paragraph about a past event, what word should you use instead of these two?
   a. will: _____   b. can: _____

3. Read the following paragraphs, and find five faulty tense shifts. Correct the errors.

   EXAMPLE: Kaitlin diets because she ~~wanted~~ *wants* to look thinner.

   In 2010, college student Amy Heller became severely malnourished. In an attempt to lose weight, Heller ingested diet pills, and she severely restricts her intake of food. When others suggested that she had a problem, Heller will deny it. By July 2011, she weighs only 88 pounds. Heller finally sought treatment, and soon she can eat regular meals.

In 2013, Heller decided to speak about her condition. She went to a treatment center and offers her services. Today, she works with patients who suffer from eating disorders.

FINAL REVIEW

Underline and correct fifteen faulty tense shifts.

EXAMPLE: Last year, there was an election, and many people vote.

voted

1. During America's 2012 election, about 60 percent of eligible citizens registered and vote. The turnout was lower than in the 2008 and 2004 elections. According to CNN, the lowest turnout is in Hawaii, where only 43 percent bothered to visit their polling stations. That November 4, Hawaiian citizens Michael and Donna Ellison don't vote because they disliked the candidates.

2. In the United States, voting is not compulsory. However, about thirty nations have a voting law. In Greece, Thailand, and Italy, everybody of legal age must vote, but the laws are not strict. During typical elections, officials did not arrest nonvoters. Additionally, Mexico and Panama do not enforce the compulsory voting law, so voter turnout remained low.

3. Many other nations, including Turkey, Uruguay, and Argentina, have very strict voting laws. Officials sometimes punish nonvoters with fines or even imprisonment. For example, during Argentina's 2003 election, Ileana Guerera decided that she will not vote in the election because she disapproved of the candidates. She receives a fine, and she had to pay it. Her brother also stayed home on April 27, 2003, but he has a doctor's note. He knew he will not receive a fine. He had a legitimate excuse, so he can stay home that day.

4. In the early 1920s, many Australian citizens were apathetic, and close to 50 percent do not participate in elections. Then in 1924, government officials

passed a law making voting compulsory. In the election of 1925, people rushed to the polling stations and vote. They worried that they can be arrested if they refused to vote. Today, the voter turnout in Australia is about 95 percent.

5.   There are many people who support compulsory voting. They believe that voting was a civic duty. However, others consider voting a civil right rather than a duty. They regarded compulsory voting laws as an infringement on personal rights. Do you support compulsory voting?

READING LINK

To learn more about college issues, read the following essays.

"The Wonders of PowerPoint" by Karine Godin (page 204)
"Homophobia" by Dominic Chartrand (page 209)
"The Importance of Music" by Christine Bigras (page 228)
"It's Class, Stupid!" by Richard Rodriguez (page 518)

MyWritingLab™
Complete these writing assignments at mywritinglab.com

THE WRITER'S ROOM

Write about one of the following topics. Ensure that you have no faulty tense shifts.

1. Describe your college campus. You might describe an interesting building or area of the campus.

2. What is your opinion of compulsory voting? Should everybody have to vote in elections? Explain why or why not.

THE WRITERS' CIRCLE   Collaborative Activity

Work with a team of students, and create a short survey. Form at least five interesting questions about college life. For example, you can ask about food services, course selection, transportation, student fees, extracurricular activities, fashions, student study habits, or any other topic that you can think of.

For each question that you create, include a list of possible choices. It will be much easier to compile your results if all students choose from a selection. Do not give open-ended questions. Finally, if a question asks about student knowledge, give an "I don't know" choice. Otherwise, students may simply make a guess, and that would skew your results.

After you have completed your survey questions, one team member should remain seated, and the other team members should split up and sit with other groups in the class to ask the questions. After each member has gathered information, the original group should get together and write a summary of the results.

Chapter 27

28 Nouns, Determiners, and Prepositions

SECTION THEME: Our Environment

LEARNING OBJECTIVES

LO 1 Identify singular and plural nouns. (p. 376)

LO 2 Identify count nouns and noncount nouns. (p. 380)

LO 3 Define determiners. (p. 382)

LO 4 Define prepositions. (p. 385)

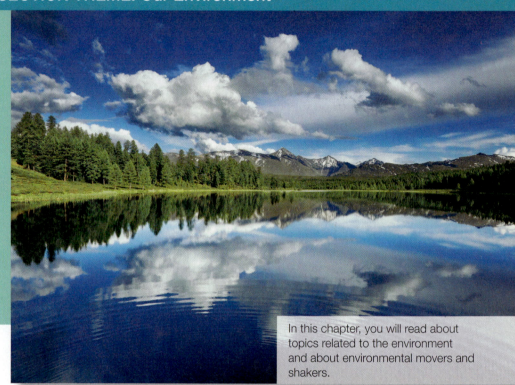

In this chapter, you will read about topics related to the environment and about environmental movers and shakers.

THE WRITER'S JOURNAL

Think about our world. Many things seem wrong in it, yet other things give us hope. Write about what is going right in the world.

LO 1 Identify singular and plural nouns.

Singular and Plural Nouns

Nouns are words that refer to people, places, or things. Nouns are divided into common nouns and proper nouns.

♦ **Common nouns** refer to general people, places, or things and begin with a lowercase letter. For example, *books, computer*, and *city* are common nouns.

♦ **Proper nouns** refer to particular people, places, or things and begin with a capital letter. For example, *Rachel Carson, Greenpeace*, and *Love Canal* are proper nouns.

Nouns are either singular or plural. A **singular noun** refers to one of something, while a **plural noun** refers to more than one of something. Regular plural nouns end in *-s* or *-es*.

	Singular	**Plural**
People	inventor	inventors
	writer	writers
Places	town	towns
	village	villages
Things	computer	computers
	box	boxes

HINT ◀ Adding *-es*

When a noun ends in *s*, *x*, *ch*, *sh*, or *z*, add *-es* to form the plural.

business/business**es**   tax/tax**es**   church/church**es**

Irregular Plural Nouns

Nouns that do not use *-s* or *-es* in their plural forms are called **irregular nouns**. Here are some common irregular nouns.

Singular	**Plural**	**Singular**	**Plural**
person	people	woman	women
child	children	tooth	teeth
man	men	foot	feet

Some nouns use other rules to form the plural. It is a good idea to memorize both the rules and the exceptions.

◆ For nouns ending in *f* or *fe*, change the *f* to *v* and add *-es*.

Singular	**Plural**	**Singular**	**Plural**
knife	kni**ves**	thief	thie**ves**
wife	wi**ves**	leaf	lea**ves**

Some exceptions: belief, beliefs; roof, roofs; safe, safes

◆ For nouns ending in a consonant + *y*, change the *y* to *i* and add *-es*.

Singular	**Plural**	**Singular**	**Plural**
lady	lad**ies**	baby	bab**ies**
berry	berr**ies**	lottery	lotter**ies**

If a vowel comes before the final *y*, then the word retains the regular plural form.

Singular	**Plural**	**Singular**	**Plural**
day	day**s**	key	key**s**

◆ Some nouns remain the same in both singular and plural forms.

Singular	**Plural**	**Singular**	**Plural**
fish	fish	deer	deer
moose	moose	sheep	sheep

◆ Some nouns are thought of as being only plural and therefore have no singular form.

Plural Form with a Plural Verb

clothes	goods	pants	scissors
eyeglasses	proceeds	savings	shorts

Plural Form with a Singular Verb

news	economics	politics	physics

◆ Some nouns are **compound nouns**, which means that they are made up of two or more words. To form the plural of compound nouns, add -s or -es to the last word of the compound noun.

Singular	Plural	Singular	Plural
bus stop	bus stops	artificial heart	artificial hearts
air conditioner	air conditioners	jet airplane	jet airplanes

In hyphenated compound nouns, if the first word is a noun, add -s to the noun.

Singular	Plural	Singular	Plural
senator-elect	senators-elect	runner-up	runners-up
sister-in-law	sisters-in-law	husband-to-be	husbands-to-be

◆ Some nouns that are borrowed from Latin or Greek keep the plural form of the original language.

Singular	Plural	Singular	Plural
millennium	millennia	paparazzo	paparazzi
datum	data	phenomenon	phenomena

HINT ◂ *Persons* versus *People*

There are two plural forms of *person*. *People* is the most common plural form.

Some <u>people</u> take the bus to work. Many <u>people</u> ride their bikes to work.

Persons is used in a legal or official context.

The crime was committed by <u>persons</u> unknown.

PRACTICE 1

Fill in the blanks with either the singular or the plural form of the noun. If the noun does not change, put an *X* in the space.

EXAMPLES:

Singular	Plural
man	men
X	goggles

1. person _____
2. _____ mice
3. brother-in-law _____
4. lady _____
5. _____ jeans
6. sheep _____
7. _____ binoculars
8. _____ shelves
9. _____ sunglasses
10. alarm clock _____

PRACTICE 2

Underline and correct ten errors in singular or plural noun forms.

EXAMPLE: Rachel Carson started writing about wildlife in her early twentys.
twenties

1.   After World War II, Americans became aware of the need to protect nature.

Many persons turned their attention to environmental issues. One of the most

important womans in the early green movement was Rachel Carson.

2.   Carson was born in Pennsylvania in 1907. She trained as a marine biologist

and wrote many articles about wildlife such as deer, wolfs, and fishes. In the

1950s, Carson became concerned about the use of pesticides. In the late 1940s,

the government had started spraying pesticide with DDT to halt the progress

of fire ants. The pesticide turned tree and shrub leafs brown. It also killed birds

because they ate berrys that were covered with chemicals.

3.   Carson collected a lot of datas on the harmful effects of pesticides. She wrote

to all politicians, from the president to senator-elects, about the negative effects

of DDT. She also wrote a book, *Silent Spring*, about her discoverys. The book

became an international best-seller, and the environmental movement became

a global phenomena.

Key Words for Singular and Plural Nouns

Some key words will help you determine whether a noun is singular or plural.

◆ Use a singular noun after words such as *a, an, one, each, every*, and *another*.

As **a** <u>young mother</u>, Dorothy Gerber prepared homemade baby food for her daughter.

Gerber tried to sell her product to **every** <u>grocery store</u> in her town.

◆ Use a plural noun after words such as *two, all, both, many, few, several*, and *some*.

Very **few** <u>companies</u> produced food targeted to children.

Today, **many** <u>babies</u> eat Gerber's baby food.

HINT ◀ **Using Plural Nouns After *of the***

Use a plural noun after the expressions *one (all, two, each, few, lots, many, most, several) of the* . . .

One of the easiest **methods** to reduce pollution is recycling.

Chapter 28

PRACTICE 3

Underline the correct noun in each set of parentheses.

EXAMPLE: Many (visitor / <u>visitors</u>) are astounded by the extraordinary beauty of
national (park / <u>parks</u>).

1.   Every (year / years), millions of (person / people) visit national parks.
During the late 1700s, George Catlin was one of the first (artist / artists) to
travel the American wilderness. He painted lots of (landscape / landscapes)
in the Dakotas and Montana. At that time, many (settler / settlers) were
moving westward. Catlin believed that new (settlement / settlements) would
have a negative (impact / impacts) on American Indian culture and on the
environment. In the nineteenth century, few (American / Americans) worried
about protecting nature. In the 1830s, Catlin lobbied the government to
preserve some (area / areas) of the wilderness.

2.   Several (decade / decades) later, Congress made the Yosemite Valley into a
state (park / parks). Then, in 1872, the government passed a (law / laws) that
allowed land to be preserved for the enjoyment of the public. The Yellowstone
(sector / sectors) became one of the first national (park / parks) in the United
States. Today, there are over 187 (region / regions) designated as national
parks. Each national (park / parks) is unique. The (area / areas) have great
natural beauty. So for your next (vacation / vacations), why not visit a national
(park / parks)? But be sure to make a reservation if you want to stay overnight!

LO 2 Identify count nouns
and noncount nouns.

Count Nouns and Noncount Nouns

In English, nouns are grouped into two types: count nouns and noncount nouns.
Count nouns refer to people or things that you can count, such as *engine, paper,* or
girl. Count nouns usually can have both a singular and plural form.

She read a <u>book</u> by Rachel Carson. She read five <u>books</u> about water management.

Noncount nouns refer to people or things that you cannot count because you cannot
divide them, such as *electricity* and *music*. Noncount nouns usually have only the
singular form.

Michael uses new <u>software</u> to track global weather patterns.

Biologists take samples of <u>air</u> to monitor pollution levels.

To express a noncount noun as a count noun, refer to it in terms of types, varieties,
or amounts.

Environmentalists use **a variety of** <u>equipment</u> for their research.

Dr. Morgan Schule examines **four test tubes of** <u>water</u> for each experiment.

Here are some common noncount nouns.

Common Noncount Nouns

Categories of Objects   ### Food   ### Nature   ### Substances

Categories of Objects		Food	Nature	Substances	
clothing	machinery	bread	air	chalk	paint
equipment	mail	fish	earth	charcoal	paper
furniture	money	honey	electricity	coal	
homework	music	meat	energy	fur	
jewelry	postage	milk	radiation	hair	
luggage	software	rice	water	ink	

Abstract Nouns

advice	effort	information	progress
attention	evidence	knowledge	proof
behavior	health	luck	research
education	help	peace	violence

PRACTICE 4

Change the italicized words to the plural form, if necessary. If a plural form would be incorrect, write X in the space. If the word ends in *y*, you may have to change the *y* to *i* for the plural form.

EXAMPLE: Greenpeace *member*___s___ distribute environmental *information*

___X___ to the *public*___X___.

1.   In 1971, the United States was planning to conduct underground nuclear

*test*_____ in Amchitka, Alaska. The *island*_____ is on the West Coast. It

is home to many *type*_____ of sea *otter*_____, *eagle*_____, *fish*_____,

and other *animal*_____.

2.   Environmental *activist*_____ from Vancouver, Canada, decided to protest

peacefully. They rented a *ship*_____, bought some camera *equipment*_____,

and stocked up on enough *rice*_____, *meat*_____, and *vegetable*_____

for their long *journey*_____. Their *boat*_____ was intercepted by the U.S.

Navy, but their *luck*_____ held out. They took *photo*_____ and gathered

*evidence*_____ of Amchitka's fragile *ecosystem*_____. Since the *protestor*_____

did not use *violence*_____, their *activity*_____ received international

*attention*_____, and the United States abandoned nuclear testing on the island.

Chapter 28

3.   Within a few *year*_____, the environmental *movement*_____ had spread,

and several *country*_____ started their own Greenpeace *branch*_____.

These *day*_____, Greenpeace is one of the largest environmental action

*group*_____ in the *world*_____.

LO3 Define determiners.

Determiners

Determiners are words that help a reader figure out whether a noun is specific or general.

Arthur Scott used **his** imagination and created **a** new invention, **the** paper towel.

You can use many words from different parts of speech as determiners.

Articles	a, an, the
Demonstratives	this, that, these, those, such
Indefinite pronouns	any, all, both, each, every, either, few, little, many, several
Numbers	one, two, three
Possessive nouns	Jack's, the teacher's, a man's
Possessive adjectives	my, your, his, her, its, our, their, whose

Commonly Confused Determiners

Some determiners can be confusing because you can use them only in specific circumstances. Review this list of some commonly confused determiners.

a, an, the

A and *an* are general determiners, and *the* is a specific determiner.

general   specific
I need to find a new **car**. The **cars** that I looked at were electric.

◆ Use *a* and *an* before singular count nouns but not before plural or noncount nouns. Use *a* before words that begin with a consonant (*a man*), and use *an* before words that begin with a vowel (*an invention*).

An extraordinary **woman** created a very profound **documentary** on nature.

Exceptions:

When *u* sounds like *you*, put *a* before it (*a unicycle, a university*).
When *h* is silent, put *an* before it (*an hour, an honest man*).

◆ Use *the* before nouns that refer to a specific person, place, or thing. Do not use *the* before languages (*he studies Greek*), sports (*we played football*), and most city and country names (*Biro was born in Hungary*).

Forests cover one-third of the **world's surface**.

many, few, much, little

♦ Use *many* and *few* with count nouns.

<u>Many</u> **environmentalists** lobby the government, but <u>few</u> **politicians** are open to suggestions.

♦ Use *much* and *little* with noncount nouns.

Manu Joshi spent too <u>much</u> **money** on very <u>little</u> **research**.

this, that, these, those

♦ Use *this* and *these* to refer to things that are physically close to the speaker or at the present time. Use *this* before singular nouns and *these* before plural nouns.

<u>This</u> **computer** in my purse measures three by five inches. <u>These</u> **days**, computers are very small.

♦ Use *that* and *those* to refer to things that are physically distant from the speaker or in the past or future. Use *that* before singular nouns and *those* before plural nouns.

In the 1950s, computers were invented. In <u>those</u> **years**, computers were very large. In <u>that</u> **building**, there is a very old computer.

Near the speaker:
this (singular)
these (plural)

Far from the speaker:
that (singular)
those (plural)

PRACTICE 5

Write *a*, *an*, or *the* in the space before each noun. If no determiner is necessary, write *X* in the space.

EXAMPLE: I read ___an___ interesting biography on James Lovelock.

1. James Lovelock was born in 1919 in _____ England. After graduating in

    _____ medicine, he worked as _____ researcher at Harvard University.

    Eventually, he left _____ university and took _____ position at _____

    NASA, where he looked for signs of life on _____ Mars. While working on

    his research, he had _____ inspiration. He developed _____ theory, which

    he called _____ Gaia hypothesis. Gaia was _____ name for _____ Earth

    goddess in ancient Greek mythology. _____ Gaia hypothesis suggests that our

    planet is composed of _____ single supersystem that regulates conditions for

    _____ life to continue.

2.   Lovelock argues that _____ human beings are badly damaging our planet's ability to maintain life. Global warming, _____ deforestation, and other types of pollution will force _____ ecosystem to break down. _____ Environmental activists support _____ Gaia theory. But sometimes Lovelock surprises his fans. He supports _____ nuclear power because he believes it can reduce _____ global warming.

PRACTICE 6

Underline the appropriate determiner in parentheses. If the noun does not require a determiner, underline *X*.

EXAMPLE: Most innovations begin with (X / <u>a</u> / the) great idea.

1.   (A / The) weather is (a / the) common topic of discussion for (many / much) people. According to meteorologists, global warming affects weather patterns. (Few / Little) phenomena are as exciting or as scary as extreme weather. For example, (the / X) tornadoes are seasonal in (the / X) North America. (A / The) tornado lasts about fifteen minutes. In 2011, there were over six hundred tornadoes in (the / X) Mississippi and other southern states. In (this / that) year, tornadoes caused (much / many) property damage and (much / many) fatalities.

2.   (Many / Much) people are fascinated by thunderstorms. (An / A) interesting fact about (the / X) Empire State Building is that it is struck by lightning approximately five hundred times per year. During thunderstorms, (the / X) golfers should spend as (few / little) time as possible outdoors if there is lightning. (A / The) thunderstorm can produce a few hundred megawatts of electrical power.

3.   (The / X) United States launched its first weather satellite in 1961. In (these / those) days, satellite photos amazed climatologists. Today, (much / many) research about global warming is being done by meteorologists. (These / this) days, satellites are crucial for gathering (a / an / X) information about global weather systems.

PRACTICE 7

Correct fifteen errors in singular nouns, plural nouns, and determiners.

EXAMPLE: Biologists do a lot of ~~researches~~ ^{research} to develop better conservation
methods.

1.   Conservationists refer to the passenger pigeon as a example of nature's fragility.

   In past centuries, the passenger pigeon was one of the most common bird in

   the North America. Until the twentieth century, the birds were seen all over a

   Western Hemisphere. Unfortunately, the species is now extinct.

2.   When the first Europeans started to colonize the New World, there were little

   hunting regulations. In these days, settlers would often hunt passenger pigeons for

   their feathers. Ladyes wanted to wear feathers in their hairs. In 1878, in Petoskey,

   Michigan, fifty thousand passenger pigeons were killed each days. Furthermore,

   as farmers cleared much forests for agriculture, many passenger pigeons lost their

   nesting grounds. Citizens had very few information about the decline of the species.

3.   Conservationists noticed the decline of the bird population, and they made a

   lot of efforts to limit the slaughter. At this time, politicians did not pay much

   attentions to conservation. By the 1890s, almost all of the passenger pigeon had

   been hunted. Martha, the last passenger pigeon, died in the Cincinnati Zoo in

   1914. The only positive outcome of the passenger pigeon's extinction was

   that peoples became interested in creating conservation laws.

Prepositions

LO 4 Define prepositions.

Prepositions are words that show concepts such as time, place, direction, and manner.
They show connections or relationships between ideas.

   The public protested the use of DDT <u>during</u> the 1960s.

   I saw an interesting book on the Amazon River <u>in</u> the bookstore.

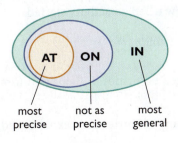

Prepositions	Prepositions of Time	Prepositions of Place
at	at a specific time of day (at 8:30 P.M.) at night at breakfast, lunch, dinner	at an address (at 15 Maple Street) at a specific building (at the hospital)
on	on a day of the week (on Monday) on a specific date (on June 16) on a specific holiday (on Martin Luther King Day) on time (meaning "punctual") on my birthday	on a specific street (on 17th Avenue) on technological devices (on TV, on the radio, on the phone, on the computer) on a planet (on Earth) on top
in	in a year (in 2010) in a month (in July) in the morning, afternoon, evening in the spring, fall, summer, winter	in a city (in Boston) in a country (in Spain) in a continent (in Africa)
from . . . to	from one time to another (from 6 A.M. to 8 P.M.)	from one place to another (from Las Vegas to Miami)
for	for a period of time (for six hours)	for a distance (for ten miles)

Commonly Confused Prepositions

to and at

Use *to* after verbs that indicate movement from one place to another.

> Each morning, Albert <u>walks</u> **to** the library, he <u>goes</u> **to** the coffee shop, and he <u>returns</u> **to** his office.

Exception: Do not put *to* directly before *home*.

> Albert returned ~~to~~ home after he won his prize. He didn't go to his friend's home.

Use *at* after verbs that indicate being or remaining in one place (and not moving from one place to another).

> In the afternoon, he <u>stays</u> **at** home. He <u>sits</u> **at** his desk and <u>looks</u> **at** his books on the environment.

for, during, and since

Use *during* to explain when something happens. Use *for* to explain how long it takes to happen. Use *since* to show when an activity started.

> **During** <u>the month of August</u>, the animal protection society office closes **for** <u>two weeks</u>.

> The government sprayed pesticides in fields and forests **for** <u>many years</u> **during** <u>World War II</u>.

> **Since** <u>World War II</u>, many countries have experienced environmental problems.

PRACTICE 8

Write the correct preposition in each blank. Choose *in, on, at, to, for, during,* or *from.*
If no preposition is necessary, write *X* in the space.

EXAMPLE: The International Year of Forests was _____in_____ 2011.

1. _____ the beginning of the twentieth century, many parts of

    the world have experienced deforestation. Kenya has been experiencing

    deforestation _____ many years.

2. Wangari Muta Maathai was born _____ April 1, 1940 _____

    Ihithe village, Kenya. _____ school, she was a good student.

3. _____ 1960 _____ 1966, she studied _____ the United States.

    _____ her studies, she became aware of Kenya's environmental problems.

    When she returned _____ home, she started working for the United Nations. She

    organized the Green Belt Movement _____ 1977, which encouraged community-

    based organizers to plant millions of trees _____ rural areas of Kenya.

4. Professor Maathai never thought her idea would become so successful.

    _____ 2004, one morning _____ October, she received a phone

    call _____ 9:00 A.M. A voice _____ the phone said that she had

    received the Nobel Peace Prize for environmental activism. She became the

    first African woman to win the prize. _____ the start of the program,

    Green Belt Movement supporters have planted over 40 million trees. Professor

    Maathai died _____ September 25, 2011, of ovarian cancer.

PRACTICE 9

Underline the correct preposition in the parentheses.

EXAMPLE: (During / <u>Since</u>) the end of the last century, global warming has
become an important environmental issue.

1. (In / On / At) 2006, the documentary film *An Inconvenient Truth* received

    good reviews (in / on / at) the Sundance Film Festival. The film also opened

    (in / on / at) May 24 (in / on / at) New York City. (For / During / Since) its

    release, the film has earned around $49 million.

2.   Al Gore has been a champion of environmental causes
(for / during / since) many years. (On / From / In) 1993 (to / in / on) 2001, Al
Gore was vice president of the United States. (For / During / Since) the Clinton
administration, Gore encouraged a carbon tax on energy sources.

3.   (In / On) the film, Gore, the narrator, argues that global warming is a serious
threat to life (in / on) Earth. (For / During) the film's premiere, audiences were
captivated by the film's message. Gore's other idea, The Climate Reality Project,
was launched (on / at) the same time as the film. (For / During / Since) that
time, both projects have inspired people to take climate change seriously.

Common Prepositional Expressions

Many common expressions contain prepositions. These types of expressions usually
convey a particular meaning.

verb   preposition

EXAMPLE: The company <u>complied</u> <u>**with**</u> the regulations.

Here is a list of common prepositional expressions.

accuse (somebody) of	deal with	introduce to
acquainted with	decide on	jealous of
add to	decide to	keep from
afraid of	depend on	located in
agree with	be disappointed about	long for
angry about	be disappointed with	look forward to
angry with	dream of	opposed to
apologize for	escape from	participate in
apply for	excited about	patient with
approve of	familiar with	pay attention to
argue with	feel like	pay for
ask for	fond of	pray for
associate with	forget about	prepared for
aware of	forgive (someone) for	prepared to
believe in	friendly with	prevent (someone) from
belong to	good for	protect (someone) from
capable of	grateful for	proud of
care about	happy about	provide (someone) with
care for	hear about	qualify for
commit to	hope for	realistic about
comply with	hopeful about	refer to
concern about	innocent of	related to
confronted with	insist on	rely on
consist of	insulted by	rescue from
count on	interested in	responsible for

(continued)

Chapter 28

sad about	succeed in	upset about
satisfied with	take advantage of	upset with
scared of	take care of	willing to
search for	thank (someone) for	wish for
similar to	think about	worry about
specialize in	think of	
stop (something) from	tired of	

PRACTICE 10

Write the correct preposition in each blank. Use the preceding list of prepositional expressions to help you.

EXAMPLE: Dr. Singh succeeded ___in___ helping the villagers conserve water.

1.   In 1984, Dr. Rajendra Singh traveled from New Delhi to the district of Alwar.

Alwar is located _____ Rajasthan, a desert state in India. Dr. Singh was

looking forward _____ starting a health clinic for villagers in the district.

When he arrived there, he was confronted _____ a difficult problem. The

water supply in the area had dried up. The villagers had to walk for miles to

search _____ water. Eventually, Dr. Singh was responsible _____ changing

people's attitudes about water usage.

2.   Dr. Singh thought _____ how to help the

villagers. He realized that the villagers no longer relied

_____ traditional methods to store water. He decided

_____ convince them to go back to ancient practices of

collecting water. He showed the villagers how to build small

dams or *johads* to collect rainwater.

3.   In seven months, the johads were full of water, and the rivers were flowing.

The villagers were grateful _____ Singh's ideas. The district has also benefitted

from the water collection system. The water table has risen; forests have

regrown; and antelopes, leopards, and birds have returned to the region to take

advantage _____ the water. Other drought-ravaged areas also depend _____

Dr. Singh's system of water management to increase their water supply.

Reflect On It

Think about what you have learned in this chapter. If you do not know an answer, review that concept.

1. Make the following nouns plural.

   a. tooth: _____

   b. backseat driver: _____

   c. bride-to-be: _____

   d. kiss: _____

   e. homework: _____

   f. loaf: _____

2. Correct the errors in the following sentences.

   much
   John Muir spent ~~many~~ time in the wilderness.

   a. He had much ideas for environmental conservation.

   b. On 1892, he helped to found the Sierra Club.

   c. He was one of the most dedicated environmentalist in the United States.

   d. Few peoples were as passionate about conservation as Muir was.

FINAL REVIEW

Correct twenty errors in singular or plural forms, determiners, or prepositions.

disasters
EXAMPLE: The depletion of the Amazon rainforest is one of the greatest ~~disaster~~ of our time.

1.   The Amazon rainforest is one of the most important forest in the world. It is home to a great variety of reptiles, birds, insects, and mammals. Tribal persons also live in the forest. The rainforest plays a vital role in regulating a global climate. But the Amazon has been in trouble since a long time. Since the beginning of the 1970s, humans have cut down around 232,000 square miles of the forest. Even though the issue of deforestation is receiving international attention, environmentalists are confronted about a complicated problem to solve.

2.   There are several reason for the deforestation. During the early 1900s, farmers cleared much trees to plant crops and to graze cattle. In these days, politicians spent few time worrying about the environment. Presently, loggers and miners are continuing to contribute to the problem. This days, many companys use heavy equipments to build roads to seek mineral deposits and mature trees. In addition, corporations use too many water and electricities for their activities.

3.   On 2008, Brazilian president Luiz Inácio Lula da Silva created the Amazon Fund. The Brazilian government wants other countrys to help raise billions of dollars to save the forest. Norway has agreed to donate millions of dollars. Each years, Norway will pay Brazil to stop logging in the Amazon forest. However, Norway's donation is controversial because the nation is responsible at mining and logging in the Amazon.

4.   Most people are deeply concerned for the problems confronting the environment. Politicians need to commit on policies that will balance economic growth and environmental responsibility.

THE WRITER'S ROOM   MyWritingLab™

MyWritingLab™
Complete these writing assignments at mywritinglab.com

Write about one of the following topics. Then review your nouns, determiners, and prepositions.

1.   Are you concerned about the environment? Why or why not?

2.   Describe at least three actions you can take to reduce your carbon footprint.

Chapter 28

29 Pronouns

SECTION THEME: Our Environment

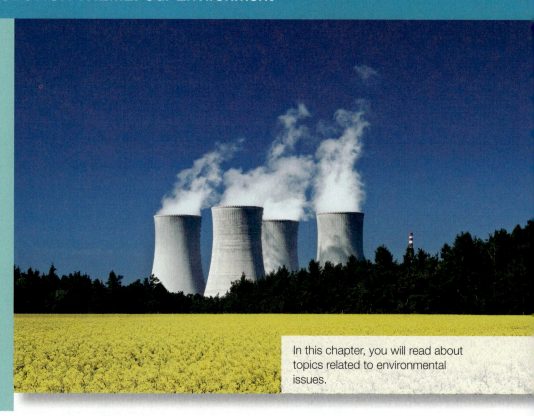

In this chapter, you will read about topics related to environmental issues.

LEARNING OBJECTIVES

LO 1 Define different pronoun cases. **(p. 392)**

LO 2 Identify relative pronouns. **(p. 397)**

LO 3 Identify reflexive pronouns. **(p. 399)**

LO 4 Maintain pronoun–antecedent agreement. **(p. 400)**

LO 5 Identify indefinite pronouns. **(p. 402)**

LO 6 Avoid vague pronouns. **(p. 404)**

LO 7 Avoid pronoun shifts. **(p. 406)**

MyWritingLab™
Complete this Writer's Journal activity at mywritinglab.com

THE WRITER'S JOURNAL

Are cars absolutely necessary? Write about why cars are or are not a necessity for modern life.

LO 1 Define different pronoun cases.

Pronoun Case

Pronouns are words that replace nouns (people, places, or things), other pronouns, and phrases. Use pronouns to avoid repeating nouns.

> It
> The Aral Sea is shrinking rapidly. ~~The Aral Sea~~ used to be one of the largest lakes in the world.

Pronouns are formed according to the role they play in a sentence. A pronoun can be the subject or object in a sentence, or it can show possession. The next chart shows the three main pronoun cases: subjective, objective, and possessive.

Pronouns

Singular	Subjective	Objective	Possessives	
			Possessive Adjective	**Possessive Pronoun**
1st person	I	me	my	mine
2nd person	you	you	your	yours
3rd person	he, she, it, who, whoever	him, her, it, whom, whomever	his, her, its, whose	his, hers
Plural				
1st person	we	us	our	ours
2nd person	you	you	your	yours
3rd person	they	them	their	theirs

Subjective Case

A **subject** performs an action in a sentence. When a pronoun is the subject of the sentence, use the subjective form of the pronoun.

She has seen many oil spills.

We asked questions about the spills.

Objective Case

An **object** of a verb receives an action in a sentence. When a pronoun is the object of a verb in the sentence, use the objective form of the pronoun.

Rose gave **him** a book about old growth forests.

My brother told **us** about the documentary.

Possessive Case

A possessive pronoun shows ownership.

◆ **Possessive adjectives** are always placed before the noun that they modify. In the next sentences, *her* and *their* are possessive adjectives.

She finished **her** book about invasive species, but they did not finish **their** books.

◆ **Possessive pronouns** replace the possessive adjective and noun. In the next sentence, *her* is a possessive adjective and *theirs* is a possessive pronoun.

She finished **her** book about invasive species, but they did not finish **theirs**.

Problems with Possessive Pronouns

When using the possessive pronouns *hers* and *theirs*, be careful that you do not add an apostrophe before the *s*.

The book on biodiversity is ~~her's~~ hers. The map is ~~their's~~ theirs.

GRAMMAR LINK
For more information about apostrophes, see Chapter 35.

Some possessive adjectives sound like certain contractions. When using the possessive adjectives *their, your,* and *its,* be careful that you do not confuse them with *they're, you're,* and *it's.*

Their is the possessive adjective.	<u>Their</u> flight to Mexico City was late.
They're is the contraction of *they are.*	<u>They're</u> looking forward to going to Cancun.
Your is the possessive adjective.	<u>Your</u> tour guide has a map of the conference center.
You're is the contraction of *you are.*	<u>You're</u> going to lecture on carbon emissions.
Its is the possessive adjective.	The documentary will be shown, and <u>its</u> director will give an interview.
It's is the contraction of *it is.*	<u>It's</u> going to win first prize.

HINT ◄ **Choosing *His* or *Her***

To choose the correct possessive adjective, think about the possessor (not the object that is possessed).

- If something belongs to a female, use *her* + noun.

  Cecilia read <u>her</u> report.

- If something belongs to a male, use *his* + noun.

  Tony booked <u>his</u> flight.

PRACTICE 1

Underline the correct possessive adjective or possessive pronoun in each set of parentheses.

EXAMPLE: Some of the rescue workers had (<u>their</u> / theirs / they're) own equipment.

1. On March 24, 1989, the oil tanker *Exxon Valdez* and (it's / its / their) captain became infamous when the ship hit a reef in Prince William Sound, Alaska. The tanker leaked crude oil because (it's / its / their) holding tanks were damaged. The oil spill was the second largest in U.S. history. The oil leaked in a very remote location. The area and (its / it's / her) ecosystem were destroyed. According to reporters, Captain Joe Hazelwood and (her / his) crew made some critical errors. The ship was not using the shipping lanes due to icebergs. Moreover, the third mate, Gregory Cousins, did not carry out (her / its / his) orders to move the ship back into the shipping lane near the reef.

2.   From March to June 2010, oil spilled into the Gulf of Mexico because of an explosion during deepwater drilling by British Petroleum. The spill and (it's / its / his) consequences were grim for the environment. Thousands of workers were needed to clean up the oil. The people of the region used all of (their / theirs) resources for the cleanup. The fishers still talk about the destruction of (their / they're / theirs) livelihood because the oil spill destroyed the commercial fishing industry.

3.   Fiona Phillips, a journalist, has written about (her / his) research into the accident. Fiona has posted (his / her / hers) photos of oil spills on a Web site, and other photojournalists have posted (their / they're / theirs). Many people have visited the site. They post (their / theirs) comments, and Fiona adds (her / hers). We should create (our / ours) own Web site about the 2010 BP oil disaster. You can write (your / you're / yours) opinions, and I will post (my / mine).

Pronouns in Comparisons with *than* or *as*

Avoid making errors in pronoun case when the pronoun follows *than* or *as*. If the pronoun is a subject, use the subjective case, and if the pronoun is an object, use the objective case.

   If you use the incorrect case, your sentence may have a meaning that you do not intend it to have. For example, people often follow *than* or *as* with an objective pronoun when they mean to follow it with a subjective pronoun. Look at the differences in the meanings of the next sentences.

objective case

I like environmental studies as much as **him**.
(I like environmental studies <u>as much as I like him</u>.)

subjective case

I like environmental studies as much as **he**.
(I like environmental studies <u>as much as he likes environmental studies</u>.)

HINT   **Complete the Thought**

If you are unsure which pronoun case to use, test yourself by completing the thought. Look at the following examples.

   He likes to watch documentaries more than **I** (like to watch documentaries).

   He likes to watch documentaries more than (he likes to watch) **me**.

Chapter 29

Pronouns in Prepositional Phrases

In a prepositional phrase, the noun or pronoun that follows the preposition is the object of the preposition. Therefore, always use the objective case of the pronoun after a preposition.

> <u>To</u> **them**, learning about the environment is not important.

> <u>Between</u> **you** and **me**, our environmental ethics class is very interesting.

Pronouns with *and* or *or*

Use the correct case when nouns and pronouns are joined by *and* or *or*. If the pronouns are the subject, use the subjective case. If the pronouns are the object, use the objective case.

	He and I
Subjective	~~Him and me~~ had to do a presentation on icebergs.
	him and me
Objective	The instructor asked ~~he and I~~ to present first.

HINT ◄ **Finding the Correct Case**

An easy way to determine whether your case is correct is to say the sentence with just one pronoun.

The librarian asked her and (I, me) to speak quietly.

Choices	The librarian asked I . . . *or* The librarian asked me . . .
Correct	The librarian asked her and <u>me</u> to speak quietly.

PRACTICE 2

Correct any errors with pronoun case. Write *C* in the space if the sentence is correct.

EXAMPLE: Last summer, my friend and ~~me~~ attended an environmental conference. _____I_____

1. Recently, my friend Larry Huang and me toured China. _____

2. He and I are interested in environmental issues. _____

3. He wanted to see the Three Gorges Dam more than me but convinced me to go along. _____

4. The guide, Leena, told we visitors that the completed dam would produce large amounts of electricity for China. _____

5. Leena took photos of Larry and me near the dam. _____

6. We didn't have our camera, so we used her's. _____

7. Between you and I, Leena should have explained some of the environmental problems caused by the dam. _____

8. Usually, Larry or me give presentations on China's
   environmental problems.   _____

9. Larry is as aware as me of how the dam has triggered deforestation
   and pollution.   _____

10. Larry said goodbye to Leena because him and me had to
    catch our train.   _____

Relative Pronouns (*who, whom, which, that, whose*)

LO 2 Identify relative pronouns.

Relative pronouns can join two short sentences. Here is a list of relative pronouns.

who	whom	which	that	whose
whoever	whomever			

- *Who* (or *whoever*) and *whom* (or *whomever*) always refer to people. *Who* is the subject of the clause, and *whom* is the object of the clause.

Subject	The <u>lawyer</u> **who** specializes in environmental law is speaking today.
Object	The <u>lawyer</u> **whom** you met is my mother.

- *Which* always refers to things.

  The ancient city of <u>Machu Picchu</u>, **which** receives two thousand visitors every year, is being slowly eroded by tourists' feet.

- *That* refers to things.

  Elizabeth Cartwright wrote a <u>book</u> **that** is about pesticides.

- *Whose* always shows that something belongs to or is connected with someone or something. It usually replaces possessive pronouns such as *his*, *her*, or *their*. Do not confuse *whose* with *who's*, which means "who is."

  The geographer traced the route. <u>His</u> maps were on the table.

  The geographer, **whose** maps were on the table, traced the route.

> **GRAMMAR LINK**
> Clauses with *which* are set off with commas. For more information, see Chapter 34, "Commas."

HINT ⟩ **Choosing *Who* or *Whom***

If you are unsure whether to use *who* or *whom*, test yourself in the following way. Replace *who* or *whom* with another pronoun. If the replacement is a subjective pronoun such as *he* or *she*, use **who**. If the replacement is an objective pronoun such as *her* or *him*, use **whom**.

I know a man **who** works at the Environmental Protection Agency.
(<u>He</u> works at the Environmental Protection Agency.)

The man to **whom** you gave your portfolio is the director of the Environmental Protection Agency.
(You gave your portfolio to <u>him</u>.)

PRACTICE 3

Write the correct relative pronoun in each blank. Choose *who, whom, which, whose,* or *that.*

EXAMPLE: The Love Canal story, _____which_____ has been made into a film, is very tragic.

1.   William T. Love, for _____ the Love Canal community was named, wanted to build a canal joining the Niagara River with Lake Ontario. The project, _____ was started in the 1890s, was abandoned due to many zoning obstacles. In the 1940s, the Hooker Electrochemical Company, _____ owned the Love Canal land, dumped toxic chemicals on the site.

2.   In the early 1970s, some Niagara Falls town councilors _____ wanted to build housing on the site offered to buy the land from the Hooker Company. Company managers refused to sell the land because of toxic chemicals. The owners, _____ knowledge about the site was important, told city officials about the toxic chemicals. But some city officials _____ were members of the planning committee ignored the warning. The soil _____ the houses and school stood on was polluted.

3.   The school _____ all the local children attended shut down because its water supply contained toxic chemicals. Children _____ had been healthy before started to become ill. Two journalists _____ investigated the situation were shocked. The mothers _____ the journalists interviewed told them about a high number of birth defects in newborn babies. A local resident _____ son developed epilepsy became the spokesperson for the community.

4.   It took a long time for the government to deal with the tragedy of Love Canal. Residents _____ lives were destroyed eventually received compensation from the government. The law _____ Congress passed requires polluters to be responsible for any damage.

Reflexive Pronouns (-*self* or -*selves*)

Use **reflexive pronouns** when you want to emphasize that the subject does an action to him- or herself.

I asked **myself** many questions.

History often repeats **itself**.

Do not use reflexive pronouns with the verbs *wash*, *dress*, *feed*, and *shave*. However, you can use reflexive pronouns to draw attention to a surprising or an unusual action.

The little boy fed **himself**.

(The boy probably could not feed himself at a previous time.)

The next chart shows subjective pronouns and the reflexive pronouns that relate to them.

Pronouns That End with -*self* or -*selves*

Singular	Antecedent	Reflexive Pronoun
1st person	I	myself
2nd person	you	yourself
3rd person	he, she, it	himself, herself, itself
Plural		
1st person	we	ourselves
2nd person	you	yourselves
3rd person	they	themselves

HINT ◄ **Common Errors with Reflexive Pronouns**

Hisself and *theirselves* are not accepted in standard English. These are incorrect ways to say *himself* or *themselves*.

                                            themselves
The children made the recycling video by ~~theirselves~~.

                                        himself.
Franklin wrote about solar energy by ~~hisself~~.

PRACTICE 4

Fill in the blanks with the correct reflexive pronouns.

EXAMPLE: I introduced _____myself_____ to the famous climatologist, Dr. Saleem Khan.

1. Dr. Saleem Khan attended the meeting on climate change in Cancun, Mexico,

    by _____. His colleague Radhika Ketkar was supposed to attend but

    had to cancel. The day before, she had fallen and hurt _____.

2.   The agenda of the meeting was to develop policy on reducing greenhouse gas emissions. The international members could not agree among _____ on the details of the policy. Some nations criticized the United States for not taking a stronger stand on reducing carbon emissions. The government was quick to defend _____.

3.   I was at the meeting with a group of other journalists. We attended the talks and saw for _____ that governments could not agree on many issues. I told my colleagues that I was going to go by _____ to interview some of the protesters. "Don't go by _____," they advised. So we went together to talk to the activists.

LO 4 Maintain pronoun–antecedent agreement.

Pronoun–Antecedent Agreement

Antecedents are words that pronouns have replaced, and they always come before the pronoun. A pronoun must agree with its antecedent, which is the word to which the pronoun refers. Pronouns must agree in person and number with their antecedents.

My instructor took us on a field trip to the wetlands. **He** took **his** family with **him**.
(*My instructor* is the antecedent of *he*, *his*, and *him*.)

China has many dust storms. **They** originate in the Gobi Desert.
(*Dust storms* is the antecedent of *they*.)

Compound Antecedents

Compound antecedents consist of two or more nouns joined by *and* or *or*. When the nouns are joined by *and*, use a plural pronoun to refer to them.

The scholar and her husband brought **their** son to the bird sanctuary.

When the nouns are joined by *or*, you may need a singular or a plural pronoun. If the antecedents are plural, use a plural pronoun. If both nouns are singular, use a singular pronoun.

Either the men or women completed **their** research first.

Does England or France have **its** own environmental policy?

Collective Noun Antecedents

GRAMMAR LINK
For a list of collective nouns, see page 364 in Chapter 26.

Collective nouns refer to a group of people or things. Generally, the noun acts as a unit; therefore, it is singular.

The government tried to implement **its** policies.

PRACTICE 5

Fill in the blank spaces with the appropriate pronouns or possessive adjectives.

EXAMPLE: Oil companies want to increase _____*their*_____ profits.

1.   Does Saudi Arabia or Canada export more of _____ oil to the

   United States? The United States imports more oil from _____

   neighbor Canada than from any other country in the world. Canada has oil

   deposits equal to all of the world's crude oil reserves. However, acquiring

   Canadian oil is problematic and expensive because _____ is found

   in sandy deposits in Alberta. Extracting oil from sand greatly pollutes the

   environment. Therefore, either Canadian government ministries or Canadian

   oil companies send _____ lobbyists to promote Canadian oil

   exports to the United States.

2.   Bobby Hinds and _____ sister Beth work in the Canadian

   tar sands industry. _____ are engineers, and _____

   company is one of the largest oil companies in the world. Sometimes the

   company asks Beth or _____ brother to solve public relations

   problems for the company.

3.   Each month, either environmentalists or oilmen send _____

   representatives to meet with Bobby and Beth to inform _____ about

   the environmental issues. The oil company and _____ supporters

   meet with Alberta politicians to discuss the economic importance of the

   oil industry. Janice Cole is an environmentalist. She and _____

   colleagues also lobby the Alberta government. The government says that

   _____ mandate is to provide jobs for citizens. The government, the

   oil companies, and the environmentalists stick to _____ own points

   of view. _____ all know that there is a tradeoff—economic progress

   versus environmental responsibility.

Indefinite Pronouns

Use **indefinite pronouns** when you refer to people or things whose identity is not known or is unimportant. The next chart shows some common singular and plural indefinite pronouns.

Indefinite Pronouns

Singular	another	each	nobody	other
	anybody	everybody	no one	somebody
	anyone	everyone	nothing	someone
	anything	everything	one	something
Plural	both, few, many, others, several			
Either singular or plural	all, any, some, none, more, most, half (and other fractions)			

Singular

When you use a singular indefinite antecedent, also use a singular pronoun to refer to it.

> <u>Everybody</u> feels shocked when **he or she** sees China's air pollution.

> <u>Nobody</u> should forget to visit China's northern forests in **his or her** lifetime.

Plural

When you use a plural indefinite antecedent, also use a plural pronoun to refer to it.

> The two documentaries are new, and <u>both</u> have **their** own point of view.

> The world has many illegal logging sites; there are <u>several</u> operating in China, but **they** cannot be controlled.

Either Singular or Plural

Some indefinite pronouns can be either singular or plural, depending on the noun to which they refer.

> Many geologists came to the site. <u>All</u> were experts in **their** field.
> (*All* refers to geologists; therefore, the pronoun is plural.)

> We excavated <u>all</u> of the site and **its** surrounding area.
> (*All* refers to the site; therefore, the pronoun is singular.)

HINT   **Using *of the* Expressions**

In sentences containing the expression *one of the . . .* or *each of the . . .* , the subject is the indefinite pronoun *one* or *each*. Therefore, any pronoun referring to that phrase must be singular.

> <u>One</u> of the reports is missing **its** appendix.

> <u>Each</u> of the men has **his** own map.

PRACTICE 6

Identify and correct eight errors in pronoun–antecedent agreement. You may change either the antecedent or the pronoun. If you change any antecedents, make sure that your subjects and verbs agree.

EXAMPLE: Everybody was worried about ~~their~~ ^{his or her} children.

1. One of the worst industrial accidents happened in December 1984 in Bhopal, India. Union Carbide manufactured pesticides at its plant in the city. One night, water leaked into a storage tank and released poisonous gas into the air. Nobody could have predicted that their life was in danger.

2. Factory workers lived near the plant. The workers and his neighbors were very poor. When the leak occurred, one of the employees tried to reach members of their family. Someone ran to their local police station to inform the authorities. Over one hundred thousand people lost their lives. Others lost his vision.

3. Journalists reported the news quickly. When the reporters arrived at the scene, he expressed shock. The public blamed Union Carbide and the Indian government for the tragedy. Both had not done its job well. Each of the victims had their life disastrously altered.

HINT ◄ **Avoid Sexist Language**

Terms like *anybody*, *somebody*, *nobody*, and *each* are singular antecedents, so the pronouns that follow those words must be singular. At one time, it was acceptable to use *he* as a general term meaning "all people." However, today it is more acceptable to use *he or she*.

Sexist	Everyone had to leave his home.
Solution	Everyone had to leave his or her home.
Better solution	The citizens had to leave their homes.

Exception: If you know for certain that the subject is male or female, then use only *he* or only *she*.

PRACTICE 7

Underline the correct pronouns in the following paragraphs.

EXAMPLE: Many people have lost (his or her / <u>their</u>) homes because of wildfires.

1. In 2012, more wildfires raged across the southern United States than in past years. Almost everybody in the path of the fires had (his or her / their) home destroyed. Police and firefighters had to use all of (they're / their) training to fight the fires. The army sent (its / his / their) water bombers to help put out the fires. Katrina Hobbart and (his / her / their) husband fled minutes before flames engulfed the road. Others also had to save (theirselves / themselves). Ronald, (who / whom) is a reporter, stated that he had never seen wildfires burn with such speed.

2. My friend Petra and (I / me) volunteered to help rebuild communities that were destroyed. I directed traffic in my part of town, and Petra directed traffic in (her's / hers). I also collected donations. Petra's boss, to (who / whom) I sent the money, gave it to community organizers. Between you and (I / me), other volunteers were just as committed to rebuilding as (I / me).

3. Climate change and (its / their / it's) consequences are severe. For example, a rise in temperature might cause drought or wildfires. Nature is often more powerful than (us / we) are. Therefore, we must work together to reduce our carbon footprint.

LO 6 Avoid vague pronouns.

Vague Pronouns

Avoid using pronouns that could refer to more than one antecedent.

Vague	Frank asked his friend where <u>his</u> book on environmental statistics was. (Whose book is it: Frank's or his friend's?)
Clearer	**Frank** wondered where **his** book on evironmental statistics was, so he asked his friend about it.

Avoid using confusing pronouns such as *it* and *they* that have no clear antecedent.

Vague	<u>They</u> say that people should get vaccines before traveling to certain countries. (Who are *they*?)
Clearer	**Health authorities** say that people should get vaccines before traveling to certain countries.
Vague	<u>It</u> stated in the magazine that scientists were collaborating on research. (Who or what is *it*?)
Clearer	**The magazine article** stated that scientists were collaborating on research.

This, that, and *which* should refer to a specific antecedent.

Vague	The teacher told us that we should study hard for our ecology exams because they were going to be difficult. <u>This</u> caused all of us to panic.
	(What is *this*? The word(s) that *this* refers to is not explicitly stated; it is only implied.)
Clearer	The teacher told us that we should study hard for our ecology exams because they were going to be difficult. **This information** caused all of us to panic.

HINT ◄ **Avoid Repeating the Subject**

When you clearly mention a subject, do not repeat the subject in pronoun form.

The Sahara Desert ~~it~~ is growing.

The book ~~it~~ is really interesting.

PRACTICE 8

Each sentence has either a vague pronoun or a repeated subject. Correct the errors. You may need to rewrite some sentences.

EXAMPLE: ~~They~~ Politicians say that we have to develop a precise policy on nuclear power.

1. It said on the news that nuclear power generates about 14 percent of the world's electricity.

2. Professor Tate told his student Michael that his paper on nuclear energy will be published.

3. It stated in the textbook that nuclear energy is a controversial topic.

4. Proponents they believe that using nuclear energy is better for the environment than burning fossil fuels.

5. Critics they say that relying on nuclear power may have dangerous effects, such as radiation poisoning, on humans.

6. In Japan, the Fukushima Daiichi nuclear plant it was destroyed by an earthquake and tsunami.

7. They claimed that the disaster was caused by poor enforcement of safety standards.

8. Politicians and the public passionately debate this.

LO 7 Avoid pronoun shifts.

Pronoun Shifts

If your writing contains unnecessary shifts in person or number, you may confuse your readers. Carefully edit your writing to ensure that your pronouns are consistent in number and person.

Making Pronouns Consistent in Number

Pronouns and antecedents must agree in **number**. If the antecedent is singular, then the pronoun must be singular. If the antecedent is plural, then the pronoun must be plural.

> singular   her
> The **director** of the laboratory encouraged ~~their~~ employees to be on time.

>   plural   they
> When the **activitists** protested, ~~he~~ carried signs.

Making Pronouns Consistent in Person

Person is the writer's perspective. In some writing assignments, you may use first person (*I, we*). For other assignments, especially most college and workplace writing, you may use second person (*you*) or third person (*he, she, it, they*).

When you shift your point of view for no reason, your writing may become unclear, and you may confuse your readers. If you begin writing from one point of view, do not shift unnecessarily to another point of view.

>   we
> If ~~one~~ considered the expenses involved in visiting another country, **we** would probably never travel.

>   we
> **We** visited the dam, but ~~you~~ could not enter it.

> **HINT** ◀ **Avoiding Pronoun Shifts in Paragraphs**
>
> Sometimes it is easier to use pronouns consistently in individual sentences than it is in larger paragraphs or essays. When you write paragraphs and essays, always check that your pronouns agree with your antecedents in person and in number. In the next example, the pronouns are consistent in the first two sentences; however, they shift in person in the third sentence.
>
> **We** went to Mexico City last year. **We** traveled around on the subway.
>   we
> Sometimes the subway was so crowded that ~~you~~ could barely move.

PRACTICE 9

Correct six pronoun shift errors.

                                           they
EXAMPLE: When scientists study climate change, ~~you~~ have to consider natural causes as well as human causes.

1.   There are two clear sources that cause climate change: natural and human.

Climatologists often state that you have limited historical data on weather patterns. Scientists know that one must take natural forces into account. For instance, in the past, climate changes have caused many ice ages.

2.   We are working on computer models of weather systems. We collect data on environmental events. For example, we study volcanic eruptions, and you can see that ash affects global temperatures. We need to have complete statistics before you can make predictions about climate change. We analyze the statistics very carefully because one must be accurate.

3.   Politicians need to craft a clear policy to tackle climate change because if one does not, the problem will become more critical.

Reflect On It

Think about what you have learned in this chapter. If you do not know an answer, review that concept.

1. Write a sentence that includes an objective pronoun. _____

    _____

2. When do you use possessive pronouns (*my, mine, his, hers*, etc.)? _____

    _____

3. Circle the best answer: In a sentence, *whom* replaces
    a. the subject.   b. the object

4. What is an antecedent? _____

    _____

5. Circle the best answer: Pronouns must agree with their antecedents
    a. only in number.   b. only in person.
    c. both in number and in person.   d. neither in number nor in person.

Final Review

Correct fifteen errors with pronouns in the next paragraphs.

EXAMPLE: Susan wants to heat ~~his~~ *her* home with geothermal energy.

1.   Our society has depended economically on oil for the past two hundred years.

    We know that oil is a nonrenewable energy source and that you must reduce

Chapter 29

our dependence on it. Politicians and they're advisors react badly to suggestions on reducing oil consumption. They're concerned about economic progress. Yet environmentalists they believe that burning fossil fuels is causing temperatures around the world to become warmer. Scientists whom are interested in climate change are trying to develop alternative energy sources.

2. Nuclear energy is one alternative source of energy. This is a cause for concern. Many environmentalists with who I have spoken talk about a need for caution when discussing nuclear power. Dr. Cynthia Malick and his students are studying the effects of nuclear disasters. There have been many, such as Chernobyl and Three Mile Island. The worst was the Fukushima nuclear accident caused by the 2011 tsunami in Japan. Everybody has their own opinions about nuclear energy.

3. Another source of alternative energy is geothermal. The United States produces the greatest amount of geothermal electricity in the world. Either the Philippines or Indonesia is also developing their geothermal production.

4. My professor, Dr. Lam Ping, and me are researching wind energy. Currently, turbines who use wind power produce about 2.5 percent of the world's electricity. Between you and I, Dr. Ping knows more about wind-generated electricity than me. Dr. Ping does much of the research on wind energy by hisself. However, the university asked both him and I to give a presentation on the subject. Our government needs to develop and promote energy alternatives.

THE WRITER'S ROOM   *My*WritingLab™

MyWritingLab™
**Complete these
writing assignments at
mywritinglab.com**

Choose one of the following topics. Make sure that pronoun case and pronoun–antecedent agreement are correct.

1. What are the different types of pollution? Divide types of pollution into different categories.

2. How would you organize an environmental awareness event?

READING LINK

To learn about environmental issues, read the following essays.

"Roaring Waves of Fire" by Christi Lester (page 200)
"The Purpose of Pets" by W. Stephen Damron (page 215)
"Mother Nature's Melting Pot" by Hugh Raffles (page 537)
"The Beeps" by Josh Freed (page 548)

THE WRITERS' CIRCLE   Collaborative Activity

Work with a group of three to five students.

Imagine that you are having a dinner party. You can invite any five people that you want. The guests can be historical figures or living people. As a team, write three sentences about each person and explain who the person is and what he or she will contribute to the party. After you finish, underline the pronouns in your sentences and verify that they have been used correctly.

30 Adjectives and Adverbs

SECTION THEME: Health Care

LEARNING OBJECTIVES

LO 1 Define adjectives. (p. 410)

LO 2 Define adverbs. (p. 412)

LO 3 Identify comparative and superlative forms. (p. 416)

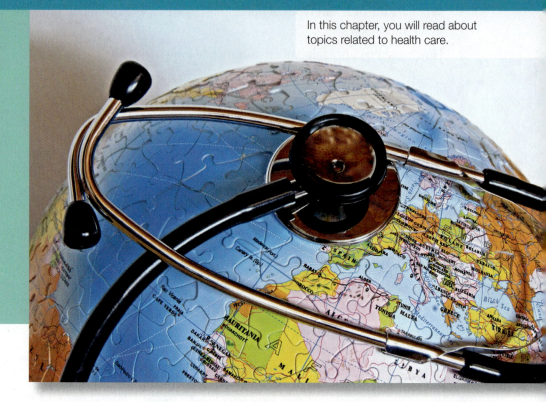

In this chapter, you will read about topics related to health care.

MyWritingLab™

Complete this Writer's Journal activity at mywritinglab.com

> ## THE WRITER'S JOURNAL
>
> Write a short paragraph describing how people can best protect their health. List several examples in your paragraph.

LO 1 Define adjectives.

Adjectives

Adjectives describe nouns (people, places, or things) and pronouns (words that replace nouns). They add information explaining how many, what kind, or which one. They also help you appeal to the senses by describing how things look, smell, feel, taste, and sound.

The **dynamic** <u>doctor</u>, Christiaan Barnard, completed a **complicated** <u>surgery</u>.

He performed the **first heart transplant** <u>operation</u> in 1967.

Placement of Adjectives

You can place adjectives either before a noun or after a linking verb such as *be, look, appear, smell,* or *become.*

Before the noun The **young unemployed** man received a scholarship for **medical** school.

LV LV

After the linking verb He was **shocked**, but he was **happy**.

PRACTICE 1

Underline the adjectives in the next sentences.

EXAMPLE: American politicians debate the soaring prices of brand-name drugs.

1. Self-employed entrepreneurs and small-business owners struggle to get adequate health care.
2. Also, certain groups of elderly Americans cannot afford sufficient, reliable medical treatment.
3. Furthermore, prescription drug costs are higher in the United States than they are in other countries, such as England, Switzerland, Canada, and Sweden.
4. Where the average American citizen pays one dollar for a prescription drug, a British citizen pays only sixty-four cents and a Canadian citizen pays only fifty-seven cents.
5. The average annual profit of the top ten drug companies is over three billion dollars.
6. Drug companies argue that they do groundbreaking research on new drugs.
7. In 2010, politicians passed what they hope is decent and fair legislation about health-care issues.

Problems with Adjectives

You can recognize many adjectives by their endings. Be particularly careful when you use the following adjective forms.

Adjectives Ending in *-ful* or *-less*

Some adjectives end in *-ful* or *-less*. Remember that *-ful* ends in one *l* and *-less* ends in double *s*.

Alexander Fleming, a **skillful** scientist, conducted many **useful** experiments.

His work appeared in **countless** publications.

Adjectives Ending in *-ed* and *-ing*

Some adjectives look like verbs because they end in *-ing* or *-ed*.

- When the adjective ends in *-ed*, it describes the person's or animal's expression or feeling.

The **overworked** and **tired** scientist presented her findings to the public.

◆ When the adjective ends in *-ing*, it describes the quality of the person or thing.

Her **compelling** and **promising** discovery pleased the public.

HINT ◄ Keep Adjectives in the Singular Form

Always make an adjective singular, even if the noun following the adjective is plural. In the next example, "year" acts as an adjective.

                      year
Paul was a nine-~~years~~-old boy when he broke his arm while playing with
other
~~others~~ children.

PRACTICE 2

Underline and correct eight adjective errors. The adjectives may have the wrong form, or they may be misspelled.

                      surprising
EXAMPLE: Many <u>surprised</u> medical findings happen by accident.

1.   One of the world's amazed scientifics discoveries happened by pure chance.

   Born in 1881, Alexander Fleming was a tireles medical doctor. He worked in

   his small London clinic, where he treated famous people for venereal disease.

   He also conducted many biologicals experiments.

2.   One day in 1928, he put some *Staphylococcus* bacteria in a culture dish. Two

   weeks later, Fleming, who was a carefull researcher, discovered that a clear

   ring encircled the yellow-green mold on the dish. A mold spore had flown into

   the dish from a laboratory on the floor below. At that point, Fleming made an

   insightfull observation. He had an astounded revelation. He realized that the

   mold somehow stopped the growth of bacteria in the culture dish.

3.   Fleming named the new product penicillin. During World War II, the drug

   saved millions of lives, and it continues to be used today to treat differents

   infections.

LO 2 Define adverbs.

Adverbs

Adverbs add information to adjectives, verbs, or other adverbs. They give more specific information about how, when, where, and to what extent an action or event occurred.

verb _____ adverb
Doctors in ancient Rome <u>performed</u> surgeries **skillfully**.

Chapter 30

adverb adverb

These surgeons could remove cataracts **quite** quickly.

adverb adjective

The ancient Romans were **highly** innovative.

Forms of Adverbs

Adverbs often end in *-ly*. In fact, you can change many adjectives into adverbs by adding *-ly* endings.

◆ If you add *-ly* to a word that ends in *l*, then your new word will have a double *l*.

scornful + ly

Many ancient Romans viewed surgeons **scornfully**.

◆ If you add *-ly* to a word that ends in *e*, keep the *e*. Exceptions to this rule are *truly* and *duly*.

extreme + ly

Doctors were **extremely** careful when they operated on patients.

HINT ◄ Some Adverbs and Adjectives Have the Same Form

Some adverbs look exactly like adjectives. The only way to distinguish them from adjectives is to see what they are modifying or describing. The following words can be either adjectives or adverbs.

early	fast	high	often	right
far	hard	late	past	soon

adjective   adverb
Dr. Greenbay has a **hard** job. She works **hard**.

PRACTICE 3

Underline the correct adjectives or adverbs in each sentence.

EXAMPLE: In 1980, the World Health Organization (official / officially) stated that it had eradicated smallpox.

1.   The worldwide eradication of smallpox was one of the most important accomplishments in modern medicine. Smallpox was a (high / highly) contagious global disease. Throughout history, smallpox epidemics were a (frequent / frequently) occurrence. People who contracted the disease had (painful / painfully) sores. Around 30 percent of smallpox victims suffered (horrible / horribly) deaths. In the Americas, smallpox (severe / severely) weakened native populations.

2.   In the mid-twentieth century, in North America and Europe, smallpox

outbreaks were (rapid / rapidly) controlled with the use of vaccinations.

However, in other parts of the world, the illness occurred (regular / regularly).

In the early 1960s, the former Soviet Union proposed a (global / globally)

initiative to eliminate smallpox. Health-care workers knew they would have

to work (careful / carefully) to help identify regions where the disease still

occurred. They (patient / patiently) educated people about the malady and

inoculated those at risk. With great effort, the World Health Organization

eradicated the (terrible / terribly) disease. Since 1977, there has been no

(natural / naturally) recurrence of smallpox anywhere in the world.

Placement of Frequency Adverbs

Frequency adverbs are words that indicate how often someone performs an action or
when an event occurs. Common frequency adverbs are *always, ever, never, often,
sometimes,* and *usually.* They can appear at the beginning of sentences, or they can
appear in the following mid-sentence locations.

◆ Place frequency adverbs before regular present tense and past tense verbs.

Medical doctors **always** <u>recite</u> the Hippocratic oath.

◆ Place frequency adverbs after all forms of the verb *be (am, is, are, was, were).*

My patients <u>are</u> **usually** punctual for appointments.

◆ Place frequency adverbs after helping verbs.

I <u>have</u> **never** broken any bone in my body.

PRACTICE 4

Correct eight errors in the placement of mid-sentence frequency adverbs.

                      often

EXAMPLE: Chronic pain is treated ~~often~~ with narcotics.

1.   Almost two million Americans are prescribed painkillers every year. Patients

fail often to recognize that they are addicted to painkillers. Doctors label

sometimes this problem the "silent addiction."

2.   Many patients usually have started taking painkillers after an accident. For

example, Emma was suffering from chronic back pain. She took painkillers to

reduce her pain but found soon that she needed a stronger dose. So she doubled quickly the dose of her prescription. Her personality started to change, and she found that she was critical often of people around her. She realized that she was addicted to painkillers and spoke to her doctor about her problem. Now, she reads always bottle labels and she takes never pain medication.

Problems with Adverbs
Use the Correct Form

Many times, people use an adjective instead of an adverb after a verb. Make sure that you always modify your verbs using an adverb.

                                                     really quickly
    Ancient Greek medicine advanced ~~real quick~~ after the time of Homer.

                                      slowly
    However, patients recovered very ~~slow~~.

PRACTICE 5

Underline and correct eight errors in adjective and adverb forms.

                                  really
EXAMPLE: Mental illness is a <u>realy</u> important issue.

1.   Mental illness is a disorder that slow inhibits a person's ability to cope with the ordinary demands of life. When a person has severely mental illness, he or she has trouble dealing with day-to-day activities. Mental illness can affect anybody, but young people are particular affected. Some people may feel acute depressed, while others may show signs of anxiety, bipolar disorder, phobias, and so on. Sometimes, the mentally ill are stigmatized very quick.

2.   Mental illness should be taken real seriously. The World Health Organization states that four out of ten causes of disability in the United States are due to mental illness, and around 46 percent of the population will suffer from some form of mental illness. If mental illness is left untreated, people can suffer tragically consequences, such as unemployment, homelessness, and imprisonment. Doctors can use different types of treatment on their patients. For example, doctors may treat patients with medication or talk therapy very successful.

Chapter 30

Using *good* and *well, bad* and *badly*

Good is an adjective, and *well* is an adverb.

Adjective	Louis Pasteur had a **good** reputation.
Adverb	He explained his theories **well**.

Exception: Use *well* to describe a person's health: I do not feel **well**.

Bad is an adjective, and *badly* is an adverb.

Adjective	My father has a **bad** cold.
Adverb	His throat hurts **badly**.

PRACTICE 6

Underline the correct adjectives or adverbs.

EXAMPLE: Wash your hands (good / well) before you prepare food.

1. Food poisoning can damage the (good / well) reputations of food companies.

2. Recently, the Bird's Nest Food Company gave the public some (bad / badly) news.

3. After eating the company's hamburgers, many people did not feel (good / well).

4. Many consumers complained of having a (bad / badly) case of indigestion, and they reacted (bad / badly) to the company's news.

5. Fortunately, public health inspectors investigated the case really (good / well).

6. The company workers stated that they had taken (good / well) care when handling the food.

7. The company showed its (good / well) intentions by recalling the food quickly.

8. To avoid food poisoning, authorities warned consumers to cook their food (good / well).

LO 3 Identify comparative and superlative forms.

Comparative and Superlative Forms

Use the **comparative form** to show how two persons, things, or items are different.

Adjectives	Dr. Jonas Salk was a <u>better</u> researcher than his colleague.
	Dr. Sabin is <u>more famous</u> for his research on the polio virus than Dr. Enders.
Adverbs	Dr. Salk published his results <u>more quickly</u> than Dr. Drake.
	Dr. Salk debated the issue <u>more passionately</u> than his colleague.

Use the **superlative form** to compare three or more items.

Adjectives	Dr. Salk was the <u>youngest</u> scientist to receive funding for polio research at the University of Michigan.
	Polio was one of the <u>most destructive</u> diseases of the twentieth century.
Adverbs	Dr. Parekh talked the <u>most rapidly</u> of all the doctors at the conference.
	She spoke the <u>most effectively</u> of all of the participants.

How to Write Comparative and Superlative Forms

You can write comparative and superlative forms by remembering a few simple guidelines.

Using *-er* and *-est* endings

Add *-er* and *-est* endings to one-syllable adjectives and adverbs.

Adjective or Adverb	Comparative	Superlative
tall	tall**er** than	the tall**est**
hard	hard**er** than	the hard**est**
fast	fast**er** than	the fast**est**

Double the last letter when the adjective ends in one vowel + one consonant.

hot	hot**ter** than	the hot**test**

Using *more* and *the most*

Add *more* and *the most* to adjectives and adverbs of two or more syllables.

Adjective or Adverb	Comparative	Superlative
dangerous	**more** dangerous than	**the most** dangerous
effectively	**more** effectively than	**the most** effectively
nervous	**more** nervous than	**the most** nervous

When a two-syllable adjective ends in *y*, change the *y* to *i* and add *-er* or *-est*.

Adjective	Comparative	Superlative
happy	happ**ier** than	the happ**iest**

Using Irregular Comparative and Superlative Forms

Some adjectives and adverbs have unique comparative and superlative forms. Study this list to remember how to form some of the most common ones.

Adjective or Adverb	Comparative	Superlative
good, well	better than	the best
bad, badly	worse than	the worst
some, much, many	more than	the most
little (a small amount)	less than	the least
far	farther, further	the farthest, the furthest

> **GRAMMAR LINK**
> *Farther* indicates a physical distance. *Further* means "additional." For more commonly confused words, see Chapter 33.

PRACTICE 7

Underline the appropriate comparative or superlative form of the words in parentheses.

EXAMPLE: Some vaccination programs are (<u>more</u> / most) effective than others.

1. Polio causes paralysis and sometimes death in infected people. Although the virus has menaced human beings for thousands of years, it became (more / most) dangerous in the twentieth century than in previous centuries.

The 1910s had the (worse / worst) epidemics of all time. Until scientists developed a polio vaccine in the 1950s, the disease was one of the (more / most) frightening of all human diseases.

2.   In 1962, Czechoslovakia and Cuba began the two (earlier / earliest) immunization programs in the developed world. Most countries in the Americas were polio free by the late 1980s. Peru was the (further / furthest) behind in its vaccination program in the Americas, but in 1991, it reported the last case of polio.

3.   Since 1988, the World Health Organization (WHO) has been implementing one of the (greater / greatest) global health campaigns in history. It aims to eradicate the polio virus. The (bigger / biggest) hurdle for eradication is the lack of basic health care in the (poorer / poorest) countries in the world, such as India, Nigeria, and Pakistan. As another obstacle, certain minority groups in developing countries oppose taking the vaccine. These groups are (less / least) knowledgeable about the positive aspects of immunization than other sectors of society. Therefore, they are suspicious of the polio vaccine program.

4.   Since the eradication initiative, doctors have reported (fewer / fewest) cases of polio than in previous years. In 2012, the (less / least) amount of polio outbreaks was reported since the eradication campaign. In that year, only Afghanistan, Pakistan, and Nigeria reported polio cases among their citizens.

PRACTICE 8

Complete the sentences by writing either the comparative or superlative form of the word in parentheses.

EXAMPLE: Some drugs produce (good) _____*better*_____ results than others.

1.   Our bodies need small amounts of vitamins and minerals to keep us healthy. Micronutrients are the (less) _____ exciting of all health-care topics. But the (small) _____ deficiency in micronutrients can lead to some of the (bad) _____ problems in human health.

2.   Many people in Africa and Asia lack iodine in their diets. The shortfall can cause one of the (serious) _____ birth defects—brain

damage. Countries that have the (great) _____ number of

hungry people have the (high) _____ rates of infant mental

slowness. Mental deficiency is (common) _____ in smaller

villages in remote areas than in (large) _____ cities because

villagers lack a varied diet.

3.   The Micronutrient Initiative is one of the (important) _____

but (little-known) _____ health-care organizations in the world.

Based out of Ottawa, Canada, it delivers micronutrients to the (vulnerable)

_____ citizens of the world—the malnourished. It costs

(little) _____ than any other health-care program. The

Micronutrient Initiative started to deliver iodized salt in the early 1990s. Initially,

doctors were (frustrated) _____ than they had expected

to be because villagers thought that putting iodine in salt would make people

sterile. But the benefits became (clear) _____ after people

started adding iodized salt to their food.

Problems with Comparative and Superlative Forms

Using *more* and *-er*

In the comparative form, never use *more* and *-er* to modify the same word. In the
superlative form, never use *most* and *-est* to modify the same word.

                                          better
Some people thought that Salk's vaccine was ~~more better~~ than Sabin's vaccine. The

                           best
polio vaccine was one of the ~~most best~~ discoveries of our times.

Using *fewer* and *less*

In the comparative form, never use *less* to compare two count nouns. Use *less* to
compare two noncount nouns. (Noncount nouns are nouns that cannot be divided,
such as *information* and *music*.) Use *fewer* to compare two count nouns.

            fewer
Today, ~~less~~ people get vaccinated than in previous decades because some question

                                     Less
the safety of certain vaccinations. ~~Fewer~~ information about vaccines was available

in the 1950s than is available today.

GRAMMAR LINK
For a list of noncount nouns, refer to page 381 in Chapter 28.

HINT ‹ Using *the* in the Comparative Form

Although you would usually use *the* in superlative forms, you can use it in some two-part comparatives. In these expressions, the second part is the result of the first part.

      action   result
The more you exercise, the better your health will be.

PRACTICE 9

Underline and correct fifteen adjective and adverb errors.

                               really
EXAMPLE: Some Americans are <u>real</u> suspicious about organ transplants.

1.   One of the most greatest miracles of modern medicine is organ transplants. Organ transplants save most lives than ever before. With donor organs, many recipients can lead more better lives than previously imagined. However, a public debate about organ transplants is growing rapid.

2.   The source of donor organs is a controversial issue. Given the scarcity of organs, some individuals who need transplants quick have obtained organs through unscrupulous methods. For instance, some have bought organs from the most poorest segments of the population in developing countries. Destitute people sometimes sell their organs to rich buyers because they need money real badly.

3.   Who should receive an organ transplant? Given the scarcity of supply, should a person who smokes heavy or drinks too much receive a lung or liver transplant? Obviously, the more a person smokes, the worst his or her health will be. Should such people be refused access to organ transplants?

4.   In addition, money is an issue in this debate. Hospital administrators are concerned about the high cost of transplants. Less people have adequate medical insurance than ever before. Should those with health insurance be treated more better than those without? According to most experts, the richest a patient is, the best his or her chances are to receive a transplant.

5. Waiting for an organ transplant is one of the worse experiences anyone can go through. Hopefully, in future years, the number of people who sign donor cards will be more higher than it is now.

Reflect On It

Think about what you have learned in this unit. If you do not know an answer, review that concept.

1. What is an adjective? _____

    _____

2. What is an adverb? _____

    _____

3. Underline the correct word in parentheses.

    a. My doctor treats her patients (good / well). She is one of the (better / best) eye surgeons in Berlin.

    b. My brother has (less / fewer) work experience than I do, but he also has (less / fewer) responsibilities.

4. The following sentences contain adjective or adverb errors. Correct each mistake.

    a. We had a real nice time at the medical conference.

    b. Everyone was dressed casual.

    c. My sister changes often her mind about her career.

    d. The advancing medical textbook is my sister's.

FINAL REVIEW

Underline and correct twenty errors in adjectives and adverbs.

1. Health care is one of the most fastest growing fields in the world. In our nation, the aging population is making the demand for nurses more and more intenser. According to *Health Affairs*, an online magazine, there is an acute

nursing shortage. Less people enter the nursing profession than in the past. In fact, the number of people in their early twenties entering the nursing profession is at its lower point in forty years. The shortage is worldwide. Canada, England, and many other nations have a more greater shortage than the United States has. As a possible career, more people should consider the nursing profession.

2.   First, nurses have greater responsibility and a more diversely role than most people realize. In states such as California, nurses can write prescriptions and nurse midwives can deliver babies. Forensic nurses treat traumatizing victims of violent crime. Furthermore, hospitals are not the only places where nurses can work. Nursing jobs are available in walk-in clinics, schools, vacation resorts, and medical equipment firms. Even film studios hire sometimes on-set nurses.

3.   Also, nursing can be an extreme rewarding career. Joan Bowes, a nurse in Oregon, says that she feels as if she is doing something usefull each day. Occasionally, her actions help to save lives. Last month, a young patient who had been injured really bad was admitted to the hospital where Joan works. A few days later, Joan noticed that the patient was unable to move his head as easy as before. She quick alerted a specialist who then diagnosed a meningitis infection. Joan's observation helped to save the patient's life. Joan's husband, Keith, is a home-care nurse. He is compassionate, and he interacts good with his patients. As one of a growing number of men in the profession, Keith feels that entering nursing was the better decision he has ever made.

4.   Nurses are more better compensated than in the past. In the 1970s, salaries for nurses were much worst than they are today. In fact, nurses were paid the less among health-care professionals. Nowadays, because nurses are in such high demand, many hospitals give signing bonuses, decent schedules, and real good salaries.

5.   Potential nurses should enjoy helping people. For those who want to have a

rewarding career with decent benefits, nursing is an excellent career choice. The

more society appreciates nurses, the best health care will be.

THE WRITER'S ROOM

MyWritingLab™

Write about one of the following topics. Underline adjectives and adverbs.

1. What steps can you take to motivate yourself to exercise regularly?

2. Prescription drugs are very expensive. How do the high prices affect
    ordinary people? List some effects of the high drug prices, and provide
    specific examples to support your point.

MyWritingLab™
**Complete these
writing assignments at
mywritinglab.com**

Mistakes with Modifiers

SECTION THEME: Health Care

LEARNING OBJECTIVES

LO 1 Avoid misplaced modifiers. **(p. 424)**

LO 2 Avoid dangling modifiers. **(p. 428)**

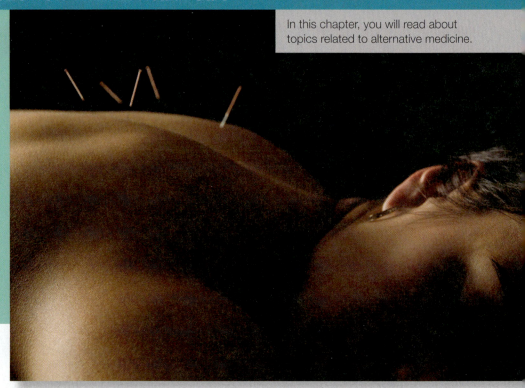

In this chapter, you will read about topics related to alternative medicine.

MyWritingLab™

Complete this Writer's Journal activity at mywritinglab.com

THE WRITER'S JOURNAL

Have you ever hurt yourself or had an accident? What happened?

LO 1 Avoid misplaced modifiers.

Misplaced Modifiers

A **modifier** is a word, phrase, or clause that describes or modifies nouns or verbs in a sentence. For example, *holding the patient's hand* is a modifier. To use a modifier correctly, place it next to the word(s) that you want to modify.

modifier   words that are modified

Holding the patient's hand, **the doctor** explained the procedure.

A **misplaced modifier** is a word, phrase, or clause that is not placed next to the word it modifies. When a modifier is too far from the word that it is describing, then the meaning of the sentence can become confusing or unintentionally funny.

> I saw a pamphlet about acupuncture sitting in the doctor's office.
> (How could a pamphlet sit in a doctor's office?)

Commonly Misplaced Modifiers

As you read the sample sentences for each type of modifier, notice how the meaning of the sentence changes depending on where the modifier is placed. In the examples, the modifiers are underlined.

Prepositional Phrase Modifiers

A prepositional phrase is made of a preposition and its object.

Confusing   Cora read an article on acupuncture written by reporter James Reston <u>in a café</u>.
(Who was in the café: James or Cora?)

Clear   <u>In a café</u>, Cora read an article on acupuncture written by reporter James Reston.

Present Participle Modifiers

A present participle modifier is a phrase that begins with an *-ing* verb.

Confusing   James Reston learned about acupuncture <u>touring China</u>.
(Can acupuncture tour China?)

Clear   While <u>touring China</u>, James Reston learned about acupuncture.

Past Participle Modifiers

A past participle modifier is a phrase that begins with a past participle (*walked, gone, known*, and so on).

Confusing   <u>Called meridians</u>, acupuncturists claim there are two thousand pathways on the body.
(What are called meridians: the acupuncturists or the pathways?)

Clear   Acupuncturists claim there are two thousand pathways <u>called meridians</u> on the body.

Limiting Modifiers

Limiting modifiers are words such as *almost, nearly, only, merely, just,* and *even*. In the examples, notice how the placement of *almost* changes the meaning.

Almost all of the doctors went to the lecture that disproved acupuncture.
(Some of the doctors did not attend, but most did.)

All of the doctors **almost** went to the lecture that disproved acupuncture.
(The doctors did not go.)

All of the doctors went to the lecture that **almost** disproved acupuncture.
(The lecture did not disprove acupuncture.)

HINT ◀ Other Types of Modifiers

There are many other types of modifiers. For example, some modifiers begin with relative clauses and some are appositives. Ensure that your modifier is near the word it is describing.

Relative Clause

Confusing	The treatments involved acupuncture needles <u>that were expensive</u>. (What was expensive: the treatment or the needles?)
Clear	The treatments <u>that were expensive</u> involved acupuncture needles.

Appositive

Confusing	<u>A very sick man</u>, Monica helped her uncle find a doctor. (How could Monica be a very sick man?)
Clear	Monica helped her uncle, <u>a very sick man</u>, find a doctor.

PRACTICE 1

Circle the letter of the correct sentence in each pair. Underline the misplaced modifier in each incorrect sentence.

EXAMPLE: ⓐ With interest, Lara noticed students meditating.

   b. Lara noticed students meditating <u>with interest</u>.

1. a. Lara does an exercise called meditation to focus her mind.

    b. Called meditation, Lara does an exercise to focus her mind.

2. a. Based on ancient practices, Lara's teacher explains meditation techniques.

    b. Lara's teacher explains meditation techniques based on ancient practices.

3. a. Lara became curious about meditation vacationing in Korea.

    b. While vacationing in Korea, Lara became curious about meditation.

4. a. Lara spent a weekend in silence at a Buddhist temple.

    b. Lara spent a weekend at a Buddhist temple in silence.

5. a. A recent survey showed that nearly twenty million Americans practice meditation.

    b. A recent survey showed that twenty million Americans nearly practice meditation.

6. a. Scientists found a connection between meditation and a change in people's blood pressure who were doing clinical studies.

    b. Scientists who were doing clinical studies found a connection between meditation and a change in people's blood pressure.

7. a. Dr. Grey will study Lara, an expert on meditation research.

    b. Dr. Grey, an expert on meditation research, will study Lara.

HINT ◄ **Correcting Misplaced Modifiers**

To correct misplaced modifiers, do the following:

- Identify the modifier.

  The orderly pushed the wheelchair <u>in sneakers</u>.

- Identify the word or words that are being modified.

  Who wore sneakers? **The orderly**

- Move the modifier next to the word(s) being modified.

  <u>In sneakers</u>, **the orderly** pushed the wheelchair.

PRACTICE 2

Underline the misplaced modifiers in the following sentences. Then, rewrite the sentences. You may have to add or remove words to give the sentence a logical meaning.

EXAMPLE: Louisa, a hypnotherapist, suggested some exercises to help Rodney relax his mind <u>with a smile</u>.

With a smile, Louisa, a hypnotherapist, suggested some exercises to

help Rodney relax his mind.

1. Hypnotism seems to be a mysterious form of mind control for audiences in television programs.

   _____

   _____

2. Recently, scientists have found that their subjects have free will who study hypnosis.

   _____

   _____

3. Rodney Booker had tried many different methods to help him sleep feeling worried.

   _____

   _____

4. Understanding the problem, hypnotherapy was suggested by Rodney's mother.

   _____

   _____

5. Feeling scared, Dr. Louisa Aziz explained hypnotherapy to Rodney.

   _____

   _____

6. Dr. Aziz reassured Rodney that she has almost had success with 98 percent of her patients.

   _____

   _____

LO 2 Avoid dangling modifiers.

Dangling Modifiers

A **dangling modifier** opens a sentence but does not modify any words in the sentence. It "dangles" or hangs loosely because it is not connected to any other part of the sentence.

To avoid having a dangling modifier, make sure that the modifier and the first noun that follows it have a logical connection.

Confusing	While talking on a cell phone, the ambulance drove off the road.
	(Can an ambulance talk on a cell phone?)
Clear	While talking on a cell phone, the ambulance **technician** drove off the road.
Confusing	To get into medical school, high grades are necessary.
	(Can high grades get into a school?)
Clear	To get into medical school, **students** need high grades.

PRACTICE 3

Circle the letter of the correct sentence in each pair. Underline the dangling modifier in each incorrect sentence.

EXAMPLE:
    a. Having taken a pill, the results were surprising.

    b. Having taken a pill, I was surprised by the results.

1. a. With the patient's budget in mind, the least expensive drugs were prescribed.

    b. With the patient's budget in mind, the doctor prescribed the least expensive drugs.

2. a. Believing in their effects, placebos are often given to patients.

    b. Believing in their effects, Dr. Zimboro sometimes gives placebos to patients.

3. a. After taking a sugar pill, patients often feel relieved.

    b. After taking a sugar pill, there is often a feeling of relief.

4. a. Surprised, the word *placebo* means "to please."

    b. Surprised, I read that the word *placebo* means "to please."

5. a. Thinking about the mind–body relationship, scientist Esther Sternberg conducted an experiment.

    b. Thinking about the mind–body relationship, an experiment was conducted.

6. a. Frustrated, Sternberg's temptation was to give up.

    b. Frustrated, Sternberg was tempted to give up.

7. a. Using laboratory rats, Sternberg discovered a link between the mind and body.

    b. Using laboratory rats, a link was discovered between the mind and body.

8. a. Given an antidepressant, the arthritis disappeared.

   b. Given an antidepressant, some rats no longer had arthritis.

9. a. Excited about her discovery, Sternberg wrote an article for a medical journal.

   b. Excited about her discovery, an article was written for a medical journal.

HINT ◀ **Correcting Dangling Modifiers**

To correct dangling modifiers, do the following:

- Identify the modifier.

    To teach yoga, a flexible body is needed.

- Identify the word or words that are being modified.

    Who needs a flexible body? **The yoga instructor**

- Add the missing subject and, in some cases, also add or remove words so that the sentence makes sense.

    To teach yoga, **the instructor** needs a flexible body.

PRACTICE 4

In each sentence, underline the dangling modifier. Then rewrite each sentence, adding or removing words to provide a logical meaning.

EXAMPLE: Worried about their health, laughter yoga is practiced.

    Worried about their health, people practice laughter yoga.

1. When exercising, getting bored is common.

   _____

   _____

2. Gathering in a park in Mumbai, India, laughter yoga was practiced.

   _____

   _____

3. Muscles are gently stretched while chanting "Haha hoho" in unison.

   _____

   _____

4. To take a laughter yoga class, $20 is needed.

   _____

   _____

5. Doing laughter yoga, stress is reduced.

   _____

   _____

6. When experimenting with laughter yoga, the advice of a professional is helpful.

   _____

   _____

PRACTICE 5

Some sentences in this practice have dangling or misplaced modifiers. Write *M* next to misplaced modifiers, *D* next to dangling modifiers, and *C* next to correct sentences. If the modifier is misplaced, move it. If the modifier is dangling, add words to make the sentence complete.

> *people try different therapies*

EXAMPLE: Hoping to live a long life, ~~different therapies are tried~~.   _D_

1. Called Ayurveda therapy, ancient Indians developed a school

   of medicine.   _____

2. Originally written on palm leaves, researchers found

   2,000-year-old texts.   _____

3. Possibly causing diseases, Ayurvedic medicine teaches about

   an imbalance in mental and physical energies.   _____

4. Ayurvedic medicine is widely followed by people in India.   _____

5. Doing meditation and yoga, essential parts of this alternative

   therapy are learned.   _____

6. Called homeopathy, India has produced a therapy that uses

   plants, animals, and minerals to cure a patient's illness.   _____

7. Later, a German doctor organized the rules of homeopathic

   treatment wearing glasses.   _____

8. In the 1800s, homeopathy became popular in the United States.   _____

9. Feeling skeptical, the merits of homeopathy are questioned.   _____

10. In fact, many conventionally trained doctors do not believe

in alternative medical therapies. _____

Reflect On It

Think about what you have learned in this unit. If you do not know an answer, review that concept.

1. What is a misplaced modifier? _____

_____

2. What is a dangling modifier? _____

_____

3. What type of modifier error is in each sentence? Write *M* for "misplaced" and *D* for "dangling." Then correct the sentence.

  a. Overeating, a weight problem was developed.

  _____

  b. The doctor examined the X-ray in the lab coat.

  _____

FINAL REVIEW

Underline ten dangling or misplaced modifier errors in the next selection. Then, correct each error. You may need to add or remove words to ensure that the sentence makes sense.

EXAMPLE: Manipulating her neck, <s>a surprising result occurred</s>. ~the chiropractor had a surprising result.~

1.   There are many fraudulent claims in alternative medicine. In fact, feeling

desperate, fortunes are spent on suspect therapies. It is difficult for members of

the public to determine which therapies are valid and which are pure quackery.

At an important medical conference, some doctors discussed chiropractic neck

treatments eating lunch together.

2.   Based on spinal adjustments, Dr. Daniel Palmer developed a new healing

technique. Born in Canada, Palmer did his first treatment in 1895. A janitor

complained that he had lost his hearing after straining his back. Manipulating

the janitor's neck, the man's hearing was restored. Using the therapy all over

America, neck manipulations are actively promoted.

3.   In 2006, a young mother went to see a chiropractor with severe headaches. Misdiagnosing the patient's illness, a mistake was made. Pierrette Parisien died following her neck treatment. The coroner recommended a review of chiropractic procedures speaking to the media.

4.   Many medical doctors have questioned the safety of neck manipulations. Chiropractors refute the criticism feeling angry. According to Dr. Rick Morris, chiropractors pay low malpractice insurance rates because injuries are so rare. Having confidence in chiropractors, neck manipulations continue to be popular.

MyWritingLab™
Complete these writing assignments at mywritinglab.com

READING LINK

To learn more about health care, read the following essays.

"Guy Chores" by Tom Keenan (page 192)
"Chicken Hips" by Catherine Pigott (page 201)
"Don't Worry, Act Happy" by Albert Nerenberg (page 224)
"Musicophilia" by Oliver Sacks (page 531)

MyWritingLab™
THE WRITER'S ROOM

Write about one of the following topics. Include some modifiers and make sure that your sentences are formed correctly.

1.   Have you ever been to an acupuncturist, a massage therapist, a naturopath, a homeopath, or any other alternative healing practitioner? Describe the treatment that you received.

2.   Give your opinion about alternative therapies.

THE WRITERS' CIRCLE **Collaborative Activity**

Work with a group of students and create an advertisement for an alternative medical treatment. You can even invent a new medical treatment. For example, you can make an advertisement to cure warts, reduce acne, or help back pain.

In your ad, include some adjectives and adverbs. In some of your sentences, include phrases that begin with *who*, *that*, and *which*. When you finish, exchange advertisements with another team. Check that the other team's advertisement contains correct adjectives, adverbs, and modifiers.

In this chapter, you will read about topics related to property crimes.

LEARNING OBJECTIVES

LO 1 Use specific and detailed vocabulary. **(p. 433)**

LO 2 Avoid wordiness and redundancy. **(p. 435)**

LO 3 Avoid clichés. **(p. 437)**

LO 4 Identify standard English versus slang. **(p. 438)**

THE WRITER'S JOURNAL

Write a paragraph that summarizes the events of a well-known crime. Describe what happened.

MyWritingLab™

Complete this Writer's Journal activity at mywritinglab.com

Use Specific and Detailed Vocabulary

LO 1 Use specific and detailed vocabulary.

Great writing evokes an emotional response from the reader. Great writers not only use correct grammatical structures, but they also infuse their writing with precise and vivid details that make their work come alive.

When you proofread your work, revise words that are too vague. **Vague words** lack precision and detail. For example, the words *nice* and *bad* are vague. Readers cannot get a clear picture from them.

Compare the following sets of sentences.

Vague	The movie was bad.
Precise	The predictable film included violent, gory scenes.
Vague	In France, thieves stole some paintings.
Precise	In southern France, armed, masked thieves staged a brazen daylight robbery of paintings by Claude Monet.

433

Creating Vivid Language

When you choose the precise word, you convey your meaning exactly. Moreover, you can make your writing clearer and more impressive by using specific and detailed vocabulary. To create vivid language, try the following strategies.

◆ **Modify your nouns.** If your noun is vague, make it more specific by adding one or more adjectives. You could also replace the noun with a more specific term.

Vague	the man
Vivid	the taxi driver the thin, nervous soldier

◆ **Modify your verbs.** Use more vivid and precise verbs. You could also add adverbs.

Vague	walk
Vivid	saunter stroll march briskly

◆ **Include more details.** Add detailed information to make the sentence more complete.

Vague	Several signs foretold Caesar's death.
Precise	Several ominous signs, such as Caesar's horses getting loose and a soothsayer's warning, foretold Caesar's impending murder.

HINT   **Use Imagery**

You can make your writing come alive by using **imagery**, which is description using the five senses: sight, sound, smell, touch, and taste. In the examples, the underlined words add details to the sentence and contribute to a more exact description.

Wearing a blond wig, the armed robber smashed the glass display case and pocketed the luxury watches.

WRITING LINK
You can find more information about appealing to the five senses in Chapter 6, "Description."

PRACTICE 1

Replace the familiar words in parentheses with more vivid words or phrases, and add more specific details. Use your dictionary or thesaurus if you need help.

EXAMPLE: Graffiti artists (write) _____scrawl words and pictures_____ on walls.

1. Many cities spend a lot of money (cleaning graffiti) _____

    _____

2. (Youths) _____ spray paint on many (places)

    _____

3. They worry about getting caught by (someone) _____

    _____

4. Some cities permit graffiti artists to paint on (certain locations) _____

    _____

5. Sometimes graffiti artists write (bad words) _____

    _____

6. Governments could combat the problem (with many solutions) _____

_____

7. Some people think graffiti artists should be (treated harshly) _____

_____

PRACTICE 2

Underline all the words in the paragraph that add vivid details to the description.

EXAMPLE: Paul bounded upstairs, <u>scrubbed the greasy odor of the dishwater from his hands</u> with the <u>ill-smelling soap</u> he hated, and then <u>shook over his fingers a few drops of violet water</u> from the bottle he kept hidden in his drawer.

The east-bound train was plowing through a January snowstorm; the dull dawn was beginning to show grey when the engine whistled a mile out of Newark. Paul started up from the seat where he had lain curled in uneasy slumber, rubbed the breath-misted window-glass with his hand, and peered out. The snow was whirling in curling eddies above the white bottom lands, and the drifts lay already deep in the fields and along the fences while here and there the tall dead grass and dried weed-stalks protruded black above it. Lights shone from the scattered houses, and a gang of laborers who stood beside the track waved their lanterns.

—Willa Cather, "Paul's Case"

HINT ◢ Adding Appositives

An appositive is a word or phrase that gives further information about a noun or pronoun. You can write sentences that are more exact and detailed by adding appositives.

appositive   appositive

Sherlock Holmes, <u>the famous detective</u>, was helped by his friend, <u>Dr. Watson</u>.

Avoid Wordiness and Redundancy

LO2 Avoid wordiness and redundancy.

Sometimes students fill their writing assignments with extra words to meet length requirements. However, good ideas can easily get lost in work that is too wordy. Also, if the explanations are unnecessarily long, then writing becomes boring.

To improve your writing style, use only as many words or phrases as you need to fully explain your ideas.

The police department was ~~a distance of~~ two blocks from the municipal library.

(A block is a measure of a distance, so it is unnecessary to repeat that information.)

Correcting Wordiness

You can cut the number of words needed to express an idea by substituting a wordy phrase with a single word. You could also remove the wordy phrase completely.

Because ~~of the fact that~~ the security guard was alone, the thieves easily overwhelmed him.

Some Common Wordy Expressions and Substitutions

Wordy	Better	Wordy	Better
at that point in time	then, at that time	great, few in number	great, few
big, small in size	big, small	in order to	to
in close proximity	close *or* in proximity	in spite of the fact	although, even though
a difficult dilemma	a dilemma	in the final analysis	finally, lastly
due to the fact	because	past history	past *or* history
equally as good as	as good as	period of time	period
exactly the same	the same	personal opinion	opinion
exceptions to the rule	exceptions	reason why is that	because
final completion	end	return again	return
for the purpose of	for	still remain	remain
gave the appearance of	looked like	a true fact	a fact

PRACTICE 3

In the next sentences, cross out all unnecessary words or phrases, or modify any repeated words.

EXAMPLE: ~~A great number of~~ Many thefts occurred in Beverly Hills, California.

1. In August 2007, five men entered an art museum on the French Riviera for the purpose of stealing paintings.

2. In spite of the fact that there were security guards, the masked thieves managed to take four masterpieces.

3. At that period of time, the thieves stuffed the paintings in bags.

4. In order to escape, the robbers used a motorcycle and a car.

5. The whole entire robbery lasted for ten minutes.

6. The thieves cannot sell their treasures on the open market due to the fact that the Monet and Bruegel paintings are well known.

7. It is a true fact that many paintings are stolen for wealthy private collectors.

8. The paintings still remain missing, and the thieves have not been caught.

9. The FBI estimates that, on a yearly basis, the market for stolen art is $6 billion annually.

Avoid Clichés

Clichés are overused expressions. Because they are overused, they lose their power and become boring. You should avoid using clichés in your writing.

                                    cliché
The defense attorney was <u>fit to be tied</u> when his client confessed.

                                 direct words
The defense attorney was <u>extremely upset</u> when his client confessed.

Some Common Clichés

a drop in the bucket	break the ice	jump in with both feet
as light as a feather	butter someone up	keep your eyes peeled
as luck would have it	cost an arm and a leg	top dog
axe to grind	drop the ball	under the weather
between a rock and a hard place	easier said than done	work like a dog

Correcting Clichés

When you modify a cliché, you can change it into a direct term. You might also try playing with language to come up with a more interesting description.

Cliché	She was as busy as a bee.
Direct language	She was extremely busy.
Interesting description	She was as busy as an emergency room nurse.

PRACTICE 4

Underline twelve clichéd expressions, and then replace them with fresh or direct language.

                                 stay alert
EXAMPLE: Jack Garcia had to <u>keep his eyes peeled.</u>

1. Cuban-born Jack Garcia is recognized as the best undercover agent in the FBI's history. During his career, he was a mover and shaker in more than a hundred different operations. For instance, some of Florida's largest drug smugglers are now in the big house thanks to Garcia. The agent's work also led to the arrest of some corrupt Florida police officers. Playing the role of "Big Frankie" or "Big Tony," Garcia would bribe officers. The officers were bent out of shape when they were arrested.

2. Garcia was able to infiltrate New York's Gambino crime family by pretending to be "Jack Falcone." To prepare for his role, Garcia had to jump into Sicilian culture with both feet. For example, he learned about Italian food.

He knew he was playing with fire whenever he sat with the crime boss Greg DePalma, and he had to be convincing. If he dropped the ball, he could find himself six feet under.

3. Garcia played DePalma like a fiddle. He constantly buttered up the boss. Also, Garcia provided DePalma with the finer things in life such as jewelry, iPods, and televisions. The FBI agent was so convincing in his role as "Big Jack" that the crime boss offered to promote Garcia in the crime family.

4. Jack Garcia's job was no piece of cake. One day, when Mafia members became suspicious of Garcia, the FBI pulled the plug on the operation. Today, thirty-one members of the Gambino crime family are in jail, and Garcia has retired from the FBI.

LO 4 Identify standard English versus slang.

Standard English Versus Slang

Most of your instructors will want you to write using **standard American English**. The word *standard* does not imply "better." Standard American English is the common language generally used and expected in schools, businesses, and government institutions in the United States.

Slang is nonstandard language. It is used in informal situations to communicate common cultural knowledge. In any academic or professional context, do not use slang.

Slang	My friends and I <u>hang</u> together. Last weekend, we watched a movie that was <u>kinda weird but also pretty sweet</u>. It was called *Safe House*.
Standard American English	My friends and I <u>spend a lot of time</u> together. Last weekend, we watched a movie that was <u>unusual but fascinating</u>. It was called *Safe House*.

> **HINT** ◀ **Do Not Use Slang in Academic Writing**
>
> Slang is very informal and should be avoided in academic writing. Keep in mind that slang changes depending on generational, regional, cultural, and historical influences. For example, rather than saying "I have to *leave*," people in one group might say *scram* or *split* while those in another group might say *bail* or *bounce*. Avoid using slang expressions in your writing because they can change very quickly—so quickly, in fact, that you might remark that this textbook's examples of slang are "lame."

PRACTICE 5

Substitute the underlined slang expressions with the best possible choice in standard American English.

EXAMPLE: Every day, the cops deal with gangs. ___police officers___

1. Gang members can be guys or chicks. _____

2. Some young people think that gangs are cool. _____

3. It takes a lot of guts to refuse to join a gang. _____

4. Someone may join a gang because he or she does not want to look spineless. _____

5. Others join gangs because they want to earn serious coin. _____

6. Sometimes people hang with gangs because they feel more protected. _____

7. It is dicey to be in a gang. _____

8. Police try to keep their cool when they deal with gangs. _____

9. Gang members are often on the lookout for narcs. _____

10. Many gang members end up in the slammer. _____

Reflect On It

Think about what you have learned in this unit. If you do not know an answer, review that concept.

1. What is vivid language? _____

_____

2. Edit the following sentences for wordiness, clichés, and overused expressions. Modify them to make them more concise.

   a. The suspect lived in close proximity to the bank that he had robbed.

   b. Peter will be in for a rude awakening if he does not study for his law-enforcement exams.

   c. Peter is feeling under the weather today.

3. Edit the following sentences for slang. Replace the slang words with standard American English.

   a. Replacing the contents of a stolen wallet is such a drag.

   b. I read a cool biography about Al Capone.

FINAL REVIEW

Edit the following paragraphs for slang, clichés, and vague language.

PART A

In the next paragraph, four vague words are underlined. Replace these words with specific details to make the paragraph more interesting. Also correct four wordy expressions.

EXAMPLE: It is estimated that the Bling Ring managed to steal about $3 million

cash and belongings

worth of <u>stuff</u>.

At the end of 2008, Rachel Lee was rebellious. Small in size, she was the daughter of successful business owners. Perhaps, as a result of the fact that celebrity culture is so strong, Lee wanted to dress like a movie star. In order to feed her cravings, Lee convinced her shy friend, Nick Prugo, to help her rob the home of Paris Hilton. For the next eleven months, Lee led a group of teen house burglars. They managed to steal clothing and money from rich <u>people</u> in Hollywood. They wanted to have a <u>good</u> life. But in 2009, the police captured the gang. At this point in time, <u>the girl</u> has finished her four-year prison sentence. Filmmaker Sofia Coppola has made a movie about the <u>interesting story</u>.

PART B

Underline and replace twelve slang or clichéd expressions.

young man

EXAMPLE: Nick Prugo was a nervous <u>dude</u>.

1.   Rachel Lee was able to mess with people's heads and get them to follow her. For their first robbery, Lee and Prugo wondered who would leave the front door unlocked and some dough lying around. They targeted Paris Hilton because they thought the celebrity was as dumb as a bag of rocks. Sure enough, Hilton's house was unlocked. They robbed Hilton several times before the celebrity realized that something was missing. They also ripped off Audrina Patridge, Rachel Bilson, and Lindsay Lohan. Of course, the gang's victims were bummed after realizing that they had been robbed.

2.   Nick Prugo claimed that he was a bit of a wimp, and he would sometimes freak out during the robberies. Rachel Lee, on the other hand, was super chill, even stopping to use a celebrity's bathroom during one burglary. As the gang expanded, the female members especially targeted the designer clothing of their celebrity victims. Lee and the others often dressed to the hilt and wore lots of stolen bling.

3.   Eventually, a schoolmate told authorities that Lee and Prugo had robbed Lindsay Lohan. The police had a surveillance camera photo of Prugo. A whiz cop had the idea of searching Prugo's Facebook page, where he found Rachel Lee's name. Police noticed the designer clothing that the thieves wore in their Facebook photos. Quickly, the gang's sweet gig came to an end.

THE WRITER'S ROOM   MyWritingLab™

MyWritingLab™
Complete these writing assignments at mywritinglab.com

Write about one of the following topics. Make sure that you use exact and concise language.

1. List some steps that parents can take to prevent their children from joining gangs or breaking laws.

2. What are some different categories of crimes? Classify crimes into three different types.

33 Spelling and Commonly Confused Words

SECTION THEME: The Legal World

LEARNING OBJECTIVES

LO 1 Follow spelling rules. **(p. 442)**

LO 2 Review 120 commonly misspelled words. **(p. 449)**

LO 3 Distinguish look-alike and sound-alike words. **(p. 451)**

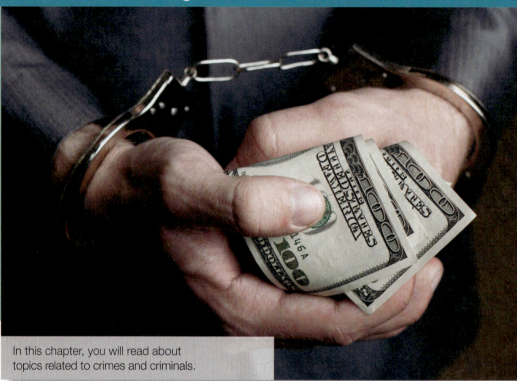

In this chapter, you will read about topics related to crimes and criminals.

THE WRITER'S JOURNAL

What are some reasons that people commit crimes?

LO 1 Follow spelling rules.

Spelling Rules

It is important to spell correctly. Spelling mistakes can detract from good ideas in your work. You can become a better speller if you always proofread your written work and if you check a dictionary for the meaning and spelling of words about which you are unsure. Here are some spelling rules that will help you improve your spelling.

HINT ⟩ Using a Dictionary

If you are unsure about the spelling or meaning of a word, consult a dictionary. Try to use a recent edition. Also, get to know the features of your dictionary.

Writing *ie* or *ei*

Remember the following rule so that you know when to use *ie* or *ei*. Write *i* before *e*, except after *c* or when *ei* is pronounced *ay*, as in *neighbor* and *weigh*.

i before *e*	niece	field	grief	
ei after *c*	ceiling	conceive	perceive	
ei pronounced *ay*	beige	vein	weigh	
Exceptions:	efficient	either	foreigner	height
	leisure	neither	science	seize
	society	species	their	weird

PRACTICE 1

Underline the correct spelling of each word.

EXAMPLE: recieve / receive

1. decieve / deceive
2. foreigner / foriegner
3. friend / freind
4. hieght / height
5. vien / vein

6. science / sceince
7. efficient / efficeint
8. theif / thief
9. deciet / deceit
10. chief / cheif

> **READING LINK**
> For more information about using a dictionary, see pages 506–507 in Part V, "Reading Strategies and Selections" (Chapter 38).

Adding Prefixes and Suffixes

A **prefix** is added to the beginning of a word, and it changes the word's meaning. For example, *con-*, *dis-*, *pre-*, *un-*, and *il-* are prefixes. A **suffix** is added to the ending of a word, and it changes the word's tense or meaning. For example, *-ly*, *-ment*, *-ed*, and *-ing* are suffixes.

When you add a prefix to a word, keep the last letter of the prefix and the first letter of the main word.

un + **n**atural = **unn**atural   **dis** + **s**atisfaction = **diss**atisfaction

When you add the suffix *-ly* to words that end in *l*, keep the *l* of the root word. The new word will have two *l*'s.

personal + **ly** = persona**lly**   actual + **ly** = actua**lly**

HINT ‹ Words Ending in *-ful*

Although the word *full* ends in two *l*'s, when *-ful* is added to another word as a suffix, it ends in one *l*.

careful   successful   hopeful

Notice, however, the unusual spelling when *full* and *fill* are combined: fulfill.

PRACTICE 2

Read the following words and decide if they are correctly spelled. If the word is correct, write C in the space provided. If the word is incorrect, write the correct word in the space.

EXAMPLES: factualy _factually_   untrue _C_

1. ilogical _____
2. continually _____
3. imoral _____
4. unecessary _____
5. mispell _____

6. beautifull _____
7. iresponsible _____
8. unusual _____
9. carefuly _____
10. fulfilled _____

Adding -s or -es

Add -s to nouns and to present tense verbs that are third-person singular. However, add -es to words in the following situations.

◆ When words end in s, sh, ss, ch, or x, add -es.

> **Noun:** church–church**es**   **Verb:** fix–fix**es**

◆ When words end with the consonant y, change the y to i and add -es.

> **Noun:** berry–berr**ies**   **Verb:** marry–marr**ies**

◆ When words end in o, add -es in most cases.

> **Noun:** hero–hero**es**   **Verb:** do–do**es**

> **Exceptions:** piano–piano**s**; radio–radio**s**; logo–logo**s**; patio–patio**s**

◆ When words end in f or fe, change the f to v and add -es.

> leaf–lea**ves**   knife–kni**ves**

> **Exceptions:** belief–belief**s**; roof–roof**s**

PRACTICE 3

Add -s or -es to each word, and adjust the spelling if necessary. Write the new word in the space provided.

EXAMPLE: reach _reaches_

1. hero _____
2. crutch _____
3. fix _____
4. echo _____
5. carry _____
6. tomato _____

7. potato _____
8. miss _____
9. fly _____
10. teach _____
11. scarf _____
12. candy _____

Adding Suffixes to Words Ending in -e

When you add a suffix to a word ending in e, make sure that you follow the next rules.

◆ If the suffix begins with a vowel, drop the e on the main word. Some common suffixes beginning with vowels are -ed, -er, -est, -ing, -able, -ent, and -ist.

hope–hop**ing**	encourage–encourag**ing**	sue–su**ing**

Exceptions: For some words that end in ge, keep the e and add the suffix.

courage–courage**ous**	change–change**able**

◆ If the suffix begins with a consonant, keep the e. Some common suffixes beginning with consonants are -ly, -ment, -less, and -ful.

sure–sure**ly**	like–like**ness**	hope–hope**ful**

Exceptions: Some words lose their final e when a suffix is added.

argue–argu**ment**	true–tru**ly**	judge–judg**ment**

HINT ◀ American and British Spelling

American and British spelling conventions are not identical. Canadian English generally follows British spelling.

United States	**Great Britain and Canada**
color center judgment	colour centre judgement

PRACTICE 4

Rewrite each word with the suggested ending.

EXAMPLE: use + ed _____used_____

1. achieve + ment _____
2. strange + est _____
3. argue + ment _____
4. love + ing _____
5. true + ly _____

6. endorse + ment _____
7. argue + ing _____
8. nine + ty _____
9. write + ing _____
10. change + able _____

Adding Suffixes to Words Ending in -y

When you add a suffix to a word ending in y, make sure that you follow the next rules.

◆ If the word has a consonant before the final y, change the y to an i before adding the suffix.

beauty–beaut**iful**	supply–suppl**ied**

♦ If the word has a vowel before the final *y*, if the word is a proper name, or if the suffix is *-ing*, do not change the *y* to an *i*.

day–days   try–trying   the Vronsky family–the Vronskys

Exceptions: Some words do not follow the previous rule.

day–da**i**ly   lay–la**i**d   say–sa**i**d   pay–pa**i**d

PRACTICE 5

Rewrite each word with the suggested ending.

EXAMPLE: try + ed   *tried*

1. happy + est   _____
2. play + er   _____
3. pretty + er   _____
4. Connolly + s   _____
5. lonely + ness   _____
6. lazy + er   _____

7. envy + able   _____
8. angry + ly   _____
9. day + ly   _____
10. say + ing   _____
11. dirty + est   _____
12. stay + ed   _____

Doubling the Final Consonant

Sometimes when you add a suffix to a word, you must double the final consonant. Remember the next tips.

One-Syllable Words

♦ Double the final consonant of one-syllable words ending in a consonant–vowel–consonant pattern.

jog–jo**gg**er   plan–pla**nn**ed   prod–pro**dd**ed

♦ Do not double the final consonant if the word ends in a vowel and two consonants or if it ends with two vowels and a consonant.

cool–coolest   park–parking   clean–cleaner

Words of Two or More Syllables

♦ Double the final consonant of words ending in a stressed consonant–vowel–consonant pattern.

pre<u>fer</u>–prefe**rr**ed   oc<u>cur</u>–occu**rr**ed

♦ If the word ends in a syllable that is not stressed, then do not double the last letter of the word.

<u>hap</u>pen–happened   <u>vis</u>it–visiting

PRACTICE 6

Rewrite each word with the suggested ending.

EXAMPLES: **Add -ed**   **Add -ing**

stop   _____stopped_____   try   _____trying_____

1. slip   _____   6. smile   _____

2. load   _____   7. stay   _____

3. mention   _____   8. enter   _____

4. plan   _____   9. begin   _____

5. commit   _____   10. refer   _____

PRACTICE 7

Underline and correct twelve spelling mistakes in the next selection.

EXAMPLE: Business owners react <u>angryly</u> *angrily* when they are criticized.

1.   For a democracy to be successfull, citizens must be able to speak freely about

issues. A strategic lawsuit against public participation (SLAPP) permits an

individual or company to act agressivly toward critics. Unfortunatly, private

citizens have very little protection against such lawsuits.

2.   For example, in 2004, Serge Galipeau and Christine Landry complained about

the strong odors from a nearby dump. Whenever they openned their windows,

they developped headaches. Their nieghbors had the same problems. Feeling

frustrated, Galipeau and Landry gathered a petition of thousands of signatures

and spoke to local news media. The dump retaliated by sueing the homeowners

for $1.25 million.

3.   Some governments have introduced anti-SLAPP legislation. For example,

Texas, Washington, and Pennsylvania have such laws. Perhaps companies are

begining to take responsibility for their mistakes instead of attacking critics,

and there will be fewer unecessary lawsuits. However, many people have questionned the effectiveness of anti-SLAPP laws. Definitly, there are some problems. For example, Galipeau and Landry won their case, but they spent a lot of time and all of their savings defending themselves. Their lifes are no longer the same.

Spelling Two-Part Words

Some one-word indefinite pronouns sound as if they should be two separate words, but they are not. Here are some examples of one-word indefinite pronouns.

Words with *any*	anything, anyone, anybody, anywhere
Words with *some*	something, someone, somebody, somewhere
Words with *every*	everything, everyone, everybody, everywhere

> **HINT** ◀ **Spelling *another* and *a lot***
>
> ***Another*** is always one word.   Bonnie committed <u>another</u> crime.
>
> ***A lot*** is always two words.   She robbed <u>a lot</u> of banks.

PRACTICE 8

Underline and correct twelve spelling errors in the next paragraphs.

EXAMPLE: <u>An other</u> scandal occurred last year.
Another

1.   Alot of politicians have been involved in scandals. Some times a public figure takes bribes. For instance, in 2006, Representative William J. Jefferson was convicted after police found $90,000 in his freezer. In 2009, Governor Rod Blagojevich tried to sell a senate seat to some one. Senator John Edwards is an other politician who made imoral choices. At first, no body knew about the married politician's girlfriend. When a tabloid published a photo of Edwards with his mistress, he denyied the rumors, but eventualy he had to tell the truth.

2.   When politicians act in an unnethical manner, they hurt their families, and they usualy destroy their own careers. Often, citizens discover that their heros, especially in the political world, are capable of just about any thing.

120 Commonly Misspelled Words

The next list contains some of the most commonly misspelled words in English.

LO 2 Review 120 commonly misspelled words.

absence	curriculum	loneliness	responsible
absorption	definite	maintenance	rhythm
accommodate	definitely	mathematics	schedule
acquaintance	desperate	medicine	scientific
address	developed	millennium	separate
aggressive	dilemma	minuscule	sincerely
already	disappoint	mischievous	spaghetti
aluminum	embarrass	mortgage	strength
analyze	encouragement	necessary	success
appointment	environment	ninety	surprise
approximate	especially	noticeable	technique
argument	exaggerate	occasion	thorough
athlete	exercise	occurrence	tomato
bargain	extraordinarily	opposite	tomatoes
beginning	familiar	outrageous	tomorrow
behavior	February	parallel	traditional
believable	finally	performance	truly
business	foreign	perseverance	Tuesday
calendar	government	personality	until
campaign	harassment	physically	usually
careful	height	possess	vacuum
ceiling	immediately	precious	Wednesday
cemetery	independent	prejudice	weird
clientele	jewelry	privilege	woman
committee	judgment	professor	women
comparison	laboratory	psychology	wreckage
competent	lawyer	questionnaire	writer
conscience	ledge	receive	writing
conscientious	leisure	recommend	written
convenient	license	reference	zealous

HINT ◀ Spelling Strategies

Here are some useful strategies to improve your spelling.

- Keep a record of words that you commonly misspell in your spelling log, which could be in a journal or binder. Have a friend read from your list of misspelled words to give you a spelling quiz. See Appendix 7 for more information about spelling logs.

- Use memory cards or flash cards to help you memorize the spelling of difficult words.

- Write down the spelling of difficult words at least ten times to help you remember how to spell them.

Chapter 33

PRACTICE 9

Underline the correctly spelled word in each pair.

EXAMPLE: <u>foreigner</u> / foriegner

1. noticable / <u>noticeable</u>

2. echos / <u>echoes</u>

3. writting / <u>writing</u>

4. <u>accommodate</u> / accomodate

5. <u>definitely</u> / definitly

6. <u>running</u> / runing

7. appealled / <u>appealed</u>

8. comittee / <u>committee</u>

9. <u>recommend</u> / recommand

10. <u>absence</u> / absense

11. <u>niece</u> / neice

12. personallity / <u>personality</u>

13. <u>exaggerate</u> / exagerate

14. butterflys / <u>butterflies</u>

15. <u>responsible</u> / responsable

16. efficeint / <u>efficient</u>

17. <u>independent</u> / independant

18. <u>appointment</u> / apointment

PRACTICE 10

Underline and correct twenty spelling mistakes in the next selection.

EXAMPLE: Forensic television shows <u>definitly</u> influence jurors.
definitely

1.   Last Febuary, Ladonna Reed called the police to report a robbery at her house. The crime scene investigator was very carefull as he dusted for prints, but Ladonna remained unimpressed with his performance. She was familar with the television show *CSI*, and the investigator did not use tecniques from the show.

2.   Jurors sometimes have unrealistic expectations about forensic science. Police, lawyers, and judges call this phenomenon "CSI syndrome." In the *CSI* television shows, investigators use tests that give instant results. While police departments rely on similar tests, it takes time to analyze evidence in a labortory. In addition, jurors who watch shows like *CSI* may think they have a high level of expertise and may prejedice other members of the jury.

3.   CSI syndrome has created an unexpected dillema for police departments and the courts. For example, in June 2005, all three hundred prosecutors from Maricopa County in Arizona filled out a questionaire. Around 38 percent of the prosecutors sincerly believed that they had at least one embarrasing acquittal

because of lack of forensic evidence. In such cases, the prosecutors thought that

sceintific evidence was unecessary for a conviction. In one case, police officers

found a bag with ilegal drugs and a handwriten note. The accused admitted that

the drugs were his. However, the jury found him innocent because prosecutors

had no DNA or fingerprints from the bag.

4.   Lawyers and judges acknowlege the CSI effect in trials. Lawyers often

change opening and closing arguements to prevent juror bias. Judges

sometimes recomend to jurors not to rely on television shows as a yardstick for

their jugment of the evidence.

HINT ◄ Using a Spelling Checker

The spelling checker tool on a computer will highlight most misspelled words and provide suggested corrections. However, be aware that a spelling checker's abilities are limited; it cannot verify that you have used commonly confused words accurately. For example, it cannot determine whether you should use *your* or *you're*.

Because a spelling checker is not 100 percent reliable, remember to proofread for spelling errors before you submit your final work.

Look-Alike and Sound-Alike Words

LO 3 Distinguish look-alike and sound-alike words.

Sometimes two English words can sound very much alike but have different spellings and different meanings. For example, two commonly confused words are *defiantly*, which means "to resist or challenge something," and *definitely*, which means "finally" or "decisively." Dictionaries will give you the exact meaning of unfamiliar words. Read the next list to get familiar with many commonly confused words.

Word	Meaning	Example
accept	to receive; to admit	The police sergeant <u>accepted</u> an award for outstanding work.
except	excluding; other than	None of his colleagues, <u>except</u> his wife, knew about the award.
affect	to influence	Writer's block <u>affects</u> a person's ability to write.
effect	the result of something	Writer's block can have bad <u>effects</u> on a person's ability to write.
been	past participle of the verb *to be*	Patrick Fitzgerald has <u>been</u> a prosecutor for many years.
being	present progressive form (the *-ing* form) of the verb *to be*	He was <u>being</u> very nice when he signed autographs.

(continued)

Word	Meaning	Example
by	preposition meaning *next to*, *on*, or *before*	The defendant sat by her lawyer. By 10:00 A.M., the jury was getting restless. Everyone hoped the case would be over by the weekend.
buy	to purchase	The lawyer will buy a new car with her fees from this case.
complement	to add to; to complete	The car will be a nice complement to her other possessions.
compliment	to say something nice about someone	Chicago's mayor complimented the detectives.
conscience	a personal sense of right and wrong	The robber had no conscience.
conscious	being aware or awake	The robber was conscious of his terrible crime.
disinterested	to be impartial	The trial judge was disinterested, favoring neither side.
uninterested	to lack interest in something	The robber looked uninterested when told of his sentence.
elicit	to get or draw out	The police tried to elicit a confession from the gang member.
illicit	illegal; unlawful	The police found evidence of the gang's illicit activities.
everyday	ordinary; common	Crime is an everyday occurrence.
every day	during a single day; each day	The police watch the gang members every day.
imminent	soon to happen	The police stated that an arrest was imminent.
eminent	distinguished; superior	Patrick Fitzgerald is an eminent prosecutor.
imply	to suggest	The reporter implied that the police need more time to investigate.
infer	to conclude	The police inferred from the clues the gang's whereabouts.
its	possessive case of the pronoun *it*	The judge's desk is large, and its legs are ornate.
it's	contraction for *it is*	It's generally known that he is very good at solving crimes.
knew	past tense of *know*	Fitzgerald knew that the newspaper executive was guilty.
new	recent; unused	He had new evidence to present to the court.
know	to have knowledge of	Many people know about Fitzgerald's work.
no	a negative	The police made no arrests.
lose	to misplace or forfeit something	The police did not want to lose track of the stolen money.
loose	too big or baggy; not fixed	Detectives sometimes wear loose clothing as part of their disguises.
loss	a decrease in an amount	The company experienced a serious loss when the money was stolen.
peace	calm sensation; a lack of violence	The two rival gangs finally made peace. They felt a sense of peace when hostilities stopped.
piece	a part of something else; one item in a group of items	The thieves ate a piece of cake to celebrate the successful heist.

Word	Meaning	Example
personal	private	The criminal has a lot of personal problems.
personnel	employees; staff	The police must hire new personnel.
principal	primary (adj.); director of a school (n.)	The principal detective talked to the principal of our school.
principle	a rule or standard	The police try to follow the principle of law.
quiet	silent	The thieves remained quiet when arrested.
quite	very	The public is becoming quite angry at the increase in crime.
quit	to stop doing something	The detective sometimes wants to quit the force.
taught	past tense of *teach*	Drake taught a class on criminology.
thought	past tense of *think*	He thought his students were intelligent.
than	word used in comparisons	Fitzgerald is more determined than other prosecutors.
then	at a particular time; after a specific time	Cornwell investigated the case, and then she wrote about it.
that	word used to introduce a clause	She wrote that Walter Sickert was Jack the Ripper.
their	possessive form of *they*	The police officers went to their favorite restaurant.
there	a place	They went there by police van.
they're	contraction of *they are*	They're both interesting people.
through	in one side and out the other; finished	The police cruiser passed through a tunnel. Then they were through for the day.
threw	past tense of *throw*	Somebody threw a rock at the officer's car.
thorough	complete	They did a thorough investigation of the crime scene.
to	indicates direction or movement; part of an infinitive	I want to go to the film.
too	also; very	The robber was too young to be given a prison sentence. Her friend was, too.
two	the number after one	There were two witnesses to the holdup.
where	question word indicating location	The police knew where the diamonds were hidden.
were	past tense of *be*	The diamonds were in a safe place.
we're	contraction of *we are*	We're going to meet the detectives.
who's	contraction of *who is*	The police sergeant, who's very well known, spoke to reporters.
whose	pronoun showing ownership	Criminals, whose crimes hurt society, must be punished.
write	to draw symbols that represent words	Patricia Cornwell will write about the crime.
right	correct; the opposite of the direction left	The police arrested the right criminal. They found the diamonds in her right pocket.

Chapter 33

Chapter 33

PRACTICE 11

Underline the correct words.

EXAMPLE: The Securities and Exchange Commission (personal / <u>personnel</u>) were shocked to hear about the Ponzi scheme.

1. In December 2008, many wealthy Americans suffered a serious financial (lose / loss).

2. They had (been / being) investing for many years with a well-known financier, Bernard Madoff.

3. Madoff was considered to be an (eminent / imminent) investor.

4. However, he was investing his clients' money in an (elicit / illicit) racket called a Ponzi scheme.

5. Madoff, (who's / whose) reputation is ruined, had used money from later investors to pay off earlier investors, creating an illusion of profit.

6. Madoff's investment scheme crumpled when his clients pulled money out of investment portfolios in an effort (to / too) reduce financial risk.

7. The clients did not (no / know) that he had cheated them out of (their / there) money until they heard the news in the media.

8. Madoff's Ponzi scheme created (quit / quite) a stir when authorities claimed it was the largest fraud in the history of Wall Street.

PRACTICE 12

Underline and correct fifteen errors in the following passages. Look for the commonly confused words that are indicated in parentheses.

EXAMPLE: He is <u>to</u> busy these days. ^too

1. (affect, effect; then, that, than)

   In 1995, audiences were fascinated by a celebrity trial than caused a great stir. O.J. Simpson was accused of killing his wife and her friend. Simpson was found not guilty, but the accusation effected his reputation. In 2008, Simpson was involved in another crime. He was first accused of armed robbery, and than he was charged with kidnapping. Simpson claimed than he was trying to get back some stolen sports memorabilia. He was found guilty of the crime. The affect of the verdict on Simpson was enormous. His stature is more tarnished that before.

2. (threw, through, thorough)

   In 2006, Paris Hilton was arrested for drunk driving. Police stopped her after she drove her car threw a red light. Thorough a spokesperson, Hilton defended herself. The police made a through investigation of the crime, and the judge put her on probation. However, Hilton did not meet the terms of her probation. In 2007, a judge through the book at her and sentenced her to forty-five days in jail. Later, the sentence was changed to twenty-three days.

3. (lose, loose, loss)

Fans sometimes loose respect for celebrities when the celebrities behave badly. Some fans believe that such loss standards of behavior should not be encouraged. However, many stars think that a lose of reputation is acceptable because they profit from their notoriety.

4. (who's, whose)

The public should remember that celebrities who commit crimes are criminals. A person whose famous should not behave criminally. Celebrities who's profession puts them in the public spotlight should be aware of the influence they have, especially on young people.

Reflect On It

Think about what you have learned in this unit. If you do not know an answer, review that concept.

1. a. In a word containing *ie*, when does *i* come before *e*?

    _____

    b. When does *e* come before *i*?

    _____

2. Circle the correctly spelled words. Correct each misspelled word.

    realy   finally   unatural   illogical   plentifull

3. Correct eight mistakes in the next passage.

    Crimes are quiet a common occurrence in my nieghborhood. The police are planing to increase there surveillance in this area. The public, to, can help. Its important to report any unnusual events. Eventualy, such actions will help lower the crime rate.

FINAL REVIEW

Underline and correct twenty-five spelling errors and mistakes with commonly confused words.

EXAMPLE: The judge is to busy these days.
too

1.   In past centuries, shaming justice was quiet common. Judges often recommanded shaming penaltyes. Guilty citizens could be placed in a stockade, and the wooden structure could lock a person's hands and head in place. The goal was to humiliate the offender. Often, even the nicest citizens in town would try spiting on the criminal. Is public shaming preferable to traditionnal prison sentences? Some experts beleive public shaming has a place in the criminal justice system.

2.   Today, shaming penalties are more common then in the 1900s. For example, a judge in Wisconsin orders shoplifters to stand in front of the stores they robed holding an "I am a shoplifter" sign. In Cleveland, resident Shena Hardin drove her SUV on a sidewalk. She excepted responsability for her action and had to stand on a street corner with a sign that read, "Only an idiot would drive on the sidewalk to avoid a school bus."

3.   Some cities have developped interesting ways to deal with those who do elicit activities. For example, in some places, its common to see billboards with the names of deadbeat dads, drug dealers, and public urinators. In Kansas City, men who visit prostitutes may hear there names been broadcast on public television. Since that penalty was introduced, the number of men doing such illegal activities has definitly droped. Nobody likes to be embarased in public.

4.   There are advantages to public shaming instead of prison terms. First, prisons are overcrowded, and it's costly to house each prisoner. Also, many offenders would rather loose a day or two of work and be humiliated than spend weeks or months in prison. Raymond Garrid of Virginia stole pants. His loyier, who's

reputation was quite good, suggested that Garrid accept the public penalty.
Garrid wore the pants around his neck as he was restrained in public stocks. He
thougth that his lose of reputation was acceptable. He claims that his penalty
has not effected his life in a negative way.

5.   Some people object to the principle of public shaming. Others see the
punishment as valid, argueing that it costs less for the criminal justice system.
What is your opinion about public shaming?

READING LINK

To learn more about legal issues, read the following essays.

"My Prison Story" by Yirga Gebremeskel (page 195)

"Breaking Traffic Laws" by Lonzell Courtney (page 214)

"Robot Ethics" from *The Economist* (page 229)

"The Case for Affirmative Action" by Dave Malcolm (page 521)

"The Criminal Justice Process" by John Randolph Fuller (page 551)

"How Spies Are Caught" (page 554)

"My Relentless Pursuit" by Amanda Enayati (page 556)

Chapter 33

THE WRITER'S ROOM

MyWritingLab™
Complete these writing assignments at mywritinglab.com

Write about one of the following topics. Check for spelling errors, and verify that you have used the correct word.

1. What is your opinion about public shaming? Should shaming sentences be given more frequently?

2. Should juveniles who commit serious crimes be treated as harshly as adults?

THE WRITERS' CIRCLE **Collaborative Activity**

Work with a partner or a small group of students and compose a paragraph about the qualities of a good comic book hero. In your paragraph, tell a story about a heroic action that the superhero does. Use slang words and clichés in your paragraph. Make sure that your paragraph is double-spaced, and make sure that the writing is clear.

When you have finished your paragraph, exchange sheets with another team of students. Edit the other team's paragraph and imagine that the audience is a college instructor. Change all clichés and slang expressions into standard American English.

34 Commas

SECTION THEME: The Workplace

LEARNING OBJECTIVES

LO 1 Define a comma and what it does. **(p. 458)**

LO 2 Use a comma in a series. **(p. 459)**

LO 3 Use commas after introductory words and phrases. **(p. 460)**

LO 4 Use commas around interrupting words and phrases. **(p. 461)**

LO 5 Use commas correctly in compound sentences. **(p. 462)**

LO 6 Use commas correctly in complex sentences. **(p. 463)**

LO 7 Identify where to use commas in a business letter. **(p. 465)**

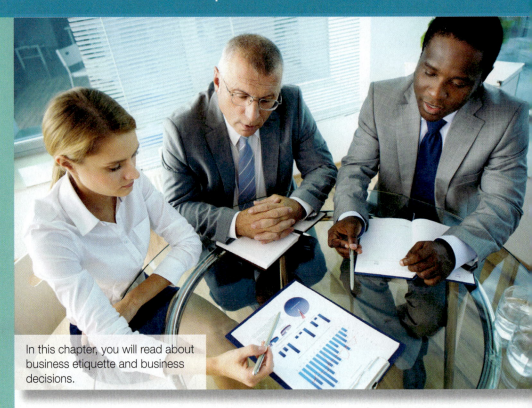

In this chapter, you will read about business etiquette and business decisions.

MyWritingLab™

Complete this Writer's Journal activity at mywritinglab.com

LO 1 Define a comma and what it does.

What Is a Comma?

A **comma** (,) is a punctuation mark that helps keep distinct ideas separate. There are many ways to use a comma. In this chapter, you will learn some helpful rules about comma usage.

Notice how comma placement changes the meaning of the following sentences. Discuss which animal is having a nap.

The dog bites, the cat runs, and then she has a nap.

The dog bites the cat, runs, and then she has a nap.

Commas in a Series

Use a comma to separate items in a series of three or more items. Remember to put a comma before the final *and* or *or*.

unit 1	,	unit 2	,	and	unit 3
				or	

Houston, Dallas, and Austin have vibrant design industries.

The job search requires courage, perseverance, and energy.

You can network, contact employers directly, or use a placement service.

HINT ◄ Punctuating a Series

In a series of three or more items, do not place a comma after the last item in the series (unless the series is part of an interrupting phrase).

Her poise, simplicity, and kindness, impressed us.

Do not use commas to separate items if each item is joined by *and* or *or*.

It is not possible to study and listen to music and have a conversation at the same time.

PRACTICE 1

Underline series of items in the next selection. Then add sixteen missing commas where necessary.

EXAMPLE: Frequent business travelers can experience physical fatigue, marital strain, and mental stress.

1. Manfred Durbar travels constantly on company business. He flies mainly to Houston Orlando and Chicago. While he thinks these cities have a lot to offer, Manfred hates the travel time. He is not alone. Pollsters surveyed people who needed to travel a lot for business, such as company executives travel agents and salesmen. According to the survey results, over 92 percent of respondents stated that they do not like to travel.

2. Business travelers gave different reasons for their lack of enthusiasm. Manfred dislikes the hassles of airport security the uncomfortable seats and the usual flight delays. He also dreads sitting next to a crying baby an overly amorous couple or a sick passenger. Businesspeople also stated concerns over hotels. They were anxious about bed bugs noisy guests and uncomfortable beds. Furthermore, respondents worried about falling behind in their work attending boring presentations and being away from their families.

3.   Senior company managers acknowledge that travel can be problematic. Many managers are trying to find ways to reduce business travel. One such solution is virtual communication. Many employees prefer sharing ideas through teleconferencing video chats or live Internet radio rather than through traditional face-to-face meetings. Also, virtual conferencing eliminates logistical problems. Employees can participate from any location such as their office desk home office or any other room. They need only a laptop or a mobile device.

LO 3 Use commas after introductory words and phrases.

Commas After Introductory Words and Phrases

Use a comma after an **introductory word**. The introductory word could be an interjection such as *yes*, *no*, or *well*, it could be an adverb such as *usually* or *generally*, or it could be a transitional word such as *however* or *therefore*.

Introductory word(s)	,	sentence.

Yes, I will help you complete the order.

Frankly, you should reconsider your customer service promise.

However, the job includes a lot of overtime.

Use a comma to set off **introductory phrases** of two or more words. The phrase could be a transitional expression such as *of course* or *on the contrary*, or it could be a prepositional phrase such as *on a warm summer evening*. The introductory phrase could also be a modifier such as *running out of fuel* or *born in France*.

On the other hand, his career was not going well.

In the middle of the meeting, I received a phone call.

Speaking to the crowd, the manager explained the stock's performance.

PRACTICE 2

Underline each introductory word or phrase. Then add ten missing commas.

EXAMPLE: In today's job market, people must remain flexible.

1.   For the first time in history workers can expect to outlive the organizations that they work for. For example many financial companies collapsed during the stock market crash of 2008. Additionally many businesses go bankrupt each year.

2.   Furthermore those working in successful companies may see their jobs become obsolete. In fact the majority of the nation's bank tellers were laid off in the 1990s. As a result many people in the banking industry have had to retrain or change jobs.

3.   According to Myriam Goldman the average person should plan for three different careers. Of course some people love their jobs and have no desire to look elsewhere. However even those in secure jobs may get bored and long for a career change down the road. Working in a volatile job market workers should remain open and flexible.

Commas Around Interrupting Words and Phrases

LO 4 Use commas around interrupting words and phrases.

Interrupting words or phrases appear in the middle of sentences. Such interrupters are often asides that interrupt the sentence's flow but do not affect its overall meaning. Some interrupters are *by the way*, *as a matter of fact*, and *for example*. Prepositional phrases can also interrupt sentences.

| Opening phrase | , | interrupting words | , | rest of sentence. |

My sister, for example, has never invested in stocks.

The market, by the way, has been down recently.

My manager, in the middle of a busy day, decided to go to a movie!

HINT ◄ Using Commas with Appositives

An appositive gives further information about a noun or pronoun. The appositive can appear at the beginning, in the middle, or at the end of the sentence. Set off appositives with commas.

beginning
A large city in Florida, Miami has a variety of public learning centers.

middle
Dr. Anex, a senior surgeon, recommends the transplant.

end
The office is next to Graham's, a local eatery.

PRACTICE 3

The next sentences contain introductory words and phrases, interrupters, and series of items. Add the missing commas. If the sentence is correct, write *C* in the space provided.

EXAMPLE: E-mail, voice mail and cell phones are changing the way that

people do business. _____

1. Jamaal Khabbaz a marketing manager, complains about high-tech gadgets in the workplace such as pagers, cell phones and personal organizers. _____

2. Many workers in his opinion break rules of basic etiquette. _____

3. He gets annoyed, for example when a lunch meeting is interrupted by a ringing cell phone. _____

4. Unfortunately, many people do not consider it rude to answer a call in the middle of a meal. _____

5. According to Kabbaz the workplace needs new business etiquette rules. _____

6. Electronic mail, a convenient way to send and receive messages is not private. _____

7. Without a doubt, it is offensive to read other people's mail. _____

8. Some people, however have no qualms about standing next to a computer and reading over the shoulder of an e-mail recipient. _____

9. E-mail junkies, those addicted to electronic messages cause the most problems. _____

10. In the middle of a busy day the e-mail addict sends cartoons, videos and messages to coworkers. _____

Commas in Compound Sentences

LO 5 Use commas correctly in compound sentences.

A **compound sentence** contains two or more complete sentences joined by a coordinating conjunction (*for, and, nor, but, or, yet, so*).

Sentence	,	and	sentence.

I want a job**,** **so** I will look in the classified ads.
Some interesting companies are nearby**,** **and** maybe they are hiring.

PRACTICE 4

Add six commas that are missing from this letter.

EXAMPLE: I am punctual ,and I am hardworking.

Dear Mr. Ruzinka,

On Craigslist, I read that you are looking for a computer technician. I am interested in the job so I have enclosed a résumé highlighting my skills and experience.

I have taken computer technology courses at El Camino College and I completed my program with distinction. I also plan to receive Microsoft certification but I have not done the final exams. Furthermore, I have worked at a bank and I have experience repairing computers at a local clinic.

I am available for an interview at any time so please do not hesitate to contact me. Thank you for your consideration and I look forward to hearing from you.

Yours sincerely,

Darius George

Darius George

Commas in Complex Sentences

L0 6 Use commas correctly in complex sentences.

A **complex sentence** contains one or more dependent clauses (or incomplete ideas). When you add a **subordinating conjunction**—a word such as *because, although,* or *unless*—to a clause, you make the clause dependent.

       dependent clause   independent clause
When the stock market opened, he sold his shares.

Use a Comma After a Dependent Clause

If a sentence begins with a dependent clause, place a comma after the clause. Remember that a dependent clause has a subject and a verb, but it cannot stand alone. When the subordinating conjunction comes in the middle of a sentence, it is not necessary to use a comma.

	Dependent clause , main clause.
Comma	After the meeting ends, we will go to lunch.

	Main clause dependent clause.
No comma	We will go to lunch after the meeting ends.

Use Commas to Set Off Nonrestrictive Clauses

Clauses beginning with *who, that*, and *which* can be restrictive or nonrestrictive. A **restrictive clause** contains essential information about the subject. Do not place commas around restrictive clauses.

No commas	The only local company that does computer graphics has no job openings. (The underlined clause is essential to understand the meaning of the sentence.)

A **nonrestrictive clause** gives nonessential information. In such sentences, the clause gives additional information about the noun but does not restrict or define the noun. Place commas around nonrestrictive clauses.

Commas	Her book, which is in bookstores, is about successful entrepreneurs. (The underlined clause contains extra information, but if you removed that clause, the sentence would still have a clear meaning.)

HINT ◄ Which, That, Who

which
Use commas to set off clauses that begin with *which*.

ImClone, **which** was founded in 1983, creates pharmaceutical products.

that
Do not use commas to set off clauses begining with *that*.

The company **that** Sam Waksal founded creates pharmaceutical products.

who
When a clause begins with *who*, you may or may not need a comma. If the clause contains nonessential information, put commas around it. If the clause is essential to the meaning of the sentence, it does not require commas.

Essential	Many people **who** buy stocks think that they will earn a profit.
Not essential	Domestic guru Martha Stewart, **who** became a multimillionaire, was convicted of obstructing justice in 2004.

PRACTICE 5

Edit the following sentences by adding eighteen missing commas.

EXAMPLE: The manager, who seems quite nice, asks very probing questions.

1. When people look for jobs they may encounter several types of interviews. The structured interview which occurs during the screening stage helps a company have a uniform hiring process. The employer, who asks a specific set of questions compares the answers of the candidates.

2. The open-ended interview which is more relaxed and unstructured allows job seekers to talk freely. If people reveal too much or ramble on they may not be hired. Anyone who wants a job should remember to maintain a business-like demeanor.

3. During panel interviews a team questions the job-seekers. For instance the supervisor the human resources manager and a coworker may all interact with the candidates. Some companies even have group interviews which are useful for judging people's communication skills.

4. The worst type of interview is the stress interview. The intense boss, who asks difficult and strange questions often unnerves the candidate. The goal which is not always apparent is to see how people handle demanding situations. Eliza Marcum for example, was asked what type of animal she would like to be. She did not understand the relevance of the question and she responded impatiently. During stress interviews, people who act upset overly nervous, or angry will probably not be hired.

Commas in Business Letters

LO 7 Identify where to use commas in a business letter.

When you write or type a formal letter, ensure that you use commas correctly.

Addresses

In the address at the top of the letter, insert a comma between the following elements.

* The street name and apartment number
* The city and state or country

Do not put a comma before the zip code.

Dr. Brent Patterson

312 Appleby Road, Suite 112

Cleveland, OH 45678

If you include an address inside a complete sentence, use commas to separate the street address from the city and the city from the state or country. If you just write the street address, do not put a comma after it.

Commas   The building at 11 Wall Street, New York, contains the Stock Exchange.

No comma   The building at 11 Wall Street contains the New York Stock Exchange.

Dates

In the date at the top of the letter, add a comma between the full date and the year. If you just write the month and the year, then no comma is necessary.

May 21, 2014   January 2014

If you include a date inside a complete sentence, separate the elements of the date with commas.

We visited Washington on Monday, July 26, 2013.

HINT ◂ **Writing Numbers**

When writing a date in a letter, it is not necessary to write ordinal numbers such as *first* (1st), *second* (2nd), *third* (3rd), or *fourth* (4th). Instead, just write the number: 1, 2, 3, 4, and so on.

February 24, 2001   October 11, 1966

Salutations

Salutations are formal letter greetings. The form "To Whom It May Concern" is no longer used regularly by North American businesses. The best way to address someone is to use his or her name followed by a comma or a colon. The colon is preferred in business letters.

Dear Ms. Lewin: Dear Sir or Madam: Dear Sarah,

Complimentary Closings

Place a comma after the complimentary closing. Notice that the first word of the closing is capitalized.

Respectfully,   Yours sincerely,   Many thanks,

Sample Letter of Application

You send a sample letter of application to an employer when you apply for a job. Review the parts of the following letter.

Seamus O'Brien
10 Santa Fe Boulevard
Seattle, WA 90001
(661) 234-5678

◄ Sender's address (name, phone, and possibly an e-mail address)

September 12, 2014

◄ Date

Avant Garde Computers
Adelaide and Sinclair Corporation
6116 Greenway Avenue
Seattle, WA 98711

◄ Recipient's address

Subject: Position of junior programmer

◄ Subject line

Dear Ms. Roebok:

◄ Salutation

I saw an ad in Saturday's *Seattle Times* stating that you need a junior programmer. I have enclosed a résumé highlighting my skills in this field. I have an aptitude for computers, and, when I was fourteen years old, I created my first game program.

I have just finished a diploma program in computer programming at Marshall College. I took courses in several computer languages. I have also completed a six-week training program, and I have enclosed a letter of reference from the owner of that company.

If you require further information, please contact me. I am available for an interview at any time and could start work immediately. Thank you for your consideration.

Sincerely,

S. O'Brien

Seamus O'Brien

◄ Closing (After the closing, put your handwritten signature followed by your typed name.)

Enclosures: résumé
          letter of reference

◄ List any documents you have included.

Chapter 34

PRACTICE 6

The next letter contains ten errors. Add seven missing commas and remove three unnecessary commas.

Good Food Solutions

2256, Kildare Avenue

Orlando, Florida 32818

June 24   2015

Sylvia Hubert

The Harvest Moon Café

1000 International Drive

Orlando, Florida, 32819

Dear Ms. Hubert:

As the new owners of the Harvest Moon Café   we would like to offer you our best wishes for your success.

Our company   Good Food Solutions, has been providing restaurant service training for many years to fine cafés and restaurants in the Orlando area. In fact   we have had a very close, and profitable business relationship with the previous owners of the Harvest Moon Café   and we hope to continue doing business with you in the very near future.

Our sales representative, Melissa Fung, would be pleased to discuss our products and services at your convenience. Ms. Fung   who has been with our company for many years, is very knowledgeable about our services. Our phone number is (407) 555-9988. We look forward to meeting with you.

Yours truly

Alwyn Scott

Alwyn Scott

Reflect On It

Think about what you have learned in this unit. If you do not know an answer, review that concept.

1. Explain the rules of comma usage in the following situations.
    a. Series of items: _____

    _____

    b. Introductory words or phrases: _____

    _____

    c. Interrupting phrases: _____

    _____

    d. Compound sentences: _____

    _____

2. What is a nonrestrictive clause? _____

_____

3. Should you place commas around nonrestrictive clauses?
    _____ Yes _____ No

4. Write three common closings for a business letter.

_____

_____

FINAL REVIEW

Edit the next essay by adding seventeen missing commas and removing three unnecessary commas.

EXAMPLE: Many countries such as Iran ‸ North Korea ‸ and Saudi Arabia censor information on the Internet.

1.   China's system of Internet control   which is the most extensive in the

    world   is often criticized. Government bureaucracies   businesses   and

    nongovernmental organizations block access to information. Web sites, that

    contain politically sensitive details are targets of government interference.

    Chinese officials not only censor Web sites   but they also monitor e-mail   cell

    phone calls   and chat room discussions.

2.   Google   the largest Internet search engine provider, started

    its full operations in China on January 27   2006. Google

    executives   who traveled to China many times, were willing to

    comply with government rules. Google management thought

    that the Chinese authorities would eventually relax censorship

rules, and Chinese clients would enjoy greater access to information. The company however limited the authorities from accessing some types of information. Because Google did not want to provide government authorities with the personal data of its users the company did not offer its clients Gmail YouTube, or Blogger. Of course the Chinese authorities were unsatisfied with Google's policy.

3.   In December, 2009, Google executives discovered that someone had hacked into the system. Citizens, who had used the search engine in China had their personal information stolen. The hackers were traced to the Chinese government.

4.   After the hacking incident Google decided to stop censorship on its Chinese search engine. It redirects users to its uncensored site in Hong Kong but the Chinese authorities have now started to censor the Hong Kong site.

Chapter 34

MyWritingLab™
Complete these writing assignments at mywritinglab.com

MyWritingLab™

THE WRITER'S ROOM

Write about one of the following topics. Verify that your comma usage is correct.

1. Are you a good money manager? Describe how you handle your finances.

2. Categorize spenders into different types. Give examples for each type.

The Apostrophe, Quotation Marks, and Titles

35

SECTION THEME: The Workplace

LEARNING OBJECTIVES

LO 1 Use apostrophes correctly. **(p. 471)**

LO 2 Use quotation marks correctly. **(p. 476)**

LO 3 Punctuate titles correctly. **(p. 478)**

In this chapter, you will read about topics related to business success and controversies.

MyWritingLab™

Complete this Writer's Journal activity at mywritinglab.com

The Apostrophe (')

LO 1 Use apostrophes correctly.

An **apostrophe** is a punctuation mark showing a contraction or ownership.

     ownership   contraction

Daymond John's business is very successful, and **it's** still growing.

Using Apostrophes in Contractions

To form a **contraction**, join two words into one and add an apostrophe to replace the omitted letter(s).

Apostrophe replaces *o*   is + **not** = isn't

Apostrophe replaces *a*   I + **am** = I'm

Common Contractions

The following are examples of the most common contractions.

◆ **Join a verb with *not*.** The apostrophe replaces the letter *o* in *not*.

are + not = aren't	have + not = haven't
could + not = couldn't	is + not = isn't
did + not = didn't	should + not = shouldn't
do + not = don't	was + not = wasn't
does + not = doesn't	were + not = weren't
has + not = hasn't	would + not = wouldn't

Exceptions: will + not = won't, can + not = can't

◆ **Join a subject and a verb.** Sometimes you must remove several letters to form the contraction.

I + will = I'll	she + will = she'll
I + would = I'd	Tina + is = Tina's
he + is = he's	they + are = they're
he + will = he'll	we + will = we'll
Joe + is = Joe's	who + is = who's
she + has = she's	who + would = who'd

Exception: Do not contract a subject with the past tense of *be*. For example, do not contract *he + was* or *they + were*.

HINT ◀ **Contractions with Two Meanings**

Sometimes one contraction can have two different meanings.

    I'd = I had or I would   ***he's*** = he is or he has

When you read, you should be able to figure out the meaning of the contraction by looking at the words in context.

    She's hiring new personnel.   **She's** seen several interesting candidates.
    (She is)   (She has)

PRACTICE 1

Add nine missing apostrophes to the next selection.

                     hadn't

EXAMPLE: Many Americans hadnt expected investment banks to collapse in 2008.

1.   In 1850, three German brothers immigrated to America and invested in cotton in Montgomery, Alabama. After the Civil War, the brothers couldve stayed in Montgomery, but they took their enterprise to New York. They werent just cotton traders. Theyd also buy and sell other items. Their company got on the New York Stock Exchange and was a successful institution for more than a hundred years.

The brothers couldnt have predicted that Lehman Brothers Holdings would be bankrupt by the start of the 21st century.

2.   The company finances didnt remain healthy. In 2007, its stock price started to fall. Investors lost confidence in the firm because it had invested in lending mortgages to risky clients. Managers shouldve been more careful. In the summer of 2008, the firm posted huge losses. The American government wasnt willing to lend the corporation money, so the company failed.

3.   Politicians criticized the company. Members of Congress felt that the top executives of Lehman Brothers shouldnt have received millions of dollars in bonuses just before the business filed for bankruptcy. When questioned about his performance, CEO Richard Fuld said that hed made the best decisions he could for the company.

PRACTICE 2

Look at each underlined contraction, and then write out the complete word.

EXAMPLE: They <u>weren't</u> ready to start a business.   <u>were not</u>

1. Carol <u>Simon's</u> very happy with her bridal gown company.   _____

2. <u>She's</u> been an entrepreneur for seven years.   _____

3. <u>She's</u> an extremely friendly, ambitious woman.   _____

4. I wish <u>I'd</u> had the same idea as Carol.   _____

5. <u>I'd</u> like to have my own company, too.   _____

Using Apostrophes to Show Ownership

You can also use apostrophes to show ownership. Review the next rules.

Possessive Form of Singular Nouns

Add -'s to a singular noun to indicate ownership, even if the noun ends in s.

Daymond's best friends joined his company.

Somebody's house became a factory.

Ross's dad has his own business.

Possessive Form of Plural Nouns

When a plural noun ends in s, just add an apostrophe to indicate ownership. Add -'s to irregular plural nouns.

Many **companies'** Web sites are down.

The four **friends'** business is very successful.

The **children's** clothing company is expanding.

Possessive Form of Compound Nouns

When two people have joint ownership, add -'s to the second name. When two people have separate ownership, add -'s to both names.

Joint ownership	Daymond and **Carl's** company is successful.
Separate ownership	**Daymond's** and **Carl's** offices are in different buildings.

PRACTICE 3

Write the singular and plural possessive forms.

EXAMPLE:

	Singular Possessive	Plural Possessive
Mr. Cohen	Mr. Cohen's	the Cohens'
1. client	_____	_____
2. boss	_____	_____
3. secretary	_____	_____
4. Mr. Ness	_____	_____
5. woman	_____	_____
6. salesperson	_____	_____

PRACTICE 4

Write the possessive forms of the following phrases.

EXAMPLE: the sister of the doctor   the doctor's sister

1. the hat of the witch   _____
2. the wands of the witches   _____
3. the profits of the company   _____
4. the directors of the companies   _____
5. the house of Jan and Ted   _____
6. the car of Omar and the car of Roy   _____

Using Apostrophes in Expressions of Time

When an expression of time (*day*, *week*, *month*, *year*) appears to possess something, use the possessive form of that word.

Singular	The customer won a **year's** supply of paper.
Plural	Mike Roy gave two **weeks'** notice before he left the company.

When writing the numerals of a decade or century, do not put an apostrophe before the final -*s*.

In the **1800s**, many immigrants arrived at Ellis Island.

Many Internet companies failed in the **1990s**.

HINT ◀ **Common Apostrophe Errors**

Do not use apostrophes before the final *s* of a verb.

       wants
Simon ~~want's~~ to open a franchise.

Do not confuse contractions with possessive pronouns that have a similar sound. For example, the contraction *you're* sounds like the pronoun *your*. Remember that possessive pronouns never have apostrophes.

          Its
The company is growing. ~~It's~~ slogan is catchy.

           theirs.
That is my idea. It is not ~~their's~~.

PRACTICE 5

Correct twelve errors with apostrophes. You may need to add, move, or remove apostrophes.

     Don't   *aren't*
EXAMPLE: ~~Dont~~ be surprised if some products ~~arent~~ as green as they claim to be.

1.   Since the 1970's, many companies' have added eco labels to products. Manufacturers say that customers wont buy products that are'nt environmentally friendly. Therefore, a company will often attach a green label to it's popular products.

2.   However, theres been controversy with green-product certification. There are over three hundred green label programs in the world. Some are fraudulent. In addition, some businesses haven't used an independent company to verify that products are actually green. For example, S. C. Johnsons house cleaning products, Shout and Windex, were labeled green by the company. Some consumers are suing the company for mislabeling. The corporations lawyers deny any wrongdoing.

3.   Most consumers are willing to pay extra for green products. But they dont want to buy items that make false claims. For example, Jeanette and Charles local grocery store sell's items with the green label. Recently, the couple discovered that the items theyd been buying were not really environmentally friendly. Now they research any product's green claim before they buy it.

LO 2 Use quotation marks correctly.

Quotation Marks (" ")

Use **quotation marks** to set off the exact words of a speaker or writer. If the quotation is a complete sentence, there are some standard ways that it should be punctuated.

* Capitalize the first word of the quotation.
* Place quotation marks around the complete quotation.
* Place the end punctuation inside the closing quotation marks.

> . . . declared , "Complete sentence."

Here is an example of a sentence with a quotation.

> Poet William Butler Yeats declared, "Education is not the filling of a pail but the lighting of a fire."

Generally, when using quotations, attach the name of the speaker or writer to the quotation in some way. Review the following rules.

Introductory Phrase

Place a comma after a phrase introducing a quotation.

> . . . says , "_____."

> Malcolm Forbes jokes, "It is unfortunate we can't buy many business executives for what they are worth and sell them for what they think they are worth."

Interrupting Phrase

When a quotation is interrupted, do the following:

* Place a comma after the first part of the quotation.
* Place a comma after the interrupting phrase.

> "_____," . . . says, "_____."

> "I don't know the key to success," Bill Cosby said, "but the key to failure is to try to please everybody."

Ending Phrase

When you place a phrase at the end of a quotation, end the quotation with a comma instead of a period.

> "_____," says _____.

> "You're fired," said Donald Trump.

If your quotation ends with other punctuation, put it before the final quotation mark.

> "_____?" says _____.

> "You can't fire me!" she shouted.

> "Why can't I fire you?" he asked.

Introductory Sentence

You can introduce a quotation with a complete sentence. Simply place a colon (**:**) after the introductory sentence.

He explains his views: **"** _____ **."**

Albert Highfield explains why businesses fail: "They try to grow too quickly."

Inside a Quotation

If one quotation is inside another quotation, use single quotation marks (**' '**) around the inside quotation.

"Main quotation,   **'**Inside quotation.**' "**

According to Shannon Dowell, "Good parents always say, 'Clean up your own mess.' "

HINT ▸ **When the Quotation Is an Incomplete Sentence**

If the quotation is not a complete sentence and you simply integrate it into your sentence, do not capitalize the first word of the quotation.

Sir Francis Bacon once said that an artist's job is to **"d**eepen the mystery.**"**

PRACTICE 6

In each sentence, the quotation is in bold. Add quotation marks and commas or colons. Also capitalize the first word of the quotation if necessary.

EXAMPLE: Comedian Bob Hope made fun of financial institutions : "A **a bank is a**

place that will lend you money if you can prove that you don't need it. "

1. According to novelist Lisa Alther **any mother could perform the jobs of**

   several air traffic controllers with ease.

2. U.S. educator Laurence J. Peter believes that everyone is useful **a miser, for**

   example, makes a wonderful ancestor.

3. Fred Delaney proclaimed **a celebrity is a person who works hard all his life to**

   become well known, and then wears dark glasses to avoid being recognized.

4. **In the future, a wall could become a computer screen** according to journalist

   Kate McNamara.

Chapter 35

5. Comedian Mel Brooks believes that humor provides people with a **defense against the universe**.

6. Muhammad Ali describes his profession as a boxer **grass grows, birds fly, waves pound the sand, and I beat people up**.

7. **Success only breeds a new goal** observed actress Bette Davis.

8. **Hard work never killed anybody** declared comedian Edgar Bergen **but why take a chance?**

9. My mother once said **remember the words of humorist Erma Bombeck do not confuse fame with success**.

LO 3 Punctuate titles correctly.

Punctuation of Titles

When using a title within a sentence, place quotation marks around the title of a short work and italicize the title of a longer work. If your text is handwritten, then underline the titles of long works. Here are some guidelines for both.

Short Works	Long Works
Short story: "The Lottery"	**Novel:** *The Grapes of Wrath*
Web article: "Music Artists Lose Out"	**Web site:** *CNET News*
Chapter: Chapter 1, "Exploring"	**Book:** *The Writer's World*
Newspaper article: "Missing in Action"	**Newspaper:** *New York Times*
Magazine article: "Young Entrepreneurs"	**Magazine:** *Forbes*
Essay: "Downsizing"	**Textbook:** *Writing Guidelines*
TV episode: "The Election"	**TV series:** *Prison Break*
Song: "Don't Panic"	**CD:** *Parachutes*
Poem: "Howl"	**Anthology:** *Collected Poems of Beat Writers*
	Movie: *Avatar*
	Blog: *Gizmodo*
	Radio Program: *Morning Edition*

Capitalizing Titles

When you write a title, capitalize the first letter of the first and last words and all the major words.

The Catcher in the Rye　　　*War and Peace*　　　"Stairway to Heaven"

Do not capitalize *.com* in a Web address. Also do not capitalize the following words except as the first or last word in a title.

Chapter 35

Articles	a, an, the
Coordinators	for, and, nor, but, or, yet, so
Prepositions	by, in, of, off, out, to, up . . .

> **HINT** ◄ **Your Own Essay Titles**
>
> When writing the title of your own essay, do not put quotation marks around the title. However, you should capitalize key terms.
>
> **A C**ultural **I**con **I**s **B**orn

PRACTICE 7

A. Add eighteen missing capital letters to the titles in the next paragraphs.

EXAMPLE: Adele contributed to a charity album called *chimes of freedom* for
          ~~C~~   *~~F~~*
Amnesty International.

1.   The British singer and songwriter Adele has gained a tremendous reputation in the music industry. Her 2008 debut album, *19*, was a huge success in the United Kingdom. In that year, she appeared on the television show *saturday night live* in the United States. With her performance of her song "Someone like you," she gained instant popularity. In fact, Adele has become so successful that she is mentioned in the *guinness book of world records*.

2.   Adele Laurie Blue Adkins was born in 1988 in Tottenham, England. When she was in high school, she saw the singer Pink perform from her album *missundaztood*. Since that time, Adele has wanted to write and sing songs. After she graduated from high school, she published two of her songs on the online magazine *platforms Magazine*. Later, Adele's friend posted the singer's songs on *MySpace*, and a star was born.

3.   In 2011, Adele released her second album, *21*. In an interview in *spin magazine*, Adele stated that her hit single "rolling in the deep" was about a former boyfriend. In an interview with *rolling stone magazine*, the singer says she is taking her success in stride.

B.   Add quotation marks or underline any titles that should be italicized. There are nine titles.

EXAMPLE: Former *American Idol* contestant Jennifer Hudson won an Academy

Award for her role in the movie <u>Dreamgirls</u>.

4.   Recently, televised American talent shows have become very popular. The

most famous show is American Idol. But other shows such as Dancing with the

Stars and The Voice have also gained fans. Such shows show ordinary people

having an extraordinary moment. Indeed, finalists of these talent shows have

become very successful. For example, Carrie Underwood's debut album, Some

Hearts, went platinum. Her first single, Inside Your Heaven, was an instant hit.

5.   Influenced by the success of the music talent show, a new genre of television

shows has developed. These are series musicals like Glee. In an article called

The Glee Effect, journalist Christopher Loudon writes that the TV show has

had an amazing impact on the entertainment industry. Fans have bought

millions of copies of the show's albums. In addition, the show has also led to

the development of other similar series. For instance, Smash portrays the lives

of characters producing a Broadway musical. Katharine McPhee, a former

American Idol contestant, plays one of the leading characters.

PRACTICE 8

Correct twelve errors. First, correctly set off three titles by adding quotation marks
or by underlining titles that should be in italics. Then look for nine more errors with
punctuating quotations, capital letters, and apostrophes.

EXAMPLE: One of Afrobeat musician Fela ~~Kutis~~ Kuti's most popular songs is called

"Army Arrangement."

1.   Frank Gossners hobby is very unusual. In an interview on the radio

program As It Happens, Gossner spoke about his passion. He hunts for old

vinyl records of African funk from the 1960's. Gossner is a leading authority of

Afrobeat, a style of music that mixe's American funk with West African music.

He often travels to West Africa to search in old shops and sidewalk markets for rotting vinyl records.

2. Many of the Afrobeat artists had recorded their music on vinyl records. The records were never digitized, so fans were'nt able to buy CDs of the recordings. As a result, much of African funk went out of style for a short time. Gossner brings his records back to the United States and posts them on his blog Voodoo Funk.

3. Gossner has reintroduced Americans to the music of El Rego et Ses Commandos, one of Benin's most famous funk bands. One of the groups most famous songs is called Djobime, which Gossner found on his recent trip to Benin. In an interview, Gossner describes how he met Theophile de Rego, the lead singer. When Gossner explained about his search for African records, he remembered the musician's reaction "well , he was amazed," Gossner says, and when I met him and played some of those old 45s for him, he was blown away".

Reflect On It

Think about what you have learned in this unit. If you do not know an answer, review that concept.

1. In contractions, which letter does the apostrophe replace in the word *not*? _____

2. Write the possessive forms of the following phrases.

    EXAMPLE: the wife of my brother: <u>my brother's wife</u>

    a. the music of Jennifer Lopez: _____

    b. the books of the professor: _____

    c. the house of Rob and Ann: _____

    d. the cases of the lawyers: _____

3. When a sentence ends with a quotation, the period should be
    a. inside the final quotation marks.
    b. outside the final quotation marks.

4. The titles of short works such as essays, articles, and poems should be
   a. underlined or italicized.
   b. set off with quotation marks.

5. The titles of longer works such as magazines, newspapers, and movies should be
   a. underlined or italicized.
   b. set off with quotation marks.

FINAL REVIEW

Edit the following paragraphs for fifteen errors with apostrophes, quotations, capitalization, and titles. Underline titles that should normally be italicized.

EXAMPLE: I downloaded Lady ~~Gagas~~ *Gaga's* song "Paparazzi" for only 99 cents.

1.   File sharing of music and films has become common in recent year's. A reporter for *Fox* news writes "An estimated 60 million people participate in file-sharing networks." Opinions about file sharing differ greatly.

2.   David Charles works in the film industry. He says that video sharing is becoming as common as music downloading. Charles' friend, Melissa Peng, often downloads songs. She says, "students don't want to buy a CD for twenty dollars when there are only one or two songs they like".

3.   There are many court cases about recording companies objections to illegal downloads. People in the music industry claim theyre losing profits. In 2007, the Wall Street Journal reported that the record industry lost 20 percent of its CD sales. The Recording Industry Association of America states its position "If you make unauthorized copies of copyrighted music recordings, you're stealing." The RIAA has sued many people for violating copyright laws. However, critics of the music industry object to such tactics. Marc Fisher is a journalist for the Washington Post. In his article, "Download uproar: Record Industry Goes After Personal Use, Fisher writes, "The RIAA's legal crusade against its customers is a classic example of an old media company clinging to a business model that has collapsed."

4.   The music and film industries know that consumers will continue to share files. Consequently, they have developed new schemes to increase profits. Apple, along with Zune, allows it's customers to download products for 99 cents. Business student Mitchel Hunt like's the new system: "I can download the videos I want very cheaply."

THE WRITER'S ROOM — MyWritingLab™

MyWritingLab™
Complete these writing assignments at mywritinglab.com

Write about one of the following topics. Ensure that your punctuation is correct.

1.   What is success? Define success and, as a supporting example, describe a successful person whom you know.

2.   What reasons do people give for downloading music and films? What are the effects of their actions? Write about the causes and effects of illegal downloading.

Chapter 35

36 Capitalization and Other Punctuation Marks

SECTION THEME: The Workplace

LEARNING OBJECTIVES

LO 1 Practice capitalization rules. **(p. 484)**

LO 2 Use other punctuation marks correctly. **(p. 486)**

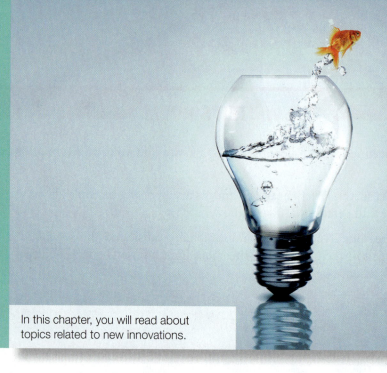

In this chapter, you will read about topics related to new innovations.

THE WRITER'S JOURNAL

Do you buy products online? Why or why not? Express your opinion about online shopping.

LO 1 Practice capitalization rules.

Capitalization

There are many instances in which you must use capital letters. Always capitalize the following words:

◆ **The pronoun *I* and the first word of every sentence**

My coworkers and **I** share an office.

◆ **Days of the week, months, and holidays**

Thursday   June 23   Thanksgiving

Do not capitalize the seasons: summer, fall, winter, spring.

◆ **Titles of specific institutions, departments, companies, and schools**

Apple Computer   Department of Finance   Daleview High School

Do not capitalize general references.

the company   the department   the school

◆ **The names of specific places such as buildings, streets, parks, cities, states, countries, continents, and bodies of water**

Market Street   Times Square   Los Angeles, California
Brazil   Asia   Lake Erie

Do not capitalize general references.

the street   the state   the lake

◆ **The names of specific planets, but not the sun or moon**

Earth   Mars   Venus   sun

◆ **The names of specific languages, nationalities, tribes, races, and religions**

Spanish   Mohawk   Buddhist   an Italian restaurant

◆ **Titles of specific individuals**

General Dewitt   President Abraham Lincoln   Dr. Blain
Professor Cruz   Prime Minister David Cameron   Mrs. Ellen Ross

Do not capitalize titles if you are referring to the profession in general, or if the title follows the name.

my doctor   the professors   Dianne Feinstein, a senator

◆ **Specific course and program titles**

Economics 201   Topics in Electrical Engineering   Nursing 402

Do not capitalize if you refer to a course but do not mention the course title.

an economics course   an engineering program   a nursing class

◆ **Major words in titles of literary or artistic works**

Washington Post   *Silver Linings Playbook*   *Lord of the Flies*

◆ **Historical events, eras, and movements**

World War II   Cubism   the Middle Ages

Chapter 36

HINT ◄ **Capitalizing Computer Terms**

Always capitalize software titles, as well as the following computer terms. Also capitalize the word "Web" in "Web site." Another common spelling for this term is "website."

Internet   World Wide Web   Microsoft Office

Chapter 36

PRACTICE 1

Add fifteen missing capital letters.

EXAMPLE: Many countries such as india want to manufacture green vehicles.

1.   In recent times, some people have produced interesting inventions including the internet. The magazine *Popular mechanics* reported on a new car. In france, Motor development International has developed a car that runs on compressed air. The car was invented by Guy Negre. He used to be an engineer on the Formula one circuit. The american distribution center is on canaan street in New paltz, New York. In a promotional video, the inventor proudly stated, "i share the same birthday as science fiction writer Jules Verne." Verne predicted that automobiles would run on air.

2.   The invention is still being perfected. At Cornell university's Department of Engineering, experts say that such a car design is possible, but it will take some time before consumers can drive the car. Many companies in europe, as well as tata motors of India, have expressed interest in producing the car. But in july 2012, one of Tata's executives said that company engineers are still working on the prototype.

LO 2 Use other punctuation marks correctly.

Other Punctuation Marks
Colon (:)

Use a colon

◆ to introduce a quotation with a complete sentence.

The writer Oscar Wilde stated his opinion: "All art is quite useless."

◆ to introduce a series or a list after a complete sentence.

The United States has produced some great writers: Emily Dickinson, F. Scott Fitzgerald, Ernest Hemingway, John Steinbeck, and William Faulkner.

◆ after the expression *the following*.

Please do the following: read, review, and respond.

◆ to introduce an explanation or example.

In 1929, investors witnessed a tragedy: the Stock Market Crash.

◆ to separate the hour and minutes in expressions of time.

The meeting will begin at 11:45.

Hyphen (-)

Use a hyphen

◆ when you write the complete words for numbers between twenty-one and ninety-nine.

twenty-six   ninety-nine   seventy-two

◆ when you use a compound adjective before a noun. The compound adjective must express a single thought.

No hyphen   The new employee must work under high pressure.

Hyphen   The new employee has a high-pressure **job**.
(You cannot say a "high job" or a "pressure job." *High* and *pressure* must go together.)

No hyphen   Our boss is thirty years old.

Hyphen   We have a thirty-year-old **boss**.
(The words *thirty*, *year*, and *old* express a single thought. You cannot remove one of those words.)

If the adjectives before a noun function independently, do *not* add hyphens.

No hyphen   They renovated an old red barn.
(The two adjectives function separately.)

HINT ◄ Nonhyphenated Compound Adjectives

Some compound adjectives never take a hyphen, even when they appear before a noun.

World Wide Web   high school senior   real estate agent

PRACTICE 2

Add eight missing colons and hyphens.

EXAMPLE: My ~~brother in law~~ **brother-in-law** is an inventor.

1.   One of the most high tech inventions of the twenty first century is Siri.

Siri serves as a personal assistant on Apple's operating system. Using voice

recognition software, Siri can perform two types of tasks answer questions and

make recommendations. She (her voice is female) was recently featured on the

well known television program *The Big Bang Theory*.

2.   Apple bought Siri in 2007 from SRI International. To develop Siri's sophisticated technology, SRI design engineers used research findings from many universities Carnegie Mellon, the University of Massachusetts, Stanford University, and more. For Apple customers, their long anticipated wait to use Siri was finally over with the launch of the iPhone 4S in 2011.

3.   Siri has been the subject of some criticism. For example, she has difficulty understanding non American accents. She cannot recognize the following accents Irish, Scottish, or Australian. Apple says that they are working on making Siri more reliable.

Ellipsis Marks (. . .)

You may want to quote key ideas from an author, but you do not always want to quote an entire paragraph. Use ellipsis marks to show that you have omitted information from a quotation. Your new sentence with an ellipses must be grammatically correct.

When you type an ellipsis mark, leave a space before and after each period. If the omitted section includes complete sentences, then add a period after the ellipses. In the next examples, notice how the quotation changes when ellipses are used.

Original Selection
Many people think that the Inuit language has ten different ways to say the word *snow*. Certainly, snow plays an important role in the daily life of the Inuit. However, this belief is a fallacy.

—Ling Park, student

> **GRAMMAR LINK**
> For more information
> about quotations, see
> Chapter 34.

Quotation with Omissions
Many people think that the Inuit language has ten different ways to say the word *snow*. . . . However, this belief is a fallacy.

—Ling Park, student

PRACTICE 3

Write quotations incorporating material from each of the next passages. Use ellipses to show where you omit words, and remember to keep important information.

1. Normal thoughts of my future (not pertaining to football), friends, family, reputation, moral status, etc., were entirely beyond me.

—From H.D.'s "Dying to Be Bigger"

According to H.D., _____

_____

_____

2. To top it off, our kids are imbued with victimology, which today has become the American way of blame. It is too routine for adults and their kids to explain all their problems as victimization. When a boy in trouble sees himself as a victim, this festers into seething anger. With easy availability of guns, it can explode as murder.

—From Martin Seligman's "The American Way of Blame"

Martin Seligman says, _____

_____

_____

_____

Reflect On It

Think about what you have learned in this unit. If you do not know an answer, review that concept.

1. List five types of words that require capitalization. For instance, the days of the week begin with capital letters.

   _____

   _____

2. Add hyphens, where necessary, to the following sentences.

   He is a twenty five year old man who carries a small red book in his back

   pocket.

   He has a high pressure job, but he remains relaxed at work.

3. Correct the six errors in punctuation and capitalization.

   The famous cuban-american actor Andy Garcia was born in havana on

   april 12, 1956. He has made many films *The Godfather*: *Part III*, *Ocean's*

   eleven, and *The Untouchables*.

FINAL REVIEW

Correct fifteen capitalization and punctuation (colon and hyphen) errors in the next selection.

EXAMPLE: Facebook developer Mark Zuckerberg is a self made millionaire.

1. MySpace and facebook have become extremely popular in recent years. Millions of people use such internet sites to reconnect with their long lost friends. Facebook's developer was a twenty-year old Harvard university student. Mark Zuckerberg launched the site in february 2004. The user friendly site fascinated the public. Researchers give three positive outcomes for people using such sites mastering new computer skills, sharing professional information, and increasing social contacts.

2. However, critics complain about privacy issues on these sites. In 2005, two Massachusetts Institute of technology students easily downloaded the personal information of around 70,000 Facebook users. In 2008, the BBC program *click* also acquired personal information of Facebook clients.

3. People should be careful when using such sites. Avoid sharing the following your birthday, phone number, school, job, and embarrassing photos. Malicious people often search for such information to steal identities. In addition, around 25 percent of employers say that they check the pages of job applicants. For

example, Luther Hudson of Wayne and smith, a marketing firm, accessed the personal information of an interviewee on friday, august 6, at 2 20 P.M., about one hour after he had read the applicant's résumé. Hudson saw an embarrassing photo of the candidate mooning her friends. He thought the applicant lacked good judgment and would not fit into the culture of the company.

THE WRITER'S ROOM

Write about one of the following topics. Ensure that your capitalization and punctuation are correct.

1. Describe your work environment.

2. What types of jobs does society place a high value on? Describe at least three different categories or types of workers who get a lot of respect.

READING LINK

To learn more about workplace issues, read the next essays.

"A Lesson in Humility" by Jeff Kemp (page 196)

"Steps to Music Success" by Jake Sibley (page 206)

"Two Jobs" by Adrianna Gonzalez (page 219)

"Why Small Businesses Fail" by Jim Baek (page 223)

"Aunt Tee" by Maya Angelou (page 540)

"Advertising Appeals" by Michael R. Solomon, Greg W. Marshall, and Elnora W. Stuart (page 542)

"Is Anything Private Anymore?" by Sean Flynn (page 545)

THE WRITERS' CIRCLE **Collaborative Activity**

Work with a partner and think about a job that would interest you. Find a job advertisement from a newspaper, a magazine, or an Internet site. You could refer to one of the following sites or look on a local jobs site.

Monster.com   *Jobs.net*   *Jobs.org*

Compose a letter of application. In the first paragraph, explain what job you want, and tell where you heard about the job. In the second paragraph, briefly detail your qualities and experience. Then, in a third paragraph, explain your availability and how you can be contacted. Ask your partner to help you compose each part of the letter.

Remember to be as direct as possible. After you finish writing, proofread your letter and ensure that you have used correct punctuation and capitalization. Exchange letters with your partner, and proofread your partner's letter.

Chapter 36

37 Editing Paragraphs and Essays

SECTION THEME: Editing Practice

LEARNING OBJECTIVE

LO 1 Practice editing different types of writing. **(p. 492)**

In this chapter, you will have opportunities to edit different pieces of writing.

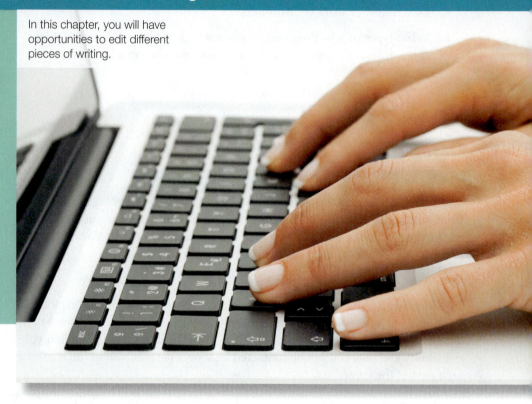

LO 1 Practice editing different types of writing.

After you finish writing the first draft of a paragraph or essay, it is important to edit your work. When you edit, you carefully review your writing to verify that your grammar, punctuation, sentence structure, and capitalization are correct. In this chapter, you can practice editing the types of written pieces that you see every day, including e-mail messages, paragraphs, essays, and business correspondence.

PRACTICE 1

Correct twenty errors in the next selection. An editing symbol appears above each underlined error. To understand the meaning of the symbol, refer to the chart at the back of this book.

1.   **wc**
   <u>Much</u> news articles focus on natural disasters such as deforestation, water

   pollution, and <u>focus on climate change</u>. **//** Such gloomy information <u>make</u> people **agr**

   very pessimistic about the future of the planet. However the environmental **p**

   movement has had some success stories.

2. In the 1980's, scientists brought a serious problem to the attention of [p]

the public who were studying the environment. They noticed that the ozone [m]

layer in the Earths atmosphere was disappearing. A hole in the ozone was [p]

getting more bigger. This phenomena was serious because the ozone protects [ad] [pl]

our planet from the sun's radiation. Chlorofluorocarbons (CFCs) from

refrigerators and aerosol sprays were damaging the ozone. Eventually, 197

countrys signed an agreement to limit CFCs in industrial products, and the [sp]

ozone hole has started to shrink.

3. By the 1970s, scientists realized that forests and lakes were dying due to acid

rain. When fossil fuels burn, they emit chemicals into the air. Causing them to [frag]

turn into acid. Acid rain damages flora and fauna. In 1990, President George

H.W. Bush signs the Clean Air Act Amendments, this act limits the amount of [shift] [ro]

air pollution companies can generate. Since then, air pollution has been reduced.

4. In 1969, the Cuyahoga River in ohio caught fire because it was one of [cap]

the most polluted river in the world. As a result, in 1972, Congress past [pl] [wc]

an important piece of legislation: the Clean Water Act. The act focuses on

stopping factories from dumping toxic chemicals into rivers. Before the act

was approved, most rivers were polluted. Since then, more then two-thirds [wc]

of all waterways have improved there water quality. Also wetlands are better [wc]

protected and soil erosion have lessened. [agr]

5.　Certainly, the United States faces many challenges to improve

the ecosystem. However, Americans will be able to find solutions for

environmental problems <u>with creative thinking</u>.
　　　　　　　　　　　　　m

PRACTICE 2

Correct fifteen errors in the next selection. An editing symbol appears above each underlined error. To understand the meaning of the symbol, refer to the chart at the back of this book.

1.　Sergeant Leung Shiu-yuk's first experience with a <u>chinese</u> triad occurred
　　　　　　　　　　　　　　　　　　　　　　　　　　　cap

when he was fourteen years old. The young Mr. Leung had an <u>arguement</u>
　　　　　　　　　　　　　　　　　　　　　　　　　　　　　　　sp

with an acquaintance. The <u>classmates</u> father aggressively claimed to be a
　　　　　　　　　　　　　　　p

triad member when he <u>comes</u> to see Mr. Leung's father about the schoolyard
　　　　　　　　　　　　　vt

brawl. At that moment, Mr. Leung decided to <u>became</u> a policeman to combat
　　　　　　　　　　　　　　　　　　　　　　　vt

organized crime in Hong Kong. Over the years, he has become <u>especialy</u>
　　　　　　　　　　　　　　　　　　　　　　　　　　　　　　sp

knowledgeable about triad operations. Mr. Leung <u>investigate</u> powerful Chinese
　　　　　　　　　　　　　　　　　　　　　　　agr

triads. He is a <u>conscious</u> expert witness for the Hong Kong police.
　　　　　　　　wc

2.　Chinese triads <u>been involved</u> in illegal activities in the United States since
　　　　　　　　　　vt

the beginning of the twentieth century. <u>There</u> business includes the drug
　　　　　　　　　　　　　　　　　　　　　wc

trade, human trafficking, and extortion. Chinese triads also defraud public and

private <u>institution</u> such as health care, insurance, and investment. The triads
　　　　pl

can manipulate and transfer financial assets across international boundaries.

                                 ad   sp

Thus, they deceive investors <u>real</u> easily. Triads are <u>responsable</u> for much

                                              wc

human misery. International police organizations are hopeful <u>than</u> they can

erase these criminal organizations. Security forces must show perseverance to

              pro

reach <u>his</u> goal.

PRACTICE 3

EDIT A PARAGRAPH

There are no editing symbols in the next paragraph. Proofread it as you would your own writing, and correct fifteen errors.

    Identity theft is the ilegal use of someones personal information. It is a serious crime, in fact, last year there was over 10 million cases of identity theft in the United States. To find identities, thieves go threw recycling bins, empty garbage cans, and stealing mail to obtain somebodys personal information. Computer hackers can even steal identities by tapping into personal information that persons keep on their computers. When a criminal has stolen a name, birthplace, address, and Social Security number, they can take out credit cards in the victim's name. For example, my coworker, Nick Matsushita. He came home one day and found a large bill from a credit card company. Somebody had use his personal information to apply for credit. Nick and me are good friends, and I know that the identity theft has caused him alot of pain. He says that if he would have known about the way identity thieves work, he would have been more careful with his personal papers. Certainly, victims of identity theft loose time and money trying to fix the problem. To avoid being a victim, be prudent when sharing personal information.

Chapter 37

PRACTICE 4

EDIT A WORKPLACE MEMO

Correct nine errors in the next excerpt from a memo.

Re: Parking

To: All Employees

It has been bought to my attention that employees are having problems parking. Because of construction of the new building. To solve a problem, the company have acquired extra parking spaces in the lot across the street. If employees wanna have a parking space, you need an entrance card. The cards are available at the front desk with names of employees. The parking inconvenience is temporary all staff members will be able to park in the regular parking lot in a few weaks.

Chad Renforth

Human Resources Department

PRACTICE 5

EDIT A PARAGRAPH

There are no editing symbols in the next paragraph. Proofread it as you would your own writing, and correct twelve errors.

Physicians overprescribe antibiotics and this practice is having a terrible effect on our health-care system. First, antibiotics are completely useless against viruses, yet alot of patients ask for and receive it when they have a simple cold. When drugs are overprescribed, some bacterial infections become drugs-resistant. Malaria and tuberculosis for example, are more difficult to treat than they were twenty years ago. The problem is especialy serious in hospitals. According to Dr. Ricki Lewis, antibiotic-resistant infections spread rapidly in a hospital environment. Furthermore, patients who are criticaly ill requires large doses of drugs who cause bacteria to mutate rapidly. We should remember that the body can fight many illnesses on its own. For instance, some common ear infections. Before accepting a prescription, consumers should ask whether antibiotics are necessary. There are problems enough in this world, the population does not need to create new illnesses by overusing antibiotics.

PRACTICE 6

Correct twelve errors in the next essay.

1.   Reid Radnor works for the American military. He, along with his wife, live on the army base in Seoul, South Korea. The base sits in the heart of the city. Everyone think that it looks like a 1950s suburb in america. It has split-level houses, schools, a movie theater, a hotel, and much more.

2.   Reid and his colleagues program computer software for the Army. In Reids office, everybody gets along. Many even socializes outside the office. Reid and his friends often play baseball at the base's baseball diamond. Occasionaly, someone proposes that they watch a movie. Sometimes, either Reid or his friends suggests lunch at the resort hotel. The food. It comes from the United States. In fact, on the base, everything originates in America. Nobody are supposed to feel homesick.

3.   The base is at the center of controversy in Korea, it symbolizes American dominance. Koreans want the military base to move away from Seoul. Some Koreans hope to built a city park on the land. Others wish to construct more housing. The Koreans have mixed feelings about American military presence in they're country.

PRACTICE 7

EDIT A FORMAL LETTER

Correct fifteen errors in the next letter.

Ari Praz

278 First avenue

New York, NY 10009

July 6, 2010

New York Department of Finance

Hearing-by-Mail Unit

P.O. Box 29201

Brooklyn, NY 11202

Subject: Ticket #4089-01411

Attention: Finance Department

I am writing to explain why am I pleading "not guilty" to a parking

ticket I recieved on the morning of friday, june 24, 2010. Please read

the following explanation and refer to the enclosed documents.

On the evening of june 23, I parked a rented car on the south side

of 18th street. I knew I could park there legaly overnight until 8:30 a.m.

At approximately 8:15 friday morning, I went to move the car from

that parking space. When I arrived, I discovered that the front tire on

the passenger side was flat. Unable to change the tire, I went to my

apartment a few blocks away to phone the rental companys hotline.

I think that I made the call at about 8:30 a.m. On the photocopies of

Continentals service records, you will see they dispatched someone

at 8:39 a.m. Unfortunately, while I was away from the car making that

call, I received a ticket, it was written at 8:40 a.m.

I'm sure you can see why I am pleading "not guilty" to this parking

offense. I have every intention of moving the car by the specified time,

I was not able to do so until roadside assistance arrived to replace the flat tire.

Yours Truly,

Ari Praz

Ari Praz

Enclosures: 2

PRACTICE 8

EDIT AN ESSAY

Correct twenty errors in the next student essay.

1. Sports surround us every day in the papers, on television, and on the radio. Some people criticize our sports-driven culture. Sports critics say that colleges' put young athletes on pedestals and do not emphasize the achievments of students in academic programs. In fact, athletes do not receive enough praise.

2. First, colleges with good sports teams gets a lot of publicity. For example, during the football season, three national television channels covers the games CBS, NBC, and ABC. During the basketball playoffs, March Madness CBS covers the games. The publicity that colleges receive from sports bring more students to the academic programs. Sports help these programs, they do not harm them.

3. In addition, colleges and universities make money from their student athletes. For example, the National Collegiate athletic association (NCAA), the organization devoted to the administration of intercollegiate athletics in the United States, showed $422.2 millions in revenue in its 2002–2003 budget. A large part of this money come from television. Most of the money is

Chapter 37

redistributed to colleges and universities. Every year, educational institutions use the funds not only for their sports programs but also are giving money to academic programs. Clearly, colleges show good long-term planning when they promote star athletes.

4. Moreover, sports are a motivation for athletes to go to college. Last year, there was about 360,000 student athletes in NCAA-affiliated colleges. Over 126,000 of thoses athletes received either a partial or a full scholarship. Therefore, they were real motivated. To attend postsecondary institutions.

5. Colleges and universities are right to pay special attention to athletes and sports programs. Because of the extra effort that student athletes must give to suceed, and because of the publicity and money that educational institutions receive from sports programs and their athletes   colleges and universities have a serious obligation to encourage there athletes.

Part V

Reading Strategies and Selections

In the first part of Chapter 38, you will learn strategies that can help you improve your reading skills. Later in the chapter, you will see a number of thought-provoking essays that present a wide range of viewpoints about topics related to popular culture and college life; psychology and health care; our environment and the workplace; and spies, hackers, and the legal world.

As you read each essay, think about how the writer achieves his or her purpose using one or more of these writing patterns: Illustration, Narration, Description, Process, Definition, Classification, Comparison and Contrast, Cause and Effect, and Argument.

From Reading to Writing 38

Aspiring songwriters and musicians study different musical styles to determine which lyrics, notes, rhythms, and so on work well together. In the same way, by reading different pieces of writing, you can observe which elements other writers use and how they use them. Then, you can try applying the same principles to your own writing.

Reading Strategies

LO 1 Practice reading strategies.

When you read, you also develop your writing skills. You expand your vocabulary and learn how other writers develop topics. In addition, you learn to recognize and use different writing patterns. Finally, reading helps you find ideas for your own paragraphs and essays.

The next strategies can help you become a more successful reader and writer. They guide you through the reading process and provide useful tips for getting specific information from a piece of writing.

Previewing

Previewing is like window shopping; it gives you a chance to see what the writer is offering. When you preview, look quickly for visual clues so that you can determine the selection's key points. Review the following:

- Titles or subheadings (if any)
- The first and last sentences of the introduction
- The first sentence of each paragraph

◆ The concluding sentences of the selection
◆ Any photos, graphs, or charts

Finding the Main Idea

After you finish previewing, read the selection carefully. Search for the **main idea**, which is the central point that the writer is trying to make. In an essay, the main idea usually appears somewhere in the first few paragraphs in the form of a thesis statement. However, some professional writers build up to the main idea and state it only in the middle or at the end of the essay. Additionally, some professional writers do not state the main idea directly.

> **HINT** ◀ **Making a Statement of the Main Idea**
>
> If a reading does not contain a clear thesis statement, you can determine the main idea by asking yourself *who*, *what*, *when*, *where*, *why*, and *how* questions. Then, using the answers to those questions, write a statement that sums up the main point of the reading.

Making Inferences

If a professional writer does not state the main idea directly, you must look for clues that will help you **infer** or figure out what the writer means to say. For example, read the next paragraph, and try to infer the writer's meaning.

> The band cost about $4,500 for the night. The hall rented for $900, and we figured we got a good deal. We had to decorate it ourselves. There were flowers on every table ($25 for each bouquet); rented china and silverware ($1,850); and tablecloths, tables, and chairs ($900). The catered food worked out to be $40 per person, multiplied by 300. This is not counting the dresses, the tuxedos, the photographer, or the rented limos. Sure, it was a special night. It is too bad the guests of honor split up three months later.

PRACTICE 1

Read the preceding paragraph. Then answer the following questions.

1. What is the subject of the paragraph? _____

2. What is the writer's relationship to the guests of honor? _____

   _____

3. What is the writer's main point? _____

   _____

Finding the Supporting Ideas

Different writers use different types of supporting ideas. They may give steps for a process, use examples to illustrate a point, give reasons for an argument, and so on. Try to identify the author's supporting ideas.

Highlighting and Making Annotations

After you read a long text, you may forget some of the author's ideas. To help you remember and quickly find the important points, you can highlight key ideas and make annotations. An **annotation** is a comment, question, or reaction that you write in the margin of a page.

Each time you read a passage, follow the next steps.

- Look in the introductory and concluding paragraphs. Underline sentences that sum up the main idea. Using your own words, rewrite the main idea in the margin.
- Underline or highlight supporting ideas. You might even number the arguments or ideas. This will allow you to understand the essay's development.
- Circle words that you do not understand.
- Write questions in the margin if you do not understand the author's meaning.
- Write notes beside passages that are interesting or that relate to your own experiences.
- Jot down any ideas that might make interesting writing topics.

Here is an annotated passage from an essay titled "Don't Worry, Act Happy" by Albert Nerenberg.

1   Robert Kall is a Philadelphia-based Positive Psychology conference organizer. While working as a therapist, he tried simple smiling as a way to treat depression. "I would put surface electrodes on the smile muscles in people's faces and, using electromyography, would measure the strength of their smiles," he said. "People who were not depressed had smile muscles that were on average four times stronger than people who were depressed," he said. This amazed him. So he began developing what could only be described as a smiling exercise program. "I would have depressed people pump 'smile' iron," he said. "I would have them do repetitions: three sets of 12 every day." By naturally triggering smiles, the "smilercizers" would seem to drive themselves to happier states.

Expert opinion

Interesting finding

Experiment suggests that happiness can be achieved by smiling.

I should try it.

"smilercizers" —made-up word

2   There's good reason why people resist the Act Happy concept. In primordial situations, fake and phony emotions might suggest a trap or danger. We're naturally suspicious around fake smiles, and forced laughter suggests fraud. We gauge our trust in others by their smiles. A put-on smile may suggest dishonesty and therefore danger, and phony laughter may signal manipulation. However, when using emotions to drive positive states, the dishonesty may not matter.

What does "primordial" mean?

Reasons humans don't like fake smiles

Writing Ideas: faking emotions, white lies

Understanding Difficult Words

When you read, you will sometimes come across unfamiliar words. You can try to guess the word's meaning, or you can circle it and look it up later.

Using Context Clues

Context clues are hints in the text that help define a word. To find a word's meaning, try the following strategies.

- **Look at the word.** Is it a noun, a verb, or an adjective? Sometimes it is easier to understand a word if you know how that word functions in the sentence.

♦ **Look at surrounding words.** Look at the sentence in which the word appears, and try to find a relation between the difficult word and the words that surround it. Maybe there is a **synonym** (a word that means the same thing) or an **antonym** (a word that means the opposite). Maybe other words in the sentence help define the word.

♦ **Look at surrounding sentences.** Sometimes you can guess the meaning of a difficult word by looking at the sentences, paragraphs, and punctuation surrounding the word. When you use your logic, the meaning becomes clear.

PRACTICE 2

1. Can you easily define the word *affluence*?   Yes   No

2. Can you easily define the word *plagued*?   Yes   No

3. If you do not understand the meanings of those two words, then read them in the context of the next paragraph. You will notice that it is much easier to guess their meanings.

John Macionis writes in his book, *Sociology*, that until a few centuries ago, the entire world was poor. But some researchers claim that it is **affluence** that demands an explanation. Affluence came within reach of a growing share of people in Western Europe during the late Middle Ages as world trade expanded. Then industrial technology created new wealth and gradually improved the living standard of even the poorest people. Poverty, which had **plagued** humanity throughout history, was finally in decline.

Now write your own definition of the words as they are used in the paragraph.

4. affluence: _____

5. plagued: _____

HINT ◂ Cognates

Cognates, or word twins, are English words that may look and sound like words in another language. For example, the English word *responsible* is similar to the Spanish word *responsable*, although the words are spelled differently.

If English is not your first language, and you read an English word that looks similar to a word in your language, check how it is being used in context. It may, or may not, mean the same thing in English as it means in your language. For example, in English, *assist* means "to help." In Spanish, *assistar* means "to attend." If you are not sure of a word's meaning, consult a dictionary.

Using a Dictionary

If you do not understand the meaning of an unfamiliar word after using context clues, look up the word in a dictionary. A dictionary is useful if you use it correctly. Review the following tips for dictionary usage.

♦ **Look at the dictionary's front matter.** The preface contains explanations about the various symbols and abbreviations.

♦ **Read all of the definitions listed for the word.** Look for the meaning that best fits the context of your sentence.

◆ **Look up root words, if necessary.** If the difficult word has a prefix such as *un-* or *anti-*, you may have to look up the root word.

Here is an example of how dictionaries set up their definitions.

Word Division
Your dictionary may use black dots to indicate places for dividing words.

Stress Symbol (´) and Pronunciation
Some dictionaries provide the phonetic pronunciation of words. The stress symbol (´) lets you know which syllable has the highest or loudest sound.

Parts of Speech
The *n* means that *deception* is a noun. If you don't understand the parts of speech symbol, look in the front or the back of your dictionary for a list of symbols and their meanings.

de•cep·tion / [di-sep´shən] / *n* 1, the act of misleading. 2, a misrepresentation; artiface; fraud.

From *The New American Webster Handy College Dictionary*
(New York: Signet, 2000), 606.

HINT **Online Dictionaries**

There are many good online dictionaries, including those that provide a pronunciation link and a thesaurus. Some good Web sites are Longman's Online Dictionary at *ldoceonline.com* and *Dictionary.com*.

From Reading to Writing

After you finish reading a selection, try these strategies to make sure that you have understood it.

◆ **Summarize the reading.** When you summarize, you use your own words to write a condensed version of the reading. You leave out all information except the main points.

◆ **Outline the reading.** An outline is a visual plan of the reading. First, write down the main idea of the essay, and then note the most important idea from each paragraph. Under each idea, include a detail or an example.

Make a Written Response

Your instructor may ask you to write about your reaction to a reading. These are some questions you might ask yourself before you make a written response.

◆ What is the writer's main point?

◆ What is the writer's purpose? Is the writer trying to entertain me, persuade me, or inform me?

◆ Who is the audience? Is the writer directing his or her message at someone like me?

◆ Do I agree or disagree with the writer's main point?

◆ What aspects of the topic can I relate to?

After you answer the questions, you will have more ideas to use in your written response.

LO2 Analyze reading selections.

Reading Selections

Themes: Popular Culture and College Life

READING 1

Being a Hyphenated American

Zaina Arafat

Zaina Arafat is a young Arab American. In the next essay, she reflects on identity and culture. As you read this definition essay, also look for elements of narration and comparison and contrast.

1   During the 1991 Persian Gulf War, I came home from school one day in tears. My classmates had been ridiculing me, and when I told my mother, she went straight to the administration. She said that during this particularly emotional time, they should make extra efforts to prevent discrimination against Arab-American students. They agreed, and assured her that they would. Months later, I came home complaining of the same torment: "They're still calling me fat! Zaina AraFAT!" Right then, my mother realized the teasing had nothing to do with my ethnic background. It was simply kids being kids. As a first-generation Arab-American, my ethnic duality has exposed me to a series of assumptions that stem from both ignorance and fear of the unknown. But these assumptions exist on both sides.

2   My parents moved to the United States from the West Bank a year before I was born. Growing up in the suburbs of Washington, D.C., my family seemed just like everyone else's, with a few variations that most wouldn't have noticed. For example, while my friends' fathers cracked open a bag of chips after work, my dad went straight for pumpkin seeds. My friends' moms drove minivans; mine, a two-seater. Their parents were big on curfews, grammar, "time outs," and seat belts. Soda was strictly forbidden in their houses, as were Cocoa Puffs for breakfast, and television was allowed only on weekends.

laissez-faire: permissive

3   I really didn't understand these rules. Since the American tendency toward overparenting contradicted my parents' Mediterranean, **laissez-faire** approach, the structure and what I saw as rigidity that existed in my friends' houses were absent in ours. Rather, our family was informal and spontaneous.

4   My friends found much in my life to be confused by, too, such as why my mom and dad called me mom and dad, as is tradition in Arab culture. They wondered why my parents and their friends seemed to be yelling at each other whenever they conversed, why every social gathering inevitably ended with dancing, and why our nicknames were longer than our actual ones: Zanzoon for Zaina; Abu Zooz for my brother, Zaid.

hummus: a spread made with chickpeas, lemon, garlic, and salt, very common in Middle Eastern cooking

5   As a kid, I was insecure about the nuances that set us apart, especially when friends asked for a bologna sandwich as soon as they saw whatever we were serving. But as I grew older, I began to appreciate my parents' attempt to assimilate while retaining our own traditions. We always had a turkey on Thanksgiving—that it was stuffed with rice and served with **hummus** seemed a fair compromise.

6   I found that while being an Arab-American in the US got better with age, the reverse applied when I visited the Middle East. As a kid, I couldn't wait for

these summer excursions. The moment I arrived in Jordan, where my extended family lives, I felt like a celebrity. I was coming from America, and that alone brought me relative fame and adoration. But eventually, things began to change. No longer able to get a free ride because of my American identity, I found there were many unspoken rules that were unfamiliar to me, such as when to put out my hand versus going for the cheek, and if the latter, two kisses or three? Also, no one wears shorts past the age of twelve. (Once on a visit to Bethlehem, my uncle had to trade me his trousers for my cutoffs.)

7   Despite the humbling, awkward moments that accompanied these lessons, I've begun to accept the potential for mistakes as an inevitable cross-cultural byproduct. And in doing so, I've realized that being Arab-American has different meanings, depending on where I am. In the Middle East, it often means having to stress that Americans shouldn't be equated with their country's foreign policy. In the US, it involves explaining that the Islamists shown on television represent a sliver of the Muslim population. It also entails reminding Americans that while **Al Jazeera** may seem oversensationalized, American media seems sanitized to Arabs.

Al Jazeera: a news network based out of Qatar

8   In many ways, "having a foot in both worlds" means having a full presence in neither. Although the phrase isn't meant to be interpreted literally, after twenty-seven years of balancing between two cultures and continents, I can say with certainty that it's far from figurative. But it's from such a vantage point that stereotypes are abolished. And as I get further away from a cultural identity crisis—and as a Kenyan-American was able to become US president—I realize that having dual ethnicity may be a great thing after all.

Vocabulary and Comprehension

MyWritingLab™

Complete additional reading comprehension questions for this selection at mywritinglab.com

1. In paragraph 5, what does the word *nuances* mean?

    a. colors   b. problems   c. subtle differences

2. Find a word in paragraph 6 that means the "second of two choices."

    _____

3a. Where are the writer's parents originally from?

    _____

3b. Where do they live presently?

    _____

4. What were some cultural differences the author mentions between her "American" friends and her own family? List at least three differences.

    _____

    _____

    _____

    _____

    _____

    _____

Critical Thinking

5. What is the significance of the title?

_____

_____

6. What example does the author use to show that her family tried to integrate into American society?

_____

_____

7. How does the author show that cultural misunderstandings are not just one-sided.

_____

_____

_____

_____

8. How does the author's attitude toward her dual heritage change?

_____

_____

_____

Writing Topics

Write about one of the following topics. Remember to explore, develop, and revise and edit your work.

1. In paragraph 8, the author writes, "'having a foot in both worlds' means having a full presence in neither." Do you agree or disagree with this statement? Give examples to support your ideas.

2. How do you define yourself: as an American or a hyphenated American? Explain your answer.

3. America promotes itself as a melting pot rather than a mosaic. In your opinion, which idea is better?

READING 2

Fads

David A. Locher

David A. Locher is an author and college professor at Missouri Southern State College. The next excerpt about fads is from his book *Collective Behavior*. As you read this classification essay, also look for elements of definition and illustration writing.

1   Fads can take a wide variety of forms. However, almost all fads have a common pattern. They always appear quickly. They seem to come from nowhere and suddenly occupy the attention of virtually everyone. Then, as quickly as they came, they fade from popularity. Most fads can be placed into one of three general categories: activity fads, product fads, and fashion or apparel fads.

2   Activity fads center on some leisure activity like breakdancing or rollerblading. People suddenly feel excited about taking part in an activity that has never seemed appealing before. Prior to the 1950s, people never felt the urge to stuff themselves into a phone booth with a large number of other people, and few have done it since then. However, it was all the rage for several years in the 1950s. Disco dancing came and (thankfully) went. Manufacturers often capitalize on these fads by producing a range of accessories to go with the activity. Often, music and movies that relate to the activity are rushed into production in an attempt to cash in on the fad before it ends. The song "The Streak," by Ray Stevens, and the film *Wheels* (a skateboarding film) are both good examples of attempts to make money from fad participants.

3   Useful product fads center on the acquisition of products that serve some purpose, however unimportant. In late 1998, "onion-bloom machines" suddenly became popular. Millions of Americans bought this kitchen tool designed to cut a large onion into a ready-to-fry "bloom" similar to the popular fried "onion blooms" served in restaurants. They were advertised on television almost every night. Stores quickly sold out their supply of the devices. The product itself is relatively useful, or at least serves some function. In this case, it makes a kind of variation of onion rings. However, the product is neither particularly necessary nor terribly important. The vast majority of onion-bloom machines are probably gathering dust in kitchen cabinets and closets all over the United States. Like many products at the center of these fads, onion-bloom machines remain on the market, but prices and demand dropped dramatically once the initial excitement wore off and people no longer felt the need for such a product in their lives.

4   Frivolous product fads may be the most interesting of all. People may stand in line for hours, fight with each other, and spend hundreds or thousands of dollars just so they can own something that is useless. The Pet Rock is the ideal example of this type of fad. In late 1975, an entrepreneur marketed a plain rock in a cardboard box called "The Pet Rock" and sold over one million at 5 dollars each. The Pet Rock was not decorated, nor did it do anything. It was, in fact, an ordinary rock. Today, it may seem difficult to understand why one million Americans would pay 5 dollars for a stone, particularly in 1975 when 5 dollars could buy a meal or two tickets to the movies. Such is the nature of useless product fads. They are always difficult to explain or understand after they end.

5   Fashion fads may or may not involve the purchase of a particular item. For example, millions of American women purchased and wore "leg warmers" in the 1980s. These wooly socks without feet were worn over pants or stockings and were used for their look, rather than practical function. Other fashion-related fads may not involve buying anything. In late 1999, at the University of Missouri in Columbia, Missouri, hundreds of young women on campus began wearing their hair loosely gathered into a small ponytail that stuck straight up from the top of their head. The only accessory required was a rubber band. No products were purchased. The rapid adoption of the unflattering look and its relatively rapid disappearance would categorize the hairstyle as a fad.

Phone booth stuffing

6   Fads usually seem strange or even ridiculous in hindsight. Looking back, it is hard to believe that hundreds, thousands, or even millions of Americans took part in bizarre fads such as pole sitting, phone booth stuffing, and breakdancing. What drives otherwise normal people to pay money for a rock, to jump from a bridge or crane attached to a bungee cord, or to stand in freezing weather for hours in order to run, push, shove, and fight over a thirty-dollar talking toy? According to Turner and Killian, in their book *Collective Behavior*, there is nothing wrong with the participants in fads. Most of them are ordinary people. It is the situation that is abnormal. Once confusion and uncertainty set in, people can potentially be led into unusual behavior.

Vocabulary and Comprehension

1. Find a slang expression in paragraph 2 that means "popular."

    _____

2. How does Locher define a fad?

    _____

    _____

3. Underline the thesis statement in this essay.

4. Locher divides one of the categories mentioned in the thesis statement into two subcategories. What are they?

    _____

5. Give examples of the characteristics of each fad Locher mentions.

    _____

    _____

    _____

    _____

    _____

    _____

MyWritingLab™

**Complete
additional reading
comprehension questions
for this selection at
mywritinglab.com**

Critical Thinking

6. Locher clearly dislikes some of the fads. Which fads does he directly criticize?

    _____

    _____

7. Who benefits the most when a product becomes a fad?

    _____

8. Why do fads disappear?

    _____

    _____

Writing Topics

Write about one of the following topics. Remember to explore, develop, and revise and edit your work.

1. What fads have you followed? Have you bought something silly, joined in an activity that was suddenly popular, or worn your hair in a trendy style? Describe one or more fads that you have followed.

2. Write a classification paragraph or an essay about other types of fads. Make sure the fads are linked by a common classification principle. For example, you might write about types of body improvement fads or types of hair fads, or you might break down fashion fads or activity fads into categories.

3. Why do you think some people are motivated to create or follow fads?

READING 3

This Boat Is My Boat

Drew Hayden Taylor

Drew Hayden Taylor is a playwright and author. His writings include essays and short stories about First Nations cultures and concerns. As you read this comparison and contrast essay, also look for elements of argument and cause and effect.

1   F. Scott Fitzgerald once wrote, "The rich are different from you and me," to which everybody usually responds, "Yeah, they've got more money." On a similar theme, it's been my Ojibwa-tainted observation over the years that "middle-class white people are different from you and me." They're insane. Much has been written over the years about the differences between native people and nonnative people, and the way they view life. There's no better example of this admittedly broad opinion than in the peculiar world of outdoor recreational water sports and the death wish that inspires them.

2   As a member of North America's indigenous population, I've cast a suspicious glance at all these waterlogged enthusiasts for several reasons. The principal one is the now familiar concept of cultural appropriation—this time of our methods of water transportation. On any given weekend, our rivers are jam-packed with plastic and fiberglass kayaks and canoes, hardly any of them filled with authentic Inuit or First Nations people, all looking to taunt death using an aboriginal calling card.

3   Historically, kayaks and canoes were the life's blood of Inuit and native communities. They were vital means of transportation and survival, not toys to amuse bored weekend warriors. For instance, there is a brand of gloves used by kayakers to protect their hands from developing calluses, called Nootkas. To the best of my knowledge, the real Nootka, a West Coast First Nation, neither kayaked nor wore gloves.

White-water kayaking

4   Let's examine the different ways these two cultural groups react to a single visual stimulus. A group of native people and white people sit in two separate canoes before a long stretch of roaring rapids—with large pointy rocks and lots and lots of turbulent white water. Watch the different reactions. Granted, I'm generalizing, but I think I can safely say the vast majority of native people, based on thousands of years of traveling the rivers of this great country of ours, would probably go home and order a pizza, or possibly put the canoe in their Ford pickup and drive downstream to a more suitable and safe location. Usually, the only white water native people enjoy is in their showers. Hurtling toward potential death and certain injury tends to go against many traditional native beliefs. Contrary to popular assumption, "portage" is not a French word—it is Ojibwa for "Are you crazy? I'm not going through that! Do you know how much I paid for this canoe?" When sunburned Caucasian canoeists are in the same position, their natural inclination is to aim directly for the rapids, paddling as fast as they can toward the white water.

5   Recently, for purely anthropological reasons, I risked my life to explore the unique subcultures of white-water canoeing and sea kayaking. There is also a sport known as white-water kayaking, but I have yet to put that particular bullet in my gun. So for three days, I found myself in the middle of Georgian Bay, during a storm, testing my abilities at sea kayaking. With me were a former Olympic rower, a Quebecois lawyer, a leading diabetes specialist, and a six-foot-seven ex-Mormon. We bonded over four-foot swells and lightning. The higher the waves, the more exciting they found the experience.

Sami: indigenous people inhabiting the Arctic area of Sápmi

6   Various indigenous populations developed other sports that have been corrupted and marketed as something fun to do when not sitting behind a desk in a high-rise office building. The Scandinavian **Sami** were instrumental in the development of skiing, though I doubt their motivation was to hurl themselves down as fast as gravity and snow would allow. The same could be said of bungee jumping. Originally a coming-of-age ritual in the South Pacific, young boys would build platforms, tie vines to their legs, and leap off to show their bravery and passage into adulthood. The same motivation doesn't drive today's bungee jumpers.

7   I have brought up the issue of recreational cultural appropriation many times with a friend who organizes these outdoor adventures. The irony is she works at a hospital, and she chews me out for not wearing a helmet while biking. She says there is no appropriation. If anything, her enthusiasm for the sports is a sign of respect and gratefulness.

8   People should pay a royalty of sorts every time they try to kill themselves using one of our aboriginal cultural legacies. Of course, no aboriginal group has ever sought a patent or copyright protection for kayaks or canoes—that was not part of the treaty negotiations. But somebody should definitely investigate the possibility. Or better yet, every time nonnatives go white-water canoeing or kayaking, they should first take an aboriginal person to lunch. That is a better way of showing respect and gratefulness, and it involves much less paperwork.

Vocabulary and Comprehension

MyWritingLab™
**Complete
additional reading
comprehension questions
for this selection at
mywritinglab.com**

1. What is the ethnic background of the author of this text?

   _____

2. In your own words, describe the author's thesis? Write a thesis statement.

   _____

   _____

   _____

3. What examples does the author use to support his thesis?

   _____

   _____

   _____

   _____

   _____

   _____

4. In paragraph 2, what is *cultural appropriation*?

   _____

   _____

Critical Thinking

5. What does the author think about white middle-class people who borrow native traditions?

   _____

   _____

6. In which paragraph does the author acknowledge the opposition when he discusses *cultural appropriation*? What point does he make?

   _____

   _____

7. What is the general tone of the author toward his subject?

   a. angry   b. sad   c. amused   d. serious

8. What does the author want the nonnatives to understand?

   _____

   _____

Writing Topics

Write about one of the following topics. Remember to explore, develop, and revise and edit your work.

1. Compare and contrast one of the following: two risky sports, two different holidays, two different brands of the same product, two different cultural traditions, or two different vacations.

2. Do you have a favorite activity or pastime? Describe it. It could be a sports activity or a leisure activity.

3. Drew Hayden Taylor uses humor to make fun of an ethnic group: Caucasians. What are some positive and/or negative effects of ethnic humor?

READING 4

Gone with the Windows

Dorothy Nixon

Dorothy Nixon, a freelance writer, has written for *Salon.com*, *Chatelaine*, and *Today's Parent* magazine. She is also the author of *Threshold Girl*, which can be read on Amazon's Kindle. In the next essay, she compares how information today is stored or lost compared to the past. As you read this comparison and contrast essay, also look for elements of cause and effect and narration.

1   The other day, I had trouble accessing Photoshop through our home network. The program was on my other computer, so I had to whip downstairs to see what the problem was. I discovered that my back-up computer was in pieces. My eighteen-year-old had pulled its hard drive apart, no doubt for some mischievous reason, and left the cannibalized carcass to air in the middle of the room.

2   When I asked, "What's up?" he said he needed a component to be able to play a computer game in his room with his friends—and some other people in Japan. Of course, my son has the most advanced computer in the house, by far. My son also visits all the usual Web sites so popular with teens and gets a lot of viruses on his computer. So he is always "wiping his hard drive," as he puts it.

3   I know this because he and his dad like to discuss such things. (That's definitely a good thing.) I seldom butt in on these conversations, but the other day I overheard a remark that distressed me. My son was oh-so-casually explaining to my husband how he had inadvertently erased all of his photographs from his grade 11 trip to Europe. The images had evaporated into the ether. All gone. Not to worry, he said, "Lots of other kids still have theirs."

4   Now, he had taken hundreds of pictures of Baroque fountains, messy hotel rooms, and bleary-eyed teens—and shown me the snapshots just once upon his return. I had intended to print out the best ones and mail them to his grandmother. Now she will never see that picture of her grandson Mark with that "gladiator" in front of the Roman Coliseum.

5   Digital technology makes it all just so easy. We can instantly capture our most intimate and spontaneous moments and effortlessly pass these images on to friends and family by e-mail or snail mail or post them on Web sites for the entire wired world to see. And, still, my son's record of his once-in-a-lifetime experience is lost forever.

6   I have a different perspective on things: About two years ago, I found some old documents saved by my husband's ancestors from Richmond, Quebec, in a trunk in my father-in-law's basement. There was a direct-mail ad for Crisco Shortening from 1915, when butter was getting costly. I found a National Drug Company promotional brochure with ads for bizarre remedies such as white liniment for ailments like "brain worry" and "fag" (what we might refer to as chronic fatigue) and impotency.

7   There were family documents, too. Hundreds of letters were tied up in ribbons. Great Uncle Herb's letters reveal he was always in debt. A newspaper clipping described British militant suffragette Barbara Wylie's arrival in Montreal in 1912. Reporters couldn't believe how attractive a feminist could be!

8   I also discovered booklets containing detailed household accounts. For the 1883 marriage, it cost 5 dollars for a lady's ring and 50 cents for a frying pan. In 1884, after the baby's arrival, a toy cost 5 cents, but the doctor's bill was 51 dollars! In 1896, a house built in pseudo-Scottish Baronial style went for 2,712 dollars. Family expenses for the era averaged between 300 and 500 dollars a year. Wood for heating and dentist and medical bills (outside of childbirth) were the big expenses.

9   We're talking a lot of history here, of interest to family as well as to historians. I posted my findings on the Web, and the information has been very well received by the academic community. Some scholars have actually thanked me for making the effort. It was just luck, I tell them, just luck that one day while I was waiting for the washing machine to end its spin cycle, my gaze rested on an old Victorian trunk in a basement where I'd been hundreds of times before. I got curious.

10   Will future amateur historians be as lucky as I was? With all the runaway digital documentation going on in homes today, will today's family history be available or accessible to future inquiring minds like mine? We just recently transferred our baby videos to CD, but it's possible that in a few years the CD format will be as impenetrable as a **cuneiform tablet**. My son's experience with his high school pictures suggests that a lot of twenty-first century family history could be, well, gone with the windows. And that will indeed be ironic—and a great big shame.

cuneiform tablet: a stone tablet with the earliest known writing system in the world

Vocabulary and Comprehension

1. In paragraph 1, what does *cannibalized carcass* refer to?

   _____

2. In paragraph 10, find a word that means "puzzling."

   _____

3. What event happened that made the author think about technology?

   _____

   _____

4. Nixon compares the present with the past. What comparison pattern does she use?

   a. point by point   b. topic by topic

MyWritingLab™

Complete additional reading comprehension questions for this selection at mywritinglab.com

Critical Thinking

5. Nixon actually compares more than the present to the past. List other topics she compares.

   _____

   _____

   _____

   _____

6. Why did the author put the information she found in a trunk on her Web site?

   _____

   _____

7. How does the author see the relationship between history and technology?

   _____

   _____

   _____

Writing Topics

Write about one of the following topics. Remember to explore, develop, and revise and edit your work.

1. Compare one of the following: two decades, two discoveries, or your past to your present.

2. Imagine that you could time-travel to a period in your past. Where would you go and why? Would you change what happened?

3. Write about an event in history. Narrate what happened.

READING 5

It's Class, Stupid!

Richard Rodriguez

Richard Rodriguez is a writer and an essayist who published the novel *Days of Obligation*. He also writes for the *Los Angeles Times* and *Harper's*. The next selection is an argument essay about affirmative action that originally appeared in the online magazine *Salon.com*. As you read, also look for elements of the comparison and contrast writing pattern.

1   Some weeks ago, a law professor at the University of Texas got in trouble for saying that African Americans and Mexicans are at a disadvantage in higher education because they come from cultures that tolerate failure. Jesse Jackson flew to Austin to deliver a fiery speech; students demanded the professor's **ouster**.

ouster: dismissal

2   It was all typical of the way we have debated affirmative action for years. Both sides ended up arguing about race and ethnicity; both sides ignored the deeper issue of social inequality. Even now, as affirmative action is finished in California and is being challenged in many other states, nobody is really saying what is wrong with affirmative action: It is unfair to poor whites.

3   Americans find it hard to talk about what Europeans more easily call the lower class. We find it easier to sneer at the white poor—the "rednecks," the trailer-park trash. The rural white male is Hollywood's politically correct villain **du jour**.

du jour: French term meaning "of the day" or "at the present time"

4   We seem much more comfortable worrying about race; it's our most important metaphor for social distinction. We talk about the difference between black and white, not the difference between rich and poor. American writers—Richard Wright, James Baldwin, Toni Morrison—are brilliant at describing what it is like to be a racial minority. But America has few writers who describe as well what it is like to be poor. We don't have a writer of the stature of D.H. Lawrence—the son of an English coal miner—who grew up embarrassed by his soft hands. At the University of Texas, it was easier for the Sicilian-born professor Lino Graglia to notice that the students who dropped out of school were Mexican American or black than to wonder if they might be poor.

5   At the same time, the angry students who accused the law professor of racism never bothered to acknowledge the obvious: Poor students *do* often come from neighborhoods and from families that tolerate failure or at least have learned the wisdom of slight expectations. Education is fine, if it works. I meet young people all the time who want to go to college, but Mama needs her oldest son to start working. It is better to have a dollar-and-cents job working at Safeway or McDonald's than a college diploma that might not guarantee a job.

6   Anyone who has taught poor children knows how hard it is to persuade students not to be afraid of success. There is the boy who is mocked by male classmates for speaking good English. There is the girl who comes from a family where women are not assumed to need, or want, education.

7   We also don't like to admit, though we have argued its merits for twenty years, that the chief beneficiaries of affirmative action—black, brown, female— are primarily middle class. It still doesn't occur to many progressives that affirmative action might be unfair to poor whites. That is because poor whites do not constitute an officially recognized minority group. We don't even notice the presence or, more likely, the absence of the poor white on college campuses. Our only acknowledgment of working-class existence is to wear fashionable working-class denim.

8   A man I know, when he went to Harvard, had only a pair of running shoes to wear and had never owned a tie. He dropped out of Harvard after two years. I suppose some of his teachers imagined it was because he was Hispanic, not that he was dirt poor. The advantage I had, besides my parents, were my Irish nuns—who themselves had grown up working class. They were free of that middle-class fear (typical today in middle-class teachers) of changing students too much. The nuns understood that education is not an exercise in self-esteem. They understood how much education costs, the price the heart pays.

9   Every once in a while, I meet middle-class Americans who were once lower class. They come from inner cities and from West Texas trailer parks. They are successful now beyond their dreams, but bewildered by loss, becoming so

different from their parents. If only America would hear their stories, we might, at last, acknowledge social class. And we might know how to proceed, now that affirmative action is dead and so many poor kids remain to be educated.

MyWritingLab™

**Complete
additional reading
comprehension questions
for this selection at
mywritinglab.com**

Vocabulary and Comprehension

1. Find a word in paragraph 6 that means "made fun of."

   _____

2. What does the word *constitute* in paragraph 7 mean? Circle the best answer.

   a. govern   b. appoint   c. represent

3. Look in the first two paragraphs and underline the thesis statement.

4. According to the author, what prevents many poor people from attending college? Give at least three reasons.

   _____

   _____

   _____

5. Who benefits the most from affirmative action, according to the author?

   _____

   _____

Critical Thinking

6. Explain why Rodriguez disagrees with affirmative action.

   _____

   _____

   _____

   _____

7. The author compares the English writer D.H. Lawrence with American writers such as Toni Morrison. How is this comparison relevant for this essay?

   _____

   _____

   _____

   _____

8. In paragraph 1, Rodriguez includes an anecdote about a University of Texas law professor. Explain why the author agrees or disagrees with the professor.

   _____

   _____

   _____

   _____

9. The author writes that his teachers, Irish nuns with working-class backgrounds, "understood how much education costs, the price the heart pays." What does he mean? (Look in paragraphs 8 and 9 for clues.)

_____

_____

_____

_____

_____

Writing Topics

Write about one of the following topics. Remember to explore, develop, and revise and edit your work.

1. In your employment or education, have you had any positive or negative experiences because of your economic, gender, ethnic, or racial background?

2. Do you agree or disagree with the author's argument? Support your point of view with specific examples.

3. The writer James Baldwin once said that being poor has high costs. What are the costs? Give examples or anecdotes to support your ideas.

READING 6

The Case for Affirmative Action: An Open Letter to Five Justices

Dave Malcolm

Dave Malcolm is a professor in San Diego. In 1995, the following letter was entered into the Congressional Record by U.S. Representative Esteban Torres in response to anti–affirmative action decisions by the Supreme Court. As you read this argument essay, also look for elements of illustration, definition, and comparison and contrast.

1   On Monday, June 12, 1995, at 10:50 a.m., I left the office of my cardiologist having just been informed that my aortic valve implant was "leaking" and that replacement surgery would be required within the next three to six months. At 10:55 a.m., on the same date, I heard on my car radio about two new Supreme Court 5–4 decisions, each apparently placing serious additional limitations on programs of affirmative action. I drove homeward, feeling sick at heart—not from feelings of anxiety about my imminent open-heart surgery but from feelings of dismay at the direction in which the country seems to be moving, especially in regard to affirmative action.

2   You see, I know a lot about affirmative action. I count myself an expert on the subject. After all, I have benefited from it all my life. That is because I am white, I am male, I am Anglo, and I am Protestant. We male WASPs have had a great informal affirmative action program going for decades, maybe centuries. I am not speaking only of the way our "old boy networks" help people like me get into the right colleges or get jobs or get promotions. That is only the surface.

Underneath, our real affirmative action is much more than just a few direct interventions at key moments in life. The real affirmative action is also indirect and at work twenty-four hours a day, seven days a week, year in and year out. Because it is informal and indirect, we tend to forget or deny just how all-important and pervasive it really is.

3   However, far be it from me to put the direct "old boy" surface stuff down. I was admitted without difficulty to the Ivy League college my father had attended. This was back in the days when the only quotas were quotas to keep certain people out, not to help them get in. There were no limits on reasonably bright kids like me—the admissions people spoke of the children of alumni as "legacies," but whether this was because the college was inheriting us as students or because the college hoped to inherit money from our families, I was never quite sure. I got a teaching job right out of college in the heart of the Depression—my father was a school superintendent well liked among his colleagues.

4   After World War II, when I became a university professor, I received promotion and tenure in minimum time, more quickly than many of my female colleagues. Of course, the decision makers knew me better; I was part of the monthly poker group and played golf every Friday afternoon. Yes, direct affirmative action—direct preferential treatment because of my gender and my color and good connections—have been good to me.

5   But, like other white males, I have benefited less obviously but far more significantly from indirect preferential treatment. Indirect affirmative action is at work to a greater or lesser degree on behalf of virtually all white males, whether one is aware of it or not. It is what did not happen to me. There were destructive, painful experiences that I did not have to endure. Early in life, I knew that boys were more important than girls and so did the girls. I have never had to worry about whether my skin color was light enough or dark enough.

6   For two of my long-time colleagues and closest personal friends, it has been a very different story. Raymond was the lightest skinned member of his family. He recalls that he was the only one who could get his hair cut downtown—but the family had to drop him off a block away from the barber shop. He once told me that he had probably spent more time worrying about his light skin than any other one thing in life. Would his fellow African Americans think he was black enough? When whites thought he was East Indian or South American, should he let them think so?

7   Maria had the opposite problem. As a child, she was called *la prieta* ("the little dark one"). Even though she knew the **diminutive** was a mark of affection, she still was aware that the label was no compliment. When she became a young woman, well-meaning whites told her, "You don't look Mexican," meaning that she looked more Spanish and hence almost white. The message always hurt deeply not simply because the speakers personally so clearly believed that there was something inferior about being Mexican but also because they had unhesitatingly assumed that she did, too, and hence would consider such a statement to be a compliment.

8   I have never had to endure "what-is-he-doing-here?" looks any time I walked along a residential street in a suburban area. I have not had to notice white women clutching their purses more tightly when they meet me walking along the street. I have never seen the "For Rent" or "For Sale" signs **figuratively** snatched out of the window as I walked up to the front door. I cannot even begin to imagine the insults, large and small, that send a five- or six-year-old running tearfully home to ask Mommy or Daddy, "Why can't I be white?"

diminutive: affectionate nickname

figuratively: symbolically; not literally

9   Out of the dozens of times I have crossed the border from Tijuana to San Diego, the one time I was pulled over to have my car inspected was when returning with my friend, Raymond, and another African American male as passengers. I was furious, but my friends restrained me, assuring me it was no big deal and that it happened to them all the time. That day I got some small sense of the rage and fury and helplessness and frustration that some people experience daily and are forced to smother.

10   I have never been so bombarded by negative messages that I began to internalize them and to suspect they might in part be true. As a professional person, I have never had to carry the burden of knowing that the slightest mispronunciation or grammatical error on my part will be seized upon by some people as validation of their negative stereotypes, not only about me but also about my people. But entire populations of my potential competitors have labored and are still laboring under disadvantages of this very sort as they compete with me. This is white male "affirmative action" at its most effective—the flip side of destructive life-long bombardment by negative messages.

11   Yes, affirmative action for some folks remains alive and well and unthreatened by court decisions. I ought to know. All my life I have been an indirect beneficiary because indirect affirmative action has been so effective at crippling or eliminating so many of those who might have been my competitors. As a white male, I have never had to compete with them on a level playing field.

12   The promise of the American dream is a society which is color-fair, not color-blind. Formal affirmative action programs play a dual role. They make the playing fields a bit more level, and they remind us that we still have far to go. It is no solution for society to trash its current formal efforts to make opportunity a little more equal as long as so many powerful informal barriers to equality of opportunity still persist. Think about it.

Vocabulary and Comprehension

MyWritingLab™
Complete additional reading comprehension questions for this selection at mywritinglab.com

1. What introduction style does the author use? Circle the best answer.
   a. general background
   c. opposing position
   b. definition
   d. anecdote

2. Using your own words, describe the main idea of this essay.

   _____

   _____

   _____

3. How has the author benefited from indirect affirmative action? List some examples.

   _____

   _____

   _____

   _____

   _____

4. What examples does the author give to illustrate that members of less-favored groups have to live with destructive, painful experiences?

_____

_____

_____

_____

_____

Critical Thinking

5. Why was Malcolm promoted more quickly than his female colleagues?

_____

_____

6. Explain how a "For Rent" sign could be "figuratively snatched from a window" (paragraph 8).

_____

_____

7. What are Malcolm's main arguments for supporting affirmative action?

_____

_____

_____

_____

8. Who is Dave Malcolm? What have you learned about him after reading this text? List characteristics that describe him, and make some educated guesses about his personality.

_____

_____

_____

_____

_____

_____

Writing Topics

Write about one of the following topics. Remember to explore, develop, and revise and edit your work.

1. Compare Malcolm's view of affirmative action with the view expressed by Richard Rodriguez in the essay titled "It's Class, Stupid!" With whom do you agree, and why?

2. List examples of ways in which people are stereotyped. You can discuss age, appearance, race, and so on.

3. What is your view about equality? Should laws protect some members of society to ensure equal access to work, education, and housing? Why or why not?

Themes: Psychology and Health Care

READING 7

The Catcher of Ghosts

Amy Tan

Amy Tan is an American writer. One of her most well-known novels is *The Joy Luck Club*. She has explored themes such as mother–daughter relationships and cultural issues. As you read this descriptive story, which appeared in her book *The Bonesetter's Daughter*, also look for elements of narration and cause and effect.

1   When we returned home, Mother and Father, as well as our aunts and uncles, were bunched in the courtyard, talking in excited voices. Father was relating how he had met an old Taoist priest at the market, a remarkable and strange man. As he passed by, the priest had called out to him: "Sir, you look as if a ghost is plaguing your house."

2   "Why do you say that?" Father asked.

3   "It's true, isn't it?" the old man insisted. "I feel you've had a lot of bad luck and there's no other reason for it. Am I right?"

4   "We had a suicide," Father admitted, "a nursemaid whose daughter was about to be married."

5   "And bad luck followed."

6   "A few calamities," Father answered.

7   The young man standing next to the priest then asked Father if he had heard of the famous Catcher of Ghosts. "No? Well, this is he, the wandering priest right before you. He's newly arrived in your town, so he's not yet as well known as he is in places far to the north and south. Do you have relatives in **Harbin**? No? Well, then! If you had, you'd know who he is." The young man, who claimed to be the priest's acolyte, added, "In that city alone, he is celebrated for having already caught one hundred ghosts in disturbed households. When he was done, the gods told him to start wandering again."

8   When Father finished telling us how he had met these two men, he added, "This afternoon, the famous Catcher of Ghosts is coming to our house."

9   A few hours later, the Catcher of Ghosts and his assistant stood in our courtyard. The priest had a white beard, and his long hair was piled like a messy bird's nest. In one hand he carried a walking stick with a carved end that looked like a flayed dog stretched over a gateway. In the other, he held a short beating stick. Slung over his shoulders was a rope shawl from which hung a large wooden bell. His robe was not the sand-colored cotton of most wandering monks I had seen. His was a rich-looking blue silk, but the sleeves were grease-stained, as if he had often reached across the table for more to eat.

Harbin: a large town in northeastern China

10   I watched hungrily as Mother offered him special cold dishes. It was late afternoon, and we were sitting on low stools in the courtyard. The monk helped himself to everything—glass noodles with spinach, bamboo shoots with pickled mustard, tofu seasoned with sesame seed oil and coriander. Mother kept apologizing about the quality of the food, saying she was both ashamed and honored to have him in our shabby home. Father was drinking tea. "Tell us how it's done," he said to the priest, "this catching of ghosts. Do you seize them in your fists? Is the struggle fierce or dangerous?"

11   The priest said he would soon show us. "But first I need proof of your sincerity." Father gave his word that we were indeed sincere. "Words are not proof," the priest said.

12   "How do you prove sincerity?" Father asked.

13   "In some cases, a family might walk from here to the top of Mount Tai and back, barefoot and carrying a load of rocks." Everyone, especially my aunts, looked doubtful that any of us could do that.

14   "In other cases," the monk continued, "a small offering of pure silver can be enough and will cover the sincerity of all members of the immediate family."

15   "How much might be enough?" Father asked.

16   The priest frowned. "Only you know if your sincerity is little or great, fake or genuine."

ingot: pieces of metal historically used as currency

17   The monk continued eating. Father and Mother went to another room to discuss the amount of their sincerity. When they returned, Father opened a pouch and pulled out a silver **ingot** and placed this in front of the famous Catcher of Ghosts.

18   "This is good," the priest said. "A little sincerity is better than none at all."

19   Mother then drew an ingot from the sleeve of her jacket. She slid this next to the first so that the two made a clinking sound. The monk nodded and put down his bowl. He clapped his hands, and the assistant took from his bundle an empty vinegar jar and wad of string.

20   "Where's the girl that the ghost loved best?" asked the priest.

21   "There," Mother said, and pointed to me. "The ghost was her nursemaid."

22   The priest said to me, "Fetch me the comb she used for your hair."

23   My feet were locked to the ground until Mother gave me a little knock on the head to hurry. So I went to the room Precious Auntie and I had shared not so long before. I picked up the comb she used to run through my hair. It was the ivory comb she never wore, its ends carved with roosters, its teeth long and straight. I remembered how Precious Auntie used to scold me for my tangles, worrying over every hair on my head.

24   When I returned, I saw the assistant had placed the vinegar jar in the middle of the courtyard. "Run the comb through your hair nine times," he said. So I did.

25   "Place it in the jar." I dropped the comb inside, smelling the escape of cheap vinegar fumes. "Now stand there perfectly still." The Catcher of Ghosts beat his stick on the wooden bell. It made a deep kwak, kwak sound. He and the acolyte walked in rhythm, circling me, chanting, and drawing closer. Without warning, the Catcher of Ghosts gave a shout and leapt toward me. I thought he was going to squeeze me into the jar, so I closed my eyes and screamed, as did **GaoLing**.

GaoLing: the girl's younger sister

26   When I opened my eyes, I saw the acolyte was pounding a tight-fitting wooden lid onto the jar. He wove rope from top to bottom, bottom to top, then all around the jar, until it resembled a hornet's nest. When this was done, the

Catcher of Ghosts tapped the jar with his beating stick and said, "It's over. She's caught. Go ahead. Try to open it, you try. Can't be done."

27   Everyone looked, but no one would touch. Father asked, "Can she escape?"

28   "Not possible," said the Catcher of Ghosts. "This jar is guaranteed to last more than several lifetimes."

Vocabulary and Comprehension

MyWritingLab™
Complete additional reading comprehension questions for this selection at mywritinglab.com

1. Find a word in paragraph 7 that means "helper."

    _____

2. Why do Mother and Father need the services of the Catcher of Ghosts?

    _____

    _____

3. Who is the ghost and what relationship did it have with the family?

    _____

4. A simile is a comparison using *like* or *as*. Underline an example of a simile that the author uses to describe the priest.

5. The author uses imagery in this essay. Give an example of the following:

    sight: _____

    _____

    sound: _____

    _____

    smell: _____

    _____

    touch: _____

    _____

Critical Thinking

6. Who is Precious Auntie?

    _____

    _____

7. What can you infer, or guess, about the Catcher of Ghosts when he asks for "proof of sincerity?"

    _____

    _____

8. What can you infer about the characters of Mother and Father from their actions?

    _____

    _____

    _____

Writing Topics

Write about one of the following topics. Remember to explore, develop, and revise and edit your work.

1. Describe an incident from your childhood or the childhood of your parents or grandparents. Try to use descriptive imagery.

2. Describe a family tradition. Give as many details as possible using the five senses.

3. What are some examples of superstitions that people have?

READING 8

The Sanctuary of School

Lynda Barry

Lynda Barry is a cartoonist, writer, and playwright. Her work includes graphic novels and the syndicated comic strip *Ernie Pook's Comeek*. As you read this narrative essay, also look for elements of description.

1   I was seven years old the first time I snuck out of the house in the dark. It was winter, and my parents had been fighting all night. They were short on money and long on relatives who kept "temporarily" moving into our house because they had nowhere else to go.

2   My brother and I were used to giving up our bedroom. We slept on the couch, something we actually liked because it put us that much closer to the light of our lives, our television. At night when everyone was asleep, we lay on our pillows watching it with the sound off. We watched Steve Allen's mouth moving. We watched Johnny Carson's mouth moving. We watched movies filled with gangsters shooting machine guns into packed rooms, dying soldiers hurling a last grenade, and beautiful women crying at windows. Then the sign-off finally came, and we tried to sleep.

3   The morning I snuck out, I woke up filled with a panic about needing to get to school. The sun wasn't quite up yet, but my anxiety was so fierce that I just got dressed, walked quietly across the kitchen, and let myself out the back door.

4   It was quiet outside. Stars were still out. Nothing moved, and no one was in the street. It was as if someone had turned the sound off on the world.

5   I walked the alley, breaking thin ice over the puddles with my shoes. I didn't know why I was walking to school in the dark. I didn't think about it. All I knew was a feeling of panic, like the panic that strikes kids when they realize they are lost.

6   That feeling eased the moment I turned the corner and saw the dark outline of my school at the top of the hill. My school was made up of about fifteen nondescript portable classrooms set down on a fenced concrete lot in a rundown Seattle neighborhood, but it had the most beautiful view of the Cascade Mountains. You could see them from anywhere on the playfield, and you could see them from the windows of my classroom—Room 2.

7   I walked over to the monkey bars and hooked my arms around the cold metal. I stood for a long time just looking across Rainier Valley. The sky was beginning to whiten, and I could hear a few birds.

8   In a perfect world, my absence at home would not have gone unnoticed. I would have had two parents in a panic to locate me, instead of two parents in a

panic to locate an answer to the hard question of survival during a deep financial and emotional crisis.

9   But in an overcrowded and unhappy home, it's incredibly easy for any child to slip away. The high levels of frustration, depression, and anger in my house made my brother and me invisible. We were children with the sound turned off. And for us, as for the steadily increasing number of neglected children in this country, the only place where we could count on being noticed was at school.

10   "Hey there, young lady. Did you forget to go home last night?" It was Mr. Gunderson, our janitor, whom we all loved. He was nice and he was funny and he was old with white hair, thick glasses, and an unbelievable number of keys. I could hear them jingling as he walked across the playfield. I felt incredibly happy to see him.

11   He let me push his wheeled garbage can between the different portables as he unlocked each room. He let me turn on the lights and raise the window shades, and I saw my school slowly come to life. I saw Mrs. Holman, our school secretary, walk into the office without her orange lipstick on yet. She waved. I saw the fifth-grade teacher, Mr. Cunningham, walking under the breezeway eating a hard roll. He waved.

12   And I saw my teacher, Mrs. Claire LeSane, walking toward us in a red coat and calling my name in a very happy and surprised way, and suddenly my throat got tight and my eyes stung and I ran toward her crying. It was something that surprised us both.

13   It's only thinking about it now, twenty-eight years later, that I realize I was crying from relief. I was with my teacher, and in a while I was going to sit at my desk, with my crayons and pencils and books and classmates all around me, and for the next six hours I was going to enjoy a thoroughly secure, warm, and stable world. It was a world I absolutely relied on. Without it, I don't know where I would have gone that morning.

14   Mrs. LeSane asked me what was wrong, and when I said "Nothing," she seemingly left it at that. But she asked me if I would carry her purse for her, an honor above all honors, and she asked if I wanted to come into Room 2 early and paint.

15   She believed in the natural healing power of painting and drawing for troubled children. In the back of her room, there was always a drawing table and an easel with plenty of supplies, and sometimes during the day she would come up to you for what seemed like no good reason and quietly ask if you wanted to go to the back table and "make some pictures for Mrs. LeSane." We all had a chance at it—to sit apart from the class for a while to paint, draw, and silently work out impossible problems on 11×17 sheets of newsprint.

16   Drawing came to mean everything to me. At the back table in Room 2, I learned to build myself a life preserver that I could carry into my home.

17   We all know that a good education system saves lives, but the people of this country are still told that cutting the budget for public schools is necessary, that poor salaries for teachers are all we can manage, and that art, music, and all creative activities must be the first to go when times are lean.

18   Before- and after-school programs are cut, and we are told that public schools are not made for baby-sitting children. If parents are neglectful temporarily or permanently, for whatever reason, it's certainly sad, but their unlucky children must fend for themselves. Or slip through the cracks. Or wander in a dark night alone.

19   We are told in a thousand ways that not only are public schools not important, but that the children who attend them, the children who need them most, are not

a thousand points of light:
a spirit of volunteerism encouraged by former president Bush

important either. We leave them to learn from the blind eye of a television or to the mercy of "**a thousand points of light**" that can be as far away as stars.

20   I was lucky. I had Mrs. LeSane. I had Mr. Gunderson. I had an abundance of art supplies. And I had a particular brand of neglect in my home that allowed me to slip away and get to them. But what about the rest of the kids who weren't as lucky? What happened to them?

21   By the time the bell rang that morning, I had finished my drawing, and Mrs. LeSane pinned it up on the special bulletin board she reserved for drawings from the back table. It was the same picture I always drew—a sun in the corner of a blue sky over a nice house with flowers all around it.

22   Mrs. LeSane asked us to please stand, face the flag, place our right hands over our hearts, and say the Pledge of Allegiance. Children across the country do it faithfully. I wonder now when the country will face its children and say a pledge right back.

MyWritingLab™

Complete additional reading comprehension questions for this selection at mywritinglab.com

Vocabulary and Comprehension

1. Find a word in paragraph 6 that means "uninteresting."

    _____

2. What type of narrator is telling this story?
    a. first person   b. third person

3. When and where does the story take place?

    _____

    _____

4. Why did the author sneak out of her house and go to the school?

    _____

    _____

Critical Thinking

5. Describe the author's family life. You will have to infer or guess.

    _____

    _____

    _____

6. In paragraph 6, the author writes that she stopped feeling anxious when she saw the school. What are some reasons that she felt secure at the school?

    _____

    _____

    _____

7. In paragraph 9, the author writes, "We were children with the sound turned off." What does she mean?

    _____

    _____

8. What role did Mrs. LeSane play in the author's childhood?

_____

_____

_____

9. According to the author, how does the public school system of her childhood compare to the public school system of today?

_____

_____

_____

10. The author uses imagery—description using the senses—to depict her environment. Give an example of each of the following types of imagery.

Sight: _____

_____

_____

Sound: _____

_____

_____

Touch: _____

_____

_____

Writing Topics

1. Narrate an event that happened in your childhood at school. How did you feel?

2. Who was your childhood role model? Was it a parent, teacher, or another adult? Explain why you respected this person.

3. Describe what the ideal classroom would look like. Mention the space, the type of teachers, and the activities in an ideal classroom.

READING 9

Musicophilia

Oliver Sacks

Dr. Oliver Sacks is professor of neurology and psychiatry at Columbia University. He has written several best-selling books on case studies of people with neurological disorders. His book *Awakenings* (1973) was made into a film in 1990, starring Robin Williams. This excerpt is taken from his book, *Musicophilia*. As you read this definition essay, also look for patterns of cause and effect and narration.

1   In 1994, Tony Cicoria, a forty-two-year-old orthopedic surgeon, was at a lake for a family gathering. It was a pleasant and breezy afternoon, but he noticed a few storm clouds in the distance. He went to a pay phone outside the pavilion to make a quick call (this was before the age of cell phones). He still

remembers every single second of what happened next: "I was talking to my mother on the phone. I heard thunder in the distance and hung up. The phone was a foot away from where I was standing when I got struck. I remember a flash of light coming out of the phone. It hit me in the face. Then I was flying backwards. Baffled, I looked around. I saw a woman position herself over my body and give it **CPR**. I saw a blue light and my own body on the ground."

CPR: cardiopulmonary resuscitation, a method used to restart the heart and restore breathing

2   After Cicoria's near-death experience, he awoke to great pain from the burns on his face and left foot, where the electrical charge had entered and exited his body. The police came and wanted to call an ambulance, but Cicoria refused, delirious. They took him home instead, where he called his own doctor. His cardiologist suspected a cardiac arrest but could find nothing amiss. Cicoria also consulted a neurologist—he was feeling sluggish and having some difficulties with his memory. A couple of weeks later, when his energy returned, Dr. Cicoria went back to work. There were still some lingering memory problems—he occasionally forgot the names of rare diseases—but all his surgical skills were unimpaired. In another two weeks, his memory problems disappeared, and that, he thought, was the end of the matter. Another month went by.

3   What happened next still fills Cicoria with amazement. Life had returned to normal, seemingly, when "suddenly, over two or three days, there was this insatiable desire to listen to piano music." It was completely unlike anything in his past. He did not own a piano, and the only music he occasionally listened to was rock music. With this sudden longing for piano music, he began to buy recordings and became especially enamored of Chopin's pieces. Cicoria said, "I had the desire to play them. I ordered all the sheet music. At that point, our babysitter asked if she could store her piano in our house—so just when I craved one, a piano arrived. I could hardly read the music, but I started to teach myself." At first, his fingers seemed stiff and awkward.

4   And then, on the heels of this sudden desire for piano music, Cicoria started to hear music in his head. "The first time," he said, "it was in a dream. I woke up, and the music was still in my head. I jumped out of bed and started trying to write down as much as I could remember." This was not too successful—he had never tried to write or notate music before. But whenever he sat down at the piano to work on Chopin, his own music would come and take over: "It had a very powerful presence."

5   The music came from deep inside him. He said, "It's like a radio frequency. If I open myself up, it comes." Now he had to struggle not just with learning to play the Chopin, but to give form to the music continually running in his head, and to try it out on the piano. He said, "I would get up at four in the morning and play until I went to work, and when I got home from work, I was at the piano all evening. My wife was not pleased. I was possessed."

6   By the third month after being struck by lightning, Cicoria—once an easygoing family man who was almost indifferent to music—was inspired, even possessed, by music, and rarely had time for anything else. The music often came in "an absolute torrent" of notes with no breaks and no rests between them, and he would have to give it shape and form. Cicoria continued to work on his piano playing and his compositions. He got books on notation, and soon realized that he needed a music teacher.

7   Some years passed, and this new inspiration never deserted him. He continued to work as a surgeon, but his heart and mind were centered on music. In 2004, he got divorced, and the same year, he had a terrible motorcycle

accident. He made a complete recovery and was back at work two months later. Neither the accident nor his divorce affected his passion for music.

8   After a few years of practicing and playing, Cicoria took part in a ten-day retreat for amateur and professional musicians. He prepared two pieces for his concert: Chopin's "B-flat Minor Scherzo" and his own first composition, which he called "Rhapsody, Opus 1." His playing, and his story, electrified the audience. Many expressed the fantasy that they, too, might be struck by lightning. Concert pianist Erica V. Feidner said that he played with "great passion" and with skill, an astounding feat for someone with virtually no musical background who had taught himself to play at forty-two.

9   What caused Dr. Cicoria's remarkable access of musicality and his sudden love of music? Patients with degeneration of the front parts of the brain sometimes develop a startling release of musical talents as they lose the powers of abstraction and language—but clearly this was *not* the case with Dr. Cicoria. He was articulate and highly competent in every way. There was nothing to suggest that Tony Cicoria had experienced any significant brain damage.

10   So why was there such a delay in the development of Cicoria's musicophilia? What was happening in the six or seven weeks that elapsed between the lightning strike and his sudden eruption of musicality? Changes were presumably occurring in the weeks after the lightning strike, when his brain must have started reorganizing—preparing for musicophilia. New tests of brain function have been developed since Cicoria had his injury in 1994, and he agreed that it would be interesting to investigate this further. But after a moment, he reconsidered, and said that perhaps it was best to let things be. He felt that he had a lucky strike, and the music was a blessing—not to be questioned.

Vocabulary and Comprehension

1. Find a word in paragraph 2 that means "remaining." _____

2. In paragraph 3, what does *insatiable* mean?

    a. unsatisfactory   b. unstable   c. uncontrollable

3. In your own words, what happened to Tony Cicoria? Answer *who*, *what*, *when*, *where*, and *how* questions.

    _____

    _____

    _____

    _____

4. Why was it so astounding that Cicoria became a pianist?

    _____

    _____

    _____

5. According to the author Oliver Sacks, what are some physical causes that may lead someone to become a musicophile?

    _____

    _____

MyWritingLab™
Complete
additional reading
comprehension questions
for this selection at
mywritinglab.com

Critical Thinking

6. Did Cicoria experience any negative effects because of his musicophilia?

_____

_____

_____

7. Who is the audience for this essay?

_____

8. The general purpose of this text is to entertain and inform. What is the specific purpose?

_____

Writing Topics

1. Write about a turning point in your life. Narrate what happened.

2. Argue that music or another art form is important in people's lives.

3. Write about a song that is really important to you. Explain what the song makes you think about or feel.

READING 10

Why We Make Mistakes

Joseph T. Hallinan

Joseph T. Hallinan was a journalist for the *Wall Street Journal*, and he has won the Pulitzer Prize for Investigative Reporting. As you read this illustration essay from his book, *Why We Make Mistakes*, also look for elements of narration and cause and effect.

1   We all know the cliché "To err is human," and it is true enough. When something goes wrong, the cause is overwhelmingly attributed to human error: airplane crashes (70 percent), car wrecks (90 percent), workplace accidents (also 90 percent). You name it, and humans are usually to blame. Many of our most common errors can be attributed to three things: not really seeing, not really paying attention, and trying to do too many things at once.

2   Every day, we look, but we do not always see. In fact, we often have startling kinds of blindness. One type is called "change blindness." About ten years ago, Daniel Simons and Daniel Levin, of Cornell University, designed an experiment. They had "strangers" on campus ask pedestrians for directions. The experiment involved a twist. As the stranger and the pedestrian talk, they are rudely interrupted by two men who pass between them while carrying a door. The interruption is brief—lasting just one second. But during that second, something important happens. One of the men carrying the door trades places with the "stranger." When the door is gone, the pedestrian is confronted with a different person who continues the conversation as if nothing had happened. Would the pedestrians notice that they were talking to someone new? Only seven of the fifteen pedestrians noticed the change. When the actor dressed as a construction worker, and he was changed for another person dressed in the

same clothing, even fewer people noticed the change. Seeing, it turns out, is very hard work.

3   Seeing is especially difficult when people are asked to look for things that usually aren't there. Dr. Jeremy Wolfe, a professor of ophthalmology at Harvard Medical School, has done experiments showing that observers have "quitting thresholds." He asked volunteers to look at busy, packed images and to find a tool, such as a wrench or hammer. If the tool was in the image 50 percent of the time, the volunteers were correct 93 percent of the time. When the tool was rarely present—in one out of a hundred images, their error rate soared. They sped up and quit earlier, spending less time on each image. According to Wolfe, humans are hardwired to quit early when the target is unlikely to be there. And most of the time that response works well enough.

4   So, what happens if someone's job is to find a gun or a tumor? Both baggage screeners at airports and radiologists at hospitals spend the bulk of their time looking for things they rarely see. In the case of radiologists, routine mammograms reveal tumors just 0.3 percent of the time. In other words, 99.7 percent of the time, radiologists won't find what they are looking for. Not surprisingly, radiologists have considerable error rates. Several studies suggest the "miss" rate hovers in the 30 percent range. In one study, doctors at the Mayo Clinic went back and checked the previous "normal" chest X-rays of patients who subsequently developed lung cancer. What they found was horrifying: Up to 90 percent of the tumors were visible in the previous X-rays. The researchers also noted that the cancers had been visible "for months or even years." The radiologists had simply missed them.

5   Finally, another reason we make mistakes is because of **multitasking**. The term, cribbed from the computer word, describes a technique by which a computer can split up its work into many processes or tasks. This allows us to run, say, Microsoft Word while downloading something from the Internet. Most of us think our brains can work in the same way. But multitasking is, for most of us, a mirage. Although we think we are focusing on several activities at once, our attention is actually jumping back and forth between the tasks. There are strict limits to the number of things we can do at one time. Not even a computer, by the way, can multitask; it actually switches back and forth between tasks several thousand times per second, giving us the illusion that everything is happening simultaneously.

multitasking: performing several jobs at once

6   The consequences of multitasking can be deadly. Consider the case of Captain Robert Loft, the pilot of Eastern Airlines Flight 401. While making his final approach to Miami International Airport, he noticed that the landing gear was down, but the indicator light didn't come on. He circled around, leveled off at one thousand feet, and decided to have a look. He couldn't figure it out, so he called in the first officer, and then the flight engineer. Even a flight mechanic from Boeing was flying that day and he, too, came to take a look. Soon, nobody was flying the plane. It went lower and lower. Suddenly, the captain shouted, "What's happening here?"

7   Those were his last words. Five seconds later, the plane plowed into the Everglades and burst into flames, killing everyone on board. A study later determined that the crew had become so engrossed in the task that they had lost awareness of their situation, all because of a $12 light bulb.

8   The crash wasn't a fluke. The experience of flying a perfectly good airplane into the ground is so common that an engineer from Honeywell coined a term for it: "Controlled Flight into Terrain" (CFIT). It is one of the most lethal

hazards in aviation and accounts for 40 percent of all aircraft accidents. Why? Pilots had "task saturation"—trying to do too many things at one time.

9   Divided attention can produce a dangerous condition known as inattention blindness. In this condition, it is possible for a person to look directly at something and still not see it. For instance, a bus driver near Washington, D.C., was talking on a cell phone to his sister when he drove into a bridge and sheared the top of the bus off. Glass and metal rained down on the passengers. The driver later told investigators that he had failed to see the bridge.

10   There are small things we can do to become less error prone. First, we should get enough sleep. Sleepy people make mistakes. It also helps to change our habits and try to look at things afresh. Habit saves us time and mental effort, but it can kill our ability to perceive novel situations. After a while we see only what we expect to see. Finally, we need to slow down. Multitasking is one of the great myths of the modern age.

MyWritingLab™

Complete additional reading comprehension questions for this selection at mywritinglab.com

Vocabulary and Comprehension

1. What introductory style does the author use?
   a. general background   b. anecdote   c. historical

2. Find a word in paragraph 8 that means "an unlikely occurrence." _____

3. Highlight the thesis statement.

4. Underline the topic sentence in paragraphs 2, 3, 5, and 6. Be careful because the topic sentence may not be the first sentence in the paragraph. Look for a sentence that sums up the main idea of the paragraph.

5. Provide an example from the text for each of the following problems.

   a. Change blindness: _____

   _____

   _____

   b. Looking for something that is rarely there: _____

   _____

   _____

   c. Multitasking: _____

   _____

   _____

Critical Thinking

6. Using your own words, define the term "quitting threshold." Also, explain how the phenomenon might be dangerous.

   _____

   _____

   _____

   _____

7. What are some possible rules or strategies that could reduce car and plane accidents? Use your imagination and come up with two or three ideas.

_____

_____

_____

8. What is the general tone of the author toward his subject?
   a. serious and neutral   b. passionate   c. sarcastic   d. sad

9. What is the specific purpose of the text?

_____

_____

Writing Topics

Write about one of the following topics. Remember to explore, develop, and revise and edit your work.

1. What types of mistakes have you made? List some and provide specific examples.

2. What are some types of multitasking that students do? Are you and other students effective at multitasking? Provide evidence to support your answer.

3. Explain the value of making mistakes. What do people learn?

Themes: Our Environment and The Workplace

READING 11

Mother Nature's Melting Pot

Hugh Raffles

Hugh Raffles is an anthropologist and author who writes about the relationship between humans and animals. His most recent book is *Insectopedia*. As you read this cause and effect essay, also look for patterns in illustration and comparison and contrast.

1   The anti-immigrant sentiment sweeping the country, from draconian laws in Arizona to armed militias along the Mexican border, has taken many Americans by surprise. It shouldn't—nativism runs deeply in the United States. Just ask our nonnative animals and plants: They too are commonly labeled as aliens, even though they also provide significant benefits to their new home. But just as America is a nation built by waves of immigrants, our natural landscape is a shifting mosaic of plant and animal life. Like humans, plants and animals arrive unannounced, encounter unfamiliar conditions, and proceed to remake each other and their surroundings.

2   Designating some species as native and others as alien denies this ecological and genetic dynamism. It draws an arbitrary historical line based as much on aesthetics, morality, and politics as on science, a line that creates a mythic time of purity before places were polluted by interlopers. What's more, many of the species we now think of as natives may not be especially well suited to being here. They might be, in an ecological sense, temporary residents, no matter how

permanent they seem to us. These "native" species can have serious effects on their environment. Take the mountain pine beetle: Thanks to climate change, its population is exploding in the West, devastating hundreds of thousands of square miles of forest.

3   It's true that some nonnative species have brought with them expensive and well-publicized problems; zebra mussels, nutria, and kudzu are prime examples. But even these notorious villains have ecological or economic benefits. Zebra mussels, for example, significantly improve water quality, which increases populations of small fish, invertebrates, and seaweeds—and that, in turn, has helped expand the number of larger fish and birds. Indeed, nonnative plants and animals have transformed the American landscape in unmistakably positive ways. Honeybees were introduced from Europe in the 1600s, and new stocks from elsewhere in the world have landed at least eight times since. They have succeeded in making themselves indispensable, economically and symbolically. In the process, they have made us grateful that they arrived, stayed, and found their place.

4   But the honeybee is a lucky exception. Today, a species' immigration status often makes it a target for eradication, no matter its effect on the environment. Eucalyptus trees, charged with everything from suffocating birds with their resin to elevating fire risk with their peeling bark, are the targets of large-scale felling. Yet eucalyptuses are not only majestic trees popular with picnickers, but are also one of the few sources of nectar available to northern Californian bees in winter and a vital destination for migrating monarch butterflies.

5   There are plenty of less controversial examples. Nonnative shad, crayfish, and mud snails provide food for salmon and other fish. Nonnative oysters on the Pacific Coast build reefs that create habitat for crab, mussels, and small fish, appearing to increase these animals' populations. The ice plant, a much-vilified Old World succulent, spreads its thick, candy-colored carpet along the California coast. Concerned that it is crowding out native wildflowers, legions of environmental volunteers rip it from the sandy soil and pile it in slowly moldering heaps along the cliffs. Yet the ice plant, introduced to the West Coast at the beginning of the twentieth century to stabilize railroad tracks, is an attractive plant that can also deter erosion of the sandstone bluffs on which it grows.

6   Efforts to restore ecosystems to an imagined pristine state almost always fail. Once a species begins to thrive in a new environment, there's little we can do to stop it. Indeed, these efforts are often expensive and can increase rather than relieve environmental harm. An alternative is to embrace the impurity of our cosmopolitan natural world and, as some biologists are now arguing, to consider the many ways that nonnative plants and animals—not just the natives—benefit their environments and our lives.

7   Last month, along with 161 other immigrants from more than 50 countries, I attended an oath-swearing ceremony in Lower Manhattan and became a citizen of the United States. In a brief speech welcoming us into a world of new rights and responsibilities, the presiding judge emphasized our diversity. It is, he said, the ever-shifting diversity that immigrants like us bring to this country that keeps it dynamic and strong. These familiar words apply just as meaningfully to our nation's nonnative plants and animals. Like the humans with whose lives they are so entangled, they too are in need of a thoughtful and inclusive response.

Eucalyptus trees

Vocabulary and Comprehension

1. Find a word in paragraph 1 that means "harsh." _____

2. Underline the thesis statement of this essay.

3. What are some positive effects that at least two nonnative species might have on the environment?

   _____

   _____

   _____

4. What measures do well-meaning eco-volunteers take to protect the landscape from nonnative species?

   _____

5. Why do such measures usually fail?

   _____

   _____

   _____

Critical Thinking

6. Why does the author compare anti-immigrant sentiment to plants and animals?

   _____

   _____

7. Why does the author think it is wrong to categorize some species as nonnative and others as native?

   _____

   _____

   _____

   _____

8. What lessons about human immigration can we learn from animal and plant migration?

   _____

   _____

Writing Topics

Write about one of the following topics. Remember to explore, develop, and revise and edit your work.

1. What are some causes and effects of natural disasters?

2. What are some reasons that people move to other countries?

3. Most Americans are descendants of immigrants. Luis Gutierrez, a politician, once said that the older immigrants fear the newcomers. Write a response. For instance, you can define a "real American" or discuss fear of outsiders, or you could explain how you are a descendant of immigrants.

READING 12

Aunt Tee

Maya Angelou

Maya Angelou is a poet, historian, civil rights activist, and writer. In this next essay from her collection *I Wouldn't Take Nothing for My Journey Now*, Angelou writes about an important person in her life. As you read this description essay, also look for elements of narration and comparison and contrast.

1   Aunt Tee was a Los Angeles member of our extended family. She was seventy-nine when I met her, sinewy, strong, and the color of old lemons. She wore her coarse, straight hair, which was slightly streaked with gray, in a long braided rope across the top of her head. With her high cheekbones, old gold skin, and almond eyes, she looked more like an Indian chief than an old black woman. (Aunt Tee described herself and any favored member of her race as Negroes. *Black* was saved for those who had incurred her disapproval.)

2   She had retired and lived alone in a dead, neat ground-floor apartment. Wax flowers and china figurines sat on elaborately embroidered and heavily starched doilies. Sofas and chairs were tautly upholstered. The only thing at ease in Aunt Tee's apartment was Aunt Tee.

3   I used to visit her often and perch on her uncomfortable sofa just to hear her stories. She was proud that after working thirty years as a maid, she spent the next thirty years as a live-in housekeeper, carrying the keys to rich houses and keeping meticulous accounts. "Living in lets the white folks know Negroes are as neat and clean as they are, sometimes more so. And it gives the Negro maid a chance to see white folks ain't no smarter than Negroes. Just luckier. Sometimes."

4   Aunt Tee told me that once she was housekeeper for a couple in Bel Air, California, and lived with them in a fourteen-room ranch house. There was a day maid who cleaned, and a gardener who daily tended the lush gardens. Aunt Tee oversaw the workers. When she began the job, she cooked and served a light breakfast, a good lunch, and a full three- or four-course dinner to her employers and their guests. Aunt Tee said she watched them grow older and leaner. After a few years, they stopped entertaining and ate dinner, hardly seeing each other at the table. Finally, they sat in a dry silence as they ate evening meals of soft scrambled eggs, melba toast, and weak tea. Aunt Tee said she saw them growing old but didn't see herself aging at all.

5   She became the social maven. She started "keeping company" (her phrase) with a chauffeur down the street. Her best friend and her friend's husband worked in service only a few blocks away.

6   On Saturdays, Aunt Tee would cook a pot of pigs' feet, a pot of greens, fry chicken, make potato salad, and bake a banana pudding. Then, that evening, her friends—the chauffeur, the other housekeeper, and her husband—would come to Aunt Tee's **commodious** live-in quarters. There the four would eat

commodious: large; spacious

and drink, play records and dance. As the evening wore on, they would settle down to a serious game of bid whist. Naturally, during this revelry, jokes were told, fingers were snapped, feet were patted, and there was a great deal of laughter.

7   Aunt Tee said that what occurred during every Saturday party startled her and her friends the first time it happened. They had been playing cards, and Aunt Tee, who had just won the bid, held a handful of trumps. She felt a cool breeze on her back and sat upright and turned around. Her employers had cracked her door open and beckoned to her. Aunt Tee, a little peeved, laid down her cards and went to the door. The couple backed away and asked her to come into the hall, and there they both spoke and won Aunt Tee's sympathy forever.

8   "Theresa, we don't mean to disturb you," the man whispered, "but you all seem to be having such a good time."

9   The woman added, "We hear you and your friends laughing every Saturday night, and we'd just like to watch you. We don't want to bother you. We'll be quiet and just watch."

10   The man said, "If you'll just leave your door ajar, your friends don't need to know. We'll never make a sound." Aunt Tee said she saw no harm in agreeing, and she talked it over with her company. They said it was OK with them, but it was sad that the employers owned the gracious house, the swimming pool, three cars, and numberless palm trees, but had no joy. Aunt Tee told me that laughter and relaxation had left the house; she agreed it was sad.

11   That story has stayed with me for nearly thirty years, and when a tale remains fresh in my mind, it almost always contains a lesson which will benefit me. I draw the picture of the wealthy couple standing in a darkened hallway, peering into a lighted room where black servants were lifting their voices in merriment and comradery, and I realize that living well is an art which can be developed. Of course, you need the basic talents to build upon: They are a love of life and the ability to take great pleasure from small offerings, an assurance that the world owes you nothing, and awareness that every gift is exactly that, a gift. Because of the routines we follow, we often forget that life is an ongoing adventure.

Vocabulary and Comprehension

1. What is a *social maven* in paragraph 5?

    _____

2. What is the meaning of *revelry* in paragraph 6?

    _____

3. Angelou uses descriptive imagery. Descriptive imagery includes active verbs, adjectives, and other words that appeal to the senses (sight, smell, touch, sound, taste). Underline at least six examples of descriptive imagery.

4. Why was it so important for Aunt Tee to be neat and tidy?

    _____

    _____

Critical Thinking

5. Why does Angelou call her aunt's apartment *dead* in paragraph 2?

   _____

   _____

6. In paragraph 3, Angelou quotes Aunt Tee. Why does the author use the slang word *ain't*?

   _____

   _____

7. What can you infer about the lives of Aunt Tee's wealthy employers? What types of people are they?

   _____

   _____

   _____

8. In paragraph 4, Aunt Tee says that she does not see herself aging. Why does she say this?

   _____

   _____

Writing Topics

Write about one of the following topics. Remember to explore, develop, and revise and edit your work.

1. Write about a time when you saw an event that changed your perception of someone.

2. Angelou tells a story to make a point about living life to the fullest. Write about a moment in time when you felt that you were living life to its fullest. Use descriptive imagery in your writing.

3. Do you live in a clean, organized environment or a messy one? Describe a clean or messy room in your home. (You might reread Angelou's depiction of Aunt Tee's home to get some ideas.)

READING 13

Advertising Appeals

Michael R. Solomon, Greg W. Marshall, and Elnora W. Stuart

The next essay, which appeared in *Marketing: Real People, Real Choices*, focuses on advertising. As you read this classification essay, also look for the illustration and argument writing patterns.

1   An advertising appeal is the central idea of the ad. Some advertisers use an emotional appeal, complete with dramatic color or powerful images, while others bombard the audience with facts. Some feature sexy people or stern-looking experts—even professors from time to time. Different appeals can

work for the same product, from a bland "talking head" to a montage of animated special effects. Although an attention-getting way to say something profound about cat food or laundry detergent is more art than science, there are some common appeals that are highly effective.

2   Testimonials are a useful type of endorsement. A celebrity, an expert, or a "man in the street" states the product's effectiveness. The use of celebrity endorsers is a common but expensive strategy. It is particularly effective for mature products that need to differentiate themselves from competitors, such as Coke and Pepsi, which enlist celebrities to tout one cola over another. For example, Michael Jackson and Shakira have been in Pepsi ads, and Bill Cosby and Bill Gates have endorsed Coke. Makeup and perfume companies also hire well-known faces to promote their brands. For instance, Penelope Cruz advertises L'Oreal mascara, and Nicole Kidman promotes Chanel.

3   A slice-of-life format presents a dramatized scene from everyday life. Slice-of-life advertising can be effective for everyday products such as peanut butter and headache remedies that consumers may feel good about if they see "real" people buying and using them. Tide, for instance, regularly depicts ordinary kids playing a rough and tumble game and arriving home covered in dirt and grass stains. Old El Paso shows a family of four sitting around the kitchen table enjoying their tacos.

4   Fear appeal ads highlight the negative consequences of not using a product. Some fear appeal ads focus on physical harm, while others try to create concern for social harm or disapproval. Mouthwash, deodorant, and dandruff shampoo products play on viewers' concerns about social rejection. Also, life insurance companies successfully use fear appeals, as do ads aimed at changing behaviors, such as messages discouraging drug use or encouraging safe sex. Axe, for instance, has a humorous ad depicting a young man with very dirty, messy hair. The young fellow gets ambushed by a group of girls who wash his hair with Axe shampoo. Election campaigns make particular use of fear advertising. For example, during the country's health care debate, many political ads warned about seniors dying and about socialized medicine. Senators regularly warn voters about their opponents' tax plans.

5   Advertising creative types, including art directors, copywriters, photographers, and others, work hard on a "big idea"—a concept that expresses the aspects of the product, service, or organization in a tangible way. The best ads are attention-getting, memorable, and appealing to consumers.

Vocabulary and Comprehension

1. Find two words in paragraph 2 that mean the same thing as "promote."

   _____   _____

2. Highlight the thesis statement in the essay.

3. What introduction style does the author use? Circle the best answer.
   a. general background   b. anecdote   c. definition

4. Underline the topic sentence in paragraphs 2 to 4.

5. What is the author's purpose?
   a. to persuade   b. to inform   c. to entertain

MyWritingLab™

Complete additional reading comprehension questions for this selection at mywritinglab.com

Critical Thinking

6. Add an appropriate transitional word or phrase to the beginnings of paragraphs 2 to 4. Write your ideas here.

    Para. 2 _____

    Para. 3 _____

    Para. 4 _____

7. Include an additional example of each type of ad. Think about some ads that you have seen.

    testimonial _____

    _____

    _____

    slice-of-life _____

    _____

    _____

    fear appeal _____

    _____

    _____

8. What are ethical problems with fear-appeal ads? Think of examples to support your point.

    _____

    _____

    _____

    _____

9. Which type of advertising is most effective, in your opinion? Which type of ad is least effective? Explain your answers.

    Most effective: _____

    _____

    _____

    Least effective: _____

    _____

    _____

Writing Topics

Write about one of the following topics. Remember to explore, develop, and revise and edit your work.

1. Develop another way to classify advertising into at least three categories. List characteristics and examples of each category.

2. Describe a very effective advertising campaign. Include details to support your point.

3. What products have been elevated into necessities when they are actually quite useless? Have you ever been influenced to buy a useless item because of a really good advertisement? Write about the power of advertising to influence people.

READING 14

Is Anything Private Anymore?

Sean Flynn

Sean Flynn has written for *Parade* magazine, *Esquire*, and *GQ*. Notice that some newspaper and magazine articles contain short, one-sentence paragraphs. As you read this cause and effect essay, also look for elements of illustration.

1   Kevin Bankston was a closet smoker who hid his habit by sneaking cigarettes outside his San Francisco office. He expected anonymity on a big city street. But in 2005, an online mapping service that provided ground-level photographs captured him smoking—and made the image available to anyone on the Internet. This year, Google's Street View project caught him again.

2   Coincidence? Absolutely. Yet Bankston's twice-documented smoking highlights a wider phenomenon: Privacy is a withering commodity for all of us.

3   What you buy, where you go, whom you call, the Web sites you visit, the e-mails you send—all of that information can be monitored and logged. "When you're out in public, it's becoming a near certainty that your image will be captured," says the newly nonsmoking Bankston.

4   Should you care? I've interviewed numerous people on all sides of the privacy debate to find out just how wary we should be.

5   One thing is clear: In today's world, maintaining a cocoon of privacy simply isn't practical. Need a mortgage or a car loan? A legitimate lender is going to verify a wealth of private information, including your name and address, date of birth, Social Security number, and credit history. We all make daily trade-offs for convenience and thrift: Electronic tollbooths mean you don't have to wait in the cash-only lane, but your travel habits will be tracked. The Piggly Wiggly discount card saves you $206 on your annual grocery bill, but it counts how many doughnuts and six-packs you buy. MySpace posts make it easy to keep in touch with friends, but your comments live on.

6   So how do you live in a digital world and still maintain a semblance of privacy? Experts say it's crucial to recognize that those bits of data are permanent—a trail of electronic crumbs that is never swept away, available to anyone with the skills and inclination to sniff it out.

7   Privacy may not feel like much of an issue for those in their teens and twenties. They've grown up chronicling their lives on popular social networking sites like Facebook for easy retrieval by friends and strangers alike. But some young people don't realize that what was funny to college buddies might not amuse a law-firm recruiter. Employers regularly research job applicants on the Internet. Some colleges are helping students prepare: Duke University hosts seminars on how to clean up a Facebook account. "You learn why posting pictures of you riding the mechanical bull at Shooters is a bad idea," says Sarah Ball, a senior whose own page is secure and clean.

8   Amy Polumbo, twenty-two, restricted her page on Facebook to a hundred or so people who knew her password. "It was a way for me to keep in touch with friends all over the country," she says. But after she was crowned Miss New Jersey in June, someone downloaded pictures of her and threatened blackmail. She thwarted the attempt by releasing the photos herself (they're quite innocent) but suffered weeks of embarrassment.

9   "I know how easy it is for someone to take advantage of you on the Internet," says Polumbo. "The Web is a place where people can destroy your reputation if you're not careful."

10   In fact, all kinds of transgressions now are easily retrievable. An employee at a New York City bank watched his reputation shrink when his colleagues pulled up an article from a small-town newspaper about his drunk-driving arrest two years earlier. Divorce lawyers have been issuing subpoenas for electronic tollbooth records to use in custody cases. (You say you're home at 6 p.m. to have dinner with the kids, but Fast Lane says you're getting off the Massachusetts Turnpike at 7 p.m.) Abbe L. Ross, a divorce lawyer in Boston, finds a gold mine in computers: financial data, e-mails, what Web sites a soon-to-be-ex spouse looks at and for how long. "I love to look through hard drives," she says.

11   Details about you already are stashed in enormous databases. Unless you pay cash for everything, data brokers almost certainly have compiled a profile of you that will be bought and sold dozens of times to marketers and direct-mail firms. "There's almost nothing they can't find out about you," says Jack Dunning, who worked in the junk-mail business for thirty-five years. Right now, there are roughly 50,000 such lists for sale in a $4 billion a year industry. Now junk mail is going digital: Companies can use personal profiles and records from Internet search engines to tailor advertising—both what you see and precisely when you see it—to individual consumers.

12   And new databases are being created all the time. Most of the major proposals for health-care reform, for example, include compiling medical records into easily and widely accessible digital files. In July, the FBI requested $5 million to pay the major phone companies to maintain logs of your calls—information the Feds can't legally stockpile themselves but might find useful later.

ubiquitous: everywhere   13   Surveillance cameras are increasingly **ubiquitous** in our post-9/11 world. Indeed, New York City plans to ring the financial district with them, as central London did several years ago.

14   Of course, there are upsides. London's network of cameras helped capture failed car bombers in June. And streamlined electronic medical records would make health care safer and more efficient.

15   Still, most experts say we need to be vigilant about the increasing encroachments on our privacy.

16   The ability to collect information and images has outpaced the security available to protect them. Since January 2005, nearly 160 million personal records have been stolen or inadvertently posted online.

17   And even if information stays secure, the big question remains: Who should be allowed to access these databases? The FBI might find evidence against a few bad guys in millions of phone records, but the government could track all

of your calls too. (President Bush has acknowledged that the National Security Agency tapped phone calls, though whose and how many is unknown.)

18   Even more disturbing: All of those data files can be linked and cross-referenced. At the 2001 Super Bowl in Tampa, fans were scanned with cameras linked to facial-recognition software in a hunt for suspected terrorists. Some privacy advocates worry that police could videotape anti-war marches and create a library of digital faces or start mining Web pages for personal information.

19   Kevin Bankston was only caught smoking, but he's worried about larger implications: "The issue isn't whether you have anything to hide," he says. "The issue is whether the lack of privacy would give the government an inordinate amount of power over the populace. This is about maintaining the privacy necessary for us to flourish as a free society."

Vocabulary and Comprehension

MyWritingLab™

Complete additional reading comprehension questions for this selection at mywritinglab.com

1. In paragraph 8, what does the word *thwarted* mean?
    a. helped   b. answered   c. prevented

2. Highlight the thesis statement.

3. This essay was written in a journalistic style with very short paragraphs. Revise this essay by drawing lines to indicate where paragraphs could be joined.

4. Why do we accept invasions of privacy? Sum up the main idea of paragraph 5.

    _____

    _____

5. Which sentence best sums up the main idea of paragraph 7?
    a. Privacy may not feel like much of an issue for those in their teens and twenties.
    b. But some young people don't realize that what was funny to college buddies might not amuse a law-firm recruiter.
    c. Duke University hosts seminars on how to clean up a Facebook account.

6. According to paragraph 11, why do companies pay for information about you?

    _____

    _____

Critical Thinking

7. Why do people put potentially embarrassing photos and information on sites such as Facebook? Use your own ideas.

    _____

    _____

8. According to the essay, what are three possible consequences of posting personal photos online of partying, etc.? Provide examples from the text.

   _____

   _____

   _____

   _____

9. Why does this essay begin and end with a reference to Kevin Bankston? What does his example show?

   _____

   _____

   _____

Writing Topics

1. At the end of the essay, Bankston says, "The issue is whether the lack of privacy would give the government an inordinate amount of power over the populace." Write a cause and effect essay about the possible consequences if the government compiles private information about citizens.

2. Reflect on how social networking sites serve to make everybody feel famous in their own social circles. Illustrate how this is true with examples from your life.

3. How has technology changed during your lifetime? Trace some of the technological advances that you have witnessed, and explain whether they are positive or negative.

READING 15

The Beeps

Josh Freed

Josh Freed is an award-winning journalist and documentary film writer. In the following example of an illustration essay, also look for elements of comparison and contrast and cause and effect.

1   Uh-oh. Something in the house is beeping—but what? Is it the stove announcing that dinner is cooked? Or is the dryer proclaiming my clothes are ready? Is the fridge defrosting, the thermostat adjusting, the smoke alarm dying, or is my cell phone dead? I'm living in an electronic jungle, trained to leap at every beep—if I could just figure out which beep it is.

2   I grew up in a time of easier-to-identify sounds, when telephones ding-a-linged, cash registers ka-chinged, and typewriters clacked; when school bells clanged, fire alarms rang, and ambulance sirens wailed—instead of today's digital whooping. Now they are all being replaced by the beep-beeps and bing-bings that are the frantic soundtrack of the twenty-first century.

3   Many of these high-pitched beeps are strangely hard to locate, even when they are right beside me. I usually fumble around for my cell phone when it rings because I can't figure out which pants pocket it's in—or which pants.

Maybe it's lost under the armchair again? Several times a week, a mystery beeping goes off somewhere in our house, and I run around like a lunatic trying to find whatever it is. I listen to our bookshelves, to our laundry piles, and even to the inside of the fridge. But the beeping always stops long before I crack the mystery.

4   Meanwhile, I am bombarded on every side by other urgent electronic sounds. My car beeps constantly, nagging me to put on my seat belt, or turn off the lights, or lock the trunk, or whatever else it's trying to tell me—probably: "Wipe your shoes before you mess up my floor, mister!" My printer beeps identically when it's out of paper, or out of toner, or when something is jammed—but which is it? My microwave beeps all the time, just for fun.

5   Out in the world, elevators and ATM machines beep constantly. TV shows beep when they bleep out swear words. Store machines beep when they swipe your groceries, or you try to swipe theirs without paying. Then there are security beeps: the loud BEEEEP . . . BEEEEP . . . BEEEEP that says you're about to be run down by a city street cleaner that's backing up; the shrill beep-beep-beep-beep that says you have 15 seconds to punch in the house alarm code or an old-fashioned siren will go off alerting a security firm that you are an intruder in your own home. The simple but dreaded beep of an airline security wand means it's time to start your striptease act.

6   Even life itself is measured in beeps. Hospitals are full of machines whose soft beeps indicate you are still alive. "I beep, therefore I am." We are born into the world in a noisy jungle of beeping medical monitors and wires. We will probably leave it the same way—for most of us, the world will end with a beep, not a bang.

7   Who would have guessed the sound of the twenty-first century would be the cry of the cartoon Road Runner, the fast-stepping bird that was always pursued by Wile E. Coyote, crying beep-beep as it ran? Today we are all Road Runners, frantically beeping as we run for our lives, chased by our own high-speed machines and hectic lifestyles.

8   Beep-beep! Fasten your seat belt. Beep-beep! You have another new e-mail . . . NOW. "BEEP! BEEP! Hello, we value your call, but we can't be bothered to take it now, so please don't speak until the beep." Electronic sounds have become so widespread, ornithologists report many birds are now mimicking our beeps, buzzes, and chirps as part of their mating songs. There are parrots that sound like cell phones, mockingbirds that mimic microwaves, and white-bellied caiques that do perfect car alarms.

9   Will the entire animal kingdom eventually chirp, roar, and growl electronically? Or will a new generation of humans choose more soothing sounds, like a phone ring that sounds exactly like birdsong, instead of vice-versa? Or an alarm clock that sounds like a rooster? Or a cash register that once again makes a genuine ka-ching? Perhaps we will all have truly personalized ring tones made by gentle New Age mechanical voices that show some respect for our space: "Jossshhh . . . This is your sto-o-ove speaking. Dinner is ready whenever you are, but don't rush—I'll keep it warm. Sorry if I disturbed you." "Suu-ssan . . . This is your phone ringing. Suu-ssan. I'm in your brown purse, under your make-up and your dirty gym socks. Will you take the call . . . or should I?" To beep or not to beep? That is the question future generations must face. But for now, I've got to run. That beeping just started again, and I've just figured out what it is: my computer.

Vocabulary and Comprehension

1. Find a word in paragraph 8 that means "imitating." _____

2. Freed states that he is "living in an electronic jungle." What does he mean?

    _____

    _____

3. The author discusses three main locations where he is bombarded with electronic beeps. List at least three locations and give examples of some noise-making machines in each category.

    _____

    _____

    _____

    _____

    _____

4. How has new office technology affected nature?

    _____

    _____

Critical Thinking

5. Why is the author frustrated with the new technology? Give at least two reasons.

    _____

    _____

    _____

6. What is the tone of the essay? Circle the best answer.
    a. serious   c. humorous
    b. angry   d. neutral

7. The author is indirectly comparing two worlds. What are they?

    _____

    _____

Writing Topics

Write about one of the following topics. Remember to explore, develop, and revise and edit your work.

1. In your daily life, what actions or objects frustrate you? List some examples to support your point.

2. What is your most valuable possession? Give examples of why it is valuable.

3. Does modern technology make life easier or was life better when technology was simpler? Use examples to support your point of view.

Themes: Spies and Hackers and The Legal World

READING 16

The Criminal Justice Process

John Randolph Fuller

John Randolph Fuller teaches criminology at the University of West Georgia. He has also been a parole officer and criminal justice planner. This excerpt is taken from his book *Criminal Justice Mainstream and Crosscurrents*. As you read this process essay, also look for elements of illustration and cause and effect.

1   In April 1983, the pelvic portion of a female torso was found on the banks of the Mississippi River near Davenport, Iowa. In an autopsy, the pathologist estimated that the victim was between eighteen and forty years old, had probably given birth, and had likely been dismembered with a chainsaw. With the help of techniques considered cutting-edge at the time, including DNA evidence, investigators matched the woman's characteristics to those of Joyce Klindt, a Davenport woman who had gone missing the month before. Eventually, her husband admitted murdering her, cutting her up with a chainsaw, and dumping her remains in the river.

2   The criminal justice system is extremely complex. It is clear to most observers of the system that only a very small percentage of the crimes committed result in someone going to prison. The criminal justice system is frustrating not only for the general public, but also for those who work in the system, as well as for victims, offenders, and their respective families because it is close to being overloaded. It is useful to envision the criminal justice system as a large funnel in which cases move downward toward their final disposition. The problem with the funnel is that it is too small to hold all the cases, and so a considerable amount of leakage occurs. Police officers, prosecutors, and judges use discretion to decide which cases are pushed further into the funnel of the criminal justice system and which ones are kicked out.

3   Processing criminal cases begins with reported crimes. At the wide mouth of the funnel are all the crimes committed in society, such as murder, rape, burglary, insurance fraud, shoplifting, and car theft. It includes all the acts that can be defined as crime whether they have been reported or not. Many, maybe even most, crimes are never reported, or if they are, they get handled informally and never make it into the official crime reporting systems. Criminologists call these unreported acts the dark figures of crime. A bit lower and at a point narrower in the funnel are crimes known to the police. These are the behaviors that the police include in their reports and are officially measured. However, individual police officers or police administrators can exercise considerable discretions in determining just how a behavior will be categorized for reporting purposes.

4   After a crime has been reported, police investigate and try to solve the crime. The investigation into the death of Joyce Klindt has been cited as a classic example of good investigation, and it set precedents for the use of scientific evidence in courts. But such success stories are not the norm. In probing the 1996 murder of JonBenet Ramsey, a local police detective was accused of making crucial mistakes in the investigation. The investigation into the little girl's death is ongoing with no clear results to date. In other less sensational cases, police investigate to the best of their abilities but must deal with limited resources, poor physical evidence, a cold trail, or just bad luck. Typically,

police gather tissue samples and fingerprints, talk with witnesses and victims, and examine police records of potential suspects. Sometimes, the evidence is gathered quickly, and a suspect is apprehended at once. Other times, cases languish and are solved years later or never solved at all.

5   Once the police have enough evidence of a crime, they make an arrest. It should come as no surprise that the police do not make an arrest for every crime they detect. In fact, clearance rates can vary widely, depending on the type of crime and the priorities of the police department. For instance, most Driving Under the Influence (DUI) offenses go undetected, but proactive police practices such as sobriety checkpoints can greatly increase the arrest statistics for a police agency. Arrests are an important measure in our crime funnel because they provide a good indication of what will happen in the rest of the criminal justice system. Arrests provide the system with the cases it must handle.

6   After a suspect is arrested, the police must make an official report of the charges. Booking occurs at the police station, where a suspect's name, age, and address are recorded, as well as information on the time, place, and reason for arrest. Usually, a photograph and fingerprints are taken, and the suspect's clothing and personal effects are stored. The suspect is usually placed in a holding cell until he or she can be questioned further. The suspect is advised of her rights and signs the report that she understands her rights.

7   Of all the arrests made by the police, only a percentage result in a person being charged with a crime by the prosecutor and funneled deeper into the criminal justice system. The discretion used by the prosecutor to decide which cases to eliminate is determined by a number of factors. The first factor is resources. The decision to prosecute is dependent on personnel, budget, space, and agency priorities. The prosecutor may have too many other cases deemed more important, or may decide there is insufficient evidence to charge a suspect. The prosecutor may think that the police made too many procedural errors. Finally, the prosecutor may have personal or agency priorities concerning what types of cases will be pressed. Political corruption cases may be encouraged or discouraged depending on the part affiliation of the state attorney versus the defendant.

8   Suspects must be brought before a judge within a reasonable time of their arrest for an initial appearance. At this stage, the defendant is formally charged with a crime and will respond by pleading guilty, not guilty, or **no contest** at a first court hearing or arraignment. The defendants then have a preliminary hearing where the prosecutor presents evidence to show that the defendant has committed the crime, also known as probable cause. The judge decides if the defendant will be granted bail. Bail is money paid to the court to ensure that a suspect who is released from jail will appear in court.

9   Few cases actually make it to the trial phase of the criminal justice process. Many cases get resolved by plea-bargaining, a negotiation between defense attorneys and prosecutors that results in some type of punishment. Of the cases that go to trial, only a small percentage end up in guilty verdicts that require further processing of the case. Some defendants are acquitted or found not guilty. Sometimes a case is dismissed because the prosecution is unable to present a viable case against the defendant. Most of the legal decisions are made behind the scenes, and the excitement and drama in the courtroom are actually quite rare.

no contest: the defendant does not admit guilt or proclaim innocence

10   The criminal justice system is very complex from the initial police investigation to the final verdict in a trial. The funnel analogy serves to point out how the numbers of cases dwindle drastically as they go through the criminal justice system.

Vocabulary and Comprehension

1. What are *the dark figures of crime*? See paragraph 3.

    _____

2. Highlight the thesis statement.

3. What are some obstacles police face when they investigate a crime?

    _____

    _____

4. What are some factors that prosecutors must consider before deciding to prosecute a case?

    _____

    _____

    _____

    _____

    _____

5. What type of introductory style does the author use?
    a. opposing position   b. anecdote   c. definition

Critical Thinking

6. Using your own words, explain how criminal cases are processed in the criminal justice system.

    _____

    _____

    _____

    _____

    _____

7. Why does the author refer to a funnel when explaining the criminal justice system?

    _____

    _____

8. In paragraph 2, the author mentions that many crimes are never reported. Using your own ideas, give some reasons why a victim may not want to report a crime.

   _____

   _____

   _____

9. In paragraph 9, the author states that many cases may get resolved through plea bargain. Think of some reasons why a defense attorney and a prosecutor might want to avoid a court trial, and therefore, want to plea bargain.

   _____

   _____

   _____

   _____

Writing Topics

1. Have you or someone you know ever been a victim of crime or conducted a criminal act? What did you do? Describe the process you went through.

2. Describe some steps people should take to be safer on their college campus or in their neighborhood.

3. Argue that certain types of criminals are treated too leniently or too harshly.

READING 17

How Spies Are Caught

This process essay recounts how spies are caught. As you read the text, also look for definition and cause and effect writing patterns.

1   Espionage is a high-risk criminal offense. The traitor must fear arrest for the rest of his or her life, as the statute of limitations does not apply to espionage. Former National Security Agency employee Robert Lipka was arrested in 1996—thirty years after he left NSA and twenty-two years after his last contact with Soviet intelligence. There are four principal ways by which spies are detected: Reporting by U.S. sources within the foreign intelligence service, routine counterintelligence monitoring, a tip from a friend or spouse, or the traitor's own mistakes.

2   Of the Americans who held a security clearance who have been arrested for espionage, about half were caught as a result of information provided by a defector from the foreign intelligence service or an agent or friend within the foreign service that the spy was working for. People who betray their country often have little fear of being caught because they think they are smarter than everyone else. They think they can easily get away with it. However, no matter how smart or clever a spy may be, he or she has no protection against U.S. Government sources within the other intelligence service.

3   If the spy is not reported by sources within the other intelligence service, there is a strong likelihood of detection through routine counterintelligence

operations. Of the cleared Americans arrested for espionage or attempted espionage during the past twenty years, 26 percent were arrested before they could do any damage, and 47 percent were caught during their first year of betrayal. This is not surprising, as counterintelligence agents know many of the foreign intelligence officers active in the United States and know where they work, where they live, where they hang out, and how they ply their trade. Any would-be spy who doesn't know how the counterintelligence system works is likely to be caught in the counterintelligence web.

4   Espionage usually requires keeping or preparing materials at home, traveling to signal sites or secret meetings at unusual times and places, a change in one's financial status with no corresponding change in job income, and periods of high stress that affect behavior. All of these changes in the normal pattern of behavior often come to the attention of other people and must be explained. Other people become suspicious and pass their suspicions on. This sometimes comes out during the periodic security clearance reinvestigation.

5   Spying is a lonely business. To explain these changes in behavior, or because of a need to confide in someone else, spies often confide in a spouse or try to enlist the help of a friend. The friend or spouse in whom the spy confides often does not remain a friend or loyal spouse after he or she realizes what is going on.

6   Most people who betray their country are not thinking rationally, or they would not be involved in such a self-destructive activity. They are driven, in large part, by irrational emotional needs to feel important, successful, powerful, or to get even or to take risks. These emotional needs are out of control, so the same emotional needs that lead them to betray also cause them to flaunt their sudden affluence or to brag about their involvement in some mysterious activity. Because they are so mixed up psychologically, they make mistakes that get them caught.

Vocabulary and Comprehension Questions

1. Find a word in paragraph 6 that means "to show off." _____

2. What are the four ways in which spies are usually caught?

   _____

   _____

   _____

   _____

3. Give an example of the following types of support.

   Statistic: _____

   _____

   Anecdote: _____

   _____

4. How might a friend or coworker suspect that someone is a spy?

   _____

   _____

MyWritingLab™
Complete additional reading comprehension questions for this selection at mywritinglab.com

Critical Thinking

5. Give at least three reasons that people betray government secrets.

   _____

   _____

   _____

6. By making inferences, determine some consequences of espionage on the individual spy.

   _____

   _____

   _____

7. In your opinion, how does treachery affect a country?

   _____

   _____

   _____

Writing Topics

Write about one of the following topics. Remember to explore, develop, and revise and edit your work.

1. Many people feel insecure in this post-9/11 society. What steps can people take to feel safe in their own homes? Explain.

2. Most people value their privacy. Should government agencies in the United States have the right to spy on citizens by any means?

3. These days, citizens can use social media tools to spy on each other. For example, teachers and police officers have been caught on cell phone videos doing misdeeds. Ordinary people have also been humiliated if they have done something embarrassing and it was caught on video and posted online. What are some benefits or disadvantages of citizen spying?

READING 18

My Relentless Pursuit

Amanda Enayati

Amanda Enayati's work has appeared in the *Washington Post* and *Detroit News*. Her writing also appears in *Let Me Tell You Where I've Been: New Writing by Women of the Iranian Diaspora*.

1   In the first twenty-four hours after someone broke into my car in my own driveway, I was mostly mad at my husband. Who leaves a backpack with a BlackBerry and a wallet full of cash and credit cards in the car overnight, with a GPS visible on the dashboard and the freaking car doors unlocked? We might as well have hung a sign on the door that read, "Suckers live here. Welcome!"

2   I had canceled four credit cards and ordered a new BlackBerry before I thought to check Craigslist. It occurred to me that the savvy modern thief would

hock stolen wares online. I did a search in a 40-mile radius of my neighborhood. My GPS was the first thing that popped up. Well, to be honest, I wasn't certain that Garmin Nuvi 265W was my GPS; I didn't remember the model number. Still, it was awfully suspicious. It was the only Garmin on Craigslist that morning.

3   My hands shook as I tapped out what I hoped was a casual e-mail query: "Hi!! I could TOTALLY use a GPS. Is this one still available? Where are you located? Thanks!!! Jasmine."

4   The reply came in less than minute. The seller described accessories that were painfully familiar: the dash mount and the auto charger—no box, no manual, and no receipt. He listed an address for pickup at an outdoor mall in San Mateo, about five miles away, and asked for my telephone number so he could call me. He signed his name "John," but the name listed in the parenthesis next to his email address read, "Harry Sham." *The nerve.*

5   At this point, I hadn't called the cops. Our car was unlocked, after all, so it was almost as if we deserved to get robbed. But then something peculiar happened. A woman who lived a few blocks away e-mailed to say she found some papers from my wallet, including my business card, in her front yard. She wanted to return them to me, thinking I might have dropped them accidentally. I had to wonder: What else might be dumped around my neighborhood? My kids and I set out on foot for a scavenger hunt. We found my book buyers' card among some bushes and my backpack in someone's driveway, with the BlackBerry still inside. For about a mile up the road, I found pieces of my life, snatched and discarded. I suppose I should have been glad to get my things back. But finding fragments of my private life in people's yards and scattered on the street, in the shrubs and gutters, is a unique kind of psychological torment. Suddenly a routine violation started to feel *really* personal.

6   Aspiring thief, you just never know what you're stepping into when you hit up a random car on a random street. However badass you think you may be, there is someone on the other side of the robbery. And in this particular case, it was someone who had escaped the Iranian Revolution as a child, who had roamed the world alone for five years because her parents couldn't get out, who had watched from a dozen blocks away as the twin towers crumbled, who had just barely clawed her way out of that concentration camp known as late-stage cancer, if only because she was intent on raising her babies, come hell or high water. And all of this before she even turned forty. Can you see how that someone might be way more twisted than you?

7   By the end of that first day, I knew what the thief looked like. I ran his e-mail address through a reverse e-mail finder, which cost me about 15 bucks for a month's worth of "surveillance." He used that same e-mail address to sign up for a low-rent dating site, uploading three pictures of himself and three pictures of his girl Amberley, with a heart tattoo on her right boob. He was a tall linebacker type with an emerging belly, a blond buzz cut, and piercing blue eyes that seemed to issue a dare. He had not posted his whole name, but I knew what I had to work with: John F, Caucasian, twenty-three years old, from San Mateo. His moniker was Johnny Boi.

8   At the time, I was still dabbling. Then two events on Wednesday pushed my hand. That morning, an elderly woman a few blocks away had found some more papers in her yard, one of them particularly embarrassing. Then, around 9:30 p.m., I received a Facebook message from someone who lived in my old apartment. A good Samaritan had put an envelope through her mail slot that

contained my driver's license with the old address and my now-canceled credit cards. That person included a note saying she had found my stuff on the ground in the San Mateo Caltrain station.

9   That sealed it: I called the police. They were over in fifteen minutes. I filed a report, handed over Johnny Boi's Craigslist ad and his photos from the dating site. The following day, I met a detective I'll call Inspector Vargas. He was not the touchy-feeliest man in the world, but he seemed competent and was hunky in a Marlboro-man sort of way. If my amateur sleuthing impressed him, he did not utter a word about it.

10   He sent a reply to Johnny's now-several-days-old Craigslist ad. I doubted Johnny Boi would respond, and I was right. Inspector Vargas also insisted I find the GPS model and serial number. Without it, he said, there was no way to connect the thief to my stuff. You might suspect someone who has not cleared out her wallet in two years probably didn't record her GPS model and serial number. And you would be correct. Hard as I tried, I couldn't find either. But here's what I did instead. I called all my credit card companies to see if Johnny Boi had managed to slip in any charges in those two or three hours before I shut down the cards. The answer was no, no, no, and yes, McDonald's.

11   Inspector Vargas told me later that credit card thieves will head someplace like a McDonald's or a gas station first to see if the card is still working. *Smart move, Johnny Boi.* Actually, no, it was not smart at all, and here's why: McDonald's has developed one of the best restaurant surveillance systems in the entire world. Now I didn't know this either, but Inspector Vargas did. Because as soon as I got him the time and place Johnny had used my Amex, he went on down to that McDonald's in San Mateo and looked through its surveillance tapes. And there, in his full glory, was my boy. The hat he was sporting didn't even come close to covering him up.

12   By now it was Friday afternoon, and Inspector Vargas does not work weekends or Mondays. I knew if we were to find out anything else about Johnny in the next several days, it would have to be all me. That's when I started to hang out on Johnny's dating site. He hadn't logged on in ten days, and I was hitting a dead end. After more searches, I couldn't find him—but Johnny's girl Amberley came up on a social networking site. Actually her cleavage did, complete with the heart tattoo. Her profile was very public, and prominent among her list of BFFs was, well, you know who. And his profile was public.

13   It was the mother lode: his first and last name, his birth date and birth place, his height, and his high school. I faxed the information to Inspector Vargas. I made sure to point out Johnny Boi's friend Tatiana's comment from three months back: "Dude!!! How do you not work? You win the freak'n lotto? If yes, you need to be spreadin the love." The writer in me could not resist checking out Johnny's two or three angry poems posted on his MySpace. They were pretty good.

14   Two days later, I got a call at 7 a.m. Inspector Vargas had run Johnny Boi's photo by the San Mateo police. They recognized him immediately because our boy was on probation. According to Inspector Vargas, Johnny Boi went on the run soon after the police visited his apartment. That night, Amberley took her man's photo collage off her Web page. The following day someone named Paula wrote on Amberley's page, "Tell your friend that his parents are being harassed by the police. He ought to DO THE RIGHT THING and turn himself in!!" Poor Paula's mood was listed as "anxious." The next day, Inspector Vargas told

me Johnny Boi was in jail. A couple weeks later, Johnny Boi pleaded guilty and served a two-year sentence.

15   I've told this story many times since. I get a lot of reactions because it's a strange tale—to think anyone can find out so much online about a thief. But what took me a long time to realize, what I missed amid my drama of violation and vengeance, was the remarkable displays of kindness I experienced from absolute strangers—people who retrieved scraps of paper from lawns, picked up piles of discarded cards from a dirty train station floor, drove miles to restore someone's belongings, and searched Facebook to find me. If I were mathematically inclined, I might even observe that in my tale, the good guys outnumbered the bad guys, by about ten to one.

Vocabulary and Comprehension

1. In paragraph 2, the word *savvy* means

   a. well-informed   b. misunderstood   c. enthusiastic

2. In paragraph 2, find a word that means "to pawn." _____

3. What type of narration is used?

   a. first person   b. third person

4. The writer survived some traumatic events. List three of them.

   _____

   _____

   _____

   _____

5. Describe three of the writer's personality traits.

   _____

6. What stolen items did the writer get back?

   _____

   _____

Critical Thinking

7. What strategies did the writer use to find out the identity of the thief? List at least six steps that she took.

   _____

   _____

   _____

   _____

   _____

   _____

   _____

MyWritingLab™

Complete additional reading comprehension questions for this selection at mywritinglab.com

8. Why was she so determined to find the thief?

9. In this essay, the thesis is implied but not stated directly. Which sentence best sums up the main idea of the essay?

   a. Thieves should be careful when they steal from people's cars.

   b. I used some ingenuity and online sleuthing to find the man who had robbed me.

   c. There are some horrible people in the world.

   d. Strangers showed remarkable kindness after I was robbed, returning items that they had found.

10. What lessons about human nature did the writer learn from her experience?

Writing Topics

Write about one of the following topics. Remember to explore, develop, and revise and edit your work.

1. Have you ever lost something or had something you valued stolen from you? Narrate what happened.

2. Write about a time when you felt conflicted and had to make a difficult decision. Describe what happened.

3. What is your impression of human nature? Are people essentially good or bad? Provide examples of people you know.

Grammar Glossary

The Basic Parts of a Sentence

Parts of Speech	Definition	Some Examples
Adjective	Adds information about the noun	cautious, cold, easy, happy, slow, strange
Adverb	Adds information about the verb, adjective, or other adverb; expresses time, place, and frequency	cautiously, coldly, easily, happily, slowly, strangely, sometimes, usually, never
Conjunctive adverb	Shows a relationship between two ideas	also, consequently, finally, however, furthermore, moreover, therefore, thus
Coordinating conjunction	Connects two ideas of equal importance	for, and, nor, but, or, yet, so
Determiner	Identifies or determines if a noun is specific or general	a, an, the, this, that, these, those, any, all, each, every, many, some
Interjection	A word expressing an emotion	ouch, yikes, oh
Noun	A person, place, or thing	singular: man, dog, person plural: men, dogs, people
Preposition	Shows a relationship between words (source, direction, location, etc.)	at, to, for, from, behind, above
Pronoun	Replaces one or more nouns	he, she, it, us, ours, themselves
Subordinating conjunction	Connects two ideas when one idea is subordinate (or inferior) to the other idea	after, although, because, unless, until
Verb	Expresses an action or state of being	action verb: run, eat, walk, think state of being or linking verb: is, become, seem

PRACTICE 1

Label each word with one of the following terms.

adjective	noun	verb	adverb
conjunction	preposition	pronoun	interjection

EXAMPLE: easy _adjective_

1. human _____
2. with _____
3. below _____
4. herself _____
5. wow _____
6. was _____
7. whispered _____
8. quickly _____
9. because _____
10. children _____
11. they _____
12. ouch _____

Types of Clauses and Sentences

Other Key Terms	Definition	Example
clause	An **independent clause** has a subject and a verb and expresses a complete idea.	The movie is funny.
	A **dependent clause** has a subject and a verb but cannot stand alone. It "depends" on another clause in order to be complete.	although it is violent
phrase	A group of words that is missing a subject, a verb, or both, and is not a complete sentence	in the morning after the storm
simple sentence	One independent clause that expresses a complete idea	The movie is funny.
complex sentence	At least one dependent clause joined with one independent clause	Although the movie is violent, it conveys an important message.
compound sentence	Two or more independent clauses that are joined together	Some movies are funny, and others are deeply moving.
compound-complex sentence	At least two independent clauses joined with at least one dependent clause	Although the movie is violent, it is very entertaining, and it conveys an important message.

PRACTICE 2

Identify the types of sentences. Beside each sentence, write one of the following:

S   simple sentence
C   compound sentence
CX   complex sentence
CCX   compound-complex sentence

1. I took a university course that was very interesting.   _____

2. In the course, I read a book about a famous women's rights crusader, and I finished the book in an hour.   _____

3. Elizabeth Cady Stanton was born in 1915, and her father was a lawyer, judge, and congressman.   _____

4. When Elizabeth was a young girl, she heard about an unfair law.   _____

5. The law restricted a woman's right to own property.   _____

6. One day, she took a pair of scissors, and she cut out the law from her father's law book.   _____

7. She thought that the law would be cancelled.   _____

8. Her plan didn't work, of course, but her father had an unusual reaction to her act.   _____

9. He put down his pen and looked at Elizabeth.   _____

10. With a serious expression on his face, he told Elizabeth that she could change things, and he asked her to think about his words.   _____

Appendix 2 Irregular Verbs

Irregular Verbs

Base Form	Simple Past	Past Participle	Base Form	Simple Past	Past Participle
arise	arose	arisen	feel	felt	felt
be	was, were	been	fight	fought	fought
beat	beat	beat, beaten	find	found	found
become	became	become	flee	fled	fled
begin	began	begun	fly	flew	flown
bend	bent	bent	forbid	forbade	forbidden
bet	bet	bet	forget	forgot	forgotten
bind	bound	bound	forgive	forgave	forgiven
bite	bit	bitten	forsake	forsook	forsaken
bleed	bled	bled	freeze	froze	frozen
blow	blew	blown	get	got	got, gotten
break	broke	broken	give	gave	given
breed	bred	bred	go	went	gone
bring	brought	brought	grind	ground	ground
build	built	built	grow	grew	grown
burst	burst	burst	hang*	hung	hung
buy	bought	bought	have	had	had
catch	caught	caught	hear	heard	heard
choose	chose	chosen	hide	hid	hidden
cling	clung	clung	hit	hit	hit
come	came	come	hold	held	held
cost	cost	cost	hurt	hurt	hurt
creep	crept	crept	keep	kept	kept
cut	cut	cut	kneel	knelt	knelt
deal	dealt	dealt	know	knew	known
dig	dug	dug	lay	laid	laid
do	did	done	lead	led	led
draw	drew	drawn	leave	left	left
drink	drank	drunk	lend	lent	lent
drive	drove	driven	let	let	let
eat	ate	eaten	lie**	lay	lain
fall	fell	fallen	light	lit	lit
feed	fed	fed	lose	lost	lost

*When *hang* means "to suspend by a rope, as in a form of capital punishment," then it is a regular verb. The past form is *hanged*.

**Lie* can mean "to rest in a flat position." When *lie* means "tell a false statement," then it is a regular verb: *lie, lied, lied*.

Base Form	Simple Past	Past Participle	Base Form	Simple Past	Past Participle
make	made	made	speed	sped	sped
mean	meant	meant	spend	spent	spent
meet	met	met	spin	spun	spun
mistake	mistook	mistaken	split	split	split
pay	paid	paid	spread	spread	spread
prove	proved	proved, proven	spring	sprang	sprung
put	put	put	stand	stood	stood
quit	quit	quit	steal	stole	stolen
read	read	read	stick	stuck	stuck
rid	rid	rid	sting	stung	stung
ride	rode	ridden	stink	stank	stunk
ring	rang	rung	strike	struck	struck
rise	rose	risen	swear	swore	sworn
run	ran	run	sweep	swept	swept
say	said	said	swell	swelled	swollen
see	saw	seen	swim	swam	swum
sell	sold	sold	swing	swung	swung
send	sent	sent	take	took	taken
set	set	set	teach	taught	taught
shake	shook	shaken	tear	tore	torn
shine	shone	shone	tell	told	told
shoot	shot	shot	think	thought	thought
show	showed	shown	throw	threw	thrown
shrink	shrank	shrunk	thrust	thrust	thrust
shut	shut	shut	understand	understood	understood
sing	sang	sung	wake	woke	woken
sink	sank	sunk	wear	wore	worn
sit	sat	sat	weep	wept	wept
sleep	slept	slept	win	won	won
slide	slid	slid	wind	wound	wound
slit	slit	slit	withdraw	withdrew	withdrawn
speak	spoke	spoken	write	wrote	written

Appendix 3 A Quick Guide to Verb Tenses

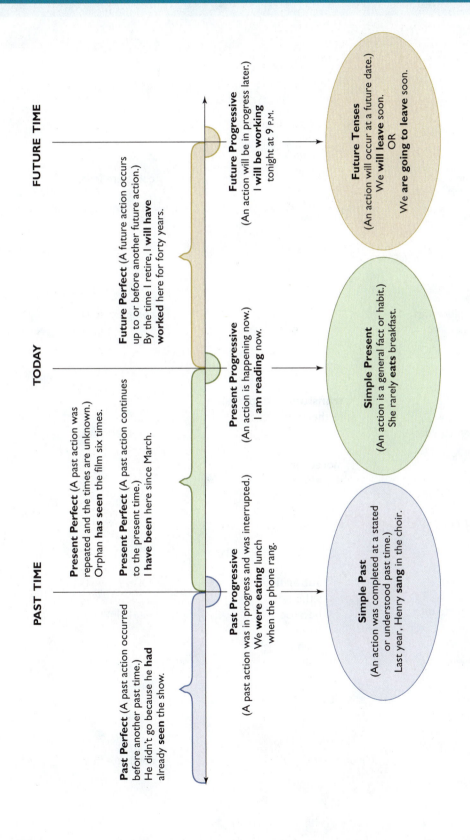

PAST TIME

Past Perfect (A past action occurred before another past time.) He didn't go because he **had** already **seen** the show.

Present Perfect (A past action was repeated and the times are unknown.) Orphan **has seen** the film six times.

Present Perfect (A past action continues to the present time.) I **have been** here since March.

Past Progressive (A past action was in progress and was interrupted.) We **were eating** lunch when the phone rang.

Simple Past (An action was completed at a stated or understood past time.) Last year, Henry **sang** in the choir.

TODAY

Present Progressive (An action is happening now.) I **am reading** now.

Simple Present (An action is a general fact or habit.) She rarely **eats** breakfast.

FUTURE TIME

Future Perfect (A future action occurs up to or before another future action.) By the time I retire, I **will have worked** here for forty years.

Future Progressive (An action will be in progress later.) I **will be working** tonight at 9 P.M.

Future Tenses (An action will occur at a future date.) We **will leave** soon. OR We **are going to leave** soon.

Combining Ideas
in Sentences

Making Compound Sentences

A.

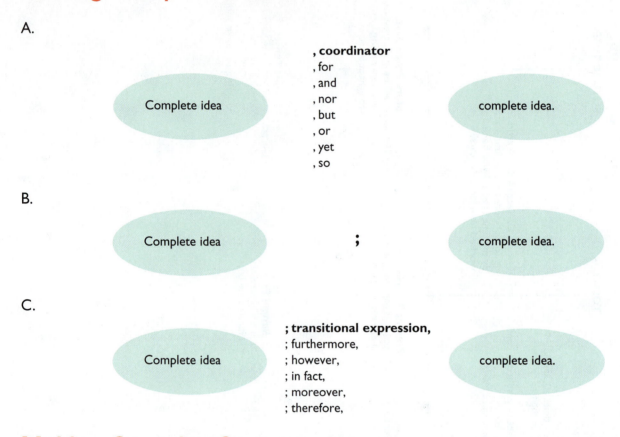

| Complete idea | **, coordinator**
, for
, and
, nor
, but
, or
, yet
, so | complete idea. |

B.

| Complete idea | ; | complete idea. |

C.

| Complete idea | **; transitional expression,**
; furthermore,
; however,
; in fact,
; moreover,
; therefore, | complete idea. |

Making Complex Sentences

D.

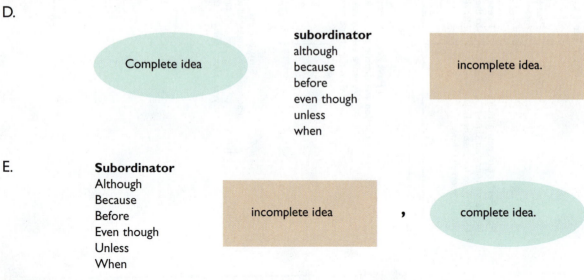

| Complete idea | **subordinator**
although
because
before
even though
unless
when | incomplete idea. |

E.

| **Subordinator**
Although
Because
Before
Even though
Unless
When | incomplete idea | , | complete idea. |

Appendix 5 Punctuation and Mechanics

Apostrophe (')

Use an apostrophe

- to join a subject and a verb together.

  We're late.

- to join an auxiliary with *not*.

  I **can't** come.

- to indicate possession.

  Ross's computer is new.

Comma (,)

Use a comma

- to separate words in a series (more than two things). Place a comma before the final *and*.

  The doctor is kind, considerate, and gentle.

- after an introductory word or phrase.

  In the evenings, Carson volunteered at a hospital.

- around interrupting phrases that give additional information about the subject.

  Alan, an electrician, earns a good salary.

- in compound sentences before the coordinator.

  We worked for hours, and then we rested.

- around relative clauses containing *which*.

  The documents, which are very valuable, are up for auction.

- in quotations, after an introductory phrase or before an ending phrase.

  Picasso said, "Find your passion."

  "Find your passion," Picasso said.

Note: Do not join two complete sentences with a comma!

Colon (:)

Use a colon

- after a complete sentence that introduces a list, or after *the following*.

  The course has the following sections: pregnancy, labor, and lactation.

- after a complete sentence that introduces a quotation.

  Picasso's advice was clear: "Find your passion."

- before an explanation or example.

  Carlos explained what he really needed: a raise.

- to separate the hours and minutes in expressions of time.

  The mall opens at 9:30 A.M.

Semicolon (;)

Use a semicolon to join two independent but related clauses.

  Mahatma Gandhi was a pacifist; he believed in nonviolence.

Quotation Marks (" ")

Use quotation marks around direct speech. When a quotation is a complete sentence, capitalize the first word in the quotation. Place the end punctuation inside the closing quotation marks.

  In his essay, Levi said, "We were interchangeable."

If the end of the quotation is not the end of your sentence, end the quotation with a comma. If your quotation ends with other punctuation, put it inside the closing quotation marks.

  "We were interchangeable," according to Levi.

  "You can't be serious!" she shouted.

  "What did you call me?" he replied.

Integrated Quotations

If you integrate a quotation in a sentence, add quotation marks around the words the speaker quoted.

  Dorothy Nixon calls herself a "terrible mother."

"Inside" Quotations

If one quotation is inside another quotation, add single quotation marks (' ') around the inside quotation.

  Sondra explained, "My mother said, 'Your teacher wants to meet me.'"

Citing Page Numbers

If you are using MLA style, write the page number in parentheses and place it after the quotation. Place the final period *after* the parentheses if the quotation ends the sentence.

  In his essay, Levi says, "We were interchangeable" (4).

Capitalization

Always capitalize

♦ the pronoun *I* and the first word of every sentence.

♦ the days of the week, months, and holidays.

    Tuesday   May 22   Labor Day

♦ the names of specific places, such as buildings, streets, parks, public squares, lakes, rivers, cities, states, and countries.

    Kelvin Street   Lake Erie   White Plains, New York

♦ the names of languages, nationalities, tribes, races, and religions.

    Spanish   Mohawk   Buddhist

♦ the names of specific planets (but not the sun or moon).

    Venus   Saturn   Earth   moon

♦ specific course or program titles (but not when the course is mentioned without the title).

    Economics 201   Nursing 411   an economics course

♦ the titles of specific individuals.

    General Dewitt   Dr. Franklin Mr. Blain

♦ the major words in titles of literary or artistic works.

    The Great Gatsby   *The Diviners*   *Crime and Punishment*

♦ the names of historical eras and movements.

    World War I   Cubism   the Middle Ages

Punctuating Titles

Place the title of short works in quotation marks. Capitalize the major words. Short works include songs, short stories, newspaper and magazine articles, essays, and poems.

    The Beatles' worst song was "Help."

Italicize the title of a longer document. If the title is in handwritten text, underline it. Long works include television series, films, works of art, magazines, books, plays, and newspapers.

Handwritten	We watched the classic movie <u>West Side Story</u>.
Typed	We watched the classic movie *West Side Story*.

Appendix 6   Writing Paragraphs and Essays in Exams

In many of your courses, you will have to answer exam questions with a paragraph or an essay. Although taking any exam can be stressful, you can reduce exam anxiety and increase your chances of doing well by following some preparation and exam-writing strategies.

Preparing for Exams

Here are some steps you can take to help prepare for exams.

- Before you take an exam, make sure that you know exactly what material you should study. Do not be afraid to ask the instructor for clarification. Also ask what materials you should bring to the exam.
- Review the assigned information, class notes, and the textbook, if any.
- Read and repeat information out loud.
- Take notes about important points.
- Study with a friend.

HINT ◁ Predict Exam Questions

An effective study strategy is to predict possible exam questions. Here are some tips:

- Look for important themes in your course outline.
- Study your notes and try to analyze what information is of particular importance.
- Look at your previous exams for the course. Determine whether any questions or subjects are repeated in more than one exam.

After you have looked through the course outline, your notes, and previous exams, write out possible exam questions based on the information that you have collected. Then practice writing the answers to your questions.

Writing Exams

Knowing your material inside and out is a large part of exam writing; however, budgeting your time and knowing how to read exam questions are important, too. When you receive the exam paper, look it over carefully and try these test-taking strategies.

Schedule Your Time
Determine Point Values

One of the most stressful things about taking an exam is running out of time. Before you write, find out exactly how much time you have. Then, plan how much time you will need to answer the questions.

As soon as you get an exam, scan the questions and determine which questions have a larger point value. For example, you might respond to the questions with the largest point value first, or you might begin with those that you understand well. Then go to the more difficult questions. If you find yourself blocked on a certain answer, do not waste a lot of time on it. Go to another question, and then go back to the first question later.

Carefully Read the Exam Questions

It is important to read exam instructions thoroughly. Follow the next steps.

Identify Key Words and Phrases

When you read an exam question, underline or circle key words and phrases in order to understand exactly what you are supposed to do. In the next example, the underlined words highlight three different tasks.

<u>Distinguish</u> between Paleolithic, Mesolithic, and Neolithic. <u>Place these</u>

<u>periods in chronological order</u> and <u>describe</u> how the people lived during

those times.

1. Discuss how each time period differs from the other.

2. Organize the essay according to each period's date.

3. Discuss what people did for shelter, food, and leisure activities.

Examine Common Question Words

Exam questions direct you using verbs (action words). This chart gives the most common words that are used in both paragraph- and essay-style questions.

Verb	Meaning
describe discuss review	Examine a subject as thoroughly as possible. Focus on the main points.
narrate trace	Describe the development or progress of something using time order.
evaluate explain your point of view interpret justify take a stand	State your opinion and give reasons to support your opinion. In other words, write an argument paragraph or essay.
analyze criticize classify	Explain something carefully by breaking it down into smaller parts.
enumerate list outline	Go through important facts one by one.
compare contrast distinguish	Discuss important similarities and/or differences.
define explain what is meant by	Give a complete and accurate definition that demonstrates your understanding of the concept.
explain causes	Analyze the reasons for an event.
explain effects	Analyze the consequences or results of an event.

Verb	Meaning
explain a process	Explain the steps needed to perform a task.
summarize	Write down the main points from a larger work.
illustrate	Demonstrate your understanding by giving examples.

PRACTICE 1

Determine the main type of response that you would use to answer each essay question. Choose one of the following essay patterns.

narrate	explain a process	explain causes/effects	define
argue	classify	compare and contrast	

EXAMPLE: Discuss the term *affirmative action*.

    define

1. Distinguish between the interest rate and the rate of return.

    _____

2. Describe what happened during the Tet Offensive.

    _____

3. List and describe five types of housing.

    _____

4. What steps are required to improve your city's transportation system?

    _____

5. List the reasons for global warming.

    _____

6. Give a short but thorough description of narcissism.

    _____

7. Discuss whether religious symbols should be banned from schools.

    _____

Follow the Writing Process

When you answer paragraph or essay exam questions, remember to follow the writing process.

Explore
- ◆ Jot down any ideas that you think can help you answer the question.

Develop
- ◆ Use the exam question to guide your topic sentence or thesis statement.
- ◆ List supporting ideas. Then organize your ideas and create a paragraph or essay plan.
- ◆ Write the paragraph or essay. Use transitions to link your ideas.

Revise and edit   ◆ Read over your writing to make sure it makes sense and
that your spelling, punctuation, and mechanics are correct.

PRACTICE 2

Choose three topics from Practice 1 and write topic sentences or thesis statements.

EXAMPLE: Discuss the term *affirmative action.*

Topic sentence or thesis statement: _Affirmative action policies give_
certain groups in society preferential treatment to correct a
history of injustice.

1. _____
   _____
   _____

2. _____
   _____
   _____

3. _____
   _____
   _____

PRACTICE 3

Read the following test material and answer the questions that follow.

Essay Exam

You will have ninety minutes to complete the following test. Write your answers
in the answer booklet.

A. Define the following terms (2 points each).

1. Region
2. Economic geography
3. Territoriality
4. Spatial distribution
5. Gross national product

B. Write an essay response to one of the following questions. Your
essay should contain relevant supporting details. (20 points)

6. Define and contrast an open city with a closed city.
7. Discuss industrial location theories in geography, and divide
   the theories into groups.
8. Explain the steps needed to complete a geographical survey.
   List the steps in order of importance.

Schedule Your Time and Determine Point Values

1. What is the total point value of the exam? _____

2. How many questions do you have to answer? _____

3. Which part of the exam would you do first? Explain why. _____

   _____

   _____

4. Schedule your time. How much time would you spend on each part of the exam?

   Part A: _____   Part B: _____

   Explain your reasoning. _____

   _____

   _____

Carefully Read the Exam Questions

5. Identify key words in Part B. What important information is in the instructions?

   _____

6. What two things must you do in question 6?

   a. _____   b. _____

7. What type of essay is required to answer question 7?

   a. Comparison and contrast   b. Classification   c. Process

8. What type of essay is required to answer question 8?

   a. Comparison and contrast   b. Classification   c. Process

Spelling, Grammar, and Vocabulary Logs

In the first few pages of your writing portfolio or on the next pages, keep spelling, grammar, and vocabulary logs. The goal of keeping spelling and grammar logs is to help you stop repeating the same errors. When you write new assignments, you can consult the lists and hopefully break some ingrained bad habits. The vocabulary log can provide you with interesting new terms that you can incorporate into your writing.

Spelling Log

Every time you misspell a word, record both the mistake and the correction in your spelling log. Then, before you hand in a writing assignment, consult your spelling log. The goal is to stop repeating the same spelling errors.

EXAMPLE:

Incorrect	Correct
realy	really
exagerated	exaggerated

Grammar Log

Each time a writing assignment is returned to you, identify one or two repeated errors and add them to your grammar log. Then, before you hand in writing assignments, consult the grammar log in order to avoid making the same errors. For each type of grammar error, you could do the following:

- Identify the assignment and write down the type of error.
- In your own words, write a rule about the error.
- Include an example from your writing assignment.

EXAMPLE: Illustration Paragraph   (Feb. 12)   Run-On

Do not connect two complete sentences with a comma.

Bad drivers cause accidents, other drivers do not expect sudden lane changes.

Vocabulary Log

As you use this book, you will learn new vocabulary words. Keep a record of the most interesting and useful vocabulary words and expressions. Write a synonym or definition next to each new word.

EXAMPLE: Exasperating means "annoying."

Spelling Log

Grammar Log

_____

_____

_____

_____

_____

_____

_____

_____

_____

_____

_____

_____

_____

_____

_____

_____

_____

_____

_____

_____

_____

_____

_____

_____

_____

_____

_____

_____

_____

Vocabulary Log

Credits

PHOTOS

Index

Revising Checklist for a Paragraph

Does the topic sentence

☐ make a point about the topic?

☐ express a complete thought?

☐ make a direct statement and not contain expressions such as *I think that* or *I will explain*?

Does the body

☐ have **adequate support**? Are there enough details to support the topic sentence?

☐ have **coherence**? Are ideas presented in an effective and logical manner?

☐ have **unity**? Is the paragraph unified around one central topic?

☐ have **style**? Are sentences varied in length? Is the language creative and precise?

Does the concluding sentence

☐ bring the paragraph to a satisfactory close?

☐ avoid introducing new or contradictory information? (Note: Not all paragraphs have concluding sentences.)

Revising Checklist for an Essay

Does the introduction

☐ contain a clearly identifiable thesis statement?

☐ build up to the thesis statement?

Does the thesis statement

☐ convey the essay's controlling idea?

☐ make a valid and supportable point?

☐ appear as the last sentence in the introduction?

☐ make a direct point and not contain expressions such as *I think that* or *I will explain*?

Do the body paragraphs

☐ have **adequate support**? Does each body paragraph have a topic sentence that clearly supports the thesis statement? Are there enough details to support each paragraph's topic sentence?

☐ have **coherence**? Are ideas presented in an effective and logical manner? Do transitional words and phrases help the ideas flow smoothly?

☐ have **unity**? Is the essay unified around one central topic? Does each body paragraph focus on one topic?

☐ have **style**? Are sentences varied in length? Is the language creative and precise?

Does the conclusion

☐ bring the essay to a satisfactory end?

☐ briefly summarize the ideas that the writer discusses in the essay?

☐ avoid introducing new or contradictory ideas?

☐ possibly end with a quotation, suggestion, or prediction?